SEVENTH EDITION
SMALL BUSINESS MANAGEMENT AND ENTREPRENEURSHIP

DAVID STOKES AND NICK WILSON

CENGAGE

United States

Small Business Management and Entrepreneurship, 7th Edition
David Stokes and Nick Wilson

Publisher: Annabel Ainscow

Development Editor: Lauren Cartridge

Content Project Manager: Phillipa Davidson-Blake

Manufacturing Buyer: Elaine Bevan

Marketing Manager: Victoria Pavlicic

Typesetter: MPS Limited

Cover design: Cyan Design

Text design: Design Deluxe

For product information and technology assistance,
contact **emea.info@cengage.com**.

For permission to use material from this text or product,
and for permission queries,
email **emea.permissions@cengage.com**.

British Library Cataloguing-in-Publication Data
A catalogue record for this book is available from the British Library.

ISBN: 978-1-4737-2973-5

Cengage Learning EMEA
Cheriton House, North Way, Andover, Hampshire, SP10 5BE
United Kingdom

Cengage Learning products are represented in Canada by Nelson Education Ltd.

For your lifelong learning solutions, visit
www.cengage.co.uk

Purchase your next print book, e-book or e-chapter at
www.cengagebrain.com

Printed in China by RR Donnelley
Print Number 01   Print Year 2016

This book is dedicated with love' to Florence the mother and Florence the daughter.

This book is dedicated with love to Florence the mother and Florence the daughter

Brief contents

Contents

Case studies

About the authors

PROFESSOR DAVID STOKES

Professor David Stokes is Emeritus Professor of Entrepreneurship, in the Small Business Research Centre (SBRC), Kingston Business School, Kingston University, London. Following education at Oriel College, Oxford and the City University Business School, his management career has been with large and small enterprises in the private and public sectors. He combines an academic and a practical involvement with small and medium-sized enterprises. The subject of his Ph.D. thesis was small enterprise development in the public sector, and he has been involved in many research studies into diverse aspects of small business management, including marketing, critical survival factors and raising finance. As a director of WestFocus, a consortium of seven universities, and Chair of the Higher Education Entrepreneurship Group (HEEG), he developed and promoted entrepreneurship education amongst students and staff of all disciplines. Some of these programmes have been adopted by other organizations, including 'Enterprising Ethiopia', which works with young people to help alleviate poverty through developing their entrepreneurial skills. Personally involved in four business start-ups, he believes in a hands-on involvement to understand fully how enterprises work. He is director and co-founder of a company that manufactures scientific instruments, and has been directly involved in a management buy-out and the development and sale of three businesses in which he held shares. He is co-author of *Entrepreneurship* and *Marketing: A Brief Introduction* by the same publishers, and has written numerous book chapters and journal articles.

DR NICK WILSON

Dr Nick Wilson is Reader in Creativity, Arts & Cultural Management at the Department of Culture, Media and Creative Industries, King's College London, where he founded the MA in Arts & Cultural Management. He was previously Principal Lecturer in Entrepreneurship and Small Business at Kingston University, and Course Director of the Programme of Master's courses in the Creative Industries & the Creative Economy. He studied music at Clare College, Cambridge and went on to train as a singer at the Royal College of Music, London, and the Hochschule der Künste, Berlin, before moving into music management, working for a leading artist management and concert promotions company. During this period, he was also an executive director and company secretary of a family business in corn and milling. After completing his MBA, he joined the Small Business Research Centre, Kingston University, as a researcher and lecturer, where he completed his doctoral thesis on the emergence of the early music performance labour market in the UK. He has undertaken a wide range of research and consultancy projects focusing on small business management and entrepreneurship in the creative industries. His current research and teaching combines a particular interest in (everyday) creativity, art and aesthetics, arts and cultural management, and the philosophy of critical realism. Nick is also co-author of *Entrepreneurship*, by the same publishers.

Preface

Purpose of this book

The principal aim of this book is to provide a course of study in entrepreneurship and the management of the smaller business. It is intended to be used on a variety of business and management courses at undergraduate and postgraduate level. It can also be used by those who wish to study the subject on their own. The material in the book has been developed from the teaching of small business and entrepreneurship components in HND, BA (Business Studies), Certificate in Management, Diploma in Management Studies and MBA courses, as well as workshops and masterclasses for non-business students who wish to start a business, or for practising small business managers and entrepreneurs.

Need

This book aims to fill a gap. There are many publications targeted at would-be entrepreneurs and existing small business owners which give general and detailed advice on how to set up and run a small enterprise. There are also many articles and books of a more academic nature which investigate important topics such as the role of the entrepreneur and the small business in the economy and society.

This book is intended to give the student one main source of reference for both the theory and practice of small business management and entrepreneurship. It has three principal learning objectives for its readers:

- to develop a general understanding of entrepreneurial behaviour in any context, and the potential outcomes and benefits of entrepreneurship with particular reference to the small enterprise;
- to evaluate the specific issues involved in creating, planning, developing and managing the entrepreneurial small business;
- to encourage individual learning through theory and practice by facilitating access to research findings and participation in practical activities such as case studies.

Approach and structure

Although a considerable amount of information is given in the book, the approach is to impart skills and knowledge by engaging the reader in interesting tasks and activities which build on existing understanding.

There are 14 chapters organized in three parts:

PART I UNDERSTANDING SMALL BUSINESS AND ENTREPRENEURSHIP: CHAPTERS 1–5

Part I gives the reader the necessary information to understand the relevance of entrepreneurship and the small business sector in a wider economic and social context, and to explore the environment in which entrepreneurs operate and the processes they employ.

PART II CREATING THE ENTREPRENEURIAL SMALL BUSINESS: CHAPTERS 6–10

Part II investigates the theories and practicalities of creating and planning an entrepreneurial small business. It also introduces the diversity of small business types, including start-ups, franchises, buying a business and the legal forms.

PART III MANAGING THE ENTREPRENEURIAL SMALL BUSINESS: CHAPTERS 11–14

Part III evaluates how entrepreneurial businesses work in practice, focusing on the development, growth and exit stages through the key functions of managing people, resources, marketing and money.

Each chapter contains activities to be completed during and at the end of the reading of the chapter:

- *Activities:* these are intended to provoke thoughts around the subject matter before it is read so that the reader discovers as much as possible for themselves.
- *Case studies:* at the end of each chapter, we use case studies to illustrate real business issues that relate to some of the themes of the chapter. These fall into two types:
  (a) A fictional case study based on actual events. In Chapters 1–5, an ongoing case study – 'A tale of two entrepreneurs' – illustrates the process which would-be or nascent entrepreneurs might go through before starting up a small business. The story is developed through the five chapters so that each situation can be followed through to subsequent stages.
  (b) A factual case study of real-life entrepreneurs and their businesses, reflecting some of the themes and learning objectives of the chapter. In some cases, these are also broken into sections to reflect the evolution of a particular business or to illustrate different learning objectives.

- *Extended tasks:* an activity is suggested at the end of each chapter which is designed to develop understanding of the subject of the chapter through observation of small enterprises in action.
- *Planning a new venture:* each chapter concludes with an ongoing activity that progresses an entrepreneurial venture through the various stages, from opportunity identification to the full planning of the business. The reader is asked at the end of each chapter to undertake a particular step in this process, linked to the subject matter of the chapter. These steps are illustrated in Figure 1, Planning a new venture. In summary, they are:
  (a) develop an opportunity from a category of *unknown risk* to *reasonable prospects* by the end of Chapter 5. At this stage, the reader will be invited to write up an initial *evaluation of the opportunity;*
  (b) define the business strategy and select a *suitable route* to market by the end of Chapter 10. At this stage, the reader will be invited to complete a *feasibility study;*
  (c) plan the operation of the business as an *acceptable risk* including an exit plan by Chapter 14. At this stage, the reader will be invited to complete a *business plan.*

Thus, there are three incremental outputs from these stages: the evaluation of the opportunity, the feasibility study and the business plan. These can form the basis of assessed work, if required.

Note to the seventh edition

This new edition of the text continues to extend its coverage of small business management and entrepreneurship, drawing on contemporary theory and practice in equal measure. While the structure and format of the chapters remains broadly the same as the previous edition, the book includes many new examples and current references drawn from a wide variety of industrial, social and cultural contexts, bringing our knowledge of small business management and entrepreneurship up to date.

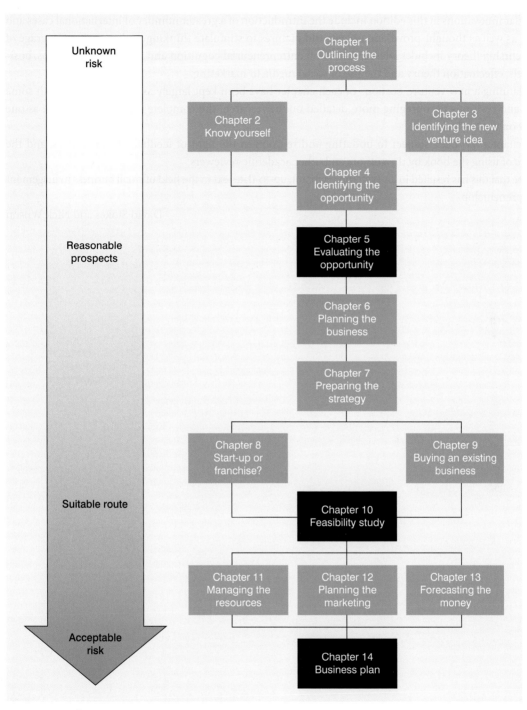

Figure 1 Planning a new venture

Particular innovations in this edition include the introduction of a greater number of international cases and examples, as well as thought-provoking images and pictures to stimulate thinking on key topics. Coverage of entrepreneurship theory includes latest thinking on entrepreneurial cognition and intent, lean start-ups, business models, effectuation theory and the use of social media in marketing.

The 'Planning a new venture' sections of each chapter have been kept largely as before, though with some additions and revisions encouraging more detailed online research; the complete exercise is available as one document on the book's website.

Every chapter has been subject to updating and revision in the light of feedback from readers, and the experience of using the book by the authors and other academic reviewers.

We hope that this has resulted in an even more vibrant, up-to-date text in the field of small business management and entrepreneurship.

David Stokes and Nick Wilson

Acknowledgements

We would like to thank Dr Mathor Mador, Dwain Reid and the Enterprise team of Kingston University for learning materials on entrepreneurship education as well as Stephen Whaley of Enterprising Ethiopia for case study material.

The publisher would like to thank the following reviewers for their comments which have helped to strengthen the book:

Dr EK Agbobli, Central University of Technology, Free State

Dr Simon Hill, Coventry University

Dr Philip Ely, Portsmouth University

Gosekwang Setibi, University of Botswana

Anastasia Mutorwa, University of Namibia

CENGAGE
Learning®

Digital
Support
Resources

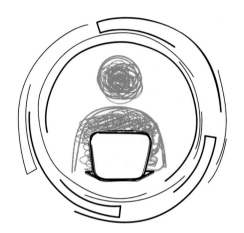

All of our Higher Education textbooks are accompanied by a range of digital support resources. Each title's resources are carefully tailored to the specific needs of the particular book's readers. Examples of the kind of resources provided include:

- A password protected area for instructors with, for example, a testbank, PowerPoint slides and an instructor's manual.

- An open-access area for students including, for example, useful weblinks and glossary terms.

Lecturers: to discover the dedicated lecturer digital support resources accompanying this textbook please register here for access: login.cengage.com.

Students: to discover the dedicated student digital support resources accompanying this textbook, please search for **Small Business Management and Entreprenueurship 7th edition** on: cengagebrain.co.uk

Understanding small business and entrepreneurship

1 **Small business in the economy**
2 **Entrepreneurship, the entrepreneur and the owner-manager**
3 **The small business and entrepreneurial environment**
4 **Innovation and the marketplace**
5 **Information and help**

PART I

- This Part consists of five chapters which evaluate the role that small businesses and entrepreneurship play in our economy and society, the environment in which entrepreneurs operate and how they are supported and helped.

- The activities and cases studies throughout this book are designed to stimulate your thoughts and experiences of the topic under discussion. Understanding and retention of information is more likely if it is related to what you already know or have experience of, so it is important to undertake the activities either in the text, or at the end of each chapter.

- At the end of each chapter, it is important to consolidate the learning by tackling the relevant step in 'Planning a new venture' (see Figure 1 of the Preface). In this Part, the five chapters represent the process of taking an opportunity from a position of unknown risk to a reasonable prospect. By the end of Chapter 5, you will be able to complete an initial evaluation of the opportunity.

1 Small business in the economy

Learning objectives

By the end of this chapter you will be able to:

- Define small and medium-sized businesses.
- Understand the significance of the small business sector to national economies.
- Appreciate the historical evolution of the sector.
- Examine the dynamics of this turbulent sector and assess the global trends.

Introduction

In this opening chapter, we assess the significance of small, entrepreneurial businesses to national economies and society. Small businesses form a very diverse sector that varies considerably by region and industry so that it is difficult to define and measure precisely, but it is important to set some general parameters for what we are studying. After a period of relative decline and neglect, the small business sector and entrepreneurship are recognized today as key elements in national economic growth. Comparisons of the profiles of the business population in developed countries indicate a clear and continuing trend towards a larger number of smaller firms with a corresponding reduction in the numbers of larger companies. The underlying structural, technological and social reasons for this trend are identified and discussed. Despite the growth in numbers, small businesses remain a turbulent part of the economy with large movements in and out of the sector each year. The entrepreneurial path is not an easy one to follow.

1.1 What is a small business?

1.1.1 PROBLEMS OF DEFINITION

What exactly is a small business, and when does it become medium-sized or large? We use the terms Small and Medium-sized Enterprise (SME), 'small business sector' and 'small business management' to describe a certain group of enterprises and how they are run. This implies that these enterprises have certain characteristics and management issues in common that distinguish them from other organizations. In practice, it is hard to define these characteristics, and even harder to draw a precise line that separates small from large firms.

Activity 1
What is a small business?

CoolLED Ltd designs and manufactures LED illumination systems for microscopes. Since its incorporation in 2011, it has grown rapidly, selling over €3 million of its innovative products annually around the world, employing 25 people and achieving a net asset value of €1.5 million on its balance sheet.

Poqués International sells discounted clothes on the internet that it sources from other manufacturers. Sales exceeded €3 million last year although it employs only 7 people. Low margins keep profits tight so its balance-sheet value is under €0.5 million.

How would you categorize each of these businesses: Micro, Small or Medium-sized?

Once you have decided, check your assessment with the definitions adopted by the European Union below.

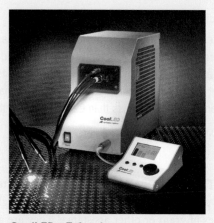

CoolLED pE-1 unit
Source: Courtesy of Liz Stark, CoolLED Ltd.

'Management' is generally understood to refer to a particular mode of activity in an organizational context; but it is helpful to remember that we all manage (our work, our families, our lives, etc.) on a daily basis. On one level, the ability to manage, in a small business or otherwise, is a universal human capacity, not a job description reserved for a privileged few.

'Entrepreneurship' is also an elusive term. It is commonly linked to small business management because it involves the processes of recognizing opportunities and the development of new ventures, but entrepreneurs operate in a range of contexts including larger corporations and the public sector, not just small businesses. Definitions of entrepreneurship and those involved in managing small businesses are explored in Chapter 2, where we consider the differences between an 'owner-manager' and an 'entrepreneur'.

This chapter focuses on the role of small businesses in terms of their contribution to society in general, but we should not forget the crucial role of the people that create and manage these enterprises.

Small businesses do not conform to any neat parameters. Much depends on the industry in which they operate and the personalities and aspirations of those that run them. These factors vary from manufacturers to retailers, professional managers to husband and wife teams, high growth, high-tech start-ups funded by venture capitalists to self-financed tradesmen content just to make a living. It is this diversity that makes generalizations of any kind, including a definition of the sector, extremely difficult, and often unwise.

1.1.2 QUANTITATIVE DEFINITIONS

Some definitions focus on numerical parameters in order to differentiate between smaller and larger business types. The European Commission (EC) initiated an important set of definitions of the small and medium-sized enterprise (SME) that introduced a further category of the 'micro' enterprise to reflect the growing importance of very small businesses. These definitions are based on headcount, and turnover or balance-sheet value, as shown in Table 1.1.

Table 1.1 SME size thresholds adopted by the European Commission

Category	Headcount	Turnover	Balance sheet total
Medium	50–249	<€50m	<€43m
Small	10–49	<€10m	<€10m
Micro	0–9	<€2m	<€2m

Note: if a firm qualifies on two of the three measures it is in that category as turnover and balance-sheet are alternative measures. So, in the examples cited in Activity 1, CoolLED Ltd would qualify as a *small* business because it employs more than 10 people and its turnover is more than €2 million even though its balance-sheet total is less than €2 million. Poqués International is a *micro* business because it employs 7 people and has a balance sheet value less than €2 million, even though its turnover exceeds €2 million.

Source: The European Union (ec.europa.eu)

These quantitative thresholds are important because they are used throughout the European Union **(EU)** for policy purposes. For example, they might be used to determine the eligibility of a business for certain types of grant or other assistance. They are also widely used by national government institutions such as the Department for Business, Innovation and Skills (BIS)[1] in the UK.

There are obvious attractions in using such definitions. They seem objective and relatively simple to apply, facilitating statistical analysis of the sector. But such measures have important limitations. The number of people employed is very dependent on the industry involved and this makes generalized comparisons across sectors difficult. For instance, 49 employees may constitute a small manufacturer, but they probably count as a medium-sized consultancy or retailer, and would be considered large as compared to most businesses operating in the cultural and creative industries. According to Curran and Blackburn (2001), the use of numbers employed is even more problematic as full-time employment has become less common, with increasing numbers of part-time, project-based, casual and temporary workers.

Financial measures, such as the turnover and balance-sheet value of a business used by the EC, present similar sector problems. For example, wholesalers tend to have high levels of sales but operate with very low margins, and this would distort comparisons with higher-margin service companies with similar turnovers. Moreover, inflation and exchange rate changes make comparisons over time and between countries more difficult. The EC acknowledged this in 2005 by revising upwards the turnover and balance-sheet thresholds for each classification to the current levels from those originally set in 1999. It regularly monitors the implementation of the SME definition and a report recently concluded that no further change is needed at present (Centre for Strategy & Evaluation, 2012).

In the USA, some of these concerns are recognized in the way that the Small Business Administration (SBA)[2] defines small businesses for the purpose of government funding. Size standards are set for each type of industry to reflect the differences between trades. Commonly, a small business is defined as having fewer than 500 employees in manufacturing industries and 100 employees in wholesale operations.

1.1.3 NON-QUANTITATIVE DEFINITIONS

To overcome some of these difficulties, non-quantitative definitions have been proposed that try to single out the essence or differentiating characteristics of a small business. Small firms may be difficult to define precisely on paper, but most are easy to recognize once they are seen in operation. There seem to be fundamental differences in practice that enable us to distinguish between small and large firms.

The Committee of Inquiry on Small Firms set up by the UK government recognized this in an influential report which became known as the Bolton Report (1971). The Report proposed that a small firm has three essential characteristics:

- A small firm is managed by its owner(s) in a personalized way.
- It has a relatively small share of the market in economic terms.
- It is independent in the sense that it does not form part of a larger enterprise and its ownership is relatively free from outside control in its principal decisions.

However, Bolton supplemented these general qualities by more specific, quantitative measurements depending on the industry type. For example:

Small firm type	Definition used
Manufacturing	200 employees or less
Construction	25 employees or less
Road transport	5 vehicles or less

Although these definitions formed the basis of much research in subsequent years, they are open to several criticisms, including:

- Low market share is not always a characteristic; small firms typically operate in highly specialized niches, or limited geographic markets, where they have a relatively high share.
- Independence is difficult to measure. For example, Bolton's definition excluded franchises that are organized by a larger enterprise, but included subcontractors who were very dependent on one customer.

Wynarczyk *et al.* (1993) identified three key aspects in which small and large firms differ: uncertainty, innovation and evolution.

- Uncertainty is a persistent feature of small firms which tend to have small customer bases and limited resources.
- Innovation of either very new products, or marginal differences to well established ones, is a key factor in the success or failure of new business start-ups.
- Evolution refers to the state of constant structural and market changes which small firms are likely to experience as they struggle to survive and develop.

This definition has not been widely used because it lacks clarity and clear differentiation from larger companies. It could very well be argued that uncertainty, innovation and evolution are also a crucial part of the business environment of large corporates in today's fast-changing world.

Curran *et al.* (1991) have argued against over-general notions of the 'small firm sector' because it consists of an exceptionally mixed bag of businesses, engaged in a wide range of activities, whose managers often have little in common with each other. Instead they used more detailed, pragmatic definitions derived from sources within a trade or activity type. Thus, a 'small' public house (free house) business is defined as having one outlet, an unspecified number of employees but not brewery owned, while a 'small' employment agency can have up to two outlets and ten employees.

1.1.4 DEFINITIONS USED IN THIS BOOK

Small business management is different in several respects to management in larger organizations, because of social structures and relationships, and because of the levels of resources available. While these differences may derive from the numbers of employees and size of turnover, it is their management implications that will be our primary concern. For example, the manager who has no specialist departments to turn to for advice, who takes messages from creditors seeking payments because of a cash shortage and who has to choose between keeping an appointment with a client or attending to an important production issue, is facing situations typical of the management of small, rather than large, businesses.

While quantitative measures such as the EU definitions oversimplify matters, they do reflect the changing management environment of an enterprise as it reaches key stages in its growth. Businesses with fewer than ten employees rarely need a middle management structure, but over that size there is often pressure on the owner-manager to delegate more of the decision-making. In this sense small business management can be extended to small enterprise management to bring in the many types of small organizations which are not traditionally regarded as businesses, but which share many of the management issues of a small firm. Small non-profit-making units (including charities, theatres, sports clubs, health centres, arts organizations, even schools) may be influenced by the 'smallness' of their operation in ways which are similar to small businesses. A doctor in a small medical practice, the head teacher of a primary school, or the manager of a small charity may work in a similar management environment, and face similar management decisions as the owner-manager of a small firm. While such organizations may not fit with accepted definitions of a small business, the management environment can still be typical of a small enterprise.

It is this peculiar management environment of the small enterprise which defines the parameters of this book, rather than any precise threshold level above which a small firm automatically becomes medium-sized or large. While those that operate in larger organizations can still act entrepreneurially and entrepreneurship is not limited to small business (see Chapter 2), entrepreneurs working in small enterprises have significant additional issues that are related to the size of the operation.

Activity 2
Why are small businesses important to the economy?

Which of the following factors help small businesses make a positive contribution to the health of the economy?

(a) Small firms provide a seedbed from which larger businesses grow
(b) They can be cheaper than rivals if you pay cash
(c) They improve the availability of different products and services
(d) They increase the size of the 'black economy'
(e) They provide employment for enterprising individuals
(f) They don't have to obey all the regulations

Which of these are positive economic factors and which negative? Try and think of other positive factors before checking your answers with the factors listed by the Bolton Report below.

1.2 Why bother with small businesses?

1.2.1 SHIFTING PERCEPTIONS OF SMALL BUSINESSES
Guided by politicians and management theorists, public perceptions of the small business have shifted over the last half century or so between the extremes of neglect and ignorance to hype and over-expectation. In the 1950s and 1960s, small firms were written off as out-of-date forms of economic activity. By the late 1970s and

1980s, they were hailed as the new saviours of ailing Western economies and, by the 1990s, SMEs were recognized as the key to fuller employment. In the 2000s and up to the present day, new ventures and small business have become synonymous with economic success.

Politicians are invariably keen to encourage a more entrepreneurial economy. It is even fashionable to become an entrepreneur as television and other media feature inventors struggling to raise money or the stories of those who have succeeded.

Small firm neglect

After centuries in which the small enterprise had been the basic economic unit, the viability of many small businesses came under threat during the industrial upheavals of the nineteenth and twentieth centuries. The importance of small businesses in terms of manufacturing output and employment began to decline and fell until the second half of the twentieth century. In the 1920s and 1930s, small manufacturing firms accounted for 45 per cent of employment in the UK, but by the 1960s and 1970s this had fallen to 30 per cent (Greene and Mole, 2006). Technological and market changes seemed to be working in favour of larger industrial units during this time:

- Economies of scale lowered costs for manufacturers big enough to use mass production techniques.
- New products from electrical goods to pharmaceutical drugs were transforming the buying habits of society but the research and development costs were very high and affordable only by larger companies.
- Protectionist trade barriers fell away as the marketplace became increasingly global to the advantage of big businesses with international marketing and distribution resources.

Social scientists and policy makers devoted their attention to large units of production, which they believed would be the increasingly predominant form of industrial organization. There was a widespread belief that the small firm was rather superfluous to economic growth and the spate of mergers and takeovers in the 1950s and 1960s seemed to confirm this view. Global marketing had handed the key to economic prosperity to the multi-national corporation and modern technology demanded a concentration of resources, confining small firms to a peripheral role supporting the dominant position of larger organizations.

Management theory and education focused its attention on the manager working in a large company. Small firm owners were seen in a rather inferior light, managing limited resources with backward technologies in an amateur way. The major publications on business disciplines such as marketing, finance and strategy were written in the context of large organizations and the new business schools which began to develop at this time used case studies of large firms, almost exclusively (Curran and Stanworth, 1987).

The 'entrepreneurial economy'

During the late 1970s and 1980s, the situation changed. Research into the behaviour of small businesses and entrepreneurship increased dramatically. The literature boomed, with written material published on virtually every aspect of the small business. Regular newspaper columns[3] began to give advice to small business owners and information on their environment.

Politicians of differing ideologies in many countries developed a remarkable enthusiasm for the small firm. All three major political parties in the UK supported policies promoting small businesses. In the 1980s, leaders on both sides of the Atlantic proclaimed the dawn of a new age of enterprise, led by an army of entrepreneurs working in small firms.

Peter Drucker (1986), one of the most influential writers in an era when management theory was based on big business practice, acknowledged the new climate by welcoming the shift from a managerial to an entrepreneurial economy in which growth was being fuelled by small and medium-sized enterprises.

1.2.2 THE BOLTON REPORT

In the UK, a watershed in the perceptions of the small firm was the highly influential Bolton Report (1971), the outcome of the Committee of Inquiry on Small Firms. During its two years of research, it commissioned many reports which have formed the basis for the large body of work carried out since, and represented one of the first significant attempts to assess the importance and functions of the small firms sector.

The report recognized that small enterprises made a special contribution to the health of the economy, identifying eight important roles:

- a productive outlet for enterprising and independent individuals (some of whom may be frustrated under-achievers in a larger, more controlled environment);
- the most efficient form of business organization in some industries or markets where the optimum size of the production unit or sales outlet is small;
- specialist suppliers, or subcontractors to larger companies;
- contributors to the variety of products and services made available to customers in specialized markets, too small for larger companies to consider worthwhile;
- competition to the monopolistic tendencies of large companies;
- innovators of new products, services and processes;
- the breeding ground for new industries; and
- the seedbed from which tomorrow's larger companies will grow, providing entry points for entrepreneurial talent who will become the industrial captains of the future.

These important roles were underpinned by the conclusion of the Committee that small firms could be extremely efficient, having the advantage of the commitment of their owner-managers, plus the ability in certain circumstances to exploit business opportunities better than their larger brethren.

However, the Committee provided evidence of the decline of the small business sector in the economy, concluding that further weakening of small firms was inevitable due to the economies of scale of larger firms. In view of the actual and potential contribution of small firms to the overall health of the economy, the major recommendation of the Report was the creation of a Small Firms Division under a Minister for Small Firms. This was implemented by the establishment of the Small Firms Service within the Department of Industry.

The particular concern of the Report was that government policies should encourage and support the sector, not accelerate its decline through an unfair burden of regulations, paperwork and taxes:

> We believe that the health of the economy requires the birth of new enterprises in substantial numbers and the growth of some to a position from which they are able to challenge and supplant the existing leaders of industry... This seedbed function, therefore, appears to be a vital contribution of the small firm's sector to the long-run health of the economy. We cannot assume that the ordinary working of market forces will necessarily preserve a small firm sector large enough to perform this function in future (Bolton Report, 1971).

Activity 3
Small business data

In 2014, the business population of the UK exceeded 5 million for the first time.

(a) What percentage of these businesses do you think are small (employing fewer than 50 people)?
(b) What percentage are micro (employing fewer than 10)?

(c) What percentage of employment do small businesses account for?
(d) What percentage of national turnover do you think they account for?

1.3 The revival of the small enterprise

In fact, the Bolton Report proved unduly pessimistic about the immediate future for small firms. If their survival as an organizational form was the issue in 1971, the concern today is that the expectations have been too high. Small firms are now heralded as leaders in providing employment and growth in a restructuring of advanced economies. In retrospect, we can see that the tide was turning before the Bolton Report.

1.3.1 THE AMERICAN EXPERIENCE

In the USA, small enterprises began their revival in the 1960s. From the late 1960s, the creation of new jobs shifted from the country's largest organizations, to small and medium-sized firms, many of them new businesses. The growth in employment in the USA between the mid-1960s and mid-1980s was phenomenal. The total workforce grew from 71 million in 1965 to 106 million in 1985, an increase of 50 per cent, or 35 million new jobs. Yet at the same time the traditional powerhouses of the American economy, the largest businesses (the Fortune 500), were actually shedding jobs, an estimated loss of 5 million permanent jobs by 1985. In other words, taking into account this loss, 40 million new jobs were created in the two decades to 1985 by small and medium-sized businesses. Much of the growth came from new enterprises, with an estimated 600 000 new businesses being started every year during the boom times of the 1980s (Drucker, 1986).

1.3.2 THE UK STATISTICS

The pick-up of small enterprises in the UK may have come later but was no less impressive. Between 1980 and 1990, the total number of firms in the UK rose by over 50 per cent in the decade (Bannock and Daly, 1994). Although the number of firms fell slightly in the recession of the early 1990s, it had risen to 3.5 million by 2000. Since then numbers have continued to grow. Even the recession following the 2008 banking crash only caused a temporary dip in growth. From 2010 to 2014, they surged upwards from 4.5 to 5.2 million (see Figure 1.1).

The profile of the business population shows that the great majority of firms are micro enterprises, employing either no one else or only a handful of people each. Table 1.2 shows that, of the 5.2 million businesses in

Figure 1.1 Total UK business population 2000–2014

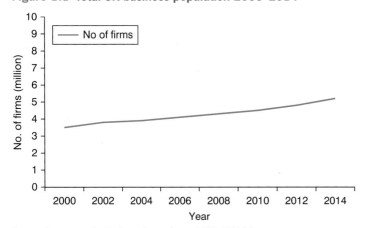

Source: Department for Business, Innovation and Skills (2014a).

Table 1.2 Profile of the UK business population, 2000 and 2014, by percentage

Size (No. of employees)	Percentage of total					
	No. of businesses		Employment		Turnover	
	2000	2014	2000	2014	2000	2014
None	69.6	75.7	13.5	17.3	7.4	6.5
1–9	25.3	19.9	16.7	15.5	15.4	12.0
10–49	4.1	3.7	13.3	15.1	14.4	14.6
50–249	0.6	0.6	11.4	12.2	13.9	13.5
250+	0.2	0.2	44.9	39.9	48.8	55.3

Source: Department for Business Innovation and Skills (2014b).

the UK in 2014, nearly 96 per cent, or 5 million firms, had fewer than 10 employees. Of these, 3.9 million businesses, 76 per cent of the total, had no employees at all, representing the increasingly large number of one-person businesses. As Table 1.2 and Figure 1.2 show, micro firms of under 10 employees accounted for one-third of employment in the private sector in 2014. Small businesses employing under 50 people accounted for nearly half (48 per cent) of all jobs in the UK private sector and one-third of turnover.

Although there are only approximately 10 000 large enterprises employing over 250 people, they make up 40 per cent of employment and nearly 55 per cent of turnover. Conversely, the total SME sector of firms employing less than 250 people now contributes 60 per cent of employment (15.2 million jobs) and 47 per cent of turnover (£1.6 trillion) in the UK.

The SME sector, which had been largely ignored or dismissed as an out-of-date irrelevance by business and management analysts in the 1960s, has grown to represent nearly half of total UK sales, and nearly 60 per cent of total private-sector employment. Moreover, the current trend is towards an even broader base of very small businesses. Between 2000 and 2014, the number of businesses employing over 250 people declined from 7500 to 6000 while the businesses employing no one except the owner increased from 2.6 to 3.9 million.

With only 1.3 million (25 per cent) of the UK's 5.2 million firms employing other people, it is important to make a distinction between types of self-employment and the creation of a small business. Self-employment can be just another form of working for larger organizations with no prospects of directly creating employment for others. For example, many professional specialists or skilled workers have become self-employed as consultants or tradespeople. Often, they work for larger firms on a fee or a subcontract basis. This has become a particular feature of recessionary times when employers try to maintain the maximum flexibility over the costs of employment, by using self-employed labour. Some welcome the opportunity for self-employment in this way. Others – it has been suggested up to one-third (Hakim, 1989) – accept self-employment reluctantly because of redundancy or lack of alternative employment.

Figure 1.2 Contribution to total UK employment by firm size (number of employees)

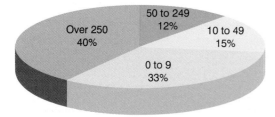

Source: Department for Business Innovation and Skills (2014b).

It is also important to recognize that many businesses do not even employ the owner on a full-time basis. Many ventures are started as a part-time activity to supplement employment elsewhere, either because the owner regards them as a sideline activity, or because they are testing out a business idea before committing to it fully by leaving their job. For this reason, mainstream firms, defined as 'full time sole occupation businesses', were estimated to total 2.8 million in 2003, considerably fewer than the total stock of 4 million at that time (Barclays Bank, 2004).

Activity 4
Why the revival?

Do you think small enterprises increase in number because:

- It's too difficult to get a job with a big company?
- Television programmes such as *Dragons' Den* encourage everyone to think of a business idea?
- It's easier to be your own boss than work for someone else?

List other factors that you think would lead to the formation of more small businesses before reading on. Which is the most important factor in your list?

1.4 Interpretations of the small business revival

1.4.1 THREE THEORIES OF SMALL BUSINESS AND SOCIETY

By the 1980s, the small firm found itself at centre stage of a political and economic debate which offered radically different interpretations over its role and its recent revival. The contenders in this debate have been classified by Goss (1991) into three distinct camps.

Free market theory

Right-wing governments in the UK and the USA simultaneously seized upon the small firm as a symbol of the new order of **'Enterprise Culture'**, which was ushering out an age of collectivism and government economic intervention. President Reagan hailed the small business as the economic saviour of America, while Prime Minister Thatcher pronounced them a barometer of freedom, insisting that 'the freer the society, the more smaller businesses there will be'.

The **free market** economy promoted by the Right relies on the widespread competition provided by new ventures and smaller companies to prevent the monopolistic distortions of large organizations. Entrepreneurial action, stemming from an 'on your bike', self-sufficient philosophy, is seen as the antidote to the adversity of job loss and regional economic realignment. The virtues of innovation and job creation in small enterprises are contrasted to the lethargy and stagnation of large nationalized industries.

Marxian analysis

According to Marxist theory, capitalism degenerates into economies dominated by a small number of monopolistic companies, as society polarizes between those that own the large units of production and those that work in them. Far from being inconvenient evidence, the revival of the small firm is explained as part of this inevitable tendency. Small firms represent a subtler form of economic domination by the large firms, and another instrument for the exploitation of labour. Central to this argument is the dependent status of small business on larger organizations which only allow them to thrive when it is more profitable that way.

So, for example, the growth in numbers of small firms in the 1980s is seen as part of a strategy by which large firms effectively subcontract their less profitable activities to smaller firms in difficult times. These can operate on a lower cost base because of their lack of unionization, and poorer terms and conditions of work. The tendency for small-firm formation to increase during recessions illustrates that the core sector of big business is merely using small business as a secondary sector, to cushion itself against market fluctuations. Moreover, this secondary sector only survives because it can exploit its unorganized, non-unionized labour with lower pay and poorer working conditions and safety records.

The green movement

Over-production, bureaucracy, centralization and short-term material gain are symptoms of a deepening crisis in industrial society which only a return to a more natural order can reverse. This is the language of many 'alternative' **green movements** which have also put small business to the forefront of their ideology. The 'small is beautiful' slogan of Fritz Schumacher (1974) has been taken up, representing the feeling that the quality of life must come before the materialistic motives of big business. Small enterprises are seen as more democratic and responsive to society than large remote organizations following strategies of high growth, which take little account of their effects either on the world environment or local communities.

1.4.2 REASONS FOR THE SMALL BUSINESS REVIVAL

Whatever the political interpretations, several interlinking factors have influenced the growth of small businesses.

Growth of the service sector

The vast majority of all small firms operate in the service and construction sectors of the economy. Eighty-five per cent of UK firms employing less than 50 people are in the **service sector** and construction (Curran, 1997). There has been a strong structural shift in the economy away from manufacturing-based industries and towards services; services have expanded to over 70 per cent of gross domestic product (**GDP**, a measure of the total outputs of an economy). Hence, small firms are most active in the most dynamic sector of the economy.

Small firms have competitive advantages in many service sectors, which accounts for their strong representation in this area of business. Many services, such as communications and professional advice services (e.g. advertising, accounting, computer services and other consultancies), rely on a personalized, tailor-made service, very suited to the flexibility and responsiveness of small business.

Other services involve consumption at the point of purchase (restaurants, wine bars, free houses), which favours smaller, localized outlets, requiring individual management. (See also Chapter 3, The small business and entrepreneurial environment, for a more detailed discussion of the influence of sectors on the small business population.)

Technological change

Many new small firms owe their creation to technological developments. A key growth area in the formation of new ventures recently has been in computers, the internet and related services such as web design and applications. As the industry is relatively young, the enterprises involved tend to be small. In the first half of the twentieth century, there was an upsurge in the numbers of companies supplying and servicing the new products of that era – motor cars, radios and other electrical goods, chemical and pharmaceutical products. As these industries matured and consolidated into fewer, larger organizations in the latter part of the century, new technology has provided the opportunity for new enterprise to develop and spread once again. This cyclical view of industrial development infers that the new businesses of today will also tend to amalgamate into larger units as markets mature – until new technologies and other developments give rise to new markets which shift the balance towards smaller businesses again.

Flexible specialization and networks

A further interpretation of these trends considers changes to patterns of demand as well as supply. Consumers now expect individual preferences to be catered for in detail as business managers have learned the value of segmenting markets to differentiate their products. The growth of the so-called 'experience economy' (Pine and Gilmore, 1999), which caters to ever-more specialist demand for particular experiences, is also significant here. A walk down any high street, past shops specializing in underwear, expensive chocolates, doorknobs and cake-making equipment confirms this point. Fundamental changes have happened in the economy as the mass production methods of large companies become less appropriate to new patterns of demand.

At the same time, new technology has reduced the fixed costs of some manufacturing processes, so that production can profitably be based in smaller, more flexible units. For example, traditional printing methods involved capital-intensive equipment, operated by expensive skilled labour, which became very uneconomic for short-run or one-off jobs. New digital, computerized printing technology has allowed instant printing to flourish by offering shorter economic print quantities and faster availability.

It has also been claimed that co-operation between networks of specialized small businesses can make them even more competitive. Some 'industrial districts' have emerged in which independent small firms operating in the same geographic area and industrial sector combine by performing one or two stages of the production process to offer a highly competitive, flexible service. Small firms manufacturing footwear and textiles in northern Italy and the high-tech and software companies around Cambridge in the UK have been held up as models of the **flexible specialization** approach. These local economic networks of small businesses which can deliver flexibly while retaining the economies of larger organizations have been seen by some commentators as the natural successor to the old industrial model which depended on scale economies from the production of standardized products. At first, the limited number and impact of these industrial districts indicated that these high hopes had not been fulfilled (Curran and Blackburn, 1994). More recently, it has been recognized that small firms do not need physical co-location to act collaboratively but are adept at using the latest communications technology to this end (OECD, 2015).

This flexible specialization model of economic development implies a long-term trend in favour of small business. Driven by consumer preferences, the marketplace has become increasingly specialized into niches of one-off products and services which small businesses using technological advances and collaborative networks can now deliver.

Subcontracting and fragmentation

The cycle of recessions since the early 1980s has stimulated a fragmentation of production and services as larger firms reorganized themselves. Leaner and fitter became the watchwords as companies adjusted to the new economic realities. In an effort to reduce fixed costs and develop flexibility to cope with fluctuations in demand, some larger organizations have subcontracted part of their activities to smaller enterprises. In other cases, large companies have withdrawn altogether from some activities to concentrate on what they see as their core business, selling off or closing down peripheral businesses. This is fundamentally different to the flexible specialization interpretation as it denies there is a long-term shift towards small business. Large organizations still retain primary control over economic activity but it has served their interests to shift some employment and output to smaller firms. It does not therefore represent a fundamental, long-term realignment of forces in favour of smaller business, but a strategy to increase the profitability and flexibility of larger ones (along the lines of Marxian analysis described in Section 1.4.1). This fragmentation model of industry sees small firms as still very dependent on larger ones.

Deregulation and privatization

Internationally, there has been a move to deregulate some markets and to privatize the provision of public services. This has provided opportunities for entrepreneurs to enter markets that were previously closed to them. The public sector in the UK has been subject to constant reorganizations, some of which have provided opportunities for SME involvement. A variety of measures has caused public bodies to open up some of the services they purchase to private-sector involvement. The creation of internal markets – a clearer distinction between departments that purchase services and those that provide them – and compulsory competitive tendering for some functions hitherto provided internally, has meant more **subcontracting** possibilities for small firms. For example, grounds maintenance and cleaning and catering services in schools and hospitals are now contracted out to the lowest bidder. Independent architects, solicitors, trainers and consultants have all benefited from additional work from public bodies that have cut back their internal departments which previously provided these professional services. Private/public partnerships have been seen as a way to improve the efficiency of the public sector and thereby reduce the burden on taxpayers.

Privatization and deregulation have become common themes in other economies, too, as governments have considered the levels and effectiveness of public expenditure. For example, New Zealand went even further than the UK with its radical reforms in the public sector. First, the Labour government from 1984 privatized large parts of the state sector, and then the National Party government from 1990 required central and local government to put more services out to contract to the private sector.

Unemployment

The revival of self-employment and small business ownership in developed countries coincided with a period of recession and high levels of unemployment from the late 1970s through to the early 1980s. There does seem to have been a link between the rate of unemployment and entry into business ownership in the UK. Redundancy, especially with a golden handshake, pushed many reluctant entrepreneurs into self-employment, and provided the stimulus for others who had already considered starting their own business but were reluctant to give up the security of their employment.

While this does seem to have been a factor in the early 1980s, unemployment has since fallen with little slackening in the rate of new business formations.

The enterprise culture

A rare consensus has emerged in British politics, as all three major political parties have proclaimed their support for a healthy small business sector and the encouragement of entrepreneurial attitudes. In keeping with their market economy ideology, the Conservative administration which came to power in 1979 introduced a series of measures designed to stimulate new businesses. These ranged from investment incentives to information and advice (see Chapter 5, Information and help).

As the revival of the small firm was well under way before 1979, this policy served to further stimulate or prolong growth, not initiate it. But the estimated £1 billion spent by the Exchequer between 1980 and 1985, through over 200 policy measures in support of small firms, clearly had a positive effect on the growth of the sector. The Labour administrations from 1997 continued these policies with attempts to concentrate fragmented support agencies under the single umbrella of the Small Business Service (SBS) and Business Link. How far the government succeeded in establishing an 'enterprise culture' which encouraged and valued entrepreneurial attitudes and self-employment, is more debatable. One survey found that although young people were very aware of entrepreneurial opportunities they were cautious over the risks involved (Blackburn and Curran, 1989). The number of graduates who establish their own business has caused particular concern. Although a significant minority would be willing to consider entrepreneurship as an alternative form of employment, the number who actually do is low (Hannon, 2005). It was estimated that only 4 per cent of the 224 000 first degree UK graduates in 2002 became self-employed (ISBA, 2004). More recently the pace has accelerated; in 2012/13 graduates founded 3500 new companies, an increase of 68 per cent over the 2000 founded four years previously, according to one survey (Department for Business Innovation and Skills, 2014c). The amount of support for entrepreneurial activities within universities has increased substantially and seems to be producing results.

Environmental and alternative movements

The growth in numbers of small firms has coincided with an increased awareness of environmental and lifestyle issues, heralded as a **New Age** in the values of society. Struggling to meet their carbon emission targets, government bodies have encouraged the development of environmentally friendly businesses. Endorsing the philosophies of the Green movement, 'eco-preneurs' have sought to further the cause through new products and services. A variety of business opportunities have been developed including:

- recycling materials and waste;
- eco-friendly products made from local and sustainable materials;
- alternative medicine products and practitioners;
- health and organic food producers, wholesalers and retailers;
- trainers, writers, publishers and retailers selling materials on alternative themes; and
- producers and retailers of alternative beauty products.

While no statistics are available on the level of entrepreneurship created by the popularity of these activities, their impact has been noticeable in some small business areas; for example, the growth in number of worker co-operatives is partially explained by 'alternative' movements (see Chapter 10).

Activity 5

Which of the following statements about international small business trends do you think are true and which false?

(a) The numbers of one-person businesses are decreasing.
(b) Small firms create more jobs than big ones.
(c) European countries bordering the Mediterranean tend to have fewer small businesses than northern Europe.
(d) Employment in the USA is more concentrated in larger firms than in Europe.
(e) Entrepreneurship is not encouraged in China.

1.5 International comparisons

1.5.1 GLOBAL REVIVAL

International comparisons of statistics on small firms are very difficult because of the lack of common definitions and data sources (Storey, 1998). However, the increase in employment in small firms seems to have been a common feature of the economies of industrialized countries from the 1980s just as most had shown a decline in the sector prior to 1970. Small firms of fewer than 100 employees increased their overall share of total employment in France, Germany, Italy, Japan, the UK and the USA, which 'signifies the reversal of a substantial downward trend in the employment shares of small units that had prevailed for many decades' (Sengenberger, Loveman and Priore, 1990), although the rate of increase varied by country and industrial sector. There is evidence for this trend in all areas of the world. In Australia, there are an estimated 2.1 million businesses of which over 97 per cent are small or micro. Of the half million firms in New Zealand, 97 per cent are small (fewer than 20 employees) providing 54 per cent of total employment, although larger firms have increased their share in recent years. The numbers of self-employed in all of the Organization for Economic Co-operation and Development (OECD) countries declined as a percentage of total employment until the late 1970s, from which time they have increased steadily.

Global estimates indicate that SMEs account for over 95 per cent of enterprises, generate two-thirds of employment and are the main source of new jobs; new firms in any year account for around 5 per cent of all jobs in that year (OECD, 2005). As well as creating jobs, small businesses drive economic growth through their contribution to innovation and productivity improvements, particularly though the activities of entrepreneurial, knowledge-based firms (OECD, 2015). In most developed economies today, the small business population is continuing to grow in importance.

A current international trend is that small firms are getting smaller. Within the business population, there has been a steady increase in the numbers of firms who employ no other people, or which fall into the micro category of fewer than 10 employees. In the UK, there has been an increase in the number of firms comprising only the self-employed owner which now make up over 70 per cent of all businesses. These micro enterprises are also particularly common in Denmark, France, Ireland and New Zealand, where they make up at least 90 per cent of all businesses (OECD, 2000).

1.5.2 EUROPE

In 2013, there were almost 22 million[5] enterprises in Europe[6], providing over 130 million jobs.

Within the EU states there are variations in the relative contributions of SMEs to national economies (Eurostat, 2011). The relative importance of SMEs is particularly high in the Mediterranean states of Cyprus,

Table 1.3 **Profile of the European business population, 2013**

Size	No. of businesses%	Employment%	Added value%
MICRO	92.4	29.1	21.6
SMALL	6.4	20.6	18.2
MEDIUM	1	17.2	18.3
SME total	99.8	66.9	58.1
LARGE	0.2	33.1	41
TOTAL NUMBER	21.6 million	132.9 million	€6.4trillion

Source: European Commission, 2014.

Greece, Italy, Portugal and Spain, plus the Baltic states (Estonia, Latvia and Lithuania) and Bulgaria. In each of these countries, SMEs accounted for more than 75 per cent of the workforce, compared to the European average of 67 per cent. Some of these differences may be explained by the relative importance of particular sectors in each national economy, or by cultural preferences for family-run businesses and self-employment. Countries where employment is more concentrated in larger firms than the European average include Finland, France, Germany, Romania, Sweden and the UK (Eurostat, 2011).

The Bolton Report showed that the concentration of resources in large companies had gone further in the UK than anywhere else in Europe. The increase in small firms and in self-employment in the UK has subsequently been greater than in most of Europe but a comparison between employment and output measures of SMEs shows that the UK still lags behind the European average. Figure 1.3 indicates that although SMEs are overwhelmingly the most common business size (99.8 per cent of all business in Europe and the UK), they provide relatively less employment and added value in the UK.

Despite these variations within individual states, the overall picture, as summed up by the Observatory of European SMEs (2002, p. 4), is that SMEs are the 'real giants of the European economy'.

1.5.3 USA AND JAPAN

Employment in the USA is also more concentrated in larger companies than in Europe and Japan. The comparison of total number of SMEs shown in Table 1.4 indicates that there are a similar number in the USA (18.2 million) and Europe (21.6 million) with a smaller number in Japan (3.9 million). When this is adjusted to take into account the relative sizes of the three economies, the pattern looks similar with Japan behind the USA and Europe. This is largely a reflection of the numbers of micro firms which are less common in Japan (where 79 per cent of SMEs are micro compared to 95 per cent in the USA and 93 per cent in Europe). However, when it comes to employment, Japan is much more dependent on its SMEs, which account for 86 per cent of the workforce compared to 66 per cent in Europe and 52 per cent in the USA.

This has led to some debate about why the USA seems to exhibit a different profile to other developed countries (see Greene and Mole, 2006). A key factor that emerges is the importance of *dynamism* as well as the size distribution of the business population. The USA has higher numbers of fast-growth businesses helped by the size of the economy and a positive regulatory environment that encourages enterprise development. In the 1980s, Birch (1981) found that rapidly growing firms which he called 'gazelles' were responsible for most of the

Figure 1.3 Comparative profiles of SMEs in Europe and the UK[6]

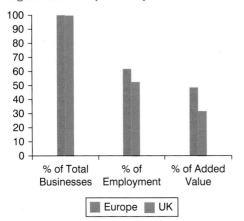

Sources: European Commission, 2014; Department for Business Innovation and Skills (2014a).

Table 1.4 SMEs in the USA, Japan and Europe

	USA	Japan	Europe
Total number of businesses (millions)	18.2	3.9	21.6
No. of SMEs per million GDP	1.6	0.9	1.65
Employment in SMEs per million GDP	4.4	7.2	6.8
SME % of total employment	52%	86%	67%

Source: European Commission, 2014.

national growth in employment. These findings were confirmed in a subsequent study that found that a small number of 'high impact firms' accounted for almost all the employment and revenue growth in the economy, yet represented only 2–3 per cent of all firms (Acs, Parsons and Tracy, 2008). This demonstrates that it is not only the number of SMEs that are important to an economy, but also their growth rates.

1.5.4 TRANSITION ECONOMIES

We have so far considered the role of small businesses mainly in the context of mature economies such as Europe, the USA and Japan. What role do SMEs play in economies at different stages of evolution?

Smallbone and Welter (2009) cite the following characteristics of a 'transition economy':

- economic assets and activities shift from predominantly public to private ownership;
- markets are opened up to competition rather than dominated by state-owned monopolies; and
- a supportive environment for business development is created including bank finance, intellectual property protection, and advice and help for new business entrants. Such changes assume that the necessary regulatory and legal framework exists to govern commercial activities such as business formation, contacts, competition and liquidation.

The countries of the former Soviet Union have been going through such changes since the fall of the Berlin Wall in 1989, with differing degrees of progress. East Germany was subsumed into West Germany's economic framework and now operates as part of the enlarged state of Germany, where the *Mittelstand* of small and medium-sized enterprises is a dominant economic force. In Poland and two-thirds Estonia, the private sector of largely small businesses now contributes three-quarters or more of national GDP in largely market-based economies.

In Russia and Ukraine, market reforms have been more mixed although the private sector now contributes two-thirds of the GDP and small businesses are encouraged and supported (Smallbone and Welter, 2009). However, SMEs still contribute only 20–25 per cent to Russia's GDP, much less than in other developed countries. The problems stem from the over-reliance on large organizations exploiting natural resources and the under-development of small business outside the European part of Russia (European Investment Bank, 2013). This has not gone unnoticed; the government announced a significant stimulus package for SMEs in 2014 and the sector is now growing more strongly. Belarus has made least changes to its economy with only one-quarter of its GDP contributed by the private sector and with few market reforms.

1.5.5 EMERGING ECONOMIES

According to the World Bank, there are 125 million 'formal' SMEs in 132 economies around the world. Of these, 89 million are in emerging economies in Africa, Asia and South America. Countries with higher income per capita tend to have relatively more SMEs; in all of sub-Saharan Africa, there are only an estimated 13 million

(Kushnir, Mirmulstein and Ramalho, R., 2010). A good indicator of a growing economy is an increase in the small business population, as evidenced by the two most populous nations on earth.

China emerged from the economic disasters of the Cultural Revolution from 1978 when party leaders decided to undertake gradual reform of the system, not by abandoning communism as the Soviet bloc later did, but by increasing the role of market mechanisms within a controlled communist state. A key decision was the creation of Special Economic Zones in the coastal cities to encourage the expansion of international trade and co-operation (Anyansi-Archibong, 1989). These helped the industrialization process that saw the number of businesses in China increase from less than 500 000 in 1986 to 3.6 million in 2003 with a further 27.9 million individuals running their own household business in the country. Between 2003 and 2013, SMEs increased their contribution from 56 to 60 per cent of GDP and from 75 to 80 per cent of jobs (Small Business Trends, 2004; Ping, 2013). Although corporate governance amongst Chinese SMEs is still cited as a problem, in 2015 the government re-confirmed their support with specific strategies for the sector in the 12th Five Year Plan.

India initially put its faith in the public sector to tackle its huge poverty problems after it gained independence in 1947. However, extensive bureaucratic controls stifled enterprise with an industrial licensing system that required approval from the Ministry of Industries before individual investments in new ventures could be made. The New Industrial Policy of 1991 changed the system radically, encouraging the private sector and liberalizing the economy. This has allowed entrepreneurs to flourish such as Rata Tata of Tata Motors; Narayana Murthy, a co-founder of Infosys; Sunil Mittal of the Bharti Group, originator of the mobile phone industry in India; and M.S. Oberoi, who transformed the hotel industry. Through the National Institute for Entrepreneurship and Small Business Development (NIESBUD), the government is now actively promoting the growth of entrepreneurship though training and support. SMEs now contribute 40 per cent of India's GDP and they are the second-largest source of employment after agriculture.

THE CASE OF BHUTAN

Bhutan, a tiny kingdom of 700 000 people wedged high up in the Himalayas between China and India, has initiated a new way of gauging successful development. Alongside economic measures such as Gross National Product (GNP), the Bhutanese government considers the impact of its activities according to an index of Gross National Happiness (GNH). This concept has attracted international interest since it was first announced by Bhutan's fourth King, Jigme Singye Wangchuck, in the 1970s because it focuses on non-economic aspects of well-being such as preserving cultural values, conservation of the natural environment and good governance. As a result, the country has declared it will be carbon neutral and 100 per cent organic with afforestation levels above 60 per cent of the landmass for all time to come. The King also renounced his absolute power and introduced a parliamentary democracy when he abdicated in favour of his son Jigme Namgyel Wangchuck, who thus became head of a new constitutional monarchy in 2008.

Such initiatives are normally the preserve of wealthier nations that can afford the luxury of environmental protection and social welfare. Yet Bhutan has one of the world's smallest and least-developed economies. Until a few decades ago, it was largely agrarian, with few roads and little electricity. Today it is undergoing rapid changes that could threaten its adherence to GNH. Its traditional economy based on agriculture was changing slowly with the introduction of private-sector service enterprises such as eco-tourism. But the development of hydro-electric power sold to India from its mountainous rivers and lakes has accelerated the pace of change. An ambitious plan to build 74 dams by 2020 could give Bhutan the industrial export base it needs to develop

(Continued)

strong economic growth. Inevitably it will also add to pollution and impact on the environment. It will increase dependency on India as the projects are undertaken mainly by large companies, using Indian labour, financed by Indian banks. This may distort the business population with more reliance on large power corporations rather than dynamic small enterprise. So far the developments have done little to alleviate the high levels of unemployment amongst the country's young people. The country may soon face difficult choices as GNH and GDP collide. Could this potential conflict be alleviated if the country's entrepreneurs develop more small businesses, or would this exacerbate the problems with even faster economic development?

1.5.6 AFRICA

It was not by accident that the visit by American President Barak Obama to Africa in 2015 began with his attendance at a Global Entrepreneurship Summit in Kenya. He wanted to emphasize the critical role that SMEs can play in stimulating development and alleviating poverty in the continent. Historically, the private sector has not been well developed in Africa where economies have suffered from over-dependence on agriculture, poor governance and centralized control. For decades, Africa has been plagued by protracted crises that have exacerbated unemployment and poverty and ushered in a vicious cycle of under-development. Economic growth rates of sub-Saharan African countries were around 2 per cent in the 1970s but plummeted into decline during the 1980s and 1990s as Africa's share of world trade dropped from 2.7 per cent in 1990 to 2.0 per cent in 2002 (Edoho, 2015).

As President Obama emphasized, Africa is now 'on the move', home to several of the fastest growing economies in the world such as Kenya, Nigeria and Ethiopia. After decades of negative or stuttering growth, SMEs have recovered to comprise over 90 per cent of African business operations and contribute to over 50 per cent of African employment and GDP (Ramukumba, 2014). For this growth to become sustainable, the problem of the 'missing middle' will need to be solved. Africa's business environment consists mostly of informal micro-enterprises operating alongside large firms, with insufficient small and medium-sized businesses in between. For example, in South Africa, one of the more developed economies, micro and large enterprises provide nearly 90 per cent of GDP while small and medium-sized firms account for just over 10 per cent. This weakness stems from small, localized markets that suffer from a lack of regional integration and a difficult business environment that does not encourage significant investment. It also leads to a less robust SME sector with an exceptionally high failure rate; as many as 70 per cent of the country's SMEs fail in their first year (as reported by the Minister of Trade and Industry in SBP, 2014).

ENTERPRISING ETHIOPIA

Ethiopia was thrust into the consciousness of Western society when images of starving children were shown on television during the droughts of 1985 and prompted Bob Geldof to launch Live Aid, a fundraising venture by musical superstars. Three decades later, the International Monetary Fund (IMF) ranks Ethiopia as one of the fastest-growing economies in Africa with an annual GDP growth rate averaging 10.8 per cent (African Economic Outlook, 2015). However, large and better-established firms are more important as net job creators than small and younger firms. Many small businesses sell the services of one individual rather than creating jobs. As a result, Ethiopia's young people find it hard to get jobs, even in an economy that is growing quickly.

Enterprising Ethiopia was founded to teach entrepreneurial and business start-up skills to young, tech-savvy workers and an increasing number of graduates who aspire to create jobs rather than just be given one. It works to enable the country's current and future entrepreneurs to create growth companies, providing jobs for others as well as themselves through training and support.

Mussie Gebremedhn tells his story:

I am 41 years old and have completed my training with Enterprising Ethiopia and I will get my 1st degree (BSc.) in law in the summer of 2014. But I also own a coffee and pastry shop and in addition I have a shop that sells building materials. So I consider myself to be a business entrepreneur. My businesses are successful, especially the coffee shop and now my wife is exercising to run the business. I have pushed her to get a diploma in accounting and now she is continuing to degree level. So she is better at account-ing than me. The building materials shop is OK but it needs huge investment to be able to provide all kinds of building materials. It is time for change. The most important thing I have learned from Enterprising Ethiopia is the importance of growing my business. The mindset in Ethiopia is mostly thinking inside the box: you open a business, you get an amount of money and you are satisfied. There is no ambition. But the Enterprising Ethiopia training taught me that through differentiation and through good management you could grow and develop your business in new ways. And I have learned how to be visionary. The number of things I can do have increased and now there are no limits. I have a lot more self-confidence; I can travel to different countries in Europe and Asia and import materials; I have learned the importance of saving up money and investing in the business, how to handle customers and how to make the business sustainable.

Activity 6
A rough ride?

The next section describes the 'churn' rate in the small business sector. Do you think this means:

(a) The degree to which small businesses milk their customers?
(b) The amount of agitation felt by an owner about their small enterprise?
(c) The number of small businesses that leave the sector?

1.6 Entrepreneurial churn in the business population

1.6.1 BUSINESS CHURN

The total number of businesses active in an economy is crucially affected by the number of new ventures being created on the one hand and the number of businesses that close down on the other – referred to as business **churn**. At any one time, a large number of new ventures are in the process of being formed and many others are being shut down: as many as 50 million new businesses may start each year around the world and a similar number may close (Bosma *et al.*, 2009). The total population of businesses in an economy can be relatively stable for considerable periods of time. In the UK, the business population was relatively stable around 3.5 million for the decade 1992–2002. But even in such a long period when the total population was neither growing nor declining, there was turbulence beneath the surface. This is happening in most developed economies at relatively high rates. In the UK, there were 425 000 start-ups (9.5 per cent of the total population) and 490 000 closures (10.9 per cent) in 2007 so that the business population contracted slightly during the year (Barclays Bank, 2008). From 2008 this trend continued as the recession in the economy developed but in 2013 births rose to 14 per cent and closures fell to 10 per cent signalling the end to the downturn and a return to strong growth of the sector. This pattern was particularly marked in London which recorded 84 000 births that year and 50 000 closures (Rhodes, 2015).

Start-up and closure rates of around 10 per cent of the total population are fairly typical of most developed economies in normal economic conditions. Some countries are higher: the USA has typically had a high start-up and closure rate of around 15 per cent (Headd, 2003); Australia exhibited a 17 per cent start-up rate and a 15 per cent closure rate in 2007 in a total business population of 2 million (Australian Bureau of Statistics, 2007). Several European countries, including Italy, Portugal, Finland and Sweden, have had somewhat lower start-up rates of 6–7 per cent (Vale, 2006). Developing economies often exhibit higher closure rates; for example, South Africa has an exceptionally high closure rate, with as many as 70 per cent of SMEs not surviving after one year (SBP, 2014). The percentages may vary but in total it means that a very large number of enterprises start up and close down every year. Small business is a turbulent sector with huge movements in and out.[6]

1.6.2 ENTREPRENEURIAL INTERPRETATIONS OF CHURN

This movement in and out of the business population is central to the role of the small business sector in the economy. (It is also crucial to the process of entrepreneurship as discussed in the next chapter.) Interpretations of the effects of churn vary according to one's standpoint as there is a trade-off between negative socio-economic consequences of business closure and the positive competitive effect of new ventures that replace less efficient existing firms. Thus, churn can be viewed in different ways:

- *Negative effects* At the social and micro-economic levels of individual business owners, large numbers of closures may be a turbulent process for firms and employees with job losses and personal trauma for those involved. At a more macro-economic level, business closures are also disruptive to supply chains, business networks and the labour market. However, not all closures can be considered failures and it is important to distinguish between businesses that close leaving indebtedness and those that close for more positive reasons. This is a theme which is developed in Chapter 3.
- *Positive benefits* From the viewpoint of the regional and national economy, business churn helps to renew and improve the competitiveness of the business stock. A process of natural selection operates in competitive markets. High-performing firms take market share and customers away from other businesses which may be forced to close as a consequence. If businesses survive and thrive because they are more innovative and efficient and they provide superior customer service, a healthier population of businesses and managers should result from this increased competition. In this way, churn is desirable as it is a sign that market mechanisms are working in favour of better-performing, innovative firms and against those that are less productive and unwilling to change.

A low churn rate with a small percentage of business start-ups and closures is often a sign of restricted competition, lack of incentives to invest and innovate and high barriers to new business entry. On the other hand, a high churn rate is usually symptomatic of a more entrepreneurial economy in which new ventures with novel products and processes force out complacent competitors or stimulate them to improve and innovate in order to remain competitive. As this indicates, high rates of churn are often associated with stronger economic growth. An economy that is growing relatively quickly exhibits a higher start-up rate; more start-ups lead to more closures as many new ventures do not last very long and so churn is increased. For example, Australia exhibited relatively high rates of churn (over 15 per cent start-up and closure rates) at a time when its GDP was growing at 3–4 per cent per annum from 2003–07 (Australian Bureau of Statistics, 2007). In times of economic downturn, closures continue at high rates or accelerate while start-ups slow down so that the total business population declines and economic growth is depressed further.

Another important influence on the health of an economy is the *rate of growth* of firms once they have been launched. This was first mentioned in Section 1.5.2 above as a factor that possibly explains why US firms have a larger average size than their European counterparts. In a multi-country comparison, Bartelsman *et al.* (2005) found that survival rates for new entrants were low in all countries but in the USA surviving new firms tended to grow faster than European firms. This may have been the result of a business environment which encouraged greater experimentation in the USA with easier availability of finance for risky projects, lower costs to set up a business and lower exit costs (e.g. reducing staff numbers) for firms whose experiments did not succeed.

1.7 Summary and activities

This chapter has investigated the importance of small businesses in macro-economic terms. Although small businesses are notoriously difficult to define from an external perspective (for example, in compiling meaningful statistical data on the sector), it is easier to identify the social and resource issues that differentiate running a small enterprise from those of a larger corporation. In the early days of the development of management theory, small businesses were overlooked in favour of large companies capable of taking advantage of international markets and mass production. Today, there is a much greater emphasis on the entrepreneurial economy. Small businesses have proven to be the key to economic growth and fuller employment since the 1980s. During that time, the numbers of micro and small businesses have increased substantially, and their share of national sales and employment has grown accordingly. Many factors have contributed to this: the growth of the service economy, the use of information technology that has enabled smaller firms to match some of the economies of scale and international reach of the larger corporations, customer expectations for flexible products and services tailored more precisely to their needs, the use of subcontractors by large corporates refocusing on their core competencies, the reorganization of public services to include more private provision of services, the encouragement of an enterprise culture and the influence of New Age thinking. SMEs are playing an increasingly important role in the transition economies of the former Soviet Union and developing economies such as China and India.

However, the small business sector remains turbulent with high levels of churn in the business stock. Large numbers of small businesses start up every year and an equally large number close down. High churn rates cause individual disruption but are indicators of an entrepreneurial economy.

Case study
A tale of two entrepreneurs: Part 1

INTRODUCTION

This is an ongoing case study to illustrate the processes which nascent (would-be) entrepreneurs might go through before starting up a small business. The story is developed through the next five chapters so that each situation can be followed in its subsequent stages. While this continuation of the story may indicate what happened next, do not assume that

(Continued)

the decisions described are examples of best practice, or that they are the best possible decisions in the circumstances. Your advice may well be wiser!

Andrea thinks small

Andrea Clarey had a decision to make about her career. She was the manager in charge of the payroll function in the accounts department of a government authority. Although no formal announcement had been made, it was strongly rumoured that the authority would soon be contracting out more of its central services, and that the payroll would be one of them. When this had happened in other areas, the options for individuals in Andrea's position were usually either to seek transfer to another department within the authority, take redundancy and look for employment elsewhere, or form an organization to put in a bid for the work that was being contracted out. Andrea had been employed by the authority for a few years and would qualify for a redundancy payment. However, she was a qualified bookkeeper and her management qualities were appreciated by other departmental heads, some of whom had already approached her unofficially to see if she would be interested in moving into their departments. While she liked the security of her monthly pay cheque, pension scheme, health insurance and other benefits, Andrea found her current work lacking in real challenges and she disliked the impersonal, bureaucratic methods of the organization and its political infighting. The independence of running her own business had some real attractions for her, especially if she could win the authority's contract to give her a flying start.

To Andrea's surprise, when she discussed the idea with her husband, John, he was immediately supportive of it.

'It's about time you got out of the rut you're in at work. If I could get a big enough redundancy package, I'd join you myself. Quite a few of my colleagues have become self-employed as consultants or specialist suppliers to large organizations. It's a major trend in the way we work – the days of working for large organizations and multinational corporations for life are over. Now we can become entrepreneurs, putting our own ideas into action, creating work for ourselves – not waiting for someone else to do it for us', John said.

'Yes, but I'll be earning less to begin with', Andrea had started to explain when her father came in to see them.

After Andrea had outlined her options to him, he took a less sympathetic line towards self-employment. 'It's out of the frying pan into the fire. You'll end up working for a big organization whatever you do – either as supplier or employee. Either way they stay in control of you, small business or not. The only difference working in a small firm is that you'll get paid less for it, and have to work harder. No unions. No negotiating power if your suppliers want to put up their prices or the bank calls in its overdraft. Big business will have you where they want you.'

Andrea was further confused when she met an old school friend who had started her own business. 'My only advice is don't do it unless you can test the idea in some way to make sure it will work. Otherwise it's just not worth the risk. I am just about making ends meet now, and this is my second attempt. All that I have to show from my first business is a much larger mortgage.'

Andrea began to realize that small business could lead to some big issues.

Kit thinks beautiful

Kit Hugos was a sales engineer in a large company supplying electronic components. Previously he had worked for a small business, TronTech, involved in the design and manufacture of specialized electronic circuitry. Although he had enjoyed the flexibility and informality of the working environment, he had become very uncertain of the longer-term viability of TronTech after a failed diversification attempt and a struggle for power between the two principal shareholders. Rather than wait for what he considered to be the inevitable collapse of the business, Kit had decided to try a more conventional career in a large blue chip organization.

But his past revisited him when Robin Davidson rang one day. He was one of the founders of TronTech, who had evidently been ousted by the other shareholders. 'Are you interested in running your own business?' Davidson asked. 'I want to set up in business again but I need a partner, someone to run the business on a day-to-day basis, as I am going to take a less active role.'

The two agreed to meet to discuss the idea. It had always been Kit's long-term aim to have his own business – but with a difference. He had seen how groups of high-tech companies in some areas worked together to compete with larger companies. These networks of small firms each provided a complete stage in the production process, but their individuality and small size made them more flexible in responding to customers' requirements. When he explained this concept to Davidson, he was less enthusiastic. 'In principle it's a nice idea. But in my experience it doesn't work as ideally as you describe. There can be co-operation between small firms, but in our industry we still tend to work for larger companies who make and market the final product. It's with them you have to co-operate first and foremost. Anything else is a bonus.'

Kit had another ideal. He wanted his own business to operate in an environmentally friendly way and not use some of the damaging processes he had seen elsewhere. Again, Davidson took a more pragmatic approach. 'Sure – as long as it doesn't push our prices up and lose business.'

Kit wondered if small was going to be less than beautiful.

Activities

(a) From these two cases draw up a 'balance sheet' of the pros and cons of running a small business. List on one side what you consider to be the positive aspects and on the other, the negative.

(b) Advise Andrea and Kit on what to do next. How should they go about assessing their various options?

(c) If you were in their positions what would your decision be – to stay in large organizations or to make the move into small business?

Case study
Workspace Group plc

INTRODUCTION

Many businesses and not-for-profit organizations exist because of what they offer or sell to small businesses. In this sense, the small business sector has itself stimulated the creation of many new ventures. The business-to-business service sector has grown rapidly to become one of the largest areas of the national economy, partly fuelled by the increase in numbers of small businesses that require services of many different types.

One example is Workspace Group plc, home for many new and growing companies in London. Its development reflects many of the changes in the fortune of the small business sector that it serves. Established in 1987 from the privatization of the former Greater London Council's property portfolio, Workspace was an experimental venture to provide much-needed, affordable working space for smaller businesses from

(Continued)

under-utilized, industrial buildings. The experiment succeeded. The company developed rapidly, acquiring new properties to provide homes for small businesses at a time when their numbers were growing fast. In 1993, Workspace joined the London Stock Exchange and used its capital base to expand its portfolio of commercial estates focused on London. Today, Workspace has some 90 properties that house 4000 business customers in London that in turn employ over 30 000 people, and the company has a healthy pipeline of new projects to ensure it is constantly responding to the needs of its small business customer base.

In some respects, the Workspace Group represents a microcosm of the small business universe. Of the UK's 5.2 million enterprises, London, alone, is home to nearly one million of them. The vast majority are very small businesses: 78 per cent of London's business population employs no one except the owner; 14 per cent have between 1 and 9 employees. Almost all Workspace's tenants are micro businesses although most have at least 1 employee. Research in 2005 identified that 60 per cent employed between 1 and 9 people, and most were young firms for whom Workspace offered the 'flexible, affordable workspace' that they required as they grew.

More recently, the company has responded to a further shift in the London business base and its needs. The relative importance of the various industrial sectors in London is changing with the rapid growth of digital businesses that have helped the regional economy grow at a faster rate than other areas of the country. Recognizing that new and growing businesses in the digital economy have different needs to traditional small firms, Workspace has revisited its service delivery model so that it can provide space 'where customers grow faster'. Clients are no longer seen just as individual tenants but members of a vibrant business community that thrives on interconnections amongst themselves as well as the outside world. Typical Workspace premises now centre on communal spaces and cafés where entrepreneurs can meet and network with fellow business owners. As a result, 12 per cent of tenants purchase from each other and 17 per cent sell to other businesses in the same centre. Digital platforms provide communal Wi-Fi and IT support while regular events provide opportunities for networking and business support. The centre managers, who traditionally spent half their time looking after the premises, now spend all of their time with tenants as a facilities team has taken over the buildings. Start-ups can share facilities at 'Club Workspace', incubator spaces for creative, co-working businesses that take off rapidly or disappear just as fast; (members of the club have a 110 per cent churn rate compared to 25 per cent across the rest of the tenant base).

Many of the tenants have created new ventures that are typical of the hundreds of thousands of small businesses that start up in the economy every year. Two of these illustrate some of the issues involved.

Dave Chaplin – ContractorCalculator.co.uk

Dave Chaplin has lived and breathed contracting since becoming a professional contractor in 1997 and spent seven years working as an IT contractor in the City of London on critical, cutting-edge IT infrastructure and development projects. He launched ContractorCalculator.co.uk, an online advice and support resource for contractors and freelancers, in 2004. He describes his experiences in starting and growing his business as follows:

> The initial catalyst was the proposed introduction of new tax legislation (called IR35) in November 1999 which sought to tax contractors as if they were employees. At the time I was an IT contractor and figured that other contractors would want to know the effect on their finances of the legislation. So I created the first ever 'IR35 Tax Calculator' and released it on IR35Calc.co.uk. The scope of the site expanded over the years and was rebranded as ContractorCalculator.co.uk in 2004.
>
> At school I started a record-selling business and car-washing business, amongst others. After graduating with an MSc aged 22 I was an employee for just three years before deciding to do my own thing and

go contracting. I'm much happier as captain of my own ship and being in charge of my own professional destiny. That pretty much means I can't have a boss!

There was little initial investment required, other than buying a web space for a few hundred pounds. The main outlay was my time to do the website development. The site was a hobby site for a few years before I decided to turn it into a proper business. For six months I worked eight hours a day for clients as an IT contractor, and another eight hours a day (including every weekend) on building the business. Then I quit contracting and had enough money saved to cover the first six months. It took two years before I was earning the same as contracting. It was hard graft for years, but the reward was worth it. Initially the site was marketed by word of mouth. Its uniqueness and demand for information meant that our audience spread the word.

The biggest challenges were:

- *Learning business skills: Sales, marketing, account management, accounting, financial planning and accounting. I read an awful lot of books, and learnt from many experiences along the way. In later years we hired consultants to help us on some processes.*
- *Maintaining focus and drive: Working solitarily from a home office with no one else setting deadlines can result in drifting. From day one I set annual and quarterly targets across all areas of the business, and made sure I stuck to them. I've told myself off a few times!*
- *Finding time: Regular monthly tasks for running a business increase as it grows, leaving little time for further growth-based tasks. Typically, a business will hire employees. Instead I became obsessed with process and automated anything and everything I could.*

Clippy McKenna – Clippy's

Clippy McKenna founded Clippy's in 2008, one of the UK's fastest growing food brands that supplies leading UK stores including Tesco, Morrisons, Asda, John Lewis, Harvey Nichols, Fortnum & Mason and Ocado. The company offers a range of British apple-based jellies, conserves, chutneys and relishes. She was named Entrepreneur of the Year in the 2012 Inspiring Women Awards.

Food has always been part of my life. At school I was drawn to the smells, tastes and sights of home economics classes and I loved working at the food counters in Woolworths. At university, I worked in the food halls at Selfridges and Harvey Nichols and my essays and dissertations were always focused on food-based subjects. Clippy's came to be when I was in the process of applying to Manchester University to study a PhD in sustainability and food networks; the focus of the PhD was the British apple and why we have lost two-thirds of British orchards to commercial properties and 'cash crops'. I thought

(Continued)

to myself at the time, who is going to read an 80 000-word dissertation when I could actually make products with British apples and sell them myself.

My vision from day one was for the Clippy's brand to become a UK household name. I wanted to create products to invigorate sleepy categories, such as jam and chutney, with innovative flavour combinations which are naturally versatile. I wanted to create a company that was not faceless but had a real story to tell. This explains why my face and the Clippy story are on every jar, and partly why I think we have been so successful.

As a young business we do not have the fiscal power of the heavyweights to compete on the same sort of scale. We do not have the multi-million pound resources to pay for TV adverts or double page spreads in magazines and national newspapers. However, what we do have is a core mission to ensure that we are not another faceless brand but instead a breath of fresh air for what has been a very stagnant market. We have to be clever with our campaigns to engage our audiences through the likes of our JamJamboree – a celebration of all things jammy and our commitment to championing the British apple.

The business is 100 per cent self-funded. It started with two apple trees from my back garden and £100 to purchase a preserves recipe book, a pan and a wooden spoon. I knew that in order to survive I would need to grow the company substantially from day one. I purchased Sage accounts to run the business and barcodes from GS1-UK. At the time it was a lot of hard work, you take it for granted that all these things take time to implement. I also persuaded my fiancé Paul to give up his well-paid job and commit his time to help grow the business and we haven't looked back since.

The biggest challenge facing the industry is that the sector is completely stagnant; there is no innovation so we've taken it upon ourselves to take the market by the scruff of the neck and develop a totally unique brand as well as a versatile, fashionable product.

If anything the downturn has worked in our favour. With people less inclined to eat out, consumers look for those special products available in supermarkets that give their dishes a much needed boost in days of such gloom. In addition, we wholeheartedly support British apples, have a fair price point and our product is a great healthy alternative to the sugar-laden options available on the shelves. Our conserves have more fresh fruit than any other jam, conserve or fruit spread. When people buy Clippy's they know they are getting a wholesome treat from a British family business using quality British apples.

The biggest and most long-established challenge is one of belief. Time and time again, I find that getting people to take me and the product seriously is a common hurdle. As the business grows and develops this becomes less of an issue as the results speak for themselves. The most powerful way to defy the cynics is to present them with your accomplishments then they quickly pipe down!

Clippy's started at the height of the 2008 recession, a year in which I also became pregnant! I joked at the time that it would be lovely to be pregnant and cook jam in my cauldron, how wrong I was – Clippy's took off and took over. It is not a working job; it is a lifestyle.

Activities

(a) In what respects are the Workspace tenants a microcosm of the small business sector? What are some of the similarities and differences to the national profile of the small businesses population? Do they differ from international trends?

(b) How do the case histories of the two tenants:
  (i)   demonstrate the differences between small and larger businesses; and
  (ii) illustrate the reasons for the growth of the small business sector?

Below is an activity which, unlike earlier tasks, is not designed to be done while reading the book or sitting at a desk. It extends beyond the classroom or home and requires you to investigate the world of small enterprise in your local environment by investigating your local community and the small businesses within it.

Extended activity
Food and drink

Consider the local community with which you are most familiar. Draw up a list of the types of businesses which provide food and drink to this community. This should include take-away food and drink which is to be consumed in the home or elsewhere, as well as food and drink consumed on the premises. For example, your list should include such categories as supermarkets, fast food restaurants, off-licences and other business types.

In each of the categories you have listed, write down the names of some of the businesses actually operating in this category.

Now try to divide them into small or large enterprises (you may also need a medium-sized category).

This data can be used in subsequent activities, so try to include as many local businesses as possible. Now try to answer the following questions:

(a) In each of your categories, which is the predominant business size – small or large? What are the trends in terms of size – towards smaller or larger enterprises?

(b) What are the particular contributions those small businesses make to the local economy? Are these contributions increasing or decreasing in importance in your experience?

(c) Try and talk to some of the small business owners and ask for their views on the competition they have from larger companies (for example, the corner shop trader's view of the major supermarkets).

Through this activity, we invite you to develop an idea for a new business into a full business plan by the end of the book. At the end of each chapter, this activity can be used to progress your own entrepreneurial venture through the various stages from opportunity identification to the full planning of the business. You are asked at the end of each chapter to undertake a particular step in this process, linked to the subject matter of the chapter. Worksheets to help you complete each step are available on the website.

Planning a new venture
Outlining the process

These steps are illustrated in Figure 1, Planning a new venture, in the Preface. In summary, they develop an opportunity in three principal stages linked to the three Parts of the book.

- By the end of Chapter 5, you will have completed an initial *evaluation of your opportunity* that takes it from a position of unknown risk to one of reasonable prospects.
- By the end of Chapter 10, you will have defined the business strategy and selected a suitable route to market. This is summarized as *a feasibility study*.

(Continued)

- By the end of Chapter 14, you will have planned the details of operating and managing the business as an acceptable risk. This is summarized as *the business plan*.

In Chapters 2–5, you will be taken first through the process of improving your understanding of your personal aims and abilities in relation to entrepreneurship.

This is linked to the identification of an idea for a new venture to ensure there is a good match. The specific opportunity is clearly identified and evaluated through research in order to establish if it has reasonable prospects. You will, meanwhile, be encouraged to adopt a creative mindset that can tolerate further change (and associated uncertainty) as you progress with your idea.

It is important to undertake these activities at the end of each chapter in order to reinforce the learning of the chapter and to ensure that the opportunity is developed progressively through the entrepreneurship process.

1.8 Notes, references and recommended further reading

Notes and further information

1 The UK government's Department for Business, Innovation and Skills (BIS) was formed in 2009 as a result of a reorganization of two former departments – the Department for Business, Enterprise and Regulatory Reform (BERR), and the Department for Innovation, Universities and Skills (DIUS) – which themselves were created from the former Department of Trade and Industry (DTI) that existed from 1983–2007. In July 2016, BIS was changed to the Department for Business, Energy and Industrial Strategy.

2 The USA Small Business Administration (SBA) is the agent of the federal government with the responsibility to 'aid, counsel, assist and protect the interests of small business concerns, to preserve free competitive enterprise and to maintain and strengthen the overall economy of our nation' (see the website www.sba.gov).

3 For example, in the UK the *Guardian* introduced a 'New Business' section every Monday, edited by Clive Woodcock in the 1980s. Today, many papers including the *Sunday Times* and the *Daily Mail* run a small business section and become involved in national awards and promotions for entrepreneurs.

4 This number illustrates the confusion in international comparisons of SME data as it includes fewer UK enterprises than reported in the UK government's statistics. The difference is likely to be in the definitions of what constitutes an enterprise (e.g. the use of part-time businesses in the UK data versus full-time sole occupation businesses in the European data).

5 'Europe' here comprises 28 states following a number of processes of EU enlargement. The UK voted to leave the EU in the summer of 2016.

6 Governments around the world are increasingly providing statistical data on the business population which can be accessed via websites. For example:
- UK: the Enterprise Directorate, now part of BIS (see note 1) at: data.gov.uk/dataset/small_and_medium_sized_enterprise_statistics_sme_for_the_uk_and_regions. It contains SME data including the annual survey 'Small and Medium Enterprise (SME) Statistics for the UK and Regions' which gives a breakdown of the business population by business size, employment and turnover (as shown in Table 1.3). This includes estimates of one-person businesses and self-employment not commonly found elsewhere.
- Europe: The European Commission collects data which can be accessed from their website ec.europa.eu/growth/smes/index_en.htm. It has an Executive Agency for Small and Medium-sized Enterprises (EASME) to manage several EU programmes.
- USA: The Small Business Administration acts as a source for statistics as well as the office of advocacy for small businesses at: www.sba.gov/advo/research/
- Australia: Australian Bureau of Statistics at www.abs.gov.au/AUSSTATS
- New Zealand: New Zealand Ministry of Economic Development at www.med.govt.nz

References

Acs, Z., Parsons, W. and Tracy, S. (2008) High impact firms: Gazelles revisited, *Small Business Research Summary*. No. 328, June, Small Business Administration, USA.

African Economic Outlook (2015) www .africaneconomicoutlook.org/en/country-notes/east -africa/ethiopia/

Anyansi-Archibong, C. B. (1989) Small business in China's special economic zones. *Journal of Small Business Management*, 27, 1989.

Australian Bureau of Statistics (2007) *Counts of Australian Businesses*, 2003–2007, (www.abs.gov.au/AUSSTATS).

Bannock, G. and Daly, M. (1994) *Small Business Statistics*, PCP.

Barclays Bank (2004) *Small Business Survey: Start-ups and Closure, 2003,* Barclays Commercial, London.

Barclays Bank (2008) *Business Customer Economic Focus,* Barclays Commercial, London. www.business .barclays.co.uk/BBB/A/Content/Files/EconomicFocus .pdf.

Bartelsman, E., Haltiwanger, J. and Scarpetta, S. (2005) Measuring and analysing cross-country differences in firm dynamics, Paper presented to *NBER Conference on Research in Income and Wealth*, 8–9 April 2005.

Birch, D. (1981) Who Creates Jobs?, *The Public Interest*, 65: 3–14.

Blackburn, R. and Curran, J. (1989) The Future of the Small Firm: Attitudes of Young People to Entrepreneurship, Paper to *12th UK Small Firms Policy and Research Conference.*

Bolton Report (1971) *Committee of Inquiry on Small Firms*, HMSO, Cmnd 4811.

Bosma, N., Acs, Z.J., Autio, E., Coduras, A. and Levie, J. (2009) *Global Entrepreneurship Monitor 2008 Executive Report,* Babson College, Universidad del Desarrollo, London Business School, www.gemconsortium.org /download/1233669410187/GEM_Global_08.pdf

Centre for Strategy & Evaluation (2012) *Evaluation of the SME Definition*, Final Report, Sevenoaks, UK, September.

Curran, J. (1997) *The Role of the Small Firm in the UK Economy,* SBRC, Kingston University.

Curran, J. and Blackburn, R. A. (1994) *Small Business and Local Economic Networks*, PCP.

Curran, J. and Blackburn, R. A. (2001) *Researching the Small Enterprise,* Sage Publications.

Curran, J., Blackburn, R. A. and Woods, A. (1991) *Profiles of the Small Enterprise in the Service Sector,* ESRC Centre for Research on Small Service Sector Enterprises, Kingston Polytechnic.

Curran, J. and Stanworth, J. (1987) The Small Firm – A Neglected Area of Management. In: Cowling, A., Stanworth, M., Bennett, R., Curran, J. and Lyons, P. (eds) *Behavioural Sciences for Managers,* Edward Arnold.

Department for Business Innovation and Skills (2014a) *Business Population Estimates for the UK and Regions 2014: Detailed Tables*, London, November.

Department for Business Innovation and Skills (2014b) *Business Population Estimates for the UK and Regions 2014: Statistical Release*, London, November.

Department for Business Innovation and Skills (2014c) *Higher Education – Business and Community Interaction Survey 2012–13*, HEFCE May 2014/10.

Drucker, P. (1986) *Innovation and Entrepreneurship*, Heinemann.

Edoho, F. M. (2015) Entrepreneurship paradigm and economic renaissance in Africa, *African Journal of Economic and Management Studies*, 6(3): 2–16.

European Commission (2014) *Annual Report on European SMEs 2013/2014 – A Partial and Fragile Recovery*, Final Report, July.

European Investment Bank (2013) *Small and Medium Entrepreneurship in Russia*, 7th November, Luxembourg.

Eurostat (2011) *Key Figures on European Business with a Special Feature on SMEs,* Eurostat Pocketbooks, European Commission.

Goss, D. (1991) *Small Business and Society,* Routledge. See ch. 1, Theories of Small Business and Society

Greene, F. and Mole, K. (2006) Defining and Measuring the Small Business. In: Carter, S. and Jones-Evans, D. *Enterprise and Small Business*, 2nd edn, Financial Times/Prentice Hall.

Hakim, C. (1989) New Recruits to Self-employment in the 1980s. *Employment Gazette*, HMSO, June.

Hannon, P. (2005) The Journey from Student to Entrepreneur: A Review of the Existing Research into Graduate Entrepreneurship. *IntEnt Conference Conference Proceedings,* University of Surrey.

Headd, B. (2003) Redefining business success: Distinguishing between closure and failure. *Small Business Economics*, 21: 51–61.

ISBA (2004) The Journey from Student to Entrepreneur. *Report to the National Council for Graduate Entrepreneurship*, ISBA and UCE, September.

Kushnir, K., Mirmulstein, M. L. and Ramalho R. (2010) *Micro, Small, and Medium Enterprises Around the World: How Many Are There, and What Affects the Count?* MSME Country Indicators, The World Bank.

Levie, J. and Hart, M. (2009) *Global Entrepreneurship Monitor: UK 2008 Monitoring Report,* Aston Business School.

Observatory of European SMEs (2002) *SMEs in Focus: Main Results from the 2002 Observatory of European SMEs,* European Commission.

Observatory of European SMEs (2003) *SMEs in Europe* Observatory of European SMEs 2003, No. 7, European Commission.

OECD (2000) Small and Medium Enterprise Outlook, OECD Publishing, Paris.

OECD (2005) *OECD Small and Medium Enterprise Outlook,* OECD Publishing, Paris.

OECD (2015), *Financing SMEs and Entrepreneurs 2015: An OECD Scoreboard*, OECD Publishing, Paris.

Pine, J. and Gilmore, J. (1999) *The Experience Economy*, Harvard Business School Press, Boston.

Ping, S. J. (2013) *China SME Finance Report*, Mintai Institute of Finance and Banking, Beijing.

Ramukumba, T. (2014) Overcoming SMEs challenges through critical success factors: A case of SMEs in the Western Cape Province, South Africa, *Economic and Business Review*, 16(1): 19–38.

Rhodes, C. (2015) *Business Statistics*, House of Commons Briefing Paper No. 065152, May.

SBP (2014) Examining the challenges facing small businesses in South Africa, *Alert*, Issue Paper 1, www.sbp.org.za.

Schumacher, F. (1974) *Small is Beautiful,* Abacus.

Sengenberger, W., Loveman, G. and Priore, M. (1990) *The Re-emergence of Small Enterprises: Industrial Restructuring in Industrialized Countries,* International Labour Organization, Geneva.

Smallbone, D. and Welter, F. (2009) *Entrepreneurship and Small Business Development in Post-Socialist Economies,* Routledge.

Small Business Trends (2004) Snapshot of China's small business marketplace, available at smallbiztrends.com /2004/07/snapshot-of-chinas-small-business.html

Storey, D. (1998) *Understanding the Small Business Sector,* International Thompson Business Press.

Vale, S. (2006) *The International Comparability of Business Start-up Rates Final Report,* OECD Statistics Working Paper Series, OECD Statistics Directorate, www.oecd .org/std/research.

World Bank. (2015) *SME Finance in Ethiopia: Addressing the Missing Middle Challenge*, Washington, DC: World Bank Group.

Wynarczyk, P., Watson, R., Storey, D. J., Short, H. and Keasey, K. (1993) *The Managerial Labour Market in Small and Medium-sized Enterprises*, Routledge.

Recommended further reading

Burns, P. (2010) *Entrepreneurship and Small Business,* Palgrave. Chapter 1.

Carter, S. and Jones-Evans, D. (eds) (2012) *Enterprise and Small Business: Principles, Practice and Policy*, 3rd edn, Pearson, chs 2–4.

Goss, D. (1991) *Small Business and Society*, Routledge, ch. 2, The Empirical Investigation of UK Small Business.

Government departments around the world publish data on the SME sector of their country or region. These can be accessed via websites such as those referenced in Note 6 above.

Storey, D. J. (2010) *Understanding the Small Business Sector*, Cengage Learning, ch. 2.

2 Entrepreneurship, the entrepreneur and the owner-manager

Learning objectives

By the end of this chapter you will be able to:

- Understand the difference between the entrepreneur and the small business owner-manager.

- Appreciate the importance of entrepreneurship as a process of social and market change.

- Realize that entrepreneurs operate in large as well as small enterprises and in the not-for-profit, public and private sectors.

- Identify a number of different motivations for starting a new business.

- Assess the entrepreneurial management behaviours that lead to a successful enterprise.

Introduction

Those who manage small firms come from all sectors of society and exhibit a vast range of demographic and personality profiles. In this chapter, we focus primarily on one set of owners who appear to display certain characteristics that give them the specific label of *entrepreneur* because they follow the path of *entrepreneurship*, a transformational process of innovation and market change undertaken by this particular breed of manager.

After introducing definitions of entrepreneurship and the entrepreneur, the chapter considers the various motivations for starting a business and discusses the personality traits considered desirable for entrepreneurial management. The characteristics of the entrepreneur are highlighted to see if a model of an ideal 'entrepreneurial type' exists. The chapter concludes with a summary of the key building blocks of entrepreneurship and the particular entrepreneurial management behaviours required to drive the market process.

2.1 Entrepreneurship and the entrepreneur: some definitions

The terms 'entrepreneurship' and 'entrepreneur' are used extensively today. Entrepreneurship is something that all national governments are keen to cultivate, and we are increasingly being encouraged to become more entrepreneurial.

Activity 1
Entrepreneurship and the entrepreneur

What have an entrepreneur and an owner-manager in common? Have they both:

(a) Started a business?
(b) Managed a small business?
(c) Made lots of money?
(d) Innovated a new product or service?
(e) Taken risks?

What do you think the terms owner-manager and entrepreneur and entrepreneurship actually mean?

2.1.1 IS THERE A BUSINESS IN YOU?[1]

'Business in You', a major initiative seeking to inspire nascent entrepreneurs to start their own businesses and to encourage existing small businesses to grow, was launched in the UK in 2012, featuring entrepreneurial case studies to convey the message that there is a 'business in everyone'.

Launching the campaign, Prime Minister David Cameron said, ' Small business and entrepreneurs are the lifeblood of the British economy and I am determined that we, working with the private sector, do everything we can to help them to start up and to grow in 2012. I want to encourage people to go for it and make this the year of enterprise – whether that is fulfilling their dream of starting a new business or taking the leap to grow their business, to employ more staff, or to start exporting' (January, 2012).

Entrepreneurship is seen as a fundamentally important part of modern economic and social life and entrepreneurs play a key role in our lives. Yet there is a lack of clarity concerning what entrepreneurship is and exactly what entrepreneurs do that sets them apart from other managers. Although we make the distinction between the terms 'entrepreneur' and 'owner-manager', they are often used interchangeably to describe somebody who is engaged in the management of a small business. Anyone who starts up in business is labelled an entrepreneur, and entrepreneurship is inextricably linked to small business management, but these terms have different meanings. It is necessary to define how we label them more clearly and to do that we need to look back at the origins of the terms.

2.1.2 ENTREPRENEURSHIP: A BRIEF HISTORY

Contrary to common belief, entrepreneurship is not a new phenomenon. People have been referring to entrepreneurs for hundreds of years. The word 'entrepreneur' derives from the French, literally meaning someone who takes between or goes between. The earliest use of the term reflected this sense of the middleman who directed resources provided by others. In the Middle Ages, an entrepreneur was someone who managed large projects on behalf of a landowner or the Church, such as the building of a castle or a cathedral.

In the seventeenth century, the concept was extended to include some element of risk and profit. Entrepreneurs were those who contracted with the state to perform certain duties, such as the collection of revenues or the operation of banking and trading services. As the price was fixed, the entrepreneur could profit – or lose – from their performance of the contract.

Richard Cantillon introduced the word into economic literature in 1734 when he described three types of agents in the economy: the landowner, who as the proprietor of land provided the primary resource; entrepreneurs, including farmers and merchants who organized resources and accepted risk by buying 'at a certain price and selling at an uncertain price'; and hirelings who rented out their services. J. B. Say, a French economist writing in the early 1800s, distinguished between the profits of those who provided capital and the profits of entrepreneurs who used it. He defined an entrepreneur as 'someone who consciously moves economic resources from an area of lower, and into an area of higher, productivity and greater yield'. In other words, the entrepreneur takes existing resources, such as people, materials, buildings and money, and redeploys them in such a way as to make them more productive and give them greater value.

This definition implies changing what already exists; it sees the entrepreneur as an instrument of change, someone who does not seek to perfect, or optimize existing ways of doing things, but searches instead for new methods, and new markets – different ways of doing things. In the mid-twentieth century, Joseph Schumpeter (1934) took up this theme of the entrepreneur as a necessary destabilizing force. According to Schumpeter, economic equilibrium, which optimizes what already exists, does not create healthy economies. Referring to the concept of 'creative destruction', Schumpeter suggested that a dynamic economy takes as its norm the disequilibrium brought about by the constant change of innovation and entrepreneurship.

In other words, we need entrepreneurs and entrepreneurship to encourage and introduce change into our lives, from which new (and better) goods and services are born. Peter Drucker (1986) developed these earlier ideas, seeing the emergence of an entrepreneurial economy in the USA as a 'most significant and hopeful event'. He defined an entrepreneur as someone who 'always searches for change, responds to it and exploits it as an opportunity'. He, like Schumpeter, made innovation a necessary part of entrepreneurship. In doing so, he focused on the management processes involved in what an entrepreneur does. Others have taken up this theme of entrepreneurship as a process, an action-oriented management style which takes innovation and change as the focus of thinking and behaviour.

2.1.3 ENTREPRENEURSHIP: CREATING VALUE FOR INDIVIDUALS AND FOR SOCIETY

The Austrian economist, Kirzner, defined entrepreneurship as the 'competitive behaviours that drive the market process' (Kirzner, 1973, pp. 19–20). This definition focuses attention on both the outcomes of entrepreneurship (what happens to markets and to society in general) and the process through which market change occurs (what individuals specifically do). It is also a perspective that emphasizes the 'discovery' of entrepreneurial opportunities (see Mole and Mole, 2010; Shane and Venkataraman 2000), as opposed to the 'creation' of opportunities brought into existence through the actions and sense-making of entrepreneurial actors (see Dimov, 2007, 2011; Sarason et al., 2006, 2010; Sarasvathy et al., 2003; Venkataraman et al., 2012). Debate continues concerning the objective vs. subjective nature of opportunities referred to in terms of the 'weak' and 'strong' premises of entrepreneurship, respectively (Sarasvathy, 2008). However, there is now general consensus that entrepreneurship involves a transformative process of social and market change that creates value for individuals and for society. This process can take place in a wide variety of contexts, but generally follows a progression from *opportunity identification* through to *realizing value*, as illustrated in Figure 2.1.

Figure 2.1 Overview of entrepreneurial process

This value can take many forms – personal wealth, family security, social inclusion or perhaps cultural and aesthetic pleasure. Most modern definitions of entrepreneurship entail some aspect of this process:

- **Entrepreneurship** is a way of thinking, reasoning and acting that is opportunity-based, holistic in approach and leadership balanced. Entrepreneurship results in the creation, enhancement, realization and renewal of value not just for the owners but for all participants and stakeholders (Timmons and Spinelli, 2004, p. 47).
- **Entrepreneurship** is the process of creating something new of value by devoting the necessary time and effort, assuming the accompanying financial, psychological and social risks, and receiving the resulting rewards of monetary and personal satisfaction and independence (Hisrich and Peters, 2002).
- **Entrepreneurship** is the process by which individuals – either on their own or inside organizations – pursue opportunities without regard to the resources they currently control (Stevenson and Jarillo, 1990, p. 23).

The results of this process of change can be categorized according to two perspectives. The first considers how, by whom, and with what effects opportunities to create future goods and services are discovered, evaluated and exploited (see Shane and Venkataraman, 2000, p. 218). The second focuses on the creation of new organizations (see Gartner, 1988).

In this book, our approach to entrepreneurship embraces both these perspectives, with a particular emphasis on small, innovative businesses as opposed to entrepreneurship in the context of larger organizations. Entrepreneurship is an emergent process of recognizing and communicating creativity so that the resulting economic value can be appropriated by those involved (Stokes, Wilson and Mador, 2010). We characterize entrepreneurship as a societal phenomenon (see Davidsson, 2003) or process of change, comprising the following three behavioural components:

1 the identification, evaluation and exploitation of an opportunity;
2 the management of a new or transformed organization so as to facilitate the production and consumption of new goods and services;
3 the creation of value through the successful exploitation of a new idea (i.e. requiring both creativity and innovation).

This in turn leads to a set of definitions for the entrepreneur and what they do:

- the *entrepreneur* is the individual who acts as principal mediator of the process of change described, through undertaking a specific project based on an opportunity that requires the implementation of a new and valuable idea (or ideas);
- the *entrepreneurial firm* is a particular type of organization which emerges as the result of the entrepreneurship process: this could either be a totally new firm or the transformation of an existing organization;
- *entrepreneurial management* involves the specific management behaviours that entrepreneurs engage in to drive the market process and produce innovation.

ENTREPRENEURSHIP FROM THE ENTREPRENEUR'S PERSPECTIVE

Scott Mitchell set up Core Electronics (now employing 220 people and with a turnover of £63 million) in 2001. He recalls how the business got started;

it went something like this:

> One day this guy woke up in the morning and said to himself, 'I'm going to become an entrepreneur.' So he went to the best computer programmer in the company where he was working and whispered, 'Would you like to join my company? Then, be there … my place … ten o'clock Saturday – and bring some bagels.' Then he goes to the best guy in the finance department and says, 'Bring some coffees.' And then he goes to the best marketing guy and the best IP lawyer with the same invitation. Ten o'clock Saturday comes around.
>
> They ask, 'Hey, what is your company going to do?' The guy replies, 'Build a new computer program.' An hour later, and the business plan is done. The finance guy says he knows where he can get some money. Then they say to their host, 'So what have you done?'
>
> What indeed? He didn't provide the coffee. It wasn't him who brought the bagels. He didn't even provide the idea. But he was the entrepreneur. He made it happen.

Entrepreneurship is not a process confined to the small profit-making enterprise. Entrepreneurship takes place in a wide variety of contexts. We consider some of these in the next section.

2.1.4 THE ENTREPRENEUR AND THE OWNER-MANAGER

Entrepreneurship is most commonly linked directly to small business management. However, the majority of small business owners do not innovate or seek out change in a continuous or purposeful way in line with the definitions of entrepreneurship. Some do, of course. There are many inventive people who seek to exploit new ideas through commercial activity. But these are the exceptions; most small businesses are founded on existing ideas and practices. The couple that open their own wine bar, the redundant employee who forms a training consultancy or the craftsman who starts up a joinery firm, are all taking risks but only by doing what has been done many times before. They do not necessarily attempt to innovate or seek out change, but base their business on hopes of increased consumption of the same products or services also on offer elsewhere.

Many small firms lack what might be thought of as creative spirit. The majority of start-ups are based on established industries. Research into the choice of product for a new business in relation to the owner-manager's previous experience showed that the vast majority stuck to the same industry. In one survey only 4 per cent had innovated a new product or technique (Binks and Jennings, 1986). There seems to be a natural tendency to play safe, staying with known business areas, when considering a new business.

Once established, small firms can also lack innovation. Owner-managers are invariably close to the day-to-day problems of their business as it grows – often too close to see opportunities or the need for change. Small business management can easily become a reactive process in which new ideas are pushed out by the need to cope with more pressing realities. In these circumstances, the owner-manager has to adapt and react, rather than direct and create. Such constant manoeuvring to fit the circumstances of the day has led to entrepreneurship being equated with a wheeler-dealer image in which creativity is used only for survival rather than progress.

The owner-manager is typically someone who is involved in running a small business who also has some form of ownership of the business. As we have seen, the majority of small businesses are very small, micro firms, with fewer than ten employees. The owners of these firms are predominantly the managers as well, and likely to be the only manager. The term owner-manager therefore describes the reality for a large number of small firms which are totally reliant on, and dominated by, their owner. That owner-manager may or may not be an entrepreneur.

Activity 2

(a) What is an 'intrapreneur'? How do they differ from an entrepreneur?
(b) Can a head teacher act in an entrepreneurial way? Give some examples if you think they can.
(c) What is meant by a social enterprise? How does it differ from a private business?

2.2 Entrepreneurship in different contexts

There is a perception, to some extent confirmed by research, that small, private-sector businesses are more innovative, and therefore more entrepreneurial, than larger corporations or publicly owned organizations. (The role of innovation in small business is discussed more fully in Chapter 4.) The lack of policy and rules in a small, informal structure can provide a more creative environment than a large, hierarchical organization.

However, the small business sector does not have a monopoly of entrepreneurial talent. Entrepreneurs can exist in large as well as small economic units, and in the public as well as the private sector. Many large enterprises, public bodies and not-for-profit organizations exhibit more entrepreneurial tendencies than some small businesses. Companies such as Virgin, Google, Amazon and eBay have deliberately tried to remain entrepreneurial by encouraging managers to innovate rather than administer. iPod, iTunes, iCloud, Gmail, driverless cars, Virgin Galactic, PlayStation, Post-It Notes, Java – these world-leading innovations are all born of individual employees being given time to work on their own projects in big companies (see, for example, Google's 'Innovation Time Off' programme). Social enterprises such as *The Big Issue* and the Grameen Bank thrive on an entrepreneurial spirit linked to a social mission. In providing leadership and resources for their state-funded schools, head teachers may act more entrepreneurially than owner-managers.

2.2.1 CORPORATE ENTREPRENEURSHIP

Historically, entrepreneurs may have seemed out of place in large companies. The development of mass manufacturing techniques relied on meticulous planning to improve efficiencies and lower costs. Planners could ensure manufacturing processes were repeated many times in the same way to produce the necessary economies of scale. Entrepreneurs, by definition, encourage change which tends to disrupt carefully planned efficiencies so that their role in large companies was perceived to be limited.

A number of factors, including the decline of the manufacturing sector and growth of service industries, led to a change in emphasis signalled in 1976 by Norman Macrae (1976: p. 42) who foresaw that 'methods of operation in business are going to change radically in the next few decades, in a direction opposite to that which most businessmen and nearly all politicians expect'. His survey – 'the coming entrepreneurial revolution' – claimed that the world was probably drawing to the end of the era of large corporations, because it was nonsense to have hierarchical managements sitting in offices trying to arrange how 'brainworkers' (who in future would be most workers) could best use their imaginations. Big businesses have survived, although there are fewer of them, but this prediction was partly accurate in that they have done so mainly by acting more like smaller enterprises. Today, many large organizations deliberately try to remain entrepreneurial by encouraging managers to innovate and think 'out of the box'. This has been made even more necessary by the intensity of global competition and the speed of technological change (Ramachandran *et al.*, 2006).

As the word entrepreneur has been so linked to small business, the term 'intrapreneur' was coined to describe someone who behaves in an entrepreneurial fashion in a larger organization. 'Intrapreneurship', or **'corporate entrepreneurship'**[2] in an existing business structure, has been encouraged by developments such as downsizing and delegation of powers to smaller, strategic business units (SBUs).

Large organizations need intrapreneurs for two main reasons:

- first, to improve the performance of the core business through innovative developments and modifications to existing products and processes; and
- second, to guard against market obsolescence through the creation of new ventures (Gautam and Verma, 1997).

Corporate entrepreneurship represents the company's efforts at renewal through innovation and new business development through venturing, allowing existing firms to revitalize by providing an antidote to fossilization. Although entrepreneurship and intrapreneurship share many common characteristics, entrepreneurship is 'developmental' while intrapreneurship is 'restorative' (Kirby, 2003: p. 300). Entrepreneurs develop new ventures from scratch; intrapreneurs aim to restore innovation and counter stagnation in an existing organization, which often involves overcoming a corporate culture that resists change and avoids risk.

Intrapreneurs do not necessarily appear unbidden in an organization – it requires entrepreneurial leaders to encourage and foster them in an existing organization. Entrepreneurial leadership is therefore the ability to encourage an entrepreneurial culture within a larger organization so that it continues to seek opportunities and encourage innovation and to adopt new ways of doing business.

The barriers to developing an entrepreneurial culture in larger organizations are considerable – and sometimes needed to prevent the excesses that inventiveness linked to the vast resources of a large organization can lead to. Research by Kingston University (Wilson, Stokes and Athayde, 2009) found that there was a general belief amongst corporate leaders that entrepreneurs are difficult to manage although they were necessary in order to prevent stagnation. They regarded the intrapreneur as a necessary evil who has to be given sufficient space to perform well but who needs watching carefully in case they take too many risks.

Given the events behind the global financial crash of 2007–8, they were perhaps right to be cautious. The actions of financial managers who extended credit to the sub-prime housing market on the basis that value increases in property would overcome mortgage repayment problems were probably considered innovative at the time. The decision to package these loans into new securities with a triple A credit rating for onward sale to investors may have been thought of as entrepreneurial. However, when the whole system unravelled as property prices collapsed, there was international condemnation of risk-taking, 'casino' banking and calls for a return to safe, predictable financial management. No one wants an entrepreneurial bank manager anymore.

BP'S CORPORATE ENTREPRENEURSHIP MODEL

In attempting to re-invent itself as a socially responsible supplier of all forms of energy, including solar and wind power, BP adopted a corporate entrepreneurship model with four key components to guide and control entrepreneurial action:

- *Direction* – the company's strategy, its goals, markets and overall positioning as a socially responsible corporation.
- *Space* – the freedom given to business unit managers to deliver on their objectives including the freedom to experiment and innovate.

(Continued)

- *Boundaries* – the legal and moral limits within which the company operates as laid down in policy documents or implicitly understood.
- *Support* – information systems, training and work/life balance services to help the managers do their jobs.

The four elements are intended to create an organizational environment of controlled freedom in which individuals can act entrepreneurially within constraints determined by the company. If one element is missing or out of balance, the model breaks down – without space and support, entrepreneurial initiative is stifled, but without direction and boundaries it can get out of hand.

Unfortunately, things did get out of hand and safety corners were cut. The Deepwater Horizon oil rig explosion of 2010 was the result. It killed 11 people and injured 17 others and caused the largest marine oil spill in history as more than 200 million gallons of crude oil were pumped into the Gulf of Mexico, affecting 16 000 miles of coastline.

2.2.2 THE VIRTUOUS CIRCLE OF CORPORATE ENTREPRENEURSHIP

Despite the problems experienced by intrapreneurs, entrepreneurial cultures do exist and thrive in the corporate environment. It is not only entrepreneurs who want to work in an entrepreneurial environment, but most employees who find that such environments give greater job satisfaction and rewards. The Kingston research found that executives were more likely to stay in an organization that was entrepreneurially supportive, even if they did not claim to be entrepreneurs or to act entrepreneurially. A key factor in the development of an entrepreneurial culture would seem to be the employment of entrepreneurial people who in turn encourage other staff to thrive in this environment. This indicates that entrepreneurial activity can lead to a 'virtuous circle' as illustrated in Figure 2.2. This suggests that the development of an entrepreneurially supportive culture is itself contingent on the employment of entrepreneurial executives. The more entrepreneurially supportive the organization the more likely the executives will display entrepreneurial behaviour and so on.

This book is primarily about entrepreneurial *small* businesses but entrepreneurial management is not something that necessarily stops when a firm reaches a particular size.

Figure 2.2 Corporate entrepreneurship virtuous circle

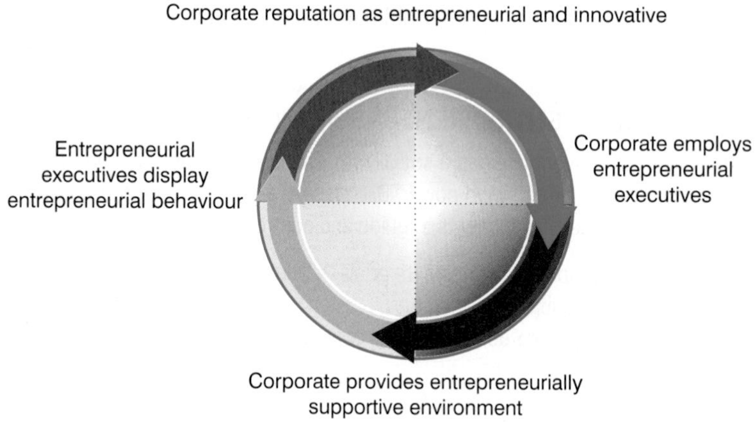

Corporate reputation as entrepreneurial and innovative

Entrepreneurial executives display entrepreneurial behaviour

Corporate employs entrepreneurial executives

Corporate provides entrepreneurially supportive environment

Source: Wilson, Stokes and Athayde, 2009.

2.2.3 SOCIAL ENTREPRENEURSHIP

Social entrepreneurship has the primary objective of adding value to society rather than to the individuals behind the entrepreneurial venture. Social entrepreneurs do not have profit or other personal needs as their primary aim but use the entrepreneurial processes to fulfill the social or economic needs of others. Like entrepreneurs generally, social entrepreneurs operate in a variety of contexts. Some form ventures that have a social aim as their main purpose, and so form a 'social enterprise'. Others run a private sector, profit-making enterprise but with distinct social values and objectives. Whatever the context, social entrepreneurs make a positive difference to the lives of others by emphasizing the social responsibility of their ventures before the need to maximize profits. They identify a social problem (which may or may not also be a business opportunity) and use entrepreneurial processes to create solutions to tackle the problem.

THE SOCIAL FACE OF BANKING

Mohammed Yunis identified that a key problem for the poor of Bangladesh was to raise very small amounts of money for projects that would help them out of poverty. But the traditional banks were not interested in making tiny loans at reasonable interest rates to the poor due to high repayment risks and administration costs. Yunis set up the Grameen Bank (or 'Village Bank') for this very purpose, believing that the poor would repay the borrowed money given the chance. The success of his venture proved that 'microcredit' could be a viable business model. Not only was the bank commercially viable, but the social impact has been so great worldwide with the model copied in hundreds of countries that Yunis and his bank were awarded the Nobel Peace Prize in 2006.

Reference: www.grameen-info.org

It has been argued that social entrepreneurs are no different to traditional entrepreneurs except that they do not prioritize the making of profits and put more emphasis on social rather than commercial results (Leadbeater, 1997). Research suggests that this also leads to different ways of operating: social entrepreneurs tend to have longer time horizons and they place more emphasis on resource acquisition as they often operate in fields where resources are scarce (Johnstone and Basso, 1999).

Many, but not all, social entrepreneurs create a social enterprise: that is, 'a business with primarily social objectives whose surpluses are principally reinvested for that purpose in the business or in the community, rather than being driven by the need to maximise profit for shareholders and owners' (Department for Trade and Industry, 2005). This means that a social enterprise creates value of a non-financial kind; for example, by regenerating local neighbourhoods, delivering public services such as healthcare, or providing employment to those disadvantaged by traditional job markets. The development of the green agenda has given social enterprise a new impetus as many have developed with aims to protect the environment. This has given rise to the 'triple bottom line' of social enterprise in which the three aims of profit (for reinvestment in a cause), social good and environmental sustainability all feature.

Social enterprise has been a growth sector recently. According to Social Enterprise UK, the national body for social enterprise, there are some 62 000 social enterprises employing over 1 million people in the UK. The growth of the sector has led to the formation of a number of social enterprises to help others develop social enterprises including the School for Social Enterprise (SSE) in the UK, Canada and Australia.

ENACTUS [FORMERLY SIFE (STUDENTS IN FREE ENTERPRISE)] – A HEAD FOR BUSINESS, A HEART FOR THE WORLD

ENACTUS is an international organization that mobilizes university students around the world to make a difference in their communities while developing the skills to become socially responsible business leaders. The students, guided by university and business advisers, form a student-led team to develop sustainable projects which create economic opportunity for others. Students take what they are learning in their classrooms about business and use it to solve real world problems for real people. Business executives support the programme through corporate donations, personal contributions and the gift of their time.

The students are led by faculty advisers who challenge them to develop projects that specifically meet the unique needs of their communities. Their efforts help rising entrepreneurs, struggling business owners, low-income families and children experience success.

The ENACTUS programme concentrates on five areas: market economics, success skills, entrepreneurship, financial literacy and business ethics. Some examples include:

- A team from the Technical University in Dresden, Germany helped to improve the marketing of a bike shop that had a workshop employing mentally disabled individuals.
- The Unified Teaching Centre of Teresina in Brazil worked with a group of disadvantaged women to develop a handmade chocolate business.
- The University of Pretoria, South Africa team sought to alleviate food shortages through their 'Paradise Fruits and Vegetables' scheme that reprocessed and packaged leftover produce from a local market as a means to provide economically feasible and nutritious food.

ENACTUS teams present the results of their community projects annually at regional, national and international competitions.

EN entrepreneurial – having the perspective to see an opportunity and the talent to create value from that opportunity;

ACT action – the willingness to do something and the commitment to see it through even when the outcome is not guaranteed;

US us – a group of people who see themselves connected in some important way; individuals that are part of a greater whole.

2.2.4 PUBLIC-SECTOR ENTREPRENEURSHIP

Services provided by the state have been through an era of upheaval in how they are managed in many developed economies. The introduction of market forces and increased delegation of management responsibilities have been common themes in these changes that have tended to encourage more entrepreneurial management behaviour. For example, head teachers of schools in the English state education system have a double reason to become more opportunistic and innovative: they have won much more control over the funds allocated to their

AN ENTREPRENEURIAL BUREAUCRACY?

Bureaucracy or 'rule by office' may have had origins in Confucianism which has permeated Chinese life for centuries and includes compliance with authority as one of its guiding principles. It is often contrasted to entrepreneurship as bureaucracy provides structures, stability and specialization whereas entrepreneurship tends to destabilize and operate outside of established organizational structures. In modern China, however, the bureaucracy of a socialist state has been supporting entrepreneurial ventures. Local government played a significant role in encouraging Township and Village Enterprises (TVEs) which have been significant contributors to the growth of the Chinese economy and entrepreneurship.

Following the death of Mao Zedong in 1976, Deng Xiaoping gradually emerged as China's new leader. Until his retirement in 1992, he took his country on a path of economic and social reform that has enabled China to emerge as a world economic super-power. The first step was the de-collectivization of agriculture which created the impetus for the rapid development of the TVEs which, by 1990, accounted for 20 per cent of China's gross output. These enterprises were not owned by the state but collectively owned under local governments. Although not strictly entrepreneurs as they were on a contract system, the managers of TVEs demonstrated many entrepreneurial characteristics and freedoms; they chose the products, raised their own funding, labour, raw materials and distribution channels and endeavoured to make profits. TVEs can, therefore, be seen as the beginnings of modern Chinese entrepreneurship (see Liao and Sohmen, 2001).

school; these funds are mainly dependent on the numbers of pupils they attract – direct incentives to become more entrepreneurial in their acquisition of resources and marketing activities.

Public-sector organizations are usually large and exist to meet the needs of society rather than make a profit, so that they can take on many of the characteristics of corporate and social entrepreneurship. However, they are owned by the state or general public and so have distinctive entrepreneurial characteristics and challenges because of the nature of the public-sector environment:

- *Restricted markets:* public services exist in markets subject to ongoing regulation and direction from one or more sources, which restrict the freedom of action of potential entrepreneurs or intrapreneurs. For example, the educational programme delivered by schools is subject to the demands of a national curriculum that prescribes much of what happens in the classroom. However, market conditions of perfect competition rarely, if ever, exist even in the private sector. Restricted markets may limit market entry by new competitors and therefore restrict the number of opportunities for entrepreneurial development in the public sector, but entrepreneurs are adept at using whatever environment exists to pursue new opportunities.
- *Multiple constituencies:* entrepreneurs who wish to innovate in the public sector will often find that progress is impeded by the complexities of the market relationships. More than one group of people can lay claim to being the 'customer' of public services because of the separation between those that pay for the service, those that choose it and those that use it. In education, there is a clear split between those that ultimately pay for the service (taxpayers), agencies that control the purse-strings (central or local government bodies), people who decide the parameters of a service (education service, inspectors, teachers, governors), those who decide which particular institution to attend (perhaps a

mixture of parents and pupils) and those that directly receive the service (pupils). Entrepreneurs have to address the needs of multiple groups such as these, often with conflicting interests, if they wish to develop an idea which is accepted in the public-sector marketplace.

- *Open access:* entrepreneurs are adept at seeking opportunities in market niches, or highly targeted groups of customers with specialist needs. In principle, most public services are available to all and have to take account of the needs of a very diverse range of people. The opportunities within a public service to target segments of users may therefore be limited: health authorities have a responsibility to provide services ranging from emergency admissions to maternity care; the police and fire services have a duty to protect all citizens irrespective of location and socio-economic group.

- *Public service ethos:* the need for public services has been explained in terms of the need to atone for the failure of market forces to safeguard the public good by providing welfare to those disadvantaged by the interactions of the marketplace. This notion that a benevolent public realm is needed to compensate for the excesses of the private domain does not sit easily with the encouragement of entrepreneurial practices that are most commonly associated with the private sector. Some public-sector managers resist entrepreneurship on the basis that it represents concepts that are alien to the ethos of their service.

- *Public accountability and scrutiny:* public services are overseen and scrutinized by the public or their political representatives in a way that does not exist in private-sector entrepreneurial enterprises that are typically controlled by one person. The speed and adaptability with which an entrepreneur can act can be severely restricted as a result. This can reduce initiatives in the public sector to cautious and inflexible activities in contrast to the creative, opportunistic processes typical in different entrepreneurial contexts.

GOVERNMENT GOLF BALLS: A CAUTIONARY TALE

UKTI, a government department charged with promoting UK exports, was upbraided for using wasteful marketing techniques in pursuit of its goals. It produced some UKTI-branded golf balls for use in the USA and Japan as part of an international marketing exercise for the department. When this became public knowledge, the press were quick to jump on this as an example of waste. The new Chancellor of the Exchequer, George Osborne chose 'the UKTI golf ball scandal' as a prime example of the previous government's waste when he presented his first budget in 2010, even though it had cost only £4000 a year for three years and possibly did raise awareness of Britain's export efforts. In the face of strong political, press and public-sector condemnation, UKTI was forced to promise never to brand golf balls again.

Reference: Cahn and Clemence (2011).

In summary, entrepreneurial activity can be found in many different sizes and types of private and non-profit organizations. It is neither exclusive to, nor always present in, small businesses. However, the management of small enterprise in the private, not-for-profit or public sector is the particular focus of this text and so will be the default context to be considered.

> ## Activity 3
> ### Why become an entrepreneur?
>
> **W**hy do you think people start their own business? Write down a list of possible motives, indicating which you consider to be positive reasons and those that you consider to be more negative.

2.3 Motivations for starting a business

2.3.1 THE HEROIC ENTREPRENEUR

There is a widely shared view that entrepreneurs are in some way rather special, even heroic individuals. Asked to picture an entrepreneur, we tend to think of an individual who masters the odds stacked against them, single-handedly overcoming traditional barriers until, by sheer force of personality, they manage to change what exists and offer the customer 'the something different' that they really wanted all along. The enterprise culture promoted by many governments has encouraged this portrayal based on the premise that, if individuals are given the right environment to become entrepreneurs, the economy can be led by heroic individuals whose entrepreneurial talent will lead the way to a new era of growth. One of the UK government's responses to the global recession, for example, was to turn to an entrepreneur for advice when Sir Alan Sugar (now Lord Sugar) was appointed as a new 'Enterprise Tsar' in 2009. In an effort to increase entrepreneurship amongst disadvantaged people, the government appointed Michelle Mone (founder of the underwear company Ultimo, who left school at 15 with no qualifications) to lead an enquiry into barriers to setting up new ventures in areas with high unemployment in 2015.

The reality is that while large numbers of new small businesses have been started, only a tiny minority will grow into substantial enterprises. Many will cease after only a few years' trading, as the heroic vision fades. The substantial growth in numbers of small businesses has masked an even greater amount of activity in and out of the sector. The growth in overall numbers has only been achieved through a high level of new entrants to small business, some of whom quickly return to other types of employment, or sadly unemployment. (See Chapter 3 for more detail.)

The decision to set up a new business is always a bold and courageous one which should caution us against the hype of becoming an 'heroic' entrepreneur.

There are many reasons for starting up a new business which can be divided into **push and pull influences**.

2.3.2 PULL INFLUENCES

Some individuals are attracted towards small business ownership by positive motives such as a specific idea which they are convinced will work. Pull motives include:

- *Desire for independence:* this features prominently in several research studies as the key motivator (see Mason and Lloyd, 1986; Binks and Jennings, 1986). The Bolton Report singled out the need to gain and keep independence as a distinguishing feature of small business owner-managers. A study of female entrepreneurs in Britain found that women were motivated particularly by the need for autonomy which had been frustrated by the individuals' prior training and background (Watkins and Watkins, 1986).
- *Desire to exploit an opportunity:* the identification of a perceived gap in the marketplace through personal observation or experience is a very common reason for starting a business. For example, a study of new

manufacturing firms in south Hampshire (see Scott *et al.,* 1986) reported that 60 per cent of founders quoted their desire to exploit a perceived market. While other studies have shown lower percentages, the wish to satisfy a perceived market gap remains a powerful motive. Entrepreneurs may seek to exploit this opportunity through specialist knowledge or product development, or they may hire the appropriate technology and skills.

- *Turning a hobby or previous work experience into a business:* many new entrepreneurs seek fulfillment by spending more time involved in a cherished hobby, or part of their work that they particularly enjoy. Although research confirms that founders tend to establish businesses in activities of which they have direct prior experience, this is often precipitated by a push motive, such as redundancy, rather than part of a considered decision process.
- *Financial incentive:* the rewards of succeeding in your own business can be high, and are well publicized by those selling 'how to succeed' guides to would-be entrepreneurs. The promise of long-term financial independence can clearly be a motive in starting a new firm, although it is usually not cited as frequently as other factors by founding entrepreneurs.

2.3.3 PUSH INFLUENCES

Many people are 'pushed' into founding a new enterprise by a variety of factors, including:

- *Redundancy:* this has proved a considerable push into entrepreneurship, particularly when accompanied by a generous handshake in a locality where other employment possibilities are low. The global recession that started in 2008 has generated thousands of redundancies across many of the most affluent societies in the world. Men and women who had known nothing but secure employment all their working lives were suddenly faced with the prospect of no job and no income. For some, this was the push required to set up on their own. The reality for many individuals is that economic recession brings hardship and strains on basic living conditions. To begin an entrepreneurial venture at this time demands a 'nothing to lose' or distinctly positive outlook on life. The support of family and friends also helps.
- *Unemployment (or threat of):* job insecurity and unemployment varies in significance by region, and by prevailing economic climate. A study reported that 25 per cent of business founders in the late 1970s were pushed in this way, while later research showed a figure of 50 per cent when unemployment nationally was much higher (see Scott *et al.,* 1986).
- *Disagreement* with previous employer: uncomfortable relations at work has also pushed new entrants into small business.

In research on entrepreneurship in different countries (Reynolds, Bygrave and Autio, 2004), push/pull influences are discussed in terms of **necessity-based** and **opportunity-based entrepreneurship**. The necessity-based entrepreneur has little choice but to start their own business, given the lack of alternative possibilities for employment. Typically, therefore, one might expect to see higher levels of such entrepreneurship in poorer, less developed countries where job opportunities may be few and far between. The opportunity-based entrepreneur, on the other hand, is characterized as one that seeks out a new opportunity in a more proactive manner.

However, we should avoid easy stereotyping of such founding activities. The dividing line between those pulled and those pushed is often blurred. Many people considering an opportunity or having a desire for independence still need some form of push to help them make their decision. Equally, many of those becoming entrepreneurs out of necessity act with extraordinary vision and tenacity to achieve their objectives.

SOUTH AFRICAN ENTREPRENEURSHIP

An examination of the state of entrepreneurship in South Africa in 2014 by the Small Business Development Ministry found that the motivations involved in new venture creation was a vital weakness in the economic development. Closure rates of SMEs are very high and the conclusion was that many unemployed people were starting a business out of desperation rather than a genuine motivation to become an entrepreneur:

'The World Bank reports that the viability of micro-enterprises is closely linked to the motivation for starting the business – successful businesses with potential for growth tend to be started by choice, as entrepreneurial ventures. Survivalist micro-enterprises, motivated by a lack of other employment options, seldom turn into successful, larger firms. For the most part, these business owners would prefer to give up their businesses and become an employee, if the opportunity arose. They are not hiring, or growing their businesses. Most of South Africa's SMEs fall into the latter category.' (SBP, 2014, p. 2).

Entrepreneurial capability

Research on the well-being of individuals has focused on the freedom to choose to act. The Capabilities Approach or Human Development Approach (Nussbaum 2000, 2011; Nussbaum and Sen, 1993) is framed around the central premise that individuals have the capacity 'to do and be' many things, though they do not always choose or have the freedom to follow these things through. Recent research by Wilson and Martin (2015) focuses on the freedoms individuals have to pursue entrepreneurship. *Entrepreneurial capability* is defined as a person's freedom to pursue and develop an entrepreneurial opportunity within their environment (Wilson and Martin, 2015, p. 99). Importantly, this capability is dependent upon a mix of internal and external conditions (discussed in more detail later, e.g. Chapter 3).

Entrepreneurial intent

An important variable in understanding the formation of new business ventures is the 'intentionality' of would-be entrepreneurs (Katz and Gartner, 1988, p. 431). Intent in the context of entrepreneurship means a conscious and planned resolve that drives the actions necessary to launch a business (see Thompson, 2009, p. 671). The concept is useful for researchers as it can be measured, although there is debate over how good a proxy it is for the level of entrepreneurship in an economy. The term 'nascent entrepreneur' is often used synonymously for entrepreneurial intent.

Activity 4
Origins of the owner-manager

Are some origins and backgrounds more likely to produce entrepreneurs or induce self-employment than others? Give your responses to the possible factors below before reading on.

- Age: which age group most commonly enters self-employment or owner-management?
- Gender: are men or women more likely to start a small business?
- Marital status: does marriage help or hinder owner-management?
- Social class: which social class provides most owner-managers?
- Education: are owner-managers above or below average education levels?
- Ethnicity: which immigrant groups have the highest propensity towards self-employment in your country?

2.4 Profiling the owner-manager

There has been considerable research interest in the backgrounds of those who start their own businesses. While the results reveal some interesting similarities overall, there are significant differences in the circumstances of owner-managers.

2.4.1 DEMOGRAPHICS
Age

Early research on small business creation in the UK pointed to two age windows for self-employment and owner-management: the first is in the 35–50 age group and the second after normal retirement at 65 (Curran and Burrows, 1988). More recent data indicates that owner-managers are still grouped in the 'mature' stages of life: 35 to 44-year-olds – 25 per cent of owners; 45 to 54 – 31 per cent and 55 to 64 – 26 per cent. The proportion in older cohorts is smaller at 7 per cent over 65 years-of-age. Although business ownership is a growing career choice for younger people, only 9 per cent of owners are aged under 35.

Types of enterprise will influence age ranges. Research into the profiles of small enterprises in different service sectors found that newer sectors such as computer and IT services attracted relatively younger owner-managers, whereas established business types such as plant and equipment hire, free houses, wine bars and restaurants were owned by relatively older managers (Curran, Blackburn and Woods, 1991).

For those researchers that consider entrepreneurship to be about discovering and exploiting opportunities (see Shane, 2003), *age* is significant. This is because it takes time for people to collect much of the information and skills necessary to exploit opportunities. Additionally, age provides credibility when it becomes necessary to transmit that information to other people in the course of obtaining resources or building organizations (Freeman, 1982). They also are more likely to have access to capital to invest in a business. As people become older, their willingness to bear uncertainty declines, perhaps because their time horizons become shorter.

However, more recent research in the UK suggests that entrepreneurs overall are becoming younger; entrepreneurs in the 25–34 age range are now more common (Harding, 2003). The development of entrepreneurship education across the world may be a factor in this. Certainly, the growth in digital businesses has been fuelled mainly by young entrepreneurs under 30.

AGE NO BARRIER FOR GATES[3]

Bill Gates was a 13-year-old student at Lakeside School in Seattle when he first began programming a computer with his young friend Paul Allen. Aged 14, the two budding entrepreneurs had developed a scheduling programme for their school which they were able to sell for $4200. By the time Gates was in his early 30s he was a multi-billionaire. Subsequently, he topped the Forbes list of 'The World's Richest People', from 1995–2006, with his net worth surpassing $100 billion. Retiring from Microsoft in 2008, he reinvented himself as a social entrepreneur. With his wife, he founded the 'Bill and Melinda Gates Foundation' that has contributed billions of dollars to fighting poverty and disease. He is a good example of how the entrepreneurial spirit can continue through several life-stages; in October 2016, he celebrated his 61st birthday.

Marital status

Marriage, it would seem, is good for small business ownership as single people are less likely to be owner-managers or self-employed than those who are married. This reflects not only the more mature age range of small business owners, but also the possibilities of either husband and wife teams in business partnership, or one supporting the other while a new venture is formed. Several studies have shown that being married increases the chances that an individual will be self-employed (see Taylor, 1996).

Social and class backgrounds

Generally speaking, the lower-middle classes have provided more small business owners than other social backgrounds. This is partly explained by attempts at upward mobility by manual and routine white collar employees, who may see self-employment as the means for advancement in society, especially if they lack formal educational qualifications.

It is also influenced by the fact that those born into families of small business owners tend to follow in their parents' footsteps. This overall trend is, however, subject to considerable variation by types of business; longer established forms of small enterprise such as free houses, wine bars and restaurants are much more likely to be owned by the children of self-employed parents, than more recent types of small business such as advertising and computer services (Curran, Blackburn and Woods, 1991). Other research has shown that individuals in the highest third of the income distribution are more than twice as likely to be entrepreneurs as those in the lowest third (8.1 per cent compared to 3.0 per cent) (Harding, 2003).

2.4.2 GENDER

Internationally, the profiles of female entrepreneurs show some striking similarities:

- women still constitute a lower proportion of business owners than men;
- they are starting new ventures at a higher rate than men so they are catching up; but
- they tend to be owners of smaller, less high-growth firms than men.

Despite the fact that the number of women entrepreneurs has increased dramatically in recent years (DeBruin, Brush and Welter, 2006), nearly twice as many men as women become entrepreneurs (Acs *et al.*, 2005). In the UK, only 18 per cent of SMEs are majority women-led,[4] although this has improved since 2005 when just 12 per cent of start-ups were led by women (BIS, 2013). Entrepreneurship, it seems, is a gendered profession. Does this mean that women entrepreneurs are so different to male entrepreneurs that we need a distinctive set of theories and conceptual models for female entrepreneurship? There are some interesting differences, but many similarities (Brush, 2006).

Similarities include:

- *Demographics:* other demographic variables such as ethnicity and social background play a greater role in business ownership than gender.
- *Motivations:* women become involved in entrepreneurial ventures for similar reasons to men, such as the need for independence and achievement.
- *Business issues:* female-owned enterprises seem to face similar issues to those of men, and have similar survival rates. Male- and female-owned businesses that grow substantially tend to end up with similar structures and practices.

Differences include:

- *Market sector:* female-owned enterprises tend to be concentrated in the retail and service sectors while male-owned firms are more widely spread.
- *Entrepreneurial process:* lack of equal opportunities in employment may influence the way in which women approach entrepreneurship. If they are disadvantaged in gaining access to managerial posts and higher salaries while employed, women may have less human and financial capital when starting up their own ventures, which in turn may make them more cautious and less ambitious for the growth of their venture.

- *Access to resources:* women tend to start up in business with less capital than men and are less likely to use equity finance. While this can be partly explained by lower finance requirements of female owners because of the sectors they tend to concentrate on, there does seem to be a 'finance gap' in relation to female entrepreneurs.

Both liberal and social feminist perspectives explain these differences by reference to the inequalities in the business and economic environment rather than in the inherent characteristics of female compared to male entrepreneurs. It is the uneven playing field, rather than the entrepreneurial potential of the players, that counts.

Gender differences have been well documented in the literature (see Gatewood *et al.*, 2003; Reynolds, Bygrave and Autio, 2004). Some researchers draw attention to the way in which socially constructed and learned ideas about gender and entrepreneurship might be limiting the ability of women to develop the cultural, social, financial and human capital required (see Carter and Rosa, 1998; Marlow and Patton, 2005). It is likely these factors influence the type of enterprise that women entrepreneurs set up, being generally smaller, less profitable and slower growing (typically in the retail and service sectors).

When discussing female entrepreneurship, it is important to distinguish between male/female biological and physiological differences and gender divisions that are constructed through social, cultural and psychological means (Gupta *et al.*, 2009). In particular, gender stereotypes play a key role in understanding the difference in entrepreneurial activity. For example, the stereotypes that women have more communal activities expressed through connectedness and supportiveness and that men are associated with more agentic properties such as autonomy, independence and aggressiveness may not only describe how men and women *are* (descriptive stereotypes) but also how they *should be* (prescriptive stereotypes). Both men and women see entrepreneurship as a male-type occupation (Gupta *et al.*, 2009). As such, women may be put off from entrepreneurship not because they do not see entrepreneurship as consistent with feminine characteristics, but because people close to them do not associate entrepreneurship with feminine characteristics, and therefore do not support them.

The lower level of female entrepreneurship in the UK is a particular area of policy interest. The government has seen this as a significant area of potential growth and development and has instigated several initiatives to encourage more women to become entrepreneurs.[5]

2.4.3 EDUCATION

There is a traditional view that small business management requires an aptitude for practical activities in which formal educational qualifications are less relevant. In this sense, owner-management was seen as an alternative route for advancement for those who had more practical and less academic skills. The Bolton Report (1971) quoted data that supported this view by suggesting that small business owner-managers were less well educated than the average in the population.

Recent research has painted a very different picture as this qualification gap seems to have disappeared with changing attitudes towards small business and the growth of knowledge-based small enterprises in the service sectors. Studies have identified that people who have stayed in education longer are more likely to be self-employed and to be successful in self-employment, and an individual will be more likely to exploit an opportunity if they are better educated (Shane, 2003). In the UK and the USA, people with more education in general and more enterprise education in particular are significantly more highly represented among entrepreneurs than others (Harding, 2007). Research also suggests that education is particularly important for female entrepreneurs (Bates, 1995). Today, a more educated society seems to produce more entrepreneurs.

People with access to enterprise education are twice as highly represented among entrepreneurs in the UK as those without such access (Harding, 2007). There has been a very significant growth in enterprise and entrepreneurship education in recent years both at school and university levels, and this is likely to have had an impact on the attitudes of young adults towards the possibilities of an entrepreneurial career path (see Athayde, 2009).

2.4.4 ETHNICITY

From the earliest times, there has been a strong relationship between migration and entrepreneurship. Economies that are thriving attract entrepreneurs who have an eye for an opportunity, and the early rise of industrialization in the UK attracted many immigrant entrepreneurs.

ENTREPRENEURS OF THE EMPIRE

Marc Brunel was born in Normandy but was forced to flee his native country in the 1790s during the French Revolution. He went first to the USA and then to England to marry an English woman, Sophia Kingdom. There, he developed innovative methods of manufacturing ships' parts that helped defeat his country of birth during the Napoleonic wars. In pioneering the first tunnel under the Thames, he invented the method that was used nearly two hundred years later to build the Channel Tunnel that linked his adopted country with his place of birth. Most notably, he and Sophia parented one of the greatest of Victorian entrepreneurs, Isambard Kingdom Brunel.

Groups of immigrants also had significant impact. In the late nineteenth century, the British government in India encouraged some of the Indian population to go to East Africa to develop the railways and commerce there. They had a major impact on the Kenyan economy especially in areas such as banking, textiles and retailing. In 1972, President Idi Amin expelled them, many fleeing to the UK where they also had a disproportionate effect on business creation.

Ethnic minority people are among the most entrepreneurial in society (Ram and Smallbone, 2001). They are believed to be responsible for 10 per cent of business start-ups in the UK and own over 6 per cent of SMEs, some 300 000 in total that contribute about £30 billion a year to the British economy (BIS, 2014).

However, there are significant variations among immigrant groups. Those of Afro-Caribbean origin have a self-employment rate of 7 per cent compared to 14 per cent from the Indian sub-continent while those originally from the Mediterranean region have typically topped the list as the group with the highest propensity towards self-employment (SBS, 2003).

Basu (2006) summarized the factors that 'push' or 'pull' ethnic minorities into entrepreneurship as follows:

- Discrimination in the labour market may push some into self-employment as the only option.
- Cultural heritage and family influences may pull others into starting a business, although there is inconsistency in the evidence for this; for example, the Indian population in Silicon Valley has displayed greater entrepreneurial potential than those with similar backgrounds in other countries including India itself.
- 'Ethnic enclaves' offer trading opportunities for specialist goods and services specific to a minority population – for example, types of food and clothes.
- Access to ethnic resources such as relatively inexpensive labour, finance, information and advice from within the local community, and access to external ethnic networks internationally.

The growth of the economies of the places of origin of immigrant entrepreneurs, especially in Asia, has led to a worldwide circulation of entrepreneurial talent as some see opportunities in their home countries and return. The increasing trend to global entrepreneurship favours ethnic minorities who are more likely to have international networks to take advantage of trading across borders.

SILICON VALLEY'S IMMIGRANT ENTREPRENEURS

Silicon Valley in California where the integrated circuit, the microprocessor and the microcomputer were born, is perhaps the best-known cluster of hi-tech companies in the world. The development of the Stanford Industrial Park by Stanford University was one of the catalysts, home for example to Hewlett Packard in its early days. The growth of high-technology industries in Silicon Valley coincided with a change in USA immigration policies that allowed significant new immigration into the region. Between 1975 and 1990, Silicon Valley's hi-tech companies created more than 150 000 technically skilled jobs of which 30 per cent were filled by immigrants, mostly engineers from China and India. The new immigrants proved highly entrepreneurial. Jerry Yang was born in Taiwan and moved to California when he was eight years old, knowing only one word of English (shoe). While studying at Stanford University in 1994, he and Gerry Filo set up a web portal that acted as a directory of internet websites. Originally called 'Gerry's Guide to the World Wide Web', it was re-named Yahoo! of which Yang was the CEO until 2009. Sabeer Bhatia lived in India until he went to study at Stanford University in 1989. From there he joined Apple, after which he and Jack Smith created an email system called HoTMaiL (the uppercase letters spelling HTML, the language of the webpage).

Launched as a free service in 1994, it attracted over 1 million subscribers in 6 months. These two well-known success stories are only the tip of the iceberg. Around 50 of the largest, publicly quoted technology companies in Silicon Valley were started by Chinese or Indian immigrants and nearly one-quarter of private companies are also run by immigrants. There is evidence that they retain and develop ties back home, strengthening trading relationships between Silicon Valley and China and India in particular. The economic and social effects of this mobile entrepreneurship are not just regional but global.

2.4.5 TYPES OF OWNER-MANAGERS AND ENTREPRENEURS

The wide range of motivations for taking the entrepreneurial path is demonstrated in the variety of types of entrepreneurs that emerge as a result. Early studies by industrial sociologists simply split them into craftsmen and opportunists, to reflect the different backgrounds and aspirations of these types (see Smith, 1967). Later work (Hornaday, 1990) extended this to three distinct types:

- *The craftsperson* – small business owners ranging from joiners to hairdressers who themselves directly provide a product or service, and who enjoy doing it.
- *The promoter* – the archetypal 'wheeler-dealer' who does deals, often starting, growing and selling several different businesses in the pursuit of personal wealth.
- *The professional manager* – the owner who adopts a more structured approach to building an organization on the lines of a 'little big business'.

This basic typology has been further developed by other writers to lengths that more accurately indicate the great diversity of entrepreneurs and owner-managers. Figure 2.3 is an illustration of this diversity.

Figure 2.3 Entrepreneurial types

1	Soloist	A self-employed person operating alone; e.g. in a specific trade or profession.
2	Key partner	One stage on from the soloist, as an autonomous individual but with a partner in the background, sometimes as a financial backer only.
3	Grouper	Those who prefer working in small groups with other partners who share the decision-making; e.g. craftsmen working in their own firm as equals.
4	Professional	Self-employed experts; for example, traditional professionals (accountants, solicitors, doctors, architects, etc.). While not traditionally considered to be entrepreneurs they do tend to work in small firms.
5	Inventor-researcher	Creative inventors who may, or may not, have the practical skills to turn creativity into innovation.
6	High tech	New technological developments have created opportunities for those with the right technical expertize; e.g. in bio-science developments or digital technology.
7	Workforce builder	The delegator who manages the labour and expertize of others in an effective way; e.g. in the building trade.
8	Serial entrepreneur	The start-up expert who only really enjoys the challenge of initiating new enterprises, then loses interest, often selling the business in order to start another.
9	Concept multiplier	Someone who identifies a successful concept that can be duplicated by others; e.g. through franchising or licensing arrangements.
10	Acquirer	Those that prefer to take over a business that already exists, rather than start from scratch.
11	Speculator	There are many property-based opportunities to buy and sell at a profit, as well as collectables such as art, stamps and antique furniture which have spawned many dealers as owner-managers of small firms.
12	Turn-about artist	An acquirer who buys small businesses with problems, but which have potential for profit.
13	Value manipulator	An entrepreneur who acquires assets at a low price and who then, through manipulation of the financial structure, is able to sell at a higher price.
14	Lifestyle entrepreneur	Small business is a means to the end of making possible the good life, however this is defined. Consistent cash flow is the primary business requirement rather than high growth which might involve too much time commitment.
15	Committed manager	The small business is regarded as a lifetime's work, something to be built up carefully. Personal satisfaction comes from the process of nurturing the fledgling firm through all its various stages of growth.
16	Portfolio entrepreneur	An entrepreneur who builds up a portfolio of ownership in small businesses, sometimes using shares or assets of one company to provide the financial base to acquire another, in parallel rather than sequentially (like a serial entrepreneur).
17	Capital aggregator	A business owner with the necessary financial leverage to acquire other substantial attractive businesses.
18	Matriarch or patriarch	The head of a family-owned business, which often employs several members of the family.
19	Going public	Entrepreneurs who start up in business with the clear aim of achieving a quotation on the stock exchange, usually via an unlisted securities market in the first instance.
20	The alternative entrepreneur	Alternative New-Age beliefs in a return to simpler, more environmentally sound lifestyles may be expressed in a wish to avoid conventional employment. Commercial activities have developed in areas such as health foods, alternative healing and medicines, alternative beauty products and New-Age publications and audiotapes.

Source: Adapted from Gray, D. (1987).

Activity 5
What do entrepreneurs have in common?

Consider what you know about three of the most famous British entrepreneurs: Richard Branson, Alan Sugar and Michelle Mone.

For each of them, list what you consider to be their main characteristics.

- What do they have in common?
- How do their personalities differ?
- Do they share any characteristics that are really important for a successful entrepreneur?

2.5 The search for the entrepreneurial archetype

2.5.1 ENTREPRENEURIAL TRAITS

Is there a typical person who becomes a successful entrepreneur, an archetype on whom we can base our judgments about someone's aptitude for entrepreneurship? Can anyone become an entrepreneur, or does it require a certain type of person to make it really work? If it does require certain attributes, are they innate or can we acquire them – in other words, are successful entrepreneurs born or made?

The influence of the founder (or *nascent entrepreneur*)[6] on a small business is crucial. Particularly in the early days, enterprises are inseparable from their founders; they are conceived by them, born of their labours and survive because of their dedication. In later stages of growth, a management team may emerge which makes the enterprise more autonomous, capable of continuity without the originating force. But it is the nascent entrepreneur who has to grow the enterprise to the stage where it has the critical mass to survive as an entity in its own right. As this impact is so vital, it would be very helpful to identify personality types who are more likely to succeed in order to encourage those who are the right fit and discourage others who do not have the necessary characteristics. Recent theory has sought to address this question by considering the nature–nurture debate in terms of the psychological conditions necessary in order for entrepreneurship to flourish (see Chell, 1999).

We should not overstate the role of specific personality types and characteristics. As Shaver and Scott observed, 'not even the most resolute advocate for "enduring personality differences between entrepreneurs and non-entrepreneurs" would argue that a complete map of the human genome will reveal a specific gene that can separate new venture founders from everyone else' (Shaver and Scott, 1991, p. 32).

2.5.2 THE BIG FIVE

Nevertheless, a number of general traits or personality characteristics have been put forward as important influences in entrepreneurship. Five traits known as the **'Big Five' personality dimensions** (Vecchio, 2003) have received particular attention: need for achievement; need for autonomy; locus of control; risk taking and entrepreneurial self-efficacy.

1 **Need for achievement** A well-known investigation into the entrepreneurial personality, by McClelland (1961), concluded that the driving force is need for achievement. This desire to achieve a goal is linked with the ability to see and act on opportunities – although being *too* goal oriented can end up in failing to spot

opportunities as they emerge. Parental influences are significant in the development of this 'basic' need-for-achievement personality. According to this study, entrepreneurs are likely to have parents who expected them to be self-reliant at an early age, while remaining supportive of and not rejecting their offspring.

Kets de Vries (1985) also concluded that family background and experiences were significant in forming an entrepreneurial personality, but from a very different perspective. He painted a picture of hardships endured in childhood which leave an adult troubled by images of the past, leading to low self-esteem, insecurity and lack of confidence. Such people often exhibit driving ambition and hyperactivity, but linked to a non-conformist and rebellious nature. The entrepreneur who comes from such a background is driven by a need to escape from their roots, but their aggressive, impulsive behaviour which does not accept the authority of others means they have to create their own organization to succeed. They are forced into self-employment through lack of acceptance in conventional employment. While an inner compulsion may lead to some business success, longer-term problems are likely to emerge as a result of these deviant personality traits.

An entrepreneur's need for achievement manifests itself in a number of ways:

- risk taking
- confidence of success
- desire for independence
- energy in pursuing goals
- measurement of success by wealth.

Entrepreneurs have been shown to possess higher achievement motivation than both corporate managers and small business owner-managers (Stewart *et al.*, 1998). However, there is a lack of convincing evidence to prove the case conclusively. A need for achievement is a characteristic shared by many individuals, not just entrepreneurs.

2 **Need for autonomy** A trait which is commonly recognized as prevalent among entrepreneurs and owner-managers alike is their strong desire for independence, the freedom to create their own futures. The desire to be independent and self-directing has been seen as a predictor of the successful 'fit' of an individual with an entrepreneurial position. Wu (1989) argued that entrepreneurs must make decisions contrary to the opinions of the majority in order to identify opportunities so that the tendency to do things their way is an important factor. Again, there is a lack of credible empirical evidence to support any firm association between a desire for independence and entrepreneurial behaviour. Much of the interest in this particular attribute results from the strong rhetoric that surrounds the notion of 'going it alone' or 'doing your own thing'.

3 **Locus of control** The desire for independence is closely related to this next personality attribute – namely, the belief that we can influence the environment in which we find ourselves (Rotter, 1966). Successful entrepreneurs, according to some research studies, are convinced that they can control their own destinies. Behavioural scientists describe those who believe they have the ability to control their environment as having an *internal locus of control* compared to others with an *external locus of control*, who believe that their lives are dominated by chance and fate. One study (Brockhaus and Horwitz, 1986) concluded that small business survival and success is linked to the internal locus of control beliefs of the owner-managers. The stronger commitment to self-determination has enabled some owner-managers to overcome difficulties which defeated others. Once again, there is limited empirical evidence to support a direct link to entrepreneurial behaviour. However, it is commonly believed amongst entrepreneurs that success comes from an inner determination to succeed (or self-determination) linked to a willingness to look externally for help and support – which is not the same as a belief in being controlled by external

forces (or pre-determination). An important personality component of entrepreneurship is therefore an inner determination underpinned by an external focus (Stokes, Wilson and Mador, 2010).

4 **Risk-taking propensity** Without a significant level of belief in themselves and their ideas, owner-managers are unlikely to have taken the initial risk of starting their own business. Entrepreneurs are often characterized as risk takers who instinctively know that gains do not accrue to those who always play safety first.

Differences in the levels of risk taken highlight a distinction between the entrepreneur and the owner-manager. At one extreme there is the opportunist entrepreneur who is cast as relentlessly pursuing every possibility with little regard to the resources available to them at the time. According to the Kets de Vries (1985) version of their personality, this compulsive competitiveness stems from their deep insecurity, which drives them to prove themselves time and time again by taking risks. Others might argue that their internal locus of control gives them the self-confidence to take on any challenge.

At the other end of the spectrum is the conservative owner-manager, who took some risk to establish their business, but whose only aim now is to preserve what they have achieved. Risks are to be avoided for this type of small business manager, whose traits match those of an administrator more than an entrepreneur.

In between there are many shades of risk taking, from the reckless to the calculated, which depend on the context as well as an individual's character. Those with a high risk-taking propensity have a decision-making orientation that can accept a greater likelihood of loss in exchange for greater potential reward. What appears as a risk for some people might actually represent a real opportunity for others. There is a balance between risk and reward which can be determined in terms of probabilities. As such, entrepreneurs may not actually perceive risk as such because they have determined the probability of success and are prepared to accept it in view of the possible rewards within a given business scenario (see Palich and Bagby, 1995). Why entrepreneurs see opportunities where others see only uncertainty is itself something of a mystery. It may be linked to their creativity, vision or perhaps their possession of some form of information regarding the particular business venture (see Casson, 1982). To the extent that entrepreneurship entails 'creative practice' or the pursuit of something 'new' and 'valuable' prior to it being recognized, entrepreneurs are driven by a 'will to believe'. This brings us to the fifth dimension – entrepreneurial self-efficacy.

5 **Entrepreneurial self-efficacy (ESE)** Self-efficacy describes an individual's belief in their ability to undertake and accomplish some particular task or activity (see Bandura, 1982; 1997). Self-efficacy, when viewed as a key antecedent to new venture intentions, is referred to as **entrepreneurial self-efficacy** (ESE) (Boyd and Vozikis, 1994). Self-belief would appear to characterize the entrepreneur at all stages of the entrepreneurship process. As an innovator, the entrepreneur is by definition dealing with new situations and outcomes. Whereas many management tasks are carried out according to some existing formula or expectations, the entrepreneur is breaking new ground. Identifying a good business opportunity (i.e. one that no one else has already spotted) requires self-belief. The pursuit of opportunity regardless of the resources to hand often demands even greater self-belief. The entrepreneur is not daunted by rejection. There are many examples of innovations that were originally regarded as crazy or cranky ideas: aeroplanes, open-heart surgery, the personal computer, the telephone and countless other innovations we now take for granted.

There is considerable interest in ESE in the entrepreneurship literature, particularly in terms of refining a measure for this construct which could be applied in practice (see McGee *et al.*, 2009). Although there remain some key problems associated with measuring ESE, it is perhaps the most convincing of the 'Big Five' attributes of the entrepreneurial personality, especially when linked to the self-confidence that comes from an inner locus of control (the third attribute explained above).

2.5.3 INNOVATION

A further characteristic of the entrepreneur is their ability to innovate. Can this be learned or are we born with, or without, an ability to innovate? Drucker (1986) insists that we can develop our innovation skills.

He regards entrepreneurship and **innovation** as tasks that can and should be organized in a purposeful, systematic way. In other words, they are part of any manager's job, whether he or she works in a small or a large enterprise. The entrepreneurial manager is constantly looking for innovations, not by waiting for a flash of inspiration, but through an organized and continuous search for new ideas. Drucker presents entrepreneurs not as people who are born with certain character traits, but as managers who know where to look for innovation, and how to develop it into useful products or services once they have found it (see Chapter 4, Innovation and the Marketplace).

Drucker's entrepreneurship is not so much a knack that you either have, or you don't, but rather a practice which you constantly follow or you choose to ignore. It can thus be developed, and learned; its core activities are innovation and a continuous, purposeful search for new ideas, and their practical applications.

There are other related personality traits associated with the entrepreneur:

- proactive approach
- self-motivation
- tolerance of uncertainty and ambiguity
- opportunistic behaviour
- creative
- visionary
- manipulative
- impatient
- energetic
- charismatic.

2.5.4 LIMITATIONS OF THE TRAIT APPROACH

Although the search for a single personality trait that characterizes entrepreneurs provides insights into some entrepreneurial types, none can claim general application. Specific criticisms of the so-called 'trait approach' include:

- Over-emphasis on finding the one key trait which characterizes all entrepreneurs. Some writers (see Timmons, 1990) have tried to overcome this problem by looking for clusters of desirable attitudes and behaviours. The most widely used scale of entrepreneurial activity, developed by Covin and Slevin (1988), is based around three behavioural dimensions of risk taking, innovation and proactive response.
- The implication that entrepreneurial traits are formed during childhood, so that the would-be adult entrepreneur either has them, or not, and cannot acquire them later.
- The lack of recognition that the needs of a business venture change during its life cycle, and so the characteristics of successful entrepreneurship will likewise change. The personal attributes which can bring a new venture to life are unlikely to be the same as those which can manage it as a more mature business. As a firm grows, other managers have a greater impact on the likelihood of success, as the influence of the original founder diminishes.

2.5.5 LEARNING AND COGNITIVE THEORY

If we agree with Drucker that innovation is something that can be learned and practised, then it follows that entrepreneurship is *not* limited to a few special individuals who are born with certain personality traits. This empowering observation receives further empirical support from cognitive behaviour theory (CBT). Entrepreneurship from the CBT perspective can be better understood by looking at the impact of personality, environment, experience, acquired attitudes *and* learning. All of these factors combine to create the competitive behaviours required by the entrepreneur to drive the market process. The focus of debate then shifts to consider the cognitive processes of the entrepreneur (Baron, 1998; Shepherd and Krueger, 2002) and the entrepreneurial mindset (McGrath and MacMillan, 2000). How do entrepreneurs make sense of the world around them and take the decisions that will result in innovative new products and services being successfully launched? Researchers have highlighted the potential importance of cognition research as a lens through which to 're-examine the people side of entrepreneurship' by investigating the memory, learning, problem identification and decision-making abilities of entrepreneurs (Mitchell *et al.*, 2002, p. 93).

Haynie and Shepherd (2009) draw attention to cognitive adaptability – the ability to effectively and appropriately change decision policies (i.e. to learn) given feedback from the environmental context in which cognitive processing is embedded. This is clearly linked to the ability of entrepreneurs to have the vision and the drive to identify and exploit opportunities, while remaining flexible enough to re-think and re-direct opportunities in different directions, as and when required.[7]

We still know little of the specific social processes that may enhance the ability to recognize or exploit entrepreneurial opportunities (Davidsson and Honig, 2003). For example, over 50 years ago, one commentator suggested that formal education increased an entrepreneur's cognitive abilities to better evaluate opportunities (Schultz, 1959). Whether or not this is the case remains an open question, as attributes, character traits, demographic background and experience all play a role. But exactly what role these factors play is still the subject of debate and ongoing research. There is no 'identikit' of a successful entrepreneur – as the entrepreneurial portraits in the next section demonstrate.

2.5.6 PORTRAITS OF THREE BRITISH ENTREPRENEURS[8]

The history of well-known entrepreneurs can provide clues and inspiration for those that wish to follow the entrepreneurial path. The following examples of well-known British entrepreneurs illustrate that successful entrepreneurship can spring from very different personal backgrounds.

Sir Richard Branson was born in 1950 into the privileged classes of the English establishment. Three generations of judges on his father's side laid the foundations for his secure and comfortable early years in a leafy Surrey village. He showed little inclination for academic studies during his years at private boarding schools and he left with six 'O' levels at the age of 17 to start his first venture, which was the magazine *Student*. An extrovert with a liking for practical jokes and a flair for publicity, he has proven to be a restless entrepreneur. After the success of Virgin Music, he sold the company in 1992 to concentrate on his airline, Virgin Atlantic. He has been involved in ventures as diverse as commercial radio, video games, insurance, space travel and condoms (his only business not to bear the Virgin brand). As well as his much publicized successes, he has also experienced failure – movies produced by Virgin Visions, the sinking of his powerboat, Challenger 1, in its attempt on the Blue Riband, and an embarrassing public flotation and private repurchase of Virgin shares. He has become as well-known for his personal exploits as for his business ventures, including various world record attempts in balloons, boats and other vehicles (some successful). Branson thrives on public recognition and his smile and dress habits are as recognizable as any film star's. An advocate for electric-powered cars (he sponsors the Formula E racing championships), he has predicted that, in 20 years' time, all cars will be electric. He is involved in a number of charitable activities including the Branson School of Entrepreneurship in South Africa, set up in 2005 to support start-ups and micro-enterprises with skills, mentors, networks and finance in collaboration with a Johannesburg university. Branson was worth nearly $5 billion in 2015 according to Forbes. He resides on his own island, Necker, part of the British Virgin Islands in the Caribbean, for 'health reasons' although it does also put him safely out of reach of the British tax authorities.

Sir Alan Sugar (Baron Sugar of Clapton) was born in 1947 into a working-class Jewish family in Hackney, in London's East End. The devastation of the war and the aftermath of rationing and shortages made his childhood on a council housing estate tough and devoid of luxuries. His father was a semi-skilled worker in the garment trade, a very insecure job where lay-offs without pay at a moment's notice were common. After failing his 11+ exam for a state grammar school, Sugar attended a secondary technical school where he was described by his teachers as quiet, introverted and 'very average'. He left at 16 with a few 'O' levels to become a civil servant in the statistics department of the Ministry of Education and Science. His entrepreneurial inclinations soon led him out of this bureaucratic environment to a job selling tape recorders, and then into his own one-man business selling car aerials and other electrical goods to London retailers. Through Amstrad (Alan Michael Sugar's Trading Company) he developed a consistent formula which made him Britain's most successful seller of electrical consumer goods: design simple products by cutting out unwanted features, have them produced by the cheapest source of supply worldwide and use large-scale advertising campaigns and extensive distribution to develop mass markets for them. He became an icon for popular capitalism in the 1980s through his self-confident belief in value-for-money goods, made possible by hard work and lack of frills – a reflection of his own values and lifestyle. He developed a love–hate relationship with established institutions from the City of London to the Football Association through his attitude towards anyone whom he believes owes their position to privilege rather than to hard work, or to working the system rather than making a valid contribution to it. Sugar has gained widespread public recognition through his appearances in the TV reality show *The Apprentice* (first produced in 2005). The management style he portrays on the programme has been criticized as 'old-fashioned and confrontational' and one anti-bullying charity claimed that the public humiliations that he metes out represent a poor management role model and give credibility to bullies. In 2009, Prime Minister Gordon Brown offered him the role of 'Enterprise Tsar' in his government, and he was subsequently ennobled, taking the title of Baron Sugar of Clapton. He had long been a member of the Labour Party and was one of its biggest donors, but he resigned prior to the 2015 general election because he claimed the party had become 'anti-business'. In May 2016, the Conservative government appointed Lord Sugar Enterprise Tsar, once again, in a drive to encourage more young people to start their own business.

Michelle Mone (Baroness Mone of Mayfair) was born in 1971 in a poor, tough district of Glasgow. Her first ambition was to become a model and she left school aged 15 to follow her dream. The vision faded when she became pregnant at 18 and she married Michael Mone. 'Exaggerating' her qualifications on her CV, she got a marketing job with Labatt, the brewing brand, where she rose quickly to become head of marketing in Scotland. Her business idea apparently came when she was wearing a low-cut dress at a dinner dance and found her cleavage-enhancing bra very uncomfortable. Made redundant from her job, she and her husband set up MJM International in 1996 with the aim of developing a bra that was both comfortable and good-looking while creating more cleavage. It took three years of research, design and development to

(Continued)

perfect her underwear using a new silicone material that she licensed. Her patented Ultimo bra was launched at Selfridges in London using actors playing plastic surgeons protesting that her new bra would put them out of business, accompanied by models wearing her lingerie outside the store. Acclaimed as the most successful launch of its kind, Selfridges sold their entire stock within 24 hours. The brand went on to become well-known internationally, helped by the use of celebrity endorsements, and, by 2011, the business was thought to be worth £20 million. The acrimonious breakdown of her marriage kept her in the media and Mone left the company in 2013. She soon returned, buying out her husband and going into partnership with a Sri Lankan-based lingerie company. Selling down her stake in Ultimo, she has recently invested in other businesses including the skin tan company UTan. Michelle Mone has always been a high-profile entrepreneur. She won the World Young Business Achiever Award in 2000; the following year she joined the board of The Prince's Scottish Youth Business Trust at the invitation of Prince Charles and, in 2010, she was given an OBE. A longstanding Labour supporter, she left the party in 2009 in protest at their handling of the economy. In 2015, the Conservative government announced that she was to lead the 'Mone Review' into entrepreneurship and small businesses, focusing on setting up businesses in deprived areas, and she was created a Life Peer as Baroness Mone of Mayfair, in September 2015.

Activity 6
Branson, Sugar and Mone

Consider the brief portraits of Richard Branson, Alan Sugar and Michelle Mone above. List the similarities and contrasts in their personal backgrounds and approach to business. Can you make any generalized comments about what makes a successful entrepreneur from these examples?

- Consider first *who* they are. Do they share any similar personality traits or attributes?
- Consider next *how* they did what they did. Are there skillsets and management behaviours that they have in common?

2.6 The 'model' entrepreneur

While no clear model of a successful entrepreneur emerges, a list of skills, attributes and behaviours which form the building blocks of successful entrepreneurship can be attempted. Figure 2.4 summarizes these into four categories: technical skills, management competencies, personal attributes and entrepreneurial behaviours. While it can be argued that certain technical skills and management competencies are required in any business context, the difference between the successful entrepreneur and the also-rans lies in respect of their particular combination of personal attributes and entrepreneurial management behaviours.

Edward De Bono, the originator of lateral thinking, has imaginatively equated business competence such as cost control to the 'water' that makes up the main ingredient in 'soup'.[9] However, he points out that a bowl of

Figure 2.4 The building blocks of successful entrepreneurship

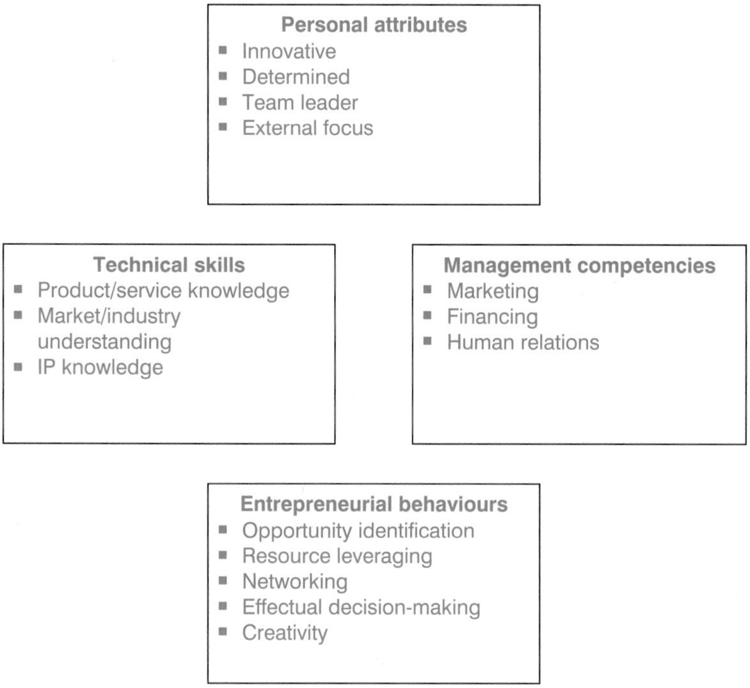

Personal attributes
- Innovative
- Determined
- Team leader
- External focus

Technical skills
- Product/service knowledge
- Market/industry understanding
- IP knowledge

Management competencies
- Marketing
- Financing
- Human relations

Entrepreneurial behaviours
- Opportunity identification
- Resource leveraging
- Networking
- Effectual decision-making
- Creativity

water is not a bowl of soup. It is what you add to the water that gives the 'value' of soup. In the same way, a business realizes value by adding the particular ingredients that are represented by the entrepreneur's management behaviour and personal attributes.

2.6.1 PERSONAL ATTRIBUTES

We have already discussed the 'Big Five' attributes associated with entrepreneurial behaviour. Such attributes are manifested in a variety of different ways in any one individual. While we concluded that no one personality type emerges as the ideal entrepreneur, certain qualities are universally beneficial.

Innovative

To be truly entrepreneurial, an *innovative* mindset is required to come up with something new, or different ways of doing things. This is linked to creativity which is discussed more fully in 2.6.4 Entrepreneurial Behaviours below.

Determined

Tom Peters (Peters and Waterman, 1988) suggested that innovation sometimes stems from an unreasonable conviction based on inadequate evidence. This flavour of energetic perseverance and decisiveness flows from a wholehearted belief in a new idea and the determination to make it work in practice – which is what differentiates an *innovative* from an *inventive* person. A single-minded determination to ride the inevitable ups and downs gives the necessary motivation and self-belief to cope with the inevitable risks, hard work and failures that follow. It demonstrates itself in an enthusiasm to make the enterprise succeed, and a determination to organize the resources necessary for success. It also manifests itself in the high energy levels and proactive, rather than reactive, decision-making which flow from a sense of purpose and personal motivation.

Team leader

While some owner-managers seem lonely figures relying only on their own abilities, successful entrepreneurs know that long-term growth relies on leading a team of people who influence the enterprise. The lone owner-manager is unable to develop a business beyond a certain size, if it is reliant totally on his or her efforts. Effective delegation and training of others are important prerequisites for sustained growth. The team does not stop at the internal members of an enterprise; other stakeholders in the business, such as financial backers, banks, suppliers, key customers, the immediate family of both entrepreneur and employees all exert an influence, which have to be managed and encouraged in positive directions. The entrepreneur requires leadership qualities to maintain this team, supporting the individuals within it, to ensure successful outcomes for the tasks in hand.[10]

External focus

Entrepreneurs who start a successful venture, and continue to grow it, maintain an external focus in what they do. Alan Sugar developed new electrical products not from formalized research into consumer needs, but through his knowledge of the trade which he built up while selling to retailers.

Richard Branson was presented with the plans for Virgin Atlantic by Randolph Fields, who developed the idea following the collapse of Laker Airways in 1982 and thought Branson would be the best person to exploit his concept. Michelle Mone has always encouraged a media presence; she has over one million followers on Twitter.

The pressure on owner-managers in the early years is on the day-to-day running of the enterprise. This may become so all-consuming that they take their eye off the external environment as they concentrate on internal operations and become internally focused. An external focus maintains the foresight to discover and exploit new opportunities on a continuous basis. It helps retain flexibility in the face of changing market forces.

2.6.2 TECHNICAL SKILLS

Technical skills relate to an understanding of the products or services on offer and the market and industry environment in which they exist. While the successful entrepreneur may not be a technical expert in their chosen field, they have an intuitive feel for their chosen marketplace and develop business relationships with those who do have the necessary expertize. James Dyson attributes his success to making products that people want to buy, a simple rule of thumb that applies to all businesses.

A 'technical skill' that should not go without particular mention is the entrepreneur's ability to operate effectively within an increasingly sophisticated and global intellectual property (IP) environment. Though entrepreneurs cannot necessarily be expected to be experts in IP law themselves, and would therefore do well to employ the services of IP/patent lawyers when required, it would be a mistake for them to simply delegate all matters of IP to others. IP is increasingly seen as the currency of the global knowledge economy. As such, being able to generate an IP strategy, which ensures both the protection and subsequent investment in IP, represents a key requisite for most entrepreneurial small business owners (for more on intellectual property management, see Chapter 10).

2.6.3 MANAGEMENT COMPETENCIES

Management competencies relate to managing key functions of the enterprise in order to achieve the enterprise's objectives. Traditionally, the essence of management is summarized in terms of four functions – planning, organizing, leading and controlling (see Tsoukas, 2000). Research indicates that strategic problems in young firms are most likely to arise in the areas of the management of people, and in marketing and finance (see Chapter 7, Successful Small Business Strategies, for a fuller discussion). The competency to deal with these areas depends particularly on the owner-manager in the early years of their venture when they are less likely to employ specialists. The model entrepreneur has all-round competency in these key management functions. However, this competency is augmented by a set of particular management behaviours which are characteristic of the entrepreneur.

2.6.4 ENTREPRENEURIAL BEHAVIOURS

We observed earlier that entrepreneurship is a societal process in which an opportunity is identified, evaluated and exploited, involving the creation of a new or significantly transformed organization, and the emergence of innovation. Such a process requires a specific set of management behaviours in order to be undertaken successfully. These include opportunity discovery and exploitation, resource acquisition and coordination, networking, effectual decision-making and creativity.

Opportunity discovery and exploitation

Entrepreneurial management requires being alert to opportunities (see Kirzner, 1973) and their potential to create new business streams either for a new venture or within an established organization. An entrepreneurial opportunity can be thought of as 'a situation in which a person can create a new means-ends framework for recombining resources that the entrepreneur believes will yield a profit' (Shane, 2003, p. 18). Success in opportunity identification comes not only from understanding the market and customers' changing needs, but also by having a wider view of potential industry transformations from the advent of new technology. Wilson and Martin (2015) outline seven antecedent conditions necessary for pursuing entrepreneurial opportunities, in any context:

1 the possibility of recombining resources
2 the possibility of transactional (market) exchange
3 the possibility of appropriating profits or value
4 entrepreneurial reflexivity (such as mulling over, deciding, planning)
5 entrepreneurial performance (turning ideas into action)
6 entrepreneurial creativity (recognizing novelty and value)
7 entrepreneurial intent (to pursue the entrepreneurial project).

Most entrepreneurs begin with a new venture idea which has yet to be proved in terms of whether it really represents a new business **opportunity**. There is usually a period of reflection and research (sometimes lasting months or even years), during which the entrepreneur establishes whether or not the 'good idea' is a viable opportunity. It is clearly important for the entrepreneur to become practised in spotting an opportunity when one arises. We discuss how to do this in more detail in Chapter 4.

Resource acquisition and co-ordination

One of the defining characteristics of new or young small businesses is that they are usually lacking the resources they require to achieve their objectives. Resources can take many forms, including money (financial capital), or key skills and employees (human capital), or perhaps the necessary relations (with bank managers, lawyers, accountants, etc.) required to oil the wheels of business (social capital). Small businesses are therefore described as being resource constrained. The ability to leverage resources from outside of the firm in order to overcome internal firm resource constraints is a key skill and hallmark of entrepreneurs/intrapreneurs (see Stevenson and Jarillo, 1990). As a firm grows, the ability to marshal the appropriate resources to create innovative responses to a changing environment – known as **dynamic capability** – becomes essential (Teece, Pisano and Shuen, 1997). Where such dynamic capabilities do not exist there is the tendency for the business to become bound by core rigidities (Leonard-Barton, 1995) which stifle its ability to cope with change.

CHANGING FASHIONS: ABERCROMBIE & FITCH[11]

The fashion retailer Abercrombie & Fitch was launched in 1892 by David Abercrombie, a trained civil engineer and topographer. His first modest store, built on the values of outdoor living, was on the waterfront in downtown Manhattan, New York. One hundred-plus years later, this small business has turned into a controversial fashion giant with stores around the globe. Some long-established companies fall into the 'competency trap' and fail to move with the times. Abercrombie & Fitch cannot be accused of ignoring modern tastes. It has become well-known for its use of youth-oriented loud music in stores and sensual photography which has been described as sexually explicit and racist. Its employment practices of using predominantly under 25-year-olds called 'models' with an emphasis on physical appearance, caused particular criticism in Europe, especially when it was claimed it paid extra for male staff to work shirtless. For an organization to possess a *dynamic capability* it is not enough just to do something different; it also has to evaluate the value of that change in different contexts and a constantly changing environment.

Entrepreneurial networking

The idea of **networking**, in which owner-managers give each other mutual support, collaborate with larger organizations and gain assistance from local institutions such as Chambers of Commerce and Business Links, has been put forward as a fundamental behaviour of the small business manager and a means of overcoming internal resource constraints (see Carson *et al.*, 1995). For the entrepreneur, networking is very often the key to realizing some other important competitive behaviours.

- Entrepreneurial alertness – the ability to scan the external environment for opportunity – is maintained through networking.
- Essential resources are located and acquired through networking. Very often the entrepreneur uses the network to leverage the required resources in the most cost-effective (or parsimonious) way.
- Networking provides the entrepreneur with a potential route towards achieving innovation without the need for expensive R&D departments.
- Early marketing within the smaller business relies extensively on the personal contacts of the owner-manager (Stokes, 2006).

The importance of maintaining an extended network of weak ties is highlighted in Granovetter's (1973) classic work on social relations. **Weak ties** are loose relationships between people, as opposed to the close

strong ties that would be found between family and friends. Weak ties are useful in respect of each of the entrepreneurial management behaviours described on the previous page. They can help in spotting new opportunities, leveraging resources which might otherwise be unavailable or too costly to locate, and carrying out innovation.

Personal contact networks (PCNs) – the relationships and alliances which individuals develop with others – are particularly useful to managers who have few, or no, colleagues internally that they can turn to for consultation and advice. PCNs can work well for owner-managers who collect information and make decisions in a relatively unstructured, intuitive way. Inter-organizational relationships (IORs) are an obvious route for small enterprises which do not have the resources to accomplish their objectives alone. While the number of support bodies available to owner-managers has increased substantially in recent years, the advantages of these networks have been minimized by another characteristic of small business owners: they are not joiners, preferring to keep themselves and their business problems to themselves. (Networking is discussed further in Chapters 4, 7 and 12.)

Effectual decision-making

A great deal of research activity has gone into working out how entrepreneurs make decisions and whether formal or informal planning is associated with new venture success. This is a particularly important area of entrepreneurship research given the conditions of uncertainty that confront the nascent entrepreneur. While managers in larger established firms expect to be able to draw upon a wide range of decision-making tools (e.g. competitor analysis; historical trends in performance, markets, etc.), entrepreneurial managers are necessarily dealing with new or emerging markets and are therefore limited in what they can use to help them make decisions. A decision to exploit an entrepreneurial opportunity is one that often must be made with little time for reflection, with limited information to go on, and in an altogether uncertain environment. In such conditions, entrepreneurs use biases and heuristics (or their gut-feel intuition) as a guide to decision-making (see Palich and Bagby, 1995; Busenitz and Barney, 1997). More fundamentally, however, the entrepreneur's decision-making process begins with the recognition of a particular set of *means* (i.e. ways of doing things; people to work with, etc.) rather than necessarily pre-judging the ends to be achieved (i.e. specific business goals). **Effectual decision-making** (see Sarasvathy, 2001) requires that the entrepreneur relies on their own ideas, networks and resources in the first instance. For more detail on effectuation, see Chapter 7, Section 7.2.2.

Creativity

Plays an integral role in the entrepreneurship process, and underpins the other entrepreneurial management behaviours discussed here. The link between creativity and entrepreneurship begins with our individual creative potential – our ability to generate and then exploit novel and valuable ideas. This is a universal feature of being human. We all come up with new and valuable ideas in the course of our everyday lives (maybe on a modest and personal scale, such as finding quicker routes for regular journeys or better ways of getting tasks done). Rather like artists, entrepreneurs need to possess an ability to tolerate complexity and contradiction. The key to long-term entrepreneurial success lies in the capacity to withstand the conflicting emotions around the performance of the entrepreneurial opportunity, from the excitement of achieving a sale to the disappointment of unfavourable feedback.

The entrepreneurial management behaviours introduced here are integral to the success of the new entrepreneurial venture. In practice, there are different degrees of entrepreneurship; some ventures show more entrepreneurship than others (see Davidsson, 2003; Tay 1998).

2.7 Summary and activities

This chapter's focus is on entrepreneurship and the entrepreneur. Entrepreneurship is understood in terms of the competitive behaviours that drive the market process. It can be seen as a transformative and creative process of social and market change that produces value for individuals and for society. In short, entrepreneurship involves the introduction of new economic activity. This is contrasted with the activities of small business owner-managers, in general, which may or may not involve *new* products, services or processes. The entrepreneur is best understood as the key mediator of this change process. Entrepreneurs draw on particular personal attributes and management behaviours. The chapter introduces the 'Big Five' personality traits (need for achievement, need for autonomy, locus of control, risk taking and self-efficacy), and outlines key entrepreneurial management behaviours including opportunity discovery and exploitation, resource acquisition and coordination, networking, creativity and decision-making.

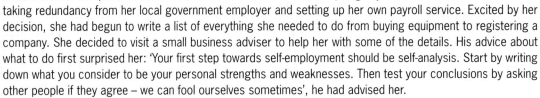

Case study
A tale of two entrepreneurs: Part 2

Andrea's strengths

Andrea Clarey was finding the first stage towards setting up her own business both unexpected and difficult. She had decided to take the plunge by taking redundancy from her local government employer and setting up her own payroll service. Excited by her decision, she had begun to write a list of everything she needed to do from buying equipment to registering a company. She decided to visit a small business adviser to help her with some of the details. His advice about what to do first surprised her: 'Your first step towards self-employment should be self-analysis. Start by writing down what you consider to be your personal strengths and weaknesses. Then test your conclusions by asking other people if they agree – we can fool ourselves sometimes', he had advised her.

Andrea had always found critical self-evaluation difficult and was reluctant to follow his advice. 'I wonder what good this navel-gazing can do', she thought. 'I'd rather just get on with the job.' She had worked in payroll services for over ten years in various types of public bodies from an education department to a local council. When she had left school at 17, she drifted through several clerical jobs until she married a few years later and started a family. Returning to work when her two children entered school, she realized that she needed more formal qualifications and studied bookkeeping on a part-time basis in the evening. Despite the pressures of raising a young family and an increasingly demanding job, she was determined to have at least one qualification to her name. This was partly to compensate for disappointing examination results at school where she had found most subjects too academic and lacking in practical application.

'My strengths are fairly obvious', Andrea thought. 'I know the payroll system inside out, and I know the public services which will provide me with at least two-thirds of the business I need to set up. I enjoy working with other people – as long as it doesn't involve too many meetings or time-wasting chit-chat. My staff have always stuck by me – I think I know how to manage my department well. But what are my weaknesses?'

Kit's weaknesses

Kit Hugos had not given too much thought to the invitation from his former employer, Robin Davidson, to set up in business on their own. He had agreed almost immediately. 'What are the next steps?' he asked, after agreeing in principle to become co-owner and managing director of a new electronics business. 'First we need to raise more money than I suspect we have between us', said Davidson. 'And to do that we need a business plan, which I have already begun to draft. One section you need to write is some details about yourself – career to date, personal strengths, that sort of thing. Banks and investors always seem to ask for it so we may as well be prepared. You joined TronTech straight from university didn't you?'

'More or less', replied Hugos. 'Although I did do some research in the electronic engineering department first. I had some interesting ideas in the field of circuit miniaturization and the university said I should register for a post-graduate degree – they even offered me a place as a Ph.D. student. But I couldn't get any grant, and my parents couldn't support me. So I came to work for you instead. I had hoped to follow up my ideas at TronTech, but you gave me too much work to do!'

'What would you cite as your strengths then?' asked Davidson.

'I'm ambitious, work hard and know the electronics trade, especially from a sales perspective.' He went on to explain that since leaving TronTech four years previously he had worked for three larger electronics companies in sales or technical support. 'I enjoy selling', he explained. 'You can work on your own without worrying about who to watch or who's watching you. And I have built up lots of good contacts on my travels – in and out of the industry.'

'Yes, quite a few people have mentioned seeing you at exhibitions and conferences. Any weakness that potential investors may pick up on?' Davidson asked.

'I'll need some financial training as I've always been hopeless at budgeting. And I can lose my temper faster than some. What do you think?'

Activities

(a) Why did Andrea's small business adviser start with self-analysis? Why is it important to Davidson's bankers and investors?
(b) Summarize Andrea's and Kit's strengths and weaknesses in relation to the technical skills, strategic management competencies, personal attributes and entrepreneurial management behaviours which they may need as owner-managers.
(c) How would you rate their chances of success in running a small business? What training or personal development needs would you suggest for each?
(d) Once they have completed their critical self-analysis, what should they do next?

Case study
Bobby and Sahar Hashemi: Coffee republic prepared for a 'Roasting'?

Bobby Hashemi grew up in a normal middle-class family in an environment that encouraged discipline and hard work. His parents' outlook on life reinforced the message that it wasn't about being the best, but doing your best that really mattered. In due course, this was to propel Bobby into a high-level professional career as an investment banker. Bobby worked hard at university, where he undertook a course in computer engineering. But he was eager to switch into the world of business and finance, for which he

(Continued)

felt much more inclined. Soon after completing his studies, Bobby started playing the stock market – he had a hunch he could make money rather more easily than working hard in an office. It didn't take long for Bobby to turn in some sound investments. However, the stakes were raised that bit higher when his father offered him £10 000 with the challenge to turn this into £100 000 by the end of the summer. With confidence riding high, and keen to prove his abilities to his father, Bobby set out to meet the challenge. But within ten days, Bobby had lost every last penny.

Having learned that there is no such thing as easy money, Bobby went on to study for an MBA at Tuck Business School in Dartmouth. The mix of hard study and outdoor sports in the Vermont countryside were a great preparation for the cut and thrust of New York city lifestyle that went with his job in Lehman Brothers. High-powered deals, red-eye flights, expense accounts, six-figure bonuses – these were the realities of living and sleeping investment banking in the late 1980s. Through all of this, Bobby and his friends talked of setting up their own businesses. They had plenty of ideas. But it always seemed that their dreams had to be put on hold while they concentrated on the business at hand.

On 23 January 1993, Bobby's father died. Bobby flew back to London straight away on hearing the tragic news. At the time, he didn't know that he was destined not to go back to New York to work. The sudden death of his father was a huge shock. Naturally, Bobby needed to take stock of his life and he also felt the need to be nearer to his mother and sister in England. Lehman Brothers gave him a six-month sabbatical followed by a transfer to London. Now back in London, Bobby started to think up options for starting his own business. Around 18 months later, the entrepreneurial opportunity had crystallized in his mind.

The hard grind of entrepreneurship

The idea of opening up a US-style coffee bar in London first came to Bobby Hashemi in November 1994. His sister, Sahar, had recently come back from her travels in South America, which were rounded off with a couple of weeks in New York on the way home. During her stay, Sahar had frequented a speciality coffee bar on Madison and 44th Street, and enjoyed such novelties as skinny cappuccinos and fat-free carrot muffins. At that time, there was nothing like it back in the UK. On getting home, Sahar had raved about these 'incredible' coffee bars to her brother. For his part, Bobby was well aware of the coffee-drinking boom taking place in the USA, having seen the prospectus for a new US coffee chain while he was in New York working for Lehman Brothers. From his own experience as a consumer, he was also well aware that London seemed to lack anything approaching the type of coffee bar Sahar was enthusing about. He became convinced that there was a genuine business opportunity here.

Sahar began to research the idea further. She toured central London, getting off at every stop on the Central Line and looking around to see what was currently available for the coffee-loving customer. It was pretty clear that a decent cup of coffee was a scarce commodity, despite the huge latent demand for a high-quality coffee experience. Though there were many sandwich bars, coffee tended to be something of a sideline.

Convinced that there was indeed a real business opportunity here, Bobby and Sahar decided that they would learn everything they possibly could about coffee and the business of coffee. Together they read, talked, drank and dreamed coffee. Soon, they attended an introductory training course on coffee making, laid on by a supplier they had met, for free. It wasn't long before they'd picked up many of the tricks of the trade, and talked to all sorts of people involved in the coffee trade.

With loads of research and first-hand experience behind them, Bobby and Sahar were in the position to write the business plan for their new coffee business. With the completed plan in hand, they set out to raise the £90 000 they needed to turn their ideas into reality. Having approached countless bank managers, and received 22 separate rejections, it would have been easy to give up. But finally, one more interview and presentation of their plan to a small branch of NatWest in Chancery Lane brought Bobby and Sahar the loan they so needed.

There was much more to be done before the business would be up and running. Finding the best location for the site; designing the coffee bar; negotiating with potential suppliers; employing staff; sourcing the right chairs, tables, door signs, coffee cups, coffee – there were many hurdles to overcome. But through sheer determination and belief, Coffee Republic opened its doors for the first time almost exactly a year after the idea had first lodged in Bobby's mind. Five years later in 2000, Coffee Republic had over 60 coffee bars and planned to open 80 more.

See Chapter 3 Case study 'The Coffee Wars' to see what happened next.

Activities

(a) What aspects of Bobby's upbringing, education and early career do you think had the most positive influence on his subsequent entrepreneurial activities?

(b) Referring to the Big Five personality attributes associated with entrepreneurial behaviour, outline any ways in which you think Bobby demonstrates the make-up of a 'typical' entrepreneur.

(c) Which human quality, illustrated in this case study, do you think is most important in preparing the nascent entrepreneur for the task of successfully exploiting an entrepreneurial opportunity?

(d) Which entrepreneurial management behaviours do you think are most clearly displayed by Bobby and Sahar in this case study?

(e) Which of these behaviours do you think was most important in the early days of this entrepreneurial journey?

Consider some small businesses with which you are familiar, and their owners and managers. (If you completed the Extended activity in Chapter 1, you can use the list of small businesses you drew up for that.)

(a) Which do you consider to be entrepreneurial? What sets them apart from other small businesses in respect of their entrepreneurship?

(b) Considering the owners, can you guestimate their ages, gender, marital status, social backgrounds, likely education and ethnicity? How do these compare to the information given in Section 2.2.3, Profiling the owner-manager/entrepreneur?

(c) What do you consider were the main influences which pushed or pulled these owners to set up their own business?

To answer these questions in detail it is preferable to interview some owner-managers/entrepreneurs. Where this is not possible, observation and previous knowledge can reveal a considerable amount of information.

Extended activity
Local entrepreneurs and owner-managers

Summary of what is required

Analyze yourself in terms of:

- personal objectives
- personal resources
- clues from the past
- your 'speciality'.

Know yourself: personal requirements and qualities for success

Planning a new venture
Know yourself

Starting up a new business venture on your own is not like applying for a job in an existing organization. There are no selection interviews, no one to tell you what to do or how to do it. It is a green field in which you can choose what seeds to plant, what to build and what role you wish to play.

In deciding what to do with your green field the most important influence is you: what you want from it and what you start with.

The starting point in thinking about any new venture is therefore some personal analysis which attempts to answer the following questions:

Personal objectives	How will you know if you are being successful?
	Where do you want to go in the future?
Personal resources	Where do you start from?
	What are your personal strengths, weaknesses and resources?
Clues from the past	What can you learn from your past?
	What lessons have you learned that may help take you from where you are now to where you wish to go?
Your speciality	What are your unique qualities that could help you reach your personal objectives?
	We are all different and therefore unique in some way.
	How can you use your uniqueness to give you enjoyment and satisfaction?
	Can you identify special talents you find most satisfying in practice?

Use the following worksheets to help you think about these questions. You can also find a very wide variety of self-analysis and personal professional development tools, questionnaires and profiling instruments on the internet. We provide more details of some of the most helpful of these in the context of small business management and entrepreneurship on the companion website.

It is important to establish these personal parameters for success as criteria against which to judge ideas for any new venture. As you develop ideas you will be asked to evaluate them according to your personal objectives and talents.

The level of commitment needed to make a new enterprise succeed is rooted in its ability to meet your personal requirements and in its potential for personal fulfilment through use of your special qualities. If your personal needs are not met, the motive force to make innovations succeed in practice will be lacking.

Personal objectives

Write down what you want in your life in the short, medium and long term:

	In 1 year	*In 3 years*	*In 10 years*
1. What do I want to be?			
2. What do I want to do?			
3. What do I want to have?			

Personal resources

Assess where you are now. Summarize what you have to offer (strengths) and what you need to learn or minimize (weaknesses) in terms of technical skills (what you can do, knowledge of specific products or markets, as well as intellectual property); strategic management competencies (specific business skills in areas such as finance, marketing, human relations and strategy); personal attributes (including innovativeness, determination, external focus and team leadership); and entrepreneurial management behaviours (alertness to opportunities, ability to leverage resources, networking skills and effectual decision-making).

	Strengths	*Weaknesses*
1. Technical skills		
2. Strategic management competencies		
3. Personal attributes		
4. Entrepreneurial management behaviours		

Clues from the past

Review your past life, and write down some specific moments when you felt purposeful and focused in a way that gave you satisfaction at the time and in retrospect. Also look at times when you felt less directed and adrift.

Personal qualities used/misused

Satisfying moments:

_____   _____

_____   _____

Dissatisfying moments:

_____   _____

_____   _____

What clues do these give about what you want, what you have to offer now and what you wish to avoid?

(Continued)

Your speciality

Make an assessment of your knowledge, skills and qualities to try and discover some things in you that are unique and that give you enjoyment and satisfaction. Review your personal objectives, personal resources and clues from the past. Select those qualities and talents that you feel make you stand out from the crowd. These are the talents that give you the greatest sense of enjoyment and satisfaction when you use them well.

My special talents are:

1.

_____

2.

_____

3.

_____

4.

_____

5.

_____

6.

_____

2.8 Notes, references and recommended further reading
Notes and further information

1 See nationalcareersservice.direct.gov.uk/aboutus /newsarticles/Pages/News-BusInYou.aspx, accessed 16 December 2015.

2 Corporate entrepreneurship is the sum of the company's venturing and innovation activities (see Zahra, 1993).

3 For a profile of Gates and other famous entrepreneurs, see: www.evancarmichael.com/

4 Majority women-led businesses are those where women make up more than 50 per cent of the partners or directors in day-to-day control of the business, or where the sole proprietor is a woman.

5 See Kepler and Shane (2007), for more discussion on the differences between male and female entrepreneurs.

6 'A nascent entrepreneur is defined as someone who initiates serious activities that are intended to culminate in a viable business startup' (Aldrich, 1999, p. 77).

7 For more discussion relating to cognitive adaptability, see Higgins (1997) on Regulatory Focus Theory;

Shane (2000) on 'entrepreneurial cognitions' based on knowledge; and Alvarez and Busenitz (2001) on heuristics.

8   Reading about entrepreneurs is a good start to becoming one. For more about these three: see Brown (1992) and Branson (1998), for more about Richard Branson; see Thomas (1991) and Burden (2009), for more about Alan Sugar; see Mone (2015), for more about Michelle Mone.

9   See De Bono, E. 'Water is Not Soup', *Space for Ideas*, East of England Development Agency, available at www.spaceforideas.uk.com (accessed 5 January 2009).

10 For more on leadership in an entrepreneurial context, see Chapter 11; Wickham (2004), ch. 27 on Leadership, Power and Motivation in the Entrepreneurial Venture; and Kirby (2006).

11 Sources: en.wikipedia.org/wiki/Abercrombie _%26_Fitch Abercrombie & Fitch, (accessed on 17 December 2015).

12 This case study is based on the account of the start-up of Coffee Republic in Sahar and Bobby Hashemi's book *Anyone Can Do it* (2002, Capstone Publishing Ltd, Chichester) and subsequent events in the news.

References

Acs, Z. J., Arenius, P., Hay, M., and Minniti, M. (2005) *Global Entrepreneurship Monitor: 2004 Executive Report*, GEM, available at www.gemconsortium.org, accessed 7 September 2006.

Aldrich, H. (1999) *Organizations Evolving*, Sage.

Altinay, L. and Wang, C. L. (2011) The influence of an entrepreneur's socio-cultural characteristics on the entrepreneurial orientation of small firms, *Journal of Small Business and Enterprise Development*, 18(4): 673–694.

Alvarez, S. and Busenitz, L. (2001) The entrepreneurship of resource-based theory, *Journal of Management*, 27(6): 755–776.

Armengot, C. R., Parellada, F. S. and Carbonell J. R. (2010) The immigrant entrepreneur in the international change: A managerial analysis according to demographic profile, *Journal of Organizational Change Management*, 23(4): 377–395.

Athayde, R. (2009) Measuring enterprise potential in young people, *Entrepreneurship Theory and Practice*, March: 481–500.

Bandura, A. (1982) Self-efficacy mechanism in human agency, *American Psychologist*, 37: 122–147.

Bandura, A. (1997) *Self-efficacy: The Exercise of Control*, Freeman.

Baron, R. (1998) Cognitive mechanisms in entrepreneurship: Why and when entrepreneurs think differently than other people, *Journal of Business Venturing*, 13(4): 275–295.

Bates, T. (1995) Self-employment entry across industry groups, *Journal of Business Venturing*, 10: 143–156.

Binks, M. and Jennings, A. (1986) New Firms as a Source of Industrial Regeneration. In: Scott, M., Gibb, A., Lewis, J. and Faulkner, T. (eds) *Small Firms' Growth and Development*, Gower.

BIS (2013) *Small Business Survey 2012: Estimates for Women-led, Minority Ethnic Group (MEG) led and Social Enterprises in the UK*, URN BIS/13/886, Department of Business, Innovation and Skills.

Bolton Report (1971) *Committee of Inquiry on Small Firms*, HMSO, Cmnd 4811.

Boyd, N. and Vozikis, G. (1994) The influence of self-efficacy on the development of entrepreneurial intentions and actions, *Entrepreneurship Theory and Practice*, 18(4): 63–77.

Branson, R. (1998) *Losing My Virginity: How I survived, had fun, and made a fortune doing business my way*, Crown Business.

Brockhaus, R. and Horwitz, P. (1986) The Psychology of the Entrepreneur. In: Sexton, D. and Smilor, R. (eds) *The Art and Science of Entrepreneurship*, Ballinger.

Brown, M. (1992) *Richard Branson, The Inside Story*, Headline.

Brush, C. G. (2006) Women Entrepreneurs: A Research Overview. In: Casson, M. *et al.* (eds) *The Oxford Handbook of Entrepreneurship*, Oxford University Press: 611–628.

Burden, C. (2009) *Sir Alan Sugar: The Biography*, John Blake.

Busenitz, L. W. and Barney, J. B. (1997) Differences Between entrepreneurs and managers in small firms: Biases and heuristics in strategic decision-making, *Journal of Business Venturing*, 12: 9–30.

Cahn, A. and Clemence, M. (2011) *The Whitehall Entrepreneur: Oxymoron or Hidden Army?*, Institute for Government.

Carson, D., Cromie, S., McGowan, P. and Hill, J. (1995) *Marketing and Entrepreneurship in SMEs*, Prentice Hall.

Carter, S. and Rosa, P. (1998) The financing of male- and female owned businesses, *Entrepreneurship and Regional Development*, 10(3): 225–242.

Casson, M. (1982) *The Entrepreneur*, Barnes & Noble.

Chell, E. (1999) The entrepreneurial personality – Past, present and future, *Occupational Psychologist*, 38: 5–12.

Covin, J. G. and Slevin, D. P. (1988) The influence of organizational structure on the utility of an entrepreneurial top management style, *Journal of Management Studies,* 25: 217–237.

Curran, J., Blackburn, R. and Woods, A. (1991) *Profile of the Small Enterprise in the Service Sector,* ESRC Centre for Research on Small Service Sector Enterprises, Kingston Business School.

Curran, J. and Burrows, R. (1988) *Enterprise in Britain: A National Profile of Small Business-Owners and the Self-Employed,* Small Business Research Trust.

Davidsson, P. (2003) The Domain of Entrepreneurship Research: Some Suggestions. In: J. Katz and S. Shepherd (eds) *Advances in Entrepreneurship, Firm Emergence and Growth,* 6.

Davidsson, P. and Honig, B. (2003) The role of social and human capital among nascent entrepreneurs, *Journal of Business Venturing,* 18.

De Bruin, A., Brush, C. G. and Welter, F. (2006) Introduction to the special issue: Towards building cumulative knowledge on women's entrepreneurship, *Entrepreneurship Theory & Practice,* 30: 585–592.

Department for Communities and Local Government (2013) *Ethnic minority businesses and access to finance,* July, www.gov.uk.

Department for Trade and Industry (2005) *Social Enterprise: A Strategy for Success,* DTI.

Dimov, D. (2007) Beyond the single-person, single insight attribution in understanding entrepreneurial opportunities, *Entrepreneurship Theory and Practice,* 31(5): 713–731.

Dimov, D. (2011) Grappling with the unbearable elusiveness of entrepreneurial opportunities, *Entrepreneurship Theory and Practice,* 35(1): 57–81.

Drucker, P. (1986) *Innovation and Entrepreneurship,* Heinemann.

Freeman, J. (1982) Organizational life cycles and natural selection processes, *Research in Organizational Behaviour,* 4: 1–32.

Gartner, W. B. (1988) 'Who is an entrepreneur' is the wrong question, *American Small Business Journal,* Spring: 11–31.

Gatewood, E. J., Carter, N. M., Brush, C.G., Greene, P. G. and Hart, M. M. (2003) Women Entrepreneurs, Their Ventures, and the Venture Capital Industry: An Annotated Bibliography, ESBRI.

Gautam, V. and Verma, V. (1997) Corporate entrepreneurship: Changing perspectives, *Journal of Entrepreneurship,* 6(2): 233–247.

Granovetter, M. (1973) The strength of weak ties, *American Journal of Sociology,* 78: 1360–1380.

Gray, D. (1987) *The Entrepreneur's Complete Self-Assessment Guide,* Kogan Page.

Gupta, V. K., Turban, D. B., Wasti, S. A. and Sikdar, A. (2009) The role of gender stereotypes in perceptions of entrepreneurs and intentions to become an entrepreneur, *Entrepreneurship Theory & Practice,* March.

Harding, R. (2003) *Global Entrepreneurship Monitor United Kingdom 2003,* London Business School.

Harding, R. (2007) *Global Entrepreneurship Monitor 2006, UK Report,* London Business School and Babson.

Haynie, M. and Shepherd, D. A. (2009) A measure of adaptive cognition for entrepreneurship research, *Entrepreneurship Theory & Practice,* May.

Higgins, E. (1997) Beyond pleasure and pain, *American Psychologist,* 52: 1280–1300.

Hisrich, R. D. and Peters, M. P. (2002) *Entrepreneurship,* 5th edn, McGraw-Hill.

Hornaday, R. (1990) Dropping the E-words from small business research, *Journal of Small Business Management,* 28(4): 22–23.

Jackson, C. (2015) *Lessons From The Kauffman Index: Immigrants are Infused with Entrepreneurial Energy,* www.kauffman.org/blogs/growthology, Kauffman Foundation.

Johnstone, H. and Basso, G. (1999) Social Entrepreneurs and Community Development. *Proceedings of the Atlantic Schools of Business Conference.*

Katz, J. and Gartner, W. B. (1988) Properties of emerging organizations, *Academy of Management Review,* 13(3): 429–441.

Kepler, E. and Shane, S. (2007) *Are male and female entrepreneurs really that different?,* U.S. Small Business Administration Office of Advocacy, available at www.sba.gov/advo/research/rs309tot.pdf, downloaded on 25 June 2009.

Kets de Vries, M. (1985) The dark side of entrepreneurship, *Harvard Business Review,* November–December: 160–168.

Khosa, R.M. and Kalitanyi, V. (2015) Migration reasons, traits and entrepreneurial motivation of African immigrant entrepreneurs: Towards an entrepreneurial migration progression, *Journal of Enterprising Communities: People and Places in the Global Economy,* 9(2): 132–155.

Kirby, D. (2003) *Entrepreneurship,* McGraw-Hill Education.

Kirby, D. A. (2006) Leadership, Entrepreneurship and Management of Small Businesses. In: Carter, S. and Jones-Evans, D. (eds) *Enterprise and Small Business,* 2nd edn, Financial Times/Prentice Hall: 291–302.

Kirzner, I. M. (1973) *Competition and Entrepreneurship,* University of Chicago Press.

Leadbeater, C. (1997) *The Rise of the Social Entrepreneur,* Demos.

Leonard-Barton, D. (1995) *Wellsprings of Knowledge,* HBS.

Liao, D. and Sohmen, P. (2001) The development of modern entrepreneurship in China, *Stanford Journal of East Asian Affairs,* 1, Spring.

Macrae, N. (1976) The coming entrepreneurial revolution, *The Economist,* 25 December (16pp).

Marlow, S. and Patton, D. (2005) All credit to men? Entrepreneurship, finance and gender, *Entrepreneurship Theory & Practice,* 29: 717.

Mason, C. and Lloyd, P. (1986) New Manufacturing Firms in a Prosperous UK Sub-region: The Case of South Hampshire. In: Scott, M., Gibb, A., Lewis, J. and Faulkner, T. (eds) *Small Firms' Growth and Development,* Gower.

McClelland, D. (1961) *The Achieving Society,* Van Nostrand.

McGee, J. E., Peterson, M., Mueller, S. L. and Sequeira, J. M. (2009) Entrepreneurial self-efficacy: Refining the measure, *Entrepreneurship Theory & Practice,* July.

McGrath, R. and MacMillan, I. (2000) *The Entrepreneurial Mindset: Strategies for Continuously Creating Opportunity in an Age of Uncertainty,* Harvard Business School Press.

Mitchell, R., Busenitz, L., Lant, T., McDougall, P., Morse, E. and Smith, B. (2002) Toward a theory of entrepreneurial cognition: Rethinking the people side of entrepreneurship research, *Entrepreneurship Theory and Practice,* 27(2): 93–105.

Mitchell, R. K., Smith, J. B., Morse, E. A., Seawright, K. W., Peredo, A. M. and McKenzie, B. (2002) Are entrepreneurial cognitions universal? Assessing entrepreneurial cognitions across cultures, *Entrepreneurship Theory and Practice,* 26(4): 9–33.

Mole, K. F., and Mole, M. (2010) Entrepreneurship as the structuration of individual and opportunity: A response using a critical realist perspective. Comment on Sarason, Dean and Dillard, *Journal of Business Venturing,* 25(2): 230–237.

Mone, M. (2015) *My Fight to the Top,* Blink Publishing.

Nussbaum, M. C. (2000) *Women and Human Development: The Capabilities Approach,* Cambridge University Press.

Nussbaum, M.C. (2011) *Creating Capabilities. The Human Development Approach,* Belknap, Harvard University Press.

Nussbaum, M. C., and Sen, A. (1993) *The Quality of Life,* Clarendon Press.

Palich, L. E. and Bagby D. R. (1995) Using cognitive theory to explain entrepreneurial risk-taking: Challenging conventional wisdom, *Journal of Business Venturing,* 10: 425–438.

Peters, T.J. and Waterman, R. (1988) *In Search of Excellence,* Grand Central Publishing.

Ram, M. and Smallbone, D. (2001) *Ethnic Minority Enterprise: Policy in Practice,* SBS.

Ramachandran, K., Devarajan, T. P. and Sougata, R. (2006) Corporate entrepreneurship: How? *Vikalpa,* 31(1): 85–97.

Reynolds, P. D., Bygrave, W. D., Autio, E. (2004) *GEM 2003 Executive Report,* Babson College and London Business School.

Rotter, J. B. (1966) Generalized expectancies for internal versus external control of reinforcement, *Psychological Monograph,* 80: 1–28.

Sarason, Y., Dean, T., and Dillard, J.F. (2006) Entrepreneurship as the nexus of individual and opportunity: A structuration view, *Journal of Business Venturing,* 21(3): 286–305.

Sarason, Y., Dillard, J. F. and Dean, T. (2010) How can we know the dancer from the dance? Reply to 'Entrepreneurship as the structuration of individual and opportunity': A response using a critical realist perspective, *Journal of Business Venturing,* 25(2): 238–243.

Sarasvathy, S. (2001) Causation and effectuation: Toward a theoretical shift from economic inevitability to entrepreneurial contingency, *Academy of Management Review,* 26(2): 243–263.

Sarasvathy, S. D. (2008) *Effectuation,* Edward Elgar.

Sarasvathy, S., Dew, N., Velamuri, R. and Venkataraman, S. (2003) Three Views of Entrepreneurial Opportunity. In: Acs, Z. and Audretsch, D., eds, *Handbook of Entrepreneurship,* Kluwer.

SBP (2014) Examining the challenges facing small businesses in South Africa, *Alert,* Issue Paper 1, www.sbp.org.za.

SBS (2003) *A Government Action Plan for Small Business: Making the UK the Best Place in the World to Start and Grow a Business. The Evidence Base,* Small Business Service.

Schein, V. E. (2001) A global look at psychological barriers to women's progress in management, *Journal of Social Issues,* 57: 675–688.

Schultz, T. (1959) Investment in man: An economist's view, *Social Service Review,* 33(2): 69–75.

Schumpeter, J. (1934) *The Theory of Economic Development,* Harvard University Press.

Scott, M., Gibb, A., Lewis, J. and Faulkner, T. (eds) (1986) *Small Firms' Growth and Development,* Gower.

Shane, S. (2000) Prior knowledge and the discovery of entrepreneurial opportunities, *Organization Science,* 11: 448–469.

Shane, S. (2003) *A General Theory of Entrepreneurship: The Individual-Opportunity Nexus,* Edward Elgar.

Shane, S. and Venkataraman, S. (2000) The promise of entrepreneurship as a field of research, *Academy of Management Review,* 25(1): 217–226.

Shaver, K. G. and Scott, L. R. (1991) Person, process, choice: The psychology of new venture creation, *Entrepreneurship Theory & Practice,* 16(2): 23–45.

Shepherd, D. and Krueger, N. (2002) An intentions-based model of entrepreneurial teams' social cognition, *Entrepreneurship Theory and Practice*, 27(2): 167–185.

Smith, N. (1967) *The Entrepreneur and His Firm: The Relationship between Type of Man and Type of Company*, Michigan State University Press.

Stevenson, H. H. and Jarillo, J. C. (1990) A paradigm of entrepreneurship: Entrepreneurial management, *Strategic Management Journal: Special Edition Corporate Entrepreneurship*, 11.

Stewart, W. H., Watson, W. E., Carland, J. C. and Carland, J. W. (1998) A proclivity for entrepreneurship: A comparison of entrepreneurs, small business owners, and corporate managers, *Journal of Business Venturing*, 14: 189–214.

Stokes, D. (2006) Marketing and the Small Business. In: Carter, S. and Jones-Evans, D. (eds) *Enterprise and Small Business*, Financial Times/Prentice Hall, pp. 324–337.

Stokes, D., Wilson, N. and Mador, M. (2010) *Entrepreneurship*, Cengage.

Stopford, J. M. and Baden-Fuller, C. W. F. (1994) Creating corporate entrepreneurship, *Strategic Management Journal*, 15: 521–36.

Tay, R. S. (1998) Degree of entrepreneurship: An econometric model using the ordinal probit model, *Journal of Small Business and Entrepreneurship*, 15(1): 83–99.

Taylor, M. (1996) Earnings, independence or unemployment: Why become self-employed?, *Oxford Bulletin of Economics and Statistics*, 58: 253–266.

Teece, D., Pisano, G. and Shuen, A. (1997) Dynamic capabilities and strategic management, *Strategic Management Journal*, 18(7): 509–533.

Thomas, D. (1991) *Alan Sugar, The Amstrad Story*, Pan Books.

Thompson, E. R. (2009) Individual entrepreneurial intent: Construct clarification and development of an internationally reliable metric, *Entrepreneurship Theory & Practice*, May.

Timmons, J. (1990) *New Venture Creation*, Irwin.

Timmons, J. A. and Spinelli, S. (2004) *New Venture Creation Entrepreneurship for the 21st Century*, 6th edn, McGraw-Hill.

Tsoukas, H. (2000) What is Management? An Outline of a Metatheory. In: Ackroyd, S. and Fleetwood, S. (eds), *Realist Perspectives on Management and Organizations*, Routledge.

Vecchio, R. P. (2003) Entrepreneurship and leadership: Common trends and common threads, *Human Resource Management Review*, Summer, 13(2): 303–328.

Venkataraman, S., Sarasvathy, S. D., Dew, N. and Forster, W. R. (2012) Reflections on the 2010 AMR decade award: whither the promise? Moving forward with entrepreneurship as a science of the artificial, *Academy of Management Review*, 37(1): 21–33.

Watkins, D. and Watkins, J. (1986) The Female Entrepreneur in Britain. In: Scott, M., Gibb, A., Lewis, J. and Faulkner, T. (eds) *Small Firms' Growth and Development*, Gower.

Wennekers, S. and Thurik, R. (1999) Linking entrepreneurship and economic growth, *Small Business Economics*, August, 13(1): 27–55.

Wickham, P.A. (2004) *Strategic Entrepreneurship*, 3rd edn, Financial Times/Prentice Hall.

Wilson, N. and Martin, L. (2015) Entrepreneurial opportunities for all? Entrepreneurial capability and the capabilities approach, *Entrepreneurship & Innovation*, 16(3): 97–110.

Wilson, N., Stokes, D. and Athayde, R. (2009) *Entrepreneurs in the Corporate Workplace*, Final Report for Cripps Sears & Partners, March.

Wu, S. (1989) *Production, Entrepreneurship and Profit*, Basil Blackwell.

Zahra, S. A. (1993) A conceptual model of entrepreneurship as firm behaviour: A critique and extension, *Entrepreneurship Theory and Practice*, 17: 5–22.

Recommended further reading

Chell, E. and Karatas-Özkan, M. (2014) *Handbook of Research on Small Business and Entrepreneurship*, Edward Elgar.

Carland, J. W., Hoy, F. and Carland, J. A. C. (1988) Who is an entrepreneur? is a question worth asking, *American Journal of Small Business*, Spring, 33–39.

Hashemi, S. and Hashemi, B. (2002) *Anyone Can Do It: Building Coffee Republic From Our Kitchen Table*, Capstone.

Say, J. B. (1964) *A Treatise on Political Economy: Or, the Production, Distribution and Consumption of Wealth*, A. M. Kelly, New York (reprint of original 1803 edition).

3 The small business and entrepreneurial environment

Learning objectives

By the end of this chapter you will be able to:

- Understand the influence of external environmental factors on small business survival and success.

- Assess the factors impacting the rate of new firm formation, including when, where and in which sector small businesses are set up.

- Recognize the differences between the more traditional small firm and the digital, web-based small business.

- Critically evaluate the influence of structural and regulatory issues on the small business's ability to compete in different industries.

Introduction

In Chapter 2, we discussed the different kinds of motivations that compel people to set up their own small businesses and the specific personal attributes and management behaviours required to undertake entrepreneurship successfully. In this chapter the focus shifts to the external forces that impact on an entrepreneurial venture. Among the questions we consider are:

- What conditions are favourable for setting up a new business?
- Which factors in the environment influence the likelihood of success (given the low survival rates of new small businesses)?
- What are the critical success factors for small business survival?
- What can we learn from looking at the pattern of small business start-up and closure?

Underlying these enquiries, the focus on small business environment also encourages us to think more carefully about what constitutes the 'entrepreneurial opportunity'. In Chapter 2, we noted that entrepreneurship involves the 'identification, evaluation and exploitation of an opportunity'. This implies that such opportunities exist 'out there', just waiting to be discovered by the entrepreneur. If this is the case, then the more we understand about the small business environment the more likely it is that we will be able to spot an entrepreneurial opportunity, and then go on to exploit it.

Activity 1
External influences

Which factors that are external to a new venture (such as the state of the economy and the political climate) are most likely to influence:

(a) the likelihood of a new venture starting up?
(b) its chances of survival thereafter?

3.1 A matter of life and death

In Chapter 1, we saw that small businesses form a turbulent part of the national economy because of the large-scale movements in and out of the sector. Many new ventures are created every year but an almost equally large number of businesses close.

In Chapter 2, we considered the backgrounds and personalities of entrepreneurs and owner-managers whose skills and characteristics play such a significant role in determining the fate of these businesses. They provide the motive force for the establishment of a new venture, and strongly influence how it is managed thereafter.

In this chapter, we consider factors in the business environment which affect the births and deaths of small firms but which are to some extent beyond the control of the owner-managers.

It is a combination of these less controllable, external factors together with the more controllable, internal factors, arising from the personal attributes, technical skills, strategic management competencies and behaviours of the owner-manager/entrepreneur, which influence:

- the likelihood of a new firm starting up – there are many environmental as well as personal influences on the formation of small firms;
- its chances of survival – once established it is vulnerable to circumstances beyond its control as well as the possibility of internal mismanagement.

This is illustrated in Figure 3.1.

Internal influences stem from the motivations, attributes, skills, competencies and behaviours of the individual(s) who sets up the business in the first instance. As we saw in Chapter 2, motives vary from those which 'pull' someone into starting their own business, such as a desire for independence, to other motives which 'push' a person into self-employment, such as the lack of employment alternatives elsewhere. Once set up, the founder's personal skills and management behaviours largely determine how the firm is managed in crucial functional areas. A review of research into the management problems faced by young, small firms revealed that they experience problems particularly in the areas of marketing, accounting and finance, and the management of people (Cromie, 1991).

External influences can be considered in two main categories – the macro- and micro-environment.

- The **macro-environment** consists of factors which tend to have an impact on all firms nationally and sometimes internationally. It includes:
    (a) Political and regulatory factors, such as levels of taxation, and health and safety regulations. Setting up a business in different countries, even within Europe, can have major implications for the entrepreneur.

Figure 3.1 Influences on small firm formation and survival

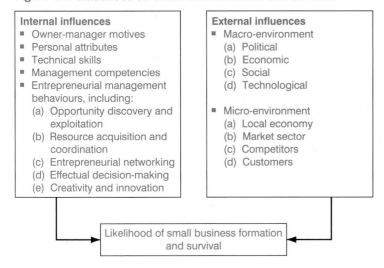

Internal influences
- Owner-manager motives
- Personal attributes
- Technical skills
- Management competencies
- Entrepreneurial management behaviours, including:
  - (a) Opportunity discovery and exploitation
  - (b) Resource acquisition and coordination
  - (c) Entrepreneurial networking
  - (d) Effectual decision-making
  - (e) Creativity and innovation

External influences
- Macro-environment
  - (a) Political
  - (b) Economic
  - (c) Social
  - (d) Technological

- Micro-environment
  - (a) Local economy
  - (b) Market sector
  - (c) Competitors
  - (d) Customers

Likelihood of small business formation and survival

(b) Economic conditions such as the rate of inflation or levels of unemployment.

(c) Social and demographic influences such as cultural and religious views on the role of women in society and business, or the age profile of the population. Western approaches to the fashion industry, for example, are incompatible with cultures in many countries of the world where women are required to dress in traditional clothing.

(d) Technological changes, for example, in information handling and communications. The impact of **electronic commerce**, in which products, services, and/or information is bought, sold, transferred or exchanged via computer networks, including the internet, has been incredibly far-reaching over recent decades and the rate of change is unlikely to get any slower. These advances have not just impacted the types of products and services available, but also the relationships between buyers and sellers and who is involved in the process. The distinction between producers and consumers is increasingly blurred as technology enables 'prosumers' to create their own 'user-generated content' (UGC). For some, this is an enabling technology as entrepreneurs now only need access to the internet to kick-start a new venture. Others see it as a tool for powerful conglomerates to dominate the market (see Smiers, 2003).

- The **micro-environment** refers to more local factors which influence firms operating in particular markets and competing in certain industries. It includes:

(a) local socio-economic conditions, such as the relative prosperity and population profile of a specific catchment area;

(b) the development and growth potential of a particular market;

(c) customer needs and the structure of demand for individual products and services;

(d) the competitive environment across specific industries.

These factors are obviously dynamic – their impact changes over time. They do not necessarily apply in the same way to the formation of new ventures as they do to their likelihood of survival.

Some factors which are crucial to the setting up of a small business may not be such a significant consideration in whether or not it survives (see Storey, 1998, chs 3 and 4). We shall therefore consider the 'births' and 'deaths' of small businesses separately in the following sections.

Activity 2
Birth rates

The birth rates of new firms vary considerably according to the time period, location and the industrial or market sector in which they are set up. Can you give examples of when, where and in which sectors you would expect to see high rates of small business births? Conversely, when would you expect to see low birth rates?

3.2 The birth of new businesses

3.2.1 DATA ON BUSINESS BIRTHS

In 2012, the 28 member states of the European Union counted 25.6 million active enterprises between them, of which 2.3 million were newly born enterprises (Eurostat, 2014). Birth rates in Europe tend to be around 10 per cent of the total business stock so that a significant percentage of the total stock of firms in the economy are very young.

The rates of new business formation are by no means uniform (see Keeble, Walker and Robson, 1993). Birth rates of small firms vary according to:

- *When* – the time period in which they are set up.
- *Where* – the geographic location.
- *Which sector* – the market and industry in which they are set up.

When: the rate of new venture creation varies over time. Business birth rates in the UK and across Europe were relatively low in the 1960s and 1970s but grew rapidly in the 1980s. After peaking at over 450 000 in the UK in 1996, they dropped to just 364 000 in 2001, before picking up again to 465 000 new business starts in 2003 (Bank of England, 2004). This fluctuating picture is illustrated in Figure 3.2. Once the impact of the financial crises had eased, the business formation rate picked up and the number of UK business births increased by 28.5 per cent from 270 000 to 346 000 between 2012 and 2013.

Where: births also vary according to location. Rates differ by geographic regions both across national boundaries and within more local areas.

Within Europe, some countries have higher rates of new business formation than others: in 2013, the birth rates ranged from 5 per cent in Belgium to 25 per cent in Lithuania (Eurostat, 2014). Although the overall UK business birth rate was 14.1 per cent, London was the top performing region at 17.9 per cent. This confirms previous regional analysis that revealed that London, and more especially inner London is both qualitatively and quantitatively different in entrepreneurial activity from the rest of the UK (Levie and Hart, 2009). Londoners were twice as likely as residents of other regions of the UK to expect to start a business in the period 2008–11.

Which sector: some industries attract more new firms than others. For example, in the UK the highest rate of business births just before the financial crisis in 2007 was in the property and business services sector (17.1 per cent birth rate as compared with 8.4 per cent in production, wholesale and health sectors). This all changed as the international crisis began to have a deep impact on start-up rates in general, and particularly those in the property and business services sector. By 2013, property start-ups had recovered somewhat to 11.1 per cent while business administration and support services had the highest business birth rate at 20.7 per cent of any UK sector (Office for National Statistics, 2014).

Figure 3.2 UK business starts and closures

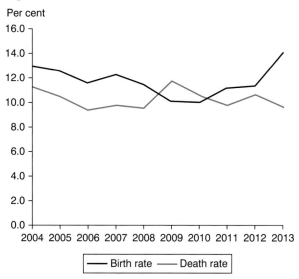

Source: Office for National Statistics (2014) *Statistical Bulletin: Business Demography, 2013*, www.ons.gov.uk.

A sector in the UK that has achieved significant growth over the last 20 years is that of creative industries. Employment in the creative economy increased from 1.81 million to 2.62 million jobs in the period 1997–2013 (DCMS, 2015a). This was equivalent to a rise of 2.3 per cent each year, which is four times greater than the 0.6 per cent increase each year in the number of jobs in the UK economy. The creative industries accounted for 5.0 per cent of the UK economy in 2013 (gross value added of £76.9 billion). This followed growth in the sector of 5.8 per cent each year (since 1997), as compared with 4.2 per cent in the UK economy as a whole. On the surface, this constitutes a 'success' story but these figures do not tell the whole story. The project-based nature of creative industries makes for a particularly uncertain sector for those that work in it, with high levels of short-term freelance work and uncertainty in terms of where 'the next job' will come from (Gill and Pratt, 2008; Oakley, 2009).

3.2.2 WHEN TO SET UP

Small firms are most vulnerable in their early years. Tracking of newly born enterprises in Europe reveals that 83 per cent survive the first year, so that 17 per cent close within one year of opening (Eurostat, 2014). Sweden had the highest one-year survival rate (95 per cent) and the UK, Netherlands, Belgium and Cyprus were all above 90 per cent. The lowest rate was in Lithuania (66 per cent) and Denmark, Hungary and Portugal were also well below average.

After the first year, survival rates gradually improve but after five years less than half (45 per cent) are still doing business. Enterprises born in 2007 in Sweden, Belgium and Austria were most likely to survive up to the fifth year after their birth, while Lithuania ran the greatest risk of non-survival (Eurostat, 2014).

The timing of business closures is strongly affected by movements of the economic cycle; for example, one-year survival rates were higher in 2000, a year of relative economic prosperity, than they were a decade earlier in the recessionary years of the late 1980s and early 1990s. In 2014, survival rates were better than in 2008. Therefore, in order to have the best possible chance of long-term survival, a new venture is best formed at a time when economic conditions are most helpful. Established firms have a much better chance of surviving recessions than young firms whose vulnerable early years need the benefit of a favourable business climate (Hall, 1995).

In a review of research into influences on the timing of new business births, Storey (1998) identified several possible factors:

- *Levels of unemployment.* As we saw in Chapter 2, unemployment, and lack of alternative employment possibilities, is an important factor which pulls people into self-employment and so times of relatively high unemployment are associated with higher rates of new firm formations.
- *Government policies.* Successive governments in the UK and elsewhere have introduced measures to encourage new business start-ups (these and other aspects of government policy are described more fully in Chapter 5. See also Table 3.1 which compares the ease of setting up in business in various states).
- *Profitability.* When income from self-employment is higher, more people will be attracted by this option.
- *Interest rates.* When real interest rates are high, new owner-managers find it more difficult to obtain finance and are less willing to borrow.
- *Personal savings and assets.* Personal savings or borrowings guaranteed by personal assets are the most common form of finance for a new business. Periods when the value of houses, the most common form of personal guarantee, are high favour business start-ups.
- *Consumer expenditure.* The highest number of new firms is in consumer services, so during times of growing consumer expenditure more opportunities for new ventures appear in this sector.
- *Structural change.* Some structural changes in the economy favour the small business, such as the movement from manufacturing to service industries. When these changes occur, more new firms are likely to appear.

While these factors may induce more new business start-ups, they do not all represent positive forces in the business environment which are likely to help the new owner-manager. Some are potentially negative factors which can push people into new ventures for the wrong reasons.

- *Potential negative factors.* Unemployment and government initiatives to reduce unemployment through self-employment may encourage many people into a new venture, but this is no guarantee of a friendly

Table 3.1 Ease of starting a business

Ranking	Country
1	New Zealand
2	Macedonia, FYR
3	Canada
4	Hong Kong SAR, China
5	Armenia
6	Georgia
7	Azerbaijan
8	Lithuania
9	Jamaica
10	Singapore
17	United Kingdom
49	United States
136	China

Source: World Bank Group 'Doing Business', June 2015
(www.doingbusiness.org/rankings).

business environment. The opposite is more likely to be true as high unemployment is likely to depress levels of demand, and therefore potential customer expenditure with a new business. High house prices, which make more finance available through personal bank guarantees, can increase the penalty for failure through the potential loss of a key personal asset without necessarily reducing the risks of it happening.

- *Potential positive factors.* Periods when real interest rates are low and consumer expenditure is growing are likely to be good times to start a new business, providing demand is not too dependent on a healthy economy. The high failure rates in the early 1990s in the UK indicate that many young firms were only viable in a strong economy and were not flexible enough to deal with more recessionary times. Times of structural change create opportunities for new ventures; for example, new types of business services have emerged to support changing work patterns following the development of new methods of communication and information processing. The successful entrepreneur is alert to underlying structural changes which can be rich sources of innovation and new business ideas (see Chapter 4, Innovation and the marketplace).

3.2.3 WHERE TO SET UP

Much is made of the fact that we live in an increasingly global community in which developments in travel and communication have radically changed the environment for business creation and self-employment. The increasing use of the internet for business information and the growth of electronic commerce enables people to set up a new venture virtually anywhere, even if the locality is not well-suited to their particular business. Global penetration of internet usage has increased from 15 per cent in 2005 to 40 per cent in 2015 as users exceed 3 billion of the world's 7 billion population (www.internetusage.com). Furthermore, more than 85 per cent of the world's internet users have purchased something online (The Nielson Company, 2007). The growth is not restricted to business-to-consumer (B2C) transactions, but is also coming from business-to-business (B2B) and other transaction types (including so-called 'collaborative commerce' where individuals or groups communicate or collaborate online). In the UK, the government set out its *Digital Communications Infrastructure Strategy* in 2015 with the ambition that 'ultrafast broadband of at least 100Mbps should become available to nearly all UK premises' (DCMS, 2015b). This is great news for the majority, but not so good if you are running your business from a cold spot where broadband coverage remains poor.

Despite the lowering of communication and trading barriers between geographic areas, there remain significant differences between countries, regions, cities and rural locations in terms of entrepreneurial activity. In particular, there has been a rise in the specialization of various regions within economies such as Silicon Valley in the USA and the Cambridge Science District in the UK. This concentration of specific knowledge and skills has a significant influence on business formation in the area. Highlighting the importance of creativity in modern economies, Richard Florida (2003) drew attention to the many individuals (he suggests over one-third of the national workforce in the USA) who 'create' for a living. This 'creative class' forms a dominant group in some societies that shapes economies, regions and cities. Florida (2008) argued against the widely held view that in an age of globalization where you live does not matter, and suggests that, on the contrary, 'place' is more important than ever.[3] The choice of where we live could be the most important decision we make in terms of the entrepreneurial path we take.

This could be caused by structural characteristics embedded in a country or region (Acs *et al.*, 2005). Storey (1998) cites eight possible factors that may lead to higher rates of new firm formation within a given geographic area:

1 *Population growth* – high population growth or high levels of immigration into an area.
2 *Unemployment* – higher levels of local unemployment.

3 *Wealth* – a high-income area with more disposable income to spend, especially on services.
4 *Workforce qualifications* – more managerial qualifications, leading to more wealth and more confidence to go it alone.
5 *Business size* – large numbers of small firms already existing in an area may indicate low entry barriers into the predominant business types of the area. A local small business culture may also encourage more of the workforce into their own new venture by example and familiarity.
6 *Housing* – high levels of owner-occupancy and house prices in a region, giving more access to capital.
7 *Local government* – higher levels of spending by local authorities which create more demand in the region.
8 *Government policy* – some small business incentives and development schemes are targeted regionally.

These factors, with the possible exception of unemployment, can represent positive influences on the new venture. Historically, most small businesses began trading within a very limited area (see Binks and Jennings, 1986) although the ease of access to the global market afforded by the internet has widened their geographic reach. Most owner-managers still select the area in which to establish their business based on where they live, not on considerations of which location represents the most favourable business environment.

This may be for good reason. Entrepreneurs use networks to seek out innovation and leverage resources and, in the early days of new venture creation, such networks are built almost exclusively around personal contacts. Whether strong (family and friends) or weak ties (indirect relations), these contacts are likely to be locally based (see Granovetter, 1973; 1985). The optimum business location on paper may disappoint in reality if the nascent entrepreneur is not socially embedded in a viable network of relationships. SMEs also tend to rely on employees living near the location of the enterprise, with 90 per cent of the workforce usually living locally (European Commission, 2007). Moving location as a business grows may risk losing valuable in-house experience and skills. These factors, with the possible exception of unemployment, can represent positive influences on the new venture (see Table 3.2 for regional differences).

Table 3.2 Ease of doing business

Ranking	Country
1	Singapore
2	New Zealand
3	Denmark
4	Korea, Rep.
5	Hong Kong SAR, China
6	United Kingdom
7	United States
8	Sweden
9	Norway
10	Finland
188	Libya
189	Eritrea

Source: World Bank Group 'Doing Business' June 2015.
(www.doingbusiness.org/rankings).

3.2.4 WHICH INDUSTRY AND MARKET TO CHOOSE

Starting a new business is more difficult in some industries and markets than others. Without the demand side or **market** there would be no customers and therefore no one to buy the competing products and services produced by those firms that together make up the supply side or **industry**. The data on new business start-ups discussed above (see Section 3.2.1, Data on business births) indicates trends favouring some industry sectors over others. Anyone wishing to start up in a given marketplace encounters a series of issues, or potential problems, whose impact varies according to the industry sector. These form barriers to entry for the small business which help determine the attractiveness of a specific sector to a potential new entrant. They are summarized in Figure 3.3. Before a small firm can do business with its chosen customer group, it must face the following competitive, structural and regulatory issues, as illustrated in Figure 3.3.

Activity 3
Barriers to entry

An entrepreneur wants to open a wine bar. Which particular barriers to market entry do you think will be encountered?

Economies of scale

Where significant cost reductions result from high levels of output in an industry, small firms find it difficult to compete. Prior to the 1970s, it was believed that the increasing existence of such economies in mass markets would lead to the inevitable decline of smaller firms. Certainly, a large firm enjoying economies of scale can use this cost advantage in a number of ways:

- By establishing low market prices, large companies can force competitors to operate on low margins which make it an unattractive market to new entrants.
- If prices are kept up, then the additional profits enjoyed by the supplier can be reinvested in marketing, or research and development of new products, again reducing the competitiveness of new entrants.

Such economies of scale created by automation in car manufacturing have effectively blocked entry to smaller companies in the mass market. However, although an industry may be subject to economies of scale, particular operations or processes within it may not. Many small firms exist as suppliers to car manufacturers that find it more efficient to subcontract some specialized areas, such as design and development.

Figure 3.3 Barriers to market entry for a small firm

Small business → Industry characteristics → Target customers

Economies of scale
Product differentiation
Capital requirements
Switching costs
Access to distribution
Other cost advantages
Government policy

In relying on **economy of scale**, the larger company can have problems which can be successfully exploited by the smaller firm. To achieve scale economies, the larger firm may have to sacrifice differentiation of products or services. It may not go as far as Henry Ford's famous restriction on the colour range of the Model T ('You can have any colour as long as it's black') but it may encourage a standardization of products or services leaving niche markets open to less uniform treatment, as the Just Kampers story below illustrates.

THE JUST KAMPERS STORY

Mark Reynolds founded Just Kampers (JK) in Surrey, UK on his 22nd birthday in 1989 because he couldn't get motor trader's insurance under that age. He was a one-man band specializing in the repair of traditional VW campervans. As the vehicles were no longer made, he had to break up old campervans for spare parts. Those parts he didn't use, he sold to a growing band of VW camper enthusiasts. As the passion for the classic vehicles grew, the availability of parts declined. He decided to source them himself and sell them from a small shop within his workshop. While on holiday in Malta, Mark discovered by chance a closed-down VW dealer that had stored a considerable stock of parts in a nearby cave. He bought all the parts and shipped them back to the UK. The retail side of the business grew rapidly and he went to the USA and South Africa to source more parts there. JK turned gradually from a repair into a parts business. The increasing popularity of the internet meant that, in 2003, they could introduce online sales. As demand picked up so the supply of second-hand parts became more difficult and some became obsolete. JK's response was to invest in the tooling to make new parts themselves to satisfy the demand as the vehicles become older and the parts harder to find. With increasing orders from around the world, they opened a branch in Australia in 2010. Recently they diversified into camping equipment to go with the classic vans. They celebrated 25 years of successful trading in 2014.

Reference: www.justkampers.com

Scale economies may be achieved by a larger firm using an existing technology, which makes them less flexible in adapting to new technologies, or blind to the changes which are taking place. Far-reaching changes in industries are often generated from without by new firms, rather than by the existing participants in the industry. The behaviour of larger firms is characterized by what has been described as 'path dependence' (David, 1992, p. 139). Established organizations seeking to bring about some change are more constrained by their past and narrow views of opportunities presented.

The move away from large, mainframe computers into smaller, high-volume personal computers was triggered not by the well-established giants, but by a complete newcomer, Apple Computers, set up by two young computer enthusiasts both named Steve – Jobs and Wozniac. A novice in the floor-cleaning industry, James Dyson, introduced an innovative carpet cleaner based on 'cyclone' technology, and his success eventually forced the established brands to abandon their

(Continued)

old methods reliant on replaceable bags. The age of the internal combustion engine may be nearly over. Some of the existing car manufacturers have introduced electric and hybrid cars, but it is a newcomer, Tesla, that is leading the way by developing an upmarket saloon with a range of 300 miles per charge. The company is run by Elon Musk who developed PayPal and had no background in the car industry.

Product differentiation

Established companies build up loyalty with customers who identify with their particular product or service. This differentiation takes time to prove the reliability of a product or service and money for advertising and branding. It therefore represents a significant barrier for any new entrant to overcome.

Direct competition with internationally branded products, supported by the resources of large companies, is not feasible for smaller firms. Nevertheless, there are always segments less affected by large-scale loyalty, and the use of viral marketing via social media can overcome some of the marketing cost barriers to entry.

The Body Shop successfully overcame the brand loyalty of the cosmetic giants by rejecting the basic ideas of beauty products on which that loyalty was based. Their cheap plastic containers and simple descriptions appealed by their contrast to the lifestyle-image approach of established brands, and provided the perfect market entry for a small firm with no resources to compete head on.

Hotmail was a fledgling email provider when they decided to reach out to the friends, family and colleagues of the small user base they had by adding a message in the footer of every email sent out that asked: *'Want a free email account? Sign-up for Hotmail today.'* The strategy laid the foundation for modern viral marketing that is widely used today on the likes of Facebook, Twitter, YouTube and LinkedIn. The principle is to ask users to share information on a large scale for free rather than use expensive advertising campaigns.

Small firms also build up their own loyalties which differentiate them sufficiently to deter new competitors. Allegiances to an existing small business are sometimes sufficiently great, and the local market sufficiently small, to make market entry impossible except by purchasing the business.

The brewing industry is a good example of large- and small-scale product differentiation. At a national and regional level, the large brewers have created differentiated, branded products which, coupled with economies of scale in production and distribution, have established high barriers. At the local level, public houses and other outlets are differentiated by location, management and environment, which often works to the benefit of an owner-manager. Well-liked publicans in small communities effectively differentiate their public houses by their own character, thereby blocking new entrants through personal loyalties.

Capital requirements

A very tangible barrier into some markets is the large set-up cost involved. Industry classifications with a low representation of small firms are usually those requiring substantial start-up investment, often those involved in production and manufacturing. This barrier can be reduced by the availability of second-hand plant and equipment. Bankruptcy and trading difficulties increase the availability of second-hand machinery often sold cheaply through auction, which is a further factor in the higher level of small business starts during times of recession.

Switching costs

When buyers switch from one company's product to another, they may incur one-off **switching costs**. These might be in the retraining of staff; for example, the most significant costs in changing computer software may be in the retraining needed for the users. Other switching costs could be incurred by a manufacturer changing supplier of raw materials which involves product redesign, or increased stock obsolescence. Where significant costs exist, the potential new supplier has to offer more than just marginal benefits to persuade a buyer to change.

Some firms deliberately exploit switching costs as a marketing ploy to attract and retain existing customers. For example, suppliers of coffee offer commercial customers the free loan of coffee-making equipment, immediately establishing a barrier to any competitors.

For small firms, switching costs often represent a real, but hidden, barrier. A concept which has been researched only hypothetically may not pass the ultimate test of being purchased in place of a competitive product, because of the emotional switching costs of severing a relationship with an existing supplier. Sales training emphasizes the need to build strong personal relationships with existing customers so these emotional switching costs will be increased, and the temptation to buy elsewhere decreased.

Access to distribution channels

Another market barrier, sometimes overlooked in the concept stage of a small business, is the need to have access to established channels of distribution.

BREAKING DOWN BARRIERS TO ENTRY THE AMAZON WAY

Traditionally, anyone wishing to publish a book would have a number of significant barriers to entry to have their creation enter the relevant distribution channel. Persuading a literary agent and then a publisher to consider a new book from an unpublished author, especially in the field of fiction, is hugely difficult and fraught with rejection. Many subsequent bestsellers were initially rejected – some many times. Robert Perzig's *Zen & the Art of Motorcycle Maintenance* is in the *Guinness Book of Records* for 121 rejections, more than any other bestseller. One way around traditional publishing was self-publishing, a route taken in desperation by Beatrix Potter with *The Tale of Peter Rabbit* as long ago as 1901. This was also unlikely to succeed for most authors until the advent of digitalization of content and the internet in the 1990s. Today, the author's proverbial pen can be linked directly to readers without the need for intermediaries. One of the key steps towards this were laid down by e-commerce entrepreneur, Jeff Besoz. He set up Amazon in 1995, having realized that the internet was going to dramatically change the way we buy things. Researching the ideal product to sell online, he came up with books; there are so many

(Continued)

of them that no shop can stock them all and they are relatively cheap to ship direct to consumers. Amazon was an immediate success as an online retailer and went on to to become a successful publisher and digital content distributor through the Kindle device that allows you to download, store and read content at home and bypass the standard distribution channels of physical books completely. That has not removed the would-be author's problems, however, as being noticed amongst over one million titles now available on the Kindle has become a significant barrier in its own right. Amazon is now attempting to overcome another significant barrier in its business model: delivery of physical goods to its millions of customers worldwide. The latest initiative is Amazon Prime Air that involves delivery by a drone.

Other cost advantages

Some cost advantages enjoyed by established companies are independent of scale. Perhaps the two most significant of these for smaller firms are:

1 *Learning curve.* Improvements come with experience, and this can be translated into cost economies. Manufacturers will often benefit from higher machine productivity, for example, as they gain production experience. A restaurant owner will learn how to reduce food waste by serving a particular menu only with time and practice. The new business can expect higher unit costs in its early days than its more established competitors.

2 *Location.* In many markets, location of premises is a crucial marketing factor. Existing firms often have good locations which will be expensive for the new entrant to equal. For example, leasehold retail premises in good locations can command a premium when they change hands; that is, the incoming tenant pays the outgoing one for the privilege of taking over the lease. Established companies may have paid no such premium because they were an original tenant, or the location had not been popular when they moved in.

Government policy and regulations

All industries are controlled by national or local government regulations, at least to some extent. **Regulations** are defined as the legal and administrative rules created, applied and enforced by government regulatory authorities – at local, national and transnational level – that both mandate and prohibit actions by individuals and organizations, with infringements subject to criminal, civil and administrative penalties (Hart *et al.*, 2008).

Regulations can create total or partial barriers to entry. Some postal delivery services have only recently been opened up to new business entrants, while other areas still remain prohibited. The licensing laws present barriers to entrants who wish to open a restaurant, run a public house or operate an off-licence.

Other regulations increase the capital costs of market entry. Conforming to Health and Safety regulations often requires expenditure in adapting premises; for example, in the provision of toilets and fire escapes. Hygiene regulations lay down strict requirements on food preparation for public consumption, which increases the start-up and ongoing costs for several types of small business, from exclusive restaurants to sandwich bars. Regulations concerning the payment of a minimum wage are by no means uniform across countries, inevitably impacting some employers (and employees) more than others (see Table 3.3).

Owners of small businesses often complain that conforming to government regulations gives larger firms an unfair economy of scale; the cost of conforming to the paperwork of tax returns, for example, is a relatively fixed cost, which the larger firm can amortize over higher sales turnover than the small firm. Governments have become increasingly aware of these problems and a number of measures have been taken to try and level the playing field (see Chapter 5, for fuller details of UK government policy).

Across Europe, 44 per cent of SMEs consider themselves as operating in an over-regulated environment (European Commission, 2007, p. 5). However, recent research cautions against the view that regulations are

Table 3.3 Minimum wage in different countries (2015)

Country	Minimum wage $ per hour
Denmark	18.00 (but limited to collective bargaining agreements)
France	12.75
Germany	11.28
UK	11.02
Canada	9.22
Brazil	1.90
Pakistan	0.62
South Africa	No minimum wage

Source: Official minimum wage rates of United Nations member states.

necessarily a constraining influence on small business performance (Hart *et al.*, 2008). Although regulations clearly do impose costs on small businesses and their owners, performance outcomes experienced in practice are by no means a function of the regulation involved. They reflect the capacities and motivations of particular businesses and the wider contexts in which they operate. For example, regulations regarding the official testing of electrical goods may help a new business to deliver the level of quality expected by customers.

REGULATIONS AND SMALL BUSINESS – THE OTHER SIDE OF THE STORY

It's probably not a good idea to mention the word 'regulation' to a group of small business owners, as it tends to provoke wrath and indignation. For many years, the 'burden of red tape' has remained at the top of the list of small businesses' list of key problem areas. However, there is another side to the story of regulation, as the case of Data X, a document storage company demonstrates. Data X was founded by Dr Ulrich Ment in 1991 and grew from just 2 employees to 160, working across 11 major city locations, and with a turnover exceeding £6 million by 2008. The regulatory environment was influential in Ulrich's decision to set up Data X in the first place, as well as in the firm's subsequent rapid growth. In true entrepreneurial fashion, Ulrich spotted the opportunity for an emerging market in document storage and self-storage. The introduction of a statutory obligation for certain businesses to maintain records (e.g. health and law firms) represented a significant market-creating opportunity, but also held the promise of long-term clients, rather than one-off transactions. Though Ulrich would be keen to point out that other regulations represent a constraining influence on his firm (e.g. the cost of compliance and high business rates), he readily admits that, in his line of business, regulations have also done him a favour.

In considering the impact of regulations on small businesses, there is a tendency to look at the immediate impact on the individual small business, rather than reflect on the bigger picture. The market context is often complex with a myriad of players involved, including suppliers, competitors, substitute industries, infrastructure and utility providers, as well as customers. While the introduction of a new regulation, such as the minimum wage requirement, will impact the individual small business directly, it will also have an effect on all the other players in the market.

Figure 3.4 Direct and indirect regulatory influences on business performance

Market system–including regulatory framework

Competitors

Suppliers

Customers

Focal
Small
Business

'Infrastructure
providers'

Employees

Indirect effects

Direct effects

Source: Hart *et al.* (2008, p. 11) Reproduced with permission.

To understand fully the impact of regulations on small business performance, therefore, policy-makers have to look in more detail at both the direct and indirect influence of the regulation on those involved, as illustrated in Figure 3.4.

This may have encouraged the European Commission to adopt the Small Business Act for Europe (SBA) in 2008 which explicitly tried to improve the environment for business creation and growth by adopting a 'Think Small First' principle in policy-making and regulation.[4]

SME REGULATION WOES IN SOUTH AFRICA

Although the South African government recognizes the need to encourage entrepreneurship in order to create economic growth, the SME sector is actually declining. GEM 2013 statistics indicate small businesses are closing down at a faster rate than new ones are being formed; only 10.6 per cent of South Africa's adult population is involved in early-stage entrepreneurship while 3 per cent operate established small businesses, putting the country in the bottom four globally for entrepreneurial activity. (In contrast, for example, 17 per cent of Brazilians are active in early-stage entrepreneurship and 15 per cent operate established firms).

According to the SBP (2014: pp. 2–3), the burden of regulation is a key factor:

'Frequent changes in the regulatory environment, the need to keep track of overlapping and sometimes conflicting regulatory requirements across multiple departments and levels of government, poor communication and access to information, and administrative inefficiencies in government departments and municipalities, mean that the SME owner spends a disproportionate amount of time dealing with regulatory compliance.'

Small firms spend an average of eight working days (75 hours) a month dealing with red tape. This regulatory compliance is estimated to cost SMEs £10 000 (R216 000) per year plus a further £1000 (R21 000)

(Continued)

to comply with tax requirements. Business owners identified labour issues as one of their top red tape headaches; small firms can spend up to 11 days per case at the Council for Conciliation, Mediation and Arbitration (CCMA) to resolve a dispute and the average SME is taken to the CCMA twice a year.

3.2.5 IMPACT OF THE INTERNET AND ELECTRONIC COMMERCE

The internet promised to offer ways in which new enterprises could bypass traditional barriers to entry and overthrow the established order in many markets. As we have already seen, internet-related technologies have begun to upset the status quo in some industries, and allowed new ventures to compete on more or less equal terms with larger firms, often exploiting new business models.

There are a wide range of electronic commerce business models which are used in many different industries and markets (see Turban, King, Lee and Viehland, 2004, pp. 14–15). Some examples include:

- *Online direct marketing* This is where the manufacturer sells online to a customer without any intermediary. This is particularly suitable for the sale of digitizable products and services (i.e. those that can be delivered electronically).
- *Viral marketing* Where an organization increases brand awareness or generates sales by inducing people to send messages to other people or to recruit friends to join certain programmes. In effect, this is web-based word-of-mouth marketing (see Chapter 12).
- *Online auctions* eBay.com, the world's largest online auction site, operates using this principle of transaction.
- *Electronic marketplace and exchanges* Although these have existed for some years (e.g. in stock and commodity exchanges) many new e-marketplaces have been introduced, bringing with them increased efficiencies to the trading process.

Clear differences are emerging between the so-called digital versus 'bricks-and-mortar' company. To some extent, these reflect an underlying shift in power (see Hartley, 2009): whereas in the industrial era concentrations of power reflected ownership and control of *capital*, power has increasingly been concentrated in control over access and distribution of *information*.

In addition to the distinctions caused by their specific business models, there are also general differences between the so-called digital and 'bricks-and-mortar' company. Digital organizations will sell goods online; bill their customers electronically; manufacture products based on their demand (*pull* production) and use a hub-based supply chain. Bricks-and-mortar organizations will sell tangible goods in shops; use paper-based billing; manufacture products so that they have stock (*push* production) and use linear supply chains. In a digital organization, there can be a perfect match of customers' value proposition (cost = value) whereas in a bricks-and-mortar organization the customers' value proposition is frequently a mismatch (cost > value).

These differences in the use of electronic commerce signal a mixture of advantages and disadvantages for the nascent entrepreneur or small business founder, which should be considered carefully:

- On the one hand, electronic commerce offers a relatively inexpensive means of advertising and conducting market and competitor research. Setting up a website is relatively easy and cheap to undertake. Arguably, a web presence can generate quick public recognition and give the small business a means of competing with larger firms. Electronic commerce offers the small business lower operating costs, more accurate and speedy information transfer and potentially closer ties with business partners.
- On the other hand, the small business rarely has sufficient financial resources to exploit the internet fully. A transaction website may require relatively high up-front fixed costs. Very often a key stumbling block

for small businesses is the lack of technical knowledge and expertise in the management of key issues associated with electronic commerce. More fundamentally, a small business using electronic commerce may have reduced contact with its customers – something that very often provides a source of competitive advantage over larger firms for the smaller enterprise.

CHANGING THE TUNE: REVOLUTION IN THE MUSIC INDUSTRY

The music industry, which has been particularly influenced by digitalization, provides an interesting case study of the influence of the internet. New technology which allows music to be copied and quickly distributed anywhere in the world threatened to destabilize the established positions of the music industry 'Majors' and create opportunities for new ventures. In the 1990s, the five big music companies (EMI, Sony, BMG, Warner Music and Polygram) tried to ignore the new technology until Napster was founded in September 1999 by Shawn Fanning to allow users to swap music files among themselves. In October 2001, the computer giant Apple launched the iPod and two years later its online iTunes store, giving rise to a new order that has shaken the dominance of the Majors to the core. Music sales halved in the decade after Napster as the internet turned the industry upside down. By 2009, the power of the 'big five' had concentrated still further so that now the duopoly of Sony and Universal effectively controlled 80 per cent of the charts and related visibility. Meanwhile, piracy had escalated to huge proportions. Figures released by the International Federation of the Phonographic Industry (IFPI) indicated that 95 per cent of all music downloads was of an illegal nature.[5]

For some, the dangers of piracy spell the demise of the industry altogether. Others see the potential of the internet to create an ever bigger, changing industry. Attention has turned to the ways in which new bands can exploit the internet to cultivate the 'fan–artist' relationship (see www.slicethepie.com which offers music fans and investors the chance to invest in new and established artists), or how online music retail can encourage consumers to discover more of the music they really love (e.g. Apple's Genius music discovery service). Bands such as the Arctic Monkeys first came to public attention via the internet through fan-based sites and helped change the way in which new bands are promoted and marketed. The drying up of royalties from reduced legitimate replays of older music has led to another benefit for music lovers. Ageing rockers have been encouraged out of retirement and back onto the stage by the financial squeeze of falling royalties. Even the bands who said they would never reform have done exactly that and gone on tour again, including the Eagles, Stone Roses, the Spice Girls, Police, Blur and Pink Floyd.

It was not only the music industry that seemed destined for a surge in new ventures. The early wave of internet entrepreneurs setting up innovative new services such as eBay and lastminute.com seemed to indicate that traditional larger organizations in many sectors could be challenged by newcomers. The domination of markets by existing brands and organizations is being threatened by a new generation of entrants. However, many of the larger players remain strong for a number of reasons:

- A high proportion of the sales made over the internet are B2B, with existing organizations adopting the internet as a purchasing mechanism. In relative terms, sales to end-users, or B2C transactions, have challenged some industries (travel, music, books) but by no means all.
- Existing major brands sold by large organizations are popular on the internet because consumers have remained concerned about internet shopping security, and choose known brands to reduce the perceived risk.
- Existing, larger companies may not have been the first to realize the potential of e-commerce, but they are likely to take advantage of subsequent developments on the internet. Well-publicized casualties among new technology companies, such as the demise of Boo.com, made investors warier of internet shares.

New investment is likely to come from existing competitors buying into the new technology. The *corporate venturing* model, where established larger firms invest in or buy up smaller innovative enterprises, remains important.

What can a small business do then to give it the best possible chance of success on the internet? Research suggests the following strategies are important to consider (Turban *et al.,* 2004, p. 593):

- **Niche or specialized product.** 85 per cent of small businesses admit they are missing out to larger competitors. However, it is difficult or impossible to compete against online giants such as Amazon.com unless you specialize in a particular niche area.
- **Flexible payment methods.** Despite improvements in security, not all customers want to give their credit card details over the internet.
- **Secure electronic payments.** This is, of course, an entry-level requirement nowadays.
- **Minimum capital investment.** It is vital to keep the company's overheads and risk low. It is for this reason that many small firms outsource their web hosting.
- **Stock control.** This is a vital aspect of any business, but no more so than in the small enterprise, where holding too much stock can tie up much-needed capital.
- **Quick and reliable logistics.** Many small businesses subcontract out their logistical services to courier or shipping firms.
- **High visibility on the internet.** The website should be submitted to directories such as Yahoo and search engines such as Google, MSN Search and Lycos and optimized for prominent search engine placement.[6]
- **Provide a comprehensive website.** The website should provide all the services required by consumers.

Activity 4
Closure rates

Ten entrepreneurs set up in business in the same year. If they suffer the average closure rates of small firms in the UK, how many would you expect to remain in business at the end of:

- Year 1?
- Year 5?

3.3 Sink or swim

3.3.1 SMALL BUSINESS CLOSURE RATES

A key feature which distinguishes small business from large business is the much higher closure rates of small firms. Statistics of the lifespan of new business and high closure rates caution against the euphoria that foresees a new wave of small business start-ups as the beginning of a new economic dawn. Figure 3.2, which charts business start-ups and closures from 2004 to 2013, illustrates that 'deaths' almost match the rate of business births as, over time, around 10 per cent of the total stock close each year. Closures increased sharply in 2009, rising above the birth rate as the financial crisis took its toll. By 2013, improving economic conditions reduced the number of closures but they still numbered 238 000 or 9.7 per cent of the total stock, equivalent to nearly 1000 for every working day of the year.

Most businesses that close are micro or small firms because these constitute the most numerous and the most vulnerable sector. Only a small percentage stay in business in the long term (Storey, 1998). As reported

Figure 3.5 Types of business closures

Discontinued		Continued	
Financial failures	Not meeting owners' objectives	Technical closures	Sold on
20%	**30%**	**15%**	**35%**
Insoluble financial problems often resulting in bad debts	Closed with neither significant debts nor sold on for a consideration	Closed for business objectives and reopened in a different form. For example, upgrade of sole trader to limited company or changes to partnership	Sold for a consideration to third parties, existing managers, family members or friends

Source: Small Business Research Centre, Kingston University, 2001.

in Section 3.2.2 (When to set up), only 83 per cent of new ventures in Europe survive the first year (Eurostat, 2014). With each year that passes, survival rates gradually improve but after five years less than half (45 per cent) of businesses are still trading.

However, we should not assume that a closed business equates to a failed business. Closures occur for a variety of reasons, some negative but others more positive, such as retirement or sale of the firm. A study carried out by Kingston University (Stokes and Blackburn, 2001) indicated that only half of closed businesses are discontinued because they have failed financially or they no longer meet their owners' objectives (see Figure 3.5). The other half are effectively continued; they are either sold on or they are businesses that close and then re-open for technical reasons such as the change of a sole trader to a limited company.

Other patterns emerge from the statistics on closed firms:

● The young are more likely to die than the old – closure rates are highest in the early months and years.
● The smallest are most vulnerable – micro firms employing less than 10 people close at a much higher rate than small firms employing up to 50 people, which in turn are more likely to close than medium-sized companies.
● Those that grow are less likely to close than those that do not. Treading water is not a good survival strategy.

In summary, as a firm becomes larger and older its chances of survival improve. Statistically, it has been calculated in one survey that a 1 per cent change in firm size leads to a 7 per cent change in the probability of survival, and a 1 per cent change in age leads to a 13 per cent change in the probability of survival (Evans, 1987).

3.3.2 ADJUSTING TO UNCERTAINTY

Small business owners are sometimes described as being at the mercy of a hostile environment which threatens them from many directions. Unfair competition from larger firms, the burden of government regulations, penal bank charges, high interest rates and the recession all contribute to make life in the small business sector a constant struggle. Smallness, and therefore lack of resources, seems to mean that small firms will always be the most vulnerable members of the business community. Certainly, the declining numbers of small firms up to the 1970s was attributed to external influences, just as their revival has been put down to changes in the social, economic and political environment. A major concern of the Bolton Committee was to protect the small business sector, which it saw as unable to sustain itself fully without government help.

Uncertainty is a key feature of the small business environment. Some researchers see it as one of the central distinctions between small and large firms (Wynarczyk *et al.*, 1993). They identify the inability to control prices because of lack of market power and dependency on a relatively small customer base as major factors which make the management environment in small firms more uncontrollable, and therefore more uncertain, than in larger organizations.

Uncertainty is also a central factor in explaining creativity and entrepreneurship. Creative practice, by virtue of producing something novel and valuable, necessarily involves a level of uncertainty for those involved. Being able to tolerate this uncertainty in a business context represents a critical success factor. Shane (2003) lists three types of uncertainty that prevent the entrepreneur knowing ahead of time whether or not their assumptions will be correct (see also Amit, Glosten and Muller, 1990):

- *Technical uncertainty:* the entrepreneur does not know if the product or service being produced will work and, if so, if it can be produced at a cost that is less than the price at which it will be sold.
- *Market uncertainty:* the entrepreneur does not know if demand will exist for the product or service.
- *Competitive uncertainty:* the entrepreneur does not know if they will be able to appropriate the profits from the introduction of the new product or service, or whether these will be reduced by the actions of competitors.

We discussed earlier (in Section 3.1, A matter of life or death) some of the influences on small business survival, dividing them into internal and external factors. The internal factors revolve around the characteristics and management behaviours of the owner-manager or entrepreneur. The external factors, which are largely outside the control of the owner-manager, were divided into the macro-environment and the micro-environment.

Key problems and issues faced by small business owners include:

- interest rates
- cash flow and payments
- low turnover
- lack of skilled employees
- total tax burden
- premises, rent and rates
- inflation
- government regulations and paperwork
- access to finance
- competition from big business
- high rates of pay.

Changes to the business environment are reflected in how important these issues are perceived to be. In the 1980s, when the economy was booming and unemployment falling, the availability of premises and skilled employees became key problems. At the end of 1990, interest rates were seen as the single biggest issue, followed by cash flow and late payments, with low turnover in third place. By the end of 1991, the effects of the recession and lowering of interest rates were reflected in a shift in the order as low turnover became the largest problem with cash flow and late payments in second place. By 2000, lack of skilled employees was back to the top of a list that reflected the key issues of the 1980s. In the early years of the twenty-first century, regulation and red tape constituted particular concerns of the small business population in the UK. Figures for 2006–07 indicate that the main constraints on business performance across European SMEs were relatively low levels of customer demand, excessive administrative regulations and the availability and cost of appropriate human resources (European Commission, 2007, p. 8) – see Figure 3.6.

Figure 3.6 Constraints on small business performance

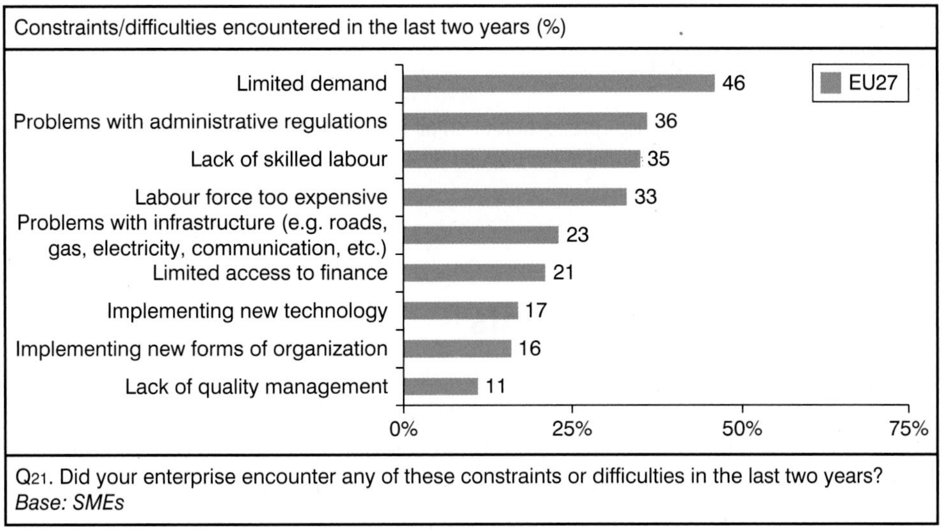

Constraints/difficulties encountered in the last two years (%)

Constraint	EU27
Limited demand	46
Problems with administrative regulations	36
Lack of skilled labour	35
Labour force too expensive	33
Problems with infrastructure (e.g. roads, gas, electricity, communication, etc.)	23
Limited access to finance	21
Implementing new technology	17
Implementing new forms of organization	16
Lack of quality management	11

Q21. Did your enterprise encounter any of these constraints or difficulties in the last two years?
Base: SMEs

Source: Observatory of European SMEs, 2006–2007, ec.europa.eu/. Reproduced with permission.

By 2008–09, the worldwide recession had again focused attention on core problems of access to finance and reduced turnover, while the international nature of the financial crisis called into question the extent to which local responses could effectively respond to global problems. In the years since the crisis, further levels of macro-economic and political uncertainty have impacted all businesses, large and small, including the de-stabilized Eurozone, revolutions and civil wars in Eastern Europe, the Middle East, Iraq, Syria, Sudan, Yemen, and worldwide acts of terrorism. These events have also forced many people to leave their homes and seek to build new lives (and small businesses) elsewhere.

Lack of resources and lack of market power make small firms particularly vulnerable. Those with least resources and market power – the very young and the very small businesses – have least defence against changes in the business environment.

How can small firms best cope with the uncertain and changing environment? Some research (Storey, 1998) indicates that adjustment is the key. Those firms that are most active in making adjustments in what they do, and how they do it, seem to have a greater chance of survival than those who carry on as before. This view is also supported by recent work on how to achieve competitive advantage in SMEs (Jones, 2003) which highlights the importance of learning at an individual and organizational level as key determinants for success.

Important adjustments to consider as part of a learning strategy include:

- market development
- production processes
- employment and labour processes
- ownership
- location.

A key adjustment was found to be in the area of market development: a continuous search for new market opportunities and broadening the customer base of the business. The nature and frequency of these market adjustments, and the potential for a small firm to make them, depends on the market sector in which the owner-manager has chosen to operate – some are more hostile than others. (These issues are discussed in more detail in Chapter 4, Innovation and the Marketplace, and Chapter 7, Successful Small Business Strategies.)

Activity 5
Popular small business sectors

Write down some industries which have a high proportion of small businesses operating within them (for example, hairdressing). Why do you think small is the popular size of business for each of the examples you have given?

3.4 Hostile and benign environments

3.4.1 STRUCTURAL ANALYSIS BY INDUSTRY

Small enterprises operate in virtually every sector, but in some industries small firms are more commonplace than others. This is not by chance. Smallness is the most appropriate size of trading unit in certain industries, where the environment, far from being hostile, favours small firms. In other areas, larger firms have distinct advantages and the small business has to find a niche in order to survive.

Table 3.4 illustrates the differences between the major sectors of the UK economy in terms of the numbers of the firms and start-up rates of new ventures. Motor trades have a low number of firms and the lowest

Table 3.4 UK business birth rates by broad industry group, 2013

	Counts given to the nearest thousand			
	Active (000s)		Births (000s)	
	Count		Count	Rate (%)
Production	158		18	11.4
Construction	309		38	12.4
Motor trades	77		7	9.0
Wholesale	117		12	10.1
Retail	220		27	12.4
Transport and storage (inc. postal)	82		12	15.1
Accommodation and food services	166		25	15.3
Information and communication	200		34	16.8
Finance and insurance	36		6	16.9
Property	95		11	11.1
Professional; scientific and technical	453		77	17.0
Business administration and support services	216		45	20.7
Education	38		5	12.5
Health	104		12	11.4
Arts; entertainment; recreation and other services	180		18	10.0
Total	2451		347	14.1

Source: Office for National Statistics, 2014.

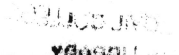

start-up rate, while business services have a much larger number and the highest start-up rate, indicative of the relative ease or difficulty of new venture creation in those sectors.

The underlying structure of an industry determines how favourable it is towards large, medium or small-sized units, and therefore whether it will provide a relatively hostile or relatively benign environment for new firm formation and survival.

Porter's (1980) well-known model of the forces which drive industry competition can be used to assess the structural features which influence an industry's suitability to the small business form. Five forces of entry, rivalry, substitutes, buyers and suppliers jointly govern the intensity of competition and profit potential for a small and large firm in a given industry sector.

Entry

The potential for a small business to enter a given industry sector is determined initially by the barriers to entry that exist, as we have already discussed more fully in Section 3.2.4. Barriers to entry work both ways for small firms: at first, high entry barriers act to keep a new venture out, but once a small firm has entered a market, they can protect it from too many new competitors.

Buyers

Buyers, or customers, 'compete' with the small firm by trying to get the best possible deal for themselves; they will try to negotiate discounts, additional services, higher quality, more after-sales support and other benefits which are added costs for the supplying business.

Buyers differ in the power they can bring to bear on a small firm, which will in turn condition the attractiveness of doing business with the buyer group of a particular industry:

- Some buyers have little choice. The costs of switching to another supplier are too great; for example, the existing supplier has locked them in by providing free on-loan equipment to use their product; or the supplier is the only stockist in town, and it is not convenient to travel elsewhere.
- Other buyers are not inclined to negotiate. The purchase is of such little significance in their cost structure that they are not sensitive to price. Graphic art suppliers, for example, are able to charge high prices because the materials they sell to a designer represent a small fraction of the price charged to the client by the designer.
- Some buyers are all-powerful. They can effectively dictate terms to a small firm which becomes dependent on them. This happens when buying is concentrated in the hands of a small number of large customers, who purchase high volumes from a large number of small suppliers. Superstore retailers have achieved this position. A small firm wishing to supply Sainsbury's or Tesco will have little choice over most marketing variables, such as product quality, packaging, delivery times and methods, and even prices.

The buyer groups, or potential customers, to which a small firm can sell, do not usually exercise equal power. Choice of buyer groups is therefore a key decision which will influence the business environment of the firm. For instance, a garment manufacturer may have a choice of selling large quantities with little marketing control to multiples such as Marks & Spencer, or lower volumes but setting their own strategies through a variety of smaller, fragmented outlets.

Suppliers

Suppliers to a small firm also influence its environment in their pricing and other marketing policies. As the small firm is now in the position of buyer, its powers in relation to the supplier mirror the factors considered already. Small firms tend to buy in a fragmented way so their power, relative to large suppliers, tends to be low. Franchising has attempted to overcome this by grouping a large number of outlets into one buying source. A franchisee can therefore expect higher discounts than an independent outlet of similar size.

Other small firms attempt to enhance their power over suppliers by coming together as formal or informal groups. For example, an office equipment company which distributed its products through a series of owner-managed agents throughout the country was able to dictate its own terms when the network was first set up. When the agents had successfully developed their territories, they used their improved negotiating position jointly to strike a better deal with the supplier.

Rivalry

Rivalry between established firms is evidenced by traditional forms of competition: selling and promotional campaigns, discount offers, new product launches, extending distribution channels and so on. Small firms may do this in spirits of rivalry which range from collaborative and co-operative to fiercely competitive.

The intensity of rivalry is affected by the exit barriers in the industry. These are the factors that keep a firm from quitting altogether, even though returns are inadequate or negative. Exit barriers for small firms can be economic – the costs of liquidation or sale and loss of income – or psychological attachment to the enterprise, loyalty to employees and pride that comes from ownership. Where these barriers are high, then a firm will continue for as long as possible before exiting, thus increasing the intensity of rivalry in the marketplace.

Threat of substitute products or services

Substitution of a firm's products or services can come in two ways:

- A substitute which performs the same function, but in a different way: a taxi service is competing not only with other taxi firms, but also bus companies, for instance; a coffee shop competes with tearooms, pubs and restaurants.
- A substitute way of spending money: the competition for disposable income comes from widely differing products and services. For example, a restaurant is competing not only with other restaurants and take-away restaurants, but also with a whole range of other leisure opportunities from the theatre to the pub.

Industries where there are fewer real substitutes tend to be more stable than those that can be easily substituted by other products or services, or those that rely on disposable income. In recessionary times, for example, taxis in areas where cheaper public transport is readily available will be affected more quickly than those that serve a more captive market, such as tourists and rural communities.

3.4.2 FRAGMENTED INDUSTRIES

In some industries, large firms will have advantages as buyers, suppliers or rivals to small firms. In other sectors, however, larger organizations will have little natural advantage, and the common form of business unit will be small.

Industries are fragmented into a large number of smaller firms for a variety of reasons:

- *Low entry barriers:* most industries with a large population of small firms have low entry barriers. These include many of the service sectors where small enterprises predominate, such as training, recruitment and secretarial agencies, household services, the 'experience economy' (Pine and Gilmore, 1998) that offers tailor-made events to consumers, and the construction industry. Low barriers on their own do not always create fragmentation, however, as there are usually other forces in favour of the small firm.
- *Diseconomies of scale:* where customer preferences necessitate constantly changing products and styles, smaller, more flexible firms can be more efficient than larger, bureaucratic companies. Women's clothes, and other industries where fashion is a major ingredient, would be typical here.
- *High creative content:* architects, interior design firms and specialist product development companies tend to be small as it is often more difficult to produce conditions of high creativity in large organizations.

- *Personal service:* where an individualized, personal service is required – for example, in consultancy, or picture framing – then small operations tend to be able to offer more responsive, tailor-made services than large firms.
- *Close local control:* restaurants, wine bars and night clubs are good examples where the close local supervision of an owner-manager often works better than the absentee management of a large company.
- *Newness:* a new or emerging industry can be fragmented because no companies have been able to take a significant market share. Technological innovations, or shifting consumer needs which create these newly formed industries are sometimes exploited first by newly formed small businesses. There are currently many small businesses operating in environmental markets such as solar heating and water filtering.

3.4.3 FRANCHISING AND FRAGMENTATION

In some markets, franchising is being used to overcome some of the forces towards fragmentation. For example, where economies of scale potentially exist in production or purchasing, an industry may still remain fragmented because the marketplace demands personal service or local sources of supply. The brewing industry overcame this problem with an early form of franchising, retaining centralized production but using tenants with some autonomy to manage the local outlet.

Format franchising has enabled parts of the retail industry to centralize production or buying, while retaining the benefits of local service and location. Fast food chains such as Burger King and KFC are able to market themselves as providing a convenient, neighbourly service while offering the low prices and uniform standards of a larger organization (see Chapter 8, for more details on franchising).

Activity 6
What counts most?

Some influences in the business environment need careful consideration before starting a new venture, as they will have a critical impact on the chances of survival. From what you have read in this chapter, which factors are the most important to take into consideration?

3.5 Critical survival factors

The previous sections point to some critical factors in the small business environment which help to determine whether a new venture will sink or swim.

3.5.1 WHERE AND WHEN

Some locations and time periods are more favourable for small business start-ups than others. At a national level, there is strong evidence to suggest that levels of entrepreneurial activity are closely associated with economic prosperity. Indeed, countries that have either very low or very high levels of entrepreneurial activity relative to their per capita GDP seem to experience lower rates of economic growth (Acs *et al.*, 2005, p. 13). The business environment is particularly hostile to the very young business, so the time and place chosen for a new venture need to be as favourable as possible in order to survive these vulnerable early days.

Growth

The business environment is least kind to very small firms. Growth is needed to give small firms more resources to deal with the inevitable environmental changes. In particular, small firms need to reach a stage of financial viability as fast as possible so they can use their limited resources to develop the business rather than supporting losses. Standing still may mean the business is going backwards.

Choice of market and industry

The market and industry in which an owner-manager chooses to operate is a decision that will have a continuous impact on the fortunes of the business. Macro-environmental forces, such as government policy and general economic conditions, are of course important, but the micro business environment largely determines how well a business can cope with changes to these more general forces.

For example, some market sectors are more sensitive to price increases than others. After an increase in VAT or other duties on alcoholic drinks, off-licences usually experience a drop in sales, while demand for wines and spirits in restaurants is hardly affected. In some sectors, such as construction, the competitive forces keep profit margins so low that relatively small changes in demand can put many small firms out of business. Prospective owner-managers can increase their chances of survival by choosing markets and industries where it is easier to ride out the storms that inevitably come. Understanding how to maximize the benefits associated with e-commerce is also important here (see Section 3.2.5).

Barriers to entry

Although owner-managers are tempted to choose a market sector which is relatively easy to enter because the barriers to small firms are low, they would do well to consider markets which are more difficult to enter. The extra initial effort may be rewarded by less competition once the business has been established.

Choice of buyer group

The choice of buyer groups, or market segments, within a sector is also a crucial decision for the owner-manager. Segments or niches of market sectors can provide a favourable business environment even if the general pattern is more hostile (see Chapter 4, for more detail on the nature of the marketplace).

For example, in the retail sector, the percentage of total sales through single outlets, i.e. small firms, has fallen to less than 28 per cent of the total as the power of the large chains has grown. But single-outlet retailers account for 62 per cent of newspapers and periodicals sold, indicating perhaps that the unsociable hours involved in this type of business do not suit the larger multiples. The construction industry was particularly hard hit during the recession of the early 1990s, but developers who targeted the elderly population by providing sheltered housing survived much better than other building companies.

Adjustments to changing conditions

The chances of survival of a small firm depend in large measure on how nimbly and skillfully it can adjust to changes in the business environment and particularly to conditions within its market sector. A new venture which is prepared to learn constantly and be flexible so that it can make continuous product and market adjustments is more likely to succeed than one which has an inflexible structure and strategy. In Chapter 2, we highlighted the importance of dynamic capabilities which enable the entrepreneur to manage with such flexibility while continuing to ensure that existing processes and procedures are carried out effectively (we shall return to this theme in Chapter 4).

3.6 Summary and activities

This chapter has focused on those factors of business activity that are beyond the powers of the small business owner to manipulate or change directly. The environment for a small business is uncertain and just surviving is a major battle for many new businesses, especially in times of economic recession. Roughly 10 per cent of the total stock of businesses in the UK start up and close each year, and this figure is broadly comparable with many other countries across Europe. This **productive churn** is an important factor in the introduction of innovation (discussed in more detail in Chapter 4) and in fostering healthy competitive forces at the level of the industry. It was noted that not all businesses that close are failed businesses. Many closures, for example, result from owner-managers moving on to set up further businesses or selling up the business to realize an investment.

It was shown that the rate of new business formation is dependent on a range of factors, including *when, where* and *which sector* small businesses are set up in. The entrepreneur therefore needs to be alert to the changes taking place at the level of the market, industry, use of technology, and national and international economies, while being ready to pursue opportunities even if the resources are not immediately ready to hand.

In discussing structural and regulatory issues affecting the small business (in relation to Porter's five forces model), the chapter also highlighted the importance of understanding the competitive nature of the particular industry being operated in and the critical success factors in managing an electronic commerce-based small business over and above those required in the traditional small firm. Finally, the importance of learning at individual and organizational levels to deal with the ever-changing nature of an uncertain environment was highlighted.

Case study
A tale of two entrepreneurs: Part 3

Andrea adjusts her ideas

Andrea Clarey was having her first doubts since deciding to set up her own business. She had defined the need she was attempting to fill as providing a cost-effective payroll service to the public sector. This seemed to fit well with her personal skills and experience but she now recognized that winning the contract for the payroll service of her existing employers, a local government authority, was not going to be as simple as she had first imagined.

'I have seen the terms of the contract they have put out to tender, and I'm not sure it is worth having', she told her small business advisor. 'It is only for a year in the first instance. So I could spend all my time and money setting up a service only to find that I lose the contract and have no business left.'

'I am also worried about the timing', she continued. 'Elections are coming up next year and if the colour of the ruling party changes so might their policies of putting administrative services out to tender.'

'What other market sectors could you consider?' the adviser asked.

'I can look at other public services', said Andrea. 'Many individual schools have become directly responsible for their payroll, for instance. Or I could consider the private sector. I would have to target small business as larger companies tend to run their own payroll. But the competition from accountants and other suppliers is fierce. Payroll software is becoming more user-friendly all the time, so it is not difficult to offer a basic service with minimal experience. I have no experience of dealing with these markets so the risks may be greater.'

Andrea was finding that the only certainty in the small business environment was its uncertainty.

(Continued)

Kit suggests a new product

Kit Hugos had an important decision to make with his partner Robin Davidson before they continued the planning of their proposed electronics business.

'We have a fundamental choice it seems to me', he explained to Davidson. 'We either act as a design and manufacture service for other companies or we make and sell our own products. If we design and manufacture for other manufacturers, they decide what the final product will be and they control all the sales and marketing to their customers. We depend totally on them to make a success of something for which we have probably come up with most of the good ideas. Alternatively, we can design our own products which we market ourselves. Then we are in charge of what we produce and sell. We don't have to rely on others to make our business work.'

'Yes, but if we produce to a customer's order, we don't carry the risk of stock – they do', countered Davidson. 'Nor do we have to bear the product development, marketing and distribution costs. Also they come up with the initial ideas – which is usually the hard part. I don't know of any products which we can develop and sell ourselves. Do you?'

'Well actually I do', said Kit. 'I have developed a personal security device. It's basically an electronic tracking system – a small transmitter which you carry on your person, and computerized receivers which can track and locate the transmitter on a digital map at all times. Any trouble, you press a button on your transmitter which alerts security who can pinpoint you straight away. I believe we could sell it direct to organizations with large, open sites – office complexes, conference centres and universities, for example – to improve their on-site security. No one else is offering anything quite like what I have in mind and the market is having to become increasingly security conscious.'

Activities

Assess the business environments in which Andrea and Kit are proposing to operate.

(a) What are likely to be the main barriers of market entry?
(b) What do you think will be some of the key macro-environmental factors in each case?
(c) Which competitive forces will be particularly influential in each case?
(d) Advise Andrea on her choice of market sector. What are the arguments for and against the sectors which she is considering?
(e) Advise Kit and Robin Davidson on their choice of market sector. What are the pros and cons of the alternatives raised by Kit?

Case study
Coffee wars: ready for a roasting Part 2

(See Chapter 2, for Part 1 of this case study which examines the founding of Coffee Republic)

Sahar and Bobby Hashemi founded Coffee Republic as a new coffee-shop brand in 1995 with high hopes that they would go on to create a substantial chain of outlets on the North American model that they admired. Today, neither Sahar nor Bobby are with the company, which has shrunk from a peak of over 60 outlets to around 25 in the UK, having gone into administration on the way. Although initially successful, it has only just survived in what became a highly competitive marketplace soon after its launch. Unforeseen external forces intervened to upset the Hashemis' well-researched plans. Three other major players entered the market at a similar time and soon carved out significant shares that severely dented Coffee Republic's ambitions.

Caffè Nero was founded in the UK by an American, Gerry Ford, in 1997. Visiting Europe to work on his PhD in US–European relations at Oxford, he also recognized a gap in the offerings of the UK's catering industry. Traditional British pubs and tea and coffee shops didn't meet his particular need to combine work, relaxation and high-quality coffee. Founding Caffè Nero in London in 1997, his aim was to bring a premium, continental-style café to Britain. He wanted it to be authentically Italian, to serve premium espresso-based coffee and fresh high-quality food, and to be a neighbourhood gathering spot. By the end of 2000, he had opened over 31 cafés and established a new national brand. Using finance raised by joining the London Stock Exchange, expansion quickened to 80 coffee-houses by the end of 2002.

By this time, the expansion of Coffee Republic had stalled as financial losses mounted. Instead of adding new coffee shops, they were forced to sell some of them to their new competitors. In 2004, they sold 12 sites to Caffè Nero and 13 sites to the American chain Starbucks which had also spotted the opportunity in the UK.

Starbucks, named after the first mate in Herman Melville's 'Moby Dick', first opened for business in Seattle in 1971, the brainchild of three partners who met while they were students at university: an English teacher, Jerry Baldwin, a history teacher, Zev Siegl, and a writer, Gordon Bowker. Early expansion was relatively slow and the three founders sold their small chain of six stores to an employee, Howard Schultz, in 1987. Expansion accelerated within the USA during the 1990s to over 100 outlets and, by 1998, they were ready to expand into Europe. Recognizing that local competition was already gaining traction, they kick-started their UK launch by buying an existing chain of over 50 outlets and a few years later they bought more stores from the stalling Coffee Republic. Today, they have 500 outlets in the UK and about 25 per cent of the coffee-shop market. There are over 17 000 Starbucks in 50 countries, making them the number one company worldwide, but, in the UK, they are second behind another British coffee house, Costa Coffee.

Like Starbucks, **Costa Coffee** was begun way back in 1971. At the time, two unemployed brothers, Sergio and Bruno Costa, who had emigrated from Italy to the UK in the 1960s, 'couldn't find a decent cup of coffee' in the cafés and tearooms of South London. They rented a property on the Vauxhall Bridge Road and opened a small trattoria, with home-made gingham napkins and dark wood tables, selling 'a taste of true Italy' to customers. In 1985, Sergio bought out Bruno's share of the company and expanded it into a chain of 41 stores. He sold his shares for £23 million to a major company, Whitbread, which acquired the burgeoning coffee-shop chain as part of their strategy of moving out of their original, but stagnant, brewing industry and into hotels and catering. Whitbread took Costa Coffee on to become the second-largest chain in the world and, by 2013, number one in the UK with around 50 per cent of the market.

Amidst all this jostling for position by major players, Caffè Nero has survived as an independent with a 15 per cent market share and over 300 UK and 600 stores worldwide. Conversely, Coffee Republic has been squeezed out of the primary coffee-shop market and forced to reinvent itself using a 'coffee-deli' approach with freshly made food as well as coffee, and using franchising to enable expansion without a large capital base. Its founders, Bobby and Sahar Hashemi, had correctly foreseen the opportunity in the market, but other players took the lion's share of what has proven to be a fast growing industry. Perhaps the likes of Costa Coffee and Caffè Nero understood better the real drivers of market growth. It is not a new-found love of coffee that has driven Britons increasingly into coffee shops; on the contrary, less coffee is drunk today than a decade ago. The key fact is that more coffee is being drunk in a social context, out of the home, as coffee shops have now filled a hole in British society that would previously have been met by pubs as a venue to meet friends and family. Women in particular use coffee shops for social gatherings, accounting for well over half of the

(Continued)

customer base. Historically, pubs as meeting places were seen to be more about males and the evening compared to coffee shops which are open all day and more female and family orientated. Online shopping has also helped increase coffee-shop usage as less time is required to shop, leaving more time for social gatherings around the high street.

Activities

(a) What factors caused the British coffee house explosion from the late 1990s onwards? What were the specific timing, location and sector-specific factors?

(b) Which specific barriers to entry (see Figure 3.2 for the list) did the entrants have to overcome? Which proved to be the more difficult ones for Coffee Republic?

(c) Examine the six critical survival factors (as summarized in Section 3.5) in relation to each of the main competitors in the coffee-shop market to explain their relative success.

Note: further research is recommended into the coffee-shop market and industry in order to complete these activities thoroughly.

Case study
Andrei Korkunov and his chocolate factory[7]

With the thawing of the Cold War in the late 1980s and the era of *perestroika* ushered in by President Gorbachev, the future of the once-mighty USSR's defence industry began to look anything but rosy. For one mid-level defence engineer working in a top-secret factory the demise of the Soviet Union brought with it a radical change in career prospects. While guaranteed a stable and secure job if he stayed put, Andrei Korkunov was bored. There was simply not enough work to do. So he left the defence industry for a co-operative that sewed clothing. Armed with some helpful management experience, Korkunov set up his own company importing a range of goods, including various food items, in 1991. Among the products he imported were expensive top-of-the-range chocolates from Italy. It wasn't long before he became set on the idea of setting up his own chocolate factory in Russia. The catalyst for action was his insight that it would be cheaper to package the chocolates in Russia rather than import prepacked boxes from Italy. One thing led to another, and soon he was negotiating the development of a new chocolate factory with his Italian suppliers.

Unfortunately, all did not go to plan. The deal with the Italian suppliers fell through, and his main partner backed out of the deal. Undeterred, Korkunov carried on. But now he was faced with what he describes as the biggest challenge – dealing with Russian bureaucracy. At the time, business owners were required to fill out endless forms and certificates relating to the production of all commodities. Korkunov remembers having to get some 40 or so permits, agreements and other forms. There was certainly enough red tape to put off the most determined of entrepreneurs. However, Korkunov's factory opened for business in 1999.

'A. Korkunov' chocolates, as they were branded, flew off the shelves in stores throughout Moscow and St Petersburg. The success of these premium chocolates took everyone by surprise. Following the 1998 financial crisis, foreign brands of chocolates had left the country and home-grown producers were concentrating on the low end of the market. Sales of his premium-brand chocolates went through the roof, even though

Korkunov's company spent only $1 million on promotion in the first five years of trading. By 2005, it had estimated sales of $100 million. The company was the leader of the expanding Russian chocolate market, but there were signs in 2006 that it was beginning to lose some of its market share. With an entrepreneurial eye for good timing, Alexander Korkunov sold an 80 per cent share of the business to American chewing-gum giant Wrigley in 2007 for $300 million.

Activities

(a) Account for how Korkunov decided upon the time to set up and exit his chocolate business.

(b) What features of the external environment would you say helped or hindered his start-up plans?

(c) To what extent do you think Korkunov's success is attributable to careful planning and market research?

You have decided to become a wine importer, bringing in wine from the producing countries and selling it on to retailers, restaurants and other licenced outlets. Using the five forces model, analyze the competitive environment you would expect to encounter as a small firm in this market sector. You may find a directory of local businesses such as *Yellow Pages* or other reference books useful in identifying potential buyers, suppliers and substitutes.

Extended activity
The five forces

Summary of what is required

- Draw up a list of problems or needs that your new venture might address.
- Assess these needs or problems through identifying supporting trends.
- Identify the one particular need or problem that will be the basis of your new venture.

The new venture need: defining the problem

The second task in planning your new venture is the broad identification of the problem or need that your idea will seek to address. This will be founded on a general area which not only has the potential to fulfill your personal requirements and use your personal strengths (evaluated in Chapter 2), but which can also give rise to new solutions to problems in the external environment or novel ways of meeting market needs.

The new venture problem or need is a focal point for developing your new enterprise. It is a single focus which concentrates creative thinking into one area. However, it is general enough to allow for plenty of different specific product or service ideas at this stage.

Planning a new venture
Identifying the new venture need or problem

(Continued)

The key criteria that you need to address at this stage:

- *Find a problem:* Einstein said, 'If I had an hour to solve a problem I'd spend 55 minutes thinking about the problem and 5 minutes thinking about solutions.' Follow his advice and think through the need that you have uncovered or the problem you are seeking to solve before coming up with too many solutions.
- *Viable need:* does the problem you are working on represent a longer-term need rooted in trends in the social, technological, economic and political environment or could it be a short-term fad?
- *Description:* define your market need or problem areas in a short sentence and link it to likely technology or resources.
- *Personal requirements:* has it potential to meet your personal objectives and aspirations identified in the section 'Planning a new venture: Know yourself?' in Chapter 2. Ideally, it will involve something you have a real passion for.
- *Personal qualities:* will it offer the opportunity to build on your personal strengths and unique qualities and not over-expose the weaknesses identified in Chapter 2?

Examples of definitions of needs or problems

- Young people are eating unhealthy food.
- The structural environment for public service managers is changing very quickly.
- Punchy, creative presentations are difficult for many managers to make.
- Elderly people lack adequate protection for themselves and their property in this neighbourhood.

Assessing the new venture need

What are the underlying trends in the environment which would make the problem or need you have identified above into a viable business proposition? What are the supporting trends in social, technological, economic, political or legal developments? Why may these provide a market opportunity? Carry out an assessment of your new venture need.

Example of assessing the new venture need: 'Personal and accommodation protection for elderly people'

- Demographic trends show an increasing percentage of the population are 75 years plus.
- Rapidly increasing crime rates against the elderly seen as soft targets.
- Conventional sheltered accommodation using permanent staff is increasingly expensive and wardens difficult to recruit.
- Increasing numbers of elderly are active and not dependent on others for normal living, but need protection and psychological support.
- Technological developments in building and personal protection devices which are expensive on an individual basis.
- The trend to decentralize emergency systems for the elderly; public services offering hotline systems for the elderly to call for help from their independent living accommodation, rather than live in homes with permanent help available.
- Increasing numbers of retired people as owner-occupiers of houses.
- Decreasing percentage of young population and therefore people resources to look after elderly.

Assessment of your new venture need

From the short list of needs and problems that you have identified, pick one that most closely meets your criteria for an industry or market that you would like to be involved in.

Do you have the necessary skills and knowledge to develop a new venture yourself in this particular industry or market environment? If no, where might you get these skills and knowledge from?

3.7 Notes, references and recommended further reading

Notes and further information

1 For more on how culture plays a role in fashioning the ways in which people live and work together, see Gateley, Lessem and Altman (1996); Bourdieu (2002).

2 Source: Office for National Statistics (ONS), 2008.

3 For more details on 'the creative class' and other aspects of Florida's work, see creativeclass.com/richard_florida

4 The Aims of the Small Business Act are to:
   - create an environment within which entrepreneurs can thrive and entrepreneurship is rewarded
   - design rules according to the 'Think Small First Principle'
   - adapt public policy tools to suit SME needs
   - facilitate SMEs' access to finance
   - help SMEs to benefit from the opportunities offered by the Single Market and third-country markets.
   Source: European Commission

5 Quoted in the article 'The future of the music industry', *The Independent,* 23 January 2009

6 See Turban *et al.* (2004) Chapter 16 for more details of how to do this effectively

7 This case study is based on an account of A. Korkunov's story in DELTA Private Equity Partners (2004) *Taming the Wild East: New Russian Entrepreneurs Tell Their Stories,* A. Osipovich, and on an article in *Kommersant,* 24 January 2007.

References

Acs, Z. J., Arenius, P., Hay, M. and Minniti, M. (2005) *Global Entrepreneurship Monitor 2004 Executive Report,* GEM.

Amit, R., Glosten, L. and Muller, E. (1990) Does venture capital foster the most promising entrepreneurial firms?, *California Management Review,* 32(3): 102–111.

Bank of England (2004) *Finance for Small Firms – An Eleventh Report,* Bank of England.

Barclays Bank Small Business Bulletin (2000) *Barclays Business Starts and Closures Survey.*

Binks, M. and Jennings, A. (1986) New Firms as a Source of Industrial Regeneration. In: Scott, M., Gibb, A., Lewis, J. and Faulkner, T. (eds) *Small Firms' Growth and Development,* Gower.

Bourdieu, P. (2002) *Distinction. A Social Critique of the Judgement of Taste,* Routledge.

Cromie, S. (1991) The problems experienced by young firms, *International Small Business Journal,* 9(3): 43–61.

David, P.A. (1992) Heroes, herds and hysteresis in technological history, *Industrial and Corporate Change,* 1(1).

Davidsson, P. and Honig, B. (2003) The role of social and human capital among nascent entrepreneurs, *Journal of Business Venturing,* 18.

DCMS (2015a) *Creative Industries Economic Estimates January 2015 – Key Findings.* Available at: www.gov.uk/government/publications/creative-industries-economic-estimates-january-2015/creative-industries-economic-estimates-january-2015-key-findings, (accessed 10 December 2015).

DCMS (2015b) *The Digital Communications Infrastructure Strategy,.* Policy paper, published 18 March, available at: www.gov.uk/government/publications/the-digital-communications-infrastructure-strategy/the-digital-communications-infrastructure-strategy, (accessed 10 December 2015).

European Commission (2003) *Green Paper Entrepreneurship in Europe,* EC.

European Commission (2007) *Observatory of European SMEs, Summary: November 2006–January 2007,* Flash Eurobarometer, EC.

Eurostat (2014) *Business Demography Statistics,* Statistics Explained, ec.europa.eu/eurostat/statistics-explained/index.php/Business_demography_statistics

Evans, D. (1987) The relationship between firm growth, size and age, *Journal of Industrial Economics,* 35(4): 567–581.

Florida, R. (2003) *The Rise of the Creative Class,* Basic Books.

Florida, R. (2008) *Who's Your City? How the Creative Economy is Making Where to Live the Most Important Decision of Your Life,* Basic Books.

Gatley, S., Lessem, R. and Altman, Y. (1996) *Comparative Management: A Trans-cultural Odyssey,* McGraw-Hill.

Gill, R. and Pratt, A. C. (2008) In the social factory? Immaterial labour, precariousness and cultural work, *Theory, Culture and Society Annual Review,* 25(7–8): 1–30.

Granovetter, M. (1973) The strength of weak ties, *American Journal of Sociology,* 78 (6): 1360–1380.

Granovetter, M. (1985) Economic action and social structure: the problem of embeddedness, *American Journal of Sociology,* 91(3): 481–510.

Hall, G. (1995) *Surviving and Prospering in the Small Firm Sector,* Routledge.

Hart, M., Kitching, J., Blackburn, R., Smallbone, D., Wilson, N. and Athayde, R. (2008) The impact of regulation on small business performance, *Report for the Enterprise Directorate of BERR,* April.

Hartley, J. (2009) *The Uses of Digital Literacy,* University of Queensland Press.

Jones, O. (2003) Competitive Advantage in SMEs: Towards a Conceptual Framework. In: *Jones, O. and Tilley, F. (eds) Competitive Advantage in SMEs. ch. 2,* Wiley.

Keeble, D., Walker, S. and Robson, M. (1993) *New Firm Formation and Small Business Growth: Spatial and Temporal Variations and Determinants in the United Kingdom,* Employment Department Research Series No. 15, September.

Levie, J. and Hart, M. (2009) *United Kingdom 2008 Monitoring Report,* Global Entrepreneurship Monitor, available to download at: www1.aston.ac.uk/EasySiteWeb/GatewayLink.aspx?alId=37199

Oakley, K. (2009) *'Art Works' – Cultural Labour Markets: A Literature Review,* Creativity, Culture and Education. Available at: www.creativitycultureeducation.org/wp-content/uploads/CCE-lit-review-8-a5-web-130.pdf, accessed 10 December 2015.

Office for National Statistics (2014) *Statistical Bulletin: Business Demography, 2013,* www.ons.gov.uk

ONS (2008) *Business Demography* 2007, Office for National Statistics, available to download from www.statistics.gov.uk/pdfdir/bd1108.pdf

Pine, J. and Gilmore, J. (1998) *The Experience Economy,* Harvard Business School Press.

Porter, M. (1980) *Competitive Strategy: Techniques for Analysing Industries and Competitors,* The Free Press.

SBP (2014) Examining the challenges facing small businesses in South Africa, *Alert,* Issue Paper 1, www.sbp.org.za.

Shane, S. (2003) *A General Theory of Entrepreneurship: The Individual-Opportunity Nexus,* Edward Elgar.

Smiers, J. (2003) *Arts Under Pressure: Promoting Cultural Diversity in the Age of Globalization,* Zed Books.

Stokes, D. and Blackburn, R. (2001) *Unlocking Business Exits: A Study of Businesses that Close,* Small Business Research Centre, Kingston University.

Storey, D. (1998) *Understanding the Small Business Sector,* International Thomson Business Press.

The Nielson Company (2007) *Global Online Survey on Internet Shopping Habits,* The Nielsen Company.

Turban, E., King, D., Lee, J. and Viehland, D. (2004) *Electronic Commerce: A Managerial Perspective,* Pearson/Prentice Hall.

Wynarczyk, P., Watson, R., Storey, D. J., Short, H. and Keasey K. (1993) *The Managerial Labour Market in Small and Medium-Sized Enterprises,* Routledge.

Recommended further reading

Bennett, R.J. (2006) Government and Small Business. In: Cater, S. and Jones-Evans, D. (eds) *Enterprise and Small Business,* FT Prentice Hall. Chapter 4 provides a good introduction to the role of government and case for its intervention on behalf of SMEs.

Bridge, S., O'Neil, K. and Martin, F. (2009) *Understanding Enterprise,* Palgrave Macmillan, chs 4, 5, 10–13 in particular.

Chell, E. and Karatas-Özkan, M. (2014) *Handbook of Research on Small Business and Entrepreneurship,* Edward Elgar, chs 13 (Social embeddedness) and 16 (Learning in small businesses) in particular.

Mellor, R.B. (2009) *Entrepreneurship for Everyone,* Sage. This book provides a useful introduction to entrepreneurship in a variety of different contexts.

4 Innovation and the marketplace

Learning objectives

By the end of this chapter you will be able to:

- Understand what is meant by the term innovation, how it relates to creativity, and how it is measured.

- Appreciate why innovative activity is important both for individual small businesses and for the economy in general.

- Assess how the small business context influences both the management and outcome of innovation.

- Consider the critical importance of understanding customer behaviour when introducing an innovative new product into the market.

Introduction

In Chapter 2, entrepreneurship was introduced in terms of three behavioural components: (i) opportunity identification, evaluation and exploitation; (ii) the management of a new or transformed organization; and (iii) the creation of value through the successful exploitation of a new idea. In this chapter, we provide more detailed analysis of entrepreneurship by focusing on one key component: innovation. The chapter begins by considering how we define and measure innovation, and assesses its fundamental importance at the level of national economies and individual small businesses. This is followed by an exploration of the nature of innovative products and services in relation to their intended markets. Although small firms have advantages in innovative activity, they also have disadvantages that some businesses overcome by co-operation and collaboration. Specific factors in the management of innovation within the small business context are introduced before the focus shifts to the innovative opportunity and the marketplace. The marketplace represents the ultimate test for innovative products, so this chapter considers two key questions for new venture owners: who will be my customers and why will they buy from me? Answering these questions accurately may well signal the difference between building a business on the basis of just 'a good idea' or on a genuine market opportunity.

Activity 1
Small versus large innovators

What advantages do small firms have over larger companies in innovating new products or services? What disadvantages do they have?

4.1 Defining innovation

The term innovation comes from the Latin *innovare,* meaning 'to make something new'. Modern-day understanding is that innovation is a process of turning ideas into new opportunities for value creation and of putting these into widely used practice. The terms innovation and creativity are often used interchangeably. In the context of small business management and entrepreneurship it is helpful to distinguish between them:

- **Creativity** is the generation of new and valuable ideas.
- **Innovation** is the successful exploitation of new and valuable ideas.

The process of entrepreneurship relies on the creativity of individuals who come up with original ideas for new products and services. This is only one side of the story, however. Entrepreneurship involves the successful exploitation of these ideas. In a market context, this involves the successful exchange of the new product or service, or what we refer to as innovation. We can only really refer to an innovation after the event (*post hoc*), because a new product or service has to prove itself in the marketplace before it can be declared to be innovative.

Innovation plays a central role in the competitiveness of countries and of business. It is a key driver of productivity and helps businesses introduce new products and services or improve the way that they are made and delivered. Research shows that 12 per cent of the turnover of EU SMEs comes from new or significantly improved products or services (European Commission, 2007, p. 5). Evidence suggests that innovating companies sustain a higher performance and grow faster than non-innovators.[1]

Innovation is a complex process that can be conceptualized in three fundamentally different ways (Tether, 2003, p. 3). These take innovation as: *achievement*; the *consequences* or impacts that arise from achievements and; the *capacity to change* or innovation as dynamic capabilities.

4.1.1 INNOVATION AS ACHIEVEMENT

According to Tether (2003, p. 6), we should consider innovations as achievements primarily in their technological and chronological context rather than their commercial or social impact. Innovations involve achieving significant leaps forward in the use of technology, or the re-conceptualization of existing problems in a way that liberates the creator from existing technological systems.

New technologies tend to evolve over time rather than in sudden leaps forward since they usually rely on cumulative and **path-dependent** associations of people, ideas and objects. One reason for this gradual evolution is because the introduction of a new technology is essentially a risky process in terms of both technological uncertainties (will it work?) and market uncertainties (will it sell?). In addition, an organization's innovation strategy is constrained by the current and likely future state of technological knowledge, and the limits of its knowledge and cognition. We return to this theme later in Section 4.5, Managing innovation – some issues.

4.1.2 INNOVATION AS THE CONSEQUENCES OF ACHIEVEMENTS

When we talk of a great innovation we mean something that has made a significant commercial and/or social impact. Very often this type of impact is unintended – and can far outreach the expectations of the original innovator. In reflecting on great innovations (such as the telephone, the car, semiconductors, the internet), we tend to think about the impact or consequences of the innovation, which were rarely anticipated at the time the innovation was first introduced. For example, Alexander Graham Bell's suggestion that his new invention (the telephone) might be useful for calling ahead to the next town to tell them a telegram was coming now seems extraordinary for the way that it completely failed to recognize the potential of the new idea. For economists, the unintended consequences that benefit everyone are called *spillovers* or *positive externalities*. Innovations often tend to have these positive externalities.

4.1.3 INNOVATION AS DYNAMIC CAPABILITIES

For many, the most compelling conceptualization of innovation focuses on the idea of its capacity for change. Innovation (like creativity and entrepreneurship) can be viewed as a process, or a mindset, that encourages a specific set of purposeful behaviours and practices that enable systematic management of change. Innovation cannot be left to chance. As Louis Pasteur said, 'Chance favours the prepared mind.' Or as Gary Player, the famous golfer, remarked, 'The more I practice the luckier I get!' The innovative small business, therefore, is one that is alive to change and flexible in its approach to it. It has 'dynamic capabilities', defined as a learned and stable pattern of collective activity through which the organization systematically generates and modifies its operating routines in pursuit of improved effectiveness (Tether, 2003, p. 10). Not only can innovation be learned but it is also dependent on the ability and willingness to learn, as Peter Drucker (1985) observed:

'Innovation is the specific tool of entrepreneurs, the means by which they exploit change as an opportunity for a different business or service. It is capable of being presented as a discipline, capable of being learned, capable of being practiced.'

Innovation can and should be managed proactively.

4.1.4 MANAGING FOR INNOVATION

Innovative work is challenging as, by definition, it is 'both novel (i.e. original, unexpected) and appropriate (i.e. useful, adaptive concerning task constraints)' (Sternberg and Lubart, 1999, p. 3). Historically, management and creativity have been considered to be in opposition to each other with managers caricatured as interested only in doing existing things efficiently whereas creativity is something to be left to creatives and artists (Wilson, 2009). This approach lies behind what has been labelled the 'heroic' model of managing creativity, in which the best thing to do to promote innovation is to let the 'creatives' in the organization get on with it unhindered (Bilton, 2010).

By contrast, the 'structural' model assumes that creativity is everywhere. The primary task is to optimize the conditions for discovering and recognizing this creativity so that it can be taken forward in the form of an innovative product or service. Unfortunately, this is easier said than done. Managing creativity and innovation can sound exciting, but as Schumpeter's phrase 'creative destruction' reminds us, it often involves a lot of upheaval, disruption and the questioning of accepted ways of doing things.

Activity 2
Defining innovations

Consider the following services and products:

- Rank Xerox copiers
- 3M Scotch Tape (Sellotape)
- easyJet
- Body Shop beauty treatments
- Apple's iPod
- Apple Pencil
- Mozilla's Firefox web browser
- TripAdvisor

(a) In what ways were they innovative? Specify for each one what differentiates them from other businesses or products.

(b) In what ways were they not innovative?

4.2 Innovation in more detail

4.2.1 MISINTERPRETATIONS OF INNOVATION

Given these different interpretations, it's not surprising that innovation is sometimes mistaken for something else. This section focuses on some of these misinterpretations to clarify what innovation is *not*.

Misinterpretation 1: innovation = invention

Innovation is strongly linked to invention but, although they overlap, they are not the same. An invention is essentially a creative idea. Innovation takes that idea, and puts it to work. Innovative activity encourages the development of new ideas, but it also turns them into useful products or services which customers need (Adair, 1990).

The British have been prolific inventors, but often failed to take their new ideas successfully to the marketplace.

Joseph Swan in England developed a light bulb at the same time as Edison in the USA. Edison thought through the system required to generate and distribute power to customers for the light bulb, and developed an industry. Swan produced a superior light bulb (Edison recognized this by buying up his patents), for which others developed a market.

The career of Sir Clive Sinclair has sometimes highlighted the distinction between invention and innovation. He left school aged 17, with only modest qualifications, starting work as a technical journalist writing handbooks for the electronics hobbyist. In 1962, he started a company, Sinclair Radionics, selling amplifier kits by mail order. It was Sinclair's innovation of cheap pocket calculators that first brought him industrial fame as his company became the UK market leader. Diversifying quickly into digital watches, pocket television sets and digital metering equipment, Sinclair Radionics ran into financial difficulties and in 1979 Sinclair left.

His innovative genius soon found another outlet when in 1980 his new company, Sinclair Research, launched the ZX81, the inexpensive home computer that temporarily gave the UK worldwide leadership in this market by selling over one million units in the first 18 months. Sinclair soon added the equally successful Spectrum and the more sophisticated QL to the range. Then the business suffered from a period of bad publicity over delivery delays, followed by a downturn in the home computer market in 1985.

Sinclair's reaction was typical – another invention, the C5 electric car. The marketing philosophy of the C5 was based on the same principles as his earlier innovations of turning technologically advanced but expensive products into something which could be afforded by mass markets. This time he misjudged the market and the C5 was a financial disaster, forcing Sinclair to sell off his computer assets to Amstrad. His inventiveness and innovations did not stop there. In 1987, his new business Cambridge Computer Company launched an early portable computer, the Z88. In 2006, Sinclair's company launched the 'A-Bike', which claimed to be the lightest folding bicycle in the world, to mixed reviews ('fabulous folder, but almost unrideable'). In 2015, he successfully used Kickstarter crowdfunding to launch an electric version, the A-Bike Electric.[2]

Misinterpretation 2: innovation = new products or services only

Innovation may result in new products or services, but it is not confined solely to their development. Certainly, the most publicized innovations are often related to new product developments. Small companies have become international giants through successful product innovation. For example, 3M's Scotch Tape, Xerox's plain paper copiers and Microsoft's computer operating system, MS DOS, turned fledgling companies into international corporations.

However, innovation does not stop at products. The Austrian economist Joseph Schumpeter (1934) identified five types of innovation through which an entrepreneur can change a market:

1 New products or services or a new quality of existing products or services
2 The introduction of a new method of production
3 The opening of a new market
4 The conquest of a new source of supply of raw materials or half-manufactured goods
5 The carrying out of the new organization of any industry.

As well as new products, most innovations today are related to: markets, marketing and operating methods.

- *New markets*: it is innovative to take existing products or services and sell them into new markets. These new markets may be differentiated by types of end user; for example, 3M first launched Scotch Tape in 1930 into the industrial packaging market. Their second and, in terms of company sales, more important innovation came later when Sellotape was launched into the office and domestic markets – essentially the same product but complete with dispenser.

  A new market may be differentiated only by geography. Small businesses often innovate in this way by spotting a geographic market overlooked by larger companies, or using an idea from another town or country before it is widely introduced. Instant print shops, which expanded very quickly in the USA in the 1970s, are an example of this. The success was spotted by several UK entrepreneurs who suitably modified the idea to local conditions, and established a strong market position which the belated launch of the American originators failed to dent. More recently, coffee shops have undergone a similar process with several British businesses including Coffee Republic and Caffè Nero starting up in the 1990s in response to the success of Starbucks and others in North America (see the case studies Coffee Wars Part 1 and 2 at the end of Chapters 2 and 3).

- *New marketing methods:* the product or service can remain the same and the market does not change; the key innovation can come from the marketing of the product to the customer. Hotmail was just another email provider until it hit on the concept of viral marketing via its own customer base which made it the fastest growing business in the market.

Like 3M's Scotch Tape, Xerox copiers required two innovations to become successful. When the first plain paper copier was patented, many companies turned down the opportunity to market it. The first machines were expensive – the equivalent of about £50 000 today – and conventional wisdom said that no one would pay that kind of money for a gadget to help the office secretary when carbon paper cost practically nothing.

Xerox – then an obscure New York company called Halloid – thought differently. Although they helped develop the machine, their real innovation was in pricing. They sold not the machine, but what it produced – copies. Providing copiers on a rental basis for a few pennies per copy made plain paper copying widely available at a price which looked like petty cash, not a major capital investment.

Distribution, another key marketing activity, has been fertile ground for innovative change for small businesses, as they have developed more convenient ways of making goods and services available to the customer. Successful innovations in this category include the home delivery of products from pizzas to flowers, and the success of Amazon which used the development of digital technology to create new distribution channels direct to consumers.

- *New methods of operating:* an enterprise can innovate in how it operates internally. It can change its production methods or its systems or its way of doing business. Process innovations can give a business a distinct competitive edge through increased efficiency or customer knowledge. Although these changes may be internal, their influence can also be felt externally in the marketplace.

For example, technology is transforming how we pay for goods or services as we become an increasingly cashless society. Process innovations involving a combination of new technologies are changing the whole shopping experience. The integration of mobile phone technology, EPOS technology and customer database management now presents significant opportunities to businesses who are able to act as 'technology brokers' (Hargadon, 2003).

The small business world has been increasingly affected by another operational innovation – franchising. A wide range of business concepts, from fast food restaurants to energy conservation systems, have been made available in a short time to a very wide audience through the franchising concept.

For the entrepreneur, the key question becomes *how* to manage the process of innovation, given the particular constraints of the small business environment, such as the lack of resources and the 'liability of newness' (Stinchcombe, 1965).

Misinterpretation 3: innovation = original

Innovation does not take place in a vacuum. New ideas always have roots in the old; they start with what already exists, and become original from the unique way in which they combine or connect these existing ideas and knowledge. In other words, a new idea is very often the meeting of two old ideas for the first time.

The most prolific innovator of all, nature, creates and recreates using different combinations of a very small number of elements; we have so far only discovered just over 90 separate elements in the universe, and living matter (which includes us) is made from only 16 of them! Although we are all 'unique', we are made from different arrangements of these small numbers of elements.

Creative thinking starts by trying to make connections between concepts that already exist, but that are too far apart for others to see. It has been said that the secret of entrepreneurial success is to use OPB – Other People's Brains. This is not to encourage imitation, which does not create anything new: it is accepting that innovators pick up other peoples' ideas, whether old or new, and piece them together to form a unique pattern, which is only original in that no one else has put them to use in this way before.

Dai Davies, the creator of Letraset, saw the need for faster lettering for graphic artists in order to save them time in creating advertising captions and headlines. He took an existing idea, water-based transfers which had previously been used for children's products, and adapted them for use by the professional graphic artist, and Letraset's Instant Lettering was born.

Anita Roddick borrowed her ideas from traditional societies from around the world. On her travels, she watched the women in Tahiti rub their bodies with cocoa butter, and the women of Morocco wash their hair in mud. These and other natural treatments were to form the basis of the product range of the business she founded – The Body Shop.

Amazon began life doing what bookshops had done for centuries: it sold books. But it did so using a different technology, developed elsewhere. The founder, Geoff Bezos, did not invent or modify the internet but he recognized that it had the power to transform the existing publishing and other industries if it was applied appropriately.

Misinterpretation 4: innovation = one-off inspiration

Innovation does not rely on one sudden flash of inspiration to give the blueprint for a new development. Innovation is a gradual process which builds into something new and worthwhile over a period of time, through a variety of stages. We have already mentioned 3M's Scotch Tape and Xerox's plain paper copiers, which became worldwide products, not through one innovation, but several. Similarly, Letraset's development was a process, not one immediate success. The initial water transfers were messy and time-consuming to use. The company did not see real success until a second product had emerged – a dry transfer lettering system which could be easily and speedily rubbed down onto the page.

The creative process needs elapsed time to achieve genuinely creative and innovative breakthroughs. The late nineteenth-century mathematician Henri Poincaré proposed a model of the creative process that comprised four distinct stages – preparation, incubation, illumination and verification. Having a 'eureka' moment demands time spent analyzing, defining and 'incubating', where the subconscious mind works upon the problem. In the final phase of verification, the new solution is tried and tested. As shown in Figure 4.1, we propose an additional stage of 'iteration'; after all, creativity typically involves working through this cycle a number of times before the final creative outcome is achieved.

Figure 4.1 The creative process

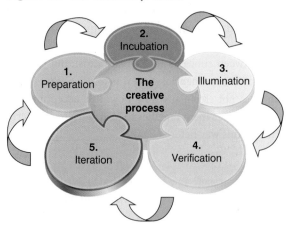

The internet is only the latest stage in the history of the development of communications technology which has taken place over many decades and has involved not just one but many innovations. The principles of linking together a decentralized network of independent computers were demonstrated as early as the 1960s. The first email software was developed in 1972 and, in 1974, a standard software protocol (TCP/IP) was made available to ensure that independent computers could all communicate together. However, users of the internet were restricted largely to researchers and academics until the development of the World Wide Web by Tim Berners-Lee in 1989. Berners-Lee did not set out to invent a contemporary cultural phenomenon; rather, he says 'it was something I needed in my work'.[3] Berners-Lee's 'user' innovation was crucial to extending internet applications as it improved and simplified the distribution and retrieval of information. But it took a further innovation before the system could become popularized. In the early 1990s, the development of a web browser, Netscape Navigator, an application programme that allows users to enter and find their way around the internet, marked the beginning of the rush for businesses and individuals to set up a web presence. Bill Gates, a key innovator in the spread of personal computing, had not played a role in the development of the internet thus far and he was caught somewhat by surprise by this explosion of internet usage. Microsoft rapidly developed its own web browser, Internet Explorer, and packaged it into Windows software, the industry standard operating system for PCs. Although the US courts subsequently ruled that this move was anticompetitive, it did allow Microsoft to catch the internet bandwagon and replace Netscape as the most popular browser system. Subsequently, Google and Firefox have overtaken Explorer as the browsers of choice as the constant search for innovation in a dynamic market continues.

The owners of many small enterprises do not follow Gates's example, but stop at the first innovation. A good marketable idea leads to a new business start-up, which meets with early success. The founding entrepreneur can perhaps be forgiven for believing that the initial innovation was all that was required. Besides, the innovator has now become a manager. Having conceived the original idea, the founder now has a business to run. Management likes order, not chaos, certainties rather than novelties. Unfortunately, creativity thrives on disorder which throws up more chances for novel combinations between hitherto unconnected parts. The danger for the small business is that the opportunity for continuous innovation becomes stifled by organized management. Policies and rules are drawn up to help keep the business on the rails in the early days but these restrict the creative thinking necessary to feed the innovative growth of the future. As Gary Hamel has observed 'Entrepreneurs must be able to produce something out of nothing. They struggle not against nature but against the hegemony of established practice' (see Hargadon, 2003).

4.2.2 HOW DO YOU MEASURE INNOVATION?

Innovation is a relative not an absolute concept so that it can only ever be understood properly in its context. The general notion of innovation as 'the successful exploitation of a new and valuable idea' begs two questions: (i) what does 'successful' mean?; and (ii) what constitutes a 'new' and 'valuable' idea? We all probably think that we would recognize an innovation if we saw one but in practice assessing the difference between a true innovation and a simpler product modification is not an easy task. However, if local or national governments wish to introduce measures to boost innovative activity, it is important to evaluate the current level of innovation in a region or country (see DTI, 2003). Over recent years a wide range of criteria has been put forward to do just that. For example, the Commission of the European Communities (2004) undertakes an annual study of innovation across European countries which is based on 20 indicators of innovation. These indicators are revealing in terms of how they reflect the variety of perspectives that are of most interest to policy-makers (see Table 4.1).

Table 4.1 The European Innovation Scoreboard (EIS) – key dimensions and indicators

ENABLERS
Human resources
Science graduates per 1000 population aged 20–29
Science doctorate graduates per 1000 population aged 25–34
Population with tertiary education per 100 population aged 25–64
Participation in lifelong learning per 100 population aged 25–64
Youth education attainment level

Finance and support
Public Research & Development expenditures (% of GDP)
Venture capital (% of GDP)
Private credit (relative to GDP)
Broadband access by firms (% of firms)

FIRM ACTIVITIES
Firm investments
Business Research & Development expenditures (% of GDP)
IT expenditures (% of GDP)
Non-Research & Development innovation expenditures (% of turnover)

Linkages & entrepreneurship
SMEs innovating in-house (% of SMEs)
Innovative SMEs collaborating with others (% of SMEs)
Firm renewal (SME entries plus exits) (% of SMEs)
Public–private co-publications per million population

Throughputs
European patents per million population
Community trademarks per million population
Community designs per million population
Technology Balance of Payments flows (% of GDP)

(Continued)

Table 4.1 (Continued)

OUTPUTS
Innovators
SMEs introducing product or process innovations (% of SMEs)
SMEs introducing marketing or organizational innovations (% of SMEs)
Resource efficiency innovators, unweighted average of:
• Share of innovators where innovation has significantly reduced labour costs (% of firms)
• Share of innovators where innovation has significantly reduced the use of materials and energy (% of firms)
Economic effects
Employment in medium-high and high-tech manufacturing (% of workforce)
Employment in knowledge-intensive services (% of workforce)
Medium- and high-tech manufacturing exports (% of total exports)
Knowledge-intensive services exports (% of total services exports)
New-to-market sales (% of turnover)
New-to-firm sales (% of turnover)

Source: Commission of the European Communities (2009) *European Innovation Scoreboard, Comparative Analysis of Innovation Performance,* 2008.

Elsewhere, four factors have been put forward as significant in respect of product innovation: (i) conceptual novelty; (ii) technological uncertainty; (iii) market uncertainty; and (iv) the extent to which a firm has committed 'sunk costs' to the project (see Tether, 2003, pp. 33–34). Of these, the first three factors require judgments based on expert knowledge. Only the fourth factor represents an aspect of business activity that can be measured readily.

Activity 3
Innovation in small businesses

Are small businesses likely to be more or less innovative than larger ones? Make a list of the advantages and disadvantages that entrepreneurs in small enterprises have over managers in large companies in relation to being innovative.

4.3 Product innovation in small firms

4.3.1 'SMALL IS INNOVATIVE'?

Small and large firms appear to have different roles to play in the innovation process (Acs and Audretsch, 1990). SMEs contribute more innovation, however it is measured, than larger firms (Audretsch, 1995), so that they are often regarded as being more innovative than large ones because of their flexibility and willingness to try new approaches (see Davis, 1991). However, it is dependent on the context: larger firms have an advantage in capital-intensive, concentrated industries where substantial resources and converging technologies are present; smaller firms appear to have the advantage in emerging industries with high levels of change.

The innovation advantages of small over large business is reinforced by well-publicized success stories of innovative entrepreneurs who were forced to start their own new business because their ideas were rejected by large, established companies. Hewlett Packard turned down Steve Wozniak's invention of a small portable computer, so he took the idea to his friend Steven Jobs and together they began making Apple computers in a garage. Hoover, Electrolux and the major floor-cleaning manufacturers rejected James Dyson's offer to licence his revolutionary technology to them, obliging him to go into production himself.

This notion that small firms contribute relatively more to innovation than larger ones was not always in vogue. In the 1960s, the UK and other European governments encouraged larger companies to form through merger and acquisition, in order to promote the research and development of new products and technologies. It was thought that only large industrial units could afford the high fixed cost of investment in research and development. The monopoly power and economies of scale of large organizations were thought to be necessary to provide the resources needed for the high costs of new technology.

In practice, there are advantages and disadvantages for any small or large business involved in innovative activity. Research going back to Rothwell (1986) has established that small firms have potential advantages in creativity, management, internal communications and marketing, stemming from their flexible and opportunist behaviour influenced by entrepreneurial owner-managers. Lack of organizational constraints gives more freedom to creativity and entrepreneurial managers seek new opportunities and take risks. Internal communications can be fast and dynamic in solving problems and marketing can react quickly to changing market requirements. However, there are disadvantages. Management teams struggle with high growth and find it difficult to adjust to increased complexity; internal communications have problems linking with outside sources of expertise, and marketing lacks the capital to set up expensive distribution systems.

Large firms, on the other hand, have professional managers controlling complex organizations, which in turn attracts highly skilled personnel specialists. Communications are able to plug external sources of expertise, thus enabling marketing teams to retail existing products with comprehensive distribution and servicing networks. Despite this, managers inadvertently become administrators controlled by risk-averse accountants; internal communications become slow to react; and the marketing management become remote from the marketplace.

In summary, small firms have potential advantages in creativity, management, internal communications and marketing, stemming from their flexible and opportunist behaviour influenced by entrepreneurial owner-managers. The vital task of holding open the space for creativity in the absence of guaranteed returns can be more readily achieved in a small, adaptive business (see Martin and Wilson, 2014). However, they have the disadvantages of lack of in-depth resources of qualified people and finance. They are also likely to succumb to particular biases based around the interests and competencies of their owner-managers. Larger firms have greater material resources which give them advantages in attracting the necessary staff and funding the growth and other activities to which successful innovation can lead. They can also benefit from a wider ideas pool, provided that organizational processes and systems don't stifle creativity.

Industrial life cycles

Comparisons between large and small firms also need to take account of the development stage of a particular industry or market. In the early stages of an industry's life cycle, firms tend to be small and innovative. The **technology** of an emergent industry is often new and therefore requires participating companies to be innovative. Emerging industries also tend to be fragmented as new ventures jostle for position with existing players. Abernathy and Utterback (Utterback, 1994) developed a model that describes the changing rates of product and process innovation at different life-cycle stages (see Figure 4.2).

Early participants in new industries experiment freely with new designs and materials. The early flurry of activity eventually ends up with the emergence of a **dominant design**, which meets the market's expectations regarding a product's features, form and capabilities. A very well-known example of such a dominant design which also shows how innovation is path-dependent is the case of the typewriter keyboard (QWERTY). While there have been shown to be more 'efficient' keyboard layouts, the QWERTY design has achieved dominance, at least in part because there are now standard or institutionalized ways of learning to type, which cannot readily be revised.

Figure 4.2 The Abernathy-Utterback model – the dynamics of innovation

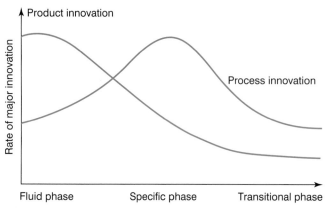

Source: Reprinted with permission of *Harvard Business Review*. From *Mastering the Dynamics of Innovation* by J. Utterback (1994/p. xvii) Copyright © 1994 Harvard Business School Publishing Corporation. All rights reserved.

Behind the variety of new products that vie with each other in the early days of a new product technology, it is likely that the processes used to produce the goods are relatively inefficient. However, as the rate of product innovation decreases and the market becomes more competitive, so it is common to observe a growing rate of process innovation.

As industries mature, the companies involved tend to become bigger through organic growth as well as consolidation among competitors. Innovation in established industries usually requires higher costs in development and marketing, thus favouring larger companies.

The microelectronics and computer industry has epitomized this process in the postwar years, moving through several phases of growth and maturity which have alternatively favoured small and large firms. In the 1950s and 1960s, the industry was dominated by a few large mainframe computer manufacturers, such as IBM, who had the resources to invest in research and development. Entrepreneurs, such as Steve Jobs at Apple, played significant roles in establishing new branches of the industry in the 1970s and 1980s. Today the shake-out in the personal computer market has swung the balance back to larger firms who are making the innovative running. Currently the world's largest manufacture of computers is a Chinese firm, Lenovo, that started in the 1980s and, in 2005, acquired the computing business of the once dominant IBM.

4.4 Innovation and the entrepreneurship dynamic

For every household name such as a Branson, Dyson or Roddick, there are thousands of unheralded owner-managers who have innovated in some way in creating their small enterprise. Their innovation may have been only to adapt existing ideas and practices to a local market; their appetite and talent for innovation may have stopped with their original idea. These 'lonely only entrepreneurs' are many times more common than the individual success story (Schoonhoven and Romanelli, 2001, p. 385). While the bestselling biographies of entrepreneurial innovators like James Dyson and Anita Roddick may inspire others to follow in their creative footsteps, it is a myth to suppose that their example can become the rule rather than the exception. Many may try, very few will succeed, and most will remain as small businesses.

To help those that remain small and yet wish to innovate, it has been suggested that cooperation and collaboration among smaller enterprises can help overcome some of their resource disadvantages. The idea of networked innovation has become increasingly popular, at least in concept. At the initiative of the European Commission, Business and Innovation Centres were set up to promote regional development. Targeted on innovative industrial activities, the aim was to promote individual projects by pooling ideas, technology and commercial experiences (Adair, 1990). The UK government encouraged collaborative innovation with the aim of making Britain 'the best place in the world to run an innovative business or service' and launched a number of initiatives including the UK Innovation Investment Fund, R&D tax credits, benchmarking tools, intellectual property advice and more.[4]

4.4.1 COLLECTIVE CREATIVITY

A growing body of research in entrepreneurship emphasizes the particular role of teams or individuals who work collectively, either formally or informally, to found new organizations and to create legitimate new market spaces (Schoonhoven and Romanelli, 2001). While new innovative heroes will undoubtedly emerge, the way forward for the majority of small businesses who wish to innovate may lie in collective creativity rather than reliance on one individual talent. The focus on the collective nature of the **entrepreneurship dynamic** has been contrasted with much of the early entrepreneurship research which focused on the attributes of individual entrepreneurs and their propensity to found new companies. To understand the mass effects of entrepreneurship – such as the creation of new industries, the pioneering of emerging markets, the development of regional economies, and even their impact on the competitiveness of nations – researchers have been developing a broader understanding of the contexts that produce the entrepreneurship dynamic. There is growing interest in the role of online social networks, user-created content and participatory media in supporting what might be thought of as 'popular productivity' (Hartley, 2009). While older generations may find it difficult to come to terms with the 'how' and the 'why' of applications such as Facebook, YouTube and Twitter, for younger 'digital natives' these tools have become commonplace and part of the normal and everyday reality of 21st Century life. Given the potential for innovation to be unleashed through the shared creativity of a digitally literate population, it is not surprising to see countries placing increasing importance on providing the infrastructure to support such activity (see the UK government's Digital Britain policy document, for example).[5]

Activity 4
Managing innovation

To what extent do you think innovation is manageable in any organization? What do you think is the main problem with introducing innovation into a small firm?

4.5 Managing innovation – some issues

As emphasized earlier, innovation is a *relative* concept and therefore can only really be understood in context. A number of key environmental variables have an impact on how SMEs manage innovation, such as the skills levels and research and development (R&D) activities that exist in their home country. The European Commission (2003) outlined the need to promote a culture of innovation in the business context.

SME owners regarded four factors as being particularly important in terms of potential barriers to innovation: (i) problems in accessing finance; (ii) scarcity of skilled labour; (iii) a lack of market demand and; (iv) expensive human resources. In addition, the protection and enforcement of intellectual property (IP) rights is seen as increasingly important for many firms.

Although SMEs have different innovation priorities and characteristics dependent on their sector, there is an inherent tension in any business between ensuring that stable systems are in place to manage operations efficiently and encouraging innovation, an activity that can destabilize existing practices and involve 'creative destruction'. There are no easy guidelines on managing this tension successfully but it has to be faced or a firm becomes stuck in a rut of its own making.

Activity 5
Finding innovations

How can we look for innovations? Suggest some clues in the business environment which may point to innovative opportunities. How can we watch out for them?

4.6 The seven sources for innovative opportunity

How can the owner-manager ensure a continuous, systematic search for innovation? The would-be innovator can look at changes in what already exists to give clues to what opportunities may appear in future.

Innovation uses and builds on changes that are already taking place. The Wright brothers' aeroplane exploited the earlier invention of the internal combustion engine by linking it to advances in the understanding of aerodynamics. The development of out-of-town superstores capitalized on changes caused by the widespread ownership of the motor car: the advantage of increased personal mobility, linked to the disadvantage of congestion in town centres. The internet has evolved from parallel advances in computing power, networked software systems and advances in telecommunications. The successful entrepreneur investigates and analyzes such change in order to find opportunities for innovation.

Drucker (1985) has identified seven sources for innovative opportunity that stem from change:

Drucker's seven sources:

1 the unexpected
2 the incongruous
3 process need
4 industry and market structures
5 demographics
6 changes in perception
7 new knowledge.

The unexpected
A very common indicator of underlying change is the unexpected result. Unexpected success, or failure, often gives clues to underlying trends which can lead to innovation.

Early computers were designed exclusively for scientific purposes. When IBM launched one of their first machines targeted at the research market, it came as something of a surprise when business customers started to express interest in the new equipment. IBM took their enquiries seriously and developed equipment and software specifically for business applications, which soon became their largest customer group.

Some years later, those computers linked to the internet were being used by businesses and consumers alike for a multitude of uses hitherto unimagined, some discovered through deliberate research that confirmed a premeditated business model (such as Amazon books), while others emerged through an unexpected outcome. TripAdvisor was first launched as a website that gave travel advice from professional travel consultants and agents to the general public. However, the site had a button that allowed private individuals to make a comment. This rapidly became the most popular feature of the website, transforming TripAdvisor into the user-driven platform that it is today rather than the professional advice website that was originally planned.

The incongruous

An incongruous event or result is a discrepancy between what is and what everyone expects; it occurs when there is a difference between reality and everyone's assumption about that reality. It is also an important source of innovation because incongruity is a further sign that changes are taking place. Unlike the unexpected it is, however, more difficult to quantify; it is not likely to show up in a report of customer enquiries or sales figures. Rather, it represents shifts in perception or attitudes.

For example, a 'wealth management' company targeted entrepreneurs who had just sold their company as potential customers for their investment vehicles in riskier secondary funds and company bonds. The response was seen to be incongruous as the entrepreneurs all declined these riskier investment strategies, saying that they wanted to invest their money conservatively, not in involving a high risk/high return strategy thought to be typical of entrepreneurs. Further research revealed that, having taken abundant risks to make their money, entrepreneurs invest it conservatively in order not to lose it.

Process need

The importance of need as a source of innovation is captured in the proverb: 'Necessity is the mother of invention'. Drucker highlights one particular need, the 'process need', as a major area of opportunity, because it is a very specific and easily identified need. Innovation from process need improves an existing process which is recognized as having significant limitations; it takes new, often unrelated, developments to revolutionize an existing process or way of doing something.

For years, there were two basic types of glass: sheet glass which was cheap but optically imperfect, and plate glass which was ground and hand polished to optical perfection and therefore expensive. There was a recognized need for cheaper, high-quality, distortion-free glass. But it was not until Alastair Pilkington developed 'float glass', allegedly inspired by a floating plate in his washing-up bowl, that the process need was met. Molten glass is floated on a bath of molten tin which keeps it flat and regular as it cools, eliminating the need for later labour-intensive polishing.

Today, there is a process need to develop economic, longer-lasting batteries. The race to develop alternative, greener sources of power is on as the potential impact of climate change becomes more obvious. Natural

(Continued)

energy sources derived from sun, wind and sea are abundant but have one common problem – storage. If the energy is not used immediately it is lost, unless stored. Hence the need for longer-lasting batteries that can economically store green energy. Around the world countless laboratories are researching to meet this latest process need. One entrepreneur who thinks he has part of the answer is Elon Musk, developer of PayPal and the Tesla electric car. He and his partners have invested $5 billion in a new facility, the 'Gigafactory' that will produce 500 000 of his new lithium ion batteries by 2017.

Sir Alistair Pilkington

Musk believes it will give the economies of scale needed to produce the powerful, economic batteries that will drive the new generation of all-electric cars that he, and many others, are confident are poised to take over the market.

Industry and market structures

Whole industry and market structures can change rapidly, sometimes after a long period of stability. Such changes offer exceptional opportunities to innovators, and considerable threat to those who incorrectly read the changes.

After a long period of stability, the basic technologies of printing changed. The preprint activities of producing artwork and printing plates, which until the 1970s relied on photomechanical methods, were increasingly replaced by computer-aided technology. At the same time, traditional printing methods using hot metal and letterpress were updated by more flexible offset lithography. Long training in the mysteries of the printer's art was no longer necessary. One effect in the marketplace was the emergence of 'instant print' shops. The lower set-up costs and skills needed to start a printing business using the new technologies allowed a new type of printer to emerge. Instant print shops were an innovation in that they were located nearer the customer and offered more flexible, faster response times. This development has in turn been challenged by the penetration of the internet and high-quality ink jet and laser printers that have removed the need for external printing in a number of business and domestic applications. The decision to print or store digitally is now in the hands of the end user, so that printing is increasingly done at the location of the user rather than the creator of the documentation.

Changing industry and market structures frequently give the small business entrepreneur opportunities to benefit from the sluggishness of larger, existing suppliers who often view structural change as threats to be resisted, rather than a chance to innovate.

Demographics

Changes to the environment of an enterprise inevitably contain many possibilities for innovation, but are often hard to see, or understand, until they are past and the opportunity missed. Demographic changes, however, are clear and unambiguous, and signalled well in advance. Statistics of population births, deaths, diseases, employment, education and income, and the trends which these figures show, are universally accepted as key indicators of demand changes within society which are often highly predictable. A high birth rate in one year will inevitably mean an increased need for first school places four to five years later. Lower death rates and longer life expectancy will be sure to create more demand for retirement homes and old-age care facilities. These new requirements create many opportunities for innovation which can be seen well in advance; yet, often, these key numbers are overlooked in the search for entrepreneurial ideas.

Changes in perception

Some changes are not really changes at all. The facts do not change, but people's perception of the facts changes, which has an equally powerful effect.

The fashion industry relies heavily on changes in perception. Clothes from an earlier generation do not change, but our perceptions of them do. We regard the trendy garments of yesterday as comically out-of-date today. Changes in perception give the entrepreneur many new openings. Today, we perceive an urgent need to protect our environment, a notion that had little following several decades ago. Anita Roddick sensed this shift in values well before it became common policy to have green products, in creating The Body Shop.

The skillful innovator will be careful to differentiate between temporary changes in perception, or 'fads', and longer-lasting developments. The entertainment industry, for example, throws up a continuous stream of new heroes, from masked cowboys to oriental warriors. Focusing an enterprise entirely on any one of these novelties would be a very short-term strategy, as young people's fidelity to any one heroic concept is extremely fickle. However, there is a well-established long-term need for heroes on which the innovators in Hollywood have built up a worldwide industry.

New knowledge

The most famous innovations are often based on 'new knowledge', or inventions. The first telephone made by Alexander Graham Bell, the light bulb demonstrated by Thomas Edison, the radio messages of Guglielmo Marconi and the early television transmissions of John Logie Baird are all well-known. Despite the publicity, such knowledge-based innovations are, in some respects, the least attractive to entrepreneurs. The time between new knowledge being available and its successful development into marketable products is long. The idea of using radio waves to transmit visual information was around in the early days of radio in the 1890s, but only became practical with the first television transmission in 1926.

Innovations based on new knowledge also require not just one independent discovery, but the bringing together of several developments. Baird's first television, itself based on earlier research on radio waves, scanned an image into lines of dots of light by a mechanical method. More sophisticated, electronic systems were required before television could become an acceptable product, a decade or so after the first transmission.

The development of the internet has followed these patterns (as described earlier in Section 4.2.1). The linking of computers to form an international communications network, or internet, has been evolving since the 1960s. But it took other advances such as an easy-to-use interface in the form of the World Wide web and web browsers for this to become practically useful. Ongoing developments such as the 'Semantic Web' and Web 3.0 will create significant advantages over the web services we already take for granted.

The so-called *ex nihilo* paradox reminds us that 'nothing comes out of nothing'. Or as Isaac Newton remarked, 'If I have seen further, it is by standing on the shoulders of giants'. As a small business manager and entrepreneur, it makes sense to pay attention to what is going on elsewhere.

Activity 6
Finding the market

Serial entrepreneur and founder of EasyGroup Sir Stelios Haji-Ioannou says that his biggest mistake was rushing ahead with a chain of internet cafes in the wake of the dot-com frenzy. Nevertheless, he remains candid about his approach to failure. He has a rule of thumb where he is 'quite happy to have a third of my businesses good, a third average and a third of them basket cases'.[6]

Ideally, how can small businesses make sure that their products are acceptable in the marketplace? In practice, how do they tend to develop new products and services?

4.7 Innovating for the marketplace

4.7.1 MISSING THE MARKET

Creativity in business is only beneficial if it has a practical application. New product ideas need to be based on the needs of customers if they are to have any use. We have already drawn the distinction between an invention – a creative idea – and innovation, which takes ideas and puts them to work. The process of implementing innovation can only happen by reference to the market or marketplace. As we identified in Chapter 3, a *market* consists of those customers who are willing and able to buy products to satisfy particular needs or wants, whereas an *industry* consists of the sellers that offer these products to current or prospective customers.

Entrepreneurs originated because of the need to shift resources from where they were under-used, or in surplus, to areas where there was demand because of relative shortages. This was done through the market-place, where those with a surplus – something to sell – could meet with those who had a shortage – a need to buy.

Business and commerce has its roots in this concept of the marketplace. The ancient bazaars of the Middle East, the medieval merchants of the Mediterranean and the shopkeepers of Victorian England, all based their trade on understanding what customers in the marketplace wanted, finding it for them and making it available in an acceptable way at the right price. They were small businesses by today's standards, whose size made regular contact with customers inevitable, helping them identify with the markets they served.

One of the most common reasons given for the failure of a small business today is that it did not identify a viable market – there were insufficient customers for its products. If the origins of entrepreneurship and the traditions of commerce over the centuries are based on understanding the needs of customers, why did modern businesses 'unlearn' this fundamental principle and need retraining in customer orientation? Some of the reasons are:

- Technology and other advances in human knowledge and skills have made many newer products or services possible. It is increasingly tempting to launch a new business based on an idea just because it becomes possible, rather than because there is an identifiable, sustainable demand from the marketplace. Larger, as well as smaller, organizations fall into this trap; the development of Concorde may have been a great technological advance, but it was a very limited business success. Successful entrepreneurs from Richard Branson to Stelios Haji-Ioannou have sometimes made the mistake of following ideas which were temptingly possible but which did not pass the ultimate test of market demand.
- Modern business has become a very complicated mixture of forces and influences. A small business manager has to consider not just the demands of customers but the requirements of many other influencers, including the government, employees, suppliers, banks, other financial partners, existing competitors and potentially new competition. The owner-manager does not have time to consider all these factors fully and sometimes it is the customer who is forgotten.
- The complex nature of modern business requires systems and policies to help manage and control the confusion. Order reduces the chaos of conflicting demands and makes the accomplishment of necessary tasks more likely. Unfortunately, order tends to create inflexibility; ways of doing things, once established, are difficult to change. The marketplace, however, is constantly changing: customers' preferences change, competitive products and services come and go, technology creates new opportunities, the law imposes new constraints. The small enterprise with limited resources can be tempted to over-organize its activities so that it fails to understand and respond to these changes.

- As an enterprise grows, it needs more levels of management. This tends to make key decision-makers, even in relatively small companies, more remote from the marketplace and the customer.

4.7.2 APPROACHES TO THE MARKET

There are two theoretical extremes in how enterprises develop products or services for the marketplace: the 'product-based' approach or the 'market-based' approach. The product-based approach implies that the enterprise is primarily concerned with product development, or the internal demands of the organization. It can lead to inflexible, even arrogant attitudes towards the ultimate buyer of the product or service ('I wish all the people who want to shop at lunchtime would realize we have to eat as well', said one store manager). It can lead also to successful products which, by chance, find a market. Many creative industries[7] businesses (e.g. music, film, performing arts), suffer from taking a product-based approach to the market (see Kotler and Scheff, 1997). This can be explained in terms of the founders' enthusiasms being based on *intrinsic* motivation (e.g. love of the music, film or art itself) rather than *extrinsic* motivation (e.g. financial reward) (see Frey and Pommerehne, 1989).

The market-based approach on the other hand seeks to find out what the customer wants and is willing to pay for. It implies that the enterprise is focused around the needs of the customer, rather than its own internal requirements.[8] It does not leave success to chance as it first researches market needs, and then develops products and services to meet them.

In practice, product development in small business is unlikely to take a totally market-based approach, however desirable that may be, for a variety of reasons, including:

- Entrepreneurs tend to take an idea first and then seek a market because they have a propensity to act once they see an opportunity rather than undertake structured research. They understand that research cannot always predict needs because sometimes customers do not know what is possible from new breakthough products and therefore cannot visualize the need for them (for a more detailed discussion, see Section 12.3.1, Market orientation: focus on the customer or the innovation?).
- Owner-managers starting a business usually have a specific skill or knowledge which they wish to exploit.
- The business is already established and wishes to add to its existing product range without diversification.
- The business has established products which it wishes to sell to new customers.

A successful approach to the market is a combination of understanding the resources available and matching them to an idea for a new product or service, which fills a gap in the marketplace. This is illustrated in Figure 4.3.

This summarizes the matching process that takes place when an idea, based on customer demand or needs, is linked to the existing or future resources of an enterprise. It acknowledges not just the importance of the customer, but also the strengths and weaknesses of the owner-manager and their small business in relation to the market opportunity.

Figure 4.3 Matching ideas to resources

Activity 7
The rifle not the blunderbuss

S mall businesses are tempted sometimes to appeal to everyone in general in order to increase sales, but they end up serving no one in particular. How can they focus what they have to offer more precisely?

4.8 Who is the customer?

4.8.1 MARKET SEGMENTS AND NICHES

It is possible for a small business to regard customers as the focal point of its activities yet still fail.

Failure can come from an inability to define precisely who is the target customer. It is always tempting to believe that products or services can have a universal appeal, or that it is safer to offer them to as wide a market as possible. However, there is overwhelming evidence that successful companies, large as well as small, carefully target customer groups. These companies identify subdivisions of markets – referred to as segments – and specialized subdivisions of segments – referred to as niches.

It is better to have a high share of a relatively small market than a small share of a relatively large market (see Section 12.3, Entrepreneurial marketing). This is particularly valid for small enterprises whose limited resources make the precisely targeted approach to the customer even more preferable. In reviewing strategy options for small firms, Storey concluded that 'innovation and the identification of a particular niche were key strategies associated with more rapid growth in small firms' (Storey, 1994, p. 149).

The purpose of segmentation

There are also dangers in identifying closely with one group of customers. Small firms can become over-dependent on one customer or over-concentrated on a small number of them. Research (Cambridge Small Business Research Centre, 1992) found that one customer accounted for over 25 per cent of the sales in one-third of the companies studied.

However, market segmentation should not be confused with customer concentration. Segmentation is based on the simple truth that customers buy similar types of products and services for different reasons, which give rise to different expectations of what they are buying.

For example, people buy books for many reasons: for pleasure, for study, for reference, for presents, even for show. Each end use will require differing qualities and specifications from the books purchased, not just in the content of the book, but also its size, appearance, durability, price and so on.

The principle of segmentation categorizes customers and consumers into groups with similar needs and expectations from their purchases. The more precise the definition of the customer group, the more precise can be the definition of their needs and requirements.

The whole purpose of market segmentation is to allow a small business to use its resources where they count most. Segmentation allows the small enterprise to look for the most promising openings for its special talents and advantages, a niche where its strengths will be of most value and its weaknesses of little account.

The process is to discover natural groupings among both customers and consumers, which match the special abilities of a small firm.

4.8.2 THE SEGMENTATION PROCESS FOR A SMALL FIRM

Definition of the target segments for a small business can be achieved in stages, as illustrated in Figure 4.4.

Figure 4.4 The segmentation process for a small business

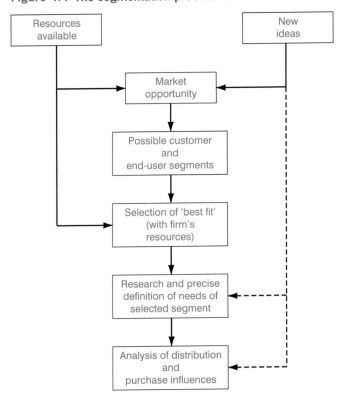

A balancing of the resources available to a small enterprise with new ideas for possible innovations establishes a general definition of a market opportunity. This is refined into possible customer and consumer segments. A selection is then made of the segment which best fits with the resources available to the firm.[9]

For example, a small business, having focused on the market opportunity of publishing books covering business subjects, decided to further specialize in students in higher and further education as the most promising way of using its special talents and strengths.

This is one of the most crucial decisions that a small business makes, influencing how it operates and where and what it sells.

Further research into the selected segment makes possible a more precise definition of the purchasing habits and requirements of the target market. This research includes considering the distribution chain and analyzing other possible major influences on the purchase decision. In some sectors, a 'decision-making unit' (DMU), consisting of a number of people playing different roles in the buying process, has to be identified in order to establish customer needs. At these stages new ideas may again be considered.

The choice of the student segment by our publishing business actually determines who will be the customer, as the firm will need to sell through the established distribution channels of wholesalers, traditional retailers and online retailers specializing in student sales. Setting up a new access system to the target market would be a much harder route. The decision also reveals other influences in the purchase decision which will need careful consideration; in this case, lecturers of business studies play an important role in determining student purchases through recommended reading lists. The DMU is therefore made up of: bookshop/retailer (the direct customer), student (the end user) and lecturer (influencer/specifier).

The segmentation process is important for a new business start-up. It is equally important for an existing small business to understand the changing needs of its target market. If the business develops beyond its initial customer groups, the segmentation process will need to be repeated.

Activity 8
Why did you buy?

Consider a small business (e.g. a restaurant, take-away food outlet, business consultancy, clothes retailer, hairdressers) that you have used on more than one occasion.

What are:
(a) the features of the products or services offered?
(b) their benefits to you?
(c) the competitive edge that attracted you back to that business?

4.9 Why will the customer buy from me?

4.9.1 THE MATCHING PROCESS

Sales are the lifeblood of an enterprise, providing the income upon which all other functions, from production to accounts, ultimately depend. The point of contact between the customer and the business will vary from a direct sales visit, to a retail shop in the high street, to electronic commerce and social media offering positive and negative recommendations. But whatever form it takes, the sales activity represents the motive force that drives the small business on, or causes it to stall, sometimes never to start again.

Selling is essentially a matching process. Customers have certain requirements or needs and an enterprise offers products or services which have certain characteristics or features. Customers compare their needs to the benefits which these features offer them, and either accept or reject the costs associated with acquiring those benefits. Figure 4.5 illustrates this process.

4.9.2 FEATURES AND BENEFITS

In the matching process, the customer's decision hinges on the **product/service benefit**, not its features.

- A *feature* is a characteristic of a product or service. For example, a student's textbook has a soft, laminated cover; this is a feature of the product.
- A *benefit* is the value of a product feature to a customer. For example, the benefits of a soft laminated cover are that it is hard-wearing, and therefore lasts well, while being light and easy to carry.

These are benefits which are relevant to students; they might be inappropriate to other customer groups, and therefore not really benefits. For example, a book that was targeted at the coffee-table market, for display purposes, would probably require the benefits of high-quality finish and attractiveness rather than lightness and durability.

A successful small business meets the needs of the targeted customer group by ensuring the features of its products or services translate into benefits appropriate to the customer.

4.9.3 PRICE: THE OVER-USED BENEFIT

Inevitably in a competitive environment, the customer has choice. The purchase decision is not based solely on an assessment of whether the benefits on offer outweigh the costs to acquire them.

Figure 4.5 The sales process in a small business

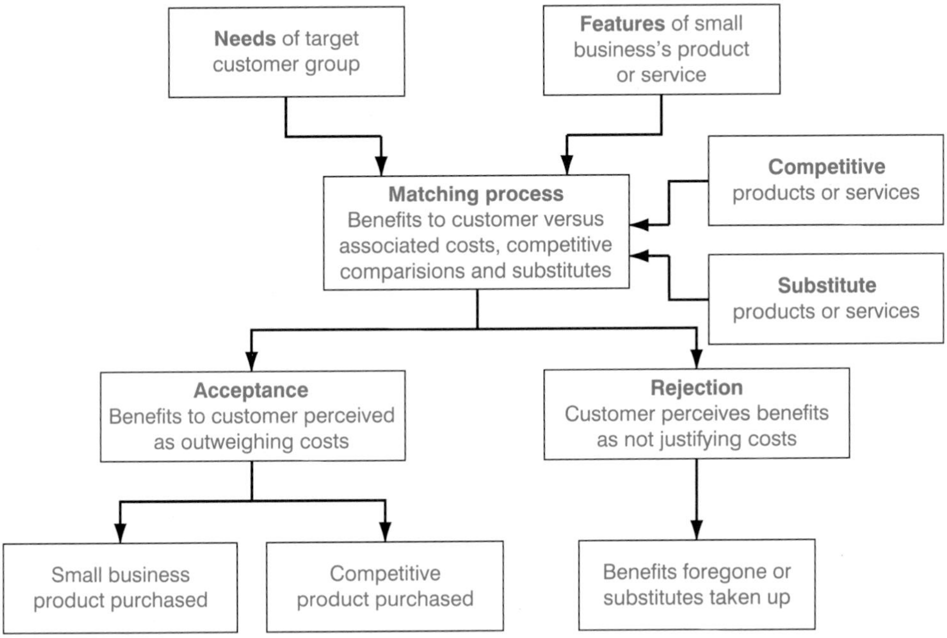

Comparisons are made with competitive products or services, and the benefits they offer. What is on offer is seldom unique, so a prospective customer usually has the opportunity to shop around and assess the purchase benefits that competitive products offer before making a choice.

Substitute products, or alternative ways of acquiring the benefits, are often also considered. Does the student purchase a book or download a chapter, for example? Can the information required be obtained from other sources; for example, videos, articles, libraries? Competition does not only come from directly comparable products or services.

To get the sale, the small business has to offer the customer more benefits than competitors and substitutes.

It is always tempting for a small business to compete mainly on price. By offering a product or service at the lowest possible price the small business helps stimulate a purchase in the first place; it is offering benefits at the lowest possible cost of acquiring them. Low prices can be an advantage over the competition for a small firm, or they may keep consideration of substitutes to a minimum.

In some instances, a small business with low overheads can compete on price in the longer term, provided they do not grow to a size where central overheads are required. A freelance bookkeeper working from home is always likely to charge significantly less than an accounting practice with premises and office staff to support.

However, there is evidence that many small businesses compete on price when they are first set up, based primarily on the cheap labour of the owner. There is even concern that government subsidies, aimed at helping a new enterprise in its early days, may be used to gain short-term advantages by undercutting the competition. This can cause problems, sometimes terminal ones, for established businesses and the new business cannot sustain its price advantage once the subsidies are removed.

Unless a business has established economies not available to its competitors, it is unlikely to gain long-term competitive advantage through pricing policies alone. As economies of scale are not usually available to a small business (because of their size), low prices are most likely to come from short-term cost savings: for example, the owner does not expect a market wage, particularly in the start-up phase of the business, or little investment is made in product development or marketing. As other businesses are likely to react by lowering their prices, the small firm may find that the only result of price competition is to reduce the profitability of the total business segment. Under-pricing has certainly been a major factor in small business failures.

4.9.4 THE COMPETITIVE EDGE

If a small firm is unlikely to gain long-term advantages over the competition through low prices, it still has to find a competitive edge if it is to survive and grow.

A competitive edge is the means by which the small firm differentiates itself from the competition. It comes ultimately from the careful selection of a target market in which the small enterprise can offer something better than anyone else. It answers the question: Why will this particular group of customers buy from me rather than anyone else?

The competitive edge of a small firm can be described in terms of benefits, with two main characteristics:

1 they are benefits significant to the target market segment;
2 in total, they amount to a greater package of benefits than those offered by competitors.

To return to our example of the book publisher, this firm considered the needs of its target customer segment – students of business studies in higher and further education – and produced the following list of desirable benefits for books offered:

- easy to understand, readable contents
- easy to follow (and memorize) layout
- affordable prices
- light and hard-wearing
- available when required
- up-to-date information
- texts aligned to courses taught.

When investigating how well existing suppliers met these needs, the small firm discovered two problem areas: many books covered broad subject areas, not necessarily in line with the content of specific courses; students complained that recommended texts were frequently out of stock at the beginning of term.

From this, the small firm developed its competitive edge. By working closely with lecturing staff, it developed innovative texts which followed courses of study, not just subject areas. By specializing in business studies it was able to concentrate on specific outlets and, by giving them a fast delivery service, to ensure adequate stocks of recommended texts at the beginning of courses.

The firm's books became the market leaders of textbooks in the limited areas covered. They gained a large share of a small market by understanding the target market better than any of their competitors, and offering products and services that were different in ways that were of significant benefit to the customer.

In the increasingly competitive global context of doing business, the strategy of competing with other firms may not always be the most successful approach for small businesses to take. More and more small enterprises work collaboratively and strive to achieve what might be thought of as **cooperative advantage** where working in partnership with others can reap significant rewards. The clustering of textile manufacturers in the north-west of Italy to form a powerful industrial district characterized by 'diffuse entrepreneurship' is a well-known example (see Amatori and Colli, 2006). Elsewhere, specific interest groups have formed entrepreneurship networks for collective advantage. For example, the South Africa Women Entrepreneurs Network (SAWEN) facilitates the socio-economic advancement of women entrepreneurs and their potential impact on national wealth-making. Supported by government, it offers a hitherto disadvantaged segment of the population the leverage of relationships with other like-minded entrepreneurs and access to business resources, opportunities and information (see sawen.org.za).

4.10 Summary and activities

In this chapter, we have identified the varied ways in which innovation is generally understood – as an achievement, as the consequences of achievements and as the capacity for creative change. For the small business manager and the entrepreneur, the most helpful concept is seeing innovation as a mindset or a process that enables change. Innovation is not the same as invention and it comes in many types (products, services, processes, organizational or market innovations). Innovations are not usually based on completely new ideas but come from the meeting of two, or more, old ideas for the first time. To the extent that innovation is something desirable in the business context, it has become increasingly important to find ways of measuring innovative activity in individual businesses, in industries and in regions or countries. As innovation is a relative concept (what is new in one field may not be so new in another), it is always important to look at innovative activity in context. Even where measures have been put forward (e.g. the European Innovation Scoreboard), these very often require some expert judgment to determine just how innovative the level of activity really is.

Small firms have been shown to display different innovation characteristics to their larger counterparts. Small businesses tend to be resource constrained, but they can benefit from flexible and informal management approaches where new ideas are welcomed. Larger firms, on the other hand, benefit from economies of scale and scope and from well-funded research and development departments, but they may be subject to higher levels of bureaucratic management which may constrain creative and innovative activity. For all businesses, the possibility of introducing new technologies (involving the recombination of people, ideas and objects) is path-dependent and will depend on a wide range of external and internal conditions. Managing innovation therefore requires a sound knowledge of these conditions, and demonstrates why those entrepreneurial management behaviours introduced in Chapter 2 (including being alert to opportunities, networking and effectual decision-making) are so important.

The chapter identifies seven key sources of innovation and emphasizes once again the fundamental importance for the small business manager of ensuring that any 'good idea' for a new product or service actually has a market. One of the ways to ensure that this is the case is to take a market-based approach to developing new products and services. Understanding who the customer is and what it is that drives their decision to buy are key factors that are sometimes overlooked by those setting up their new businesses.

Case study
A tale of two entrepreneurs: Part 4

Andrea goes back to school

Andrea Clarey decided to concentrate her efforts on the schools market for the payroll service that she was setting up. She considered that a possible large contract from the local authority where she currently worked would make her too dependent on one customer – and there was no guarantee she would win the contract despite a considerable amount of effort that would have to go into any tender for it. Her preliminary investigations into a possible market for her service among primary and secondary schools had indicated that she should further target her efforts. First, she had decided to concentrate on smaller schools, and primary schools in particular. Secondary schools were larger but there were fewer of them and those she called on used either the local educational authority or well-established accountants to handle their substantial payrolls. Second, she found out that some state schools

(Continued)

had more financial independence than others. This invariably meant they had to source their own payroll system and the smaller primary schools usually bought in the service from a local supplier.

She also felt that she could develop a competitive edge by an innovative service not offered elsewhere to her knowledge. She had stumbled upon the idea when she attended an annual meeting of parents with governors at her daughter's local school. As part of the changes in the way state schools are managed, governors had taken on more responsibilities, but also had to report back to parents once a year giving them information on such matters as the financial accounts of the school. Andrea noticed that over 75 per cent of expenditure at her daughter's school was on staff salaries and she asked the Chairman of Governors if this was normal and how it compared to other, similar-sized schools.

'Yes, quite normal', he had assured her, 'although since schools became more autonomous we get less and less comparative information from other schools – so I can't tell you, for example, how typical the amounts we spend on administrative compared to educational costs are.'

This had given Andrea an idea. The local council where she worked had just bought a benchmarking system for its services. This allowed it to compare its efficiencies in key areas such as manpower deployment and response times for enquiries with other large organizations. Andrea thought she could do something similar for schools.

'As part of my payroll service for schools, I could offer them an analysis of their costs with trends and historic comparisons', she thought. 'Then I could offer them comparative information from other schools who are also my clients – completely confidentially of course. That ought to give me an edge over the competition.'

Kit tracks an idea

Kit Hugos was trying to persuade his partner in their embryonic electronics business to give him the go-ahead to develop his new product idea – a personal tracking device. 'The principle is not new', he said. 'Basically, it's a radio transmitter which can be attached to a person so that their whereabouts can be tracked at all times. What is new is the size and power of the latest electronic components and circuitry. I can now design a device the size of a thumb nail which can be carried discreetly on a person and transmit their whereabouts up to 50 miles away. It can feed co-ordinates into a computer mapping system so that the precise location of the device – and the person wearing it – can be identified. It can also be fitted with an alarm system in case of problems.'

'Sounds very interesting', his partner, Robin Davidson, said. 'But who do you see buying it – and at what cost?'

'Every time I think about this product I can see more applications. Organizations with large sites used by lots of people find it almost impossible to provide the round-the-clock surveillance that is needed for security these days. Parents are concerned about the whereabouts of their children whether they're toddlers in the park or teenagers out at night. Now they can track them on a computer screen all the time and be alerted if there is a crisis. The actual device can be made quite cheaply. We could probably sell it for less than £50. The big cost comes with the computer mapping software, which obviously has to be very local, and would need to be developed for the locality of the users.'

Activities

Ideally, how can small businesses make sure that their products are acceptable? In the case of Andrea and Kit:

(a) Would you describe their ideas as innovative? If so, in what ways? In what ways are their ideas potentially flawed?

(b) Who will be their potential customers and what benefits will they offer them?

(c) Do their ideas amount to a competitive edge that can sustain a business?

(d) Can you think of different target markets for their ideas? Or other innovative opportunities for their chosen services?

(e) What should they do next? Advise Andrea and Kit on how they should proceed with the next stage of developing their new business.

Case study
More food for thought[11]

F ew life-changing events come any bigger than becoming a mother or a father. When Sally Preston, a former food technologist for Marks & Spencer, became a mum in 1995, life also took an unexpected commercial twist. Like many parents, Sally was soon faced with the challenge of providing her four-month-old with food she felt happy with. Balancing the hours of preparation that home-cooked baby food involves versus the sometimes necessary, if not so palatable option, of jarred baby food, Sally hit upon an idea for a new business – manufacturing frozen homemade recipe baby food.

In October 2001, Sally's company 'Babylicious' was born. Originally manufacturing frozen baby food, the company now sells a range of healthy snacks for kids under the Kiddylicious brand (part of The Kids Food Company), with a strong export strategy in Europe, the USA, Asia and Australia. But the path to this particular innovation was not an easy one. Although conceived out of a genuine need – and one shared by countless parents – Sally faced something of an uphill struggle in persuading investors and other key decision-makers that this idea was a genuine market opportunity. The banks refused to support her business and 'business angels' wanted too much equity in the business, forcing Sally to re-mortgage her home. Even when the business was up and running, there followed other challenges – not least how to persuade consumers to change their consumer habits. Things went from bad to worse when someone deliberately tried to steal her business's name, and a hoax caller spread a rumour to her retailer customers that the business was under investigation by the Advertising Standards Authority. Operating her new business from her kitchen and dining room, innovation once more came to the rescue. Sally hit upon the idea of marketing Babylicious in partnership with other baby products. Awareness of the product was raised by putting labels on nappy sacks and leaflets into baby cups.

Something of a precocious 'toddler', The Kids Food Company now runs from its own business premises in Amersham, with a turnover in excess of £4 million. As Sally has explained, 'I never wanted it to be a small cottage industry. I've always had big national and international plans, I could see the global attraction of it.'

Activities

(a) What do you think was the main source of innovation behind Sally Preston's new business idea?
(b) How did Sally overcome the barriers to her innovation?

Source: babylicious.co.uk; for their current range of products, see www.kiddylicious.co.uk

Case study
Taking the rough with the smooth[12]

I n a funny sort of a way, Innocent Drinks began life in the bath. Well, that's one way of opening the story of how three college friends came about innovating one of the most successful recent brands in the drinks market. For making fruit smoothies wasn't the first idea that Richard Reed, Adam Balon and Jon Wright had set their designs on.

(Continued)

The three friends had originally hit upon the idea of the bath that automatically filled to the desired level and temperature. The main problem with this idea wasn't that it wouldn't work – it was in convincing other people that it would, when it involved technology that neither Richard, Adam nor Jon had actually invented. So the entrepreneurs began to look at their own lives for inspiration. What they discovered, based on something they personally knew a lot about, convinced them of a genuine market opportunity. For they recognized that it had become increasingly difficult for them to take the time that they knew they should devote to staying healthy. The modern hectic urban lifestyle that they lived seemed incompatible with eating healthily or going to the gym on a regular basis. If they could only come up with a way of doing something healthy that didn't require a lot of time they would surely be on to a winning formula. It was this moment of insight that led to the launch of Innocent Drinks – a fruit smoothie that tasted good, was good for you, and that could be easily and quickly consumed.

Of course, the idea itself was not totally 'new'. People have been making all kinds of drinks from fruit for millennia. But the concept bucked the trend of mass-produced fruit drinks in terms of not relying on concentrates or using preservatives to lengthen shelf life. It was also to make inspired use of the latest ideas about packaging and presentation. Having the initial idea was one thing, but the three entrepreneurs had absolutely no experience in either fruit or the drinks market. They made up for this by undertaking their own research of the product and the market. Relying on the simple measure of what tasted good to them and their friends, they were able to narrow down the recipes they would use for the commercial product. Their initial market research then continued to demonstrate the founders' flair for creative thinking and entrepreneurial spirit. An ingenious trial tasting was held at a jazz festival. Customers were asked to place their empty cups in a 'yes' or a 'no' bin to vote on whether the friends should give up their jobs and make smoothies full-time. With the 'yes' bin recording a landslide victory, they quit their jobs the next day.

At this point in the story it would be easy to add the phrase '… and the rest is history'. But this would suggest that the transition from secure employment to entrepreneurial start-up was entirely a smooth one. The reality was rather different. Accessing the finance needed to set up the company on the scale required was no easy task – not least because this was just at the start of the dot-com era, when investors were looking at rather different kinds of business proposition. When the cash ran dry, it would have been easy to have thrown in the towel and returned to corporate life. But Richard Reed attributes their getting through this phase to the strength of their friendship and to being part of a team. This was also to see them through when distributors initially refused to stock their drinks. The team loaded a van with drinks and personally delivered them to delicatessens and health shops around Notting Hill. They presented themselves as a new local juice company and handed over free samples, asking the owners to call them if they started to sell. Sell they did, and after the first weekend, 45 companies asked for more.

Innocent Drinks has come a long way from its humble origins. The company sold 24 smoothies on their first day of business in 1999 and, ten years later, they sold approximately 2 million per week. In April 2009, Innocent sold a minority 10–20 percent share of the business to Coca-Cola for £30 million and, in 2013, the three founders sold most of their remaining shareholding to Coca-Cola – which Richard Reed described as a 'Sexit' or successful exit.

Activities

(a) What lessons can aspiring entrepreneurs take from Richard, Adam and Jon's experiences in setting up Innocent Drinks?

(b) Drawing on this case, outline what you consider to be the critical success factors in turning a good idea into an innovation?

C onsider the list of local businesses you drew up for the Extended activity in Chapter 1. (If you did not complete this activity, draw up a list of local businesses, large and small, involved in the food and drink industry which operate in a local community with which you are familiar.)

(a) Which ones do you consider to have been innovative and in what ways?
(b) Is there a noticeable correlation between the likelihood of innovation and the size of the business in the sample you have considered?
(c) Consider three or four of the smaller businesses in your sample. Who are their target markets, and why do their customers buy from them rather than other businesses?

Extended activity
Local innovation and markets

Planning a new venture
Identifying the solution

Summary of what is required:

- Build on your new venture idea with more creative, open thinking by identifying as many solutions as you can that overcome the problem you identified in this exercise in the last chapter.
- Make a shortlist using more critical thinking to evaluate the possible solutions and eliminate those that do not fit key personal and business criteria.
- Assess the competitive edge of each shortlisted solution.
- Rate the benefits sought by customers, and offered by you.
- Identify the best solution which represents a genuine business opportunity.

Build on your new venture idea

The objective of this step is to select one genuine business opportunity by first identifying as many solutions to the problem or need you discovered in the last step and then narrowing them down by reference to your own objectives and to the benefits they offer to targeted customers.

Work on the problem or need you came up with in the last chapter and identify as many solutions to the problem as possible. The aim is not to come up with the best single solution. The objective is to produce a large number of new, imaginative and innovative ideas that might solve the problem. These can be discarded later, or built on to produce something creative and practical.

Creative thinking comes from seeing or making new connections. These connections are often between existing ideas or concepts that are too far apart for one person to visualize together.

The basis of *brainstorming and open thinking* is to use a group of people to build on one another's ideas, so that these improbable connections are made. If you can work with others to develop your list of ideas, then do so. If you cannot, write down as many ideas as you can on your own.

(Continued)

Use the following guidelines if working in a group to brainstorm ideas:

- generate as many ideas as possible: the more the better;
- improve and build on each other's ideas: as well as suggesting new ideas, try and develop someone else's ideas by proposing improvements or ways of combining ideas;
- encourage long shots: crazy-sounding ideas can often spark off original and practical thoughts;
- encourage rather than criticize others: praise other group members' ideas to encourage them to come up with more rather than turning off their creative tap by adverse comments;
- always record all ideas on a sheet of paper or a flip chart.

Make a shortlist

The large number of product and service ideas that could provide a solution to a need or problem now need sorting and shortlisting.

It usually helps to group them into different categories or types. If any are still half-formed, try and build them into something practical, or group them with others to see if there are any possible new combinations. From this list, first eliminate any that you consider cannot be translated into productive use (i.e. they are totally impractical).

Examples of shortlisted solutions to meet the need for 'personal and accommodation protection for elderly people':

- personal security warning devices, from whistles to digital and online alarms;
- individual housing security devices, user-friendly for the elderly;
- impersonal sheltered housing: flats for the elderly in electronic surveillance security accommodation;
- help service for the elderly on a subscription basis, via a clearing house for approved services; for example, plumbers, transport, etc.;
- house conversion service, specialist conversions of larger premises owned by elderly, to small accommodation with rental/sale of surplus.

Next, review each shortlisted solution against the key criteria established in the earlier steps of 'Know yourself', and 'Identifying the need or problem'.

- *Personal requirements* How well does it fit with your personal objectives and requirements?
- *Personal qualities* Will it offer you the opportunity to maximize your strengths and unique qualities?
- *Innovation* Does it meet identifiable needs or overcome a problem in a new way?
- *Viability* Is it supported by longer-term trends or could it be short-lived?

Decide on a shortlist of three or four ideas which you believe will best meet these criteria.

Assess the competitive edge

Before final selection of the one idea you wish to consider for further evaluation, it is necessary to first ensure you will have a competitive edge in the marketplace by considering your target customers and the benefits you will offer them. Again, it is useful to have group feedback where possible or invite others to comment on your shortlisted ideas in relation to the marketplace.

Use the 'Domestic markets checklist' to describe your targeted customer if you are selling to domestic or consumer markets (B2C).

Use the 'Industrial markets checklist' to describe your customer if you are selling to industrial markets or other businesses (B2B). Note: it is important to identify the person(s) who makes the purchase decision. Also use these checklists to consider the benefits which these customers seek from the type of product or service you are offering. When you have identified the benefits the customer is seeking, consider how well these benefits are met by existing products or services and give them a rating between 0 and 10.

Finally, use the competitive edge checklist to identify your competitive edge: specify the benefits of your product or service, and how important these are to the customer, compared to competitive offerings.

Identifying your target customer

Decide if you will be selling to largely domestic or industrial markets. Then use the appropriate checklist to specify your customer target. (They are for guidance only; you may wish to add other parameters or you may feel some are not relevant.)

Checklist

Domestic markets: target customers

Sex	Male ☐	Female ☐

Age group

Under 15	☐
15–25	☐
26–40	☐
41–65	☐
Over 65	☐

Type of employment

Managerial ☐	Manual ☐	Office/Clerical ☐
Housewife ☐	Self-employed ☐	Retired ☐

Other (specify) _____

General

Income range _____

Householder or rented accommodation _____

Area of residence _____

Lifestyle/personality type _____

Interests and hobbies _____

Socio-economic grouping _____

Benefits target customer seeks from my product or service	*Existing product or service provision**
1. _____	☐
2. _____	☐
3. _____	☐
4. _____	☐
5. _____	☐

*For each benefit stated, how do you rate existing products or services available to the target customer? Use a scale of 0 to 10 where 0 = benefit not provided and 10 = benefit fully provided.

(Continued)

Checklist

Industrial markets: target customers

Sector/Industry type: _____

Legal identity: Limited ☐   Partnership ☐   Charity ☐

Size of organization: Turnover range _____

                           Number of employees _____

Location of companies: Geographic area: UK _____

                                             Overseas _____

Job title of decision-maker(s) for my product or service: _____

Frequency of purchase: _____

Benefits target customer seeks from my product or service	*Existing product or service provision**
1. _____	☐
2. _____	☐
3. _____	☐
4. _____	☐
5. _____	☐

*For each benefit stated, how do you rate existing products or services available to the target customer? Use a scale of 0 to 10 where 0 = benefit not provided and 10 = benefit fully provided.

Rate the benefits sought by customers, and offered by you

What are the principal features and benefits of your product or service?

Feature	*Benefit*
1. _____	_____
2. _____	_____
3. _____	_____
4. _____	_____
5. _____	_____

How do your target customers rate these benefits? Indicate for each benefit which you think is the most important in their buying decision, the second most important and so on.

In the 'Domestic markets checklist' or the 'Industrial markets checklist' you have also indicated how you rated existing products or services available in terms of benefits sought by the target customer.

Comparing these two ratings of the relative importance of benefits to customers, and your assessment of the competitive delivery of benefits, what will be your competitive edge?

What will you be offering that is better than the competition and valued by your target customer?

My competitive edge is:

1. _____

2. _____

3. _____

Identify the opportunity

Carefully evaluate each solution once again.

Consider which idea best fulfils the two key criteria of (i) your personal objectives and special talents; and (ii) a competitive edge in the marketplace.

Make a decision and select one solution or opportunity to take forward for evaluation.

4.11 Notes, references and recommended further reading

Notes and further information

1 See Lord Sainsbury, UK Government Minister for Science and Innovation, speech at London Innovation Conference, 17 March 2003.

2 See BBC News online, 'A-bike, no less', 12 July 2006, news.bbc.co.uk/1/hi/magazine/5173612.stm, accessed 22 December 2015 and www.kickstarter.com/projects /a-bike/a-bike-electric-the-lightest-and-most-compact -elec/posts/1321764, accessed 22 December 2015.

3 *MIT Technology Review,* July 1996: 34, quoted in Hargadon, 2003. It makes the distinction between two types of innovation – **user innovation** and **manufacturer innovation**. A user innovation arises when the developer expects to benefit by using it (as was the case with Berners-Lee). A manufacturer innovation happens when the developer expects to benefit by selling it (Hargadon, 2003).

4 See the Department for Business, Innovation & Skills website on Innovation, available at www.gov.uk /guidance/innovation-get-support-and-advice

5 The Digital Britain policy document is available at www.gov.uk/government/uploads/system /uploads/attachment_data/file/228844/7650.pdf

6 Mail online, 'Stelios, We'll see the worst two years of our life', 11 January 2009 (accessed 14 July 2009).

7 Creative industries are defined as 'those activities which have their origin in individual creativity, skill, talent, and which have the potential for wealth and job creation through the generation and exploitation of intellectual property' (DCMS, 1998). For more details, see www.culture.gov.uk

8 For a fuller discussion of these concepts, see one of the texts on marketing; for example, Kotler, P. T. and Keller, K.L. *Marketing Management,* 15th edn, Prentice Hall, 2015.

9 For a more detailed description of segmentation, see Stokes and Lomax (2007) *Marketing: A brief introduction,* Cengage, ch. 7.

10 See James Dyson's Dimbleby Lecture, available at www.bbc.co.uk/pressoffice/pressreleases/stories /2004/12_december/09/dyson.shtml, accessed 22nd December 2015.

11 This case study is based on material from the Babylicious website: www.babylicious.co.uk/; the business now trades under the name Kiddylicious (see www.kiddylicious.co.uk).

12 Sources: Innocent website www.innocentdrinks .co.uk/us/our-story and an interview with www .startups.co.uk

References

Acs, Z. J. and Audretsch, D. B. (1990) *Innovation and Small Firms,* MIT Press.

Adair, J. (1990) *The Challenge of Innovation,* Talbot Adair Press.

Amatori, F. and Colli, A. (2006) Models of entrepreneurship in a latecomer country: Italy. In: Cassis, Y. and Minoglou, I. P. (eds) *Country Studies in Entrepreneurship,* Palgrave Macmillan.

Audretsch, D. B. (1995) *Innovation and Industry Evolution,* MIT Press.

Bilton, C. (2007) *Management and Creativity: From Creative Industries to Creative Management,* Blackwell Publishing.

Bilton, C. (2010) Manageable creativity, *International Journal of Cultural Policy,* 16(3): 255–269.

Cambridge Small Business Research Centre (1992) *The State of British Enterprise,* Department of Applied Economics, University of Cambridge.

Commission of the European Communities, (2004) *European Innovation Scoreboard 2004: Comparative Analysis of Innovation Performance,* CEC.

Davis, W. (1991) The Innovators. In: Henry, J. and Walker, D. (eds) *Managing Innovation,* Sage Publications.

Drucker, P. F. (1985) *Innovation and Entrepreneurship,* Heinemann.

DTI (2003) *Innovation Report: Competing in the Global Economy: The Innovation Challenge*, DTI, December.

European Commission (2003) *Entrepreneurship in Europe*, Green Paper, EC.

European Commission (2007) *Observatory of European SMEs, Summary*, Flash Barometer, EC.

Frey B. and Pommerehne, W. (1989) *Muses and Markets*, Blackwell.

Gates, B. (1995) *The Road Ahead*, Viking.

Hargadon, A. (2003) *How Breakthroughs Happen*, Harvard Business School Press.

Hartley, J. (2009) *The Uses of Digital Literacy*, University of Queensland Press.

Kotler, P. and Scheff, J. (1997) *Standing Room Only: Strategies for Marketing the Performing Arts*, Harvard Business School Press.

Martin, L. and Wilson, N. (2014) Re-discovering creativity: Why theory/practice consistency matters, *International Journal for Talent Development and Creativity*, 2(1): 31–42.

Pavitt, K. (1991) Key characteristics of the large innovating firm, *British Journal of Management*, 2(1): 41–50.

Rothwell, R. (1986) The Role of Small Firms in Technological Innovation. In: Curran, J., Stanworth, J. and Watkins, D. (eds) *The Survival of the Small Firm*, Vol. 2, Gower.

Rothwell, R. and Zegveld, W. (1982) *Innovation and the Small/Medium Sized Firm*, Frances Pinter.

Schoonhoven, C. B. and Romanelli, E. (eds) (2001) *The Entrepreneurship Dynamic: Origins of Entrepreneurship and the Evolution of Industries*, Stanford University Press.

Schumpeter, J. A. (1934) *The Theory of Economic Development: An Inquiry into Profits, Capital, Credit Interest and the Business Cycle*, Transaction Publishers.

Sternberg, R. J. and Lubart, T. I. (1999) (reprinted 2007) The Concept of Creativity: Prospects and Paradigms. In: Sternberg, R. J. (ed.) *Handbook of Creativity*, Cambridge University Press. Chapter 1: 3–15.

Stinchcombe, A. L. (1965) Social Structure and Organizations. In: March, J. G. (ed.) *Handbook of Organizations*, Rand-McNally: 142–193.

Storey, D. (1994) *Understanding the Small Business Sector*, Routledge.

Tether, B. S. (2003) What is Innovation? Approaches to distinguishing new products and processes from existing products and processes, *CRIC Working Paper No. 12*, ESRC Centre for Research on Innovation and Competition, University of Manchester and UMIST.

Utterback, J. (1994) *Mastering the Dynamics of Innovation*, Harvard Business School Press.

Wilson, N. (2009) Learning to manage creativity: An occupational hazard for the UK's creative industries, *Creative Industries Journal*, 2(2): 179–190.

Recommended further reading

Christensen, C. and Raynor, M. E. (2003) *The Innovator's Solution: Creating and Sustaining Successful Growth*, Harvard Business Press.

Kelley, T. (2005) *The Ten Faces of Innovation: IDEO's Strategies for Defeating the Devil's Advocate and Driving Creativity throughout Your Organization*, Broadway Business.

Stokes, D., Wilson, N. and Mador, M. (2010) *Entrepreneurship*, Cengage, ch. 2. The Properties of Entrepreneurship, pp. 28–46.

Tidd, J. and Bessant, J. (2009) *Managing Innovation: Integrating Technological, Market and Organizational Change*, Wiley.

5 Information and help

Learning objectives

By the end of this chapter you will be able to:

- Realize the need for a learning process involving customer feedback during the start-up phase of an enterprise.

- Appreciate the market information needs of a small business.

- Understand the research processes and methods appropriate for entrepreneurs to learn about their market environment.

- Identify and implement relevant primary and secondary research.

- Assess the range of government and other help and support available to SMEs.

- Evaluate the merits of government policies that aim to help entrepreneurs.

Introduction

Nascent entrepreneurs need information and, quite often, some help to set up a new venture. Owner-managers of established businesses need market intelligence to make informed decisions to keep pace with change. This chapter considers what information both new and established entrepreneurs need about their market and their environment and how they can obtain it with limited resources. It reviews the concept of the 'lean start-up' as a way of ensuring that feedback from the market informs entrepreneurial learning in the early days of new venture creation. Although entrepreneurs traditionally rely on informal information gathering, more rigorous approaches to research can usefully be employed to reduce risk. Many sources of help and advice are available but the fragmentation of delivery through the various agencies often makes it difficult for small business owners to access what they need. Governments have increasingly invested in support for small businesses, although the returns for this investment have yet to be fully substantiated.

Activity 1
The lean start-up

The concept of the 'lean start-up' has recently become popular. What do you think is the fundamental principle of a *lean* start-up compared to any other form of new venture?

5.1 Testing the new venture – the 'lean start-up'

To survive and thrive in the marketplace, an entrepreneur needs information of different types depending on the stage of development of the business. For a start-up, the crucial question is whether there is sufficient market demand for the new product or service to enable the enterprise to establish itself as a viable business. Many owners launch their business in order to find out the answer to this crucial question but this can be a costly, time-consuming and stressful way of assessing demand, especially if the response is negative. However, the feasibility of a new venture can be assessed with the help of research on the business environment and markets in which it will operate (Bragg and Bragg, 2005).[1] This involves acquiring knowledge about potential customers, competitors and industry structures to assess the acceptability of the new idea.

This research can have two distinct objectives:

(a) To develop and confirm a strategy for market entry based upon the identifiable needs of the target customer group;

(b) To provide credibility to outside backers and financiers and convince them that the new venture is founded on the realities of the marketplace, not just the dreams of the entrepreneur.

In earlier chapters, we noted that entrepreneurial ventures exist in environments of extreme uncertainty, especially during the start-up phase; there can be few certainties in creating something that really is new. Many new ventures are born each year but an equally large number close (Chapters 1 and 3). As new ventures are now recognized as a key part of a successful capitalist economy, many governments offer assistance to help small businesses survive the uncertainty, as this chapter later explores.

First, however, entrepreneurs need to help themselves on their uncertain journey by learning as much as they can about the environment in which they travel. Starting a business has been described as a learning process that involves running experiments that allow the entrepreneur to test their idea. These experiments can be conducted according to the principles of a **'lean start-up'** (Ries, 2011).[2]

The terminology has its roots in 'lean manufacturing' concepts that evolved from Japanese car manufacturing. 'Lean' in this sense means short of anything that does not add value to the customer. It does not necessarily mean low cost or short of resources but puts emphasis only on aspects of an operation that are important to a customer and strips out anything else.

Similarly, a 'lean start-up' takes what is of value to a customer as the key measurement of success or failure during the experiments to test the viability of a new idea.

Entrepreneurship becomes a circular process, rather than linear, in which experiments or tests relating to a new business idea enable the entrepreneur to learn more about the validity of the idea and hence modify it as necessary. An idea is turned into something resembling the product (or service) and this prototype is used to gather information through contacts with potential customer groups and market tests. This is illustrated in Figure 5.1.

A key concept behind the lean start-up is to carefully measure what the customer values in any new idea. In order to do this, some representation of the product or service has to be made. Ries (2011) advocates building a *'minimum viable product'* as the first step in this process so that there is something tangible to talk about with potential customers. These can vary from screen shots of a new website to a physical model of a new product design. The closer they convey the essence of the idea, the more reliable the measure of viability back from the marketplace will be. The outcome of this process is learning how close the idea is to adding sufficient value to a potential customer to make them want to buy it.

At this stage, a decision is required. Does the feedback from the market require modifications or more drastic changes to the idea, or can the entrepreneur persevere with the concept unchanged? This needs careful thought based on the key measure of added value to a customer. Unfortunately, proto-entrepreneurs are prone to blindness when it comes to seeing the faults in their own ideas, which is why a rigorous process of evaluation

Figure 5.1 The lean start-up cycle

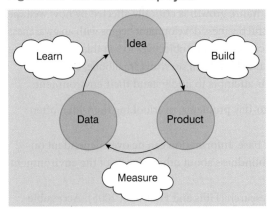

Source: Ries (2011)

is necessary. Too often, negative feedback from customers is either ignored or taken too seriously and the idea dropped altogether. The learning process requires key entrepreneurial characteristics in abundance – determination and an ability to learn from what some might call a 'failure'.

According to Ries (2011), 'pivoting' is a subtle form of change; when we change direction with our feet we tend to keep one foot on the ground and pivot the other one in the new direction. So it is with assessing a new idea: one part can change while another remains constant. Pivoting prevents throwing out the proverbial baby with the bathwater.

Entrepreneurship research that looks at how entrepreneurs make decisions (see Sarasvathy, 2001; Dew *et al.*, 2009) suggests an important fourth stage that runs parallel to this lean start-up evaluation: assessing affordable loss.

Affordable loss involves entrepreneurs 'estimating what they might be able to put at risk and determining what they are willing to lose in order to follow a course of action.' (Dew *et al.*, 2009, p. 105). The decision to 'plunge' into entrepreneurship is therefore contingent on both internal and external factors.

In summary, the four stages to the evaluation are:

1 Create a minimum viable product (MVP), a minimum version to demonstrate to customers (early adopters).
2 Measure how customers respond.
3 'Pivot or persevere' – change the parts that don't work and keep those that do.
4 Assess if this course of action constitutes an 'affordable loss'.

Activity 2
Entrepreneurial research

How do entrepreneurs tend to find out about their business environment? How do they tend to do it differently from managers in larger companies? Which methods are most effective?

5.2 Entrepreneurial networking

Successful owner-managers have a good understanding of the environment in which their enterprise operates. They know their customers well; they keep an eye on competitive activity; they are aware of underlying trends that may affect their business. For some time now, researchers have suggested that a key factor in business survival is how quickly new owner-managers can understand their environment, and then learn from their experiences of dealing with it (e.g. Watkins, 1982). Such research has also shown that future growth is critically affected by how well the owner-manager stays in touch with external influences. Successful business development begins with an awareness of the total situation surrounding an enterprise, and the modification of initial objectives to suit this ever-changing environment. Adjustment to the business environment is crucial to long-term survival (Smallbone, 1990).[3]

There are several problems facing owner-managers in their attempts to understand their environment:

- Owner-managers tend to concentrate on immediate day-to-day problems, overlooking the wider, often long-term, issues.
- Small firms often operate with a relatively small customer base. Information can be over-dependent on feedback from a small number of customers, leading to a blindness about other aspects of the environment (Chaston, 2000).
- Owner-managers seem suspicious of formalized market research (Hills and Hultman, 2005). Accessible market information is not necessarily relevant to the position of a small firm. There is reluctance to commission more relevant research because of its costs.

For these reasons, owner-managers tend to rely on informal information-gathering methods of highly variable reliability. Even successful entrepreneurs use informal networks to keep up to date, using extensive contacts to develop a rich mental map of their environment.[4]

This is an aspect of *entrepreneurial networking* in which the owner-manager seeks feedback from people they know well about decisions they are about to make. Typically, this is done face-to-face, in an unplanned and opportunistic way. It seems as though a small firm owner's approach to information gathering is often chaotic and opportunistic. They tend to shy away from planned programmes of market research. They neither have the time, nor often the skill, to sift through the mountain of data which could inform their business decisions. Instead, they tend to gather information 'on the hoof' as they go about their daily tasks. (Networking is also discussed in Chapters 2, 4, 6 and 12.)

Successful entrepreneurs have an uncanny knack of picking up the really pertinent pieces of knowledge they need, seemingly without having to process other, less relevant, information. For example, Alan Sugar took Amstrad into a wide variety of electrical household products, from videos to home computers, by trusting his personal antennae to be in tune with what the market wants, rather than using formalized research to assess customer needs (Thomas, 1991).

Activity 3
Information required

What is the key information an entrepreneur needs after the venture has been set up? Make a list of key questions that successful entrepreneurs are constantly asking about their business environment.

5.3 Market research for small firms

5.3.1 ENTREPRENEURIAL INFORMATION NEEDS

Although entrepreneurs often gather information in this informal, intuitive way, they still need to be asking the right questions even if they seek to answer them through an informal process. So what do entrepreneurs need to know about their marketplace?

- **Market information** is essentially about existing and potential customers, trends in the market sector and competitors.
- **Marketing information** is about those factors which can change the existing position of customers and competitors. It seeks to find out what will influence customers in their decision-making processes (Stokes and Lomax, 2008).

Typical questions that arise in both these categories are shown in Table 5.1.

Such information is just as important to the developing enterprise as it is to the new business start-up. Time and cost factors will restrict the volume and accuracy of answers available to these questions, but the successful owner-manager will continually be looking for answers through formal and informal methods.

Table 5.1 Marketing intelligence needs of a small business

Market information	Marketing information
• What are the *characteristics* of existing customers and potential new customers? (a) *Who* makes the buying decision? (b) *What* are the differences between customer groups? e.g. between those who buy a lot and those who buy a little. (c) *When* are purchases made? e.g. on a regular or cyclical basis.	• What benefits are the customers seeking to acquire from the product or service offered? • How will the buying decision be made? (Who will have an influence on the decision and how will this be exerted?) • Where does the customer buy existing products or services? • What distribution channels are used?
• What is the *size* of the target market? (a) The number of customers? (b) Volume of purchases? (c) Value of purchases? (d) What are estimates for the above in one year's time, and subsequently? • Who are the direct *competitors?* (a) How many? (b) How big? (c) How successful?	• What price parameters are there? • How does the customer find out about the product or service? By word of mouth? By advertising and other promotional activities? • How well do competitors meet the requirements of the target customers' group? What are their strengths and weaknesses in relation to customer preferences? • How do competitors use marketing activities in relation to the target market?
• What are the *substitutes* for the product or service? What choices does the buyer have in terms of: (a) Indirect alternatives? (b) Substitutes for discretionary expenditure?	• What is their pricing policy? • How do they promote? • How do they distribute? • What is their product strategy?

Activity 4
Primary or secondary data?

Information is sometimes categorized into primary and secondary data.

(a) What do you think is the difference between the two?
(b) What are the advantages and disadvantages of each type for an owner-manager?

5.3.2 THE RESEARCH PROCESS

Entrepreneurs tend to regard market and marketing research as long-winded and expensive (Hills and Hultman, 2005), but there are many inexpensive and uncomplicated ways in which a small business can research the marketplace.

An example of a research process which can be undertaken by a small firm is shown in Figure 5.2. The stages of this process are:

1 Describe the target customer segment. Any description of the customer group under investigation needs to be as precise as possible, to avoid wasting resources in gathering unnecessary data.
2 Define research objectives. What will the information be used for once it has been obtained? What questions, if answered, will meet the aims of the research?
3 Check existing knowledge and data. There is always a wealth of existing data available, especially in an ongoing business. Some of this may not always be obvious even to the owner-manager. Customer records, sales people, sales assistants, invoice records, sales ledgers, financial statistics: these are all very important potential sources of information about the marketplace.
4 Define new information required. What new information will be required if the questions arising from the research objectives are to be answered?

Figure 5.2 A market research process for a small enterprise

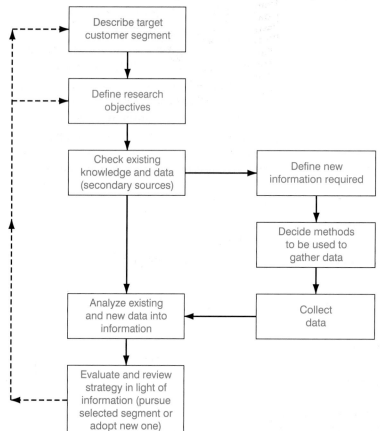

5 Decide the methods to be used to gather data. The following sections of this chapter discuss what methods are available.

6 Collect the data.

7 Analyze existing and new data. This is usually raw information which needs collating and turning into intelligent information, i.e. data which has been interpreted and summarized.

8 Evaluate and review strategy in the light of information gained through research. This is the stage at which decisions relating to the objectives of the research can be made. It may involve a rethink about the customer segment under investigation. Does the information support the targeting of the selected segment and, if so, how can this be best pursued? Should the firm's resources be concentrated on a different segment, in which case which one, and what research now needs to be undertaken?

5.3.3 RESEARCH METHODS

The questions which are posed by the research objectives will determine which methods can be used for collecting the data. Data is divided into two basic categories:

- Primary: new data specifically collected for the project, usually through field research.
- Secondary: data that already exists which can be collected by desk research.

The comparative advantages and disadvantages of each type are summarized in Table 5.2.

Activity 5
Secondary sources

Someone asks for your advice on how to find out about the market environment for their proposed new business. What secondary information sources would you advise them to investigate?

For example, an entrepreneur had decided to set up a fish restaurant specializing in healthy fish and chips. She was concerned about the rising costs of fish due to the increasing cost of fuel and fish shortages. She had also heard that some fish stocks such as cod were actually increasing. She needed more definite information about the impact of these trends on her business. Where would you suggest she look?

Table 5.2 Advantages and disadvantages of primary and secondary data

	Primary data	Secondary data
Definition	Data collected specifically for the purpose in hand	Data that already exists through other sources
Advantages	• Reflects specific need • Up-to-date • Individual control	• Lower cost • More immediate • Wide-ranging data
Disadvantages	• Expensive to collect • Time-consuming • Risk of competitors finding out intentions	• Does not meet specific needs • Often out-of-date • May be incomplete

5.4 Secondary data

Research usually considers secondary information sources first. Small firms most commonly use **secondary data** because it is immediate and either free or low cost. The main sources of information are discussed below.

Internal sources

The internal records and knowledge base of an existing small business is the obvious place to start, as it is low-cost, available data and usually reliable. Most small firms have at least basic records of customers, sales and costs; they may also keep records of prospective customers; for example, from sales visit reports. Non-written information may also exist; for example, from the knowledge of staff who have contact with customers. One of the advantages of buying an existing business for the new entrant is that this type of internal information should exist to help them assess the risks involved.

Personal contact networks

We have already referred to the importance of entrepreneurial networking – the personal contacts, relationships and alliances which owner-managers develop (see also Chapters 2 and 3). These can provide a rich source of informal information. Networks include suppliers; customers; local businesses; contacts in the trade; professional advisers such as bank managers, accountants and solicitors; former colleagues; friends and acquaintances. For someone starting up a new venture with few contacts in the trade, suppliers are often a good source of information: they are usually in regular contact with similar businesses and have a vested interest in helping a potential new customer get started.

Trade associations

These may be specific to a particular trade or industry (for example, the National Federation of Fish Fryers and the Sea Fish Industry Authority), [5] or a locality (the local Chamber of Commerce). Both may be able to provide information and contacts for the new entrant.

Competitor sources

Most businesses publish information about themselves, usually intended for customers, but also obtainable by other small firms. Accessible published information includes websites, product information leaflets, reports and accounts. Trade shows and exhibitions can be good sources of competitive information; the catalogue will provide a good summary of the existing companies in the field and literature can be collected easily from one place. Franchisers give information to prospective franchisees on the prospects in their particular market, which in some circumstances can be obtained by new entrants who are not taking up a franchise.

External secondary sources

The internet has made access to external sources of information easy and fast, provided you know what you are looking for. Other external sources include central and local government, directories, published statistics and reports, and national and trade press articles. Government statistics and those published by other official bodies can have the disadvantage of being out-of-date, and not in line with exact needs. General guides, or web portals, to the information available (listed below in Section 5.8) are a good place to start for anyone unfamiliar with the range of possible data.

Many sources of data can be referred to free of charge on the internet or in a library. Where information has to be purchased it is still relatively low-cost as the data collection is amortized over many subscribers. Trade associations, Chambers of Commerce, banks, universities, colleges of further and higher education, and research institutions are good sources of information for specific fields. Newspapers and periodicals tend to provide more general data but can be useful for background information.

An indication of published data is given in Section 5.8 (Useful sources of information for entrepreneurs) at the end of this chapter. It is not a comprehensive list but includes useful sources and more general guides. There is now a significant amount of data covering a wide range of products, markets and companies that is readily available.

Activity 6
Primary research

An owner-manager of an existing business wishes to carry out primary research into their marketplace. What inexpensive methods are available to carry out this research?

For example, the founders of a social enterprise that aimed to help homeless people wanted to find out how their fundraising methods were perceived by the general public. How would you advise them to research this?

5.5 Primary data

Most small firm owners and entrepreneurs are reluctant to undertake primary research (Carson *et al.*, 1995). Although it is invariably time-consuming to collect and collate, primary research data need not be expensive. In some instances, it can cost nothing except time. Some primary research approaches are described on the following pages.

5.5.1 SURVEYS AND QUESTIONNAIRES

Market surveys are a common source of **primary data**, but they can take many forms. A typical survey asks questions of a number of respondents selected to correspond to the target market under investigation. Its main instrument is the questionnaire, which is probably the most widely known and used market research tool. Questionnaires can be used to measure:

- buying patterns and trends (Have you purchased XYZ in past 12 months/six months/one month?);
- attitudes to products and services (How would you rate the performance of XYZ on a scale of 1 to 5?);
- expectations related to products and services (When you purchase XYZ, which of the following benefits is most/least important?);
- competitors' activities (Which of the following products have you purchased in the past 12 months?);
- media exposure and influence (Which of the following journals do you read regularly?).

Owner-managers of small firms have tended to overlook many of the opportunities of gathering information by surveys; they have been regarded as the province of bigger companies with more resources to collect large statistically valid samples. The internet has helped to change this as surveys can now be designed and hosted online at low cost. Respondents still need to be encouraged to complete the survey by various contact methods, but the use of an internet-based survey means that inexperienced researchers can design and analyze a survey at low cost.[6]

Sampling

Conclusions about a larger number of people or products can be drawn by studying a smaller number, or sample, that is taken to be representative of the whole. This is based on the cook's principle that you can find out what a dish is like by tasting a small amount and assuming the rest tastes the same. However, the sample has to be selected in such a way that it can be taken either to represent or illustrate the larger whole without bias – in the same way that a cook would want to ensure that the taste at the top of the dish was not concealing a burned portion at the bottom. Sampling methods include:

- *Probability sampling* ensures that every member of the population under consideration has an equal chance of being selected. This can be done, for example, by choosing respondents randomly from a database. However, this can make research expensive or time-consuming in making contact with those selected. *Clustering,* or dividing the sample into a smaller number of areas, can help to minimize this problem.
- *Quota sampling* involves selecting the key characteristics of the population under study (e.g. age, gender, social group, size of business), so that the complete sample matches the total population in these important respects (e.g. in terms of the percentages in each category). Data is then collected from a quota of individuals who match these criteria. This is less accurate than random sampling as bias can enter the selection procedures of the quota.
- *A convenience sample* is based on ease of access. It is used for research where a statistically valid sample is less important than finding relevant respondents quickly. Respondents may be selected on the basis of personal contacts of the interviewer or by asking one respondent to recommend another.

The number of people or units in the sample depends on the size of the total population being studied (e.g. number of businesses in a particular region, or consumers in a particular age range) and how confident you need to be that the sample represents the total population accurately. Formulae can be used to calculate the required sample numbers needed to be representative of a given population size. For example, one may wish to know the sample size required to be representative of the opinions of 1000 businesses in a particular region, or 10 000 consumers in a particular age range. Using statistical techniques for determining sample size, the answers are given in Table 5.3 as 278 and 370, respectively.

Table 5.3 illustrates the changing relationship between the size of the total population being studied and the sample size required to have a reasonable level of confidence in the generalizability of the results: as the population increases, the sample increases at a diminishing rate. This implies that, to survey small populations of less than 100, response rates have to be high to be confident that the results are representative of the whole. This decreases rapidly as the total population being studied increases.

Contact methods

The principal contact methods for surveys or other forms of research are:

- *Personal* Face-to-face interviews are usually the best way of finding out detailed knowledge and attitudes towards services or products. Such personal contact can vary from a structured completion of predetermined questions to an unstructured discussion that uses an interview guide to ensure the main topics are covered. Existing customers or visitors to business premises often form the most important yet easy-to-reach sample for such interviews. For instance, finding out about customer dissatisfaction is a major problem for restaurant owners. Most unhappy customers say nothing at the time – they just do not come back, and then complain to their friends, thereby amplifying the damage without giving the restaurant

Table 5.3 Sample size for a given population

Population size	Sample size
10	10
50	44
100	80
200	132
250	152
500	217
1 000	278
2 000	322
5 000	357
10 000	370
100 000	384

Source: Krejcie, R. (1970) *Journal of Educational and Psychological Measurement,* 30: 607–610, Chicago State University Press.

owner an opportunity to put the damage right. A simple questionnaire or an informal interview can help overcome the problem. Surveys of existing customer perceptions of a small firm can be particularly revealing and inexpensive if conducted at the point of sale.

- *Telephone* Surveys by telephone can be quick and often give high response rates if the interview is kept short. Start-ups can find out about the products and services already available by calling existing suppliers. Existing small firms can survey their competitors' prices by phoning round for quotes on a standard item or piece of work.
- *Mail* Questionnaires by post can be useful to reach a wider audience and remove many problems of bias through the interviewer. A small inducement may be necessary to provoke the quantity of response desired. However, surveys by mail should not be confused with any form of selling, which, although tempting to mitigate the costs, will inevitably bias the results. For example, a training consultant mailed a brief questionnaire to companies in his area to find out more about their perceived training needs and intentions. Although he offered a discount voucher for forthcoming workshops as an incentive to respond to the questionnaire, he resisted the temptation to confuse his research objectives with a specific sales message about his training programmes.
- *Electronic methods* In a similar way, surveys can also be sent via email to known addresses, or through websites that ask visitors for information. Electronic communications can also be used in conjunction with other contact methods – a questionnaire that has been elicited by mail or telephone can be completed electronically. Use of an internet-hosted survey that is promoted by a number of different methods including mobile phone and email communications supplemented with more traditional personal contacts and mail has become an increasingly common way for entrepreneurs to conduct research.

Which method to choose?

These contact methods have advantages and disadvantages, summarized in Table 5.4, which will determine the application to which they are best suited. If a speedy response with tight control of who is surveyed

Table 5.4 Methods of survey data collection: comparative merits

Criterion	Contact methods			
	Mail	**Email**	**Telephone**	**Personal**
Quantity of data	Poor	Poor	Good	Excellent
Interviewer effect[†]	Good	Good	Fair	Fair
Control of sample	Excellent	Good	Fair	Poor
Speed	Poor	Excellent	Excellent	Good
Response rate	Poor	Poor	Good	Good
Costs	Fair	Excellent	Fair	Poor

[†]This refers to the possibility of interviewers biasing results because of their preconceived ideas.

is a priority, then telephone and email are probably the best methods. A small firm might use this route, for instance, to find out more about competitive activity to which an immediate reaction is necessary (e.g. price cutting). If the need for confidentiality and impartiality is paramount, then a mail survey is usually the preferred route. This is likely to be the case when personal details of, for example, health or income are required. This might, therefore, be the preferred method for surveys by small firms offering financial services or computer dating.

If the survey requires a flexible approach, allowing respondents the opportunity to comment in a qualitative, open-ended manner, then a personal interview is necessary. This could be the case, for example, where a small publishing company wished to test various concepts for educational books by interviewing lecturers and teachers of the subjects concerned.

The structure of a questionnaire

The construction of the questionnaire in terms of wording and layout will largely determine how useful it is as a guide for decision-making. Although a trained researcher should be used where possible, there is nothing to stop the small business manager drafting a valid questionnaire without expert help, provided it is kept simple and basic rules are observed.

The most common approach to an overall structure is through 'funnelling'. This involves asking more general questions first and then gradually restricting the focus through more specific questions, leaving the most direct questions until last. This funnel technique is used to reduce elements of bias that might come from asking up front specific questions that would affect who might continue to complete the questionnaire.

The first consideration in designing a questionnaire is to define what information is required. The questions asked will flow from this and will be of two basic types:

- *Closed questions* are those that can attract only a limited response such as Yes/No or a rating on a scale (Do you own your own house?, or How do you rate our service: excellent, good, fair, below average or poor?). Closed questions can be used when quantitative analysis is required from the surveys and result in a very structured approach.
- *Open questions* are those which invite a freer response, such as an opinion or individual information (What do you think of the present government? Which sports do you play?). They are particularly useful in researching attitudes and buying motivations.

Questionnaires often use a mix of these styles of questions. A typical questionnaire might start with structured questions to qualify the respondent (e.g. Do you live within 5 miles of this town, 5 to 10 miles, more than 10 miles?) and finish with unstructured questions inviting comments on a key aspect of the research objectives (Why do you shop in this area?).

Bias in questions

The wording of a questionnaire needs careful examination to avoid biasing the response. This can result from social pressure on respondents to answer in a certain way because of implied expectations. For example, the question 'Do you dislike smoke from other people when you are walking in a street?' encourages a positive response, which may over-emphasize genuine objections to other people smoking in the street. One word can radically change the impact of a question. Consider the following two questions for inclusion in a survey of the parents of children at a first school:

1 'Do you think all after-school activities should be free of charge?'
2 'Do you think all after-school activities could be free of charge?'

The change of the word 'should' for 'could' switches the whole emphasis of the question: 'should be free of charge' may prompt the answer 'yes'; 'could be free of charge' may lead to more realistic replies.

Omnibus surveys

If the market to be researched is large, or there is a need for continuous information, a small enterprise can consider omnibus research. This is a service offered by research agencies who regularly conduct surveys in a specific industry or market sector. The results are then sold to subscribing companies, which spreads the costs of the research over a wider client base. Subscribers can also add their own specific requirements to the survey, which is a good way of obtaining cost-effective data providing the information needed is straightforward and can be obtained from a small number of questions.

   Omnibus surveys are either based on national samples of adult purchasers, or specialist populations; for example, regional markets or house owners. They are particularly useful if continuous consumer research is needed. If regular feedback from a large customer base is important, this can be obtained from surveys which are regularly repeated.

5.5.2 OTHER PRIMARY RESEARCH

Other types of primary research that can be used by the small firm include:

Group discussions (focus groups)

Group discussions or **focus groups** are a good example of qualitative research available to the small business. A group of people, conforming to the parameters of the target market, are invited to an informal discussion, led by a facilitator to guide the conversation around desired topics. The session is normally recorded, and may also be observed. The aim is to give insights into perceptions and motivations of potential customer groups. One of the prime uses is in testing concepts for new products or services. The results do not usually represent a statistically valid sample as the number of respondents is small. However, the qualitative data that emerges can be subtler as the facilitator probes for reactions to various propositions, or builds on the comments and reactions of the participants in the group. A small business can consider using them as they are not prohibitively expensive. The principal costs are the time of the facilitator, an interpretative report on proceedings, if required, and the recruitment of the group. For example, a small firm specializing in marketing free publications to doctors, financed by pharmaceutical advertising, conducted discussion groups of general practitioners to test the concept of a new magazine. They obtained useful feedback not only on the acceptability of the idea, but also on the proposed name, content, design and layout.

Observation

Some business opportunities lend themselves to research through observing what is happening in the marketplace. For example, a potential retailer could observe the quantity and types of shopper using locations where he or she was interested in opening a retail outlet. Competitive information can also be gained from observation; the size, staffing and activity levels of stands at exhibitions and trade shows are useful indicators of competitive strengths and weaknesses. Some entrepreneurs use more underhand observation tactics such as following a competitor's delivery van to find out where their customers are!

Where possible, observations should be quantified to ensure objectivity and comparability. For example, pedestrians can be counted at different times, in different locations, to build up a comparative audit of shopping traffic, which could give vital clues to potential demand in given areas.

Experimentation

Experiments, or tests, are sometimes conducted in the small business field to obtain live feedback from the marketplace. A small retail chain of two or three shops might vary their marketing activities in one outlet to test market promotional ideas; for instance, prices may be changed in one shop only and sales patterns compared to the other shops in an effort to gauge the effectiveness of the price change.

Geodemographic databases

The term 'geodemographic' comes from combining both geographic and demographic information about people. Research uses this concept by building a profile of the population in defined geographic areas based on the latest census and other demographic and lifestyle information. Significant socio-economic factors such as age, sex, marital status, occupation, economic position, education, home and car ownership are covered so that the population can be divided into many types of demographic and lifestyle profiles.

For example, one of the **geodemographic databases**[7] classified the population into different types ranging from 'Wealthy suburbs, large detached houses' (2.6 per cent of the UK population) and 'Private flats, elderly people' (0.3 per cent), to 'Estates with high unemployment' (1.3 per cent) and 'Multiethnic, large families, overcrowding' (0.6 per cent).

Significantly for small business, these population types are identified according to precise areas based on postcodes. As there are approximately 1.9 million domestic postcodes in the UK, or an average of 15 houses per full postcode, the geodemographic information can be targeted to very local areas.

Activity 7
Help!

A new owner-manager needs help and advice in order to set up their business. Where do you suggest they go for it? Do you know of any government schemes that might be available to them?

5.6 Help for small business

5.6.1 WHY HELP SMALL FIRMS?

The small business sector has become of such economic and social significance internationally that its development can no longer be left to chance. In the UK, successive governments formed by different political parties have followed policies aimed at supporting small firms. Non-governmental organizations give support for specific sectors and regions. Banks and financial institutions offer help beyond just the provision of finance. European governments and the European Union have instituted policies and initiatives to promote the development of SMEs, as have most governments around the world.

Help on this scale in favour of one particular business sector seems contrary to the free-market policies increasingly followed by international policy-makers. While the governments and organizations responsible have not spelt out a coherent overall strategy, the rationale for actively discriminating in favour of the small firm stems from a number of beliefs about the role of the small firm.[8]

- *Creation of jobs:* most countries encourage small firms, and particularly new firms, as a way of reducing unemployment.
- *Source of innovation:* although small firms have proved to be an abundant source of inventive ideas, they can lack the resources to put them into practice without external assistance.
- *Competition to larger firms:* as part of an anti-monopoly policy, small firms are needed to compete with larger companies by providing alternative sources of supply.
- *A level playing field:* some legislation is aimed at removing the unfair advantages that large firms might enjoy over small. These include the fixed cost of implementing government regulations in taxation, health and safety, and employing additional personnel, which are a relatively higher burden for the small firm to carry. Small firms' access to external finance is also seen as more restricted as financiers prefer lending to larger companies, where the risk is less and the returns greater. (The costs of setting up loans are similar for greater or smaller amounts – see Chapter 13.)

In the UK, successive governments since the early 1980s have been particularly active in attempting to promote small firms, with literally hundreds of measures and initiatives introduced. These have been in the three main areas of financial assistance, lightening the tax and administration load, and information and advice.

5.6.2 FINANCIAL ASSISTANCE

Various forms of direct and indirect financial assistance have been tried. Some of these have been targeted at start-up firms, but the emphasis of current initiatives is to help established businesses that need to develop. (See also Chapter 13 which explores forms of finance for small firms, including public assistance.)

Helping the unemployed and disadvantaged into business

A number of schemes have tried to help the unemployed either to set up their own business or to become employed by established small businesses. The Business Start-Up Scheme (BSUS) and its predecessor the Enterprise Allowance Scheme (EAS) encouraged people to start their own business by paying them an allowance for a limited period. (For example, the EAS was designed to offset the loss of unemployment benefit once an unemployed person was in business by paying them a weekly allowance.) These schemes attracted large numbers of participants; over 650 000 people took part in the first decade of the scheme to 1993. However, they encouraged more self-employment than small business development in that, for every participant in the schemes, only one-third of a full-time job was created for others. Attrition rates were also high: only 50 per cent of businesses started under the schemes were still trading three years later, emphasizing the dangers of using the 'push' motive to encourage the unemployed to start their own business.

The New Deal run by the Labour administration from 1997 to 2009 effectively replaced these initiatives by offering training and financial assistance for the longer-term unemployed to seek jobs, including those provided by small businesses. In doing so, it shifted the emphasis to creating jobs in established firms rather than setting up new ones. A small business taking on an unemployed person through the scheme received an allowance, plus a contribution towards training costs. However, 'jobseekers' were also supported into self-employment by being able to retain their unemployment allowances for up to 26 weeks while they 'test traded' their business.

The Coalition government ended the New Deal, claiming that the costs outweighed the benefits, and replaced it with the Work Programme in 2011 as part of an extensive reform of welfare support. This confirmed the trend away from payment incentives to start new businesses and focused on finding jobs in existing firms.

Helping small firms obtain bank finance

To obtain a bank loan, an owner-manager often needs not just a good business proposition, but also some form of collateral or guarantee to support the loan. The Small Firms Loan Guarantee (SFLG) scheme was introduced in 1981 to help owners obtain finance from banks when they would not normally be able to do so because of lack of assets to use as security. It was intended for small businesses (up to £3 million turnover) that were unable to arrange loans under normal banking policies as, in certain circumstances, the government would agree to guarantee up to 75 per cent of a bank loan, in return for which the borrowing firm paid a small amount of extra interest.

The overall effects of the scheme on the small business community were minimal. Although the scheme may have originally encouraged some clearing banks to take the small business sector more seriously, it still accounted for less than 1 per cent of total lending to small firms. It was still a central plank in the government's response to the onset of recession as they first extended the existing scheme in March 2008 and then replaced it with the Enterprise Finance Guarantee Scheme in January 2009. This opened up the scheme to medium-sized as well as small firms by increasing the maximum annual turnover criterion to £25 million and the loan size to £1 million.

The issue of bank lending to small firms became a key issue following the banking crisis of 2008. Although large amounts of public money were injected into the banking system, there were still concerns that lending to small firms had been substantially reduced, or was being made at interest rates substantially above the record-low Bank of England base rate (0.25 per cent in 2016).

Helping small firms attract venture capital

In addition to bank lending, the government is keen for private individuals and companies to act as external investors in smaller businesses, and has introduced tax incentives to encourage such investment.

The Enterprise Investment Scheme (EIS), and its predecessor the Business Expansion Scheme (BES), were designed to attract outside investment in small businesses by UK tax payers. The EIS, which has been running since 1994, gives investors tax relief on up to £1million of investment in qualifying companies and exemption from capital gains tax providing the shares are held for more than three years. To qualify, investors cannot be paid directors or employees of the business, neither may they own more than 30 per cent of its equity.

The scheme has attracted not only direct investment by individuals, but also EIS portfolios, offered by some financial institutions who selected a range of businesses for investment, thereby spreading the risk of the investment and putting it under professional management. This also has the effect of concentrating investment in larger firms and not the small businesses originally targeted by the scheme.

Venture Capital Trusts (VCTs) were introduced in 1995, as vehicles for private individuals to buy shares in a portfolio of smaller firms. VCTs are quoted on the London Stock Exchange (LSE) and invest in smaller private trading companies. Investors in VCTs benefit from tax relief on income tax from dividends and capital gains tax on disposal of shares. The Corporate Venturing Scheme gives tax incentives to larger companies to invest in new or expanding small businesses.

5.6.3 LIGHTENING THE TAX AND ADMINISTRATION LOAD

UK government policy has been to remove as much of the burden of taxation and the bureaucratic regulation of business activities as possible, claiming in the 1985 White Paper, 'Lifting the Burdens', and subsequent policy statements, that this was necessary to encourage economic development and growth.

Small business has been singled out for special treatment in several areas.

Taxation

Successive governments have used taxation policies to encourage entrepreneurial activity and improve the liquidity position of small businesses in a number of ways:

- A progressive rate of corporation tax meant that smaller firms benefited from lower corporation tax rates. The tax rates for companies with profits up to £300 000 was lower than those above (20 per cent compared to 23 per cent in 2013). Although this differential was removed from 2015 with a flat rate of 20 per cent, it was announced that Britain's corporation tax rate would fall further, to 18 per cent, in 2020. This compares to a corporation tax rate in the United States of 40 per cent, in France of 33.3 per cent, in Japan of 33 per cent, and in Germany of 30 per cent, and so represented a clear signal that the UK wants to encourage business development and entrepreneurship.
- R&D tax credits encourage SMEs to invest in innovation. A tax relief on allowable R&D costs of 230 per cent is available to small businesses employing less than 500 people, which means that for each £100 spent on R&D, an additional £130 on top of the £100 spent can be offset against taxable profits.
- Inflation accounting, rather than historic cost accounting, can now be used in assessing tax liability, with a resulting benefit for most profitable small firms.

Capital gains

Entrepreneurs have been encouraged to invest in their business through a favourable capital gains tax regime. 'Entrepreneur's relief' reduces the effective tax rate to 10 per cent of the gain on the sale of a business asset, providing the entrepreneur has held at least 5 per cent of the shares for more than one year and is an employee or director of the company. This compares to rates of 18 or 28 per cent that would normally apply. (See also Chapter 9 'Buying an Existing Business', Section 9.6.)

Tax collection

Businesses are major collectors of Pay-As-You-Earn income tax (PAYE), National Insurance Contributions (NICs), and Value Added Tax (VAT). By requiring even very small businesses to act as unpaid tax collectors, the government places a very high burden on them, which for the very smallest has been calculated to cost as much as one-third of the value of the tax collected (Sandford, Godwin and Hardwick, 1989).[9]

Although still a major burden there has been some mitigation:

- *VAT:* once a business's turnover passes a certain threshold, a business has to register for VAT, and thereby charge its customers and account for VAT. This minimum threshold for registration for VAT has been substantially increased from £25 000 in 1990 to £68 000 in 2010 and £82 000 in 2015, thereby removing many firms from the need to collect and account for VAT.

  VAT is normally accounted for quarterly, against invoiced sales and purchases. The Cash Accounting Scheme, which permits firms to pay VAT only on those transactions which have been paid for, and not just invoiced, and the Annual Accounting Scheme, which allows for one return only for the year with estimated monthly payments, have helped to reduce the financial and administrative costs of these procedures for many small firms.

- *PAYE:* employers with small monthly PAYE deductions can now account for this tax on a quarterly return, not the monthly basis which is normally required.

Health and safety at work
Like all businesses, small firms are responsible for working conditions on all their premises for employees and visitors alike. The Safety at Work Act (1974), the Offices, Shops and Railway Premises Act (1963), and the Factories Act (1961) give employers extensive responsibilities, covering such areas as fire precautions, means of escape, hygiene, temperature, toilet and washing facilities, workspace and machinery safety. The government recognized the difficulties for small firms of applying these regulations in detail, by removing the requirement to prepare a written safety policy from very small firms with less than five employees. Health and Safety Inspectors have also been encouraged to increase their awareness of smaller firms' interests.

REFIT in the EC
Increasing concerns that legislation and regulations from the European Commission (EC) placed unfair burdens on small business has led to a number of initiatives to reduce their impact. The latest of these is REFIT (Regulatory Fitness and Performance Programme) which aims to make EU law simpler and to reduce regulatory costs. Simplification and burden reduction has been improved in several areas including electronic financial reporting and patents.

5.6.4 INFORMATION AND ADVICE
The third major area in which the government has sought to help small firms is in the provision of information and advice.

Government SME services
On the recommendation of the Bolton Committee, the Small Firms Service (SFS) was set up in 1972 within the Department of Trade and Industry, to provide information through a network of 13 Small Firms Centres (SFCs). Since, there has been a long history of changes in attempts to provide an easily accessible service. In 1989/90, the responsibility for small business support was transferred to Training and Enterprise Councils (TECs) in England and Wales, and Local Enterprise Companies (LECs) in Scotland, set up with the aim of improving efficiency in delivering training and other government initiatives, directed at regenerating local economies.

Not all the TECs succeeded as businesses in their own right: in 1995, South Thames TEC went into receivership. TECs' responsibilities covered large as well as small firms in their area, and they found it difficult to reach more than a small percentage of SMEs. The TEC network was effectively replaced as a small business support mechanism by the emergence of the Small Business Service and Business Links.

The Small Business Service (SBS), which came into being in April 2000, was intended as an umbrella organization which would promote and coordinate the wide range of help, information and advice available from many sources. Reporting to the Under-Secretary of State for Small Business, it operated a number of schemes and initiatives, largely delivered through a network of Business Links in England, Small Business Gateway in Scotland and Business Connect in Wales.

This attempt at simplification had little impact and much criticism was levelled at the overlap and confusion amongst the thousands of publicly funded support schemes. Solutions for Business was launched in 2009 with a much simplified portfolio of just 30 support schemes accessible via the Business Link service. Launched in 1993, Business Link described themselves as 'a free business advice and support service, available online and through local advisers.' They operated throughout England as part of the Regional Development Agencies (RDAs), whose remit was to coordinate economic development in nine English regions with a particular aim of improving the relative competitiveness between different areas of the country and reducing the economic imbalance between and within regions. Business Link and the RDAs were finally wound up following the 2010 election.

More recent policy has been to embrace the complexity and overlap of localized support agencies as a benefit. The role of central government is seen more as a signpost to the many services on offer through the www.gov.uk portal, launched in 2012. One link from this website lists 554 schemes offering financial support and assistance to businesses in the UK.[10]

Amongst the confusion and often short-lived initiatives to help SMEs, one scheme stands out because of its longevity and success rate. Knowledge Transfer Partnerships (KTP, known as TCS until 2003) aim to provide the small business owner with the knowledge and expertise to tackle a particular problem or opportunity of strategic importance to their business. An owner-manager identifies a project vital to their development, but one which is beyond their existing technical or business competence (e.g. a design for a new product, or an export marketing strategy). A recent graduate, supervised by a university expert with the requisite knowledge base, works on the project for two years with up to two-thirds of the cost borne by a government grant[11] (see Figure 5.3).

KTPs come under the umbrella of Innovate UK[12] which gives access to a range of funding from £5000 to £10 million for SMEs that develop an innovative product or service.

Other assistance

Other public- and private-sector bodies have echoed the national government's emphasis on assistance for small firms.

- *Universities* have begun to open up their knowledge and resource base for the benefit of SMEs. Stimulated by grants from government and schemes such as KTP, many universities encourage academics to collaborate with business owners for the benefit of innovation and enterprise development. They support students and graduates as entrepreneurs through entrepreneurship clubs, teaching programmes for non-business students and business plan competitions. Coordinating bodies such as the National Centre for Entrepreneurship in Education (NCEE)[13] and the Higher Education Entrepreneurship Group (HEEG)[14] raise the profile of entrepreneurship and the option of starting your own business as a career choice among students and graduates. There is an increasing number of programmes to encourage and support young entrepreneurs at university, as well as at school or in the workplace.[15]
- *Local government* agencies offer various kinds of assistance to small firms. This can be through their Economic Development Units (EDUs) which offer cheap premises and relaxed planning controls. Some offer financial assistance in loans or grants to certain kinds of business, such as cooperatives. About two-thirds of all local authorities offer some type of advisory or information service.

Figure 5.3 Knowledge Transfer Partnerships (KTP) involve a three-way relationship to implement innovation

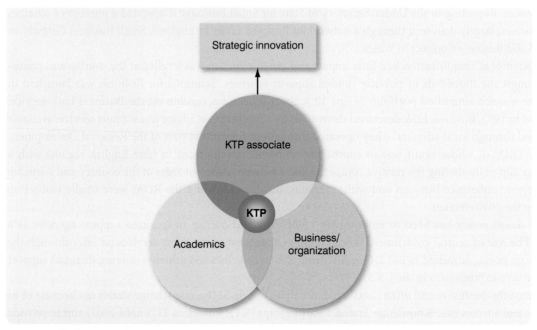

Source: Knowledge Transfer Partnerships (KTP) is a Technology Strategy Board programme: www.ktponline.org.uk.
Reproduced with permission.

- *Banks* have set up their own small business advisory units which offer a range of information and advice.
- *Chambers of Commerce* offer a variety of support services to their members, many of whom are small businesses.
- *Outside the UK* many governments have set up similar organizations to coordinate information and advice for small firms. For example:
  - Europe, the Executive Agency for Small and Medium-sized Enterprises (EASME – ec.europa.eu /easme/en);
  - United States, Small Business Administration (www.sba.gov);
  - Australia, the business services portal of the Department of Industry, Tourism and Resources (www .industry.gov.au);
  - New Zealand, the Small Business Directorate in the Ministry of Business, Innovation and Employment in New Zealand (www.mbie.govt.nz/);
  - South Africa, the Department of Trade and Industry (www.thedti.gov.za/).

Activity 8
Does it help?

Consider how the government in the UK has tried to help small firms. In what ways do you think these measures may have helped the small business sector? How do you think they could be improved?

5.7 The effects of government policy

5.7.1 CRITICISMS

Over three or more decades, there has been substantial growth in the types of assistance offered to small firms in the three major areas of financial assistance, lightening the tax and administrative load, and information and advice.

There is considerable debate over the impact and effectiveness of all this activity (Storey, 2006). In particular, there is really no conclusive evidence that these measures have induced growth in the small business sector that would not have happened anyway. Measurement of the success of policies has been largely by reference to the numbers of small firms using a particular service – the number of loans guaranteed, or the number of inquiries to a support agency, for example – without research into whether those small firms would have existed, or survived, without such assistance. This problem of assessing 'additionality' is a central challenge for evaluations of many types.

There can be little doubt that a general environment has been developed which does encourage, rather than dampen, enthusiasm for starting and growing a small business. However, a number of important criticisms have been made of the effectiveness of government policy.

Lack of objectives

One of the problems in assessing the effectiveness of government policy is the lack of overriding objectives and specific targets for measures which are aimed at helping small firms. Storey (1998) has been a strong advocate for more focused government action based on:

- clear objectives of small business policy for government as a whole, not just by department; and
- targets for each policy measure so that the effectiveness in meeting those targets could be monitored.

Regional bias

Most of the schemes described are nationally available. Historically, the major government initiatives had an equal availability in all areas and Storey (1982) was particularly critical of this policy on the basis that it was regionally divisive because it favoured areas that are already better off. New firm formation rates do vary by region. Despite government intervention, they still tend to be highest in the south-west and south-east, areas of comparatively low unemployment, and lowest in the north and Scotland, which are areas with traditionally high levels of unemployment.[15] This produces unequal benefits from such schemes as the Enterprise Finance Guarantee, which has a much higher take-up rate in the south-east, for example. Some recent initiatives did prove more popular in the north than the south, which has thrown some doubt on the extent of regional bias. However, overall, the comparatively wealthy southern areas have benefited more from financial assistance.

Backing winners or losers?

Assistance to small firms is also widely spread among all varieties of business and industries. There is some evidence that this merely encourages the unemployed to set up in competition with existing businesses, some of which are thereby reduced to marginal levels of profitability or failure through this subsidized competition. The new business can do this because the owner-managers devote their own labour to the enterprise at below-market rates and, initially, they are subsidized by government-sponsored schemes.

Some commentators have suggested that policy should be more selective in assisting 'winners' – small firms with a proven record of growth and the potential to create new jobs. Some government initiatives, such as

Business Link, did move in this direction by offering training, consultancy and advice to established businesses, rather than financial incentives for new ventures.

Confusion and overlap

A further area for concern is the sheer number of services now available to the small business owner-manager, which can result in bewilderment and inefficiency. The widespread muddle and overlap prompted Michael Heseltine, as President of the Board of Trade, to launch 'One-Stop' shops in 1992, the Labour administration to introduce the Small Business Service in 2000 as an umbrella organization to coordinate all government-sponsored initiatives as well as launching Solutions for Business. This was a simplified range of just 30 business support products in 2009, and the 2010–15 Coalition government to adopt a signposting role to the many local schemes on offer.

However, business owners perceive little progress in attempts to overcome fragmentation and confusion. As one government administration succeeds another, the constant changes and re-branding of support initiatives have continued unabated.

Government regulation seen as a barrier to growth

Perhaps the most severe indictment of central policy is that government intervention is cited more often as a barrier to growth, rather than an encouragement. When asked to rank what they perceive to be the biggest barriers to growth for their business, owners invariably give government regulation and red tape as one of the top problems working against expansion (SBRT, 2006). Despite attempts to reduce the effects of legislation and countless measures to promote business growth and entrepreneurship, small business owners and entrepreneurs remain sceptical of their benefits.

5.7.2 EUROPEAN COMPARISONS

All EU (European Union) countries follow policies in support of small firms, many similar to those in the UK. However, there are differences in both the extent and emphasis of measures in individual states.

De Koning and Snijders (1992) looked at the numbers of government measures (instruments of policy) by type of policy (policy field) and by country. A total of 236 instruments of policy were analyzed in the 12 member countries (i.e. an average of 20 per country).

- Ireland (at 28 instruments of policy), Germany (26), France (23) and the UK (23) were above average, which could be interpreted to mean they had tried to intervene in favour of small businesses at an above-average rate for EU countries.
- Luxembourg (11 instruments of policy), Denmark (14), Portugal (15), Italy (17), Greece (19), Belgium (20) and Spain (20) were below-average or average.
- Technology and research and development (R&D) is the most favoured policy field with a variety of financial, information and training initiatives. The UK and France focus more than others on start-ups, whereas Germany and Ireland concentrate more on finance. Environment and energy, and administrative simplification were the least frequent policy fields.

The authors of the study recommended that some of the policy areas, especially education, financing, information and help, technology and export policies, could be better coordinated within the EU. Subsequent attempts to follow this advice have had mixed results, as this review has illustrated.

5.7.3 IMPACT IN DEVELOPING ECONOMIES INCLUDING AFRICA

The recognition of the key role that SMEs play in the developed economies of Europe and the USA has finally been mirrored by an acceptance of their role in fighting poverty in under-developed, emerging nations including those in Africa, South America and Asia. This has, in turn, led to the development of government initiatives to help promote SME growth in those countries.

However, in contrast to European initiatives, it has been argued that help should focus more on the 'informal economy'. This represents a high percentage of the GDP of many developing and transition countries – 42 per cent in Africa, 41 per cent in Latin America and 35 per cent in the transition economies of Europe and the former Soviet Union, compared with 13.5 per cent in OECD countries (Mamman *et al.*, 2015). The informal economy provides employment and income for many who lose or cannot find work in the formal economy, and it includes a disproportionate number of women, young people and others from disadvantaged groups. For example, it has been estimated that informal employment accounts for 84 per cent of women's employment in sub-Saharan Africa (Mamman *et al.*, 2015).

The challenge in Africa is to develop the 'missing middle' between these micro firms in the informal economy, and the larger corporates that dominate at the other end of the size spectrum. Several initiatives supported by Western economies have attempted to provide help and support to encourage the informal one-person businesses to develop into growing SMEs that provide employment for others. For example, the African Guarantee Fund for SMEs, funded by the African Development Bank in partnership with Denmark and Spain, was launched in 2012 to provide guarantees to financial institutions so that they could fund small businesses and unlock their potential to deliver inclusive growth in the region. Other programmes offer information and advice such as the 'South Africa SME Toolkit' website (southafrica.smetoolkit.org) that offers help to start, manage and grow a small business.

Whether such schemes get through to those who need it most is not clear, as their impact is still relatively unknown. Piza *et al.* (2016) examined the available evidence on the effects of SME support services in lower- and middle-income countries (LMICs) on employment generation and small-firm revenues and profits. Overall, they found the results positive. Support initiatives did improve firms' business performance, help create jobs and improve productivity. However, their meta-analysis did not cover all regions equally and there was a particular paucity of evaluation studies for sub-Saharan Africa (Piza *et al.*, 2016).

5.8 Summary and activities

This chapter evaluates the information required by an owner-manager at various stages in the development of their business. New ventures need to be validated through early contact with the marketplace. Once in business, entrepreneurs tend not to gather information through formalized research but through informal networking. However, secondary and primary research is important to assess the risk of new ventures and to make adjustments to the market environment for established businesses. The wide variety of research methods and data sources that are available to small businesses and entrepreneurs are considered in detail in order to facilitate this information collection process.

This chapter also summarized the external help and support available to SMEs with particular reference to the UK. These are categorized into three types: financial assistance; lightening the tax and administrative load; and information and advice. Some of the sources of this help are considered, and the effectiveness of government support is debated.

Case study
A tale of two entrepreneurs: Part 5

Andrea investigates an old friend

Andrea Clarey wanted to find out more about her intended payroll service for schools. Her husband suggested she networked among friends and acquaintances to test out the idea. She did not want to talk to the head teacher of her daughter's local school as she felt it might be too close for comfort to discuss new business ideas. Instead, she called an old friend who had just become the head teacher of a large primary school, and arranged to meet her over coffee. When she finished explaining her idea, her friend looked rather blank.

'I am afraid I leave that to the school bursar. I don't really get involved in payroll matters. Although I do see the final costs of what staff at the school earn, the bursar liaises with the Education Authority's payroll service over calculations of tax and so forth and any queries that arise from time to time. Frankly it's an area I don't really want to get involved in.'

'What about my idea for information on payroll and other costs at the school, with comparisons to other schools? Is that of any use or interest to you?'

'Yes and no. I'm always interested in what other schools are doing, and my Chairman of Governors is always trying to find out how much money other schools get compared to us. But every school is different. The cost of staff varies according to age and experience, so one school might spend a lot more on salaries than another simply because it has older staff. So it doesn't necessarily mean the children are getting a better education just because more is being spent on staff costs at their particular school. So I don't know how valuable any comparative figures would be. Like all statistics, I suspect they could be interpreted in too many different ways.'

Kit and Robin concentrate

Robin Davidson was sure that Kit Hugos's new product idea could only work in very specific market sectors.

'The key to your security device', he told Kit, 'is not the transmitter carried on the person – that is relatively cheap and easy to make. What is difficult is the tracking software that locates the device and indicates where it is on a map. We need to digitize a map of the area to be covered, and the smaller that area is the better, in the first instance. If we try to map a town or wider area to track the general public, we are talking lots of development costs and complications. Let's look at markets where people are confined to a limited area, but are still potentially at risk.'

'I have read that university campus sites and large colleges and schools have become an increasing security risk', replied Kit. 'They are used by thousands of different students who are constantly changing in a relatively open environment. It's impossible to control tightly who goes in and out. The same could be said of conference centres and exhibition halls, which are another problem area. Large office complexes are increasingly targeted for attacks and thefts. I could go on, but where do we stop? We can't investigate all these potential markets.'

'You're right. We may need to focus our efforts – and we need some help.'

Activities

Advise both Andrea and Kit on how to research their market and where to find help.

(a) What secondary sources of information should they consider?

(b) What affordable primary research would you recommend for both of them? In each case, indicate your recommended research objectives and proposed methods.

3 Which sources of help and advice should they consider in order to take their business ideas to the next step?
4 What should they do next?

You can find out what happened next to Kit Hugos and Andrea Clarey in case studies in later chapters. See Chapter 7, Section 7.7.1 Circumspect strategies Parts 1 and 2, for Kit's progress, and Chapter 8, Section 8.8.1, You've been framed, for Andrea's next steps.

Case study
A Cool Way to Start a Business

Whenever Nick Edwards talks about setting up CoolLED Ltd, he always says it was done the wrong way round: first, he found a technology and developed a product, then he found a market for it. Ideally, he admits, he should have researched the market looking for an unfulfilled need and then found the technology to meet it. But, as he claims, if he hadn't developed the technology first, he wouldn't have found the application that proved to be a market winner.

As technical director of an electronics sub-contract manufacturer, Edwards saw many new products developed by other businesses and entrepreneurs that needed a production house like his to make their innovations. With fierce competition from the Far East, margins for any European manufacturer were very thin and his business was no different; typically, his gross profit was one-third of the selling price and from that he had to meet all the overheads of a factory unit and a skilled work force. The only way to improve on profit margins, he realized, was to design and produce his own product. As an engineer, he had plenty of ideas but none that stood the test of even a brief look at the market.

Then he began to see more and more designs from customers that used LEDs – light emitting diodes or semi-conductor devices that emit light when an electric current passes through them without using a bulb. Developing an expertise in connecting LEDs to electrical devices from customers' orders for large-scale signage, he began to play around with his own ideas. He kept away from the core LED development area of domestic and commercial lighting, but investigated the use of LEDs in more niche applications. The first one he uncovered was the potential use for LEDs in ultraviolet (UV) curing, a method of instantly curing inks, adhesives and coatings. With potential applications in many industries including printing, car manufacture and contact lenses, he thought he was onto a winner.

The first issue was that he did not have enough time to investigate and prove the technology, neither did he have one of the key areas of expertise. He overcame this problem with a government scheme that offered collaboration with a university through the intermediary of a recent graduate. This Knowledge Transfer Partnership led to the employment of Gerry Whoriskey working for Nick to develop the new LED product guided by a researcher at Southampton University with the necessary optical expertise, all underwritten by a government grant.

Two years later the new product was born – a UV LED curing device. It had potential applications in industries that cured inks or adhesives with advantages over the current technology that used mercury vapour bulbs:

(Continued)

LEDs lasted longer; they were easier to change and had instant on/off switching compared to mercury bulbs which needed to warm up and cool down; the adverse environmental effects of using mercury in an industrial process were overcome.

A separate division within the company was set up to sell the new product under the umbrella name of CoolLED. After a PR launch attracted much media interest, Nick and Gerry visited potential customers.

They met to consider the feedback they had received. They had discovered that digital printing, a growth area in an otherwise sluggish industry, was an application with definite potential. However, there were issues that prevented immediate switching to the new technology. Manufacturers cited the costs of reconfiguring plant while print customers said that the limited availability of UV LED curable inks would limit the applications in the short term. Others felt they did not want to be first into UV LEDs as they could be of variable quality, whatever their other advantages.

'There is another option,' said Gerry. 'When I visited a university research laboratory, all the microscopes were using mercury bulbs as a light source. The laboratory manager complained about their unreliability and costs. If we could develop an LED illumination system, we could be onto a winner.'

Both knew that would involve going back to the drawing board. They had a basic system but this application would require considerable adaption.

The limited resources of a small business developing a new product of its own were stretched and shareholders were asking if they should continue to fund the new division. It seemed as though they had invented something interesting but they were still looking for the right market.

Activities

(a) Compare the development of the CoolLED product to the principles of a 'lean start-up'. What have they done right and not so right?

(b) Considering the risks in developing a speculative new product, were the government right to fund part of its development? Should they be investing taxpayers' money in new ventures like this?

(c) What would you advise them to do next: persevere with developing the print industry, or pivot to the potential new market of light sources for microscopes?

CoolLED's UV LED curing pen

F ind out which organizations exist in your local area to support small enterprises. Contact as many as you can and obtain information on their services. A good starting point is services offered by central government (in the UK, this is available at www.gov.uk/business-support-helpline). There may also be local support available (for example, Chambers of Commerce).

If you were to start a small business how useful do you think you would find the services on offer?

Extended activity
Local support

Summary of what is required

- Set research objectives.
- Find out more about the customer.
- Find out more about the competition.
- Find out more about the environment.
- Summarize this research as an *evaluation of the opportunity*.

Planning a new venture
Evaluating the opportunity

In Chapter 4, you selected an opportunity and identified the target customer group. The next step is to refine the opportunity by finding out more about the target customer segment, the competition you will face and the characteristics of the environment in which the market operates.

This can only be done by carrying out some preliminary research. Use Checklists 1 to 3 to structure the research and carry it out. This can then be summarized as an initial evaluation of the opportunity.

Setting the objectives for research

The overall objective of the research is to provide you with more information to evaluate the opportunity as a viable enterprise. It is suggested that this is structured around two specific questions, to which you may wish to add more:

1   What opportunities and threats exist in the marketplace now, and in the future, for my potential business?
2   How much will the customer buy from me in my first three years of trading?

These research objectives can be looked at in relation to the customer, the competition and the environment.

Checklist 1: researching the customer

1   What specific questions do I need to ask about the target customer segment?

- What is the size of the total market?
- How many individual customers are there?
- Will I be dealing with more than one customer segment?
- How often do they buy?
- How much do they buy at one time?
- Do they buy randomly or at specific times?
- Do some customers account for a high percentage of purchases?
- If so, which ones, and what percentages?
- What percentage of the market can I expect in Year 1? Year 2? Year 3?
- What are the existing distribution channels and structure of the market?
- Other questions.

2   Which research methods can I use to find out some answers?

Secondary research:
Primary research:

Checklist 2: researching the competition

1   What specific questions do I need to ask about the competitors in my target market?

- Who are the competitors?
- What percentage of the market do they have?

(Continued)

- What is their estimated sales turnover?
- How long have they been in business?
- Is the market stable or changing, with new competitors entering and/or leaving?
- What is the competitive edge (or main benefits) of the principal competitors?
- How profitable and efficient are they?
- How do customers rate the principal competitors?
- Are they active in the marketplace?
- If yes, in what ways?
- Other questions.

2   Which research methods can I use to find out some answers?

Secondary research:
Primary research:

Checklist 3: researching the environment

1   What specific questions do I need to ask about the environment of my target market?

- What are the boundaries of my target market?
- What are the social trends?
- What are the economic factors?
- What are the political factors?
- What are the technological trends?
- What are the demographics of the market?
- What will be the key external influences in the marketplace in the next three years?
- How will these influences affect the competition?
- How will these influences affect me?
- Other questions.

2   Which research methods can I use to find out some answers?

Secondary research:
Primary research:

Summary: evaluating the opportunity

Collect together the research you have done and see how it matches up against your research objectives. In particular, answer the questions below as best you can:

- What does my information suggest will be my likely sales turnover?

	Year 1	Year 2	Year 3
Pessimistic	——	——	——
Optimistic	——	——	——
Most likely	——	——	——

- What information have I found out about the market that represents opportunities and/or threats?
- Short-term and long-term trends representing opportunities and/or threats?
- Competitive opportunities and threats?
- Customer opportunities and threats?
- Other?
- How does my information meet other research objectives that I set myself?

5.9 Useful sources of information for entrepreneurs

This is not intended as an exhaustive listing, but a general indication of where to start (with particular reference to the UK), how much information is available, and of what type. For a more comprehensive list, consult the general guides given below.

General guides can be used to find out what data exists.

- www.gov.uk provides a single entry point to over 1000 government websites containing information and details of services available. It links to areas important for a business owner.
- UK government official statistics on a wide range of topics from overseas trade to output prices can be found at www.gov.uk/government /statistics
- www.gov.uk/government/organisations /companies-house offers statutory information on individual businesses; it represents a great resource for investigating competing and complementary businesses. The online library contains all their published guidance booklets.
- The British Library Business & IP Centre at www .bl.uk/business-and-ip-centre provides support to business owners, entrepreneurs and inventors. At the centre in London, you can access a comprehensive collection of databases and publications for free, as well as attend practical workshops, one-to-one advice sessions and inspiring talks.
- www.eubusiness.com aims to be a one-stop shop for business information about the European Union with details of European law, business development and news.
- US Small Business Administration on www.sba .gov/tools/
- The Australian government's portal for business information and advice is on www.business.gov.au
- The New Zealand government's portal for business information and statistics is via www .business.govt.nz
- South Africa has a small business development agency at www.seda.org.za

- PRODCOM (Products of the European Community) at ec.europa.eu/eurostat/web/prodcom European-wide information on sales and prices of an extensive range of products from alcohol to zinc.
- *UN Demographic Yearbook,* population statistics of many countries derived from census data at unstats.un.org/unsd/demographic/products/

Non-official sources of market intelligence include:

- Market Intelligence (Mintel International, www.mintel.com), monthly reports mainly on consumer markets and products. The contents pages of reports (but not the reports themselves) are viewable on the website.
- The Economist Intelligence Unit (EIU, part of The Economist Group, www.economist.com) which publishes regular reports on specific industrial sectors.
- *Key Note Reports* (Key Note Publications, www.keynote.co.uk), detailed briefs on over 100 market sectors. Their website gives executive summaries of the reports.
- *Key British Enterprises* (Dun & Bradstreet, www.dnb.com), information on 50 000 UK companies representing 90 per cent of industrial expenditure. A list of Dun & Bradstreet's publications is available on their website.
- *Who Owns Whom* (Dun & Bradstreet), covers over 100 000 companies giving details of company ownership.
- *Kompass* (Kompass Publishers, www.kompass .co.uk), information on products and services, plus UK companies with financial data. Also available for some other countries.

Other useful websites: there are many websites targeted at small businesses or new ventures, which contain both advice and information.

- *Banks* offer advice and industry data for SMEs; see, for example, www.barclayscorporate.com/; www.business.hsbc.co.uk; www.lloydsbank.com

- *The Small Business Research Portal* at www.isbe.org.uk is useful for research and has helpful links for both advice and information.
- *Business Europe:* www.businesseurope.eu provides news, advice and case studies specifically for European SMEs.
- www.j4bgrants.co.uk offers comprehensive information on government funding for both business and voluntary groups.

- *Start-ups:* www.startups.co.uk provides articles from this magazine plus some useful start-up guides to specific businesses, and documentation templates.
- *Forum for Private Business:* www.fpb.co.uk lobbies on behalf of SMEs to create a better political and economic environment for business. Its site has useful links and information about the business environment.

5.10 Notes, references and recommended further reading

Notes and further information

1 This assumes that an opportunity for exploitation has already been identified. See Chapter 4, Innovation and the marketplace. See also Birley, S. and Muzyka, D. F. *Mastering Entrepreneurship,* Prentice Hall, 2000, ch. 2, The Opportunity, for useful sections on identifying and researching business ideas.

2 The concepts of the lean start-up were first developed by Eric Ries in his best-selling book *The Lean Start Up* and are now spread through seminars, blogs and his website: theleanstartup.com. The ideas are particularly relevant to digital start-ups with which Ries is personally familiar. The history of his own instant messaging company, IMVU, and those of other internet companies such as Dropbox and Facebook form an important part of the development of the concept. However, the model that he describes of developing a new venture idea while in close contact with the target customer group, rather than completing the development phase and then launching to the market, is valid for all start-ups.

3 See Chapter 3. Smallbone (1990) and others (e.g. Storey, 1998) make the point that firms most active in making adjustments to what they do and how they do it, especially in terms of market adjustments, are most likely to survive (as we discuss in Chapter 3).

4 Hills and Hultman (2005) cited research that gave evidence that even high-growth small firms are unlikely to use formalized market research. An investigation among small Swedish firms found that only 41 per cent used formalized marketing research activities. See also earlier evidence in Milne, T. and Thompson, M. (1986) The Infant Business Development Process. In: Scott, M., Gibb, A., Lewis, J. and Faulkner, T. (eds) *Small Firms' Growth and Development,* Gower. Their research concluded that owner-managers are 'impatient with formality

including formal market research. But the successful ones are doing the research in an extremely powerful and efficient personal contact manner.'

5 The National Federation of Fish Fryers has a long history and their website contains useful information on the industry and trends: (www.federationoffishfriers.co.uk/). The Seafish Industry Authority (www.seafish.org) also provides data and trends in the industry.

6 Several providers now offer low-cost methods to create and host a survey. Typically, they offer tutorials in survey design, web-enabled tools to help configure the survey and a hosting service so that the survey can be accessed through a simple weblink. Examples include: Survey Monkey (www.surveymonkey.com) and Survey Writer (www.surveywriter.com).

7 ACORN is one such geodemographic tool operated by CACI information services (acorn.caci.co.uk/).

8 See Storey (1998), particularly ch. 5, Public Policy, in which the author spells out his long-held view of the need for coherent policy objectives to draw together the 'patchwork quilt' of measures in support of small business.

9 See Sandford, Godwin and Hardwick (1989) whose study calculated that firms collecting less than £1000 PAYE and NIC in one year incurred costs equivalent to one-third of the tax collected. This fell to less than 1 per cent where the annual collection was more than £280 000.

10 See the website www.gov.uk/business-finance -support-finder/search

11 For fuller details of this scheme, see the KTP website (ktp.innovateuk.org). For an evaluation, see Inkpen, A. and Tsang, E. W. K. (2005) Social capital, networks, and knowledge transfer, *Academy of Management Review,* 30(1): 146–165.

12 Innovate UK is the UK's innovation agency. See: www.gov.uk/government/organisations/innovate-uk

13 The National Centre for Entrepreneurship in Education (NCEE) 'uses its networks, partners and resources to stimulate and encourage a more entrepreneurial education and support sector to create the opportunities for more individuals and organisations to develop the capacities they need for an entrepreneurial future'. (www.ncee.org.uk).

14 HEEG (Higher Education Entrepreneurship Group) is 'a collaborative network of enterprise educators and promoters, whose participants provide insight, ideas and time to develop events which are interesting and useful for our community'. (www.heeg.org.uk).

15 The many programmes that encourage and support young entrepreneurs include:

- *The Young Enterprise* programme, which offers students the opportunity to run a real company and to learn about aspects of business from the first-hand experiences of volunteers (www.young -enterprise.org.uk).
- *Shell Live WIRE* helps 16–30-year-olds to start and develop their own business (www.shell -livewire.org).
- *Step* offers project-based work to students and graduates in SMEs (www.step.org.uk).
- *The Prince's Trust* is a UK charity that helps young people overcome barriers, often through self-employment or venture creation (www.princes -trust.org.uk).

16 See Chapter 3 on regional variations in the birth of new businesses. For a more historical perspective on this enduring issue, see Whittington, R. (1986) Regional Bias in New Firm Formation. In: Scott, M., Gibb, A., Lewis, J. and Faulkner, T. (eds) *Small Firms Growth and Development,* Gower.

References

Bragg, A. and Bragg, M. (2005) *Developing New Business Ideas,* Pearson Education.

Carson, D., Cromie, S., McGowan, P. and Hill, J. (1995) *Marketing and Entrepreneurship in SMEs,* Prentice Hall.

Chaston, I. (2000) *Entrepreneurial Marketing,* Palgrave.

De Koning, A. and Snijders, J. (1992) Policy on SMEs in countries of the European Community, *International Small Business Journal,* 10(3): 39–56.

Dew, N., Sarasvathy, S., Read, S. and Wiltbank, R. (2009) Affordable loss: Behavioral economic aspects of the plunge decision, *Strategic Entrepreneurship Journal,* 3(2): 105–126.

Hills, G. E. and Hultman, C. M. (2005) Marketing, Entrepreneurship and SMEs: Knowledge and Education Revisited, *Proceedings of the 10th Annual Research Symposium of the Academy of Marketing Special Interest Group on Entrepreneurial and SME Marketing,* Southampton University, 6–7 January.

Krejcie R. (1970) Determining Sample Size for Research Activities, *Educational and Psychological Measurement,* 30: 607–610.

Mamman, A., Kanu, A. M., Alharbi A. and Baydoun, N. (2015) *Small and Medium Sized Enterprises (SMEs) and Poverty Reduction in Africa: Strategic Management Perspective,* Cambridge Scholars Publishing.

Piza, C., Cravo, T. A., Taylor, L., Gonzalez, L., Musse, I., Furtado, I., Sierra, A. C. and Abdelnour, S. (2016) the impacts of business support services for small and medium enterprises on firm performance in low- and middle-income countries: A systematic review, *International Development,*12(1).

Ries, E. (2011) *The Lean Start-up: How Constant Innovation Creates Radically Successful Businesses,* Viking.

Sandford, C., Godwin, M. and Hardwick, P. (1989) *Administrative and Compliance Costs of Taxation,* Fiscal Publications.

Sarasvathy, S. (2001) Causation and effectuation: Toward a theoretical shift from economic inevitability to entrepreneurial contingency, *Academy of Management Review,* 26(2): 243–263.

SBRT (2006) *Survey of Small Business in the UK,* Vol. 22, Issue 87, Q2, Small Business Research Trust.

Small Business Research Trust (2006) *Quarterly Survey of Small Business in the UK,* 22(87): Q2.

Smallbone, D. (1990) Success and failure in new business start-up, *International Small Business Journal,* 8(2): 34–47.

Stokes, D. and Lomax, W. (2008) *Marketing: A Brief Introduction,* Thomson Learning.

Storey, D. (1982) *Entrepreneurship and the New Firm,* Croom Helm.

Storey, D. (1998) *Understanding the Small Business Sector,* International Thompson Business Press.

Storey, D. J. (2006) Evaluating SME Policies and Programmes: Technical and Political Dimensions. In: Casson, M. *et al.* (eds) *The Oxford Handbook of Entrepreneurship,* pp. 484–510, Oxford University Press, Oxford.

Thomas, D. (1991) *Alan Sugar: The Amstrad Story,* Pan Books.

Watkins, D. (1982) Management Development and the Owner Manager. In: Webb, T., Quince, T. and Watkins, D. (eds) *Small Business Research: The Development of Entrepreneurs,* Gower.

Recommended further reading

Ries, E. (2011) *The Lean Start-up: How Constant Innovation Creates Radically Successful Businesses*, Viking. See Note 2.

Market Research for Small Business – access to research resources on the web including how to avoid common mistakes. sbinformation.about.com/od/marketresearch

Proctor, T. (2000) *Essentials of Marketing Research*, Financial Times/Prentice Hall. A good general introduction to research including some examples of questionnaires and case histories.

Stokes, D. and Lomax, W. (2008) *Marketing: A Brief Introduction*, Cengage, ch. 5 Marketing research.

Storey, D. J. (2006) Evaluating SME Policies and Programmes: Technical and Political Dimensions. In: Casson, M. *et al.* (eds) *The Oxford Handbook of Entrepreneurship*, pp. 484–510, Oxford University Press, Oxford. A summary of the international policy implications of supporting SMEs and methods for evaluating that support.

Creating the entrepreneurial small business

6 **Business planning**
7 **Successful small business strategies**
8 **Start-ups and franchises**
9 **Buying an existing business**
10 **Forming and protecting a business**

PART II

- This Part comprises Chapters 6 to 10. It considers how small businesses are created, focusing on successful strategies for start-up and growth, business planning and formation and the pros and cons of different routes to market entry. The five chapters are designed to give an introduction to the key issues that represent particular challenges for the nascent entrepreneur in setting up a small enterprise.

- As in Part 1, each chapter concludes with a practical step that guides you through planning a new venture. Here, in Part 2, the five steps represent a process of taking an opportunity from a reasonable prospect through to choosing a suitable route for market entry, as illustrated in Figure 1 in the Preface. At the end of this section, you will be able to complete a feasibility study of your own new venture.

6 Business planning

Learning objectives

By the end of this chapter you will be able to:

- Understand the factors which have an impact on the initiation of strategic planning in small businesses.

- Assess the different needs of investors in reviewing the business plan.

- Recognize the key factors for writing a successful business plan.

- Understand the similarities and differences between planning an e-business and a traditional enterprise.

- Structure a business plan according to the necessary components.

Introduction

This chapter looks at the *when, who, why* and *what* of business plans for the small enterprise:

- when they are produced or can be used
- who writes them, and for whom
- why they are produced, and the benefits that can follow
- what they look like, the topics covered and a format that can be used.

The chapter is presented as a precursor to a discussion of successful strategies for small business in Chapter 7. In reality, the processes of business planning and strategy development are inseparable. It is important to emphasize that it should be an iterative and ongoing process, not a one-off task that instantly spells out the detail of how the business will get from A to B. Planning in the early stages can only be a strategic vision with few known absolutes – the 'what' but not much of the 'how'. That comes later when initial concepts are tested in the market and estimates of demand and the costs of supply become more concrete. Planning is part of the learning process of new venture creation in which ideas are conceptualized, tested, amended, re-tested and amended again until they align with customer needs. As part of this process, plans cannot be fixed but need to flex to take account of feedback from the market and 'pivots' in the new venture strategy (see Chapter 5).

Activity 1
Planning issues

Do you agree or disagree with the following statements? Give reasons for your choices.

(a) Business plans are most important when a business first starts up.
(b) Business plans are only necessary to obtain funds from a bank or investor.
(c) Formalized planning is what managers do, not entrepreneurs.

6.1 The purpose of a business plan

6.1.1 PLANNING AND PERFORMANCE

Many entrepreneurs perceive the **business plan,** first and foremost, as a document that is produced for the bank manager, investor or venture capital fund manager, in order to raise money. Small businesses that do not have an external funding requirement, therefore, tend not to write formal business plans.

Reasons for this include:

- pressure on doing, rather than thinking or gathering information, in the small business environment
- the belief that strategic planning is for larger organizations and big business resources, and not necessary for smaller firms who can plan effectively on the back of an envelope.

The Keynesian concept of central control and planning of the economy at the macro level has been roundly rejected by most of the leading industrial economies over the last 30 years or so. This might be seen to reflect the feeling at a micro level that entrepreneurial management, of the seat-of-the-pants unstructured variety, should be encouraged, rather than criticized. This apparent victory for the 'entrepreneur' over the 'planner' helped devalue the planning process, except as the means to the end of raising finances.

In fact, entrepreneurship is not all about seat-of-the-pants risk taking and opportunism – even if some of this does also go on. Although entrepreneurs may have to rely on intuition and trial and error in the absence of any certainty of market data in order to make decisions about new and innovative products and services (Busenitz and Barney, 1997), this does not mean that they do not plan. A core element of planning is implicit in Casson's well-known definition of the entrepreneur as 'someone who specializes in taking judgmental decisions about the coordination of scarce resources' (Casson, 1982). Entrepreneurs may not always formalize their plans into written documents, but most carry ideas, tactics, strategies, even detailed proposals in their heads, which, if written down, would pass as plans. (We discuss the importance of informal and formal strategic planning for the entrepreneur in more detail in Chapter 7.)

6.1.2 ENTRENCHED CULTURAL VALUES WHICH IMPEDE STRATEGIC PLANNING[1]

Cultural values, or 'the broad tendency to prefer certain states of affair over others' (Hofstede, 1991), can have a very significant effect on whether or not strategic planning is undertaken in the first place (see Harris, 1996).

Six 'entrenched cultural values' can impede the initiation of strategic planning in businesses (Harris, 1999):

- **Stability:** *The desire to maintain the status quo is a major impediment to any longer-term strategic planning.* This desire may or may not be consciously held by the established small business owner. Often, it results from the so-called 'competency trap' where business owners find it increasingly difficult to change the way they do things because it appears that what they are doing works just fine.

- **Compartmentalization:** *As staff intentionally compartmentalize their jobs in an effort to defend their respective roles, there is little opportunity for working together in a coordinated, planned fashion.* This view of the working world is perhaps at odds with the flat, fraternalistic organizational structures that typify many technology-based and creative small businesses.

- **Short-term cost orientation:** *A preconceived view as to the effectiveness of cost-cutting as an overall strategy in management's mind negates the need for any strategic planning.* Many new ventures follow the 'parsimonious path to entrepreneurship' right from day one (see McGrath, 2000), so that the scope for a cost-cutting strategy may be limited.

- **Internal orientation:** *A company that is characterized by an internal orientation generally holds the view that all company problems are to be found via intra-company analysis. External analysis is no longer viewed as legitimate.* This raises interesting questions for the way in which business owners develop strategy on the basis of their knowledge about their internal resources, competencies and capabilities (see Chapter 7).

- **Management practices:** *The managers' style of management (particularly a 'hands-on' approach) can focus on tactical issues at the expense of strategic responsibilities. Strategic planning is therefore not carried out.* This is certainly the reality for most small business owners at some point in their careers. Where small business owners hold multiple roles and wear many different 'hats', the issues of time management and fire-fighting make strategic planning a serious challenge on a daily basis.

- **Reactiveness:** *While reactionary decision-making is a necessary component of most organizations, many managers consider reactive decisions more appropriate than proactive planning.* This ties in very closely with the notion of deliberate and emergent strategies – both of which are required in the vast majority of businesses (see Chapter 7).

Are these cultural constraints justified, or can planning really add value to a small business? Some investigations (e.g. Robinson and Pearce, 1984) point to a lack of evidence that formalized strategic planning in small firms leads to improved performance. Research by Dimov (2010) suggests that the nascent entrepreneur's 'opportunity confidence' – that is, their evolving judgment about the opportunity – positively affects venture emergence, whereas early planning only has indirect effects. Another study highlights how many entrepreneurs rarely (if ever) update business plans, or even refer to them after the initial drafting (Karlsson and Honig, 2009).

By contrast, there is a considerable weight of evidence to support the view that planning is a valuable activity in the context of business start-ups. Delmar and Shane (2003) argue that business planning is an important precursor to action in new ventures; by helping founders to make decisions, balance resource supply and demand, and turn abstract goals into concrete operational steps, business planning reduces the likelihood of a venture disbanding and accelerates the product development process. Brinckmann, Grichnik and Kapsa (2010) show how planning is beneficial, but draw attention to contextual factors such as the newness of the firm and the cultural environment, which point to the need for a 'dynamic' approach that combines planning and learning. Chwolka and Raith (2012) discuss the value of planning in terms of the possibility of evaluating alternative actions and being able to improve strategies. The main purpose of evaluation before market entry is to pursue good business ideas and terminate bad ones.

Focusing on the relationship between planning and business growth, one research study found that small businesses which grew rapidly spent more time in formally planning their activities (see Storey, 1998). This research indicated that it is more important to plan after start-up than before setting up a new venture; no significant differences in performance were found between firms who had a written business plan at start-up and those who had not, but 93 per cent of the fast-growing firms had introduced a business plan later on, compared to 70 per cent of more stagnant businesses (Storey, 1998). More recently, research carried out on 360 SMEs employing 5–249 people suggested that policy measures that promote the take-up of business plans and are targeted at younger, larger-sized businesses may have the greatest impact in terms of helping to facilitate business growth (Blackburn *et al.*, 2013).

Overall, the evidence suggests that formal planning is more common in businesses as they grow from small to larger firms. Whether it actually helps small firms develop into larger ones, or whether it is just a characteristic they tend to adopt when they become bigger, is less clear.

Activity 2
Timing of plans

Can you give some examples of situations in which it might be beneficial for a small enterprise to draw up a business plan?

6.1.3 THE WHEN, WHO AND WHY OF PLANNING
A business plan can be used at different times, with potential benefits for several audiences. This is shown in Figure 6.1 which illustrates when a business plan can be used, by whom, for whom and why.

6.2 When to plan?

There are events or reasons that trigger the need for business plans:

- *Start-up.* After the concept stage of initial idea and feasibility study a new business start-up may go through a more detailed planning stage, of which the main output is the business plan.
- *Business purchase.* Buying an existing business does not negate the need for an initial business plan. A detailed plan, which tests the sensitivity of changes to key business variables (e.g. what if sales drop by 25 per cent… what if overheads increase by 25 per cent …?), greatly increases the prospective purchaser's understanding of the level of risk they will be accepting, and the likelihood of rewards being available.
- *Ongoing review.* Ongoing review of progress, against the objectives of either a start-up or small business purchase, is important in a dynamic environment. 'If you do nothing, nothing will not happen', is a truism that should motivate any small business manager to review their business periodically in its constantly changing environment.

  To have lasting benefit, a business plan ought not to be a one-off document that gathers dust in a drawer once it has fulfilled its immediate purpose. It can be the live, strategic and tactical planning focus of how a small business responds to the inevitable changes around it (see Ramirez *et al.*, 2010, for discussion of business planning 'for turbulent times').
- *Major decisions.* Even if planning is not carried out on a regular basis, it is usually instigated at a time of major change. Again, it may be linked to a need for finance; for example, the need for major new investment in equipment, or funds to open a new outlet. It may be linked to failure, such as a recovery plan for an ailing business.
- *Online developments.* An existing 'bricks-and-mortar' business looking to scale up its online activity needs to have a plan, or what could also be called a business case, which justifies the investment in a specific project or application.

Figure 6.1 The purpose of a business plan – the when, who and why

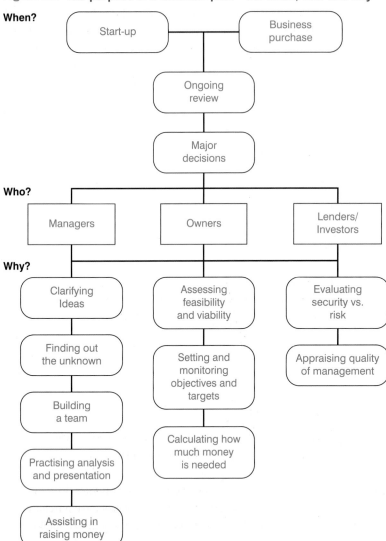

6.3 Who can benefit?

Three types of people will be interested in a business plan: the managers who run or intend to run the business on a day-to-day basis; the owners, or prospective equity investors; and the lenders who are considering loans for the enterprise.

- *Managers* are involved in small business planning both as producers and recipients of the plan. The management of a small enterprise are the only people likely to be sufficiently knowledgeable to produce a business plan; the small business equivalent to a corporate planning department does not usually exist. Business plans are also written to aid small business managers. An obvious conclusion, but one that is often overlooked, is that the managers themselves can be very important beneficiaries, not only of the plan, but also the planning process. Of course, for anyone intending to manage their own new venture it is certainly prudent to write the business plan themselves, rather than enlist the services of a third-party consultant or other professional, for this reason alone.
- *Owners*. The managers of a small enterprise may also be the owners and take a keen interest in the planning process, wearing their shareholder's hat. A plan may be intended for prospective equity partners, either a sleeping partner looking for an investment, or an active partner looking to join an existing small business. Owners may also be lenders, as in venture capital companies, who take an equity stake in return for providing loans.
- *Lenders/investors*. The traditional recipient of the business plan is the bank manager. It is true that the major banks all encourage the production of business plans to justify overdrafts and loans, offering literature and advice on putting together business plans. Other lenders of money, from private individuals to venture capital companies, will also expect to make their investment decision after the presentation of a formal business plan. Indeed, it is generally accepted that the business plan is the minimum document required by any financial source (Kuratko and Hodgetts, 2001).

Research has highlighted the important, but perhaps rather overlooked, fact that investors look for different things in a business plan (Mason and Stark, 2004). Entrepreneurs should be aware of the need to tailor their business plans according to whether they require bank funding, venture capital funds or finance from business angels (see Chapter 13, for further description of these types of investor).

The primary concern of the bank manager is that any loan issued might not be repaid (a particular concern in times of economic difficulty and recession). As a result, the banker is most interested in the finances of the business (cash flow and margins), ascertaining whether or not the business can service the debt, and determining the nature of any assets that might be used by the business or entrepreneur to secure the loan in the case of failure. The assets of a business, such as its debtors and fixed assets, are likely to be investigated for their underlying quality and not just their balance-sheet value. Although personal guarantees are frequently needed from owners, these are not necessarily a passport to successful loan negotiation. Financiers will not lend money for ideas they do not believe viable, even when fully backed by security. The higher the assessment of the risk, the greater the security needed to obtain finance. In terms of assessing risk, it is normal practice for the bank manager to compare the business plan financial information against industry averages (where they are available). It is therefore incumbent upon the entrepreneur to ensure that they explain any deviation clearly.

The finances of the business will be of particular interest to venture capital fund managers and business angels. However, their main concerns are not the same as those of the bank manager. Rather, they relate to the growth potential of the business and the potential returns that they might expect. To this end, particular attention must be given to the market – its size, growth and level of competition. Additionally, equity investors review the financials in order to assess the likely level of profitability, the potential valuation, the amount of funding required over different stages and what the money will actually be used for.

Venture capitalists and business angels themselves often share rather different perspectives on when to invest. While venture capital fund managers are exclusively oriented towards financial returns, business angels may also be seeking some kind of 'psychic income' in the form of interest, glamour and fun. As Mason and Stark (2004, p. 243) describe it:

'Whereas a business plan targeted at a venture capital fund manager needs to contain the "steak", one that is aimed at business angels needs to contain both "steak" and "sizzle". It is therefore important that the plan should attempt to engage potential angel investors on an emotional level'.

Activity 4
Why are plans beneficial?

Why might a business plan be of benefit to:

(a) owner-managers; and
(b) investors or lenders?

6.4 Why produce a plan?

These three groups will have some shared, and some separate, motives for using a business plan. *Managers, owners* and *lenders/investors* will all be seeking to investigate the following issues:

- Assessing *the feasibility and viability of the business or project*. Will it work and become commercially and financially viable? It is in everyone's interests to make mistakes on paper, hypothetically testing for feasibility, before trying the real thing.
- *Setting objectives and budgets*. What is the overall direction and financial target set by the plan? Having a clear financial vision with believable budgets is a basic requirement of everyone involved in a plan.
- Calculating *how much money is needed*. What level and type of finance is required to make the plan work? A detailed cash flow with assumptions is a vital ingredient to quantify precisely the earlier 'guesstimates' of the likely funds required.

Managers involved in producing the plan can, in addition, gain from the process itself in the following ways:

- Clarifying *ideas*. Putting together a business plan often acts as a powerful focus, bringing together generalized and random thoughts into a clearer understanding of the concept, and how it can be made to work.
- Finding out *the unknown*. The information-gathering process of a plan can uncover many interesting and relevant facts. The day-to-day pressure may obscure much in the business environment including: a new competitor about to open; opportunities for cheaper premises or suppliers; the availability of new equipment; successful marketing methods used by others; or useful ideas from staff.
- Building *a team*. Developing a plan can be a catalyst to promote a feeling of participation among all those involved in a small business. Contrary to popular belief, small enterprises do not necessarily benefit from their shorter communication lines by encouraging participation in decision-making processes. Some owner-managers are deliberately secretive about their plans; others leave insufficient time to communicate effectively with their staff. Even before a business has been launched, future partners may develop ideas themselves which remain unexpressed to each other.

The business plan provides a useful forum for all people involved in a small enterprise to express their ideas and feelings in a way which develops a spirit of teamwork among them. The separate parts can find some unity not only in the plan, but also in the process of putting it together. The business plan can also be very useful in a family business when the owner-manager is planning for succession (see Ward, 2011).

- Practice *in using analysis and presentation.* A plan can be an aid to training and management development. The research and analysis involved in a business plan, with quantification into forecast profit and loss and cash flows, is a widely used learning tool at centres of business education and also in practice elsewhere. For some would-be and practising small business managers the planning process is their first experience of market research and detailed budgeting. The presentation of a business plan to raise funds from banks or investors is good experience in selling a concept of any kind.
- *To assist in raising money.* A well-presented business plan is no guarantee of raising money, but it helps. Research into why banks decline finance for small business cites inadequate information as a common reason (Robbie, 1986). Banks and venture capital companies receive many requests for finance. A professional-looking business plan will at least help overcome the first hurdle of gaining a hearing.[2]

Lenders/investors will look to a business plan to provide them with additional information, particularly:

- *To appraise the quality of management.* A lender of loan capital will be aware that in a small business the intangible asset of the quality of its management is more important than tangible assets in guaranteeing the security of a loan. The best opportunity they have to assess the quality of that management may be in observing the production and presentation of the business plan. It is not just what the plan says, but also how it is put together and communicated, that will count for or against a lending or investing decision. In addition, three key aspects of the entrepreneurial team need to be conveyed clearly in the plan: What do they know? Whom do they know? And how well are they known? (Sahlman, 1997, p. 101).
- *To assess the overall competence of the entrepreneurial team.* There are some who argue that the numbers reported in a business plan really can't speak for very much at all. Indeed, Professor Sahlman of Harvard Business School states, 'As every seasoned investor knows, financial projections for a new company – especially detailed, month-by-month projections that stretch out for more than a year – are an act of imagination' (Sahlman, 1997, p. 98). So one might controversially suggest that the business plan is more about demonstrating a core level of competence and logical thinking and analysis, than providing a long and detailed justification of the actual forecasts and predictions contained therein.

Activity 5
What is in a plan?

What general topics should a plan cover? Suggest some specific headings which a plan might have to cover these topics.

6.5 The format of a business plan

6.5.1 OUTLINE OF A BUSINESS PLAN

The precise format of a business plan depends on the particular business and the intended audience of the plan. It is not possible to suggest subject headings for a plan which would have universal application, although the main clearing banks and other sources of help in the UK do make outline business plans available. The literature on how to write a business plan has been criticized for adopting what looks like a 'one size fits all' approach (Mason and Stark, 2004, p. 228). It is clearly important to remember that the range of people interested in reading business plans will have different perspectives and agendas. As observed earlier, bankers do not look for the same criteria as providers of risk capital. Nevertheless, most plans will be concerned with at least four main sections – the people, the opportunity, the context, and the risk and reward (Sahlman, 1997, p. 99).

Whatever the precise format adopted, it is essential that the separate sections of the plan belong together in an integrated whole. The marketing, operations and financial aspects of the plan should not be considered as free-standing components of the overall strategy. Rather, they should flow together to tell a clear and logical unified story. It may also be useful to think of the marketing section as driving the operations strategy, which, in turn, will dictate what finance is required and how this should be managed.

Critical to a successful business plan is the presentation of appropriate evidence to demonstrate to the potential investor or lender that the entrepreneurial team has thought through and has a clear understanding of the key drivers of the venture's success or failure. This could relate to profit margins, distribution channels, customer acquisition costs, or a wide variety of other factors which are specific to the particular context of industry and market (see Chapter 3, for more detail on the importance of industry and market). Behind this demonstration is the unspoken goal of the planning process when used to 'sell' the new venture – namely, to be able to display competence as the managers of the new venture (whether a start-up or the introduction of an innovation to an established firm). But it would be misleading to infer that competence was enough on its own. As we have seen in our discussion of 'steak' and 'sizzle', many investors will be looking for that extra something, a spark of creativity and flair, that cannot be captured in any textbook, guide or 'how to write the best business plan' book.

Here are some guidelines for what you should and should *not* put in your plan.

Some dos and don'ts

DO ensure that you write the best Executive Summary you can. This is the part of the plan that potential investors and others will actually read. As a guide, the summary should be no more than two or three pages (i.e. 1000 to 1500 words) and include the following key elements:

- The market
- The product or service
- The management team
- Business operations
- Financial projections
- Amount and use of finance required and exit opportunities.

Also include the company's mission statement.

- DO write the business plan yourself (or with the management team). Outsourcing it to a third party is not a good idea, and it will show.
- DO make the plan readable (with the type size ten point or above), using graphs and charts where appropriate, and avoid making it overly long.
- DO include a cover or binding and a contents page, ensuring the plan is written in email-friendly formatting if being sent by email.
- DO ensure that you keep referring back to your business plan once you've completed it. Although it is a one-off document, it is also a useful tool that can be updated and constantly revised throughout the life of your business.
- DO write a new business plan or substantially revise an existing one if and when a succession takes place in a family business.

- DO edit the plan carefully – get some friends to check it and ensure that it makes sense.
- DON'T write in the plan 'We have no competitors because this is an innovation…'. You will always have competitors.
- DON'T write in the plan 'We only need a 10 per cent market share…'. So do the other 75 new entrants get funding?
- DON'T write in the plan 'Our management team has a great deal of experience…', unless it has in the areas that really matter for your business.
- DON'T forget to justify your financial projections. Most business plans contain lots of impressive-looking numbers. The key is to make sure that your case is believable and compelling.

The business plan for an online business – a so-called 'e-business plan' (Turban *et al.*, 2004, p. 605) – differs only marginally from the traditional offline business plan. The biggest difference in e-business planning stems from the internet's power to allow businesses to get up close with their customers – what some commentators have referred to as its reach and richness (Evans and Wurster, 2000). This can lead to new and innovative business models and change business assumptions. E-business plans must take account of personalization of content, customer self-service or one-to-one marketing, for example, because the web enables them and they have the potential to act as sources of competitive advantage for firms that adopt such techniques (see Chapter 7 for more on business models and competitive advantage).

6.5.2 THE THREE KEY QUESTIONS

What should a business plan look like, and what should be included or excluded? Many outline business plans look formidable documents, running to numerous pages filled with very detailed questions. In fact, to do its job, a business plan needs to answer three straightforward questions:

- Where are we now?
- Where do we intend going?
- How do we get there?

Where are we now?
An analysis of the current situation of the marketplace, the competition, the business concept and the people involved is a necessary first step. It will include any historical background relevant to the position to date.

Where do we intend going?
The direction that is intended for the business needs to be clear and precise, if others are to share its vision for the future. As well as qualitative expression of the objectives, quantifiable targets will clarify and measure progress towards the intended goals. Identification of likely changes to the business environment will build on the opportunities outlined, and assess possible threats.

How do we get there?
Although planning is vital to have a clear sense of the chosen destination, it is also important for the entrepreneur to stay flexible and alert to opportunity. Knowing when to stay on the chosen path, and when to stray off it, is perhaps a key entrepreneurial characteristic.

Implementation of accepted aims is what all the parties to a plan are interested in as a final result. Plans for marketing and managing the business, with detailed financial analysis, are the advisable preliminaries before putting it all into practice.

Figure 6.2 The format of a business plan

Figure 6.2 suggests an outline which can be used in answering the three key questions we discussed earlier:

- Where are we now?
- Where do we intend going?
- How do we get there?

Suggested topics for each section are developed in more detail below. Two examples of business plans are also given in the Case Studies at the end of this chapter.

1. Analysis of current situation (where are we now?)	
(i) Identity of the business	
• Introduction	• relevant history and background • date or proposed date for commencement of trading/beginning of a plan
• Names	• name of business and trading names • names of managers/owners
• Legal identity	• company/sole trader/partnership/cooperative • details of share or capital structure
• Location	• address: registered and operational • brief details of premises
• Professional advisers	• accountants, solicitors, bank
(ii) The key people	
• Existing management	• names of the management team • outlines of background experience, skills and knowledge • why they are suited to the business – identifying a good management 'fit' is essential

• Future requirements	• gaps in skills and experience and how they will be filled
	• future recruitment intentions

(iii) The nature of the business	
• Product(s)/service(s)	• description and applications – in easy-to-grasp layman's terms
	• breakdown of product line as percentage of sales
	• outline of any intellectual properties (filed and pending), including patents, trademarks, design registrations, copyrights
	• online or off-line business?
	• key suppliers
	• after-sales service, or guarantees and warranties offered
	• planned developments of product or service
• Market and customers	• definition of target market – big or small?
	• trends in marketplace – potential for growth?
	• classification of customers
	• needs of customers and influences in their buying decisions
	• benefits offered by business to target customers
• Industry and competition	• description of industry and competitors
	• strengths and weaknesses of the major competitors
	• competitive edge; the uniqueness of your business compared to the competition

2. Future direction (where do we intend going?)	
(i) Strategic influences	
• Opportunities and threats in the business environment	• socio-economic trends
	• technological trends
	• legislation and politics
	• competition
• Strengths and weaknesses of the business	• in its industry
	• in the general environment
(ii) Strategic direction	
• Objectives	• general – outlining nature of value to be created in the business opportunity
	• specific – identifying where (and how) value is created and realized through potential exit routes
• Policies	• guidelines and rules
• Activities	• action plan
	• timetable of key activities

3. Implementation of aims (how do we get there?)	
(i) Management of resources	
• Operations	• managing the value chain
	• premises
	• materials
	• equipment
	• insurance
	• information and communication systems, including website

(Continued)

• People	• employment practices
	• recruitment
	• retention and motivation
	• payroll and personnel system
	• team management

(ii) Marketing plan

• Competitive edge	• unique selling point of business	
• Marketing objectives	• specific aims for product or service in the marketplace	
• Marketing methods	• innovation	• features and benefits
		• product mix
		• product development
		• e-commerce
	• incentives	• basis of pricing
		• margins
		• discount policy
	• promotion	• word of mouth and other methods to be used
		• consistency of image
		• web details and use of internet
	• distribution	• channels used
		• direct or intermediaries
• Research	• confirmation of demand	
	• future research planned	

(iii) Money: financial analysis

• Funding requirements	• start-up capital
	• working capital
	• asset capital
	• timing and source of funds required
	• risk and reward
	• security offered
• Profit and loss	• three-year forecast
	• sales
	• variable costs
	• gross profit
	• overheads
	• net profit
• Cash flow	• three-year forecast
	• receipts
	• payments
	• monthly and cumulative cash flow
• Balance sheet	• use of funds
	• source of funds
• Sensitivity analysis	• break-even point and time to positive cash flow
	• what-ifs
• Summary	• main assumptions
	• performance ratios

Although this outline suggests that business plans can be long, they should not be an unmanageable length for an external audience. Where detailed information is necessary, it should be given in appendices so that the main body of the report can be kept as concise and clear as possible. In view of the fact that a typical professional venture capital firm receives approximately 2000 business plans a year, the entrepreneur must present the plan in the best possible light, simply to ensure that it gets to the starting line.

6.5.3 COMMON MISTAKES IN PREPARING THE BUSINESS PLAN

1 Putting it off altogether.
2 Not having a clear idea of where you want to go with the business. Linked to this is the ability to communicate your pitch clearly – the so-called 'elevator pitch'.
3 Being too focused on profits and forgetting the importance of good cash management.
4 Focusing too much on the 'big idea' at the expense of the detail of how you are going to achieve it (product-focused approach). Linked to this is not clearly defining your market.
5 Over-promotion and hype. Very often there is a danger of using hyperbole and embellishment to try and sell ideas, rather than state things as they are. Linked to this is the importance of detailing how you will attract customers (rather than assuming they will just appear).
6 Too ambitious or optimistic with growth forecasts.
7 Over-reliance on one deal or customer order.
8 Failure to link the market research to your financial projections.
9 Poor presentation – particularly damaging in the context of design businesses.
10 Too much attention given to the company logo and name at the expense of the products/services and how you will sell these.

The Small Firms Enterprise Development Initiative (SFEDI) has produced Business Enterprise Standards which can be used to help you start up your business and write a successful business plan. The Standards can be used as checklists of what needs to be done and understood, as well as for learning and benchmarking once the plan is being put into place. There are 68 Standards which can be worked through (see Table 6.1).

Table 6.1 Business Enterprise Standards

Check the likely success of a business idea	Find innovative ways to improve your business	Sub-contract work for your business
Define the product or service of your business	Build relationships to build your business	Make sure people in your business can do their work
Plan where your business is going	Choose a legal format that suits your business	Develop people's skills for your business
Carry out a review of your business	Keep up to date with current legislation affecting your business	Deal with workplace problems or disputes
Carry out the plans for your business	Develop procedures to control risks to health and safety	Change job roles and handle redundancy
Make changes to improve your business	Conduct an assessment of risks in the workplace	Set up a stakeholder pension scheme
Improve the quality of products or services	Assess the environmental impact of your business	Check what customers need from your business

(Continued)

Table 6.1 (Continued)

Plan the exit strategy from your business	Decide on the financial needs of your business	Plan how to let your customers know about your products or services
Evaluate an existing business opportunity	Set and monitor financial targets for your business	Plan how you will sell your products or services
Get support for a creative business idea	Keep financial records for your business	Advertise your products or services
Monitor the social performance of a social enterprise	Manage cash flow in your business	Sell your products or services
Decide on a business location	Get customers to pay on time	Explore overseas markets for your business
Choose a business premises	Invest capital in your business	Sell your products or services on the internet
Contract for a business premises	Get finance for your business	Develop a website for your business
Create the infrastructure your business needs	Monitor borrowing for your business	Bid for work for your business
Undertake freelance work	Carry out the banking for your business	Make presentations about your business
Identify needs and suppliers for your business	Prepare wages	Decide how you will treat your business customers
Monitor the quality and use of supplies and equipment in your business	VAT registration and returns	Deliver a good service to customers
Achieve the goals for your business	Review the skills your business needs	Explore your own business motives
Win and keep customers	Plan what people your business needs	Check your ability to run your business
Make deals to take your business forward	Recruit people for your business	Improve your business skills
Seek advice and help for your business	Delegate work to others in your business	Work with a board in a social enterprise
Manage time in your business	Improve relationships with stakeholders in a social enterprise	

Source: SFEDI Business Enterprise Standards www.sfedi.co.uk

There are a wide range of issues which need to be worked through carefully before launching a business and others which arise after launch. It is particularly important that personal and business objectives are in tune with each other. In Chapter 5, we learned that the 'lean start-up' method involved a constant process of developing ideas, testing them in the market and adjusting them in line with findings. Business planning mirrors this; it is an iterative process rather than 'big design up-front' (see Blank, 2013), and it is likely that there will be many iterations of a plan while evidence for the viability of an idea is gathered. This is illustrated in Figure 6.3.

Figure 6.3 The iterative business planning process

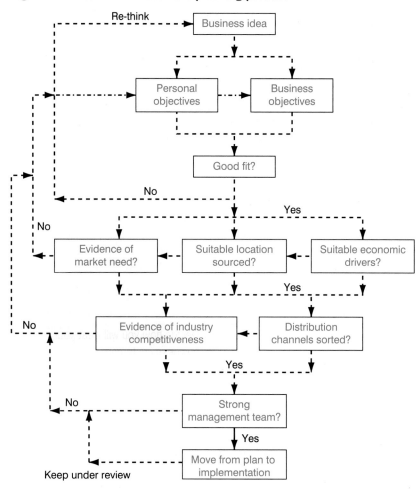

6.6 Summary and activities

This chapter looks at the process of business planning for the new and small firm. Three key questions lie at the heart of the planning process – where are we now, where do we intend going, and how do we get there? Though these questions appear straightforward enough, there are often good reasons why planning is avoided or becomes a low priority for the small business manager or entrepreneur. Strongly held cultural values can impede the planning process. Even where planning is undertaken, however, it is important to remember that time never stands still – so the answers to key questions can lose their currency, or at worst become wholly irrelevant to the reality of the business today (perhaps in the event of a significant world event such as financial crisis or a more localized loss of a key customer). The business plan represents a snapshot of the business at a particular time and place, rather than any underlying 'truth' about the nature of the business over the long term.

Business planning is a process that is undertaken for a variety of different reasons. While it can serve as an extremely useful tool for internal analysis of a small business, the most common use of the business plan is to gain finance from some external source. The chapter outlined how different investors and lenders look for different criteria in a new venture: therefore, for a business plan to be successful it needs to be tailored for the target audience.

Finally, the chapter outlines the basic format of the business plan and gives an indication of the key elements in its structure. While there is no one winning formula for writing a business plan, the entrepreneurial team should strive to display competence in their approach to managing the new venture, alongside a clear account of the particular strengths (experience, knowledge, contacts, etc.) of the individuals involved. After all, as Arthur Rock, the venture capitalist associated with the formation of Intel and Apple, among many other businesses, said, 'I invest in people, not ideas'.

Case study
Eocha Ltd: Part 1

THE BUSINESS PROPOSAL

Introduction

In the USA, Robin Poques would probably have been called a business angel. In the UK, he was better known as a private investor in small businesses. To date, his entrepreneurial activities had provided him with a reasonable living, but he was still searching for the big breakthrough – a business opportunity which would grow to a size that could be floated on the stock market and make him not only rich, but also celebrated as a successful entrepreneur. He frequently received introductions and business plans for proposed ventures from a variety of sources. The majority he rejected as not viable, or not capable of the fast growth he was looking for. Recently, he had been introduced to two business people who proposed to start up an electronics business which seemed to meet most of his criteria, and he needed to make an investment decision. He studied the written plan he had received from Eocha Ltd.

Private and Confidential
EOCHA LTD BUSINESS PLAN

Background

Eocha Ltd is a start-up product design and prototyping company. The company has been formed with significant equity funding from its founders and an opportunity exists for third-party investment. Eocha will work in certain niche areas of high-technology product design that offer opportunities for knowledgeable, independent designers. The founders' know-how will facilitate the custom design of products by utilizing all aspects of microelectronics technology. In particular, it will utilize microelectronics technology to turn low-tech products into 'smarter', high-tech innovations. All products will be custom designed and built to prototype stage for other companies in a wide range of industries. Eocha will concentrate initially on applications with smaller volumes, yet high added value, or in areas which traditionally have not used electronics extensively. The company will not attempt to compete with high-volume electronics manufacturers who have their own research and development departments. Rather, it will complement growth companies wishing to innovate by offering them a high-grade design and problem-solving service. Eocha will primarily sell a design service, rather than a product, in a way which will differentiate it from competitors and allow for high profit margins.

The people

The founders of the company are Dr Charles Appleton and Edwina Oaks. Dr Appleton will act as Chairman and Managing Director, with responsibility for the overall strategy of the company and production. Dr Appleton is well known in the academic, industrial and investment world as a leading authority in microelectronics. Edwina Oaks will act as General Manager, with specific responsibility for sales, marketing and administration. She currently has senior management responsibility for new product design in a large UK company.

The founders previously worked together in Appletech Ltd, a contract design company founded by Dr Appleton. In the three years they worked together, Appletech expanded rapidly. However, as a result of an abortive move into high-volume production of their own products, prompted by Appletech's external investors, both Dr Appleton and Mrs Oaks left that business. This plan is designed to bring their skills together again in the development of a specialist operation. A third-party investor(s) is sought both to invest in the business and contribute to its strategic planning and administration. However, it is intended that the founders are in a majority on the board of directors, to allow the company to be run by individuals who fully understand its operation. The two founders bring sufficient breadth of experience and knowledge to manage the company in the early stages.

A crucial area of development will be the recruitment of innovative staff, including engineers and designers. Individuals have already been identified and discussions are continuing concerning their joining the company. The founders' knowledge and reputation is seen as a significant factor in the recruitment of key staff within the industry.

Full curricula vitae of the founders are available on request.

The market

More and more products, from flight simulators to fishing rods, are becoming 'smarter'; that is, they can record more information, and make more decisions about their utilization, without human intervention. The development of the silicon integrated circuit (SIC or, more commonly, microchip) was the key enabling technology of this trend. But SICs, or chips, do not function on their own. For many years, there has been a thriving industry in the design of circuits that connect together SICs and other electronic devices to produce useful circuits, systems and products. For example, a SIC does not easily handle the high powers and voltages of the everyday electronics world, so specific adaptations have to be made in order for microchips to be used in many applications. The falling price and increasing power of SICs is increasing the number of applications that can successfully use them, and this trend will continue to increase the demand for smart products. Customized silicon microcircuits are now used extensively in many industries, including telecommunications, instrumentation, security, aerospace and the military. Significant demand exists for the design of new products incorporating such circuits, which has been estimated at £400–£500 million in Europe, with higher figures for North America. The increased complexity and power of the SIC has increased the demand for electronic products designed for specific customer requirements by 15 per cent per annum throughout Europe in recent years. The reduced size and price of products using electronic circuits is usually accompanied by enhanced performance and reliability, so that their integration into product design is becoming a competitive 'must' in many industries.

(Continued)

The opportunity

The opportunity is to build a substantial, medium-sized firm over the next few years. Specifically, this firm will specialize in the design and prototyping of new products utilizing the latest technologies in electronic circuitry designed for specific customer requirements. It will design such products using computer-aided design software. It will purchase the necessary components to build prototypes of such circuits and products, including the SIC and other devices. However, Eocha will add considerable value through the design and interconnection of the devices in the circuit in such a way as to meet customer specifications of the final product. The founders have extensive knowledge and expertise in this area of microelectronic applications in new product design.

Initial customers have already been identified from the founders' existing contacts. Due to the wide application of the technology, no specific industry area will be pursued above others in the longer term. In the short term, it is known that innovative applications exist in several markets, including kitchen appliances which will become increasingly smart in the next few years.

The difficulties

Although Eocha is aiming for a niche share of the overall new product development market, one of the difficulties will be the slow build-up of work inherent in custom design; 6–18 months are common lead times from initial customer contact through to design of an initial prototype. The financial projections and capital requirements reflect this.

Substantial capital investment is required for the necessary equipment and facilities. This is partly offset by a low requirement for working capital, as products are made to order and not stocked in advance. Both of these factors are reflected in the cash flow forecasts.

Increasingly, the manufacture of these innovative products takes place outside of Europe around the Pacific Rim. Strategic alliances will be sought with companies in Asia and elsewhere to provide them with the design resource at the leading edge of technology which they do not always possess themselves.

In summary

Particular strengths are:
- founders with a proven track record in the technology area
- growth demand for high-technology product design
- close links with research institutions
- low capital investment in relation to the microelectronics industry.

Particular challenges are:
- slow initial build-up of client base due to customized nature of the business
- high capital investment compared to lower technology design companies
- the need for strategic alliances with manufacturers outside of Europe.

The investment

Initially 100 000 £1 ordinary shares are being authorized. Sixty thousand will be issued at par to the executive founders (40 000 to Dr Charles Appleton and 20 000 to Edwina Oaks). An investor and non-executive director will be offered the balance of shares (40 000) at £2.00, the premium reflecting the commitment and expertise of the executive founders. A £50 000 overdraft is sought from the bank, secured against the sales ledger. In the first instance, hire purchase will also be used to purchase some capital equipment.

Summary projections

End of year	1	2	3
	£000s	£000s	£000s
Sales	120	450	700
Gross profit	96	360	560
Overheads	110	270	420
Operating profit	(14)	90	140
End of year	1	2	3
	£000s	£000s	£000s
Cash flow			
Accounts paid	197	417	610
Capital spend	141	40	75
Received	(72)	(398)	(675)
Funding required	266	59	10

Key assumptions

Sales should build up rapidly once the initial lead time is taken into account. There is no reason why this expansion should not continue after Year 3, providing the appropriate technical staff can be recruited.

Gross margins are calculated to average 80 per cent, as the costs of materials at the design and prototyping stage are low compared to the indirect costs, particularly staff costs.

Overheads include the costs of all staff and directors, as well as premises, administration, finance and marketing costs.

Cash flow assumes a time lag between invoice date and payment of approximately 60 days in the case of both debtors and creditors.

£140 000 is received from shareholders' investment in Year 1 as part of the funding of the operation.

Hire purchase is used to purchase equipment, although a percentage deposit (30 per cent) has to be found from internal funds.

The decision

Robin Poques had already had one meeting with the founders, whom he judged to make an innovative, technically competent team. He was concerned about their business management capabilities, but he felt he might himself have a role to play in this area. He also knew other investors were interested in backing them, so he did not have much time to make a decision.

Activities

(a) How well do you think the founders have presented their case? How would you advise them to improve the layout or content of their plan?

(b) How would you assess this business proposition in terms of its strengths and weaknesses as a new venture?

(c) What other information or clarification would you now seek if you were Robin Poques?

(d) Assuming you have to make a decision in principle based on what is presented here, advise Robin Poques on whether he should invest or not.

This case is continued in Chapter 11.

Planning in practice: *giftsmania*

This case study is a real-life example of a business plan. It is not suggested that this is an exemplary approach that should be followed prescriptively. As in most plans, there are some good sections but also some areas that could be improved. As you read it through, think about how *you* would have approached the task differently. Comments and questions have been inserted into the plan for you to consider as they arise, rather than at the end.[5]

EXECUTIVE SUMMARY

Have you ever wondered why people give gifts or what they look for in a gift? Is it to express an emotional connection, or do they also like to stand out and be perceived as creative and original among their friends and loved ones? We at *giftsmania* believe that giving the 'perfect' gift is priceless. We offer our customers the chance to give tailor-made, interesting and special gifts for any occasion; gifts they can't just go and buy from any store, no matter how much they pay. *Giftsmania* makes memories!

> The plan needs to provide a convincing and engaging opening paragraph while also avoiding the hype of a promotional leaflet. How successful do you think the authors have been here?

The focus of our products is on developing specially drawn caricatures and comics for our customers, based on the photographic and biographical materials they provide us with. In collaboration with our graphic illustrator and cartoonist partners, we will be able to develop storyboards with details from their real lives that they can then share with their loved ones.

We believe this business plan lays the foundations for our future business on solid ground. This document summarizes the research, brainstorming and creative planning we have done as a cohesive and creative group. We are launching in early-December, and by that date we will have our operations up and running. At this point, all of our marketing material is under development and necessary outsourcing deals have been secured.

> If you were reading only this executive summary as a potential investor, what information do you think is missing?

The Company
Mission statement

Believing in the originality of our clients, we provide them with the creativity and know-how to provide added value, and make a special impact on their loved ones' memories. Our mission is to bring new meaning to the 'gifting' experience.

> Mission statements can inspire or confuse. Do you think small businesses need mission statements at all, or are these just for large organizations?

Background

Giftsmania is a personalized and premium gift service with its focus on creating caricatures and comics tailored for the customer, to be given to a friend or loved one on a special occasion; that is, a wedding, birth of a new baby or anniversary. The personalized gift service starts with storyboarding and concept development for each project by working closely with the client, who provides the materials and details of the person receiving the gift. Typically, clients will send materials to the *giftsmania* team via the internet (though the option exists to meet with a representative face-to-face for larger projects). Our creative team will then be able to work with the supplied information

> Note that this business relies on the client providing inputs efficiently and effectively. What operational problems would you foresee and how effectively does the plan deal with them?

about the gift-receiver (image, age, style, likes and dislikes, funny aspects of his/her character, special stories and experiences that he/she shared with the gift-giver and possibly the specific event the gift is given for).

For example, our client may be someone who wants to give a gift to her brother for finally getting a new job after months of unsuccessful trials. The client, being close to her brother, will know the 'ins' and 'outs' of the job-hunting story. She will provide our team with the pictures and funny details and we will develop a storyboard around this experience and have it drawn up by our exceptional quality caricaturists and cartoonists. Upon the client's approval, we proceed with production and delivery.

The company's name (*giftsmania*) reflects the originality and creativity of the idea and relates to the main target group of young, stylish and aspirational individuals (described later). The name will also define the products' naming structure. For each project, we will add the word 'mania' and present it visually in an identical form to our logo (see the figure below).

© RUBA HATEM

alex jobmania

Project naming structure and design example

The nature of our customized and premium service inspires and demands a special level of communication with our customers. We have invested in the software and hardware to facilitate quick and hassle-free exchange of pictures in a variety of suitable formats. Our business model is a personalized service and we therefore deal with each client individually.

The team

At the heart of every good business is an exceptional management team. This is no truer than at *giftsmania*. The origins of the business stem from friendship and a desire to work together on this entrepreneurial business venture. We are a group of five innovators with extensive management and retail experience that have come together to share a common purpose and deliver an exceptional product offering with great market growth potential. We are Katryna Grimshaw (Managing Director), Penwisa Kietduriyakul (Director of IT and Operations), Ruba H. Haj Moh'D (Director of Sales and Marketing), Opeoluwa Ogundare (Director of Finance) and Bui Thi Thu Giang (Company Secretary and Human Resources). See Appendices for CVs of each of the team members. Each of the company members has an equal share of 20 per cent of the company.

This team has a unique mix of creative and business backgrounds that blend to create the solid base necessary for the

> Having a strong brand and/or logo is extremely important in an age where we rely heavily on the power of the visual image. Is this a strong brand name? What brand values does it provoke?

> What potential problems do you envisage the small business facing in dealing with this 'personalized' service?

> The business plan needs to provide enough information about the key people behind the business while avoiding filling the business plan with too much detail on individuals and their career histories. Are there any key factors which are missing here?

> So far, it is not clear whether the team have the in-house skills to produce the caricatures and cartoons which are central to the business idea. What problems might there be if the company has to outsource this particular function?

(Continued)

success of the company. The management team's personal objectives complement each other very well. Each Director has other business interests which provide them with sufficient income to allow *giftsmania* to be run (initially at least) without drawing salaries (for more details, see the finance section). The products and services offered are all managed by the team with minimal need for outsourcing. This structure guarantees minimum risk and sets potential for speedy growth in the market.

Products and services

We have designed the following (Mania Packs) to offer to our customers upon launch, either separately or in bundles:

1
Original tailor-made comic frame or strip, specially drawn, printed (framed) and delivered to the customer.

Price: £25 (unframed)
£45 (framed)

2
Eight-page comic book/A5 size, specially drawn and story boarded for the customer and presented as a funny story of the gift receiver showing the 'insider' details of the occasion.

Price: £180 (in presentation box)

3
[This product only available in addition to either frame or book mania] Specially designed (up to five pages) website for the occasion where the comics are featured to share with friends and family in addition to other personal sections with pictures and a guestbook.

Design and development: £200
Hosting and domain name: yearly payment of £54

Table 1 Products and pricing

	Products	Cost price (£)	Selling price (£)	Contribution (£)
Option 1	Frame Mania (unframed)	15	25	10
Option 2	Frame Mania (framed)	30	45	15
Option 3	Book Mania	130	180	50
Option 4	Web Mania	154	254	100

- Our initial expectations (based on detailed market research) is that the *Frame Mania* product will account for circa 65 per cent of the overall sales, with the remainder made up of 30 per cent *Book Mania* and 5 per cent *Web Mania*.
- Costs relating to the outsourced artwork and printing are estimated at 75 per cent of the stated costs of production, with the remainder being allocated to the management team to cover concept development.

Market and industry

Market

Startups (2007) states that 'it is extremely difficult to define the gift retail sector for the simple reason that it is almost impossible to restrict the definition of a gift'. In short, anything can be bought and given as a present. It also makes the point that the market is becoming increasingly fragmented. The KeyNote Giftware Market Report (2007) identified five major sectors: toys and games; jewellery and watches; ceramics; glassware; and small leather goods, such as purses and wallets.

As the market is both extremely competitive and segmented, there exist an almost incalculable number of products competing for customers' personal disposable income. In such a case, 'innovation becomes vital in the giftware industry in order to capture consumers' imaginations and encourage them to spend' (KeyNote, 2007). This is especially apparent in the toys and games market where, according to the British Toy & Hobby Association (BTHA), of the 500 best-selling toys in 2006, more than half were new products. It is crucial, therefore, that we at *giftsmania* emphasize our originality, and stay up-to-date with new trends and supportive technologies (e.g. latest design and photo editing software).

> **If you were a potential investor reading this plan, what do you think this section would have told you about the management team's knowledge of (i) the *international* market, and (ii) the *local* market for their specialized products?**

Giftmania's primary target market is young professionals (20s–40s), with disposable income – those who like to be 'different', give a truly memorable gift for a friend's wedding, christening or baby shower. Generally based in the UK, we will start out with a focus on London (within M25) and, to begin with, around the Richmond area – which has the highest household income (e.g. one-quarter of households in Richmond have an equivalent income of over £60 000 per year (GLA, Data Management and Analysis Group, PayCheck 2008). Our unique product can, however, be adapted easily for a broader, more international market as we will work primarily through the internet.

Using the ACORN classification system in the UK we will target primarily category 1, the 'wealthy achievers', and category 2, 'urban prosperity'. Together, these categories account for 27.6 per cent of the total working population. As these are the groups with the highest incomes and most disposable income, they will most likely be more willing to spend a little extra time and money on a personalized gift. We can also include in our potential market those who fall under category 3, 'comfortably off', as they may consider our product/service when looking for a gift for a very special occasion or loved-one.

> **While it might be helpful in theory to segment the market according to the ACORN classification system, how might this be done in practice?**

To establish the potential size of our target market, we begin conservatively by looking at the working population of London, estimated at around 5.037 million (see GLA, 2008). Based on an estimate of the number of young professionals working in our chosen areas as between 5–10 per cent of the population, we take our initial population to be circa 400 000 individuals, suggesting a sizeable group to focus on in the first instance.

Industry

According to the Giftware Association (GA), the national trade body for the UK gift and home industry, the sector generates an estimated £10 billion per year (Giftware Association). Wedding gift lists dominate with the British spending over £6.7 billion on wedding gifts (John Lewis Survey, 2007), and other occasions, namely anniversaries and baby showers, are becoming more lucrative.

(Continued)

Gifts and luxury goods are optional purchases; sales of such items are largely responsive to general economic circumstances.

Rising wealth facilitates expenditure on a wide range of non-essential spending, of which gift buying is one. Positive growth in PDI and consumer expenditure is indicative of rising affluence and this has, and will continue to be, a positive factor for the gift market. Being able to afford to buy better quality gifts as well as being able to afford to buy gifts on more occasions is closely linked to affluence and perceptions of economic wellbeing. (Mintel, June 2005)

The economic downturn may have a negative effect on the industry. A decline in disposable income for many UK shoppers will inevitably restrict the capacity of some of our customers to spend on the premium products offered by *giftsmania*. Having said this, however, we are confident that there are many within the target market that are relatively recession-proofed and still likely to buy gifts and luxury items. It is also encouraging that between 2002 and 2011, the giftware market is forecast to increase by 9.9 per cent to reach £4.86 billion in 2011 (KeyNote, 2007). See Figure 1.

Figure 1 Forecast for UK giftware market

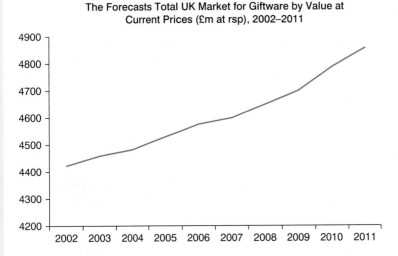

The Forecasts Total UK Market for Giftware by Value at Current Prices (£m at rsp), 2002–2011

Source: Keynote: 2007

Strategic issues
Opportunities and threats in the industry

(a) Social trends

The wedding market is particularly important to the giftware industry, especially in the jewellery and glassware sectors. According to the latest figures from National Statistics, in 2005 the number of weddings in England and Wales reached its lowest level since 1896 (KeyNote, August 2007). People are getting married older and more couples are living together before marriage. This decline in weddings will adversely affect the giftware industry as a whole but predominantly the jewellery

> One of the most compelling aspects of a good business plan is its reliance on solid market research rather than anecdote or perhaps wishful thinking. How strong is the plan in that respect?

and glassware sectors. Furthermore, the older wedded couple is more likely to have a more affluent circle of friends as gift-givers, meaning that demand for the premium gift (such as that offered by *giftsmania*) will hold up well in comparison.

(b) Technological trends

According to the Interactive Media in Retail Group (IMRG), the online store organization, 'consumers have spent £100bn online in the 12 years since April 1995 and £3.47bn was recorded for April 2007 alone' (IMRG, 2007). Jo Evans, IMRG's Managing Director, says that April's online sales in one month were worth about the same as London's West End takes in a year. Online shopping is becoming a real and growing alternative to high-street retail. These days most high-street stores offer online shopping, yet Amazon continues to lead in this field.

This online shopping boom is a great opportunity as there in no real limit to the number of companies competing online. The trend can be used to our advantage as our service is offered through our website and the ideas and product can be discussed and developed with the customer through online communication. With the proliferation of online businesses, however, effective marketing of the *giftsmania* brand and product offering will be of paramount importance.

(c) Economic trends

The global economic recession has caused tremendous hardship amongst many businesses, and retail organizations have been particularly badly hit. With less disposable income, the capacity of potential customers to spend on gift and luxury items is diminished. However, there is also evidence to suggest that the more affluent consumer has continued to buy premium products on the high street. With the record low interest rates, some better-off consumers have been able to ride the recession relatively well. Recent retail sales figures (rising 0.4 per cent in July) also hold out the promise that the recession is coming to an end.

As has been indicated earlier, the *giftsmania* range of products appeals to a young and aspirational segment of the society. We believe, in the light of detailed market research, that despite the current economic conditions, there is a bright future for *giftsmania*, with demand holding up for the launch period and increasing thereafter.

> **Note the need to state explicitly what this entailed.**

Competition

The market for gifts comprises a number of different segments. *Giftsmania's* products will stand out from the competition in terms of their bespoke and highly differentiated nature. This is particularly important in the context of a market that is generally undifferentiated, where high street stores and individuals all source their products from a relatively concentrated set of providers. Standing out from the competition is a critical success factor for *giftsmania*.

> **Where this kind of assertion is made it needs to be backed up by appropriate evidence.**

Research indicates that the highest performing sectors of the gifts market are those associated with bespoke and premium products. For example, the strongest growth in the UK greeting card market (valued at £1.4 billion in 2007) has been in handmade craft cards and through non-core retail outlets like bookstores and galleries, as well as online (see Mintel, 2007). *Giftsmania* is confident that its products are very well positioned in the market and can compete effectively with existing competition.

A list of the main competitors in the gifts market in the UK is presented in Table 2.

(Continued)

Table 2 Competitors in the UK gifts market

Sector	Competitors
(a) Toys and Games	The Character Group PLC; David Halsall International Holdings Ltd; Hasbro UK Ltd; Mattel UK Ltd and Vivid Imaginations Ltd
(b) Jewellery	Abbeycrest PLC; Baugur Group Ltd; Graff Diamonds International Ltd and Signet Group PLC
(c) Ceramics and Glassware	Portmeirion Group PLC; Royal Doulton (UK) Ltd and Waterford Wedgwood PLC
(d) Greeting cards	UK Greetings; Hallmark Cards UK; Simon Elvin and Paper House. While Remind 4u, Moonpig, charitycards.co.uk, cardsgalore.co.uk, greetigifts. co.uk and jacquielawson.com are the emerging players in the online greeting card sectors.

The scale of *giftsmania*'s operations is not expected to rival any of the competitors listed above. Rather, there is a host of direct competitors which are too numerous to name here, but none of which present particular threats to the business.

Strengths and weaknesses of the business

The main strengths of our business hinge on the uniqueness and personalization of the comics, which is complemented by the high quality of the printing. As the brainstorming of the creative concepts will be done within the team, there is a minimum need for outsourcing, only to the caricature artists and the print shop.

Other potential weaknesses in the business are our inability to copyright the idea, the danger of being copied and the effect of fluctuations in international exchange rates.

Objectives

- In the short term, to enter an extremely varied and competitive market and to generate sales sufficient to break-even by month 6 and establish a 0.5 per cent share of the target market by end of Year 1.
- In the medium term, to achieve a business turnover that can provide each director with at least £5000 income per year, after tax.
- In the longer term, to achieve and sustain a 5 per cent share of the target market by end of Year 5.

> It is helpful to distinguish between direct and indirect competitors. What is highlighted here is the difficulty of identifying who exactly is a competitor in some cases. *Giftsmania*'s product offerings compete with a wide variety of other goods and services (including 'art' of all sorts, which is not discussed here). How helpful is Table 2 in this case?

> How would you assess their assessment of direct competition?

> Would you consider it a weakness of the small business that it outsources the art-work in this case?

> One of the difficulties for the small business founder(s) is to balance a realistic and cautious appraisal of the new venture's potential with their entrepreneurial drive and vision. Is this balance struck here?

Future directions

After establishing *giftsmania* as a brand name and gaining consumer awareness, we plan to extend our product-line to include the following:

1 Specially-made board games with comics themes.
2 Customized playing cards printed with the comic strips on the back.
3 Comics printed on a range of other products, including T-shirts, posters, mugs and other mass-produced items.

More ideas can also be developed according to the nature of each project. We keep our services totally flexible to fit with the needs of our clients.

> There is a fine balance between presenting the essentials for the start-up and successful launch of the business, and indicating the future and longer-term direction of the enterprise. Given the bespoke nature of *giftsmania*'s initial product line, do you think the outlined future direction seems appropriate?

Launch date

Our company will be launched in early-December. Our initial marketing and advertising strategy has been carefully planned to maximize the potential of this date before Christmas.

Operational plan
Production

Central to the success of *giftsmania* is our ability to conceive of amusing and creative storylines for each of the mania products. It is the management team's collective creativity which will be drawn upon here. We have secured the services of a pool of five exceptional caricature artists whose work will guarantee satisfaction. Two of these artists work in London, two in Jordan and the fifth is currently based in Spain. For examples of their work, see Figures 2 and 3 below as well as Appendices.

Figure 2

Starting the Habit Early!

Source: © Mr Osama Hajjaj

(Continued)

Figure 3

Source: © Mr Osama Hajjaj

The online nature of our business model allows us to maximize the potential of this pool of artists, drawn from across the globe. The outsourcing to caricature artists (and print shops) is not foreseen to create any limitations to production in the future. We are also confident that we can use existing networks to expand the pool of artists as demand increases. By Year 5, we expect to be working with up to 20 tried and tested artists on a regular basis.

Though we are outsourcing the execution part of the business, the core of the service, the creative concepts development, is completely covered within our team. The production cycle (see Figure 4) indicates the key relationships between clients and *giftsmania*. As previously stated, the default mode of communication is by email, and we have a secured network already in place to facilitate this. However, for the *Web Mania* product we anticipate the need for face-to-face communication, if feasible (and this is built into the pricing structure if the client is based within the M25 area of London).

> A question that a potential investor (and client) would be likely to ask is 'how will you ensure the quality of the product if the caricature work is outsourced?'

Quality control

As the customers are directly involved in the creation of the products stage by stage, there is no need for a guarantee or warranty at the end of the service. We will, however, give the customer the opportunity to approve the ideas and storyboard before they go to print. In addition, the customer will not be charged until completion of the final product.

> Do you anticipate any risks involved with this strategy? It is helpful to include an analysis of these risks in the business plan.

Figure 4 The production cycle

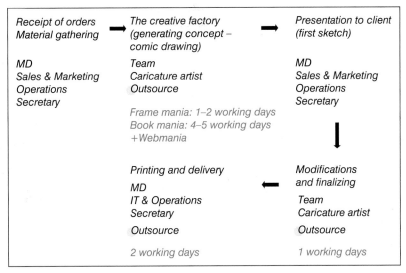

Suppliers

In order to create and develop each product quickly and efficiently, two key suppliers will be necessary. As indicated above, *giftsmania* has secured the services of five exceptionally talented caricature artists, all of whom work in a similar style (see Appendices for full details of each of these artists, together with further examples of their work).

Giftsmania has also negotiated very competitive trade rates for printing materials on a just-in-time basis (guaranteeing same-day delivery) with the print company KPrint (see Appendices for full details). *Frame* and *Book Mania* products will be printed on 300 gsm paper, chosen for its exceptional quality and performance. Agreements are in place with suppliers and credit terms have been agreed (14 days).

> Note that the plan makes no specific mention of the current 'office' and the primary location for the business. It is always important that this is clearly indicated in the plan. What other operational details have been omitted here?

Marketing Plan
Competitive edge

Many so-called 'personalized gifts' come in the form of printed names and photos/pictures on standard mass-produced items (mugs, silver chains, apparel, etc.). Our service offers a genuinely personal approach that captures and illustrates memories, inside jokes and very special aspects about the gift receiver's life and character. Looking at competition from this perspective assures us that we are introducing a unique service.

> As a general rule, beware using the word 'unique' in business plans. Arguably, all small businesses are 'unique' in some way. This does not guarantee success. How would you re-phrase this?

(Continued)

Marketing objectives

We aim to raise awareness and create a strong brand identity in a relatively short period of time through a smart marketing plan that focuses on reaching our bull's-eye target audience rather than random advertising spread widely with ineffective exposure.

Marketing methods

1 Word of mouth:

A snowball effect of satisfied customers can work as a primary (free) advertising tool. Being a service of a social nature, it is expected that people who have either tried it, known someone who has tried it, or simply heard about it from others, will be integral to creating a positive word of mouth about *giftsmania* products.

2 Giveaways:

As *giftsmania*'s main selling point concerns the originality and unique-ness of the gifting experience, we aim to market it with a 'twist'. Anything we produce to carry the identity of our service needs to stand out among regular promotion tools. We, therefore, plan to use branded giveaways instead of regular BTL material. See Figure 6.6 for an example.

> **This can be an effective strategy but giveaways cost money. Can they afford it?**

   We will distribute our items in different high-class shopping areas around Christmas time, across London (especially Richmond). When everyone is in the mood for 'gifting', a creative idea for a gift can catch people's attention.

3 The online environment:

Right where our target audience is, is where we plan to hit. Advertising online doesn't need to be expensive if thought about creatively. Thanks to the free blogs, and the social network groups (such as Facebook and Myspace and the like), we are now able to reach a considerable number of potential customers freely and at the click of a button.

> **The internet is often seen as an attractive environment for new small businesses, but it is one thing to have a fantastic website or blog, but quite another to drive clients and customers to that site. What strategies could *giftsmania* take to achieve this?**

4 Direct sales to large corporations:

Comics tell stories and share memories; they are therefore an excellent medium for employees to share their office gossip, funny stories and events. The *Frame Mania* is a unique gift for a person who was just named 'the employee of the month', for example. The *Book Mania* can be a very memorable gift for someone who is resigning after many years with her colleagues. The *Web Mania* is a great place to share comments and laughs with loved ones, especially when living

> **The experienced investor may well raise an eyebrow here, noting that this corporate market was not even mentioned in the earlier section on the 'Market'. How could they make the business plan more consistent?**

away from home due to business commitments. Therefore, we plan to target sales towards established companies, showing them samples of our portfolio and providing them with special deals to encourage them to use our service (ideally with multiple orders). The corporate gift market is potentially a lucrative area of business for *giftsmania*.

Financial strategy

Start-up capital

The proposed business is not resource intensive and start-up costs are minimal. The company will operate with a very modest authorized share capital (£1500 provided by the directors), with each director owning a 20 per cent share in the business. It is forecast that this will provide sufficient working capital to sustain the business through the launch phase, with break-even expected in Month 6. It has been agreed that salaries will not be paid among the board of directors until Year 2, with initial profits being put directly back into the business.

Sales projections

Careful market research indicates a promising outlook for *giftsmania*'s sales. We present projected sales volume for the first six-month period of trading in Table 3.

Table 3 Estimated sales volume (six months)

Sales volume	Estimated sales volume for the financial trading period					
	December	**January**	**February**	**March**	**April**	**May**
Frame Mania (unframed)	10	4	6	8	10	12
Frame Mania (framed)	5	1	2	2	2	3
Book Mania	5	2	3	5	7	8
Web Mania				1	2	2
Total	**20**	**7**	**11**	**16**	**21**	**25**

Notes and assumptions:

1 Target market share of 0.5 per cent of population (400 000) would give sales of 2000 by the end of Year 1.
2 It is assumed that sales would start off relatively weak (though with a peak for pre-Christmas interest) and build up as word of mouth strategy developed.
3 Market research (survey to 250 individuals in Richmond town centre) has indicated likely proportion of sales as Frame Mania (65 per cent) Book Mania (30 per cent) and Web Mania (5 per cent).

> **A critical factor in writing the business plan is to ensure that the financials are based on the marketing strategy (and, ideally, solid market research). It is always good practice to include 'Notes' to indicate the assumptions used to arrive at the numbers presented. What 'Notes' would be useful to insert here?**

Costs of production

Giftsmania has devised a business model that will keep costs to a minimum, while ensuring that clients receive a premium and quality product, which exceeds their expectations every time. Projected direct expenditure (i.e. covering costs of production) is outlined in Table 4, indicating the monthly contribution anticipated.

(Continued)

Table 4 Sales and cost comparison (six months)

	Sales (ex VAT) (£)	Cost (ex VAT) (£)	Contribution (£)
December	1375	950	425
January	505	350	155
February	780	540	240
March	1444	984	460
April	2108	1428	680
May	2383	1618	765
Total (6 months)	**8595**	**5870**	**2725**

Profit and loss projections (year 1)

A summary of the company's profit and loss forecast for the opening year is presented in Table 5. Costs and overheads will be kept to a minimum by using existing business premises and leveraging the directors' other business interests.

Table 5 Summary profit and loss statement (Year 1 projection)

Profit and loss	**Income (£)**	**Expenditure (£)**
Sales		
Gross	20 198	
VAT (17.5%)	3008	
Net	17 190	
Costs		
Costs of production (inc. VAT)		13 795
Costs of production (ex. VAT)		11 740
Gross profit	5450	
Overheads		
Salaries		–
Rent		1500
Rates and insurance		1000
Other costs (inc. marketing)		2000
Other costs (admin.)		300
Total overheads		4800
Net profit before tax	650	

Notes:

1 Sales figures based on achieving 0.5 per cent market share in Year 1.
2 Costs of production include outsourcing for artwork and printing costs, as well as covering concept development and liaising with the clients.

3 No salaries drawn in Year 1.
4 Rent is minimal as using existing premises.
5 Rates and insurance are minimal.
6 Costs of marketing kept low by some level of subsidization from existing business interests.

Profit figures for Years 2–5 are expected to grow significantly, achieving a 5 per cent market share by Year 5, with a turnover in the region of £250 000.

Managing the cash flow

The aspirations of the directors are modest in the first instance. We are aware that this business will start small. However, it has the potential to grow substantially as it is built on a highly scalable business model. The short-term objective is to establish a firm sales-base and we would expect to be in a position to break-even by the end of the first half of the opening year's trading (see Table 6). Careful and prudent cash flow management is an essential feature of *giftsmania's* approach.

Table 6 Cash flow forecast (first 6 months)

	DEC (£)	JAN (£)	FEB (£)	MAR (£)	APR (£)	MAY (£)
Beginning cash position	1000	−462.50	−72.50	−170	−242	− 94
Cash out						
Option 1 Frame Mania(unframed)	150	60	90	120	150	180
Option 2 Frame Mania (framed)	150	30	60	60	60	90
Option 3 Book Mania	650	260	390	650	910	1040
Option 4 Web Mania	–	–	–	154	308	308
Marketing + Utilities	1200	200	200	200	200	200
Total cash out	2150	550	740	1184	1628	1818
Cash in						
Sales	687.50	940	642.50	1112	1776	2245.50
Total cash in	687.50	940	642.50	1112	1776	2245.50
Net change in cash	−1462.50	390	−97.50	−72	148	427
Cash at month end	−462.50	−72.50	−170	−242	−94	333

Notes:

1 Costs to suppliers paid within 14 days.
2 Sales received within 30 days (assumed following month).
3 Additional marketing expenses incurred in December for launch. Thereafter, steady outgoings based on annual rent, rates, etc.
4 Negative cash-flow to be funded from directors' funds or business overdraft (depending on competitive rates).
5 Break-even anticipated for Month 6.

> The basics of the business are presented here – but what is missing?

(Continued)

For further financial details please refer to the Appendices.

References

- ACORN, New ACORN classification map, retrieved 22 November 2007 from www.caci.co.uk/acorn/acornmap.asp
- BBC News, December 2006, Online Banking Fraud Up 8000%, retrieved 19 November 2007 from news.bbc.co.uk/1/hi/uk_politics/6177555.stm
- Giftware Association (GA), retrieved 10 November 2007 from www.ga-uk.org/
- GLA, Data Management and Analysis Group PayCheck 2008, November, available at www.london.gov.uk/gla/publications/factsandfigures/dmag-briefing-2008-33.pdf
- GLA, Data Management and Analysis Group *Londoners and the Labour Market: key facts,* September, available at www.london.gov.uk/gla/publications/factsandfigures/dmag-briefing-2008-30.pdf
- Interactive Media in Retail Group (IMRG), Online Shopping – £100 and counting, retrieved 29 November 2007 from www.imrg.org/SearchList.aspx?txt=west+end&language=en-GB
- KeyNote, Giftware – UK, August 2007
- Mintel, Gift List Services – UK, January 2007
- Mintel, Gift Shopping Habits – UK, June 2005
- Mintel, Greeting Cards – UK, April 2007
- National Statistics 2005, Marriages Decrease, retrieved 28 November 2007 from www.statistics.gov.uk/CCI/nugget.asp?ID=322&Pos=&ColRank=2&Rank=448
- Startups, Gift Shop, retrieved 29 November 2007 from www.startups.co.uk/6678842909814916402/gift-shop.html
- Unity Marketing, Gifting Report, 2007

Appendices

[not included here]

Case study
The entrepreneur versus the planner

A small business owner, Richard Rodrigues, met a corporate planner, Kevin Watkins, for a social drink. The two were old friends but, as they had not met up for some time, they were anxious to catch up on each other's news.

Kevin was still working for a large utility company, as he had been when they last met. His work was to assist the line managers in his organization to produce regular business plans which reflected corporate goals.

Richard's business, by comparison, was small and changing. He had owned a publishing company, which specialized in producing magazines for the medical profession paid for by advertising from drug companies.

'Yes, I think I was doing rather nicely in publishing when we last met', Richard commented to Kevin. 'That's all changed now of course. Generic prescribing came along and wiped out that business. Doctors have to prescribe non-branded drugs where possible now, so there's little point in the drug companies advertising their branded products to them. My publications were dependent on that advertising, so the day that generic prescribing came in, I went out – of business that is.'

'You mean you've stopped publishing altogether?' asked Kevin. 'Didn't you see it coming and move into some other form of publishing?'

'Well, I heard about it of course, as it was being talked about well before it became policy', Richard replied. 'But I didn't think it would affect me the way it did. My advertising revenue dropped by 25 per cent, which was enough to make the publication unprofitable. I had hoped I could ride the storm, but there didn't seem much point once I was losing money. If I'd had more time to develop new products, I probably could have stayed in the same business. There's still plenty of money to be made in medical publishing. But once the cash is flowing out of a business, it's like taking the plug out of a bath of water; it's hard to put it back in the hole and keep what you've got. I decided to cut my losses and do something else.'

'What did you do then?' Kevin questioned.

'I decided to do something completely different. I bought a toy company, making dolls and children's games', announced Richard. 'Want to buy it? It keeps me awake at nights with its cash flow problems.'

'No thanks. Very seasonal business, I imagine. Still you would have known that before you bought it. What's been the problem?' asked Kevin.

'You're right,' said Richard, 'I did know it was a seasonal business, but I actually did a very good deal in buying it. The price was rock bottom. I didn't even have to take out any loans. It's just that so much depends on Christmas it's impossible to plan anything. My accountant checked out the reported profits and balance sheet before I bought the business, so I knew what I was getting. And the profits are there, as the previous owner said they would be. He just forgot to tell me about the cash flow. I nearly went bankrupt in the first year waiting for Christmas.'

'Didn't your business plan predict that, or at least indicate there would be some serious troughs in your cash flow?' asked Kevin.

'Like I said, I didn't need any loans, so I didn't need a business plan. I don't have a corporate planning department like yours, you know', said Richard.

'Well I don't want to push my own profession, but I think a business plan would have told you about these troubles in advance. But then I am biased', laughed Kevin.

Richard did not seem to appreciate the joke.

'If I had to put together the sort of five-year plan you produce every time I make a decision; I'd get nowhere fast. As a matter of fact, when I found out about this toy company for sale, there was another larger organization interested. It was only by going down there the next day and making an offer on the spot that I clinched the deal. I expect your equivalent in this other company is still working on the business plans!' he retorted.

'I don't think that's fair at all', responded Kevin. 'How can you know what you're doing without some sort of plan? It doesn't have to be complicated or time-consuming. And it can show how sensitive a business is to seasonal factors or more permanent changes like your last business. You know, a business plan may have helped you there too.'

'I don't think so at all', Richard said indignantly. 'What I needed then was creativity and innovation to change my business, not the straitjacket of some plan. Anyway they are only financial forecasts – crystal ball gazing. What's the point of that when you're going bust?'

'Ok, Ok, so you don't believe in planning. How about objectives? Do you believe in setting those?' asked Kevin.

'Of course I do', said Richard, 'I just don't want to spend my time writing them down, that's all. You sound like the sales manager of my toy company. He's always sending me endless statistics of how he's doing compared to last year. I tell him to get out and see the customers. Don't worry about the targets, I can set those, and I'll tell you if you're not doing well. Just get out there and sell, that's all I ask.'

(Continued)

'Well you obviously like centralized control, at least that's something you have in common with us planners', smiled Kevin.

Activities

(a) Kevin may be right to claim that business plans could have helped Richard. In what ways do you think Richard could have benefited from a business plan in both of his businesses?

(b) Richard may be right to be sceptical about planning. What are the problems, perceived and real, in writing a business plan?

(c) Richard claims that plans 'are only financial forecasts – crystal ball gazing'. What would you want to put into a business plan to make it more meaningful in his situation? Suggest some outline headings for a business plan for Richard's toy company.

Extended activity
A bank's plan

Most high street banks offer information on business plans with a suggested outline either online or in hard copy form. Obtain a business plan from a local bank and study its content (start by using the web links below). How appropriate do you think the outline plan is for most small businesses? How would you improve on the structure for your own business plan?

- *Barclays Bank* Assistance for starting up and planning available at: www.barclays.co.uk/business/starting-a-business/
- *HSBC* www.knowledge.hsbc.co.uk/

Other helpful resources on business planning can be found at: www.smallbusiness .co.uk/channels/start-a-business/

Planning a new venture
Planning the business

Summary of what is required

- Decide the format.
- Review your approach to presenting the plan.

Decide the format

Evaluate how your business plan can be organized to answer the three fundamental questions:

- Where are we now?
- Where do we intend going?
- How do we get there?

Decide on the outline headings for your plan; that is, begin by adopting the outline format given in Section 6.5.2 Outline of a business plan; or amend it, as you feel appropriate, to your specific business opportunity.

Review your approach to presenting the plan

Look at some business plans from as many sources as you can. This will include the Case Studies in this chapter, bank templates (see the Extended activity), business plan websites (e.g. bplans.org.uk and the Microsoft Office website) and business plans of firms owned by your friends and family, if possible.

Consider the following questions carefully:

- What do you like about each of the example plans you have read? What don't you like about each of the plans you have read? To what extent is each plan 'suitable for purpose'?
- For example, if the plan was written for a new design consultancy, what did the design and layout of the business plan itself convey to you about the new venture?
- If the plan was written to seek a large amount of investment, how well had the author(s) conveyed the level of possible risk and reward?

For your own new venture, outline in the form of a bullet-point summary the main messages you wish *your* business plan to convey. For example:

- a highly innovative business
- a business which will benefit from the particular enthusiasm and dedication of the management team
- a niche business operating in a specialist area
- a lifestyle business
- a business with strong revenue growth.

In each case, justify how you will get your message across in the written business plan effectively and credibly.

6.7 Notes, references and recommended further reading

Notes and further information

1 These are adapted from Harris (1999).
2 The major banks provide outline plans for finance applicants. Downloadable business plan templates are also available – see Bplans, available at www.bplans .co.uk/. The British Venture Capital Association highlights the need to write a compelling Executive Summary. They offer excellent advice as to how to write a good plan, focusing on readability, length, appearance and 'things to avoid'. See www.bvca.co.uk

3 We are grateful to the founders of *giftsmania* for allowing this business plan to be adapted and to be included as a case study.

References

Blackburn, R.A., Hart, M. and Wainwright, T. (2013) Small business performance: Business, strategy and owner-manager characteristics, *Journal of Small Business and Enterprise Development*, 20(1): 8–27.

Blank, S. (2013) Why the lean start-up changes everything, *Harvard Business Review*, May.

Brinckmann, J., Grichnik, D. and Kapsa, D. (2010) Should entrepreneurs plan or just storm the castle? A meta-analysis on contextual factors impacting the business planning-performance relationship in small firms, *Journal of Business Venturing*, 25(1): 24–40.

Busenitz, L. W. and Barney, J. B. (1997) Differences between entrepreneurs and managers in small firms: Biases and heuristics in strategic decision-making, *Journal of Business Venturing*, 12: 9–30.

Casson, M. C. (1982) *The Entrepreneur: An Economic Theory*, Martin Robertson.

Chwolka, A. and Raith, M.G. (2012) The value of business planning before start up – A decision-theoretical perspective, *Journal of Business Venturing*, 27(3): 385–399.

Delmar, F. and Shane, S. (2003) Does business planning facilitate the development of new ventures? *Strategic Management Journal*, 24(12): 1165–1185.

Dimov, D. (2010) Nascent entrepreneurs and venture emergence: Opportunity confidence, human capital, and early planning, *Journal of Management Studies*, 47(6): 1123–1153.

Evans, P. and Wurster, T. (2000) *Blown to Bits: How the New Economics of Information Transforms Strategy*, Harvard Business School Press.

Harris, L. C. (1996) The impediments to initiating planning, *Journal of Strategic Marketing*, 4(2): 129–142.

Harris, L. C. (1999) Initiating planning: The problem of entrenched cultural values, *Long Range Planning*, 32(1): 117–126.

Hofstede, G. (1991) *Culture and Organizations*, McGraw-Hill.

Karlsson, T. and Honig, B. (2009) Judging a business by its cover: An institutional perspective on new ventures and the business plan, *Journal of Business Venturing*, 24(1): 27–45.

Kuratko, D. F. and Hodgetts, R. M. (2001) *Entrepreneurship: A Contemporary Approach*, 5th edn, Harcourt.

Mason, C. and Stark, M. (2004) What do investors look for in a business plan? A comparison of the investment criteria of bankers, venture capitalists and business angels, *International Small Business Journal*, 22(3): 227–248.

McGrath, R.G. (2000) The Parsimonious Path to Profit. In: Birley, S. and Muzyka, D. (eds) *Mastering Entrepreneurship*, Financial Times/Prentice Hall: 42–46.

Ramirez, R., Selsky, J. W. and Van der Heijden, K. (2010) *Business Planning for Turbulent Times*, Earthscan.

Robbie, M. (1986) Small Business Requests for Bank Finance: Reasons for Decline. In: Scott, M., Gibb, A., Lewis. J. and Faulkner, T. (eds) *Small Firms' Growth and Development*, Gower.

Robinson, R. and Pearce, J. (1984) Research thrust and small firm strategic planning, *Academy of Management Review*, 9(1).

Sahlman, W. A. (1997) How to write a great business plan, *Harvard Business Review*, July–August.

Storey, D. J. (1998) *Understanding the Small Business Sector*, International Thomson Business Press.

Turban, E., King, D., Lee, J. and Viehland, D. (2004) *Electronic Commerce: A Managerial Perspective*, Pearson/Prentice Hall.

Ward, J. L. (2011) *Keeping the Family Business Healthy: How to Plan for Continuing Growth, Profitability and Family Leadership*, Palgrave Macmillan.

Recommended further reading

Ashton, R. (2007) *The Entrepreneur's Book of Checklists: 1000 Tips to Start and Grow Your Business*, Prentice Hall.

Blackburn, R. A., Hart, M. and Wainwright, T. (2013) Small business performance: Business, strategy and owner-manager characteristics, *Journal of Small Business and Enterprise Development*, 20(1): 8–27.

Johnston, R. E. and Bate, J. D. (2013) *The Power of Strategy Innovation: A New Way of Linking Creativity and Strategic Planning to Discover Great Business Opportunities*, AMACOM Div American Management Association.

Mason, C. and Stark, M. (2004) What do investors look for in a business plan? A comparison of the investment criteria of bankers, venture capitalists and business angels, *International Small Business Journal*, 22(3): 227–248.

Mullins, J. W. (2003) *The New Business Road Test: What Entrepreneurs and Executives Should Do Before Writing a Business Plan*, Financial Times/Prentice Hall.

Woods, C. (2007) *From Acorns: How to Build A Brilliant Business*, Prentice Hall.

7 Successful small business strategies

Learning objectives

By the end of this chapter you will be able to:

- Understand why the strategic management process is different for entrepreneurs, small business owners and large businesses.

- Explain the concept of a business model and its key elements.

- Account for small business strategy in terms of management, marketing, money and motives – the 4 Ms.

- Assess the ingredients of a successful strategy for small, entrepreneurial enterprises.

- Appreciate the importance of learning as a key factor in successful small business strategies.

Introduction

Much advice is published on how to succeed as an entrepreneur or small business owner. There is much to be gained from listening to the practical advice of those who have experience of small enterprises. But with a low probability of sustained growth, and a high risk of closure, can the entrepreneur or small business founder adopt specific strategies to improve their chances of success?

Activity 1
What is strategy?

What do you think is meant by 'strategy' in the small business context? What would be the main ingredients of a small business strategy?

7.1 Strategy and the small business

Strategy is a word more commonly associated with large organizations but strategic decisions have been found to be just as significant to the success of small enterprises. This chapter describes some of the main considerations in formulating small business strategies, taking into account the diversity of motives of entrepreneurs and owner-managers.

7.1.1 SOME DEFINITIONS
First, we need to differentiate between related terms: strategy, objectives and policies.

- The origins of **strategy** theory are based in warfare with written texts going back as far as Sun-Tzu's *The Art of War* in 500 BC. Not surprisingly, early strategic thinking adopted a competitive rather than a cooperative stance in which one side attempted to gain advantage over the other – a win–lose approach to strategy. Business strategy has tempered this with win–win approaches that emphasize collaboration as well as competition.[1] It has its origins in the early 1960s when Igor Ansoff (1965) and others advocated extensive research and information gathering as the precursor to strategy formulation (although Ansoff later criticized what he called 'paralysis by analysis').

A strategy is now defined as the actions a company takes to achieve one or more of its goals through either a plan, pattern, ploy, perspective or position.[2] It provides the direction necessary to allocate the resources of the enterprise in a unique and viable way, which takes account of internal strengths and weaknesses, and external opportunities and threats (see Campbell *et al.*, 2011; Butler, 2012). Strategic thinking synthesizes the creativity and intuition of the entrepreneur into a vision for the future (Mintzberg, 1994) suggesting that creativity and strategy have more in common than people think (Bilton and Cummings, 2010).

Strategy brings together an enterprise's major *objectives, policies* and activities into a cohesive whole (Quinn, 1980).

- **Objectives** represent what is to be achieved (but not how). Objectives can be a broad and permanent assessment of the values to which an enterprise and its chief participants aspire (e.g. to remain independent of others; to satisfy customers while doing and enjoying what we are best at; to make a large capital gain; to promote the protection of the environment; to work in a truly democratic and fair organization). Alternatively, objectives can be more narrow and less permanent, defining specific targets (e.g. to reach a turnover of £1 million; to open three outlets; to pay off the overdraft; to take on an extra partner).
- **Policies** are rules or guidelines which define the limits within which activities should occur. Again, they can be broad (borrowings should be kept to a minimum, so that our assets are not at risk), or more specific (we will not trade on a Sunday).

7.1.2 SMALL BUSINESS AND THE STRATEGIC MANAGEMENT PROCESS
The strategic management process is the way in which managers develop strategies (Marsden and Forbes, 2003; Hatten, 2015). A key theme of this book is that small firms differ from larger firms in a number of key respects.[3] These include the centrality of the owner-manager, the formality of structure, the level of resource constraints, vulnerability to external context and change, and limited product range and market focus. As the economist, Edith Penrose (1959), famously commented:

'The differences in the administrative structure of the very small and the very large firms are so great that in many ways it is hard to see that the two species are of the same genus…. We cannot define a caterpillar and then use the same definition of a butterfly.'

These and other factors have a considerable bearing on the strategic management process in a small business. For example, the vulnerability of small businesses to their external environment can lead to an inability to deal adequately with change (see Marsden and Forbes, 2003, p. 36). The introduction of new or amended regulations, for example, can have a disproportionate effect on the fortunes of small businesses, whose limited resources cannot easily be redeployed to deal with the new procedures that must be put in place. (As a result, small business lobbying groups have consistently argued for less red tape and for a reduction in the burden of legislation on small enterprises.) This has led some commentators to argue that competitive advantage in small firms is sometimes only achieved through the accidental convergence of particularly favourable circumstances (see Jennings and Beaver, 1997). In other words, entrepreneurial success relies more on opportunistic use of changes in legislation, technology, society or the economy than long-term strategies (see Ackermann and Audretsch, 2013, for detailed discussion of small business strategy and economics). This contrasts to the more corporate view that competitive advantage can be created deliberately through adopting realistic long-term objectives and plans based on thorough research into market trends. The logic that the strategic management process in small businesses is more about adapting to the uncertainties of the environment than proactively predicting, planning and controlling it, is not, however, backed up by much research evidence. Just as there are many different types of small business, so it would seem, there are a variety of modes of entrepreneurial strategic decision-making (see Sarasvathy, 2001; 2004; 2009; Read and Sarasvathy, 2005).

Activity 2
Emergent strategies

Strategy sometimes emerges as a pattern of activity, not deliberately conceived in advance. Can you give some examples where this may happen in small business? Consider also how these emergent strategies might then be converted into intended strategies. In general, how deliberate are the strategies of entrepreneurs?

7.1.3 ENTREPRENEURSHIP AND THE STRATEGIC MANAGEMENT PROCESS

Entrepreneurs actively take opportunities to implement new ideas (see Chapter 2). They are more about *doing, enacting* and *realizing* than simply planning and controlling. There is clearly a tension between being alert to opportunities and holding a vision of what is to be achieved and how this will be accomplished. Strategies can be deliberate, consciously intended courses of action. They can also emerge as a pattern with no advance deliberation. Realized entrepreneurial strategies are invariably a mixture of both.

Deliberate strategy

Strategy may be formulated as a deliberate plan of stated, or unstated, intentions. Some entrepreneurs produce a business plan before start-up which sets out their intended course of action (see Chapter 6). Others do not formally document a plan, but intentions are thought through in advance in a deliberate and purposeful way.

Emergent strategy

Some strategies are not conceived in advance but emerge as a consistent pattern during the course of events. Examples of strategies that emerge as patterns, before conversion to deliberate strategies, include:

- *Marketing approaches* that are on a reactive basis until a pattern emerges. For example, an entrepreneurial firm had no deliberate strategy about the size of its customer base. But one customer liked their products so much that they ordered more and more. There was no time to find other customers, as this one demanded so much attention. A strategy of concentrating 80 per cent of production capacity on one customer emerged. After a while, the owner realized the dangers in this and deliberately decided to follow a strategy of broadening the customer base.

- *Management of people* strategies that emerge as unplanned reactions to factors previously unknown. For example, a small business retailer employed mainly part-time staff, as they found that the best applicants for advertised vacancies were invariably those only able to work on a part-time basis. When this pattern was recognized, the owner consciously adopted a policy of seeking part-time staff.

- *Financial strategies* are sometimes difficult to plan deliberately, except in the short to medium term. For example, a small manufacturer did not intend a strategy of long-term bank borrowing. But when the entrepreneur reviewed the bank statements over a two-year period, the overdraft never fell below £30 000. A pattern of borrowing had emerged, and the bank manager advised recognition of this strategy by converting the fixed element of the overdraft into a 10-year loan. Patterns that emerge from an entrepreneur's activities become strategies, even though they are not formally designed that way.

Realized strategy

In practice, even the most carefully planned strategy is not fully implemented; there will be an emergent aspect to it. Emergent strategies, once spotted for what they are, often become subject to some form of planning. Strategies are therefore usually a mixture of deliberate and emergent approaches. Small businesses, whether or not they are entrepreneurial, will exist somewhere on the continuum between very planned, deliberate strategies to frequently unplanned, unstructured approaches. Where exactly they fit will depend on the personality of the founder and the nature of the objectives of the business. An ambitious entrepreneur, who believes in the detailed planning of every move, might operate at the deliberate end of the spectrum. At the other extreme, there may be the classic opportunist whose strategies emerge as the business environment fluctuates.

Strategy and control and value paradoxes

It would seem that successful entrepreneurship requires a management touch that can reconcile both intended and emergent strategies. A useful way of expressing this balanced approach is in the strategic management of organizational control paradoxes and value paradoxes (see Figure 7.1).

Every organization (whether newly formed or long-established) must find its own perspective with regard to these contrasting standpoints. In terms of the control paradox, Thurbin[4] contrasts the 'task perspective' with the 'exploration perspective'. If the small business veers too much towards the 'task perspective', for example, we might expect to see overly oppressive control mechanisms in place which will reduce responsiveness and flexibility. Business development in a small consultancy firm, for example, may become overly constrained if marketing and sales methods are too prescriptive (i.e. the means become more important than the ends). If, on the other hand, the enterprise is overly explorative, there is the danger of losing focus and straying from the entrepreneur's core vision. Similarly, with the value paradox, the perspective that supports management conventions stands in contrast to that which seeks opportunity and change. In this case, an organization that

Figure 7.1 Strategic management of control and value paradoxes

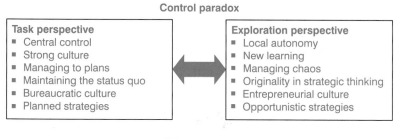

Control paradox

Task perspective
- Central control
- Strong culture
- Managing to plans
- Maintaining the status quo
- Bureaucratic culture
- Planned strategies

Exploration perspective
- Local autonomy
- New learning
- Managing chaos
- Originality in strategic thinking
- Entrepreneurial culture
- Opportunistic strategies

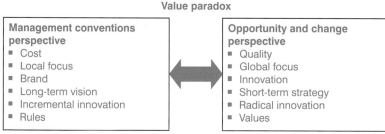

Value paradox

Management conventions perspective
- Cost
- Local focus
- Brand
- Long-term vision
- Incremental innovation
- Rules

Opportunity and change perspective
- Quality
- Global focus
- Innovation
- Short-term strategy
- Radical innovation
- Values

overly focused on management conventions would tend towards risk-averse behaviour, unwilling to take decisions where there is a high level of uncertainty and ambiguity. This can be contrasted with an organization from the opportunity and change perspective that is prone to risk taking.

While the archetypal entrepreneurial organization would demonstrate a preference for the exploration and opportunity and change perspectives, there is always a balance to be struck. The successful entrepreneurial strategy also takes account of other perspectives.

Activity 3
Seeing ahead

James Murray Wells was 22 when he set up his company in his parents' front room. It all started when his eyesight started changing and he realized he needed some reading glasses. On visiting his local optician, he was astonished to find the prescribed glasses would cost £150. As a student, this was not what he considered to be an affordable loss. It was, after all, about half his monthly rent. James was prompted to do some research and he discovered that his £150 glasses cost only about £7 to make. He realized he could make the glasses for a fraction of the price charged by the high-street retailers (who collectively held a 70 per cent share of the market). He set about learning how to carry out optometric testing and cutting lenses. Within the first year of setting up his new business, Glasses Direct had sold over 22 000 pairs.[5]

(a) What factors influenced James' decision to set up a glasses business?
(b) When James realized he could produce glasses more cheaply, what did he do next?
(c) If you were in James' position, what resources would you call upon to help you set up your own glasses business? Also, what would you do to acquire the resources you don't already have at your disposal?

7.2 New venture strategy

7.2.1 STRATEGIC CHALLENGES

Modern entrepreneurship is more of a collaborative than combative process in which working with others and networking is a key strategy (see Chapter 2). The need for *both* competition and cooperation is particularly clear for SMEs pursuing technological innovation (see Gnyawali and Park, 2009). Starting up new ventures of any kind brings particular challenges, not least of which is to overcome what has been termed the **liability of newness** (Stinchcombe, 1965) or establishing credibility in the business context. This can be difficult, especially for young entrepreneurs who do not have a previous track record in business. However, entrepreneurs overcome conventional attitudes to untried individuals and 'pursue opportunities without regard to the resources they currently control' (Stevenson and Jarillo, 1990, p. 23).

Entrepreneurs also face another significant problem when starting up a new venture: an acute shortage of resources. This forces the founder to exploit a particular strategy which has been termed **asset parsimony**. The so-called 'parsimonious path to profit' can be categorized in the following way (McGrath, 2000, p. 44):

- Never buy new what can be bought second-hand.
- Never buy what can be rented.
- Never rent what can be borrowed.
- Never borrow what can be begged.
- Never beg what can be salvaged.

The founder of the now successful Cobra Beer company, Karan Bilimoria, provides an interesting example of this principle in practice.[6] Karan and his business partner lost their would-be distributor in the very early days of their business, so ended up piling 15 cases of Cobra in the back of their 2CV and going cold-calling on Indian restaurants, grocers and off-licences. Cobra's vision was 'to aspire and achieve … against all odds'.

7.2.2 OPPORTUNITY RECOGNITION

In Chapter 3, it was noted that the birth rate of small businesses varies according to when they are set up. An opportunity 'has the qualities of being attractive, durable and timely and is anchored in a product or service, which creates or adds value for its buyer or end user' (Timmons and Spinelli, 2003, p. 82). In other words, an opportunity needs to be grabbed at exactly the right moment, neither ahead of its time nor behind it.

This can make deliberate, proactive strategic decision-making difficult. Where the window of opportunity is, only open for a brief period (perhaps following redundancy or a management takeover) there may simply not be enough time to undertake planning in any formal sense. Where this is the case, how does the entrepreneur ensure that the opportunity will create or add value? As we saw in Chapter 2, the entrepreneur's self-belief, grounded on previous experience and knowledge, becomes of key relevance. Shane highlights this aspect of the entrepreneurial new venture strategy in his description of the entrepreneurial opportunity as 'a situation in which a person can create a new means-ends framework for recombining resources that the entrepreneur *believes* will yield a profit' (Shane, 2003, p. 18). A successful new venture strategy not only reconciles deliberate and emergent themes, but also manages the tension between what is *known* through empirical evidence and what is *believed* to be true on the basis of gut instinct.

A model of the opportunity recognition process (Lumpkin, Hills and Schrader, 2004), based on a five-stage model of creativity[7] helps to explain how this tension is managed. Opportunity recognition is not limited to one 'Aha!' experience, but can be understood as an iterative process through which fresh insights are contemplated, new information is sifted and knowledge created over time (see Lumpkin and Lichtenstein, 2005).

New venture strategy is, first and foremost, an emergent activity even if it requires deliberate planning activities along the way.

7.2.3 EFFECTUATION THEORY AND THE ENTREPRENEURIAL DECISION-MAKING PROCESS

In considering an opportunity, the entrepreneur has to evaluate new markets, new enterprises and new products or services before any of these might actually exist. This makes the decision-making process difficult.

The 'normal' way that we make a decision is based on causal thinking where we begin by specifying the goal to be achieved or decision to be made, identify a set of alternative ways of achieving our goal, take into account possible constraints, and implement selection criteria for choosing between the options. However, for an entrepreneur, when the goals cannot be specified exactly before the event, a different type of thinking process is required. Sarasvathy (2001) has put forward **effectuation theory** for explaining how entrepreneurs take decisions in the context of uncertainty and ambiguity. In contrast to the traditional causal approach to decision-making outlined above, effectuation involves the following steps (Sarasvathy, 2001, p. 250):

- The decision-making process begins with the entrepreneur recognizing a given set of *means* (i.e. ways of doing things given the current resources, people and ideas to hand).
- In turn, these means can give rise to a set of *effects* or outcomes (e.g. a new market, firm, type of service or product range).
- These means are themselves constrained (and enabled) by wider aspects of the environment (e.g. market conditions, demographics, politics and culture).
- The entrepreneur makes a decision concerning the chosen effect based on the level of **affordable loss** or acceptable risk that the entrepreneur is prepared to incur.

The logic of effectuation is more than a theory of how entrepreneurs make decisions. It also directs us to four behavioural aspects of the entrepreneurship process which underpin the entrepreneur's activities (Sarasvathy, 2001, p. 252; see also Chandler *et al.*, 2011; Perry *et al.*, 2012; Fisher, 2012; and Berends *et al.*, 2014, for more discussion of effectuation in both theory and practice.):

1 The entrepreneur's behaviour is directed by affordable loss, rather than expected returns.
2 The entrepreneur seeks to form strategic alliances, rather than competitive analyses.
3 The entrepreneur relies on the exploitation of contingencies (i.e. the unexpected event or lucky accident), rather than the exploitation of pre-existing knowledge.
4 The entrepreneur seeks to control an unpredictable future, rather than predict an uncertain one.

It is important for the entrepreneur to rely on their own ideas, networks and resources in the first instance, as these will impact on their ability to generate innovative outcomes. An effectual process can be used, beginning by asking 'Who do I know?' and leading on to 'What can I do?' Interacting with people you know or meet and obtaining stakeholder commitments can create new means which expand the cycle of resources or new goals that can create new firms and markets.

To demonstrate the distinction between causal and effectuation thinking, imagine you have volunteered to cook a celebratory dinner for a friend's birthday. Following the principles of causation, you could decide to find out your friend's favourite meal (spaghetti bolognese) and set about cooking that. Your day would probably include checking to see what ingredients you already

(Continued)

have in the kitchen cupboard (e.g. spaghetti, garlic, tomatoes) and then making a trip to the supermarket to buy what else you need (e.g. tinned tomatoes, mince, Worcestershire sauce, red wine). If, on the other hand, you were following the principles of effectuation, you would start from the premise that you are going to make a birthday meal from what you already have in the kitchen cupboard (e.g. spaghetti, garlic, tomatoes, bacon, chilli, white wine). This time the outcome of your cooking is something different (spaghetti amatriciana).

7.2.4 COMPETITIVE ADVANTAGE OR PROFITABILITY?

Central to this discussion of new venture strategy is the objective of creating or adding value for the buyer or end-user (see Chapter 14, for a more detailed discussion of how 'value' is realized in the small business context). For most large firms, the driving force of their business strategy is also to provide value to shareholders. This is often held to be achieved through a management focus on those activities that contribute to a firm's relative cost position and potential for differentiation, or what is otherwise termed **competitive advantage** (see Porter, 1985, p. 33).

Where the main shareholder is the founder or entrepreneur, there are not the same pressures or constraints on business performance. Sometimes, there is no direct competitor to achieve an advantage over if an innovative product or service is being developed. Competitive advantage is not necessarily the key objective of small, entrepreneurial businesses. The primary goal may be to achieve viability and profitability – or, more simply, to survive (Ackroyd, 2002).

7.3 The business model

7.3.1 DEFINITIONS OF A 'BUSINESS MODEL'

In order to create a new venture, entrepreneurs have to make decisions first about the opportunity: what is the problem to be solved and which product or service offers the best solution? Once they have defined the opportunity, the entrepreneurs' next task is to work out if it can become a viable enterprise: can it generate sufficient revenue to support the operation that will be needed to offer the product or service? Many good opportunities fail at this second hurdle because they do not follow a viable 'business model'.

The concept of the business model first came to public awareness during the 'dot-com bubble' of 1997–2001. Over-investment by speculators in new internet companies that had unsound business models led to a financial crash when the bubble burst. Many of the new breed of online companies failed spectacularly despite fulfilling what seemed like a real need. For example, Pets.com was launched in 1998 to sell products for pets over the internet and went public on NASDAQ amid much publicity in 2000. It was liquidated only nine months later. What went wrong? The concept was sound; there are several successful pet suppliers based on the internet today including pet-supermarket.co.uk and petsmart.com. Pets.com made the mistake of over-estimating the speed at which they could convert pet owners to online shopping. Their business model was to drive customers to their website through extensive marketing campaigns and service the demand that this created through a dedicated infrastructure of giant warehouses and sophisticated processes. To work, the model required a critical mass of customers prepared to spend the necessary £200 million for the company to break even. Pet owners proved to be conservative in their shopping habits and only switched slowly to online shopping – far too slowly for Pets.com to pay its bills.

Business models are notoriously difficult for online companies to get right. Set up as a liberating service available free of charge to all, the internet has only slowly adapted to the realities of the marketplace in which payment is made for services rendered. Many internet services have been offered free of charge until a critical mass of followers can be 'monetized' through either advertising, paying for premium services or subscriptions. Some, such as Facebook, have evolved into profitable organizations; others, such as Dropbox, are still making the transition through a 'freemium' revenue model. Many others, like Pets.com, will find their business model does not deliver a viable business.

Although much of the analytical discussion of business models relates to web-based businesses, this has served to highlight the importance of the concept to enterprises in general (Hedman and Kalling, 2003). All enterprises have an explicit or implicit business model, including social and public enterprises. The following two definitions explain the concept succinctly:

> 'A business model describes the rationale of how an organization creates, delivers, and captures value.' (Osterwalder and Pigneur, 2010, p. 14)

> The 'essence of a business model is in defining the manner by which the enterprise delivers value to customers, entices customers to pay for value, and converts those payments to profit'. (Teece, 2010, p. 172)

The meaning of 'value' in this context is determined by the context. To the managers of the organization, 'value' is measured in terms of the extent to which revenues generated from customers meet or exceed the costs of running the business. However, to other stakeholder groups 'value' means more than just revenue streams. To a customer, value means the benefits of buying the product in relation to its costs: the 'value proposition'. To the owners, it is measured in terms of the value of their shares in the company. To employees, value is a function of remuneration, job security and satisfaction. To the network of players in the industry, including suppliers, collaborators and competitors, value is considered in the context of changes to the 'value chain' as goods and services are passed along the links between producer and end-user, or the 'value-web' of interconnected enterprises in creative industries or professional services.

In this way, a business model integrates various concepts and activities into a holistic overview of what makes the business tick and how it survives in a competitive marketplace. It is the 'story' which explains how the enterprise works, how it brings together customers and products, and how it harnesses technology and resources to deliver those products to the market in a financially viable way (see Amit and Zott, 2001; Chesbrough and Rosenbloom, 2002; Morris *et al.*, 2005; Baden-Fuller and Morgan, 2010).

ADELE FASHIONS

Adele is a Johannesburg-based fashion entrepreneur. She has worked in the industry for 25 years, and has extensive knowledge of the industry (designers and producers) and the market (retailers and end consumers). She sells women's fashion ranges to retail chains in South Africa. To create these ranges, she examines trends in the European fashion market, and produces ranges of clothing based on these trends, but adapted for the South African

(Continued)

market. Her business model uses her knowledge, experience and contacts to draw together resources from around the world to produce her clothing range. Her value chain consists of out-sourced labour in London, South Africa and China in the following sequence of events:

- A consultant in London identifies trends that they think are important in the mainstream retail market and buys samples which show off these trends. Photographs of these samples are emailed to Adele for consideration. The samples she thinks will work best in South Africa are then couriered to her;
- a designer in South Africa produces designs which are based on the trends in London, but tailored to South African habits, climate and price range;
- Adele shows the designs to her retail contacts and agrees a price and volume;
- a manufacturer in China produces the goods to Adele's specification and ships directly to the retailer;
- the retailer sells the clothing under their brand name, handling all promotion and display of the product.

Adele creates value by identifying international fashion design trends that can be adapted to suit needs in South Africa quickly and cheaply. Designs based on the latest trends in London can appear in South Africa for the next season, making her service particularly attractive to retailers. She employs sub-contractors on a job-by-job basis, keeping her costs and risks low, and enabling other entrepreneurs to develop businesses of their own to support hers.

Source: Mador, M. in Stokes, Wilson and Mador (2010)

7.3.2 ELEMENTS OF BUSINESS MODELS

A business model is made up key components that explain how products or services are linked to markets and customers in a sustainable manner, as shown in Figure 7.2.

Business models explain the interactions between these components, and how they work together to create value. To maximize value in an enterprise, the entrepreneur works out what drives revenue streams, how to optimize the cost structure of the operations, and how well products or services fit into the market and access routes to customers.

In mature businesses, these components operate together more smoothly, subject only to fine-tuning. But during the formation of an enterprise, they are not fixed and often have to be substantially modified and adapted according to feedback from the development of one of the other components. For example, as knowledge is gleaned about how much the customer is prepared to pay for the product or service, revenue streams can be estimated in relation to the likely cost structure of the business. This, in turn, determines the level of sophistication of the internal processes of the operations and the affordability of factors that impact on product development such as R&D and IP protection. (Such activities are dealt with in detail in Part III, 'Managing the entrepreneurial small business'.) Collectively, they form a crucial aspect of a successful small business strategy and therefore need to be defined and tested as part of a new venture creation process.

Successful and innovative business models have the capacity to change industries. Prompted by the development of the internet, a wide range of business models has emerged, some of them highly innovative.[8]

EBAY – THE ANCIENT ART OF THE AUCTION ONLINE

One of the most successful of web-based enterprises has been eBay. Founded in 1995 in the USA, it has auction sites based in dozens of countries. Although auctions have been around for thousands of years, eBay has re-invented the traditional format thanks to some of the unique characteristics of the internet, and to some innovative approaches which it pioneered.

The business model is to provide an online platform where buyers and sellers can engage in commerce. eBay charges sellers a listing fee and a small percentage of their income from each transaction; it charges them to use Skype and for payment processing through Paypal; it also sells advertising within the site. The business model relies on high usage levels being generated by several factors:

- a robust and trustworthy technology platform;
- an efficient, transparent and well-policed commercial system;
- universal availability within the national markets where the company has launched;
- a relatively low transaction cost for buyers and sellers;
- a genuine need for a marketplace existing.

These factors attract high volumes of traffic from both buyers and sellers, which are necessary to generate high revenues from what are often very small financial transactions.

The appeal of the commercial platform to both buyers and sellers has created new entrepreneurial opportunities, with sellers using it to set up shops, rather than simply auctioning a few items now and then. The company estimates there are more than 200 000 businesses that trade through eBay in the UK, in addition to millions of private sellers, with an estimated £6 billion of sales each year.

This is a new industry of small traders able to start a shop and access a large potential customer base with minimal capital outlay.

Figure 7.2 Components of a new venture business model

Components of a new venture business model				
Products/ services	**Operations**	**Fit into the market**	**Routes to market**	**Customers**
What is the product or service offering? What research and development activities are needed to create a viable product/service? How do we protect our idea? What regulations do we need to comply with?	What is needed to make the business function? Which internal processes enable: (a) customers to acquire the product/ service? (b) control of cash and profits? Which external networks will help the business to function?	What are the key features of the product/service? What problem does it solve? What are the key benefits created? How do they meet customer needs? What will make us different from competitors?	How do we communicate with customers and consumers? How do they access our products/ services in the market? What is the supply chain or web? What other enterprises are involved?	Who are the customers (who pay) and the consumers (who use)? How do they get value from the product/service offering? How big is the market? What are the relevant trends?

Cost structure What are the key cost elements of the venture? What are the fixed costs that don't change? What are the costs that vary with sales volume? What grants/sources of finance are available?	**Revenue streams** Who will pay? What will they pay for? How much do I need to sell to cover my basic costs?

Source: Stokes D., and Mador, M., Kingston University Enterprise, adapted from Osterwalder and Pigneur (2010).

Activity 4
Cause of death

In Chapter 3, we saw that closure rates among small firms are extremely high (Section 3.3.1).
What do you think are the principal internal causes of small business failure? Try to classify some specific reasons into more general strategic categories.

7.4 Survival strategy

7.4.1 CRITICAL FACTORS IN THE CLOSURE OF YOUNG BUSINESSES

Many new ventures are launched without a viable business model and fail; others face problems in their formative years that result in their closure. What do they do wrong? In order to learn from past mistakes, it is instructive to look at the evidence from the common causes of closure.

The Office of the Official Receiver in the UK lists the following causes of business failures:

- insufficient turnover
- poor management and supervision
- lack of proper accounting
- competition
- not enough capital
- bad debts
- excessive remuneration to the owners.

These factors can be further broken down according to whether they operate externally to the business or whether they exist within it:

- *External influences.* Macroeconomic conditions such as interest rates and overall levels of consumer demand, and micro-environmental factors in the local catchment area or industry sector such as the intensity of competition, are important influences on whether a new venture sinks or swims (see Chapter 3, Section 3.1, A matter of life and death). The small business environment varies from being hostile to relatively benign, dependent on the time period, geographic area and market sector in which the new venture operates. Due to the vulnerability of very young and very small firms, much depends on the owner-manager's ability to adapt to the surrounding changing circumstances (Section 3.3.2, Adjusting to uncertainty).
- *Internal factors.* The personal attributes, skills and competencies of the individual owner-manager are crucial to how well the business faces up to the inevitable crises that arise. Which particular internal issues should the owner-manager be prepared to face? The list could be very long, but researchers have attempted to identify those areas that are particularly important, as some seem more critical to survival than others.
- One study (Watkins, 1982) analyzed events which particularly threatened the survival of small ventures. The percentages of small businesses studied experienced crises in:
  - marketing (38.1 per cent)
  - finance (32.2 per cent)
  - managerial (14.3 per cent)

- personnel (13.0 per cent)
- 'acts of God' (10.4 per cent)
- no crises (18 per cent).

- A *review* of around 50 articles and five books on the subject of small business failure and bankruptcy (Berryman, 1983) revealed six major categories of failure: accounting, marketing, finance problems, the behaviour of the owner, other endogenous (internal) factors and exogenous (external) factors.

- A study of surviving small firms concluded that 'small, young organizations experience problems particularly in the areas of accounting and finance, marketing and the management of people' (Cromie, 1991).

- *Researchers* in Britain and Europe (Watkins and Morton, 1982) asked financial institutions lending to small manufacturing industries to rank their perceptions of the major threats to the survival of small firms. Their reasons were:

United Kingdom	1	Availability of finance
	2	Management capability of owner
	3	Marketing problems
West Germany	1	Availability of finance
	2	Management capability of owner
	3	Marketing problems
France	1	Management capability of owner
	2	Availability of finance
	3	Difficulty in complying with new laws and regulations.

- The judgment of individual investors in small business, or so-called business angels, is interesting in that it indicates what they have discovered to be critical factors which make a venture more likely to succeed or fail. The principal reasons given by business angels for not investing are (Harris, 1993):
  - lack of relevant experience of the entrepreneur and any associates
  - deficiencies in marketing
  - flawed, incomplete or unrealistic financial projections.

7.4.2 MANAGEMENT, MARKETING AND MONEY

From this analysis, there seems to be some consensus over the areas critical to a small enterprise's chances of survival which are controllable to some extent by the owner-manager.

Management (of resources, especially people)

The competence of the owner-manager is the ultimate determinant of survival or failure. In the early days, the founder's personal competence in selecting a viable business model and operating it will be crucial, as the firm is likely to be indistinguishable from the owner. As the business develops, growth can be prematurely curtailed by an unwillingness or inability to draw others in to help with the management of the enterprise. Management of people is particularly important as it includes not only the personnel issues of dealing with employees, but also of managing people outside the organization who are also critical to its success, such as key customers, suppliers, banks and investors.

Marketing

To have a good chance of survival, a small firm needs to answer the basic strategic question: what customers are we targeting, with what products? A common weakness in owner-managers lies in their failure to understand key marketing issues. Product and service concepts and standards often reflect only the perceptions of

Figure 7.3 Key influences in small firms for survival – the '3 Ms'

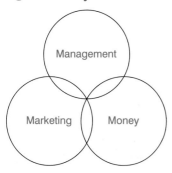

the owner, which may not be mirrored in the marketplace. Minor fluctuations in markets can topple a newly established small firm, particularly where it is reliant on a small number of customers.

Money

Financial difficulties of small firms arise either because of an inability to raise sufficient funds to capitalize the business properly, or a mismanagement of the funds that do exist (or a combination of both). Access to external funds may be difficult to achieve for the new, or young, small business with no track record, especially for owners without personal assets to offer as security. Venture capital may be inappropriate for very small enterprises. Many new owner-managers, having received funds, misuse them; small businesses have been notorious for their lack of proper financial controls and information.

While these factors do not represent a formula for a successful small business strategy, they can be used to describe the basic influences on a small business strategy in relation to the objective of survival within the controllable environment of a small firm as: management, marketing and money.

These are illustrated in Figure 7.3 as the '3 Ms'.

These influences are shown as overlapping, as clearly they do not work in isolation.

- *Management* is concerned with the efficient and effective use of resources by the enterprise, in order that it can meet its objectives. Money is one of the resources for management to use, or misuse. Marketing decisions are a crucial aspect of management.
- *Marketing* represents the relationship of the enterprise with those customers it seeks to serve. It will determine how much money flows into an enterprise via sales to customers. It will also dictate the kinds and quantities of resources that management will need to satisfy the demand it has stimulated.
- *Money* enables the whole system to work. It enables management to purchase the resources it requires; it enables marketing activities to take place.

7.4.3. STRATEGIES BEYOND SURVIVAL

Beyond survival, strategies will depend on the objectives of the enterprise. However, the quality of management and marketing and the quantity of money remain as key influences on the ability of the small firm to meet its objectives, whatever these happen to be. New strategies will need to build on, rather than detract from, these primary influences. The motives of the owner-manager(s) are therefore a fourth influence to be added to the existing three.

As we have already noted, unlike large companies where objectives arise from the influences of a variety of stakeholders, small enterprise strategy is driven by a more easily identifiable source, often one person. This additional force in any development of strategy beyond survival is shown in Figure 7.4 – the '4 Ms'.

Figure 7.4 Key influences in small firm strategies beyond survival – the '4 Ms'

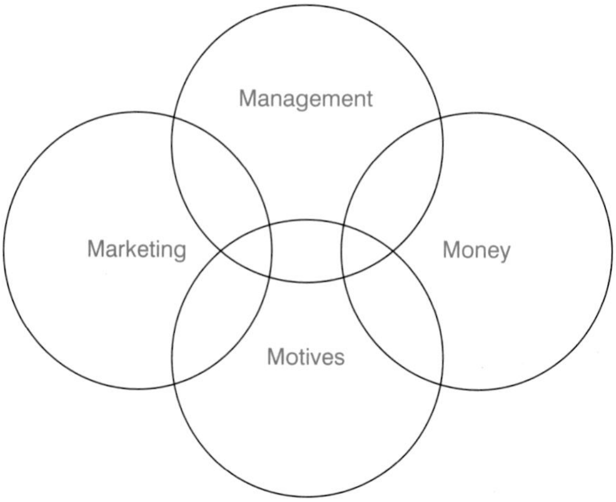

Again, the influences overlap to represent the impact they can have on each other.
For example:

- *Motives* can point to one strategy which is thwarted by money or marketing considerations. An owner may be motivated to run a business which is completely environmentally friendly, only to find that money does not permit this policy to be fully implemented. A restaurant owner may have personal motives to provide only vegetarian food, but finds that the marketplace does not support this strategy.
- *Management* considerations may indicate a strategy which is thwarted by the motives of the owner. An appropriate management structure for a growing business may never be implemented by an owner motivated by a strong desire for personal control.
- *Marketing* strategies may run counter to motives. An owner's desire to run what they perceive as a completely ethical business may prohibit certain sales approaches. Despite evidence of strong local demand, and competitive advantage, a trader may refuse to open on Sunday for personal reasons.
- *Money* influences may be diminished by personal motives. A desire to retain certain friendships may prevent rigorous pursuit of debtors. An owner with motives to promote their standing in the community may turn down the cheapest deal in favour of the local supplier.

Activity 5
Large or small?

Musician Sheila Holdsworth founded her online bra shop for smaller-busted ladies (www.knowknockers.co.uk) in 2004, as a part-time concern. She got the idea initially after listening to a radio interview with the founder of Ample Bosom, and thought that a similar idea, only for ladies with smaller busts, may be just what many women, like herself, needed.

In large businesses, growth of sales and profits is a common strategic goal, but this is not always the case in small business. Why not? What other strategic objectives might a small business have?

How would the strategies of a business with less ambitious growth plans be different to a business with high-growth plans?

7.5 Growth strategy

7.5.1 SUCCESS EQUALS GROWTH?

It is often assumed then that, to be truly successful, a small firm must manage the transition into a larger company. Small business is, after all, the seed corn for tomorrow's larger enterprises; many of our industrial giants will disappear to be replaced by today's fast-growing small firms. Success is inextricably linked to growth. The small business owner who achieves rapid growth to enter the large business category is seen in a heroic light. Examples of successful entrepreneurs are drawn from the likes of James Dyson, Richard Branson and Anita Roddick, who had humble origins in small business, but who moved on to bigger things. An analysis of successful small business strategies often starts with a large company and its founders, then works backwards to see how they got there.

Less attention is given to the owner-manager who has thrived in business, yet remained small (Curran, 1998). There are countless people who deliberately start up their own 'lifestyle' businesses with no intention of ever taking on extra staff and going for growth.

This poses an interesting conundrum for policy-makers as high-growth firms are vital to the economy, providing most employment prospects: over 50 per cent of the new jobs created by small businesses are provided by the fastest-growing 4 per cent of firms (Storey, 1998). We also know that the most vulnerable businesses are the smallest, so it is a good survival strategy to grow larger. There is, therefore, a sound logic at both macro and micro levels in encouraging new ventures to grow as this helps build a strong economy and optimize the chances of success for individual owners.

7.5.2 THE SIZE DISTRIBUTION OF FIRMS IN THE ECONOMY

The vast majority of businesses do not grow beyond their classification as a small firm. Only a few grow to become medium-sized, and even fewer grow into the new, large companies of the future. Larger firms in the UK economy account for a very small percentage of the total number of enterprises. As we saw earlier (see Chapter 1, Table 1.3), about 98 per cent of UK businesses fall into the EC 'small' category of fewer than 50 employees, and about 89 per cent are 'micro' enterprises of fewer than 10 employees.

If the size distribution of firms is visualized as a pyramid, the base is extremely broad and the apex very narrow. If success means climbing from the bottom to the top, then it is rare indeed.

7.5.3 MODELS OF GROWTH STAGES

This view of small business success or failure has been refined into various models of the growth stages of a small business. The initial model, on which most others have been based, is Greiner's (1972) model of *evolution and revolution,* which he developed in the early 1970s. A central feature of his model is that movement between stages is precipitated by some kind of crisis. For example, the first stage (which Greiner labels 'growth through creativity') leads to a 'crisis of leadership' which, through resolution, signals the start of the next stage, 'growth through direction'. Greiner's model is made up of five stages, and most subsequent models[9] are also based on this number. A composite model with five stages is illustrated in Figure 7.5.

- *Stage 1: Concept/test stage* The new business idea is conceived and planned. Full-scale operations may be preceded by detailed planning and testing in the marketplace. In some cases, the business is run as a part-time operation, before the owner places complete dependence on it.
- *Stage 2: Development/abort stage* The small business begins operation and is developed to viability, or it is aborted at an early stage. This stage is typified as the individual entrepreneur or owner-manager launching a new enterprise largely through their own efforts.

Figure 7.5 A model of the growth or decline of a small business

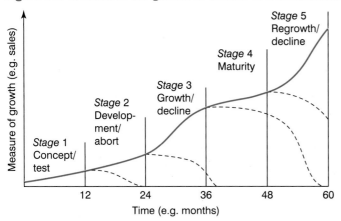

Some analyses indicate crucial periods when a small business will survive or fail. One such period is illustrated as the first 18–24 months, when a new enterprise will pass through the critical phase of start-up and grow to a viable size, or it will not develop satisfactorily and suffer an early exit. Business survival statistics[10] confirm this high level of early closures, with only approximately 60 per cent of enterprises surviving the first two years (see Chapter 3, Table 3.6).

- *Stage 3: Growth/decline stage* The third crucial stage is sometimes shown as occurring between the second and third years of operation. The growth that can occur at this time places organizational strains on the enterprise. The one-person entrepreneurial management style is inadequate to sustain growth fully. A division of managerial tasks, the recruitment of non-owner-managers and the development of a functionally organized team are seen as prerequisites to take the business through this phase, without which it will struggle and often close.
- *Stage 4: Maturity* A further stage looks at the business maturing, and going through a period of stability, when growth flattens. The small firm loses its simple structure of centralized decision-making, and becomes more sophisticated in its control systems and more bureaucratic in its procedures. In other words, it takes on some of the characteristics of a larger organization.
- *Stage 5: Regrowth/decline* The identification of a further stage, sometimes referred to as the S-curve hypothesis, suggests that once a small business has established itself in the marketplace, with a demonstrable competitive advantage, profits or external investment will follow to further exploit this early success. This will trigger a second period of high growth. Without this second surge of growth, the lack of impetus in the maturity phase can turn into stagnation and decline, as competition intensifies.

Implicit in this and other stage models of firm growth is the fact that different strategies and skills are required at different stages of a firm's life. Setting up a new business is not the same managerial task as running an existing, fast-growing one. The problems and issues seem to crop up in the same strategic areas, however. For example, Drucker (1985) puts forward four requirements for the successful development of a new venture:

1 Focus on the market;
2 Financial foresight, especially planning cash needs in advance of growth;
3 Building a top management team before it is required;
4 Careful definition of the founder's role in the enterprise.

His analysis assumes that growth is the motive force, and illustrates how the significance of marketing, money and the management of people shifts according to the stages of growth of an enterprise:

- *Marketing:* the need for a market orientation is paramount while a new firm is establishing itself. Lack of market focus is a problem typical of the very young business; failure comes quickly if there is insufficient demand, or inadequate stimulation of it.
- *Money:* inappropriate financial policies are the greatest threat to a new enterprise in the next phase of its growth. Here, the focus has to be particularly on cash, not profits, as the growing firm outstrips its capital base. The business will need to change its financial structure and improve mechanisms for controlling money if it is to move smoothly into the next phase of its development.
- *Management:* once it is established in the marketplace, and has developed the necessary financial structure and controls, the young enterprise faces a further barrier before it can progress into adulthood. By this stage, the business is too big to be managed by its founder(s) alone. It needs a management team. But a team does not form overnight; it has to be built in advance to function fully when it is needed – a brave move for a growing business with limited resources.

A corollary of the emergence of a management team is that the founder(s) then has to redefine their own role in the light of the changed circumstances. It may be that their style is not flexible enough to fit in with a broader spread of control. The only remedy may be their departure from a top executive position to an advisory role. This does seem to be the fate of many successful entrepreneurs who successfully get things going, but then find themselves increasingly sidelined by other stakeholders in the growing firm (e.g. Anita Roddick or Stelios Haji-Ioannou). These strategies for the high-growth new venture are illustrated in Figure 7.6.

While these models of the various growth stages of successful small enterprises are descriptive of how some businesses develop, they overlook the statistical evidence that most small businesses do not grow into larger organizations at all. It is true that many do close; but others simply establish themselves and survive as small businesses, without becoming larger companies in either size or organizational structure.

It is also important to follow the fate of the owners as well as the businesses. There is an assumption that most owners that close down their business have been unsuccessful. But many owners do not see it that way. In a study by the Small Business Research Centre of Kingston University (Stokes and Blackburn, 2001), owners

Figure 7.6 Phased influences in growth strategies

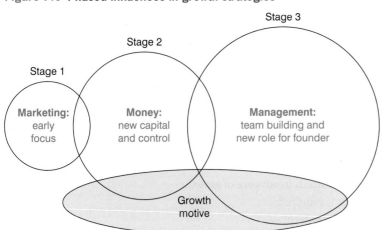

were asked to rate their success as a manager of a business that closed. Over half (54 per cent) rated themselves as successful with only 14 per cent describing themselves as unsuccessful. As a further indication of the confidence of these owners, the majority tended to remain involved in running a business. The study classified owners that had closed a business into three broad categories:

1 *Departing* (30 per cent) – owners who returned to employment, or became unemployed or out of work through ill health.
2 *Retiring* (10 per cent) – owners retiring from active involvement, having sold or closed their business.
3 *Returning* (60 per cent) – those who continued as business owners by opening or buying a new or similar business to the one closed, or through the existing ownership of another business (sometimes referred to as serial entrepreneurs).

This indicates that only a minority of owners can be described as truly departing when a business closes down, as most still wish to run their own business and are soon returning to business ownership (see Chapter 14, for a more detailed discussion on business closures). A model of the experiences of business owners would resemble more of a roller coaster ride with many peaks and troughs, rather than the neat curve of the life-cycle model of a business as shown in Figure 7.5. The crucial role of the entrepreneur/owner-manager means that success or failure of a small business can only be judged in relation to the motives and objectives of that individual, rather than any standard measure of business performance.

7.5.4 UNDERSTANDING OBJECTIVES

The general purpose of the management of any enterprise has been defined as the achievement of the organization's objectives and a continuous improvement in its performance.[11] Successful management is thus directly linked to the objectives of the organization. If the objectives of a business include high rates of growth, then this is clearly a yardstick against which success of the management can be judged. If, however, continuous strong growth is not necessarily one of the aims of an enterprise, then success has to be measured in other ways.

As many small businesses are the psychological extension of the owner-manager or entrepreneur, their personal motives and objectives will be crucial in assessing success or failure. Research has cast considerable doubt on whether growth is the common goal driving the small business owner forward. A survey of owner-managed businesses concluded that, for owner-managers, growth is only one of a number of desirable objectives and is less important than survival and staying independent (DoE, 1990). Another study reported that more than 30 per cent of owners wanted their small firms to stay at their present size (Small Business Research Trust, 1991). This echoes earlier work done at the time of the Bolton Report which suggested that many owners paid lip service to the ideal of growth, being primarily motivated by the need to preserve independence, which too much growth might threaten.[12]

Clearly, the motives of entrepreneurs and owner-managers for entering into the world of small business will vary, giving rise to different objectives for their business. Attempts have been made to classify entrepreneurs in terms of their personal values, in order to distinguish between some of the more obvious types, and their possible objectives (see Chapter 2, Entrepreneurship, the entrepreneur and the owner-manager).

The so-called social action view sees the small firm as a social grouping in which the attitude to growth is determined by the participant's social background, identity and desires.[13] Passive owner-managers, who look upon growth as a necessary evil to ensure survival, will not primarily be motivated by the prospect of high profits. They will be more concerned with the intrinsic satisfaction of the job itself (*the artisan*), or by the business's ability to deliver an acceptable lifestyle, without having to compete in the rat-race of employment in larger organizations (*the isolationist*). At the other end of the spectrum are those who conform to the capitalist model of a profit-seeking opportunist (*the classical entrepreneur*), which may involve attachment to the marketplace (*the marketeer*), or a specific product or process (*the technocentric*). Others may place emphasis on recognition from others, with security for themselves and their heirs (*the manager*), making them less likely to take the risks of high growth, while being dissatisfied with minimal growth.

Perhaps the only common motive that can be attributed to owner-managers and entrepreneurs with such differing backgrounds and desires is the survival of the business itself for a sufficiently long period to deliver the objectives sought.

7.5.5 THE ENTREPRENEUR, THE FIRM AND STRATEGY

Explaining small business performance and growth cannot be undertaken without considering a range of important contributory factors together as an integrated whole (see Wiklund *et al.*, 2009). In a review of the evidence on small business growth, Storey (1998) developed a framework of the characteristics of high-growth small firms involving three essential components:

- the starting resources of the entrepreneur
- the firm
- strategy.

The entrepreneur

The success of a business is very dependent on the characteristics of the entrepreneur, but it is difficult to isolate attributes which are more significant than others, (as we have seen in Chapter 2, Entrepreneurship, the entrepreneur and the owner-manager). Storey suggests four entrepreneurial elements which are likely to be important influences on high growth:

- *Motives.* Those 'pushed' into a small business through unemployment, or other causes, are less likely to establish high-growth firms than those 'pulled' by the attraction of a market opportunity.
- *Education and experience.* Higher levels of education and prior managerial experience help.
- *Age.* Middle-aged founders are more likely to combine the energy and experience requirements for growth.
- *Numbers.* Businesses owned by several people, rather than one individual, are more likely to have the range of skills required to cope with growth.

Other possible influences such as prior self-employment, prior business failure, gender, family history and social marginality were found to be less strong.

The firm

The characteristics of the firm itself also have an influence:

- *Age.* Younger firms grow more rapidly than older ones. A new business needs to grow rapidly to achieve a viable size.
- *Size.* Smaller firms tend to grow more rapidly than larger ones. As with age, there is pressure on small firms to reach their minimum viable size, or 'minimum efficiency scale' (MES) as quickly as possible.
- *Legal form.* Limited companies experience more rapid growth than sole traders or partnerships.
- *Location.* As small firms tend to trade in localized markets, location can be a significant influence on growth.

- *Sector.* The overall growth rate of the market or industrial sector in which the firm operates influences its development.

Strategy

Once the firm is in business, the strategic actions and decisions taken by the entrepreneur/owner-manager are what counts. The strategy-making process involves planning, analysis, decision-making and many aspects of an organization's value system, culture and mission (Hart, 1992). Many researchers have focused attention on the kind of strategy-making process, or **entrepreneurial orientation**, that provides organizations with a basis for entrepreneurial decisions and actions (Lumpkin and Dess, 1996; Wiklund and Shepherd, 2003; Wiklund *et al.*, 2009; Rauch *et al.*, 2009).

As we have seen, for small businesses the objective of growth is important, though not universal. Four strategy areas which particularly influence growth are:

- *External equity.* Growing businesses are more likely to have obtained external funds from outside individuals or organizations.
- *Market positioning.* High-growth firms tend to occupy deliberately chosen market niches where they can exploit innovations and any technological sophistication they might have.
- *Innovation.* New product or service introductions are key to small firm growth.
- Growth is restricted if *non-owning managers* are not brought in. The selection, motivation and retention of a management team is important to increase the capabilities of the business.

Internationalization

This has become an increasingly important aspect of small business strategies. This is most readily associated with exporting activities which are undertaken by fewer than 10 per cent of SMEs across Europe (European Commission, 2007, p. 5). However, over the last decade or so, internationalization has become a much more differentiated business activity which is seen as a crucial strategy for achieving competitiveness. Internationalization now includes practices such as foreign partnerships and investments, cross-border clustering and any activity that facilitates the exchange of knowledge and technology between small and medium-sized firms (and sometimes large firms, too). The most common form of internationalization is, in fact, not exporting, but the use of foreign supply relationships (used by 30 per cent of all SMEs across Europe).[14] Underlying these kinds of relationships is, on the one hand, the availability of cheaper labour and associated production costs, but also the need to increase knowledge and gain know-how in key areas of developing technology, on the other. Collaboration and cooperation are therefore key strategic approaches for many forward-looking and externally focused small businesses that see increased turnover, lean production and business growth as core objectives.

Activity 7
Successful small business strategy

How would you define a successful small business strategy? What do you think are the critical factors for successfully undertaking the strategic management process in a small business?

7.6 A composite model of successful strategies

7.6.1 SUCCESSFUL SMALL BUSINESS STRATEGIES

We have so far discussed the various influences on the likelihood of, first, the survival of a new venture and, second, its growth into a larger enterprise. These have been divided into external and internal influences, and into factors that particularly affect high-growth firms. As growth is one of the key factors in survival, many of the influences on survival are similar to those that are important for high-growth firms. A composite model of these influences is summarized in Figure 7.7.

Section 3.5, Critical survival factors, summarized the initial external factors listed in this model. Section 2.6, The 'model' entrepreneur, analyzed the building blocks of successful entrepreneurship that make up the critical internal factors. This chapter has added the important ingredient of motives. Together, these factors influence the likelihood of success or failure interdependently. For example, the importance of internal factors such as management competencies varies according to the sector in which the firm is set up, just as the decision regarding in which sector to start a new venture is influenced by personal factors and previous experience.

Figure 7.7 Critical factors in small business strategies

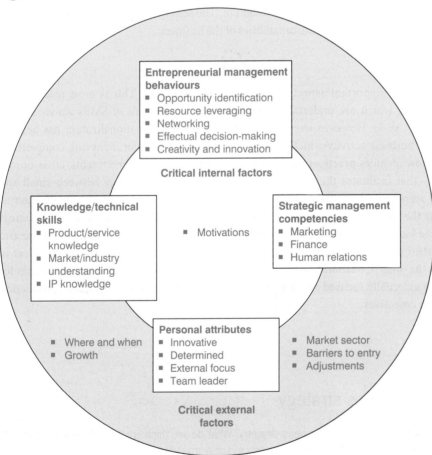

Few entrepreneurs develop a business in which all these factors are favourably disposed. If a complete set of favourable influences is not attainable, which are the most significant ones to get right? Research into successful small firms provides some guidance: evidence from several studies[16] suggests that the success of a small firm depends more upon the policies it adopts than the buoyancy of the markets in which it operates. External influences are less important than individual factors, particularly the management behaviours and competencies and the personal attributes to cope with the small business environment.

Some individuals succeed as entrepreneurs when the odds seem stacked against them, while others fail when the conditions for success are relatively good.

7.6.2 LEARNING AND STRATEGY

Making adjustments to existing strategies is an important part of small business survival and growth (see Section 3.3.2, Adjusting to uncertainty, and Section 7.1.3 in this chapter). The ability of the entrepreneur or owner-manager to learn from any problems or mistakes and rapidly to adjust their business accordingly is key to success. An important corollary to this is the importance of understanding which strategies can be adjusted quickly and which decisions, once taken, have longer-term impact.

For example, a retailer had two strategic decisions to make when opening a second branch to their original shop. The first decision was where to locate the new shop. The second was what to stock in it. The first decision is likely to be more critical than the second, as it is much harder to adjust or change if required. A shop lease may be hard to pass on, and can still remain a liability many years after the premises have been sub-let to someone else. While the stock available for sale is a crucial marketing decision, the owner-manager may have more flexibility in their decision-making, especially if they can obtain sale-or-return terms from suppliers and move stock between shops.

Regardless of the specific motivation of those involved in the setting up and subsequent development of a small business, a successful small business strategy needs to remain flexible and responsive to change. Flexibility is, in fact, a **core competence** for small business competitiveness. The ability of a firm to use both its personnel and material resources in flexible combinations to produce productive outputs is what lies at the heart of the so-called **resource-based view of the firm**.[17] As the firm grows, the entrepreneur or owner-manager will need to retain their responsiveness to the changing environment. Thus, firms need to acquire 'dynamic capabilities' or 'the ability to integrate, build and reconfigure internal and external competences to address rapidly changing environments' (see Teece, Pisano and Shuen, 1999, p. 88; Augier and Teece, 2009). In order to succeed, the small business must be prepared not only to take what might be seen as traditional actions, such as lowering costs and losing any unnecessary overheads, but also to introduce innovative actions which may involve the production of new or improved products and ever higher levels of customer service. These innovations are likely to be supported by the application of new technology, perhaps requiring the implementation of electronic commerce. This, of course, highlights once again the central importance of learning at the level of both the individual and the organization.

7.7 Summary and activities

Although the concept of strategy is more often associated with larger, fully developed businesses, it is of central importance throughout the business life cycle. The entrepreneur requires a new venture strategy that identifies a viable business model before the business can successfully move from conceptualization of an opportunity to a fully working enterprise. The strategy and business model are open to change and adaptation especially during the new venture creation phase and kept under review as the business grows, even to the point of exit. Entrepreneurs often adopt effectual thinking to deal with the uncertainty of their surroundings. Effectuation occurs when the entrepreneur seeks to control what happens in the future rather than predict future uncertainty by focusing on the means (i.e. resources, ideas, people, contingencies), rather than the ends (i.e. new markets, firms, services or products).

The different parts of the business life cycle bring different challenges for the small business owner and entrepreneur. While the nascent entrepreneur is faced with overcoming the liability of newness and possible resource constraints, the growing small business will need to acquire dynamic capabilities that allow it to adapt to change, rather than become a victim of its own success. The chapter introduces various models or frameworks for explaining small business growth.

While there can be no prescriptive small business strategy that will be successful in every context, it is possible to identify the basic influences on a small business strategy, within the controllable environment of a small firm, as *management, marketing* and *money* – the '3 Ms'. Beyond survival, a fourth 'M' – *motives* of the owner-manager – is a key factor in the strategy of the firm.

Ultimately, however, the ability of small businesses to meet the challenges they face is dependent upon reconciling deliberate and emergent aspects of the strategic management process, and ensuring that strategy is aligned with the personal and business motivations of the founders (whether this includes business growth or not). In a changing environmental context, this requires constant learning at individual and organization levels.

Case study
Circumspect strategies: Part 1

The first three years

In Part I, Chapters 1 to 5, the case studies followed the progress of Kit Hugos as he went through the process of testing the feasibility of his business ideas.
After investigating the markets more thoroughly through primary and secondary research, he discovered that another company, PS (Personal Safety) was already developing a similar product for universities and children's play areas. PS's expertise was in the software to track tagging devices. Kit Hugos and partner Robin Davidson were specialists in the miniaturization of electronic circuits and devices, and a natural partner for PS. Discussions took place, resulting in an order for Kit Hugos's new company, Circumspect, to design, develop and manufacture the electronic circuit which would be at the heart of the personal tagging transmitter to be worn. PS thus became Kit's first customer, which allowed him to invest in a design and manufacturing facility knowing that he had some business to cover initial overheads. He gradually extended the customer base over the next few years to include companies with other applications for their specialist expertise. Circumspect became a customized designer and manufacturer of specialized electronic circuitry sold to companies with applications particularly in security and communications. Military products featured heavily in the order book in the first three years.

The next five years

It took him the first three years after start-up to grow to a viable size of around £400 000 sales, with some element of profitability. This was too long for his partner Robin Davidson. Impatient with the lack of growth, he sold Kit some of his shares and became very much a non-executive director.

Then in the fourth year sales levelled off, caused, as Kit discovered, by some fundamental changes in the marketplace around him. Kit's timely investigation into the marketplace provided him with the clues to refocus his business. His initial orders had come from industries dependent on military expenditure. Determined to reduce his reliance on this vulnerable sector, he turned his attention to developing commercial-sector customers, where his technology base might be in demand. He found them in the automotive industry, which was rapidly expanding the number of electronic components in domestic and commercial vehicles.

'Whereas yesterday a car might have had 30 per cent of its equipment containing electronic components, today it is 70 per cent and tomorrow it will be 95 per cent. Even engines are going electric', one manufacturer had told him.

Focusing on this particular opportunity required extra money to buy new equipment for his factory, and, as it turned out, to finance a new surge in growth of his business as well. His market strategy paid off, as sales climbed to over £500 000 by the end of his fifth year. Unfortunately, he then almost ran out of money. The growth put increasing strains on his financial resources and systems. Debtors grew as a percentage of sales, and up-to-date, reliable accounting information was very hard to find. It took Kit some time to re-establish control of his cash flow, and put in some systems to cope with a business that was no longer very small.

With a full order book, Kit was content to spend most of the sixth year working on the efficiency of his company – first the financial aspects, and then the operating systems. Quality control was something he found particularly in need of attention, as customers were becoming more and more demanding in that area. He had little time for marketing, but sales stayed buoyant, rising to over £600 000 by the end of year six.

The improvements made meant that when he did turn his attention once again to sales in year seven, he could seek out new customers with increased confidence that he could provide an excellent service. The trouble was that the time between arousing a customer's interest and receiving and fulfilling orders was a long one in his business of electronic design. The amount of time he had spent internally and not externally began to show through in the seventh year, when his order book had a distinctly thin look about it. Shipments flattened off, and annual sales showed no real increase over the prior year. He redoubled his marketing efforts, spending long hours travelling to see customers.

After a year in which turnover had levelled off, and his business had a definite mature look about it, sales began to grow healthily in year eight. It was at this stage that Kit sat down to review where he was going. He talked to an old friend about it one day.

'The trouble is', Kit explained, 'that I seem to stagger from one extreme to the other. Every year is crucial for different reasons. When will I have a normal business that is not in some kind of crisis?'

'What exactly has been the pattern of these crises?' asked the friend.

'Stop-start-stop-start would be the best way to describe it', replied Kit. 'The order book looks thin, so I spend my time out selling. I fill up my order book, then the supervisor in the factory yells that she can't cope unless I spend time with her, to sort out production schedules and the ordering of components. Then my accountant tells me that debtors are a bit high, and I should spend some time chasing money. So I take time out to sort out these problems. What happens? You've guessed it. The order book weakens, and I have to dash off and drum up some more business. I'm not sure if I can cope with this up and down existence much longer.'

'Have you thought of getting anyone else in to help, at a senior level I mean?', suggested the friend.

'Sure, I'd love to, but the business can't afford two of us right now. A good man at director level is going to cost the company between at least £50 000 and £60 000. That's all the profit we make right now. I need to grow the business by another £200 000 in sales to afford high-level management. But I'm not sure I can do it on my own.'

(Continued)

Activities

(a) Map out the stages which Circumspect has been through so far. Try to draw this as a life-cycle graph indicating the key category of problem(s) experienced in each stage.

(b) What strategies has Kit adopted at each stage to overcome the problems?

(c) What is the principal category of problem that faces Kit right now? What do you think he should do about it? Outline the strategy you would recommend that he adopt, with some specific activities.

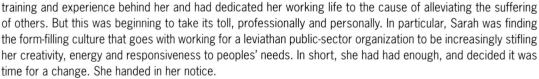

Case study
Going by the book? Part 1

The opening page

At the age of 36, Sarah Mandrake was a successful occupational therapist working in a management role in south London. She had many years of training and experience behind her and had dedicated her working life to the cause of alleviating the suffering of others. But this was beginning to take its toll, professionally and personally. In particular, Sarah was finding the form-filling culture that goes with working for a leviathan public-sector organization to be increasingly stifling her creativity, energy and responsiveness to peoples' needs. In short, she had had enough, and decided it was time for a change. She handed in her notice.

At first, Sarah felt a mixture of relief and a feeling that a heavy weight had been lifted from her shoulders. It wasn't long, of course, before the focus of her thinking centred on what she should do next. Years of training and emotional commitment in this vocational field could not simply be wiped away and replaced by something else. She needed time to take stock. But there were still bills to be paid. She had always loved burying herself in a good read, and she was sure that she could find a local job in a bookshop which involved sensible hours and, most importantly, very little responsibility. The following Saturday morning she went down her local high street and went in to the bookshop, enquiring as to whether they needed any additional staff. 'No, thanks!', said the manager, politely. This wasn't the response that Sarah had rehearsed in her mind. However, she persevered and, by lunchtime, Sarah had secured herself a new job working for Michael French's bookshop.

For the next six months, Sarah worked Tuesdays to Saturdays and earned enough to keep both her and her companion – a West Highland terrier called Maisie – fed and watered. Then the bookshop's general manager suddenly left. With Christmas sales looming, Sarah was asked if she'd take on the vacant position. It was an offer she couldn't refuse. By now, the lure of increased responsibility (and some extra money) was becoming quite attractive once again.

Things carried on, relatively incident-free (bar the annual launch of the latest Harry Potter novel), for the next three years or so. Each successive year, the bookshop increased its turnover under Sarah's management. Yet, once again, she found her energies and enthusiasm drained by other people's decisions. Michael French kept a firm control on budgets and stock-keeping. He was also beginning to take a more active role in dealing with the customers. Sarah had reached another crossroads.

This time, the stakes were much higher. She wanted to set up a bookshop of her own. This wouldn't be 'just another bookshop', however, but one that did things differently. She had a clear vision both of how she would create value for her customers, and what needed to be done to bring this about. The first time she actually said this to her family, however, she couldn't quite believe what she was saying. Reading books was one thing, running your own business based on a 'novel' business idea was quite another. Where should she set it up? Where would the money come from? What would happen if it all went wrong? A million and one questions buzzed around her head. They all boiled down to the same question, however – how was she going to make it work? She must have a strategy. But how do you just set up your own bookshop? She would have to find a suitable one to buy.

Just as before, Sarah realized that the only way to make things happen was to instigate them herself. She had heard on the grapevine that a bookshop was for sale in a small town in Norfolk – near to where she had grown up. As many of her friends still lived and worked in this area, she was drawn to relocate there. So, while she was up staying with her mother, she drove off to scout out this shop and see whether it was worth taking it further. It wasn't. As she drove back she thought about what 'might have been'. But then she passed another bookshop in another town that seemed to have everything going for it. Unfortunately, it was closed. Undeterred, she made a note of its name and address. When she got back home a few days later, she got on to the internet, found a contact email and composed a message. 'I would love to own my own bookshop in this part of the world. Would there be any chance you might be thinking of selling up soon?' Even to Sarah, this looked rather opportunistic. But then, she had nothing to lose. She pressed 'send', and thought no more about it; until the reply came: 'Thanks for your message. We are retiring later this year, and were thinking about what to do with the shop ... can we meet to discuss?'

One thing led to another. Sarah met with the owners. It was a great little bookshop, and seemed to have a good future ahead of it. There was just one problem. By their own admission, the previous owners had 'cooked the books'. They explained to Sarah, off the record, that an expensive car and other tax-deductible expenses had been run through the accounts. It was no wonder, therefore, that when Sarah's accountant came to check on the records he advised her that it was not a viable concern. 'I can't advise you to go ahead with this purchase', he said.

Sarah was faced with a dilemma. Should she listen to her head or to her heart? Looking back at where she had come from and looking forward to her years ahead, it was clear to her at least what she needed to do. Sarah Mandrake made her decision.

Activities

(a) To what extent would you consider Sarah's approach so far to be (a) deliberate, or (b) emergent?
(b) What do you think Sarah did next?
(c) What would you have done, and why?

Case study
Circumspect strategies: Part 2

End of a decade

Kit Hugos was celebrating 10 years in business with his bank manager.

'It's quite an achievement to survive a decade in your own business. Most small businesses don't make it this far. How does it feel?' asked the bank manager.

'Oh, I obviously feel very pleased to have survived. But right now I also feel quite sad. It's rather like watching one of your own children grow up, knowing that one day they have to leave you', replied Kit.

(Continued)

'Surely you're not retiring?' asked the bank manager.

'No, not exactly', explained Kit, 'but I have to change something. Young managers these days don't seem to have the same approach as our generation. Take my operations director; he's just decided to give all the shop floor workers Friday afternoon off from 3 p.m. He says that it's modern working practice, but I'd like to know how he's going to make up the lost time, and hit his production targets.

'Oh and talking of targets, my new accountant is target-mad! We joke that if anything moves, she gives it a budget, but it's almost true. Everything we do is allocated somewhere and costed against targets. It can be useful, but it's made the whole place so bureaucratic, forms for everything', complained Kit.

'You don't have to tell me about forms', said the bank manager, 'but doesn't the business need this type of organization now?'

'Well it didn't before I hired all these managers. I sometimes think they are just making a job for themselves. Now they want to bring in consultants to introduce total quality management. Why we need an outsider to come in and teach us the latest jargon I'm not sure', said Kit. 'I'm beginning to think I've got the wrong team. These MBAs don't seem very practical people for a small business.'

'You're not so small any more', commented the bank manager. 'Your turnover has certainly jumped up since you enlarged your management team. What do you think it will be this year?'

'Well we might even make £2.5 million. I suppose this is my biggest problem. We're selling more than ever, and growing by 30–40 per cent per annum, but I'm not getting any benefits personally. There's no more cash for me to pay myself, and I'm not getting the same satisfaction from my work. I feel they resent my interference except in technical matters where they're always asking for help. What do you think I should do?' Kit asked.

'Well, 48 is a bit young for retirement', joked the bank manager. 'Ever thought of selling the business?'

'My accountant tells me to wait a few more years. Although we've grown fast, the profits will not materialize for a while. We've grown the overhead very quickly and it can cope with quite a lot more volume. Just at the moment though our ratios wouldn't look too good in any sale prospectus', answered Kit.

'I'm going to have to put up with them, or put them out, I can't decide which.'

Activities

(a) Why do you think Kit is facing the problems he describes?

(b) What do you think Kit should do about his problems? If you were Kit what questions would you be asking yourself?

Case study
Going by the book? Part 2

The plot thickens

Sarah made her decision and bought the business. As a lifestyle venture, it ticked all the boxes. She had been desperate to make a move, and now she was going to live the rural idyll. Sarah devoted herself to launching the new shop. In some ways, she had never worked so hard – ordering new stock, new furniture and fittings, ensuring the shop was advertised well in the local magazines and business press and, of course, being there all day, every day, for her customers. It all took enormous effort. But the rewards gradually started to roll in. Income in the first year of trading wasn't nearly as bad as the accountant had warned. Christmas in her own home with a view over the Norfolk fields was unforgettable and made everything feel worth it. Incremental improvements followed and second-year trading surpassed expectation, reaching £120 000 by early December. Then came the global economic recession.

To some extent, the profitable years of trading masked the bigger picture. The book trade was facing substantial pressures on many sides. For the small independent retailer, the online giant Amazon had become a ferocious competitor. Sarah, and many independent bookshop owners like her, just couldn't compete with the scale and scope, to say nothing of the fast delivery options that Amazon offered. When Sarah's local books distributor started to hit difficult times, she found herself turning to Amazon to deliver key stock. Amazon wasn't the only competition, however. It was gruelling to see the prices for books offered by some supermarkets – so much so that when Sarah ran out of stock for the latest Harry Potter book launch, she found it cheaper to nip over to the supermarket and buy some extra copies than ordering more wholesale.

Sarah had had no holiday for three years now and money was becoming tight. She sat down to review her long-term options:

- Attempt to penetrate the local market further by better marketing and advertising.
- Re-focus attention on children's books, creating a niche in that area for the local market.
- Diversify her product offerings, adding gifts, more cards and stationery.
- Stretch the features offered in her book shop (perhaps by offering coffee for browsing readers, or exploring online ordering options).
- Supplement her bookshop income through other means (perhaps by taking on some online research job which could be worked on in 'quiet' times).

Sarah knew she needed to act, but just wasn't sure which of these options was the best to take right now. Looking round for inspiration her eyes came across the business section under 'reference'. She took out a book about *Small Business Management & Entrepreneurship,* and started to read about 'entrepreneurial strategy'.

Activities

(a) Compare and contrast the business model of Amazon to that of an independent retailer like Sarah.
(b) Outline possible strategies an independent retailer could adopt to survive alongside Amazon's successful model.
(c) If you were Sarah, which of these possible strategies would you opt for and why?
(d) How would you keep the possible risks involved in implementing your chosen strategy to a minimum?

C onsider a successful business which has had high growth in recent years. This may be one with which you are personally familiar, or a well-known large company that has grown from small roots in recent times (such as The Body Shop, Virgin, or easyJet, if you have been following their fortunes).

How would you summarize its overall business strategy? Try to do this by reference to the '4 Ms' of management, marketing, money and motives (or objectives of the business).

Which of its strategies would you say were intended, and which have emerged as a pattern of activities over some time?

Extended activity
A strategic case study

Summary of what is required

- Confirm personal motives for entry into a small enterprise.
- Set general objectives.
- Set specific objectives.
- Define policy.
- Draw up a timetable of key activities.
- Outline your business model.

Planning a new venture
Preparing the strategy

Completion of this step should answer the question: where do we want to be in the short and long term? It is setting out the strategic direction and parameters of the enterprise in a *deliberate* way, while allowing for the *emergent* nature of the strategic management process, as you will remain open to new ideas and influences throughout planning a new venture.

Confirm personal motives

The first step is to re-examine personal motives for entry into a small enterprise. You will have distinctive motives and expectations. Now is the time to confirm what these are, as they will be crucial in determining the strategies and objectives of the business. To check your self-analysis, and the fit with the opportunity as you have defined it, go back to the sections under the heading Planning a new venture in Chapter 2 (Know yourself: personal requirements and qualities for success), Chapter 3 (Identifying the new venture need or problem) and Chapter 4 (Identifying the solution).

Are these personal motivations still valid?

Are there new or additional factors which you should now consider before translating these into business objectives?

Set general objectives

What are the general objectives of the enterprise? General, in this context, means broad in scope and timespan. For example, general objectives could specify overall economic goals (e.g. to achieve sales in excess of £1 million and profits of £100 000), industry goals (to develop a particular process), lifestyle goals (e.g. to provide a satisfying and democratic place of work), environmental goals (e.g. to produce products which are environmentally safe), market goals (to achieve market leadership in a given segment) and so on.

Clearly, these general objectives of the enterprise will be strongly linked to your personal motives as an individual.

The general objectives are:

1 _____
2 _____
3 _____
4 _____

Set specific objectives

What are the specific objectives of the enterprise? Specific means narrow in scope and timespan. For example, specific objectives could detail sales and profit targets for years 1, 2 and 3. They could quantify the number of outlets to be opened by year, the number of employees or partners by which an enterprise grows each year, the size of the customer base, the number of new accounts to be opened in each year, the percentage market share targeted by year, the number of new products and other quantifiable goals.

The specific objectives will build into the general objectives set earlier.

Specific objectives are:

1 _____

2 _____

3 _____

4 _____

5 _____

6 _____

Define policy

What will be the policies of your enterprise? What general rules or guidelines will you set for yourself? For example, will you have money policies (e.g. to be risk averse, to extend no credit, to carry 90 days' stock, to borrow only against the assets of the business, to lease equipment rather than purchase it outright)?

Will you have management policies (e.g. to employ only young/experienced/part-time staff, to pay sales-people commission only, to allocate responsibilities between partners in a predetermined way, to operate a shift system, to pay staff bonuses)?

Will you have marketing policies (e.g. not to quote on the basis of price alone, or never be knowingly underbid, to maintain a specific product mix, to spend a fixed percentage of sales revenue on advertising, to use agents on commission, and not employ salespeople, to sell direct to consumers, to distribute via wholesalers)?

Financial policies include:

1 _____

2 _____

3 _____

Management policies include:

1 _____

2 _____

3 _____

Marketing policies include:

1 _____

2 _____

3 _____

Outline the business model

Give outline answers to the questions posed in the table below: Components of a new venture business model.

(Continued)

Components of a new venture business model

Products/ services	Operations	Fit into the market	Routes to market	Customers
What is the product or service offering? What research and development activities are needed to create a viable product/service? How do we protect our idea? What regulations do we need to comply with?	What is needed to make the business function? Which internal processes enable: (a) customers to acquire the product/ service? (b) control of cash and profits? Which external networks will help the business to function?	What are the key features of the product/service? What problem does it solve? What are the key benefits created? How do they meet customer needs? What will make us different from competitors?	How do we communicate with customers and consumers? How do they access our products/ services in the market? What is the supply chain or web? What other enterprises are involved?	Who are the customers (who pay) and the consumers (who use)? How do they get value from the product/service offering? How big is the market? What are the relevant trends?

Cost structure	Revenue streams
What are the key cost elements of the venture? What are the fixed costs that don't change? What are the costs that vary with sales volume? What grants/sources of finance are available?	Who will pay? What will they pay for? How much do I need to sell to cover my basic costs?

Draw up a timetable of key activities

The final step in setting the parameters of strategy is to timetable some activities. What are the key stages that need to be followed in setting up this enterprise, in what order and by when?

What is the target opening date?

What has to happen before this and when (e.g. negotiation of finance, registration of company, acquisition of premises/equipment/staff, training of staff)?

What has to happen immediately after this and when (e.g. marketing campaign, production initiation, further training, targeted first order, delivery and invoice date)?

Timetable of key activities

Date/Month	Activity
_____	_____
_____	_____
_____	_____
_____	_____
_____	_____

7.8 Notes, references and further reading

Notes and further information

1   It has increasingly been recognized that the competitiveness of small firms is influenced by the extent of inter-firm collaboration – see, for example, Rosenfeld, S. A. (1996) and Gnyawali, D. R. and Park, B.-J. (2009).

2   See Mintzberg, H., Ahlstrand, B. and Lampel, J. (1998) *Strategy Safari*, Pearson Education, for a discussion of different schools of strategic thought – including the design, planning, positioning, entrepreneurial, cognitive, learning, political, cultural, environmental and configurational perspectives.

3   See Penrose, E. T. (1959) *The Theory of the Growth of the Firm*, Blackwell; Jennings, P. and Beaver, G. (1997) The Performance and Competitive Advantage of Small Firms: A Management Perspective, *International Small Business Journal*, 15(1): 66–75; and Smallbone, D. and Wyer, P. (2000) Growth and Development in the Small Firm. In: Carter, S. and Jones-Evans, D. (eds) *Enterprise and Small Business: Principles, Practices and Policies*, Financial Times/Prentice Hall.

4   Thurbin, P. (1998) *The Influential Strategist*, Financial Times/Pitman Publishing. See especially pp. 225–241.

5   See www.cobrabeer.com/ for the history of Cobra's business development.

6   Csikszentmihalyi's 'stages of creativity' model (1996) includes the stages (1) preparation; (2) incubation; (3) insight, which form the discovery phase; (4) evaluation; and (5) elaboration, which constitute the formation phase.

7   Further details of Glasses Direct can be found at their website: www.glassesdirect.co.uk/about/story/

8   Professor Michael Rappa of the University of North Carolina, USA, runs a website www.digitalenterprise .org, which is a particularly useful resource in discussing business models. He provides a list of business models on the web, and continually updates the list as new models are developed. However, the models he discusses are equally likely to be available in the physical world.

9   See, for example, Scott, M. and Bruce, R. (1987) Five Stages of Growth in Small Business, *Long Range Planning*, 20(3). This describes the stages as: inception, survival, growth, expansion, maturity. They also suggest that crisis points fall before the next stage of development. See also Churchill, N. C. and Lewis, V. L. (1983) The Five Stages of Small Business Growth, *Harvard Business Review*, May–June: 30–50.

10   See Chapter 3, The Small Business and Entrepreneurial Environment, Section 3.3.1, Small Business Closure Rates, which reviewed some statistics on small business longevity.

11   According to the Management Charter Initiative (MCI), the key purpose of management is to achieve the organization's objectives and continuously monitor its objectives. *Occupational Standards*, MCI, The National Forum for Management Education and Development, 1991.

12   See especially Golby, C. W. and Johns, C. (1971) Attitudes and Motivation, *Committee of Inquiry on Small Firms*, Research Report No. 7, HMSO.

13   Identities of artisan, classical entrepreneur and manager described here are from Stanworth, J. and Curran, J. (1986) Growth and the Firm. In: Curran, J., Stanworth, J. and Watkins, D. (eds) *The Survival of the Small Firm, 2*, Gower. Identities of technocentric, marketeer and isolationist, are from Goss, D. (1991) *Small Business and Society*, Routledge.

14   See European Commission, (2003) *Internationalisation of SMEs, 2003*, Observatory of European SMEs, No. 4.

15   See Crawford, M. and DiBenedetto, A. (2006, pp. 112–16), for more details.

16   See Hall, G. (1995) *Surviving and Prospering in the Small Firm Sector*, Routledge. From his own research and a review of other studies, this author concluded that 'internal efficiency would appear more important than the general state of the environment'.

17   See, for example, Grant, R. M. (1999) The Resource-Based Theory of Competitive Advantage: Implications for Strategy Formulation. In: Zack, M. H. (ed.) *Knowledge and Strategy*, Butterworth-Heinemann.

References

Ackermann, S. J. and Audretsch, D. B. (2013) *The Economics of Small Firms: A European Challenge*, Springer Science & Media.

Ackroyd, S. (2002) *The Organization of Business*, Oxford University Press.

Amit, R., Zott, C. (2001) Value creation in e-business, *Strategic Management Journal*, 22(6–7): 493–520.

Ansoff, H. I. (1965) *Corporate Strategy: An Analytic Approach to Business Policy for Growth and Expansion*, McGraw-Hill.

Augier, M. and Teece, D. J. (2009) Dynamic capabilities and the role of managers in business strategy and economic performance, *Organization Science*, 20(2): 410–421.

Baden-Fuller, C. and Morgan, M. S. (2010) Business models as models. *Long Range Planning*. 43(2–3): 156–171.

Barrow, C., Burke, G., Molian, D. and Brown, R. (2005) *Enterprise Development*, Thomson Learning.

Berends, H., Jelinek, M., Reymen, I. and Stultiëns, R. (2014) Product innovation processes in small firms: Combining entrepreneurial effectuation and managerial causation, *Journal of Product Innovation Management*, 31(3): 616–635.

Berryman, J. (1983) Small business failure and bankruptcy: A survey of the literature, *European Small Business Journal*, 1(4): 47–59.

Bilton, C. and Cummings, S. (2010) *Creative Strategy: Reconnecting Business and Innovation*, John Wiley & Sons.

Butler, D. (2012) *Business Development: A Guide to Small Business Strategy*, Routledge.

Campbell, D., Edgar, D. and Stonehouse, G. (2011) *Business Strategy: An Introduction*, Palgrave Macmillan.

Chandler, G. N., DeTienne, D. R., McKelvie, A. and Mumford, T. V. (2011) Causation and effectuation processes: A validation study, *Journal of Business Venturing*, 26(3): 375–390.

Chesbrough, H., Rosenbloom, R. S. (2002) The role of the business model in capturing value from innovation: Evidence from Xerox Corporation's technology spinoff companies, *Industrial and Corporate Change*, 11(3): 529–555.

Crawford, M. and DiBenedetto A. (2006) *New Products Management*, McGraw-Hill.

Cromie, S. (1991) The problems experienced by young firms, *International Small Business Journal*, 3: 43–61.

Csikszentmihalyi, M. (1996) *Creativity*, HarperCollins.

Curran, J. (1988) The Small Firm: A Neglected Area of Management. In: Cowling, A., Stanworth, J., Bennett, R., Curran, J. and Lyons, P. (eds) *Behavioural Sciences for Managers*, Arnold.

Department of Employment (1990) *A Survey of Owner-Managed Businesses*, DoE, September.

Drucker, P. (1985) *Innovation and Entrepreneurship*, Heinemann.

European Commission (2007) *Observatory of European SMEs Summary*, Flash Barometer, EC.

Fisher, G. (2012) Effectuation, causation, and bricolage: A behavioral comparison of emerging theories in entrepreneurship research, *Entrepreneurship Theory & Practice*, 36(5): 1019–1051.

Gnyawali, D. R. and Park, B.-J. (2009) Cooperation and technological innovation in small and medium-sized enterprises: A multi-level conceptual model, *Journal of Small Business Management*, 47(3): 308–330.

Greiner, L. E. (1972) Evolution and revolution as organizations grow, *Harvard Business Review*, July–August: 37–46.

Harris, D. (1993) Where those business angels fear to tread, *The Times*, 13 March.

Hart, S. L. (1992) An integrative framework for strategy-making processes, *Academy of Management Review*, 17(2): 327–51.

Hatten, T. S. (2015) *Small Business Management: Entrepreneurship and Beyond*, Cengage. (See especially Part 2, Planning in small business.)

Hedman, J. and Kalling, T. (2003) The business model concept: Theoretical underpinnings and empirical illustrations, *European Journal of Information Systems*, 12: 42–59.

Jennings, P. and Beaver, G. (1997) The performance and competitive advantage of small firms: A management perspective, *International Small Business Journal*, 15(1): 66–75.

Lumpkin, G. T. and Dess, G. G. (1996) Clarifying the entrepreneurial orientation construct and linking it to performance, *Academy of Management Review*, 21(1), 135–172.

Lumpkin, G. T. and Lichtenstein, B. B. (2005) The role or organizational learning in the opportunity-recognition process, *Entrepreneurship Theory and Practice*, July: 451–472.

Lumpkin, G. T., Hills, G. E. and Schrader, R. C. (2004) Opportunity Recognition. In: Welsch, H. P. (ed.) *Entrepreneurship: The Way Ahead*, Routledge: 73–90.

Marsden, A. and Forbes, C. (2003) Strategic Management for Small and Medium-sized Enterprises (SMEs). In: Jones, O. and Tilley, F. (eds) *Competitive Advantage in SMEs*, Wiley & Sons Ltd.

McGrath, R. G. (2000) The Parsimonious Path to Profit. In: Birley, S. and Muzyka, D. (eds) *Mastering Entrepreneurship*, Financial Times/Prentice Hall.

Mintzberg, H. (1994) The fall and rise of strategic planning, *Harvard Business Review*, January/February: 107–114.

Morris, M., Schindehutte, M. and Allan, J. (2005) The entrepreneur's business model: Toward a unified perspective, *Journal of Business Research*, 58(6): 726–735.

Mullins, J. W. (2003) *The New Business Road Test*, Financial Times/Prentice Hall.

Osterwalder, A. and Pigneur, Y. (2010) *Business Model Generation*, John Wiley & Sons.

Penrose, E. T. (1959) *The Theory of the Growth of the Firm*, Blackwell.

Perry, J. T., Gaylen, N. C. and Markova, G. (2012) Entrepreneurial effectuation: A review and suggestions for future research, *Entrepreneurship Theory & Practice*, 36(4): 837–861.

Porter, M. E. (1985) *Competitive Advantage: Creating and Sustaining Superior Performance,* Free Press.

Quinn, J. (1980) *Strategies for Change,* Irwin.

Rappa, M. (2002) Business models on the web. digitalenterprise.org/

Rauch, A., Wiklund, J., Lumpkin, G. T. and Frese, M. (2009) Entrepreneurial orientation and business performance: An assessment of past research and suggestions for the future, *Entrepreneurship Theory & Practice,* May.

Read, S. and Sarasvathy, S. (2005) Knowing what to do and doing what you know: Effectuation as a form of entrepreneurial expertise, *Journal of Private Equity,* Winter: 45–62.

Rosenfeld, S. A. (1996) Does cooperation enhance competitiveness? Assessing the impacts of inter-firm collaboration, *Research Policy,* 25: 247–263.

Sarasvathy, S. (2001) Causation and effectuation: Toward a theoretical shift from economic inevitability to entrepreneurial contingency, *Academy of Management Review,* 26(2): 243–263.

Sarasvathy, S. (2004) Making it happen: Beyond theories of the firm to theories of firm design, *Entrepreneurship Theory & Practice,* Winter.

Sarasvathy, S. (2009) *Effectuation: Elements of Entrepreneurial Expertise,* Edward Elgar.

Shane, S. (2003) *A General Theory of Entrepreneurship: The Individual-Opportunity Nexus,* Edward Elgar.

Small Business Research Trust (1991) *The Quarterly Survey of Small Business in Britain,* Open University (2nd Quarter).

Stevenson, H. H. and Jarillo, J. C. (1990) A paradigm of entrepreneurship: Entrepreneurial management, *Strategic Management Journal: Special Edition Corporate Entrepreneurship,* 11: 17–27.

Stinchcombe, A. L. (1965) Social Structure and Organization. In: March, J. G. (ed.) *Handbook of Organizations,* Rand McNally: 142–193.

Stokes, D. and Blackburn, R. (2001) *Opening Up Business Closures: A Study of Businesses that Close and Owner-manager Exits,* Small Business Research Centre, Kingston University.

Storey, D. (1998) *Understanding the Small Business Sector,* Thomson International Business Press.

Teece, D. J. (2010) Business models, business strategy and innovation, *Long Range Planning,* 43(2–3): 172–194.

Teece, D. J., Pisano, G. and Shuen, A. (1999) Dynamic Capabilities and Strategic Management. In: Zack, M. H. (ed.) *Knowledge and Strategy,* Butterworth-Heinemann.

Thurbin, P. (1998) *The Influential Strategist,* Financial Times/Pitman Publishing.

Timmons, J. A. and Spinelli, S. (2003) *New Venture Creation: Entrepreneurship for the 21st Century,* McGraw-Hill.

Watkins, D. (1982) Management Development and the Owner-manager. In: Webb, T., Quince, T. and Watkins, D. (eds) *Small Business Research,* Gower.

Watkins, D. and Morton, T. (1982) Small Firms in Britain and Europe: The Perceived Environment. In: Watkins, D., Stanworth, J. and Westrip, A. (eds) *Stimulating Small Firms,* Gower.

Wiklund, J. and Shepherd, D. (2003) Knowledge-based resources, entrepreneurial orientation, and the performance of small and medium sized businesses, *Strategic Management Journal,* 24, 1307–1314.

Wiklund, J., Patzelt, H. and Shepherd, D. A. (2009) Building an integrative model of small business growth, *Small Business Economics,* 32: 351–374.

Recommended further reading

Astrachan, J. H. (2010) Strategy in family business: Toward a multidimensional research agenda, *Journal of Family Business Strategy,* 1(1): 6–14.

Blackburn, R. A., Hart, M. and Wainwright, T. (2013) Small business performance: Business, strategy and owner-manager characteristics, *Journal of Small Business and Enterprise Development,* 20(1): 8–27.

Hitt, M. A., Ireland, R. D. and Hoskisson, R. E. (2009) *Strategic Management: Competitiveness and Globalization,* 8th edn, Mason, OH: Cengage Learning.

Moore, S. B. and Manring, S. L. (2009) Strategy development in small and medium sized enterprises for sustainability and increased value creation, *Journal of Cleaner Production,* 17(2): 276–282.

Osterwalder, A. and Pigneur, Y. (2010) *Business Model Generation,* John Wiley & Sons.

Ward, A., Runcie, E. and Morris, L. (2009) Embedding innovation: Design thinking for small enterprises, *Journal of Business Strategy,* 30(2/3): 78–84.

See also www.effectuation.org for more on effectuation theory.

8 Start-ups and franchises

Learning objectives

By the end of this chapter you will be able to:

- Recognize the different options for bringing a new business idea to market.

- Assess the advantages and disadvantages of a start-up as the vehicle for exploiting an opportunity.

- Identify what is meant by franchising and the key issues involved.

- Describe the international development of franchising.

- Assess the advantages and disadvantages of franchising from the perspective of both franchisor and franchisee.

Introduction

This chapter first identifies the alternative routes for developing an opportunity from concept into business reality including start-ups, franchises, buying a business and the possible legal forms. It then considers the two main methods of beginning a new business – start-ups and franchises – in more detail. The advantages and disadvantages of each are evaluated compared to other small business forms. Chapter 9 looks at buying an existing business, and Chapter 10 at forming and protecting the new business.

Activity 1
Which route?

As well as starting a brand new business, what other possibilities are there for involvement in a small business as an owner-manager? Give some examples, where you can, of businesses in each category.

8.1 The alternative routes to market entry

A recurring theme of investigations into small businesses is that they do not represent a homogeneous sector at all.[1] The differences between the parts are sometimes so great that meaningful generalizations about the whole are difficult to make. This is particularly evident when looking at the choices facing would-be owner-managers who have decided on their preferred business concept and now wish to take it into the marketplace. Owner-managers can select from several different ways of pursuing their opportunity, from beginning a new business to buying an existing one. The legal form of the business also has to be decided. In turn, these initial choices lead to further alternatives, as illustrated in Figure 8.1.

Inevitably, there are overlaps and areas of greyness between these various forms.

Figure 8.1 Possible routes to market entry for the small firm

Beginning a new business

- *Start-up* A business start-up means creating a new business, which stands alone and which is not tied to other organizations, except in the normal course of trading. It does not mean that the idea is necessarily novel, only that the vehicle which is set up to exploit it is new.
- *Franchise* A **franchise** is a method for starting a new business within the framework of an existing, larger business entity. It is a legally separate enterprise operating in some way under the umbrella of another organization.
- *Product and trademark agreements* A franchise can mean an agency to sell another company's products in a certain way or within a certain territory. This may involve use of a registered trademark. It may involve distribution only (e.g. of cars), or it could include production under a licensed process. It includes straightforward agencies and more elaborate systems such as multilevel marketing. Some franchise agreements do not preclude other activities, and may thus form part of a business start-up's portfolio of products or services.

Activity 2
For and against a start-up

What do you think are the advantages and disadvantages of a business start-up compared to other possible routes to market entry such as franchises or buying an existing business? Write them down as a balance sheet with two columns headed 'for' and 'against'. You should notice that an advantage often has a corresponding disadvantage.

- *Format franchising* **Franchising** has come commonly to mean a system for a business to set up using a complete format developed by another company, including trading name, standardized business presentation, products or services and operating systems. Some franchises have become household names, such as McDonald's, The Body Shop and DynoRod, but outlets are operated as separate legal entities by their owners.

Buying an existing business

- *Outright purchase* This involves buying an existing business from somebody else; although there is a new owner, the business does not start from scratch but is already trading in some way.
- *Buy-out* A buy-out is buying an existing business from within, rather than from the outside. Recently, this has become an increasingly popular form, as larger corporations have sold off parts of their organizations to the existing management team. Some buy-outs, such as National Freight, are large enough not to be classified as a small business at all.
- *Buy-in* This occurs when the existing owners accept a new partner, or shareholder, who buys into a small firm which already exists.

The legal form

In addition, there is choice over the legal form the organization takes. There are four main legal forms possible for the small firm: **sole trader, partnership, limited company** or **co-operative**.

The rest of this chapter considers the relative merits of the principal ways of beginning a new business – start-ups and franchises. Chapter 9 looks at the various options for buying an existing business, and Chapter 10 evaluates the legal identities open to small businesses.

Each of these vehicles for establishing a new business has its particular advantages and disadvantages. The preferred choice will depend both on the nature of the opportunity to be exploited and the circumstances of the individuals who wish to pursue it.

8.2 The start-up

8.2.1 THE WIDE SCOPE OF START-UP

The business start-up means exactly what it says; it is a new enterprise, starting up and trading in its chosen field – a green field in which the seeds of ideas have a chance to grow and develop. For many new ideas there is no other option; existing businesses have not developed the idea that a would-be entrant wishes to exploit.

Within this category, the types of new businesses vary significantly, in line with the objectives of the founder, linked to their willingness and ability to invest in the enterprise.

The level of risk taken in a start-up ranges from virtually nothing to highly significant personal, financial and time investment. Many new entrants try to minimize risk in starting something new by only incurring significant liabilities after the idea has been tested in the marketplace – dipping their toe in the water before committing themselves to total immersion; others take the plunge immediately.

Investment in a start-up can be made by an individual on their own, as the sole owner of the business, or it can be shared with others, who are either directly involved as equal partners, or less committed but still investing money, or time, in starting the business. This can be seen as a spectrum, as in Figure 8.2.

One end of the spectrum is typified by one person who begins in business on a part-time basis. The risk, while all their own, is minimal as income is generated elsewhere and investment requirements are small. The motivation may be to turn an existing hobby or skill into financial gain, or to put that proverbial toe in the water before taking the plunge.

At a higher level of risk on the spectrum is the tradesman, or professional, who decides to become self-employed, while keeping their liabilities low by minimal investment in equipment or overheads other than their own personal drawings and expenses.

A start-up, such as a new shop or manufacturing company, may require greater investment in capital equipment, premises, office equipment or staff in addition to the owner and other overheads. If this investment is made by a sole trader it can represent a very high level of individual risk.

Such investment can be shared, again at different levels, depending on the scope of the start-up. Some new enterprises require such significant initial investment that a consortium of partners come together to share the risk. For example, a new technology-based firm (NTBF) may be formed as a partnership between the full-time founders of the enterprise, a venture capital company that contributes long-term finance and non-executive management, and a bank that provides an overdraft as working capital.[2]

Entrepreneurs do not always take on more risk in their new ventures than other types of small business creation. As discussed in Chapter 2 (Section 2.3, The search for the entrepreneurial archetype), what appears as risk for some people may actually represent a real opportunity for others.

Figure 8.2 An Illustration of the business start-up spectrum

Investment/risk	Sole risk	Scope of start-up	Examples
Minimal personal risk with low initial investment	▼	Part-time business activity	Hobby or skill used to generate additional income or to test idea
Increased initial investment required	▼	Self-employment in existing trade or profession	Consultant or plumber using home as office
High individual risk	▼	Sole trader creating new business entity	Retail outlet, restaurant, small manufacturer
	Shared risk		
Initial investment minimized	▼	Partnership or self-employment	Accounting or other professional practice, craft partnership
Increased initial investment from partners	▼	New business organization owned by two or more	Manufacturer, small hotel
High level of shared risk with significant up-front investment	▼	Consortium start-up	High-tech company with technical, management and financial partners

The scope of the start-up will be determined by the nature of the business, and the objectives of the owners. Businesses vary considerably in their investment requirements, from the self-employed plumber who has to buy some basic tools and a van, to a capital-intensive manufacturer, needing hundreds of thousands of pounds to get off the ground. The objectives of the founders in relation to the speed of anticipated growth will also influence the investment requirements. Perhaps the objectives extend only to personal self-employment with no other staff or overheads; or maybe the scope is more ambitious, foreseeing the need to develop a team of people to cope with the business activity.[3]

8.2.2 THE ADVANTAGES AND DISADVANTAGES OF THE START-UP

Some of the advantages and disadvantages of the business start-up, compared to other methods of becoming a small business owner (such as buying an existing business), are summarized in Table 8.1. Notice that, as

Table 8.1 **The advantages and disadvantages of the start-up as a small business entrant**

Advantages	Disadvantages
Creation of the owners: freedom of choice over what the business does, how it operates, and what its values are	*Unproven idea:* the idea may be creative, but will it work? Even after the most thorough research, a new business can only prove itself in practice
Control of the owners: personal decisions count, external influences can be minimized	*High failure rate:* the failure rate of start-ups is high; less than 50 per cent survive the first four years. Other methods, e.g. franchising, have better track records
Satisfaction of the owners: success due to the skill and efforts of owners, which gives them heightened sense of satisfaction when (if) success comes	*Hard, lonely work:* unsociable working hours are often linked to feelings of being alone as, even in a partnership, there are no support departments and services in the firm. Entrepreneurs do it themselves
Clean sheet: the business starts with no backlog of problems; it will create plenty, but at least they will be new ones and not inherited from the past	*No market share or goodwill:* compared to buying an existing business or franchising, the start-up has the problem of establishing its name from scratch; the goodwill in an established company name or loyalty of existing customers takes some time to build up
Help from various agencies: government assistance and help from other agencies is available to encourage new business start-ups	*Barriers to entry:* there are many barriers to market entry. One-off start-up costs can be significant. Legislation has to be considered, premises found, accounts with suppliers opened, credit worthiness proved; these and many other obstacles have to be overcome before trading begins
Match between founder and enterprise: the founders of a new enterprise can ensure that their individual strengths are well used, and their weaknesses minimized, by choosing a business well matched to their own qualities and experiences	*Difficult to forecast:* with no track record, a start-up is very hard to predict for financial and other outcomes
Less funds required: a start-up that works costs less than buying a similar franchise or existing business	*Difficult to finance:* banks and other lenders are always keener to give money to proven concepts than to new ideas

is common with this kind of 'balance sheet' analysis, advantages have corresponding disadvantages. So, for example, the advantage that a start-up is the creation of the owners, which gives them freedom of choice, has the corresponding disadvantage that it is unproven by anyone else – in the sense that no one else has done it in exactly the same way before. Many small businesses are not particularly innovative and do copy what other businesses have already done, so not all business start-ups are necessarily riskier than franchise options. The advantage of control over decision-making carries with it the disadvantage that these decisions could be misplaced, as the high failure rate of new small businesses might suggest. Starting with a clean sheet has the downside of no market share or goodwill at the outset.

While virtually anybody can decide to set up a new business, regardless of their suitability for doing so, this cannot be said of setting up as a franchise. Franchisors choose their franchisees carefully. In effect, those taking the franchise route will be pre-tested for suitability before they even start trading (see Meek *et al.*, 2011; Nijmeijer, Fabbricotti and Huijsman, 2014). On the other hand, those taking the start-up route can normally choose to close their businesses whenever they wish, whereas franchisees are often tied into contracts for several years. This is a further aspect of control that it is important to understand fully when deciding on the route to market entry.

Activity 3
Defining franchising

Franchising has been used to describe a number of business arrangements and systems. How would you define franchising? Give some examples of companies that run their business as a franchise.

8.3 What is franchising?

Franchising is a business arrangement in which one party (the franchisor) allows others (the franchisees) to use a business name, or sell products, in such a way that the franchisees can operate their own legally separate business. It is a particular business model with a wide range of possibilities: it can mean as little as a simple agreement to sell a company's products in a specified area, or it can represent a complete package which lays down exactly how the business is to be run – commonly known as business format franchising.[4]

The European Franchise Federation has adopted a definition of franchising in its Code of Ethical Conduct.[5] This highlights the importance of 'collaboration' on the one hand, allied to the issuing of a 'right' to trade under certain constraints:

> **Franchising** is a system of marketing goods and/or services and/or technology, which is based upon a close and ongoing collaboration between legally and financially separate and independent undertakings, the Franchisor and its individual Franchisees whereby the Franchisor grants its individual Franchisees the right, and imposes the obligation, to conduct a business in accordance with the Franchisor's concept. The right entitles and compels the individual Franchisee, in exchange for a direct or indirect financial consideration, to use the Franchisor's trade name, and/or trade mark and/or service mark, know-how, business and technical methods, procedural system, and other industrial and/or intellectual property rights, supported by continuing provision of commercial and technical assistance, within the framework and for the term of a written franchise agreement, concluded between parties for this purpose.

8.3.1 PRODUCT AND TRADEMARK AGREEMENTS

The early forms of franchising were agreements in which manufacturers distributed their products through licensed dealers. In the nineteenth and early twentieth centuries, the Singer Sewing Machine Company, for example, sold its product in this way. Breweries, oil companies and car manufacturers all developed the distribution of their products through different forms of licensing arrangements.

Under such arrangements, local tenants or dealers took responsibility for sales in a given territory in return for some element of the local profit. The producers developed their products and the goodwill associated with their trademarks; the local distributor contributed local knowledge, contacts and effort. Such distribution arrangements are still common, particularly for the marketing of drinks (soft and alcoholic), petrol and cars.

Certain manufacturing processes, particularly where a patent exists, are also licensed. The patent holder may wish to exploit their innovation on a wider basis than their own resources allow. They therefore permit other manufacturers to use the process under licence in return for a royalty. This is particularly common in international markets where local laws prohibit foreign ownership of production, or where local conditions make it impractical.

Some small businesses specialize as import agencies, often negotiating a number of agreements to import foreign goods, and act as the national or regional distributor.

If these goods are branded, the producer will usually attempt to protect their trademark by an agreement which not only outlines the terms and conditions of trade, but also sets minimum standards covering sales and after-sales aspects.

Other forms of agreement cover the use of registered trademarks or celebrity names. The right to use well-known names, fictional or real, can be purchased under a licensing agreement which specifies how the name is to be used, and what royalties will be paid for the privilege. Many children's products, for example, are sold in the image of the latest popular hero, manufactured and distributed under a licensing arrangement with the creator. Real live celebrities may also allow their name to be associated with a product or service under an endorsement agreement.

Although up-front payments and ongoing royalties can be onerous, the small business, with no established identity of its own, can often benefit from a relevant association with an established, known name. For example, a small manufacturer of leisure clothes and equipment may seek endorsement of their products by a local sports personality, to add stature and gain new outlets.

For some small businesses, product and trademark arrangements are essential. Many public houses are tied to a major brewery, even though the business entity that runs the pub is owned by the tenant; the publicans benefit from the national marketing by the brewery, but there are restrictions on what else they can sell. A small manufacturer of toys and games will inevitably seek licensing arrangements so that their products can be merchandized using the latest cartoon characters; sales can be dramatically influenced by the well-timed launch of a product endorsed by the latest heroes.

8.3.2 BUSINESS FORMAT FRANCHISING

Today, the word franchising is more commonly used to describe **business format franchising**. This is a more in-depth relationship between franchisor and franchisee than a simple product or trademark licensing arrangement.

The International Franchise Association[6] describes this type of franchise as:

> A continuing relationship in which the franchisor provides a licensed privilege to do business plus assistance
> in organizing training, merchandising and management in return for a consideration from the franchisee.

Curran and Stanworth (1983) explain that business format franchising consists of a contractual relationship between two independent firms in which a parent company (the franchisor), having developed a new product or service, agrees to allow another firm (the franchisee) to sell that product or service in a specific way, in a particular location, and during a given period in return for a one-off initial fee and an annual sales-based payment. This type of franchise goes beyond the supply of products and trade names, and covers many other aspects of how the business is run. The business format offered by the franchisor can cover such aspects as:

- trade name, business style, logo, house colours;
- detailed product or service specification;
- analysis of location, and lease negotiations;
- design of premises, and purchase of equipment;
- financial advice to establish the business;
- operating systems and manuals;
- management control systems;
- training and help to set up;
- continuing assistance, including research and development and management counselling;
- national and local marketing;
- centralized purchasing;
- current market research results.

This represents a complete package which allows the franchisee to use a format proven by the franchisor, while retaining independence as a business. There is an agreement between the two parties which sets out how the business will be run, and the obligations of both parties.

The major banks also offer specific advice and information on franchising; for certain proven franchises they will be able to offer loans more easily than for other types of new business with no track record.

Activity 4
Examples of franchises

Give some examples of franchises that you have heard of or may have used. What do you think it costs to become a franchisee in each case?

8.4 The franchising market

8.4.1 THE DEVELOPMENT OF FRANCHISING

Business format franchising has grown most dramatically in the USA. Originating in the nineteenth century, it took off in the 1950s, and now accounts for around one-third of all retail sales. Kentucky Fried Chicken (KFC) became one of the pioneers when Colonel Sanders travelled around America teaching people how to cook chicken his way. Today, KFC is the world's largest chain of chicken-based quick service restaurants (QSRs) with over 15 000 system units across more than 100 countries and territories, including over 850 restaurants throughout the UK and Ireland.

Another fast food chain was started in the 1950s by Ray Kroc based on the standardized hamburger production techniques developed by the McDonald brothers. McDonald's is now the largest chain of fast food restaurants in the world, serving nearly 70 million customers daily, with over 35 000 restaurants around the world.

In the UK, franchising is less significant but it is a fast-growing sector. Wimpy, a fast-food chain, was the first major franchise in the UK developed by J. Lyons and Company from 1956, alongside its ice cream brands, Lyons Maid and Mr Softee. By the 1990s, franchising had become the fastest-growing sector among retail and service outlets, accounting for almost 4 per cent of total retail sales.

According to the British Franchise Association (2014), the annual turnover of franchised companies in 2013 was £13.7 billion (as compared with £1 billion in 1984), made through over 39 000 franchised outlets operated by over 900 franchisors. There are estimated to be 22 400 franchisees in total (as one in four run multiple units). The number of people employed in franchising was 561 000. Although many franchises had their origin in the USA, today 80 per cent of the franchise systems in the country are now UK-owned and UK-run, and 25 per cent export their business model abroad.[7]

The pattern of growth has been similar throughout Europe, where there were over 100 000 franchised outlets by the 1990s with sales of over £20 billion. In some countries, penetration of franchising seems more advanced than the UK. According to the British Franchise Association,[8] franchising accounts for 0.4 per cent of GDP in the UK, 1.3 per cent in France, 1.9 per cent in Belgium and 2.5 per cent in Holland. Popular locations for operating franchises are currently Ireland, France, Germany and Spain. Canada has a very high penetration level with 40 per cent of retail sales through franchised outlets. Franchising has grown quickly in Japan and Australia, spread into eastern Europe and China (see Heung *et al.*, 2008), and recently into the Middle East, where it is emerging as a growth market.

Probably the best known franchises tend to be in the catering and retail sectors. However, there are, in fact, more franchise operations in the services sector (e.g. personal, property, business and commercial services). It is still a relatively young industry: many of the franchises on offer today are less than three years old. The internet has been a popular source of recent franchise opportunities, as well as a new promotional medium for traditional franchises. The range of franchised businesses is extremely wide.[9] Some of the more unusual franchises offered in the UK include:

- Cash Generator – retailer of new and second-hand products, cash provider and cheque cashing
- Complete Weed Control Ltd – weed control service to public and private sector organizations
- Hire Intelligence UK – short-term rental of personal computers
- Jo Jingles Ltd – music and singing club for pre-school children
- Nationwide Investigations Group – private detective agencies
- TaxAssist Accountants – accountancy franchise
- The Alternative Board – business improvement service.

8.4.2 PROFILE OF FRANCHISEES

As in making any attempt to categorize small business owners according to a particular 'type' of individual, we need to take care when profiling the typical franchisee. People go into franchising for a variety of reasons and with different motives (see Combs *et al.*, 2009; 2011; Dant, Grünhagen and Windsperger, 2011). For some, the opportunity offers a degree of freedom whilst also offering a perception of reduced risk, knowing that the business formulae is tried and tested. For others, franchising can be a means to creating something of a business empire.

FRANCHISING AND THE ENTREPRENEURIAL TALENT[10]

One of the most well-known franchises in the UK is the pizza delivery business Domino's Pizza which has more than 550 stores already and an ambitious goal of opening up 1000 by 2017. The company sponsors TV shows such as Hollyoaks (from 2015) and Britains Got Talent (to 2011), which gives the chance for talented individuals to perform in front of a live audience and millions of viewers on peak-time television. While becoming the franchisee of one of the company's stores is unlikely to bring such immediate media attention, it can certainly be a route to a change of lifestyle. Mike Groves, for example, set up his first Domino's Pizza franchised store following redundancy from a management position in a fast-food chain. From working in a corporate context for the same company for over 20 years, Mike was keen to try something new. He had long been interested in setting up his own business. Within seven years of launching his first outlet in Worthing, Mike was already planning to open up his fifth store.

It would be wrong to think that franchisors just offer franchise agreements to anyone interested. Research suggests that, on average, franchisors interview seven people before they find the right candidate for each opportunity.

We know a good deal about the profile of the 'average' franchisee in the UK from the NatWest/BFA annual surveys:[11]

- 82 per cent of all franchisees are married.
- The average franchisee is aged 47.
- The average age of new entrants is 41.
- 70 per cent of new franchisee recruits are male.
- There has been a steady increase in the number of female franchisees.
- The proportion of graduates operating franchise units is over 40 per cent.
- 17 per cent of new entrants are of Asian background.
- 4 per cent of new entrants are from the black community.

8.4.3 SOCIAL VENTURE FRANCHISING

The application of the franchising model is widespread and occurs across many different industry contexts. It has become important in the context of social enterprise (i.e. 'non-profit' and social ventures which achieve their social objectives through building businesses whose surpluses are reinvested in the enterprise, rather than being distributed to the owners). Social franchising can offer an effective strategy for encouraging growth and disseminating best practice (Tracey and Jarvis, 2007). As Piggot (2004, p. 8) observes, it 'creates a series of partnerships whereby the parent organization gets a comparatively risk-free route to rapid growth; the franchisee also enjoys reduced risks and a ready-made business model with all the benefits that this implies'.

In the context of social enterprise, the nature of the relationships between the franchisor and the franchisee must be based on mutual trust and a belief that both parties are receiving adequate 'returns'. The underlying strengths of commercial franchising (i.e. a strong brand presence; competitive products and services; the ability of the franchisor to provide ongoing and effective assistance to the franchisee) are precisely the benefits which are key to the success of the social enterprise, especially as there may be a danger of launching the enterprise too early in some cases (Tracey and Jarvis, 2007).

For example, University College Falmouth launched a social franchise, *Hidden Art Cornwall*, in 2005 to address the lack of provision and support for the local designer-maker sector. Since then, it has benefited many designer-makers through its social franchising approach.[12]

The European Social Franchising Network (ESFN) promotes and develops the concept of social franchising on a European level. Examples of social franchises include Le Mat, a social hotel chain; CASA, offering care packages and services for people in the Sunderland area; CoRE, developing renewable energy and community profits, and Villa Vägen ut! ('Way out!') which is spreading the concept of halfway houses for recovering drug addicts across Sweden.[13]

THE BIG ISSUE – FRANCHISING THE HOMELESS

The Big Issue is a novel franchise devised by Gordon Roddick and A. John Bird. It is a weekly magazine which is exclusively sold on the street across Britain by homeless people. In order to become a *Big Issue* vendor, an individual must prove that they are homeless or vulnerably housed, undergo an induction process and sign up to a code of conduct. Vendors are allocated a fixed location to sell from and issued with a number of free issues of the magazine. Once they have sold these, they can purchase further copies for £1.25 which they sell for £2.50. They are working, not begging. Since *The Big Issue* was launched in 1991, it has helped thousands of vulnerable people take control of their lives and is currently working with around 2000 individuals across the UK, offering them the opportunity to earn a legitimate income; to 'help them to help themselves'. It currently circulates around 100 000 copies every week.

The Big Issue is a social enterprise, and any profits made go into a trust which supports the homeless and campaigns for social change.

(Source: www.bigissue.com)

A. John Bird, co-founder of Big Issue

8.4.4 HOW MUCH DOES IT COST?

In addition to the usual overhead costs of running a business, the franchisee will have to find some additional funds.

Minimum start-up costs

These include an initial franchise fee as a one-off payment to the franchisor for the privilege of becoming a franchisee. In addition, other start-up investment is required to cover the costs of buying equipment, fitting out premises, trade signs, initial stocks of materials, stationery, promotional literature and all the other items which the franchisor deems necessary to run the business. There may be some element of profit to the franchisor in providing the new franchisee with these. The average initial cost of starting a franchise is around £50 000, including the franchise fee, working capital, equipment and fittings, stock and materials.

The advertised minimum finance required for some well-known, and some less well-known, franchises are, at the time of writing, as shown in Table 8.2 below.

Table 8.2 Profile of some franchises: number of outlets and costs

Franchise	Business type	£ initial investment (+ VAT)
Jo Jingles	Pre-school music classes	8000
WPA Healthcare	Health solutions	9200
Card Connection	Greetings card distribution	35 000
TaxAssist	Accounting services	37 000
actionCOACH	Business coaching organization	41 000
Signs Express	Business signs	45 000
McDonald's	Quick service restaurants	150–400 000

Reference: www.whichfranchise.com. Accessed Dec 2015.

Annual charges

Franchisors will also levy a service fee and possibly other charges on an ongoing basis. The service charge is normally calculated as a percentage of net invoiced sales, varying from 5 per cent to 15 per cent plus. On average, franchisees pay an estimated 7.7 per cent of their sales in recurring fees to their franchisors, or approximately £25 000 per annum.[14]

Where the supply of goods on a continuous basis is part of the franchise arrangement (e.g. The Body Shop and McDonald's), then the franchisor will have some level of profit in the transfer price of these goods.

Fixed charges representing a contribution to national advertising and management are also common. In taking into account the different factors involved with assessing the scale of franchise fees, it is useful to bear in mind the following key points:

- The longer the franchise contract, the larger the initial fee.
- The greater the reliance on the franchisor's efforts and support, the higher the fee.
- Where ongoing fees are absent, it is usually the case that mark-ups or rebates on products supplied to franchisees substitute them.
- Some 'special' fees may also be charged by the franchisor for services such as training in the use of new software.

Activity 5
For and against franchising

What do you think are the advantages and disadvantages of franchising:

(a) from the perspective of the franchisee; and
(b) from the perspective of the franchisor?

8.5 The pros and cons of franchising

8.5.1 SUCCESS AND FAILURE AMONG FRANCHISES

Many claims are made by the franchise industry about the supposedly higher success rates experienced by franchise chains than conventional business start-ups. According to the British Franchise Association (2014),

92 per cent of franchised businesses are at least 'marginally profitable', with 49 per cent of franchisees saying they are either quite profitable or very profitable. The BFA figures suggest that franchising is one of the more robust markets of the economy, with the overall contribution of franchising to the UK economy growing by 20 per cent from 2008 to 2013 while the overall economy shrank by 2.5 per cent over the same period. The readiness of banks to lend money to franchisees is cited as evidence for a higher likelihood of success, which is often quoted to be five times as high as start-ups.

However, it has been argued that franchisee failures are often disguised by a combination of under-reporting from the franchisors, franchise outlets changing hands and the exclusion of 'unethical' franchises from the data (Hoy, 1994). While franchise failure rates are, on average, lower than for start-ups generally, much depends on the quality of the individual franchise.

Franchises vary greatly in quality, from the well-established proven formulae of household names, to new creations that have yet to establish their viability. In the USA, franchising is regulated by legislation which ensures that franchisors have to register with the authorities and complete a 'franchise offering' circular. This is similar to a share prospectus and contains information essential for the prospective franchisee, such as details of the history and officers of the franchisor company. In the UK such disclosures are voluntary, as is the regulation of the industry. Most established franchisors are members of the British Franchise Association, whose code of conduct and accreditation rules are based on codes developed by the European Franchise Federation.

One of the key guiding principles is that the franchisor shall have operated a business concept with success for a reasonable time, and in at least one pilot unit before starting its franchise network.[15] The stages of setting up as a franchisor can be lengthy and expensive if the recommended route is adhered to (Stanworth, 1995):

1 *Establish basic business idea.* Testing the marketing, product/service and operational strategies should take at least two years with probable adjustments and modifications to the original concept.
2 *Open pilot outlet.* Another two years (minimum 12 months) is probably required to test out a replica of the business in another location with different management to verify that it is a transferable concept.
3 *Operationalize the franchise.* This involves drawing up three key documents:
   (i)   *an operating manual* – detailed guidance on how to run the business;
   (ii) *a franchise contract* – the legal document spelling out the obligations of both parties;
   (iii) *a franchise prospectus* – the marketing literature to attract franchisees.
4 *Recruitment and training of franchisees.* Advertising and attending exhibitions is a continuous exercise if the franchise is to grow.

This process can take five years, if followed correctly, before the first franchisee is recruited.

Many franchise concepts do not last the development course, or try to cut corners. A surprisingly high number fail or disappear once launched. A study (Stanworth, 1995) investigated the fortunes of franchises which had been advertised 10 years previously, in 1984. After 10 years, only 25 per cent were considered to be a generally successful franchise, a further 25 per cent were still in existence in some form but were not considered to be a franchise success story, and over 50 per cent had failed as a franchise and disappeared from view. (See Gillis and Castrogiovanni (2012), for further discussion of franchising and business growth).

These figures have implications for franchisees as well as franchisors. The vulnerability of franchise operations can put many individual operators at risk overnight, as was demonstrated by the well-publicized difficulties of the Ryman and Athena franchisees when the owning companies went into liquidation. In 2004, 6.5 per cent of franchisors withdrew, either as a result of commercial failure (1.4 per cent), dispute (0.3 per cent), or for some other reason (4.8 per cent).[16]

A prospective franchisee will clearly want to know more about these aspects to protect themselves from the possibility of taking on some of the disadvantages of franchising without the compensating advantages.

According to one commentator, there are two basic questions which prospective franchisees must be able to answer before entering an agreement (Spinelli, 2000, p. 60):

1 Is risk sufficiently mitigated by the trademark value, operating system, economies of scale and support process of the franchisor to justify sharing equity with the franchisor (via the payment of an up-front franchise fee and ongoing royalties)?

2 Are personality and management style amenable to sharing decision-making responsibilities with the franchisor and other franchisees?

With increasing numbers of franchise operations being developed on an international basis (see Gámez-González *et al.*, 2010; and the 2014 special issue of *Journal of Marketing Channels*), it is also especially important that imported trademark systems or franchise processes are sensitive to the differences in customer demand in different countries.

8.5.2 ADVANTAGES AND DISADVANTAGES FOR FRANCHISEES
Advantages for franchisees

- The business concept is proven, or should be. The British Franchise Association has laid down guidelines as to what constitutes proven, as outlined above, which includes more than just one business outlet for a short period.
- The way to operate the business has already been worked out and tested. Starting up should be easier and faster.
- Training and support is given including, technical training, business training, site selection and choice of suppliers.
- Statistically, fewer franchises fail than other business start-ups; therefore, it can be easier to obtain finance for the franchise. As discussed above, annual failure rates are difficult to establish precisely, and success is not as assured as some of the advertising material may suggest. However, one estimate is of failure rates between 5–7 per cent per annum, lower than for small firms generally (Stanworth and Curran, 1990).
- National branding will often have been established. Larger, well-established franchise operations will often have national (or international) advertising campaigns and a solid trading name.
- Research and development, and competitive analysis, will usually be undertaken by the franchisor to keep abreast of environmental changes.
- Economies of scale may apply; for example, in nationally agreed terms with suppliers which take account of the total franchised business.
- Economies of experience should apply; for example, in knowing the marketing techniques that have worked best for other franchisees.

Disadvantages to franchisees

- Not your own creation. This is someone else's idea; the franchisee is implementing, not creating. Opportunities for pursuing entrepreneurial ideas are therefore restricted.
- Lack of independence. The franchisor makes the rules which the franchisee has to follow. This is often discussed in terms of institutional theory (see Barthélemy, 2011), where, in order to survive, organizations must conform to the rules and belief systems prevailing in the environment (DiMaggio and Powell, 1983).
- The financial costs can be considerable with large up-front fees and high royalties. Set-up costs can also be higher as they have to follow a prescribed formula.
- The franchise may not be suited to your area.
- The goodwill your business builds up is never all yours, as it is dependent on a continuing franchise agreement. This could cause problems when you decide to sell the business.

- The franchisor needs to ensure regular disclosure of information by the franchisee to protect their royalties and the franchise agreement. This can become intrusive into the financial affairs of the franchisee.
- The brand image of the franchisor can become a distinct liability if things go wrong. The franchisee is dependent on the stability of the franchisor; a national problem with the franchise can dramatically affect the franchisee who has no control over events.

8.5.3 ADVANTAGES AND DISADVANTAGES FOR FRANCHISORS
Advantages for franchisors

- Franchising is a way of expanding a small business into a big business in a relatively short time. The burden of raising capital to develop a business concept is shared with franchisees and fast expansion becomes easier to fund.
- Another common barrier to expansion, the recruitment, motivation and reward of key staff, is also eased; a proven opportunity usually has a queue of potential franchisees waiting to start. Franchisees tend to be motivated individuals prepared to accept rewards in line with the results of their business.
- The franchise also offers the franchisor the possibility of learning from their franchisees, assuming that they are able to put in place knowledge management procedures that can convert tacit into explicit knowledge (Lindblom and Tikkanen, 2010; see also Weaven *et al.*, 2014).

Disadvantages for franchisors

- Franchising inevitably means loss of control compared to a conventional branch outlet. Franchisees are more independent than a branch manager.
- If the franchisor offers a franchise based on the recommended practices of the BFA, then it will take time, effort and resources to operate the concept as a pilot franchise unit.
- The franchisor may take on many obligations in the franchise agreement, such as continuing commercial and technical assistance during the lifetime of the agreement, which will necessitate developing central support resources.
- Franchisees are becoming more organized as groups in their dealings with franchisors. Their ability to exert pressure on franchisors will probably increase as the industry matures.
- Failure of a single franchisee, through no fault of the franchisor, can do considerable damage to the reputation of the franchisor.

Ultimately, the franchisor has a powerful vested interest to ensure the survival and success of its franchised outlets; without them the franchise will fail.

The self-interest of the franchisor will be best served by meeting in full its obligations to prove the idea it wishes to network, and providing the required support to ensure the prosperity of the franchisees.

Activity 6
Is it a small business?

What characteristics do franchises have in common with non-franchised small businesses? How do they differ?

8.5.4 WHY DO SMALL BUSINESS FOUNDERS CHOOSE BUSINESS FORMAT FRANCHISING?

The study of business format franchising has been advanced by two concepts that help to explain why small business owners might choose to enter into the franchise arrangement in the first place: resource scarcity theory and agency theory:

1 **Resource scarcity theory** This theory, first put forward by Oxenfeld and Kelly (1969), suggests that businesses' motivation to franchise is derived from a shortage of the necessary resources for expansion. The authors suggested that franchising allows rapid market penetration in the early stages of a firm's growth. Franchising can be seen as helping new ventures to overcome financial constraints and the nurturing of managerial talent, as well as helping in the provision of local market knowledge. Empirical evidence suggests that franchisors tend to opt for a stable level of franchised outlets over time (see Lafontaine and Shaw, 2005).

2 **Agency theory** Agency theory concerns the way in which one party (the principal) delegates responsibility for a specific set of actions to another party (the agent) (Jensen and Smith, 1985). A core assumption underlying agency theory is that the principal and the agent are likely to have different interests and attitudes towards risk. Often, the agent knows more about the particular situation than the principal, making it impossible to ensure that the agent makes decisions in the principal's best interests (Alchian and Woodward, 1988). The objective of a franchise agreement is to overcome this problem by aligning the interests of the parties more closely (see Bates, 1998; Shane, 1998). A franchisor has much at stake in ensuring that franchisees succeed in order that their royalties continue to be paid. The franchisee is dependent on the brand and format of the franchise, and so will endeavour to make the business model work and even collectively try to improve it where they can; they often demonstrate this commitment by taking out multiple franchises of the same brand.

8.6 But is it a small business?

Is a franchised outlet a small business? Or should it be classified as a form of managed branch of a larger organization?

The Bolton Committee excluded franchises from its review of the UK small business sector. One of its key criteria in defining a small business was independence from other organizations. As a franchise is not independent from the franchisor, the total franchised network could be considered as one business, rather than a collection of separate, small firms (franchisees) and one larger business (the franchisor).

In practice, all small firms exhibit differing degrees of independence. None are truly autonomous, as all will depend to some extent on forces outside their full control. Successful entrepreneurship may be attributed to independently-minded individuals but, in practice, they inevitably need to be good at networking and working with others to achieve their objectives (Schoonhoven and Romanelli, 2001).

Customers can be a powerful controlling factor, particularly if a small business is reliant on a few of them. A small producer supplying a large supermarket chain, for example, may not have full control over many important operations of its business, including quality control, delivery schedule and pricing policies. Financial backers of an enterprise may also exert considerable influence on the management of a small business, particularly one that is in difficulties.

In reality, the independence of small firms is not a fixed factor but, rather, a point on a continuum. A particular firm's position on the continuum depends on a number of influences, including the level of competitive activity in its chosen market, the power of its buyers and suppliers, and its relative financial strength.

Franchisees occupy a place on this continuum, but not necessarily at the end of minimal control. Neither will all franchisees be at the same point; some will be more controlled by their franchisors than others. The perceptions of the franchisor and its franchisees over who controls what have been shown to significantly differ. A survey of three franchise networks indicated that, while franchisors felt that their franchise contracts were strictly enforced, franchisees believed that contractual obligations were not rigorously applied (Stanworth, Curran and Hough, 1986). They did agree, however, that franchisees had the principal responsibility for hours of opening, employment of personnel, bookkeeping and quality standards, which represent a significant part of the operational running of the business.

When is a franchise a small business?

A critical ingredient in the make-up of the relationships in a franchised network is that the franchisee operates a legally separate business. This business may be constrained by the terms of the franchise contract but, in the eyes of the law, it is a separate entity. The experience of franchisors is that they need to manage their franchisees by persuasion not mandate, as the desire for independence is strong among franchisees. The degree of independence exercised by the owner of a successful franchised outlet is not so significantly different from a more conventional small business that it can be considered a totally different business type.

Many of the principles for the successful management of small businesses hold true for franchised outlets. The performance of individual outlets operating the same franchise varies more significantly than can be explained by location factors alone. Some franchisees always struggle. Others become successful owner-managers, with a chain of franchised outlets.

In recent years, the development of the internet and online technologies has enabled new forms of business activity and interdependence to develop. The example of *eBay* is a case in point.

EBAY: ORGANIZATION, NETWORK OR ONLINE ECONOMY?[17]

As with so many small businesses, eBay has its origins in the interests and needs of its founder. Pierre Omidyar, so the story goes, noticed that his fiancée (now wife) who collected Pez sweet dispensers, was having trouble in finding people to trade with, and came up with eBay as a means of bringing buyers and sellers together from across the world. From relatively humble beginnings, eBay now offers an online platform for millions of items to be traded every day. This online presence has developed to the point where over 123 000 British businesses now trade on eBay, with at least 170 of these turning over more than a million pounds each year from selling on the site.

The eBay environment offers buyers and sellers the chance to develop relationships with each other through discussion boards, and there is a Business Centre that offers advice on starting and growing an eBay business and opening eBay shops. eBay therefore challenges the conventional boundaries between the organization, a network and an economy.

It will be interesting to see whether the ever-developing opportunities for social networking and collaboration afforded by the internet will give rise to new forms of business relationships which challenge perceived wisdom on the nature of the 'small business' in the future. The very reason for firms existing in the first place – to reduce the necessary transaction costs involved when exchanging a product on the market – could disappear, if collaborative working and new forms of exchange are developed (see Williamson, 1981).

Research interest in the relationship between franchising and entrepreneurship continues – as expressed in the title of one article: 'Is franchising entrepreneurship? Yes, no, and maybe so' (Ketchen, Short and Combs, 2011). Recent research indicates that franchisees have similar levels of entrepreneurial tendencies to franchisors (Dada, Watson and Kirby, 2015). Furthermore, franchisors appear to value entrepreneurial personalities within their franchised outlets, as demonstrated by their franchisee selection process.

8.7 Summary

This chapter provides an introduction to the two main methods of beginning a *new* enterprise – the start-up and the franchise. The advantages of business start-up, as opposed to other methods of becoming a small business owner (e.g. buying an existing business) are presented. These tie in well with many of the entrepreneurial characteristics discussed in Chapter 2 (e.g. independence, autonomy, decision-making, self-efficacy, etc.). Franchising is highlighted as an alternative to the start-up. Key characteristics of the franchising process are presented, introducing the nature of the relationship between franchisor and franchisee, and including a brief guide to setting up. The pros and cons of franchising are discussed before the chapter concludes by considering whether or not we should consider the franchised outlet as a managed form of a larger organization, rather than as a particular type of small business.

8.8 Case studies and activities

Case study
You've been framed: Part 1

THE STORY SO FAR

In Part I, Chapters 1 to 5, we followed the progress of Andrea Clarey as she went through the process of evaluating her business opportunity. After investigating the market more thoroughly through primary and secondary research, she made her decision.

Andrea's investigations into her own payroll business convinced her, first, that market segments for payroll services in terms of different sectors did exist (such as schools and small businesses) but, second, that they were not large enough to sustain her business on a local basis. As her main competitive advantage was to provide a local, personalized service, this seemed to be a fundamental problem. She also had misgivings about her personal aptitude to run her own small business with the accompanying pressures and risk. When an attractive job working for the payroll department of the County Council was advertised, she applied. The Council was also tendering for outside work to supplement their internal service, and during the interview Andrea explained some of her ideas to them. This undoubtedly helped her get the job, which she was happy to take. Her investigations into the world of self-employment had helped her to understand herself and her motivations a little better, so that she felt less discontent in her new job. She also gained some insights into small business which she was able to share with a friend, Bryony Hannam, when she talked to her about her idea for a picture framing service.

Bryony Hannam's picture framing idea: start-up or franchise?

Bryony Hannam knew that her friend Andrea Clarey had recently investigated setting up her own business, so she decided to talk to her about her own idea. She had decided she was particularly suited to a picture framing business, and she was sure there was a need for the service in her home town. There were other picture framers, but Bryony reckoned they fell into one of three categories:

1 small back-street traders, often working part time, with long delivery times and poor choice of framing materials, although usually inexpensive;
2 art galleries offering a framing service. She was personally intimidated by the rarefied atmosphere of these, and she knew others who were similarly put off. They also offered limited choices and long delivery times as they normally subcontracted the work to other framers;

(Continued)

3 high street poster shops, which targeted a young market primarily interested in posters. Although they offered other types of framing, their main business was the ready-made clip frame.

Bryony was convinced that there was a need for a different type of framer – one who focused on the home-owner. She felt they wanted good quality framing which would coordinate with their interior decor. They also wanted convenience, in terms of where to shop, and a quick delivery time, with friendly helpful service from staff who related to their needs. She planned to set up in a position close to the main shopping centre, serving the local community. She also felt a location near to car parking was important as framed pictures were often bulky and awkward to carry any distance.

However, she felt constrained to go ahead because she had very little business experience and, although she was familiar with the art world, she had never framed any pictures herself.

In her investigations of the marketplace, she had discovered that she could get help from various quarters. There was no shortage of part-time business courses in the area; there were picture framing courses available, from a weekend introduction to more extensive practical training. The manufacturers of framing equipment and the suppliers of materials all offered her training and advice in setting up.

She also discovered a nationally operated franchise which initially sounded very attractive. The franchise offered her a complete package for setting up as a picture framer – from the design of the retail premises and workshop, the purchasing of supplies, the craft and techniques of framing itself, through to the marketing of the business, and the management of its cash flow and other financial aspects. They could promote her outlet as part of a national operation and help her keep up to date with the latest developments in the framing world. Their marketing literature indicated they had been operating franchises for over four years, having set up their own framing business before that.

When Bryony read through the franchise agreement, she had second thoughts. The financial implications were considerable. As well as an up-front fee of £10 000, she would have to pay them an ongoing royalty of 10 per cent of her total sales revenue. In addition, she would still have to pay for the fitting of the premises, to their exact requirements, and find the finance for equipment and working capital, which they estimated at a further £25 000. Despite assurances that finance would be readily available, Bryony wondered if she would ever be truly independent with such heavy liabilities and constraints on how she could operate the business.

When she discussed the idea with Andrea, she explained some of her investigations to date.

'This particular franchise', she said, 'is a member of the British Franchise Association, so that gives me some guarantee of their authenticity. They have proven the business by running a pilot unit, and they are now quite well-established.'

'If it's such a good deal for you, as they claim, why do they give so much away? What's in it for them?' asked Andrea. 'And if it is a good idea for you now, will it still be in three years' time when you have an established business but you will still be paying them royalties?'

Activities

1 What do you think is in it for them? What are the advantages for this particular franchisor?
2 Identify the advantages and disadvantages of Bryony proceeding with this franchise compared to starting up on her own.
3 Consider Andrea's final point. How will the pros and cons change over time? Will the balance be changed in three years?
4 What would you advise Bryony to do – start up on her own or take on the franchise?

This case is continued in Chapter 9.

Case study
Petpals

For many years, Nick Skinner had worked in sales and marketing for a family-owned construction firm specializing in the supply of materials. On the whole, he enjoyed the job, and certainly the good salary and car that went with it. But the reality of trekking up and down motorways all day and 'dancing to someone else's tune' was beginning to get to him. He began to look for a new start. As an animal lover, he was particularly interested in the idea of running his own business that would bring him into contact with some of the ever-growing population of household pets (more than 18 million in the UK).

The reality of starting up his own new business appealed – but also seemed very daunting given his lack of previous experience. He began to talk to people. He talked to his family and friends. He talked to people in the industry. At first, he received many sceptical and negative comments. But Nick was not immediately put off. In fact, he welcomed all the comments he received, and was able to better evaluate his next steps in the light of advice from all quarters.

A turning point came when Nick got in touch with the company Petpals, the first professional mobile pet care franchise service company in the UK. They supported and encouraged Nick, offering training and advice; 12 months later, he was enrolled on the company's initial training course. By this time, Nick had left his previous employer, was doing some work experience and spending time with an existing franchisee.

Finally, releasing some equity from his own home into his new franchise business, Nick took the plunge and began trading. In his first year, Nick achieved real sales of £44 000 and paid himself over £22 000 through Limited Company dividends.

For him, at least, it seems that franchising made perfect sense.

Adapted from a Petpals franchise case study available at www.whichfranchise.com/franchisee_template2.cfm? StoryID5373 (updated 17 July 2009)

Activities

(a) On the basis of this case, what advice would you give to someone thinking of buying a franchise?
(b) Under what circumstances do you think it would be inappropriate for someone wanting to set up their new business to seek the franchising route?

Consider a franchised outlet or business in your local area. Write an analysis of that franchise, with details of the format provided; that is, the products, the logo, the trademarks and image. How successful do you believe this enterprise has been compared to similar non-franchised businesses? Ideally, talk to the owner-manager of a franchised outlet for their views.

Extended activity
A local franchise

Planning a new venture
Start-up or franchise?

Summary of what is required

- Investigate the advantages and disadvantages of a new business start-up.
- Consider the possibilities of the franchise system – either as franchisor or franchisee – for your business idea.

Review start-ups

Consider a new business start-up as an option. Conduct an audit of the advantages and disadvantages of this option for your specific idea, carrying out any necessary research.

Review franchising

Consider the development of your business opportunity using a franchise network with you as the franchisor. List the advantages and disadvantages.

Consider taking up a franchise as a franchisee as a possible way of developing your business opportunity. Do suitable franchises exist? Obtain details of a franchise in a business area similar to your own, and list the advantages and disadvantages of this course of action.

Information on what franchises are on offer is available from (i) national exhibitions held each year in Birmingham, Manchester and London, (ii) magazines such as *The Franchise Magazine* and *Business Franchise*, (iii) publications such as *The British Franchise Association Franchisee Information Pack*. See recommended further reading, for more details.

8.9 Notes, references and recommended further reading

Notes and further information

1 For example, Curran, J. and Burrows, R. (1988) *Enterprise in Britain: A National Profile of Small Business Owners and the Self-Employed*, Small Business Research Trust. In many of his publications, Professor Curran emphasized in particular the diversity of small businesses and the need for caution in drawing generalizations about them as a sector.

2 The new technology-based firm (NTBF) or technology-based small firm (TBSF) has been identified by researchers looking at businesses that start up in newly emerging and fast-moving areas of technology. The role of these NTBFs is discussed, for example, in Rothwell, R. (1986) The Role of Small Firms in Technological Innovation. In: Curran, J., Stanworth, J. and Watkins, D. (eds) *The Survival of the Small Firm, 2,* Gower. Their finance needs are given particular scrutiny in Ullah and Taylor (2007), and Rannikko and Autio (2012) focus on their entrepreneurial orientation and growth.

3 This theme of diversity in types of owner-managers of small business is explored in more depth in Chapter 2, Section 2.2.4, Types of owner-managers and entrepreneurs.

4 This was the definition used by the Small Firms Service in their booklet *Franchising*, Small Firms Service, Department of Employment.

5 See www.thebfa.org/codeofethics.asp. This is part of the British Franchise Association's website which has much useful information on both the background to franchising and how to choose an opportunity.

6 The International Franchise Association, based in Washington DC, USA, was founded in 1960 as a non-profit-making body and it now provides a database of over 1000 franchise opportunities in the USA and worldwide (see www.franchise.org/). The IFA runs its own online 'university' where you can undertake a Franchising Basics course, for free (see www.franchiseuniversity.org).

7 Source: British Franchise Association (BFA), available at: www.thebfa.org

8 The British Franchise Association (BFA) was formed in 1977 by several leading franchisors in the UK, with the aim of establishing a clear definition of ethical franchising standards to help members of the public, press, potential investors and government bodies to identify sound business opportunities.

9   See the summary of the 2013 NatWest BFA Franchise Survey, www.thebfa.org/about-franchising /franchising-industry-research

10 Sources: www.businessfranchise.com/special -features/dominos-pizza-franchise, accessed 24 February 2016); and the NatWest BFA Franchise Survey.

11 See note 10.

12 See hiddenart.co.uk/

13 More details to be found at the ESFN website, www.socialfranchising.coop/

14 See note 10.

15 See Keynote Report (2008) *Franchising,* 11th edn, www.keynote.co.uk

16 The European Code of Ethics for Franchising has been adapted by an agreed Extension and Interpretation to form the Code of Ethical Conduct of the British Franchise Association. For further details, see *The Ethics of Franchising,* Martin Mendelsohn, BFA, 3rd edn.

17 Source: www.eBay.co.uk data, July 2009, available at www2.ebay.com/aw/uk/200907.shtml#2009-07 -30110910, accessed 14 December 2015.

References

Alchian, A. and Woodward, S. (1988) The firm is dead; long live the firm: A review of Oliver Williamson's 'The economic institutions of capitalism', *Journal of Economic Literature,* 26: 65–79.

Barthélemy, J. (2011) Agency and institutional influences on franchising decisions, *Journal of Business Venturing,* 26(1): 93–103.

Bates, T. (1998) Survival patterns among newcomers to franchising, *Journal of Business Venturing,* 13: 113–130.

British Franchise Association (2014) *NatWest bfa Franchise Survey,* BDRC, January, www.thebfa.org /about-franchising/franchising-industry-research, accessed 14 December 2015.

Combs, J. G., Ketchen, D. J. Jr, Shook, C. L. and Short, J. C. (2011) Antecedents and consequences of franchising: Past accomplishments and future challenges, *Journal of Management,* 37(1): 99–126.

Combs, J. G., Michael, S. C. and Castrogiovanni, G. J. (2009) Institutional influences on the choice of organizational form: The case of franchising, *Journal of Management,* 35(5): 1268–1290.

Curran, J. and Stanworth, J. (1983) Franchising in the modern economy: Towards a theoretical understanding. *International Small Business Journal,* 2: 8–6.

Dada, O., Watson, A. and Kirby, D. (2015) Entrepreneurial tendencies in franchising: Evidence from the UK, *Journal of Small Business and Enterprise Development,* 22(1): 82–98.

Dant, R. P., Grünhagen, M. and Windsperger, J. (2011) Franchising research frontiers for the twenty-first century, *Journal of Retailing,* 87(3): 253–268.

DiMaggio, P. J. and Powell, W. W. (1983) The iron cage revisited: Institutional isomorphism and collective rationality in organizational fields, *American Sociological Review,* 48:147–160.

Gillis, W. and Castrogiovanni, G. J. (2012) The franchising business model: An entrepreneurial growth alternative, *International Entrepreneurship and Management Journal,* 8(1): 75–98.

Gámez-González, J., Rondan-Cataluña, F. J., Diez de Castro, E. C. and Navarro-Garcia, A. (2010) Toward an international code of franchising, *Management Decision,* 48(10):1568–1595.

Heung, V. C. S., Zhang, H. and Jiang, C. (2008) International franchising: Opportunities for China's state-owned hotels?, *International Journal of Hospitality Management,* 27(3): 368–380.

Hoy, F. (1994) The dark side of franchising or appreciating flaws in an imperfect world, *International Small Business Journal,* 12(2): 26–38.

Jensen, M. C. and Smith, C. W. (1985) Stockholder, manager, and creditor interests: Applications of agency theory. In: E.I. Altman and M.G. Subrahmanyam (eds), *Recent Advances in Corporate Finance,* Irwin, pp. 95–131.

Ketchen, D. J., Short, J. C. and Combs, J. G. (2011) Is franchising entrepreneurship? Yes, no, and maybe so, *Entrepreneurship Theory & Practice* (Special Issue: New directions in franchising research), 35(3): 583–593.

Lafontaine, F. and Shaw, K. L. (2005) Targeting managerial control: Evidence from franchising, *Journal of Economics,* 36: 131–150.

Lindblom, A. and Tikkanen, H. (2010) Knowledge creation and business format franchising, *Management Decision,* 48(2): 179–188.

Meek, W. R., Davis-Sramek, B., Baucus, M. S. and Germain, R. N. (2011) Commitment in franchising: The role of collaborative communication and a franchisee's propensity to leave, *Entrepreneurship Theory & Practice,* 35(3): 559–581.

Nijmeijer, K. J., Fabbricotti, I. N. and Huijsman, R. (2014) Making franchising work: A framework based on a systematic review, *International Journal of Management Reviews,* 16(1): 62–83.

Oxenfeld, A. R. and Kelly, A. O. (1969) Will successful franchise systems become wholly-owned chains?, *Journal of Retailing*, 44: 69–83.

Piggot, C. (2004) Up, up and away. The possibilities of social franchising, *Social Enterprise*, 3: 8–10

Rannikko, H. and Autio, E. (2012) Entrepreneurial orientation, resource mobilization, technological distinctiveness and growth of a new technology-based firm, *Frontiers of Entrepreneurship Research*, 32(17), Article 9.

Rothwell, R. (1986) The Role of Small Firms in Technological Innovation. In: J. Curran, J. Stanworth and D. Watkins, D. (eds) *The Survival of the Small Firm*, 2, Gower.

Schoonhoven, C. B. and Romanelli, E. (2001) *The Entrepreneurship Dynamic*, Stanford University Press.

Shane, S. (1998) Making new franchise systems work, *Strategic Management Journal*, 19: 697–707.

Spinelli, S. (2000) The Pitfalls and Potential of Franchising. In: S. Birley and D. Muzyka (eds) *Mastering Entrepreneurship*, Financial Times/Prentice Hall.

Stanworth, J. (1995) Penetrating the mists surrounding franchise failure rates – Some old lessons for new business, *International Small Business Journal*, 13(2): 59–63.

Stanworth, J. and Curran, J. (1990) Franchising. In: Woodcock, C. (ed) *The Guardian Guide to Running a Small Business*, Kogan Page.

Stanworth, J., Curran, J. and Hough, J. (1986) The Franchised Small Enterprise: Formal and Operational Dimensions of Independence. In: Curran, J., Stanworth, J. and Watkins, D. (eds) *The Survival of the Small Firm*, Gower.

Tracey, P. and Jarvis, O. (2007) Toward a theory of social venture franchising, *Entrepreneurship Theory & Practice*, September: 667–684.

Ullah, F. and Taylor, P. (2007) Are UK technology-based small firms still finance constrained?, *The International Entrepreneurship and Management Journal*, 3(2):189–203.

Weaven, S., Grace, D., Dant, R. and Brown, J. R. (2014) Value creation through knowledge management in franchising: A multi-level conceptual framework, *Journal of Services Marketing*, 28(2): 97–104.

Williamson, O. E. (1981) The Economics of Organization: The Transaction Cost Approach, *The American Journal of Sociology*, 87(3): 548–577.

Recommended further reading

British Franchise Association (BFA) www.whichfranchise .com is a very useful website and the official online partner of the BFA. The NatWest/BFA Franchise Survey remains the leading study of franchising in the UK, and is also available through the BFA.

Felstead, A. (1993) *The Corporate Paradox: Power and Control in the Business Franchise*, Routledge.

Nijmeijer, K. J., Fabbricotti, I. N. and Huijsman, R. (2014) Making franchising work: A framework based on a systematic review, *International Journal of Management Reviews*, 16(1): 62–83.

Spinelli, S. (2000) The Pitfalls and Potential of Franchising. In: Birley, S. and Muzyka, F. (eds) *Mastering Entrepreneurship*, Financial Times/Prentice Hall. Section 1, Evaluating the opportunity.

Stanworth, J. and Purdy, D. (2006) Franchising and the small business. In: Carter, S. and Jones-Evans, D. (eds) *Enterprise and Small Business*, Financial Times/Prentice Hall.

See also the (2014) Special issue 'International franchising research and practice: Past, present, and future' in the *Journal of Marketing Channels*, 21(3), comprised of 7 articles.

There are also magazines sold at newsagents, or available online, which specialize in franchising and are useful resources in order to understand the scope of the system. For example, see *Business Franchise* and *The Franchise Magazine*, which also has a website, www .thefranchisemagazine.net.

9 Buying an existing business

Learning objectives

By the end of this chapter you will be able to:

- Appreciate the options that exist to purchase (or sell) an existing small business.

- Understand the possible motives of those wishing to sell a business.

- Assess the value of different types of assets of a business for sale.

- Identify possible liabilities to avoid in business purchase.

- Understand different methods of valuing a business for sale.

- Evaluate the advantages and disadvantages of buying an existing business against starting a new venture.

Introduction

Chapter 8 reviewed the options that exist for those who wish to exploit a business opportunity. This chapter is concerned with one group of these options: buying an existing business. Buying a business can have significant advantages over starting from scratch: it can overcome significant barriers to entry such as legal and planning difficulties, and gives immediate market share and turnover. However, it also carries significant potential problems including hidden liabilities, and lack of entrepreneurial satisfaction from taking over someone else's creation. Taking these factors into account, it is clear that the particular circumstances of the purchase and the motives of both buyers and sellers will be critical to how it works out. Although the principles of buying a business have worldwide application, national laws and local regulations influence some of the details; for example, the legal rules on buying commercial property or dealing with an insolvent business may differ. As this chapter deals with such matters according to UK law, the relevant regulations need to be investigated for buying a business in other countries.

This chapter may also be useful when considering *selling* a business, as the factors involved can often be deduced by considering a sale from the buyers' perspective (see also Chapter 14 Business Exits and realizing value).

Activity 1
Why are businesses sold?

Why would someone want to sell their business? Give some examples of:

(a) some different types of owners who might sell a small or medium-sized business; and
(b) their motives for sale.

9.1 The scope for buying an existing business

9.1.1 PURCHASE OPTIONS

A would-be entrepreneur does not have to start up a completely new business to exploit an opportunity. There are a range of opportunities to acquire the ownership, or part ownership, of a business that already exists. The options for buying a business depend on:

- the sellers – who range from individuals to large corporations;
- the status of the business – which may vary from a successful to a failed enterprise or franchise;
- the buyer – who may either purchase the business outright, or opt to become a partner in the business with existing managers and shareholders.

These options give rise to many permutations of ways of buying a business, as illustrated in Table 9.1.

Table 9.1 Possible purchase routes into an existing small business

	Small firm sale	Large firm sale	Franchise sale	Forced sale
Outright purchase	Yes	Yes	Yes	Yes
Buy-in	Yes	Unlikely	Yes	Yes
Buy-out	Yes	Yes	Yes	Yes

9.1.2 TYPES AND MOTIVES OF SELLERS

Small firms

Owner-managers have a variety of reasons for selling their businesses, including:

- recognition of lack of success, and low probability of success in the future;
- problems not related to the business which force its sale, including health problems, marital break-up or other personal issues (see Herbane, 2010, for discussion of small business and 'crisis management');
- other business activities which make a sale desirable; for example, the need to raise money for another failing/succeeding enterprise, or the desire to free up time for other business involvements;
- desire for a career change out of small business;
- retirement with no family succession plans (see Scholes *et al.*, 2009; Chrisman *et al.*, 2012);
- desire to cash in on the success of a business;
- a dispute which has led to the breakdown of a business partnership where one side cannot, or does not wish to, buy out the other.

The seller may own all of the business or only a part.

Larger firm

Larger companies sometimes dispose of a part of their business which, by itself, constitutes a small or medium-sized firm (Gilligan and Wright, 2014). Motivations for doing so include:

- financial targets set by the parent company are consistently not met by the small business unit. The return on the investment is considered inadequate, and there is a desire to re-invest the capital and management time elsewhere.
- The parent company adopting a new strategy, which means that the small business unit no longer contributes to meeting group objectives. Particularly in times of recession, larger companies which have diversified into new areas of higher risk may seek to return to what they consider to be their core business. This has motivated the scaling down of some companies, and the break-up of some conglomerates into parts which can be classified once again as a small business.
- The parent company needing to raise money for other activities, because of financial difficulties, or for other reasons.
- The parent company is itself being taken over, and the new owners do not see the small business unit as contributing to their overall strategy, or they may wish to sell parts of the acquisition to help fund the purchase.
- Legislation forcing a large company to sell some parts of its business.

Franchise

As well as starting a new outlet in a franchise network, it is also possible to buy either the business of an existing franchisee, or a branch outlet from a franchisor. Existing franchisees may wish to sell their business for any of the reasons given for small firms above. In addition, they may simply be disillusioned with the franchise system, because it does not provide sufficient independence to the franchisee, for instance. The franchisor will have to agree to such a sale, as the franchise agreement will need to be assigned to a new owner. However, it is usually in their interests to facilitate the change of ownership for two main reasons:

- The franchisee wishing to sell will hardly be motivated to manage the franchise properly having failed to secure a buyer because of the intransigence of the franchisor.
- It is motivational for other franchisees to see the exit possibilities from their business; they will like to feel they are building up a capital gain, as well as ongoing income from their business. Franchisors are therefore usually keen to build up a second market for the sale of franchised outlets, providing they can approve the quality of the incoming franchisee.

Franchisors may also wish to sell off an outlet which they themselves own and manage. This may have been an original pilot operation to prove the franchise concept. Or the franchisor may have developed a series of owned outlets before moving into franchising, the success of which then triggers a sale of the managed outlets to franchisees.

Forced sales

The high closure rates of small businesses gives rise to opportunities to purchase the assets of a failed enterprise from a liquidator, receiver or administrator. The **forced sale** of a business and its assets takes different forms dependent on the legal status of the failed company.[1]

- **Liquidation** describes the legal process of closing down a bankrupt company, and the sale of its assets to pay off as many debts as possible. The owner no longer controls the business; a liquidator is appointed who will sell off the assets of the business for the highest possible price. Insolvency has usually gone too far at this stage for there to be much interest in the ongoing trading of the business. The liquidator simply disposes of the individual assets as quickly and economically as possible. Liquidation is not so much a possibility to buy a business as an opportunity to buy some assets, such as equipment or office furniture, at low prices.

- Receivership allows more possibilities to acquire the ongoing business of a company in trouble. A receiver is normally appointed by a lender, such as a bank, who has secured their loan by a charge against certain of the company's assets, often the debtors. The receiver comes in to realize the assets in order to repay as much as possible of the debt.

    Unlike a liquidator, a receiver can keep a business trading if it is considered in the best interest of the creditors.

- **Administration.** The Insolvency Act of 1986 introduced a further possibility for creditors who might otherwise have had to force a company into liquidation. Before the 1986 Act, the only way of dealing with company failure where there were no specific charges on company assets was through liquidation. Potentially viable businesses were accordingly forced into liquidation because the creditors had no other process available to them for the recovery of their money. The 1986 Act introduced Administration Orders, which are court orders appointing an administrator empowered to salvage as much of the company as possible, or to sell its **assets** on a more profitable basis than under the circumstances of a liquidation. The 2002 Enterprise Act[2] further changed insolvency law by providing for a new regime for company administration and restricting the use of administrative receivership.

While it would be unwise in most circumstances to buy the shares of a company in receivership or under administration orders, it is possible to acquire those assets of the business which enable it to continue trading, thereby in effect buying the business.

OPPORTUNITY FROM CRISIS?

The 2007–08 financial crisis which brought down many well-known banks such as Lehman Brothers, also led to a record number of insolvencies around the world. The number of corporate insolvencies rose quickly as a result in the changed economic climate and the crisis in the international financial markets. In 2008, insolvencies in the USA were over 60 000, a rise of 45 per cent over the previous year. In Western Europe, there were around 169 000 insolvencies in 2008, an increase of 14 per cent. This included 63 000 in France, the highest level in Europe, and over 38 000 in the UK, a rise of 25 per cent.

In 2014, another insolvency crisis hit the UK high streets with almost three times as many shops disappearing as the year before. Notable chains collapsed, including the mobile phone retailer Phones4U, and La Senza lingerie shops (which had started life as small businesses).[3]

These high levels of failure represented pain for some and opportunity for others. In the 2007–08 crisis, there were major consolidations in the banking sector as stronger organizations stepped in to acquire those that were struggling; for example, JP Morgan Chase acquired Bear Sterns when it collapsed in 2008 and Bank of America bought Merrill Lynch. In the UK, Lloyds TSB took over the HBOS group which included Halifax and Bank of Scotland.

In 2014, the increase in usage of the internet was behind many of the retailers' problems with travel agents and traditional clothing and shoe outlets closing. However, UK consumer spending overall increased as internet shopping expanded, and the leisure and entertainment sectors such as coffee shops and betting shops increased their number of outlets.

Activity 2
Who buys small businesses?

Give some examples of:

(a) different types of buyers of small businesses.

(b) their motives for buying.

9.2 Small business buyers

The intentions of the buyer add further to the possible permutations for buying into an existing business.

9.2.1 OUTRIGHT PURCHASE

A would-be entrepreneur may choose to buy an ongoing business as a means of market entry. An existing small business owner may also decide to expand by purchasing another small enterprise. In some trades, the barriers to entry for a new start-up are sufficiently high to make the purchase of existing businesses the most common route (Gartner and Bellamy, 2008). This has been the case, for example, in the licensed trades such as restaurants, public houses and hotels.

THE CASE OF THE LICENSED TRADE

It is very difficult to obtain the necessary permission to sell alcoholic drinks from premises which do not have an existing licence, especially for a bar where this is not tied directly to the consumption of food. However, there is a well-established market in the buying and selling of existing licensed premises. Specialist licensed property agents, or transfer agents, act on behalf of owners wishing to sell the freehold or leasehold of their premises.[4]

A buyer can find vendors in any of the seller categories listed in the matrix of possibilities for entry into small business (Table 9.1):

- *Small firm:* some pubs are free houses, owned outright by the publican and not tied by contract to any one brewer. These are bought and sold much like other small firms, often with the added attraction of having a freehold property as an asset.
- *Larger firms:* corporations have also been forced to sell some public houses which they owned. A Monopolies and Mergers Commission report into the supply of beer found that large brewers controlled too many of the outlets for their products. Their recommendations forced brewers to sell off hundreds of licensed outlets.
- *Franchise:* some pubs are sold effectively as a franchise because the publican trades from licensed premises which are tied by a lease to one particular brewery.
- *Forced sales:* in the early 1990s, forced sales of public houses became commonplace. Free house prices were doubly hit by the general depression in the property market and the increase in premises for sale forced on the brewers. Owners who bought when prices were much higher were affected by high

(Continued)

interest rates and the decline in the value of their property asset, which was usually the main collateral for loans to buy the business. This also coincided with a downturn in demand for pubs' services. Increased competition from other leisure service providers, and stricter enforcement of drink drive legislation, led to a general decline in sales. These factors combined to cause a rise in the number of forced sales. A survey in 1991 suggested that one-third of free house pub sales were forced on the owners.[5] This shakeout in the industry provided opportunities for new chains of themed pub-diners to emerge, as they were able to obtain licensed properties at bargain prices.

This cycle repeated itself after 2007/08 when a combination of changing habits and recessionary pressures forced many pubs to close, especially those in limited market areas such as small villages. In 2007, over 1400 pubs closed in the UK as beer sales declined to their lowest levels since the 1930s.[6] Even the chains were affected with casualties such as the Massive Pub Company, with 33 pubs around London, going into administration and an eventual sale in 2008.

Today, pubs are thriving, not as places to drink but, rather, to eat. Half of the British population now visits a pub at least once per month, which is a higher visitor figure than instant burger restaurants or coffee shops. Pubs have even tapped the breakfast business. Visits to pubs at breakfast grew from 44 million in 2008 to 100 million in 2014.[7]

9.2.2 BUY-IN

Buyers may not wish to purchase an existing business in its entirety. They may instead **buy-in** to an existing business, and become a new partner, or shareholder, with those that already exist.

This is more commonplace in some sectors and types of small business than others. It often happens, for example, in professional practices such as accountants, solicitors, doctors and other medical practitioners such as physiotherapists. These are often large partnerships, where it is normal to have a turnover of partners who leave, or retire. In such circumstances, it is not necessary to dissolve the partnership, because the partnership agreement allows for the recruitment of another partner into the practice.

Other types of small firms, including franchises, may also wish to allow in a new partner or shareholder. A key problem for owner managers is that their own capabilities and resources will eventually limit the growth of the business unless a management team can be recruited and retained. To be effective in the longer term, managers who join a business need to share the founder's objectives and commitment through incentives including a share of the equity of the business. However, the buy-in does offer a way of promoting more 'open' innovation, where the sharing of ideas and human capital (individuals) allows more people to get the most out of limited resources (see Chesbrough, 2007).

Recognizing the importance of rewarding managers as well as owners, the UK government introduced tax incentives for employees to obtain shares in small businesses through enterprise management incentives (EMIs). EMIs are tax advantaged share options that enable small business owners to offer equity in their business to key employees at minimal cost. The grant of the option is tax free and there will normally be favourable tax allowances for the employee when the option is exercised.[8]

A similar need can also arise if a small firm has a particular problem. The addition of different skills and capital from a new partner or shareholder represents a possible recovery strategy.

For example, Anita Roddick had a problem raising funds in the early days of The Body Shop. The success of her first shop in Brighton encouraged her to open a second. She was unable to raise the necessary capital from the bank and so, instead, found a new partner who put up the necessary £4000 in return for 50 per cent of the equity of the business. It proved a very sound investment.

Buying into a business being sold off by a larger firm is also possible. This is becoming more common, especially in conjunction with buy-outs by the management (see below).

9.2.3 BUY-OUT

Buy-outs refer to the purchase of a business, or a significant part of it, by its existing management. Relatively rare in the 1970s, management buy-outs have become increasingly common since the 1980s (Gilligan and Wright, 2014). Although buy-outs can occur from small firms and franchises and have also happened as a result of a forced sale by the parent company, larger firms are usually the sellers. Indeed, many buy-outs are larger firms buying themselves out of even bigger companies; for example, MFI was bought out of Asda for £718 million. As a result, deals are normally for substantial amounts of money: in 2004, the largest management buy-out in the UK was the Automobile Association at £1.8 billion; in Europe, it was Celanese of Germany for £3.1 billion (Wright *et al.*, 2006).

Buy-outs can reward those who have worked for a company for some time without any form of ownership in the first instance. Richard Lee, who started his career on the factory floor of Jablite, a manufacturer of insulation materials, before working his way up to become managing director, helped lead a £26 million management buy-out of the business in 2015 from European owner Synbra. Commenting on the deal, he said: 'I joined the business as a 17-year-old, operating moulding machines, because I didn't know what to do for a job. When I started I used to have to hand-mix the dye we used and would come home from work absolutely blue from it and used to stain the lino in my mum's house. I never thought that I would end up as an owner of the company 28 years later.'

The company produces expanded polystyrene used in the construction industry for insulation, employing 150 staff with total revenues of £44 million and profits of £3.5 million in 2014.[9]

Management buy-outs have become an important part of industrial reorganization, and an increasingly common way for managers to become owner-managers. Although they are now a feature of most national economies, the level of buy-out activity varies widely by country (Birley and Muzyka, 2000). The USA and the UK are the biggest buy-out markets but these are growing in Europe and Asia (Wright *et al.*, 2006). In the UK, buy-outs averaged 600 each year from the mid-1990s. Although they fell away during the financial crisis, they have recovered somewhat to 416 deals in 2014. The individual value of each deal is high. They averaged over £4 million each in 2014 for a total deal value of £17.5 billion. In 2015, New Look, Virgin Active and ERM Group all had values greater than £1 billion (CMBOR, 2015a).[10]

In Europe, buy-outs reached a record number of 1526 in 2006 and a record value of €181 billion in 2007 before rapidly declining to €23 billion in 2009. Since the financial crisis, deals have slowly recovered to 902 at a total value of €23 billion in 2014 (CMBOR, 2015b).

Made possible by finance from venture capital funds, buy-outs have been fuelled by some well-publicized success stories, such as the buy-out of Premier Brands for £97 million from Cadbury Schweppes, in which 4500 of the 5000 employees bought shares at 1p each. When the company was later sold on, these shares were worth £5 each, turning a factory worker's stake of £10 into £5000, and giving the managing director a reported profit of £45 million. Such large-scale buy-outs encouraged many smaller ones.

Changes in local government legislation that introduced more competition in the provision of services stimulated some buy-outs in the public sector as well.

For example, a local council, the City and District of St Albans, subcontracted the management of its leisure facilities to a company formed by the management who had previously been employed by the council to run those same facilities. The council benefited from a fixed-cost base for the provision of leisure services, rather than unpredictable losses which they had experienced hitherto. The management team was able to market the facilities more aggressively and was financially more efficient out of local authority control.

That was in 1987; since then the company, Sports and Leisure Management Ltd, has gone on to expand this management concept to 36 different local authorities. They now manage 117 leisure facilities from Plymouth to Sunderland under the 'Everyone Active' brand.[11]

But not all buy-outs are success stories (Wright and Burrows, 2006). There have been many casualties. High interest rates and falling demand in recessionary times work against buy-outs, particularly where high levels of borrowing and expectations of rapid growth are typical. In the 20 years from 1986 to 2006, just over 1400 of the total of 12 300 buy-outs in the UK entered receivership, a failure rate of 11.5 per cent (Wright *et al.*, 2006). These included well-known names such as Magnet and First Leisure Night clubs.

9.2.4 BUY-IN MANAGEMENT BUY-OUT

A variation on the management buy-out theme is the buy-in management buy-out (or **BIMBO** as it is sometimes called), which combines outside and inside management in the purchase of a company. The risk of buying into a company from the outside can be reduced if the existing management of the company is also involved. In theory at least, it is possible to have the benefit of a fresh approach and wider experiences from the buying-in manager(s), linked to the in-depth knowledge of the company and its markets provided by the buy-out manager(s). The motives of the vendor follow the general lines of the larger firm as seller outlined above. Disposals often follow strategy changes brought on by financial problems or changes of ownership.

LETRASET AND THE STANLEY GIBBONS BIMBO

Letraset grew from a small firm in the 1960s to a quoted international company in the 1970s, and then found it difficult to sustain growth in its core graphic art business. By the early 1980s, it had diversified into toys, leisure and collectables, and quickly hit problems in these new businesses.

A recovery strategy involved selling three companies in the toy and leisure field to their existing management as buy-outs. But it was too late. Letraset was acquired by Esselte, the Swedish office products group. Wanting only the core graphic arts activities, Esselte promptly put the remaining unrelated business, Stanley Gibbons, the stamp dealing and philatelic publishing group, up for sale. Stanley Gibbons was eventually bought by a consortium of its own internal management plus some external stamp trade specialists in an early BIMBO.

Activity 3
Buying assets

When buying a business, it is common practice to buy only the assets and not the business entity itself. If you were buying a small business (such as a picture framing business):

(a) what types of assets would you wish to buy?

(b) on what basis would you value them?

9.3 Assets for sale

In buying an existing business, whoever the seller or buyer, it is important to recognize what exactly is for sale. This will depend not only on the wishes of the parties to the negotiation, but also on the legal status of the business. Sole traders and partnerships have no legal existence separate from their owners; therefore, only the assets of such businesses can be sold. Limited companies, on the other hand, are separate legal bodies; they have an existence distinct from their owners (see Chapter 10, for fuller explanations of legal entities). Once a limited company has been given birth, it can change parents. Shares can be bought and sold. However, in order to avoid inheriting unwanted or unknown liabilities it is also common for only the assets of limited companies to be acquired.

The assets of a business for sale will be the focus of attention of any prospective buyer. They are as varied as the small enterprises they belong to and so come in many shapes and sizes. However, there is nearly always a way of putting a monetary value on them (see Hubbard, 2014). Business assets can be reviewed under several headings, not all of which will appear in the balance sheet.

9.3.1 TANGIBLE ASSETS
Freehold property

The business may own the freehold of the property from which it trades. This is often the case where the position of the property is a key factor in its success in the marketplace. Hotels, restaurants, public houses, wine bars, sports clubs and other leisure facilities will all depend on their geographic location to attract customers. If location is such an important element in the marketing strategy of a small enterprise, then it is sensible to gain security of tenure over the property by buying the freehold, or at least securing a long lease, with first option to renew. Other businesses, less dependent on location, also purchase **freehold** property as a long-term investment, preferring to have a mortgage on an appreciating asset, rather than pay rent. Property owned by a small firm improves the look of its balance sheet and may make it easier to raise finance at a later date.

When such a business changes hands, the property is sometimes the most valuable asset. The bricks-and-mortar and land of a small hotel, for example, will almost certainly be of more value than the beds, furniture, kitchen equipment and other fixtures which make it possible to trade as a hotel.

Purchasing a freehold property as part of buying a business requires all the care and caution of buying any other property. In addition to the usual checks on ownership, planning permissions, restrictive covenants, mortgages and other charges, any prospective purchaser will particularly want to assure themselves of the suitability of the premises to the business. Moving from owned premises can be a long-winded affair that takes months, or even years in a slow property market.

Leasehold property

Property rented under a **leasehold** agreement can also be a valuable asset to a business. Most independent retailers, for instance, operate from leasehold premises. The situation of those premises sometimes commands a premium when the business, or even just the premises, changes hands. Commercial estate agents dealing in the transfer of such properties will quote a price for the 'benefit of the leasehold interest' which, in times of a strong market, can be considerable even for a small property with a relatively short lease if it is well situated. Any purchaser looking at the history of the leasehold property market will understand that it is, however, more volatile than the freehold market. High premiums paid for premises can disappear to nothing in times of recession, when even reverse premiums become possible. In 1990/91 and in 2007/08, the slowness of trading in high streets caused increased closures of retail firms so that existing tenants became prepared to pay prospective owners to take the liability of their lease from them. The owners of properties proving difficult to rent may offer rent-free periods to new tenants as an inducement to take on a new lease.

By its very nature a lease is a declining asset, compared to a freehold which will probably be an increasing asset over the long term. Its value as an asset in the purchase of an existing business will therefore depend on the desirability of the premises, and the state of the property market at the time of purchase. Thereafter, the value is likely to fluctuate. Other factors which will influence the value of a lease include:

- *Transferability.* Most leases are not automatically transferable. Landlords will want to control the suitability of any incoming tenants. Although most leases state that permission for transfer should not be unreasonably withheld, restrictions on transferability will devalue a lease.
- *Term of the lease.* Most commercial properties are held on shorter terms than residential properties. Ten-year leases are quite common, so that a business changing hands within the term of a lease will sometimes have only a few years left to run on the lease. However, a landlord will find it quite difficult to eject a sitting tenant, and many leases provide for the existing tenant to have first refusal on a new lease. These rights can be overridden however; for example, by a landlord wishing to redevelop, or occupy the property for their personal use.
- *Repairs and dilapidations.* Many commercial leases are on a 'full repairing' basis: that is, the tenant is responsible to pay for the upkeep not only of the interior, but also the exterior of the buildings and any surrounding land. A 'dilapidations' clause in the lease will also usually make the tenant responsible for returning the premises to the landlord in a specified condition at the end of a lease. The cost of these ongoing and end-of-lease repairs and refurbishments can constitute a considerable burden on the tenant, especially if the premises are old and near the end of the lease. Such factors will again influence the value of a lease. In some instances (for example, where a high level of dilapidations is expected soon), the lease can have a negative value, as its liabilities outweigh its usefulness.
- *Rent and provision for reviews.* Where the rent due on a property is considered to be below market levels, then this will add to the value of a lease. Most leases provide for rent reviews on a three- or five-year basis. The date of the next review, and provisions in the lease on how it is to be carried out, are also important. Many leases provide for upward only reviews, with prescribed arbitration procedures in the event of a failure to agree on a new rent. Such clauses will limit the benefit of any sub-market rent situations.

Furniture, fixtures and fittings

Buying an existing business implies that any premises from which it operates will be fitted out and furnished. A freehold or leasehold property, when taken on from new, is usually a bare shell, adaptable to the use of the incoming tenant. The cost of these fittings, whether it be shop fittings in the case of retail premises, or partitioning and modifications for manufacturing or office premises, is usually considerable. When a business is to be sold these fixtures and fittings are an asset whose value depends on their extent, condition and appropriateness.

The type of the business will determine the nature of the furniture, as well as fixtures and fittings. It is likely that those small enterprises where the customer receives a service on the premises will have a relatively high level of value in this kind of asset.

For example, a restaurant will require tables, chairs and other furnishings, and decor appropriate to its target market, which can be expensive to purchase. The value of these to prospective purchasers will depend on whether they wish to focus the business in the same way (on the same group of customers), or switch to a new theme and style which might involve a complete refit of the premises.

Those service industries where customers are not usually dealt with on the premises, and which require only a small area of office space, are likely to have a lower value in these assets. Manufacturing companies will vary, and sometimes will have spent the minimum possible on furnishings and fixtures. Higher-technology firms, however, often need to invest in sophisticated fittings; for example, to create a dust-free 'clean room' for certain processes.

Machinery, equipment and vehicles

The machinery and equipment necessary to perform the functions of a business will invariably be acquired with it. The type and extent will obviously depend on the business and could include:

- *manufacturing plant* (e.g. automated packaging machinery, testing equipment), workshop machinery and tools (e.g. lathes, compressors, saws and other small tools);
- *commercial equipment* (e.g. kitchen equipment, microscopes, exhibition stands);
- *office equipment* (e.g. computers, copiers, telephones, desks);
- *vehicles* (e.g. delivery vans, fork-lift trucks, company cars).

The alternatives for evaluating these types of assets all have flaws:

- The *written-down book value* will tend to be somewhat arbitrary depending on the depreciation policies of the business, which may have been optimistic or cautious.
- The *market value* could be a pessimistic figure, as these assets tend to be worthless when sold off individually and not as part of an ongoing business.
- The *replacement value* is a useful measure to appreciate what it might cost to start up an equivalent new business, but it will not take account of the age and useful life of the equipment.
- The *original* cost of the equipment is, again, a useful measure to have in valuing these fixed assets, but will neither take account of inflation in new prices, nor devaluation of an asset through age.

Ownership is an important consideration in the acquisition of any assets under this heading. Frequently, hire purchase, leasing or rental agreements cover such equipment, which determine who owns it and how much there is to be paid for the continued use of the equipment on an ongoing basis.

Stock and work-in-progress

The vendor of a small firm will usually wish to sell the stock of the business to the new owner. This stock can be classified into three main types:

- *Raw materials stock:* the materials a business buys in from suppliers which it then uses or converts into something else. For example, a picture framing business will have a stock of glass, mount board, and uncut lengths of wood and metal mouldings for frames.

- *Work-in-progress:* on the day of handover from one owner to the next, some jobs will be partly finished, representing work still in progress. For example, the picture framer may have frames which are not fully finished sitting on the workbench.
- *Finished stock:* there will be a stock of product which is ready for sale to the customer, but which remains unsold or unshipped and not invoiced on the day of transfer. The picture framer will have finished pictures awaiting collection by customers. There may also be unsold framed pictures displayed in a shop area, along with unsold ready-made frames and unframed prints.

The valuation of such stock is often more straightforward than other assets, with fewer negotiating points.

The basis of valuation for raw materials stock is normally the original cost paid for the stock. If there have been price rises subsequent to the purchase of the stock, the seller may wish to negotiate a higher price based on its replacement value. The buyer, on the other hand, may wish to ask for a reduced price if they consider some materials damaged, obsolete or overstocked and perishable. **Work-in-progress** is more complicated to value, but is normally valued on a similar basis to raw materials stock, with an additional amount to represent the value already added to the product.

Finished goods stock is normally valued at its selling price at the time, taking account of any overstocked positions, which may decrease the value of some lines.

Stocks are normally valued on the day of transfer of the business, so that it does not represent a fixed sum of money during the negotiations. Stocks are taken over at valuation, and it is only the method of this valuation that is negotiated prior to handover.

Some types of business may need an independent valuer, because of either the complexity or the time-consuming nature of the valuation of stock. The stock of a farm to be taken over will include crops already planted, requiring an expert to assess their value. A busy catering business, such as a restaurant or hotel, may have a large number of different items, some partly consumed, which require outside assistance to quantify on the day of the sale of the business.

Debtors

Those people or companies who still owe money to a business for sale, on account of goods received or services rendered, represent a real asset in the books of any business which extends credit to its customers. The issue in valuing debtors is whether or not they will honour the debt, and how long they will take to pay. This uncertainty over the validity of debtors is often overcome by the vendor of the business either retaining ownership of the debtors, and collecting the money themselves after the sale of the business, or guaranteeing the amount that is collected from debtors by the new owner.

As with stocks, debtors will be valued on the date of transfer of the business to represent an up-to-date figure.

9.3.2 INTANGIBLE ASSETS AND GOODWILL

A distinction is drawn between the *tangible* and *intangible* assets of a business for sale. The assets discussed so far are tangible, in that they can be physically identified and quantified. The intangible assets of a successful business will often be more important because they relate to why these physical assets have any meaning in the marketplace (Cohen, 2011; see also Nerudova and Bohusova, 2009, for related discussion of accounting principles for SMEs in Europe; Dahmash *et al.*, 2009, Australian listed companies; Oliveira *et al.*, 2010, Portuguese listed companies; and, Salamudin *et al.*, 2010, the Malaysian market). The intangible assets include the reputation and image of the company, the **goodwill** that exists between the business and its customers, the people that work for it and any know-how that can be protected. In effect, they make the tangible assets productive and give value to the business. In a manufacturing plant, they enable a mixture of buildings, equipment and stock to work together to add value to products and services in a way that is meaningful to customers and profitable to the business.

Table 9.2 summarizes the principal tangible and intangible assets of a business. In practice, the distinction is not clear-cut; there are many areas of overlap between the types of asset, some of which have been shown.

Intangible assets only have real value while a business continues to trade. Once it has ceased trading, they lose most of their meaning and their worth. An unsuccessful business will tend to have fewer intangible assets, as these represent the necessary conditions for success. But even a failed business will not have failed in every respect and can have some valuable intangibles, such as a skilled and loyal workforce. Even these assets soon evaporate once business has ceased, which is why the concept of administration was introduced to allow struggling enterprises the opportunity to reorganize their finances, or be sold while trading continued.

Table 9.2 Tangible and intangible assets of a business for sale

Tangible assets	Examples of areas of overlap	Intangible assets
Property (freehold/leasehold)	Location of premises	Goodwill
Furniture, fixtures and fittings	Signage and logo	Image and reputation
Plant, equipment and vehicles	Systems and training	Employees
Stock and work-in-progress	Research and development	Intellectual property
Debtors	Mailing list	Customers

Goodwill

In many respects, this is a summary of the value of the intangible assets of a business. It is an accountancy term which can find its way into the balance sheets of a business, but its accuracy will be determined by circumstance and not necessarily reality. If a business has recently been acquired, the tangible assets, such as property, stocks and debtors, will have an identified value which will probably not equate to the purchase price of the business and therefore the total use of funds in buying it. In these circumstances, goodwill is a balancing figure representing the difference between the book value of specific assets, less any liabilities, and the amount actually paid to acquire them. Immediately after the purchase of a business, the amount of goodwill in the balance sheet will therefore reflect the negotiated value placed on it. But any small business which has not been recently bought or sold will not have had its goodwill valued in this way, and so it will not necessarily be reflected in the accounts.

Goodwill also occurs as a balance-sheet item in relation to property. For example, an existing retail business may move premises and pay a premium over and above the value of any fixtures and fittings in order to acquire a good commercial site. This premium will be reflected in the balance sheet as goodwill or intangible fixed assets. This is a first area of overlap in distinguishing between tangible and intangible assets. The value of freehold or leasehold property is not just a function of its physical attributes and associated costs, but also its geographic location in relation to the marketplace. For some small firms this will be the key factor in determining its value. A hotel near an airport or busy seaside town will be worth far more than an identical building in an area that few people visit; if external factors cause a decrease or increase in the number of visitors, then the property value will be affected accordingly. In other circumstances, the value of a property for a small firm is less significant; a manufacturing company with a geographically spread customer base may be successfully located anywhere where there is available labour.

Goodwill is a general term which attempts to value the likelihood of success and therefore the future profitability of an enterprise. When a business is advertised for sale, goodwill is often the word used to describe the vendor's valuation of this future profitability, which is added to any market value of the tangible assets.

Image and reputation

The image and reputation developed by a small firm among its existing and potential customers will have a profound affect on its probability of success. An enterprise's image can be symbolized more tangibly in its logo style, the permanent signs used to advertise its presence and other fixtures and fittings which give the customer an impression of what the business is like.

For this reason, a franchise network will emphasize the need to portray a consistent look in the premises of franchisees by using standard images and furnishings. But, for all that, reputation is a fragile asset; the work of years to build an image of quality and reliability can be destroyed in minutes through shoddy or variable products or services.

The new owner of a small firm can become a negative influence on a well-established reputation, or provide a well-needed change to a more tarnished image.

THE VALUE OF A BRAND: THE RISE AND FALL OF WOOLWORTH

Woolworths was the retail phenomenon of the twentieth century. Started by Frank Woolworth in the 1880s as a mass-market shop that sold factory-made goods at rock bottom prices, it became one of the first global brands, with more than 3000 near-identical stores across the world. Its profitability was such that the founder was able to erect the world's tallest building in 1913, the Woolworth Building in New York, and pay for it in cash. In the UK, 'Woolies' became a household name, regarded by shoppers as quintessentially British. The business model began to fade towards the end of the century and Woolworth disappeared from the US retailing scene in 1997. In the UK, the chain of 800 shops collapsed spectacularly in the financial crisis of 2008, going from normal trading to shutdown in just over a month. The brand was still considered a valuable asset and was bought by the Shop Direct Group who used it to trade online at woolworth.co.uk until 2015, when it became 'Very'. Former Woolworths employees made several attempts to rescue parts of the chain, as many stores had valuable high street locations. A former senior manager, Andy Latham, re-opened 15 of the shops as 'Alworths'. This, in turn, went into administration in 2011 and was sold to the discount chain Poundstretchers. A Woolworths 'Saturday girl', Claire Robinson, re-opened the Dorchester Woolies as an independent, 'Wellworths', in 2009 amidst much publicity. She was forced to change its name to 'Wellchester' by the new owners of the Woolworth brand name and the store closed in 2012.

In other parts of the world, the Woolworth name has survived. A canny group of Australian entrepreneurs registered the name F.W. Woolworth & Co. Ltd in the 1920s and the US and UK parent companies objected too late. Making a successful move into food retailing in the 1960s, the Australian Woolworth is a major, thriving chain today. In South Africa, entrepreneur Max Sonnenberg pulled off a similar trick and began using the name for his stores in the 1930s with no financial connection to the parent. The chain still trades with a focus not just on value, but also the 'good business journey' of ecological and ethical considerations, including energy and water conservation, sustainable farming and fishing (see www.woolworth.co.za). Independent Woolworth stores also exist in Zimbabwe, Barbados and New Zealand.

Employees

As well as the owner, the employees of a small business can be a crucial element in its success. Their skills, experience and way of doing business will directly or indirectly impact on the satisfaction of customers.

In part, this will be truly intangible, relying on individual expertise and motivation. A more tangible aspect of this asset will be the systems which have been established to guide employees in the various operations of the business, in the use of plant and equipment, and the training offered to them to improve the quality of their work, for example.

The seller of a small business often has acted as its manager and, in this sense, may have been the key employee. Their contribution to the business, and the impact of their removal from it, will be an issue that is particularly important in the sale of a small, owner-managed enterprise.

Intellectual property

Innovation is a key ingredient in the success of a small enterprise. The results of innovation can become an important part of the intangible assets of a small business, classified as intellectual property. The four main areas of intellectual property are:

- **Patents** afford temporary protection to technological inventions.
- **Copyright** covers literary, artistic and musical creations in the longer term. Copyright is a right to prevent copying and covers items from computer software and databases to drawings and business plans.
- **Trademarks** or brand names used in trading can be registered to protect them from infringement or passing-off by other companies.
- **Design right** extends protection to registered designs of products which have original features in their shape or configuration.

Protecting this intellectual property in a small business context can be challenging (Olander *et al.*, 2009). (See Chapter 10, for more detailed explanation and discussion of these rights.)

A small business may have created an asset from such properties in two distinct ways:

1 *As the owner of a protected intellectual property.*
   For example, a small publisher usually copyrights any material which it publishes and, although this does not appear in the balance sheet, it has considerable value if the material can be reused.
2 *As the contracted user of intellectual property.*
   For example, the same small publisher also has contracted rights to publish books by certain authors who themselves own the copyright to the work.

Contracts covering licensing arrangements for products or processes protected by patents, trademarks or design rights can form an integral part of a small enterprise's activities. A new owner will therefore wish to ensure any necessary assignment of such contracts.

Past investment in research and development is a more tangible demonstration of the worth of a small firm's intellectual property, which otherwise might only be visible in its stocks of finished product, some of which may carry a brand name or be protected by patent.

Customers

Customers are perhaps the most tangible of the intangible assets of a small firm; they can be observed and are often organized into a mailing list or, appear in a schedule of debtors.

What is intangible is their loyalty and commitment to the business, especially if it changes ownership. The extent and longevity of the customer base will be important aspects in its valuation. A business which relies heavily on a small number of recently acquired customers has a very different asset to one with a large number of well-established clients.

Activity 4
Avoiding liabilities

A buyer of an existing business obviously wishes to avoid acquiring too many liabilities with the business. If you were negotiating to buy a small business, what sort of liabilities would you look out for? Which would you definitely wish to avoid? Which might you be prepared to accept?

9.4 Liabilities to be avoided

Taking on liabilities as well as assets is a significant risk in buying an existing business. While wanting to retain and build on the existing assets of a small business, a prospective purchaser will wish to avoid any liabilities arising from the past activities of the firm.

The liabilities of a small business might include:

- trade creditors;
- bank and other borrowings;
- tax, VAT, PAYE and National Insurance contributions;
- lease and hire purchase agreements;
- guarantees or mortgages on assets.

If the business being sold is a sole trader or a partnership, then only the assets can be sold. The previous owner(s) will be left to pay off trade creditors, repay the bank or other borrowings and settle outstanding tax, VAT, PAYE and National Insurance liabilities.

If the shares of a limited company are being purchased, these liabilities belong to the company and will be transferred with it. The unknown quantity of some of these liabilities, especially those involving taxation where uncertainties can exist for several years after purchase, can be dealt with by:

- arranging for the vendor to give personal indemnities and warranties on the amount of future liabilities; or
- purchasing only the assets of a limited company in the same way as though it were a sole trader or partnership. These assets can be purchased by a shell company with no previous liabilities.

There are some liabilities which cannot be avoided, even when purchasing only the assets of a business, as some of these assets will be inseparable from certain liabilities. These include:

- *Obligations to employees.* When a business is sold as a going concern, even if only the assets are transferred to a new owner, employment law regards terms of employment and the period of service of an employee as continuous. Employees' contracts specifying their terms and conditions of service, including any notice period required for termination of employment, remain valid.

    An employee's period of service with the former owner is added to that with the new owner, to form one continuous period of employment. This can increase the new owners' obligations for such benefits as redundancy payments.

    Where a business has contracted out of the state pension scheme and set up its own private pension fund, there is a continuous obligation on the employer to ensure that the fund can meet the minimum benefits of the state scheme.

- *Liabilities attached to specific assets.* An acquired asset may not be totally free of liabilities. Equipment can be subject to lease or hire purchase agreements; property or debtors may be part of a guarantee on loans. Such liabilities can be terminated by the seller before passing title to a new owner, or the buyer may agree to take on the liability with the asset.

Activity 5
What is it worth?

You own a small business (such as the picture framer already mentioned) which you wish to sell. On what basis will you decide the asking price for the business? In other words, how will you decide the price for your business?

9.5 Basis of valuation of an existing business

9.5.1 ASSETS OR PROFITS

There are two basic ways of valuing an existing business (Gilligan and Wright, 2014), which follow the nature of the assets to be valued:

1 *Market or other valuation of the assets to be acquired.* Tangible assets tend to be valued this way. Property, fixtures and fittings, equipment, stocks and debtors can all be physically, and separately, identified and valued.
2 *Multiple of annual profits.* Rather than evaluating individual assets, a buyer can consider the earning power of the business now and in the future. This is the usual way of assessing the value of intangible assets. If intangibles cannot be physically measured or counted, their effectiveness in the marketplace can be evaluated; the usual yardstick for this is profit.

The basis chosen for valuation will depend on the mix of assets of the business, as shown in Table 9.3.

Table 9.3 **The basis of valuation for a small business**

Asset mix	Tangible assets only	Mix of tangible and intangible assets	Intangible assets only
Valuation basis	Market value of assets	Assets at valuation plus goodwill valued as multiple of profits	Multiple of profits
Examples	Agricultural smallholding Freehold retail premises	Small manufacturing firm Leasehold restaurant	Training consultancy Estate agency

- Some small businesses are *asset-rich,* and profitability becomes of secondary importance in a valuation. For example, an agricultural business such as a small farm or smallholding is valued primarily on the going rate of an acre of land in the neighbourhood. Two farms of the same size would be of similar value, despite the fact that one may be farmed more efficiently, and therefore be making more profits (or fewer losses), than the other. In the same way, freehold retail shops are priced according to the market value of other similar properties in the area. If the business trading from the shop is not profitable, this has little impact on the price, which will be determined more by the potential trade of the locality for any kind of retail operation.

- At the other end of the spectrum are businesses with no real *tangible assets* at all. A consultancy operating from home can only be measured by its profitability because its assets will be overwhelmingly intangible. Other small firms valued on this basis include those operating in the experience economy (e.g. some small cultural and arts organizations), and the service industries where they act as intermediaries between buyers and sellers – for example, estate agents, import agencies and insurance brokers.
- In practice, the majority of businesses for sale are valued on the basis of a mix of tangible and intangible assets (Gartner and Bellamy, 2008). Even service industries accumulate fixed and other assets if they survive in business for long enough – fixtures, fittings and equipment for the office, and debtors and cash remaining in the business, for example. Many businesses depend on tangible assets for their processes and build intangible assets through the goodwill of a customer base. Most small manufacturing firms would come into this category. Other service-oriented enterprises also have valuable fixed assets in equipment and fittings, as well as intangible goodwill. For example, a restaurant will need considerable investment in its kitchen and decor, while its profitability will determine its full value as an ongoing business.

9.5.2 MULTIPLE OF PROFITS

If intangible assets are to be judged by profitability, how much profit should be taken into account? This is normally expressed as a multiple of annual profits; for example, a business making £30 000 per annum might be judged to have goodwill valued at £90 000, or three times annual profits. The size of the multiplier is a key negotiating point, which will consider the following factors:

- *Quality of earnings.* Where a small firm has a history of several profitable years in business (usually a minimum of three years) and can demonstrate clearly that it has a sound, continuing level of profitability and trades with a well-spread customer base, then it can be said to have good quality earnings. It will be worth a higher multiple of profits than, say, a business which has just made an annual profit of a similar amount, which was for the first time and was dependent on only one large order. This is really a measure of risk in the likelihood of profits continuing at the current level in the future. When the risk that profits will fall is low, a potential buyer will be more easily persuaded to pay for more years of those profits.
- *Interest rates.* Bank interest rates will indicate the maximum multiplier that can be paid for a business and still be worthwhile. For example, if interest rates are 5 per cent and a small firm is for sale at £100 000, representing a multiple of 20 on annual profits of £5000, then interest payable on a loan to buy the business will cancel out the annual profits.

  If a limited company uses its own shares to buy another business (i.e. the vendor receives shares in the purchasing company, rather than cash), then higher multiples are possible because money interest rates are less relevant.

  But with interest rates in the 3–8 per cent range, multiples of between 2–5 times profits are common in small firm transactions.
- *Rate of inflation.* Higher rates of inflation can operate in the same way as higher interest rates. The return or profits from an investment have to keep pace with inflation just to maintain its value. If £100 000 is paid for a business in times when inflation is running high, at say 10 per cent, then profits will have to be £10 000 per year just to maintain the value of the original investment. This fixes a maximum profit multiplier of five times earnings if the money invested is not to lose its value.

9.5.3 GEARING

A buyer of a small business commonly uses a mix of borrowed and personal funds. The relationship between the buyer's own money and borrowed funds, or **gearing**, is an important influence on the risks and rewards of a purchase and, therefore, the price worth paying.

Higher gearing enables buyers to purchase more for each pound of their own money invested. If the business is successful, this increases the reward. But it also increases the risk; if the profits of the business fall, the effect on the buyer's personal stake is magnified. For example, Table 9.4 outlines two possible options for a buyer with £50 000 of his own money to invest.

Table 9.4 The effects of gearing on a small business purchase

	Purchase A (£000)	Purchase B (£000)
Purchase price (4 × profits)	100	200
Profit (before interest, depreciation and tax)	25	50
Personal capital	50	50
Borrowings	50	150
Interest @ 6%	3	9
Profit after interest	22	41
First scenario: profits rise by 25%		
Profits	31	62
Profits after interest	28	53
Value of business (4 × profits)	124	248
Personal equity after borrowings repaid	74	98
Second scenario: profits fall by 25%		
Profits	19	38
Profits after interest	16	29
Value of business (4 × profits)	76	152
Personal equity after borrowings repaid	26	2
Third scenario: profits fall by 50%		
Profits	13	25
Profits after interest	10	16
Value of business (4 × profits)	52	100
Personal equity after borrowings	2	(50)

- *In Purchase A*, the buyer raises a further £50 000 to buy a business for £100 000, representing four times profits. After interest, the buyer is left with profits of £22 000, a rate of return on his own money invested of 44 per cent.
- *In Purchase B*, the buyer invests the same £50 000 from personal funds, but this time becomes more highly geared by raising a further £150 000 to buy a business for £200 000, again at a multiple of four times annual profits of £50 000. This time the buyer is left with £41 000 profit after interest, a rate of return of 82 per cent on the same personal investment of £50 000.
- *If the business goes well,* then the deal gets even better under Purchase B. The first scenario of profits rising by 25 per cent increases the return on investment, and the £50 000 invested is now worth £98 000, compared to £74 000 under Purchase A (assuming the business is still valued at four times annual profits).
- *If business goes badly,* the deal gets worse under Purchase B, and can become disastrous sooner than under Purchase A. A profit fall of 25 per cent will still give Purchase B higher profits at £38 000 compared to £19 000 under Purchase A, but a valuation of the business on the same basis of four times annual profits

shows that the original investment of £50 000 has virtually all been lost under Purchase B, and only half lost under Purchase A.

Under Purchase B, a profit fall of 50 per cent will not only lose the buyer his original stake, but also put him into debt by £50 000 if the business was sold. Under Purchase A, the buyer loses his personal investment but no more.

Although higher gearing improves the rewards of success, it also increases the risks in failure. A cautious buyer will want to be very convinced about the quality of earnings before accepting a high gearing in order to make a purchase.

In the mid-to-late 1980s, the easier availability of loans to buy businesses helped increase the risks involved, not only by tempting purchasers to accept higher gearing, but also by increasing the price of buying a business at a time of relatively low interest rates and a booming economy (Gilligan and Wright, 2014). Management buy-outs were particularly affected. By the late 1980s, the success of earlier buy-outs made the route more popular and more expensive for buyers. Higher prices meant higher gearing; gearing for large management buy-outs went from 1:2 (borrowings to equity) in 1981 to 5:1 by 1989.[12]

The recession in the early 1990s, the dot-com boom and bust of the late 1990s and the financial crisis of 2008 particularly hit those businesses which were purchased with high gearing, through higher interest rates and lower profits. Failures and government regulation have made banks more cautious and gearing ratios are back to levels more common in the early 1980s.

Activity 6
Tax implications

In what ways can tax affect:

(a) the purchaser of a small business, and
(b) the seller?

9.6 Taxation aspects of a small business purchase

Taxation aspects are important in buying an existing business, not only in the immediate impact they may have on the total costs of purchase, but also the ongoing level of profitability thereafter.

Once a purchase price has been agreed, the next negotiating point is often the allocation of the price to the individual assets purchased. The interests of a buyer and a seller in terms of tax minimization seldom coincide.

The buyer
When assets are purchased, some qualify for writing down allowances which are deducted from taxable profits. The amount of these allowances varies according to the asset purchased:

- *Plant, machinery and vehicles:* these normally qualify for capital allowances.
- *Property:* tax relief on buildings and land is the exception, rather than the rule.
- *Stock:* stock used in the course of trading represents a cost against sales, but it is possible to make a paper profit on the value of stocks held through inflation, or because of a low valuation of stocks bought with the business.

- *Debtors:* if debtors are acquired in a purchase which subsequently is not paid, then these bad debts can be written off against profits, and any VAT or sales tax paid can be reclaimed.
- *Patents and know-how:* from 1 April 1986, new provisions were introduced in the UK to allow payments for know-how or patent rights to be written down.

These allowances apply for sole traders, partnerships and limited companies. Therefore, careful consideration is required in allocating a purchase price to the various assets acquired, as future tax liabilities will be affected. A prudent buyer will seek the advice of an accountant in this complicated area.

The seller

The seller will also wish to give careful consideration to the taxation implications of a sale. Capital Gains Tax (CGT) may be a major concern. Capital gains for both individuals and companies are now taxed as income in the year in which they are made. In the UK, there is an individual exemption (£11 100 in 2015/16) in any one tax year, and gains are reduced to reflect changes in the retail price index.

Rollover relief can also apply. If business assets are sold, and others purchased within three years, payment of tax is deferred until the new assets are finally sold.

From the late 1990s, the UK tax regime became more favourable to those entrepreneurs wishing to realize the value of their businesses. The current 'entrepreneur's relief' on the disposal of qualifying business assets and shares gives an effective rate of 10 per cent, with a limit £10 million of gains made in a lifetime.

Tax losses

If a limited company has made trading losses which have not all been cancelled out by subsequent profits, then those losses remain with the company and are available for use by a new owner of the shares. Tax losses can thus represent an asset which makes it more advantageous to purchase the shares of a limited company, rather than just its assets. However, if the nature of the trade carried on by the company is significantly altered, the relief against future tax given by past losses may be denied. It is not possible to purchase a company solely for its tax losses, and carry on business in a totally new direction.

Activity 7
For and against buying a small business

Compared to a start-up or franchise, what are:

(a) the advantages of buying an existing business, and
(b) the disadvantages?

9.7 For and against buying an existing business

How does buying an existing business, or part of it, either as an outsider, or an existing manager, compare to other routes to market entry as a small enterprise?

Possible advantages

- *Overcomes barriers to market entry.* Where there are significant barriers to market entry for a small business entrant, buying an existing enterprise may be the most realistic alternative. For example, the planning permission and other legal permits required for restaurants, hotels, nightclubs, wine bars and public houses make market entry through acquisition the most common route.

- *Buying immediate turnover and income.* This could be important, especially when the buyer has no other sources of income.
- *Buying market share.* One of the key ingredients for a successful small business is to build a high share of a specific market. If existing businesses control a significant percentage of the desired market, then it may be advantageous to buy into them, rather than compete.
- *Existing assets of property, equipment and staff.* The costs and time required to put these into place as a start-up can be considerable, and it may be more appropriate to focus resources and energy on the market-place through an existing operation.
- *Goodwill with existing customers.* An existing customer base is evidence of the viability of a business concept, and therefore takes some of the risk out of small business ownership. It can also provide a good platform for future growth.
- *Existing track record.* The ability to look over the past performance of a company provides comfort not only to a potential buyer, but also to financial supporters such as banks. A business showing evidence of a good track record over a number of years is easier to fund than one with no history at all.
- *Insider knowledge.* This advantage only usually applies to situations where the existing management is involved in the purchase. But it may also be in the best interest of existing management to be as open as possible with prospective new owners, rather than suffer the consequences of concealment at a later date.

Possible disadvantages

- *Buying possible liabilities with assets.* Even if only assets are purchased, liabilities can still be attached to them; for example, employee liabilities. If shares in a company are bought, then liabilities will certainly exist. Liabilities can form part of an acceptable risk when they are known; the greatest problem is the possibility of liabilities, unrecognized at the time of purchase, emerging at a later date.
- *Uncertainty over records.* A business for sale will obviously be presented in the best possible light. Sole traders and partnerships are not required to have their accounts audited, so some information may be withheld. The onus is on the buyer to ask the right questions, not on the seller to provide all the information.
- *Risk in intangible assets.* The goodwill inherent in an existing business can disappear very rapidly if a new owner makes inappropriate changes. A previous owner-manager may represent a substantial part of the goodwill, which goes with them when they leave.
- *Historical problems in the business.* An existing business may have some negative goodwill which is not immediately apparent. There may be a history of poor relationships with suppliers or staff, for example, which outlives the departure of the owner.
- *Not all my own work.* Some of the satisfaction an entrepreneur gains from a new business start-up derives from taking a business idea from conception to successful implementation. Buying an existing business can diminish the sense of achievement, and therefore the motivation to make it succeed.
- *Short-term profitability.* Research also suggests that the short-term profit orientation of some private equity buy-outs can negatively influence the potential of the new ownership team to initiate and sustain entrepreneurial management (see Bruining *et al.*, 2013).

Motives for sale

The key question to ask in buying an existing business is: why is it for sale? A buyer needs to establish acceptable reasons why a business should be sold. If they cannot, there may be hidden negative factors which may apply equally to the buyer (Gartner and Bellamy, 2008).

Table 9.5 summarizes the advantages and disadvantages of buying a business.

Table 9.5 A summary of the possible advantages and disadvantages of buying an existing business

Possible advantages	Possible disadvantages
Overcomes barriers to market entry	Possibility of liabilities as well as assets
Buying immediate turnover and income	Uncertainty over records
Buying market share	Risk in intangible assets
Existing assets of property, equipment and staff in place	Historical problems in the business
Goodwill with existing customers already built up	Not all my own work
Existing track record	Short-term profitability
Insider knowledge (especially in management buy-outs)	

9.8 Summary and Activities

The options to purchase a business are varied and depend on: the status of the business (successful to unsuccessful); the motives and types of seller; the entry method of the buyer (outright purchase or buy-out/buy-in routes). The possible assets of a business to be acquired need to be carefully understood and assessed. These include tangible assets such as premises, equipment and stock. They also include intangible assets such as goodwill, intellectual property and the skill base of employees, which are more difficult to value. Equally important, the potential liabilities of a business for sale such as creditors, loans, guarantees and obligations to employees need to be evaluated.

There are two basic ways of valuing a business: the market value of its assets; and a multiple of its annual profits. Sometimes, the price of a small business for sale is based on a combination of these two measures depending on the mix of tangible and intangible assets. However, as the assets of most businesses are largely intangible, a multiple of profits is the common measurement of value. Buying a business has notable advantages over starting a new venture, including overcoming barriers to entry, gaining instant market share and income, and obtaining valuable assets such as customer lists and skilled employees. But there are problems, as significant liabilities may go with the business. Some entrepreneurs may feel incomplete in their achievements if they do not found an enterprise. Thus, the motives of both sellers and buyers are the key to understanding if this is the best route to market entry for a business owner.

Case study
You've been framed: Part 2 (of 3)

BRYONY HANNAM CONSIDERS BUYING AN EXISTING BUSINESS

While investigating her idea of a picture-framing business, Bryony Hannam discovered that a framer and picture gallery was for sale, located not far from her home town. She decided to investigate further, and asked the business transfer agent handling the sale to send her the particulars.

(Continued)

Southgate and Co.

Business agents and valuers

On the instructions of the shareholders,
FOR SALE: ART ENTERPRISES LTD trading as GRAY'S FRAMING STUDIOS

Important These particulars are confidential: staff are unaware of the impending sale.

General Established by our client some five years ago, we are now pleased to offer for sale three picture shops well-situated in market towns, and a framing workshop, giving combined sales of £300 000 gross per annum.

Price We are instructed to seek offers in the region of £150 000 (one hundred and fifty thousand pounds) for the entire issued shares of the company. Stock to be transferred at an additional valuation (approx. £50 000).

The retail premises There are three shops, all in good positions next to busy high streets in sizeable market towns.

> The premises are leasehold, with terms left to run of 12, 17 and 22 years.
> Rent review patterns are five-yearly with reviews due in two years' time.
> Each shop is staffed by a manager and an assistant.
> Each shop is furnished and fitted to a high standard, with picture and frame moulding displays, carpeting and other furnishings, a desk and an electronic cash register. Sales areas in the three shops vary at 700, 900 and 1200 sq. ft.

The workshop The workshop of 2000 sq. ft. is situated in a small industrial estate. The lease has 16 years to run, with a rent review due next year.

The premises are comprehensively equipped with all the machinery and tools needed for the provision of a successful and efficient framing service. Equipment includes:

- Mitre saws and guillotines
- Glass cutting table
- Mountboard cutter and trimmer
- Assorted small tools
- Pneumatic under pinner
- Dry mounting press
- Worktables, racks and shelving
- Large capacity air compressor

Staff: the workshop employs one manager and two framers.

The business The business was established by our client five years ago. Since that date, the business has expanded from a single unit to the current three-unit operation.

> The principal activities are those of:

1 *bespoke framing*
2 *framed and unframed pictures.*

1 Bespoke framing. The company offers a high-quality framing service for customers which accounts for approximately 60 per cent of turnover. Production, according to the customer's specification, is carried out centrally and delivered back to the retail premises within a seven-day period.

Particular strengths of this service are:
- wide choice of frames and mounts
- quality of production
- level of service provided by retail staff.

2 Pictures. The company retails a range of pictures from reproduction prints and posters, limited editions, to original oils and watercolours. The majority of stock retails for between £15 and £200. Particular strengths are:
- wide range of images available
- affordable prices.

Financial information Past trading results:

£000s	Current year	Prior year	Next year forecast
Sales (net of VAT)	260	180	325
Cost of materials	85	60	105
Gross profit	175	120	220
Overheads:			
Salaries and wages	90	75	100
Rent and rates	45	28	50
Other	10	7	15
Total overheads	145	110	165
Net profit	30	10	55

Net profit is before depreciation, interest, and director' salaries and fees.

The Purchase price The business is for sale at £150 000 comprising:

Value of leases remaining:	£35 000
Value of equipment and machinery:	£15 000
Value of fixtures and fittings:	£10 000
Goodwill:	£90 000
Total	**£150 000**

In addition, stock will be charged at valuation, estimated at £50 000.

Liabilities, including creditors, borrowings and hire purchase agreements, will be discharged prior to completion of the sale.

Future developments The sales forecast for next year includes a full year's trading by the third shop, which opened part way through the current year. Overheads are based on actual costs plus inflation so that the forecast result is considered most realistic by our clients.

Bryony's reaction

Bryony was excited after she had done some initial calculations: 'It's just what I'm looking for', she told her husband. 'And I won't have to go through all the trauma of starting up from nothing. The business is obviously successful judging by the sales figures. I know one of the shops. It's very similar to the idea I was working on; it's just not in this town, that's all. But of course, I could always open up another outlet here as I had planned to do, except that I will have a ready-made workshop and existing sales to keep me going from day one.'

'What about the price?' her husband asked. 'Your mother only left you £75 000. Where will you get the rest from?'

'I'm going to talk to my accountant about the price, but the bank manager has already said I can borrow the rest, with the house as guarantee of course. If the stock is £50 000, I will have to borrow £125 000, which will cost less than £10 000 per year. The profits more than cover that', replied Bryony.

'What about your salary? You will need something for your efforts, not to mention return on the money you're putting in', her husband persisted.

'If it makes the forecast profits next year, the business will still have profits of £40 000 after interest, which sounds a good enough return to me', argued Bryony.

The accountant's caution

The next day Bryony saw her accountant, who had been studying the particulars and the finances in more detail.

'I'm concerned about this forecast', he said. 'If the business makes the projected figures for next year it may be worth what they're asking. But part of that result will be down to you; if you buy it, you will be running it by then. Why should you pay for future profits? It's what the business earns now that they're selling, not what you can do with it tomorrow. If it is so sure to improve next year, why are they selling it now?'

'The agents told me on the phone that the shareholders were a husband and wife team who are getting divorced and want to sell the business as a result', Bryony replied.

'Well that may, or may not be a genuine reason for sale. You will need to find out more. Can you talk to the managers?'

'No, no one in the organization knows it's for sale', said Bryony.

'What about the assets, and this stock you will be buying? Do you know anything about them? How new is the equipment? Is it what you want? Is the stock right for the business when you will be running it? If not it might be better to start from scratch, and even compete with them, as it sounds from what you've said that they've lost interest in the business', suggested the accountant.

'Yes, I know I will have to check these things. The agents say I can have a tour tomorrow. I'll be introduced as a customer', said Bryony.

'The other worry I have is buying the shares. It would be better to buy only the assets, and not the company itself', continued the accountant. 'Unless there are tax losses we can use, that is.'

'I thought the particulars state that they will pay off any liabilities outside the sale', said Bryony.

'They do', replied the accountant, 'but that only applies to liabilities we know about. When you buy the shares of a company, you may be buying liabilities we don't know about – disputes with suppliers, employees, past tax claims, VAT problems – there are a lot of possibilities.'

Activities

(a) Bryony has thought of some of the advantages of buying an existing business. What others might there be for her in this proposition?

(b) What will be the problems? The accountant has mentioned several, but lists some other potential pitfalls.

(c) How can Bryony find out more information as suggested by the accountant? What else does she need to find out about and how can she go about getting the information? What other advice does she need?

(d) Do you consider the asking price for the business to be a fair one? Make an alternative valuation, and suggestions for justifying this to the owners.

Case study
Dubarry Limited

Dubarry has a long history. Local community leaders in Ballinasloe, County Galway, Ireland, established the company back in 1937 primarily as a cooperative initiative to provide local employment. They had approached a footwear manufacturer in Northampton, England, and offered it an opportunity to establish a plant in Ireland. The footwear manufacturer, which specialized in ladies shoes, had previously operated as a subcontractor in the UK but used the shift to Ireland to create its own label. A French countess, mistress of Louis XV, provided the inspiration for the brand name Dubarry, which the company believed had the necessary 'international sounding' sophistication.

For the following forty years, Dubarry built a solid reputation as a quality footwear manufacturer. Sales were helped at that time by the prevailing import duties applicable to overseas products. As the marketing director of the company pointed out: 'In those days they made shoes and people bought them'.

The company began to diversify in the 1960s and moved into the subcontracting market, making moccasins for a Danish company, which specialized in marine wear. For many years the partnership worked well and Dubarry built up considerable expertise in the production of sailing shoes. However, when the Danish company hit financial problems, Dubarry was left with a situation where they had the engineering skills and investment in place for this specialist footwear, but no market. The company then began to market itself directly to the marine sector.

By the early 1980s Dubarry itself had run into problems. Ireland had become part of the European Community, and with the disappearance of trade barriers, the company found itself in a very different competitive environment, especially as it had continued as a family run venture with little expertise to develop overseas markets.

A management buy-out changed the company dramatically. The Directors held a 60 per cent stake, with a government body, 'Enterprise Ireland' that promoted local industry, taking a 40 per cent stake to ensure ongoing employment at the company. 'Prior to that as a company it had been production-led. They were brilliant shoe-makers but they didn't have the marketing or commercial skills to exploit the new environment which had come about. After the management buy-out, the emphasis changed and Dubarry became much more marketing and export focused', the marketing director commented. In 1998 the management buy-out was completed in that Enterprise Ireland's share was bought back by current management, making Dubarry a wholly private Irish-owned company.

'That whole evolution since the first buy-out was to build up the niche market in the sailing industry. It was about recognizing that if an Irish brand was going to make it abroad, it could only be in a niche market – there wouldn't have been the resources to go too broadly into general footwear. We've continued to build on our expertise in sailing and the position today is that our export business is purely based on our sailing and outdoor products. Dubarry has become the number one performance technical footwear brand within the international sailing market. If you go to any of the major offshore sailing regattas Dubarry is the brand of choice. For example, we are the official footwear supplier to the Volvo Ocean Race which is one of the greatest ocean races', the marketing director explained. Dubarry's products compete on performance and functional benefits – specifically as waterproof, breathable, non-slip footwear. The marketing strategy since the management buy-out has been to develop the brand. 'By that I mean going out into the international environment and looking for distributors for the brand; focusing in on the niche market and getting the best we possibly can out of product performance bearing in mind that we don't have significant financial resources. It's a case of if you can't out-spend the competition you have to out-perform them technically, or out-manoeuvre them commercially. The company puts a lot of effort into making sure our products are on the world's best sailors, by hook or crook. In other words you get this pyramid approach – target the best publications, the best sailors, the best events, and this percolates down to the lower echelons. That's not rocket science but it works', said the marketing director.

(Continued)

The company's product range has now expanded to include outdoor boots, clothing and accessories so that Dubarry has become an international brand outside of its sailing origins. It has become more global in its sourcing too, working closely with partners internationally to source raw materials, designs and production.

Source: From the website Enterprise Ireland, www.enterprise-ireland.com

See: www.enterprise-ireland.com/en/Source-a-Product-or-Service-from
-Ireland/ClientProfileDetails/?Cid=328, accessed 2 January 2016.

See also the company website www.dubarryboots.com

Activities

(a) The management buy-out of Dubarry is quoted as having 'changed dramatically' the fortunes of the company. What were the main changes? Why do you think a management buy-out helped those changes?

(b) The buy-out was in two stages. What were these? Why were two stages necessary? What would have been the benefits to the company of the second stage?

Madame Du Barry, eighteenth-century French courtesan, whose name lives on as an Irish shoe and clothing brand

Case study
You've been framed: Part 3 (of 3)

BRYONY LOOKS AT A BIMBO

Bryony Hannam pursued her investigations into Gray's Framing Studios with such tenacity that she discovered some very interesting facts. Talking to one of the suppliers helped her to find out the reason why the business had been put on the market.

'It's immoral', she complained to her husband, 'all this work I've done, only to find that the workshop manager is going to buy out the couple owning the business. It seems that they have put the business on the market just to find out what sort of price it might fetch. They intended all along to sell it to the workshop manager, not an outside buyer.'

'Did the agent know?' asked the husband.

'Evidently not, I got this from a supplier who is out of favour with the manager, but who knows what he's up to', answered Bryony.

'Well you've found out quite a lot about their business, that can't be wasted effort. But there's not much else you can do now is there?' Her husband tried to console her, knowing she had grown keen on the idea.

'Well there is something. Maybe I should talk to the manager. I don't suppose he's got all the money necessary himself; it could work to my advantage if he needed a partner. After all he's got all the inside information on the business. It would be a safer bet to buy it with him', said Bryony thoughtfully.

A week later Bryony was with her accountant again.

'That's right', she explained, 'he's only raising £20 000 from his own pocket. He's been offered the rest of the money from a finance company who would buy loan stock, with the balance as an overdraft from the bank.'

'This workshop manager seems to be quite smart', mused the accountant. 'By offering loan stock, he plans to retain a majority of the ordinary shares for himself no doubt. How much does he plan to offer did you say?'

'£100 000 plus the value of the stock', answered Bryony. 'He's putting up £20 000 for shares and the finance company will buy £20 000 worth of shares, but also put in £60 000 of loan stock, which has no voting rights, but qualifies for profits at a preferential rate. He plans to raise the £50 000 or so for the stock as an overdraft. He says it's not all necessary and can soon be reduced, especially with credit from the suppliers. So he's effectively planning on buying half the company for £20 000', Bryony summed up.

'You've certainly found out a lot. Why did he tell you all this?' asked the accountant.

'I was introduced to him by this supplier as you know, and it was soon obvious he still has two problems. First, he doesn't have any experience in running anything other than the workshop, and the shop managers aren't interested. Secondly, the finance company is making lots of demands with seats on the board and monthly reports. He's beginning to think it will be rather like being part of a larger company, even though he will own half of it', said Bryony.

'So what is his solution?' asked the accountant.

'I suggested he might be better off with a working partner who will put up money in a similar way to the finance company, but help him run the business and expand it – open new outlets, look after the marketing. In other words, me! And he's accepted in principle', Bryony beamed her pleasure.

'Ah, you're talking of a BIMBO', said the accountant, quickly adding before he was misunderstood, 'a buy-in management buy-out. They're becoming more common, and do seem to have some advantages.'

Activities

(a) What do you consider to be the advantage of this approach? What are the potential problems?

(b) What finance package made it possible for the workshop manager to realize 50 per cent of the equity, for less than 15 per cent of the total consideration?

(c) What deal, if any, do you think Bryony should strike with him?

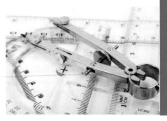

Extended activity
Garage for sale

Try to obtain particulars of businesses for sale by contacting business transfer agents in your area, or by looking at advertisements in the small business pages of publications such as the *Financial Times, Sunday Times* or *Daltonsbusiness.com*.[13]

Then, assume that you work for a business transfer agent as a negotiator responsible for finding buyers for small businesses for sale. The owners of a local garage have instructed you to sell their business. It is profitable, with a good base of customers for repairs and maintenance. It also has the agency for a Japanese car manufacturer specializing in four-wheel drive vehicles. You have interviewed the owners and gathered the information you require about the business.

Your task now is to write up the particulars of the business, using some of those you have obtained as a model. It will outline the nature of the business and give basic financial information to justify the purchase price that you have put on the business.

Summary of what is required

- Consider what type of business you could consider buying (all, or part of) that would be consistent with the development of your business idea.
- Obtain information on suitable businesses for sale.
- Evaluate the advantages and disadvantages of the specific business(es) offered for sale.
- Decide if this is the appropriate route to market entry for you and your business opportunity.

Review buying a business

Before committing yourself to a business start-up, it is worth considering buying an existing business. Consider what types of business for sale would help the development of your business idea. This does not necessarily mean that the businesses you think of buying are trading in the market or style you have chosen. For example, if your business idea is a themed cocktail bar and restaurant, it may be beneficial to buy a restaurant with a very different appeal to the one you have considered. The advantages will be that some of the barriers to entry will be more easily overcome (such as licensing permissions), and equipment (such as for food preparation and storage) could still be appropriate for a different end product. Even if you are considering a totally different business, it is worth looking for some assets that may be useful. If your business involves retail premises, you will certainly need to consider taking over the lease of an existing retail outlet, then changing it over to your use, rather than waiting for the right new premises to become available.

You may also wish to consider not just an outright purchase, but buying into an existing business, with or without the participation of the existing management.

If your original idea did not look feasible from your initial analysis, is there an established business which you could consider buying instead? Are there businesses for sale in an area of interest to you?

Information on businesses for sale

Once you have decided the type of business to look for, obtain information on suitable opportunities. There are a number of sources to consider: business transfer agents, websites and media, and organizations.

Business transfer agents: act rather like estate agents in that a seller will register with them and provide details of their business for sale; in the event of a sale, the seller pays the agent a commission. Some specialize in local businesses, others in a particular trade, with confectioners, tobacconists and newsagents (CTNs) and licensed premises being firm favourites because these change hands relatively frequently. Commercial estate agents also provide details of available commercial properties including some which are offered as going concerns.

Websites and media: Internet searches will reveal a variety of organizations offering advice and details on businesses for sale. For example: www.businessesforsale.com; www.startups.co.uk; www.mergernetwork.com.

National and local press often carry business opportunity sections. These include: *Financial Times*; *Sunday Times*; *Dalton's Weekly* (www.DaltonsBusiness.com – especially for retail outlets, pubs, hotels and restaurants).

Organizations: accountants, solicitors and government agencies all assist in the transfer of businesses.

The UK Business Angels Association is a nationwide business introduction service, which aims to put 'business angels' (individuals with capital to invest in smaller business ventures) in touch with ventures which need investment and vice versa. See www.ukbusinessangelsassociation.org.uk

Planning a new venture
Buying an existing business

Evaluate the advantages and disadvantages

Having obtained what details you can of a business for sale, or an opportunity of investing as a new partner, consider the merits of this as an option for pursuing your business idea. Use the information in this chapter on general advantages and disadvantages to help you in your evaluation.

Decide

Decide if you wish to choose this method of market entry for your particular idea and, if you do, how you will investigate it further.

9.9 Notes, references and recommended further reading

Notes and further information

1 For more information on bankruptcy and liquidation, the UK government's Insolvency Service has an informative website and a number of publications: www.gov.uk /government/organisations/insolvency-service

2 The Enterprise Act 2002, and other legislation affecting SMEs, can be read on the UK government's National Archives website: www.legislation.gov.uk/

3 From domaine-b.com, an informative online business magazine. 'Global insolvencies projected to rise in 2009', 4 December 2008, www.domain-b.com/economy /worldeconomy/20081204_global_insolvencies.html Also 'UK high street shop closures triples in 2014' 16 March 2015 on www.domain-b.com/industry /Retail/20150316_streets.html

4 Many companies specialize as agents in the buying and selling of businesses in the licensed, hotel and catering industry. One of the largest is Christie & Co which has a searchable website at www.christie.com.

5 As reported in the *Daily Telegraph*, 14 September 1991, p. 24. The article 'Private woes in the public house' summarized the business difficulties of those involved in running their own pub.

6 As reported in the Telegraph.co.uk, 10 April, 2008, 'Low sales force four village pubs to close a day' at www.telegraph.co.uk/news/uknews/1584590/Low -sales-force-four-village-pubs-to-close-a-day.html, accessed 30 December 2015.

7 As reported in 'Cask matters', 27 May 2015, at cask-marque.co.uk/cask-matters/latest-trends-in-pub -going, accessed 30 December 2015.

8 Details of enterprise management incentives (EMIs) are on the gov.uk website at www.gov.uk/tax-employee -share-schemes/enterprise-management-incentives -emis. Tax advantaged share options up to a value of £250 000 may be granted to employees under the EMI option scheme. The shares must be in an independent trading company that has gross assets of no more than £30 million (20014/15). No income tax is payable but capital gains tax applies to any uplift in value when the shares are sold.

9 As reported in the *Daily Telegraph* on 27 April 2015: www.telegraph.co.uk/finance/newsbysector/industry /engineering/11566039/Former-factory-floor-worker -helps-lead-26m-management-buyout-of-Jablite.html (accessed 2 January 2016).

10 The Centre for Management Buy-out Research (CMBOR) was founded at Nottingham University Business School in 1986 and moved to Imperial College Business School in 2011. Its objective is to monitor and analyze management buy-outs in a comprehensive and objective way. For details and report samples, see: wwwf.imperial.ac.uk/business-school/research/the -centre-for-management-buy-out-research/

11 This, together with other interesting cases, was first reported in 'The management buy-out report' in *Management Week*, Management Week Publishing Ltd, 30 October 1991. For current details of Sports and Leisure Management Ltd, see everyoneactive .com.

12 See note 8.

13 Details of businesses for sale and advice on how to buy them can be obtained from a variety of sources and websites such as: www.mergernetwork.com; ft.com /businessesforsale and uk.businessesforsale.com/.

References

Birley, S. and Muzyka, F. (2000) *Mastering Entrepreneurship,* Financial Times/Prentice Hall.

Bruining, H., Verwaal, E. and Wright, M. (2013) Private equity and entrepreneurial management in management buy-outs, *Small Business Economics,* 40(3): 591–605.

Chesbrough, H. W. (2007) Why companies should have open business models, *MIT Sloan Management Review,* Winter: January 01.

Chrisman, J. J., Chua, J. H., Steier, L. P., Wright, M., McKee, D. N. (2012) An agency theoretic analysis of value creation through management buy-outs of family firms, *Journal of Family Business Strategy,* 3(4): 197–206.

CMBOR (2015a) *UK Buy Out Report, 3rd Quarter, 2015,* Centre for Management Buy-out Research (CMBOR), Imperial College Business School, London.

CMBOR (2015b) *European Buy Outs Report, Overview, Full Year 2014,* Centre for Management Buy-out Research (CMBOR), Imperial College Business School, London.

Cohen, J. A. (2011) *Intangible Assets: Valuation and Economic Benefit,* John Wiley & Sons.

Dahmash, F. N., Durand, R. B. and Watson, J. (2009) The value relevance and reliability of reported goodwill and identifiable intangible assets, *The British Accounting Review,* 41(2): 120–137.

Gartner, W. B. and Bellamy, M. G. (2008) *Enterprise,* South-Western Cengage Learning.

Gilligan J. and Wright M. (2014) *Private Equity Demystified: An Explanatory Guide,* 4th edn, ICAEW Corporate Finance Faculty, Imperial College Business School, London.

Herbane, B. (2010) Small business research: Time for a crisis-based view, *International Small Business Journal,* 28(1): 43–64.

Hubbard, D. W. (2014) *How to Measure Anything: Finding the Value of Intangibles in Business,* John Wiley & Sons.

Nerudova, D. and Bohusova, H. (2009) The application of an accounting standard for SMEs, *International Journal of Liability and Scientific Enquiry,* 2(2): 233–246.

Olander, H., Hurmelinna-Laukkanen, P. and Mähönen, J. (2009) What's small size got to do with it? Protection of intellectual assets in SMEs, *International Journal of Innovation Management,* 13(3): 349–370.

Oliveira, L., Rodrigues, L. L. and Craig, R. (2010) Intangible assets and value relevance: Evidence from the Portuguese stock exchange, *The British Accounting Review,* 42(4): 241–252.

Salamudin, N., Bakar, R., Ibrahim, M. K. and Hassan, F. H. (2010) Intangible assets valuation in the Malaysian capital market, *Journal of Intellectual Capital,* 11(3): 391–405.

Scholes, L., Wright, M., Westhead, P., Bruining, H. and Kloeckner, O. (2009) *Family Firm Buy-Outs, Private Equity and Strategic Change,* SSRN working paper, available at SSRN: ssrn.com/abstract=2002893

Wright, M. and Burrows, A. (2006) Entrepreneurship and Management Buy-outs. In: Casson M. *et al.* (eds) *The Oxford Handbook of Entrepreneurship,* Oxford University Press: 484–510.

Wright, M., Burrows, A., Ball, R., Scholes, L., Burdett, M. and Tune, K. (2006) *Management Buy-outs 1986–2006: Past Achievements, Future Challenges,* Centre for Management Buy-Out Research, Nottingham University.

Recommended further reading

Birley, S. and Muzyka, F. (2000) *Mastering Entrepreneurship,* Financial Times/Prentice Hall, ch. 8, Buying a company.

The Centre for Management Buy-out Research (CMBOR) website details many publications on buy-outs at wwwf.imperial.ac.uk/business-school/research/the-centre-for-management-buy-out-research/

Gartner, W. B. and Bellamy, M. G. (2008) *Enterprise,* South-Western Cengage Learning, ch. 10 Purchasing a Business. (One of only a few USA entrepreneurship textbooks with a chapter devoted to this topic.)

Rooney, K. (2003) *Good Small Business Guide,* Bloomsbury Publishing. See Evaluating an existing business: 50–52.

Sperry, P. and Mitchell, B. (1999) *Selling Your Business,* Kogan Page.

Wright, M. and Burrows, A. (2006) Entrepreneurship and Management Buy-outs. In: Casson M. *et al.* (eds) *The Oxford Handbook of Entrepreneurship,* Oxford University Press: 484–510. An authoritative review of the literature on management buy-outs.

Wright, M. and Marlow, S. (2012) Entrepreneurial activity in the venture creation and development process, *International Small Business Journal,* 30(2): 107–114.

10 Forming and protecting a business

Learning objectives

By the end of this chapter you will be able to:

- Understand the key differences between the various legal forms that a business can take.
- Identify the responsibilities of the directors of a limited company.
- Assess which legal form is appropriate to a particular business opportunity.
- Evaluate the options for forming a social enterprise.
- Formulate the advantages and disadvantages of the legal options for business formation.
- Identify the various ways of protecting business ideas and intellectual property.
- Undertake a feasibility study for a new venture.

Introduction

In the pursuit of a business idea, an entrepreneur needs to form a legally recognized vehicle to exploit the opportunity and to protect the concepts as far as possible from those wishing to copy them. This chapter contains information, first, about the basic legal identities a small business can take: limited company; sole trader; partnership; and cooperative. The advantages and disadvantages of each form are identified and evaluated. Second, we discuss the nature of intellectual property that might arise during the development of a business opportunity and how to register and protect it. The legal forms described in this chapter are based on current legislation in the UK. In other countries, legal rules and regulations on business formation differ. France and Germany, for example, have a wider variety of available business structures than the UK and most of these are quite widely used. Therefore, reference to local regulations outside the UK should be made through the relevant government department. Intellectual property rights are more uniform, although reference also needs to be made to the appropriate national patent office.

Activity 1
Choice of business form

What are the main different legal forms that a business can take?

10.1 Choice of business organisation

A small business can adopt one of a dozen or more different legal forms in the UK. The choice depends on the circumstances and objectives of the owner(s) of the enterprise. Figure 10.1 summarizes the basic alternatives of sole traders, limited companies, partnerships and cooperatives. There are many varieties on these main themes; for example, social enterprises can form organizations which guarantee that their funds will be devoted to a particular purpose (see Section 10.7). But the first choice in any enterprise is between going it alone or working in co-ownership with others. A limited company can be owned by one or several persons. If this is not the desired form, then single ownership has to be achieved as a sole trader, and multiple ownership as a partnership or cooperative. Each of these forms and sub-varieties, such as limited partnerships and limited liability partnerships, are evaluated below in relation to the legal rules and regulations operating in the UK. For other countries, information on the relevant international legal structure is usually readily obtainable from the appropriate government website.

Figure 10.1 Forms of small business according to ownership

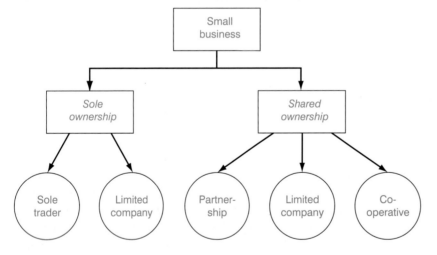

Activity 2
Company differences

A limited company is significantly different to a sole trader or partnership in several respects.

(a) What are these?
(b) What advantages and disadvantages do these differences give to the small business owner?

10.2 Limited company

A limited company (including limited liability partnerships), incorporated under the Companies Act, is a legal body which has a separate identity to that of its owners. It can be bought and sold as a whole, or in part; go bankrupt without its owners suffering the same fate; have legal documents signed on its behalf by a director; and employ staff. Putting business activities into a company literally gives them life as a separate legal entity. This is a key difference to a sole trader or partnership, in which the owners are inextricably linked to the business and not separable from it.

The concept of limited liability invariably applies in most countries, but often in different forms. The equivalent to the UK limited company (Ltd):

- in Australia is a Proprietary Limited company (Pty Ltd);
- in Germany it is a GmbH (Gesellschaft mit beschränkter Haftung);
- in France it is a Société à Responsibilité Limitée (SARL);
- in Italy it is an S.p.A. (Società per Azioni);
- in South Africa it is a Proprietary Limited company – (Pty) Ltd;
- in the USA, it is a Corporation, although there is also a Limited Liability Company (LLC) which gives limited liability but does not have shares.

A BRIEF HISTORY OF THE COMPANY

Although the concept of the company is almost as old as trade itself and an essential part of international business today, it did not emerge in its modern, limited liability form until about 150 years ago. The Romans invented some of the concepts, particularly the idea that an association of people could have an identity that was separate from that of the individuals involved (Micklethwaite and Wooldridge, 2003). This idea re-emerged in the city states of Italy in the Middle Ages when investors financed the voyages of merchants by issuing shares in 'compagnia' with joint liability for members for any losses, as well as a share in the profits of the voyage (Ferguson, 2009).

Further north, merchants formed guilds, associations of tradespeople that could be treated as separate collective bodies. The discovery of 'new worlds' to the east and west of Europe led to the establishment of 'chartered companies' such as the Dutch East India Company and the Hudson Bay Company, which sought to exploit the resources of a particular territory with a charter from the state. These evolved into 'joint stock companies' offering shares that could be traded through stock exchanges following the opening of the first such open market for shares in Amsterdam in 1611. Although this vehicle was used to fund notorious capitalist ventures such as the slave trade, it also helped build the infrastructure of early America with companies, rather than states, constructing canals, roads and water systems, and operating universities and banks.

Robert Lowe, 1st Viscount Sherbrooke.

(*Continued*)

The liberalization of trade in Victorian times gradually freed the company from state control, but one vital ingredient of the modern company was still missing – limited liability. Many feared that limited liability would pass on the risks of doing business from the owner-managers to financiers, suppliers and customers, but others argued it would allow the poor to set up in business more easily. The Joint Stock Companies Act, piloted through Parliament by Robert Lowe in 1856, finally settled the argument by granting limited liability to incorporated companies. For his pioneering work in this respect, Lowe has been called 'father of the modern company' (Micklethwaite and Woolridge, 2003, p. 57) but it was a controversial decision. One of his critics at the time suggested the following, less complimentary epitaph:

'Here lies poor old Robert Lowe;
Where he's gone to I don't know;
If to the realms of peace and love,
Farewell to happiness above;
If, haply, to some lower level,
We can't congratulate the devil.'

10.2.1 RESPONSIBILITIES

A company needs shareholders (the owners) and directors (those empowered to act on the company's behalf by the shareholders). In small companies, shareholders and directors are often the same people, but not necessarily so. Some investors in a business do not become directors. Family members and friends who put up money for a business may prefer not to take on the responsibilities of a director as well. But it is common for external investors, such as private individuals who invest as 'business angels' (see Chapter 13), or venture capital corporations, to protect their investment by taking a seat on the board as a non-executive director (Mason and Harrison, 1999).

Shareholders' responsibilities

The shareholders' responsibility for the company's debt is limited to the paid-up value of their shares. Once they are paid for, the company cannot call on shareholders for more funds (unless by way of a voluntary subscription for more shares), even if it is insolvent.

Directors' responsibilities

The responsibilities of a director extend beyond that of a shareholder.[1] Although directors can separate their own personal assets from those of the business, this is dependent on responsible business behaviour. Where directors have been deemed to have behaved irresponsibly, they can be held personally responsible for the company's debts.

Directors' duties and responsibilities include:

- *To act honestly, and in the company's best interests:* for example, a vested interest in a transaction involving the company must be disclosed to other shareholders.
- *Not to allow the company to incur debts when there is no reasonable chance of paying the debts.* Directors who knowingly allow a company to continue to trade while insolvent can be held personally responsible, without limit, for those debts.[2]
- *To have regard for the interests of employees as well as shareholders.* There are EU-inspired provisions in the Companies Act to ensure directors generally take note of employees' interests. There are also specific responsibilities under employment, industrial health, safety and training regulations; violation of these can result in proceedings against the company, and its directors in person.

- *To comply with the requirements of the Companies Act.* This, for instance, requires proper accounts and records to be kept and officially filed on a regular basis.[3]

As well as the possibility of fines and criminal proceedings because of improper behaviour or failure to execute duties and obligations, directors can be declared unfit and banned from directorships for up to 15 years.

Over and above legal compliance issues, the ownership structure of a firm has long been held to make a difference to how those involved in managing the business actually act. Jensen and Meckling's (1976) seminal paper, 'Theory of the firm: Managerial behaviour, agency, costs and ownership structure', has been very influential over the last 40 years in drawing attention to the possible dangers that arise when managers look after other people's money, rather than their own (in the context of non-profit firms, see also Eisenhardt, 1989; Nyberg *et al.*, 2010; and Van Puyvelde, 2012).

10.2.2 THE MEMORANDUM AND ARTICLES OF ASSOCIATION

Although commonly referred to as one, these are in fact two key legal documents, which set out the constitution and management arrangements of the company.

Memorandum of association

This is the company's charter, which includes:

- *The name of the company.* The name of a limited company has to be approved by the Registrar of Companies. It can neither be offensive, nor likely to be confused with an existing company. To limit its liabilities, limited must be the last word of the name of a company trading for profit.
- *Location of the registered office.* The location of the registered office effectively establishes under which laws a company trades, and where it pays its taxes. It is the address to which official and legal notices will be sent. It need not be the company's principal place of business and, for small firms, it is frequently the address of the company's solicitors or accountants.
- *The objects of the company.* The objectives for which a company has been formed, its powers and area of business, are defined in the objects clause of the **Memorandum of Association**. These are normally kept very general (as in general commercial activities) to avoid activities and transactions being declared *ultra vires* (outside of the powers of the company), which may then make them the personal liability of the directors or management. Recent legislation has abolished the *ultra vires* rules for external transactions, so that third parties can now insist a company meet the obligations to which a director or senior manager has committed the company, even if they fall strictly outside of the company's objects. *Ultra vires* still holds for internal transactions, however, between directors and shareholders, for example.
- *The limited liability of the shareholders.* This clause in the Memorandum limits the liability of shareholders to the value of their shares.
- *The share capital and structure.* The amount of authorized capital, and how it is divided into shares, is specified. Shares are normally made up of relatively small denominations (e.g. £1), to retain flexibility in transfer and issuing of new shares.
- The amount of capital subscribed for by shareholders (that is, shares issued and paid for) is the issued share capital of a company.
- Sometimes not all the authorized capital is subscribed for, some shares being authorized but not issued. Shareholders are still, however, liable for this amount but no more, in the event of liquidation.

- *The names of signatories.* At incorporation, there must be two signatories who agree to take out at least one share each. The 2006 Companies Act changed the requirement for there to be two shareholders initially and, from 1 October 2009, all the shares can be held by one individual.

Articles of association

The **Articles of Association** is a document that sets out the rules for the running and regulation of the company's internal affairs. It contains detailed information about the internal management of the company including the appointment of directors, their powers and fees, and procedures for meetings. It also deals with the relationships between the company and shareholders, and between individual shareholders. For example, the Articles usually provide for the issue of new shares to be offered, first, to existing shareholders, in proportion to their existing holding, so that they can protect their percentage stake in the company.

Likewise, it is common in small companies for shareholders to give first refusal rights to the other shareholders should they wish to sell any equity.

Formation of a limited company

Forming a new limited company can take some time. Suitable Memorandum and Articles of Association and other documents must be lodged with the Registrar of Companies, and a Certificate of Incorporation obtained.[4]

It is possible to buy a ready-made company off the shelf. This is usually a shell company which has not traded but is incorporated and, with a suitable name change, can be used by a new small firm.

The choice of company name is also subject to regulations to avoid infringing on the rights of other companies (See Section 10.7.2, Trademarks and business names).

10.2.3 TAX, NATIONAL INSURANCE AND PENSIONS

As a company is a separate legal body, owner-directors are employed by it, and are therefore employees for tax, National Insurance and pension purposes. As a corporate body, the company is the employer and taxable on its profits.

This means that:

- *PAYE* is operated for owner-director salaries. As tax is deducted at source, this has cash-flow disadvantages over the self-employed status of a sole trader or partner who pays tax on a more retrospective basis. Income tax is paid at normal rates.
- *National Insurance contributions* are paid by directors as employees, and by the company as the employer, which makes them more expensive than for self-employed owners, but entitles the director-employee to the full range of benefits.
- *Corporation tax* is paid by the company on profits it makes, after deducting all expenses, including directors' salaries. For UK small businesses, this will usually be at a lower rate (20 per cent on all profits in 2015/16 and 19 per cent in 2016/17) which can be an advantage over self-employed owners making good profits, which will be taxed as income at the higher rates. Losses can be carried forward in a company to be offset against future profits or capital gains. This can represent an asset if the company is sold.
- *Pensions* can be contributed to by both employee-directors and the company. There is no limit to the contributions which a company can make free of tax to a pension scheme on behalf of employees, subject to the life-time pension allowance of an individual (£1 250 000 in 2015/16). Director-employees can also contribute part of their salary to a pension fund,[5] with relief at their highest rate of income tax.

Self-employed sole traders and partners are more restricted, as they have no company to make contributions on their behalf.

- *Capital gains* made by a company form part of its profits, and are therefore liable to corporation tax with no relief, unlike a self-employed owner who can use personal relief to offset the tax due.

The principal advantages and disadvantages for a small business to trade as a limited company are shown in Figure 10.2.

Figure 10.2 A limited company – a summary of advantages and disadvantages

A limited company has an existence separate from its owners. As a corporate body, it has independent legal and tax status.

Advantages

- Limited liability for shareholders.
- Some formalized structures (e.g. directors' meetings) make management clearer.
- Income tax is paid only on salaries drawn; higher rates of personal tax can be avoided when profits are retained.
- Finance is easier to raise externally, especially from equity.
- Easier to widen ownership base.
- Existence not threatened by death or personal bankruptcy of one of owners.
- Possibly higher perceived status.

Disadvantages

- More time-consuming and expensive to set up.
- Complicated and time-consuming to conform to requirements of Companies Act.
- Loss of confidentiality, as some records are publicly filed.
- Audit and accounting costs higher.
- Higher National Insurance contributions.
- As employees, directors have worse cash flow of taxes under PAYE than self-employed.
- Limited liability is reduced in early days as creditors seek personal guarantees from directors.
- Directors can be held personally liable if the company trades while insolvent.

10.2.4 OTHER LIMITED LIABILITY ORGANIZATIONS

Other business types with limited liability include:

- **Public limited company (PLC)** Small businesses tend to opt for the status of a *private* limited company but it is possible to become a *public* limited company (PLC). This form is mainly intended for those that seek to raise public money on the stock markets, as private limited companies cannot do this. To become a PLC, a company must have share capital of at least £50 000, and have at least two shareholders and a company secretary. The PLC is similar to the German and Austrian *Aktiengesellschaft* (AG), which also has publicly owned shares.
- **Limited by guarantee** Limited companies protect the shareholders who own them by limiting their liability to the money they have invested and no more. But what if the enterprise does not have traditional shareholders or share capital; for example, as is the case in social enterprises? In this case,

it is possible to form a company limited by guarantee, rather than by shares. The members of the company, such as the trustees of a social enterprise, agree on the liability limits in order to limit their exposure to liabilities.

- **Limited liability partnerships** The concept of partnerships that also have limited liability was introduced in the Limited Liability Partnership Act of 2000. This status is mainly used by professions such as solicitors and accountants so that partners can limit their liability but it does impose the extra reporting requirements of limited companies, such as filing annual accounts.

Activity 3
Going it alone

What are the advantages and disadvantages to the small business owner of becoming a sole trader?

10.3 Sole trader
10.3.1 LEGAL STATUS

A sole trader is unlike a limited company in that the law considers the owner and the business to be inseparable. There is no legal separation between the assets and liabilities of the business, and the assets and liabilities of the individual who owns it.

This makes for simpler and more informal arrangements for operating a business. It can also increase the risk for an owner, whose total possessions are now on the line with their business at all times.

The sole trader can simply choose a business name, and start trading. If they use a name different from their own, they will have to put their own name on their headed paper, however. The only obligation is to inform the relevant authorities for taxation and employment status purposes (e.g. Revenue and Customs).[6]

A sole trader can invest in or draw funds from the business as they think fit. However, additional resources can only be raised by loans; it is not possible to invite outside equity participation.

10.3.2 TAX, NATIONAL INSURANCE AND PENSIONS

As the business will not have any separate status from the owner, the sole trader will be self-employed, and not an employee. This has implications for tax and pension provisions.

Tax is payable on any profits of the business, which are treated as if it were the income of the owner, whether they receive it or not. A sole trader cannot choose to reinvest profits for income tax purposes. If profits are made, the sole trader is taxed as if they were taken as income, whether they were drawn or not.

As profits increase, so tax can be payable at higher rates (45 per cent for 2015/16). Being self-employed, the sole trader will not pay tax as income is earned, but on a retrospective basis. Losses can be offset not only against future profits of the same business, but also against other income of the owner, as they are inseparable from the business. If the owner previously paid taxes under PAYE, then trading losses in the early years can be used to claw back some of these taxes paid before self-employment.

National Insurance contributions for self-employed people are payable as:

1 a weekly flat rate (Class 2 contributions payable on earnings over £5965 p.a. in 2015/16, although you can make voluntary payments);

2 a percentage of profits (Class 4 contributions) over a certain amount (set at £8060 in 2015/16). Although this usually amounts to less than the total amount payable by company director-employees the benefits, including unemployment benefit, can be less (see www.gov.uk/national-insurance).

Capital gains can be more favourably treated, as the sole trader's personal allowance for tax-free capital gains (£11 100 in 2015/16) is available in the event that the business makes a capital profit. A company does not have such allowances.

Pension payments were more restricted for the self-employed in the UK until 2006, when a single lifetime allowance and an annual cap on pension payments qualifying for tax relief was introduced for all individuals whether employed or self-employed.

10.3.3 SETTING UP AND RECORD KEEPING

Setting up is very straightforward, requiring only notifications to the local tax office of self-employment status. VAT registration is a further possible step, either on a voluntary basis, or because the business trades at above the minimum registration level (£82 000 per annum from April 2015).

HM Revenue and Customs (HMRC) requires certain financial records to be kept for taxation purposes. Apart from that, the accounting requirements of the business can be determined by internal management needs. An independent audit is not a legal requirement. Records are private, and need not be revealed to anyone other than HMRC.

The principal advantages and disadvantages for a small business to trade as a sole trader are shown in Figure 10.3.

Figure 10.3 A sole trader – a summary of the advantages and disadvantages

> The individual and the business are the same. There are no legal or tax distinctions.
>
> *Advantages*
>
> * Straightforward and easy to set up; minimal legal requirements and costs.
> * Make all the decisions and keep all the profits.
> * No audit of accounts legally required.
> * No public disclosures of records (unless registered for VAT).
> * Business losses can be offset against other income, including claw back of past PAYE.
> * Self-employment can defer payment of income tax and can reduce National Insurance contributions.
>
> *Disadvantages*
>
> * Unlimited liability, including personal assets outside of the business.
> * No additional funds possible from equity investments by others.
> * Transfer of ownership less flexible; can only sell the assets of the business.
> * Possible status problems perceived by third parties.
> * All profits taxed as personal income whether retained in business or taken out.
> * Self-employed national insurance entitlements have fewer benefits.

10.4 Partnership
10.4.1 LEGAL STATUS

Where two or more people set up in business intending to share the profits, then the law deems that they are in partnership. Regulations under the Partnership Act of 1890[7] provide a framework which applies unless partners specifically agree to the contrary (Barrow, 2006). Some of these provisions assume that:

* all partners have an equal vote in how the business should be run;
* all partners have invested equally in the business;

- all partners have an equal share of profits and losses;
- partners will not receive a salary;
- partners will not receive interest on their capital invested.

Clearly, these assumptions will not be the intentions of every partnership. But, unless there is an agreement by the partners to the contrary, the law will assume this to be the case in the event of a dispute.

Partnerships are restricted to 20 partners, except in certain professions, such as law and accountancy.

Activity 4
Joining others

What are the advantages and disadvantages to small business owners of forming a partnership with others to start a business or social enterprise?

A partnership is like a sole trader, in that it is not a legal entity. It therefore carries unlimited liability. Unlike the sole trader, partners do, however, have to look beyond just their own liabilities. Each partner is jointly and severally responsible with other partners for all the obligations and debts of the partnership, even where they exist directly as a result of another partner's actions. If one partner fails to meet their share of the liabilities, creditors can look to the rest of the partnership to make good the deficit.

Limited partnerships were made possible by the 1907 Limited Partnership Act. This effectively creates a second type of partner – a *limited partner* – whose liabilities are less onerous than the general partners. Limited partners contribute a sum of money to the partnership and they are not liable for the debts and obligations of the firm beyond this amount.

A hybrid form of limited liability partnerships (LLPs) came into effect from April 2001. The taxation treatment of individual partners is the same as ordinary partnerships but partners' exposure to the liabilities of the business is limited. A limited liability partnership is taxed and has the same organizational flexibility as a partnership but, in other respects, it is very similar to a company. (See also Section 10.2.4, Limited liability partnerships.)

The formalities to establish a partnership follow those of the sole trader; they are simple, and legally only require the names of partners on any letterhead. If one partner dies, retires or becomes bankrupt, the partnership is automatically dissolved, whether or not this is in the best interests of the other partners, unless a separate written agreement is made to the contrary.

HISTORIC PARTNERSHIPS THAT REVOLUTIONIZED INDUSTRIES

Many famous businesses were begun by two or more partners as many trademarks based on the founder's names testify: Ben and Jerry, Fortnum and Mason, Marks and Spencer, Proctor and Gamble, Smith and Wesson, and Warner Bros.

Henry Royce, an impoverished engineer who had designed a luxury car, met Charles Rolls, an aristocratic car dealer, in 1903 and the two formed a partnership in which Royce produced the cars and Rolls sold them. This was the basis of the Rolls-Royce Corporation whose primary trade today is in aircraft engines.

Bill Hewlett and David Packard graduated with engineering degrees from Stamford University and set up as a partnership in the 1930s to produce test equipment in a garage. Hewlett-Packard, the company that evolved from this partnership, has introduced countless innovations in office equipment, including laserjet printers and touch screens.

Some partnerships prove to be less than equal: Coco Chanel needed money to market her new fragrance Chanel No. 5 and turned to Pierre Wertheimer, whose family controlled the largest cosmetic firm in France. Chanel became the best selling perfume in history and, although Coco had the fame, she only had 10 per cent of the business. Today, the Wertheimer family own 100 per cent of the company and worldwide rights to the Chanel name.

10.4.2 THE PARTNERSHIP AGREEMENT

To regulate matters between the partners (and prevent dissolution as described above) a Partnership Agreement is strongly advised (Barrow, 2006). This is not a legal requirement, however; partnerships are legally, and in practice, a matter of trust between the partners. A Partnership Agreement can define some broad areas of responsibility and authority such as:

- details of the partners, and the name and nature of the business they carry on;
- duration of the partnership, date of commencement and any anticipated termination date;
- capital contributed by the partners, and any agreement on interest payable to partners for money introduced;
- calculation and division of profits: this needs to be specified, particularly where partners contribute unequally, as the 1890 Act assumes they have equal rights to profits;
- management and control of the business: this is most needed where partners put in unequal amounts of time in the partnership. Where there is a sleeping partner, management partners may need to guard against future interference, and provide for their own salaries before profits are divided;
- dissolution: what happens on the retirement, death or withdrawal of a partner has to be spelt out in order to prevent automatic dissolution of the partnership.

10.4.3 PARTNERS' RESPONSIBILITIES

A partner in a business is expected by law to behave fairly and in good faith. In practice, partners will control each other to a greater or lesser extent. As all partners act for the partnership, and therefore incur liabilities on behalf of other partners, the choice of partner is an extremely important decision. It can be a decision which has effects even beyond the life of a partner, as their estate can still be responsible for partnership liabilities, unless the partner has taken public leave of the partnership by notifying their retirement to business contacts and advertising it in the *Business Gazette*.

10.4.4 TAX, NATIONAL INSURANCE AND PENSIONS

As there is no corporate body to employ them, partners are self-employed. This confers the same advantages and disadvantages as to the sole trader. Losses in the partnership can also be used to offset taxes due on other, non-partnership income.

The principal advantages and disadvantages of operating as a partnership are shown in Figure 10.4.

Figure 10.4 Partnerships – a summary of the advantages and disadvantages

Two or more persons undertaking a business activity together are in partnership. There is no separate legal entity, and partners are personally responsible for all liabilities of the partnership.

Advantages

- Easy to set up.
- Access to the experience of other partners.
- No audit of accounts legally required.
- Confidentiality is maintained, as no public access to accounts.
- Losses from the business can be offset against other income.
- Can be relatively easily transferred to a limited company at a later stage.
- Benefits of self-employment for income tax and National Insurance purposes.

Disadvantages

- Partners are liable for debts, jointly and severally.
- Partners' estates can still be liable for their debts after death.
- Death, bankruptcy or retirement dissolves partnership, unless there are specific continuation provisions in the agreement.
- Less flexibility in transferring ownership than limited company.
- High degree of mutual trust required.
- Profits taxed as income, whether drawn or not.
- Self-employed National Insurance entitlements may have fewer benefits.

Activity 5
Some examples

Can you give some examples of the types of small business which become:

(a) limited companies?
(b) sole traders?
(c) partnerships?

Why do they choose this particular route?

10.5 Choosing the appropriate business form: sole trader vs partnership vs limited company

The choice of business identity is usually between these three forms, as cooperatives and other forms are less common. Their appropriateness depends on the circumstances of the business and the objectives of its owners.

The decision on which form a business will take may be dictated by one category only. If the nature of the business is such that uninsurable liabilities are possible on a large scale, then a limited company is the only choice. For this reason, many small firms manufacturing components for other companies wish to maintain limited liability. Lawsuits instigated by end-users over a product deficiency could involve a subcontractor not involved in the final sale. When products are exported, especially to the USA, this can increase the possibility of legal problems that are not within the control of the subcontractor.

At the other extreme, where a small business is offering an individual service which carries no real liabilities, or is covered by full indemnity insurance, then the advantages of the lack of formality in sole trader status will probably be the obvious route. Most tradesmen operate as self-employed sole traders or partners for this reason.

The developing business may wish to change status because of an altered environment. Growth can make it desirable to introduce the more formal structures and money-raising possibilities of a limited company.

The decision between these three basic forms can be evaluated on a number of criteria which are shown in Table 10.1.

Table 10.1 A checklist for the appropriate form of company

Categories	Company	Sole trader	Partnership
Liabilities	Liability limited, but personal guarantees and directors' obligations can reduce limitations	All assets liable including those not involved in the business	Liability extends to business debts of other partners
Records and accounts	Legal accounting and audit requirements Accounts filed open to inspection	No strict accounting or audit requirements Records not available for public inspection	As for sole trader
Setting up	Formalities of registration, although can buy off-the-peg	No formalities except registering as self-employed	As for sole trader, except partnership agreement strongly advised to prevent problems, especially of dissolution
Raising money	Wide choice, including further equity investments	Options limited to overdraft or loan	Overdraft, loans or new partners with money
Selling up	Flexible, as can sell part or all of shares	Can only sell assets; difficult if selling part of the business	As for sole trader
Status	Possibly higher perceived status	Possibly lower perceived status	As for sole trader
Tax, National Insurance and pensions	Employee status PAYE, high National Insurance, but full benefits Corporation Tax on company profits; losses retained in company	Insurance cheaper but fewer benefits; losses can be offset against tax on other income	As for sole trader

Activity 6
Why cooperative?

A cooperative business is owned and controlled by its employees for their mutual benefit. In what different circumstances are they formed? What are the principal motives of their founders?

10.6 Cooperatives

Cooperatives are jointly owned by their members. A consumer **cooperative** is jointly owned by its customers, a community cooperative by the community it serves. A worker cooperative, the most common form, is an enterprise owned and controlled by all the people working for it for their mutual benefit. It is an alternative form of business structure, where the emphasis is on the work environment and not the accumulation of individual wealth. Established in the eighteenth century, worker cooperatives were almost extinct until a revival began in the 1970s that has continued ever since.

10.6.1 LEGAL FORM

Cooperatives are usually limited companies, cooperative societies or, more rarely, partnerships. Governed by the Industrial and Provident Societies Acts 1965–75, registration as a cooperative requires the following principles to be adopted:[8]

- The objectives, management and use of assets are controlled by the members.
- Membership is not restricted; it must be open to anyone who fulfills the qualifications laid down.
- Each member of the cooperative has an equal vote in how it is to be run.
- Surpluses, or profits, are shared between the members, pro rata to their participation.
- Share capital remains at its original value. Members benefit from their participation, not as investors; cooperatives are not about making capital gains.
- Interest on loans, or share capital, is limited, even if profits permit higher payments.

A registered cooperative is a separate legal body, which has limited liability for its members, and which must file annual accounts. A minimum of seven members is required to register, but they do not all need to work full-time. Registration is not mandatory however, and, where cooperatives do not register, they are regarded in law as partnerships with unlimited liability.

10.6.2 BACKGROUND

In the eighteenth and nineteenth centuries, working people formed many self-help groups to cope with poverty and hardship. Cooperatives were part of this movement; they were established either from above, by those seeking to spread a philosophy of cooperation, or at the grass roots, by working people themselves in an effort to improve their conditions.

Today, the best-known cooperatives in the UK are the Cooperative Group, which operates retail and financial services as a consumer cooperative, and the John Lewis Partnership including Waitrose, a worker's cooperative. Worker cooperatives peaked at around 1000 in the early 1900s and then declined to a very small number by the 1960s. From the 1970s, they enjoyed a revival, promoted by the Cooperative Development Agency set up by the government in 1978 to give advice to anyone wishing to form a cooperative. Cooperatives[UK] is now the central organization that supports cooperative enterprises in the UK. Estimates suggest there were 7000 cooperatives in 2015 (compared to 1500 cooperatives in the late 1980s) involving 15 million people with a turnover of £37 billion (Cooperatives[UK], 2015).

They are dominated by the retail and farming sectors: over 400 cooperative retailers, including John Lewis, Waitrose and the Cooperative Group, had a joint turnover of £26 billion; farming cooperatives were more numerous at 620 but with a lower turnover of £6.2 billion.[9]

The reasons for the growth lie in the motives for establishing the various types of cooperative.

COOPERATIVE FANS, PRINTERS AND PUBLISHERS[10]

Three examples illustrate the diversity of the cooperative sector and some of the motivations of the founders.

FC United of Manchester is a cooperative football club owned and democratically run by its members who are equal co-owners, holding one voting share each in the club. The club was founded by disgruntled Manchester United fans in 2005 in protest at the takeover of the Old Trafford club by the Glazer family. But according to FC United's official website this was the last straw, not the sole reason: 'The material theft of a Manchester institution, forcibly taken from the people of Manchester, was the tip of a pyramid of destruction, with changing kick off times for the benefit of television, soulless all-seater stadia full of "new" supporters intent to sit back and watch rather than partake in the occasion, heavy handed stewarding and ridiculously priced tickets propping it all up. A group of individuals determined to continue the fight formed a steering committee and FC United of Manchester was delivered. They wanted Our Club, Our Rules and they got just that, a member owned democratic, not-for-profit organization created by Manchester United fans. A club accessible to all of the Greater Manchester community, dedicated to encouraging participation of youth whether it be playing or supporting and to providing affordable football for all' (FC United of Manchester, 2016).

The Footprint Workers Cooperative is a small printing company set up in 2006 in north-east England, currently run by five members. It prints booklets, leaflets, newsletters 'and that sort of gubbins'. According to the company website, 'We are a worker's cooperative, which means our business is owned by the workers. As we have no bosses we run it as we want, doing interesting jobs for interesting people. We want to be straightforward, friendly, responsible and responsive, rather than "aiming to deliver comprehensive multiplatform printing solutions to clients in the voluntary and vocationally challenged sectors". We do it as ethically as we can, printing on proper recycled papers, powered by a genuine green electricity tariff and using the least environmentally damaging processes we can find. We also give a percentage of the money we make to worthy projects.' (Footprint Workers Cooperative, 2016).

Zed Books was founded in 1977 'to publish books that educate people about the urgent need to make the world a more just, more peaceful, more environmentally friendly place for all humanity to live in'. The books are primarily for students, academics, campaigners and activists. It is managed cooperatively by its worker-directors and has no shareholders. In its 30-year history, it has published over 1000 titles with the common goal of giving 'voice to the people, places and issues at the margin' (Zed Books, 2016) including *Struggles for Citizenship in Africa* (Bronwen Mamby), and *Celebrity and the Environment: Fame, Wealth and Power in Conservation* (Dan Brockington).

10.6.3 TYPES OF COOPERATIVE

Like other small businesses, cooperatives do not constitute a uniform group. Research into the characteristics and objectives of cooperatives suggests that there are four main types (Goss, 1991; BIS, 2011).

- *Endowed cooperatives:* some owners transfer their business to their employees, either as a philanthropic gesture, or an attempt to keep the firm going; for example, if the owner has no heir. Shares are usually held in trust by the employees. This is a relatively uncommon form, the best-known example of which is the chemical manufacturer, Scott-Bader Commonwealth.
- *Defensive cooperatives:* if an enterprise is threatened with closure, employees have formed cooperatives in a desperate attempt to keep their company alive and their jobs with it. Cooperatives of this type have been small in number, but have often commanded considerable publicity. As Industry Minister in the 1970s, Tony Benn, encouraged some of the better-known examples, such as Triumph Motorcycles (Meriden) and the *Scottish Daily News* (formerly the *Scottish Daily Express*). The formation of FC United of Manchester in protest at the takeover of Manchester United by the American Michael Glazer could be seen as a defensive cooperative.
- *Job-creation cooperatives:* in times of high unemployment, increasing numbers of cooperatives have been set up to create new jobs. Encouragement and help from agencies such as Cooperatives[UK], with financial support from government-sponsored job schemes, have stimulated this form in recent years.
- *Alternative cooperatives:* this is the most common form of modern cooperative, arising from various alternative movements, emphasizing social and environmental needs rather than profit. Members of these cooperatives are often from the well-educated middle-classes, looking for a lifestyle that is different to what they perceive as the conventional rat race. Businesses are often in craft-related industries; health products, such as wholefood distribution; or publishing and printing. The Footprint Workers Cooperative and Zed Books could be classified under this category.

10.6.4 ADVANTAGES AND DISADVANTAGES

The recent renaissance of cooperatives has stimulated evaluation of their success or failure (Cornforth, 1986; Carlberg *et al.,* 2004; Harrison, 2013).

Advantages

There are some obvious advantages in the high level of commitment a member of a cooperative is likely to feel towards their work. Increased motivation comes from putting an ideology into practice, and from sharing equally in the control and rewards of an enterprise. Those working in cooperatives report a higher than average sense of purpose and satisfaction from their work.

Disadvantages

Cooperatives face the same problems as many other small businesses, including the lack of management experience and other appropriate skills, insufficient finance and difficulties in gaining access to the marketplace. But they also face additional problems:

- Many start in difficult economic conditions. Defensive cooperatives emerge from firms already in serious trouble. Job-creation cooperatives are stimulated by recession and high unemployment. Many alternative cooperatives operate in markets which are inherently difficult; for example, small health-food shops. Only endowed cooperatives have the benefit of a successful background as they are usually formed from a well-established business; it is not surprising therefore that their success rate is the highest among cooperative types.

- Workplace democracy requires innovative organizational structures which sometimes work, but often do not. Decision-making can become confused. Lengthy debates over the running of the cooperative can be an unproductive use of time. Finding people to join a cooperative, and keeping the ones that have, is more difficult than conventional recruitment and retention practices, and can put an effective brake on growth.

The emphasis on social and environmental factors, particularly in alternative cooperatives, often leads to inefficient, labour-intensive work practices. Despite these difficulties, the new breed of cooperative is claimed to have a survival rate better than that of a small business generally; recent data on cooperatives in the UK indicates that four out of five formed since 2010 are still in existence, an 80 per cent survival rate (Cooperatives[UK], 2015). It is not necessarily a criticism that their financial performance tends to be poorer but, rather, a reflection of the lower status accorded to making profits in many cooperatives.

10.7 Social enterprise

Unlike many small businesses, social enterprises are formed to fulfill social rather than economic needs, so that trading surpluses are re-invested into the community or social project rather than distributed to shareholders (see Chapter 2, Section 2.2.2, for discussion on social entrepreneurship and the social enterprise). However, their legal structures can be the same as a small business. A social enterprise can be set up as a limited company, a sole trader or a partnership and some are particularly suited to the cooperative legal structure.

However, social enterprises can take on other special forms:

- **Community Interest Company (CIC)** – a special type of limited company with an 'asset lock' to ensure that it only uses its assets for a specific social purpose.
- **A Charity** – this can be either incorporated (Charitable Incorporated Organization – CIO) to ensure limited liability; or unincorporated, with individual liability for the trustees as in a partnership.
- **Community Benefit Societies (BenComs)** – these are formed for the benefit of a particular community and must return surpluses to that community. Although similar in aims to a cooperative society, the key difference is that BenComs do not pay profits to the members of the society who control it but, rather, to the community it is set up to benefit (see BIS, 2011, for definition of this and other organizational forms).

INTERNATIONAL EXAMPLES OF SOCIAL ENTERPRISE[11]

- *Greyston Bakery* was founded by a Zen Bhuddist meditation group led by Bernard Glassman, in the Bronx, New York. It produces desserts and ice creams, including brownies for Ben & Jerry's ice cream. All profits go to the Greyston Foundation, which supports local community projects including childcare. Their motto is: 'Do Goodies'.
- *Dayodaya Ethical Group (DEG)* is a cooperative organization that works for animal rights in India, providing shelter to over 30 000 elderly cows, generating revenue by selling milk and producing bio-gas.
- *Township Trades*, a not-for-profit business in South Africa where young adults, most of whom have lost parents to HIV/Aids, can make soap that is sold at local markets. The business, based in the Khayelitsha

Township on the outskirts of Cape Town, employs 16 locals who are trained to use natural ingredients to make soap which is then sold at market stalls.

- *Divine Chocolate* is a Fairtrade company that is co-owned by the cocoa farmers cooperative Kuapa Kokoo in Ghana. In order to increase their market share, the farmer's cooperative combined with other companies and institutions to manufacture and market their own range of chocolate bars – Divine. It now has sales of £11 million from its range of 25 products.
- *Green-Works* is a UK recycling organization that collects unwanted office furniture from businesses and redistributes it to schools, charities and community groups. The company achieves zero landfill, creates jobs for disadvantaged people and helps businesses to fulfil their corporate social responsibility commitments. The company started with £400 and a van in 2000; by 2007, its turnover exceeded £2 million; in 2011, it was taken over by London Re-Use Ltd.

These social enterprises illustrate the diversity of legal types that they can take. Some are for-profit companies that re-invest their surplus into the community (e.g. Greyston Bakery; Green-Works). Others are cooperatives that are owned by their workers or suppliers (e.g. Divine Chocolate; Dayodaya Ethical Group). One has a specific social purpose supported by income from a traditional activity (e.g. Township Trades).

10.8 Intellectual property rights

10.8.1 WHAT IS INTELLECTUAL PROPERTY?

The development of a business normally involves the generation of ideas, inventions, designs, know-how or skills, and names associated with the business. These form 'intellectual property' (IP) that can be protected through legal processes to become **intellectual property rights (IPRs)**. Intellectual property 'allows people to own their creativity and innovation in the same way that they can own physical property.'[12] In some cases, such as copyright, protection arises automatically, without any registration or application, as soon as there is a record of what has been created. In other cases, such as patents and trademarks, intellectual property cannot be protected unless it has been applied for and granted (see Kitching and Blackburn, 1998, for discussion in the context of SMEs; Blackburn, 2007; De Rassenfosse, 2012; and Keating, 2013, for entrepreneurship and innovation management in small firms; Duening *et al.*, 2014, for technology entrepreneurship; and Richards, 2009, and McManus, 2012, for spin-outs and commercialization).

There are four main types of IP:

- *Trademarks* that identify a product or service as a brand that can be differentiated from other offerings;
- *Patents* for new and improved products and processes that are capable of industrial application;
- *Copyright* for material such as music, films, sound recordings and broadcasts, including software;
- *Designs* that specify the appearance of a product, such as its shape, texture or ornamentation.

10.8.2 TRADEMARKS, BRANDS AND BUSINESS NAMES

The name of a business, product or service is important for commercial and legal reasons. Commercially, it is important to choose a name that is memorable and tells potential customers what is on offer. Legally, it is important to protect the name once it becomes established in the marketplace. Although the choice of name should be based primarily on commercial grounds, there are legal restrictions to prevent others adopting a name that already has commercial value.

- A *trademark* is a sign or a distinctive mark associated with a product or service. This might be words, logos, colours, slogans, three-dimensional shapes and sometimes even sounds and gestures. It tells the customer that this product or service comes from a particular source.

  Trademarks have to be registered and for this they need to be represented graphically in words and/or pictures. If you wish to protect your mark in particular individual countries, you should apply to the Intellectual Property Office for that country.[13]

  However, it is possible to apply for a 'Community Trademark', which gives protection throughout the European Union.[14] There is also a World Intellectual Property Organization, part of the United Nations, that administers international treaties dealing with different aspects of intellectual property protection.

  Imitation of registered trademarks is a criminal offence. Even where names are not registered, attempts to pass off other goods for the real thing are also illegal.

- *Brands* are combinations of name, symbol and design that clearly differentiate one product from another. The *brand name* is the word used to distinguish the brand (Mars Bar, Rolls Royce, Apple). The brand mark or *logo* is the distinctive symbol or graphic representation that is associated with the brand (the red lettering of Mars, the RR of Rolls Royce, Apple's bitten apple). It is important to protect a brand early in its development through a trademark in order to prevent copying and passing off.

- *Company names:* the name of a limited company can be registered in the UK provided it is not identical to an existing company, or cannot be considered offensive or illegal. Certain words, about 80 in total, such as Royal, Windsor, National, British, University, Chemist, Trust, can only be used with the approval of the Secretary of State.[15]

  Sole traders and partnerships can use their own names without consent. If they choose to operate under a name other than their own, they are legally required to disclose their names on business letters, invoices, receipts and other stationery.

- *Domain names:* a **domain name**, or website address, has become an important asset to a business. A domain name identifies a business on the internet, and allows potential customers to find it by entering the name into the browser address box, or through a search engine such as Google or Yahoo. It is becoming increasingly difficult to find a name that has not already been registered. There were over 160 million top level domains registered by 2016 and over 100 000 names are often registered in a day, although almost as many are deleted.[16] Most countries now maintain a registry of domain names. For example, Nominet. UK[17] holds a database of domain registrations and provides neutral advice on registering and maintaining a name. Some sites carry international directories of domain registries.[18]

10.8.3 PATENTS

Inventions of products or processes, accepted as superior to what went before, can be given temporary protection by patents. A patent grants an inventor the right for a defined period of time to prevent anyone else from making or selling their invention without a licence. The UK Intellectual Property Office describes a patent as 'a deal between an inventor and the state in which the inventor is allowed a short-term monopoly in return for allowing the invention to be made public'.[19]

Contrary to common belief, patents are not usually about revolutionary breakthroughs in technology. Most patents are concerned with the evolution of existing products and processes, rather than a revolution of complex technology.

Inventions have to fulfil a number of conditions in order to be considered for a patent. These include:

- *The invention must be something new or novel in the sense that it is not already known about.* There must be no prior publication or information made public about the invention prior to the filing of the patent – even by the inventors themselves. This means that inventors have to be extremely cautious about publishing information on their work before making an application to a patent office. Making an idea public includes using, demonstrating or verbally describing it to others. For this reason, inventors need to ask anyone to whom they wish to show their invention to sign a non-disclosure agreement (NDA) which ensures that the demonstration does not constitute a public disclosure.
- *The invention must involve an inventive step.* As well as being new, the invention must not be a development that would be obvious to anyone with a good knowledge of the relevant technology. It has to represent a genuine advance, rather than an obvious modification to existing equipment, products or processes.
- *The invention must have an industrial or commercial application.* It has to have the potential to be made or used in some kind of industry in the practical form of a device, product, material, process or method of operation.
- *The invention must not be within an excluded area.* These include treatment of the human body, new animal or plant varieties, scientific or mathematical theory, literary or artistic creations, methods for doing business and computer programmes.

How to obtain a patent

The process of obtaining a patent takes place in two stages.[20] First, the inventor files an initial patent application at the Patent Office of the desired country. This is a relatively simple process and allows the inventor 12 months before completing the full patent application. Once this initial application is filed, the term 'patent pending' can be used in relation to the invention. Inventors can also disclose their inventions publicly as they now have precedence over subsequent patent applications for similar inventions.[21] They can explore the commercial potential and viability of the invention without too much hindrance, before going to the time and expense of the full application.

Second, the inventor must take steps towards a full application within 12 months or the application lapses. This involves a full description of the invention, and a set of 'claims' to define the scope of the protection, followed by a patent search and detailed examination of the invention by the Patent Office. This involves costs (which, with agent's fees, could be £2000 per application in the UK) and takes time; the whole process takes around two-and-a-half years or more, unless you choose the 'fast track' method which can reduce the process to less than 18 months.

Patents can add considerable value to a business – but at a cost. They provide protection from competitors for up to 20 years in the UK. Patents can be sold or licensed to others. But patent rights are territorial. A UK patent gives the owner the right to manufacture or sell only within the UK. It is possible to apply for a patent in other countries and there are some international treaties (such as the European Patent Convention and the Patent Cooperation Treaty) which simplify the procedure for getting a patent in more than one country.[22] This inevitably adds to the costs of obtaining a patent.

Patents also have to be defended against infringement. Often, the existence of a patent is sufficient to deter a potential infringer. If a patent owner believes an infringement has been made, a carefully worded letter asking the infringer if they are aware of the patent may be sufficient. If not, legal action may be taken and damages claimed. This, however, can be a costly and time-consuming process.

Research indicates that the distribution of patents is highly skewed in terms of company size, with a few large companies being responsible for the majority of patent applications. However, SMEs do play a vital role in terms of 'national systems of innovation' (i.e. the flow of technology and information that is critical to the innovative process on the national level) and are more active in emerging technologies (Frietsch, Neuhäusler, and Rothengatter, 2013).

10.8.4 COPYRIGHT

Where the product of a business is a literary, artistic or musical creation, it can be protected by copyright, which now, under recent legislation, also covers computer software.[23] Copyright gives two types of protection: first, the creators have financial rights over the copying or use of their material; second, they have 'moral rights' to be identified as the creator and they can object if it is distorted or changed in a detrimental way. It has become an important business consideration, especially for those enterprises operating in the creative and computing industries.

Protection covers most media in which materials can be published, including the internet.

Although copyright protects original works of various types, it does not protect the idea behind it. Neither does it protect names or titles, which are better protected as trademarks. The logo of a business or product name may be protected under copyright as an artistic creation, so it is possible that trademarks may also be covered by copyright. The length of time that copyright lasts depends on the nature of the work covered. In Europe, it normally covers the lifetime of the creator plus 70 years after their death.

You do not need to apply or register for copyright as it is an automatic right. However, it is common for a creator to mark material with the international copyright symbol © followed by the name of the copyright owner and year of publication. Although not essential, this may be useful in any infringement proceedings. It is also often prudent to ensure that you can prove that the material is yours at a certain time. For example, you can deposit a copy with a bank or solicitor, or send yourself a copy by a method that clearly dates the delivery. There are also online sites that now provide this service for a fee (e.g. copyright.co.uk).

'A Whiter Shade of Pale', the debut single of the band Procol Harum, became an international hit in 1967. But court proceedings to clarify ownership of the copyright to the music were finalized over 40 years later. The song was written by lead singer Gary Brooker who, at first, enjoyed full royalty rights until 2006. Then the band's organist, Matthew Fisher, claimed he had written the distinctive keyboard organ melody that introduces the song. He was awarded 40 per cent of the royalties but this was overturned on appeal in 2008. The Court of Appeal agreed that Fisher had contributed the organ theme but ruled that he should receive no money from past or future royalties as the judge said he was 'guilty of excessive and inexcusable delay in his claim to assert joint title to a joint interest in the work.' In 2009, a further appeal overturned this judgment, ruling that Fisher should enjoy royalties but only on future, not past, earnings.

10.8.5 DESIGN RIGHT

The design of a product can be an important asset to a business and may be synonymous with its image. As part of the intellectual property of a business, 'design' refers to the appearance of a product, especially its shape, colours, texture or materials. Designs are protected as registered designs, or through unregistered design rights.

Designs for products, either initial drawings or a prototype, can be registered. Design registration gives the owner the right for a limited period to prevent a product to which the design has been applied being sold without permission. It lasts for the first 10 years of the sale of the product. You need to register a design with the appropriate body, usually the national intellectual property office.[24] This concept of design right was first introduced in the UK by the 1988 Copyright, Designs and Patents Act.[25]

Unregistered designs may also have rights if they are original, distinctive or unusual in some way. Design right prevents deliberate copying and, like copyright, is an automatic protection that applies without registration. Like other intellectual property, it can be sold or licensed to third parties.

10.9 Summary and activities

In choosing a route to market entry for a business opportunity, an entrepreneur has to make decisions that relate to the law. The first decision relates to the basic legal form of the business: limited company, sole trader, partnership or cooperative. The second decision relates to what legal protection can be gained for the intellectual property of the business. The legal status of a business has implications with regard to the following key factors: the degree to which the owners have liabilities towards the business; the records and accounts that are required to be kept; the procedures for setting up the business; the methods possible for raising money; the ways in which the business can be sold; the image or perceived status in the marketplace; the types of taxation and National Insurance. The legal form chosen depends on the circumstances of the owner and the needs of the business in relation to these key factors. In general, if significant liabilities are likely to occur in the running of the business, then a limited liability form of business is required. If not, the flexibility and lower costs of being a sole trader or partnership probably prevail. Cooperatives benefit from the motivation of their members but are constrained by the need to ensure democracy in decision-making.

Intellectual property rights allow entrepreneurs to own their ideas and innovations, just as they can own more tangible items such as stock and equipment. There are four main types of intellectual property: trademarks, including business names, logos and domain names that identify a business or product as a brand; patents awarded to new or improved products and processes that have a commercial application; copyright that automatically protects the authors and creators of material in various media; and designs that are protected automatically, or through design right registration of the distinctive appearance of a product.

Case study
Forming a business: Part 1

JANET AND MIKE TAKE THE PLUNGE

Janet and Mike Bloomfield had come to a momentous decision. Mike had often talked of giving up his job with a large leisure group and running a small hotel in their favourite seaside town; Janet had been working as a physiotherapist for many years and wanted to set up a practice of her own. Now that the children had all left home, they were preparing to take the plunge. Mike had found the ideal hotel for sale, with under-used space on the ground floor, which would make an ideal area for Janet's physiotherapy practice.

They had found a buyer for their home and their offer on the hotel was accepted, so their move into small business was becoming a reality.

Raising the money

The hotel was for sale freehold, and they planned to live in it themselves. They had calculated that the proceeds of the sale of their house, plus a mortgage, would pay for the hotel, but not their estimate of the necessary refurbishments Mike planned, or the investment in fittings and equipment for Janet's practice.

- Estimated start-up costs were (£000s):

cost of hotel	650
refurbishment	50
physiotherapy practice conversion and equipment	40
working capital	30
Total	*770*

- Funds available were (£000s):

net proceeds of sale of house	350
mortgage on hotel	320
funding required	100
Total	*770*

Mike and Janet had talked to their bank manager about funding the difference. He had asked for a second mortgage on the property plus a business plan he could approve, before he would commit to an overdraft.

Then Janet's father offered to invest in the business. He had some spare capital which he was happy to put into their venture, provided he received a reasonable income from it.

Discussing the form

Janet had been discussing the alternative legal forms of business organization with their solicitor and she asked Mike for his views.

'We will need to make a decision soon', she urged, 'as it will affect how we buy the hotel and start to trade. Do you think we should form a company or operate as a sole trader, or in partnership?'

'Well, I assume we cannot be a sole trader as there are two of us', replied Mike.

'Not necessarily', said Janet. 'We could run our businesses totally separately, and therefore each operate as a sole trader.'

'What's the point in that, when we're both under the same roof, sharing in some of the costs?' asked Mike.

'Well', said Janet, 'I think we should know how each business is doing, and therefore keep separate records of sales and costs. If not, one might be keeping the other going without us realizing it – I'm not going to subsidize you for ever you know!'

'Seriously', Janet continued, 'if one business does not do well, we don't want it to pull down everything else with it. Suppose one business did fail. If it isn't quite separate, all our assets could be liable.'

'Then we need a company to limit our liability', suggested Mike.

'I don't think so', said Janet. 'Talking to our solicitor, she says that we can operate as sole traders, with you responsible for the hotel and me for the practice. That way there are fewer formalities and records to keep.'

(Continued)

'Yes, but if we own the property jointly', Mike interrupted, 'this means that if one of us fails, our main asset is still on the line. What happens if you are sued by one of your patients?'

'I'm covered by professional indemnity insurance for any mishaps', Janet answered.

'What about your Dad, then?' Mike continued. 'If he is going to invest in our businesses, how can he put money into a sole trader?'

'Well, I think he can make us a loan, but it may be complicated to split it between us', replied Janet. 'To avoid confusion, why don't we go through a checklist of the various aspects so that we make a structured decision?'

Activities

(a) Assess whether or not you agree with Janet, that they should operate as two separate businesses. If they were not married, would you advise differently?

(b) Consider Table 10.1, Checklist for choosing the appropriate form, in Section 10.5 above. In each category, decide which would be the most appropriate form for Janet and Mike.

(c) Decide which form(s) you would recommend they choose.

Case study
Forming a business: Part 2

JANET THINKS COOPERATIVE

Two years on, Janet and Mike Bloomfield's move to an alternative lifestyle, running their own businesses, was proving to be a success. The hotel had flourished under Mike's experienced management and was more than repaying the mortgage, loans and overheads.

Janet's business was also developing well, but in a way she had not expected. The demand for physiotherapy in their new location proved fickle. At times, Janet had more patients than she could handle, but there were lulls in which she had insufficient custom for her services. During one of these slacker periods she decided to try a diversification for her business. For some time, she had been interested in alternative forms of healing, and had several contacts practicing various types of treatment and therapy outside of the main stream of conventional medicine. She also knew that there was a growing demand for these services. What some of her practising friends lacked was proper business premises from which to operate.

The solution to her problem of fluctuating demand and their lack of accommodation seemed obvious. She invited an acupuncturist, an aromatherapist, a reflexologist, a shiatsu masseuse, a herbalist and a homeopath to use the facilities she had developed within the hotel.

The centralization of these services on one site proved a great success, generating sufficient business to provide all the practitioners with a living. Janet was now concerned to devise a working structure in which everyone could happily operate, and be fairly rewarded for their efforts.

'It's not the sort of business that we will ever be able to sell at a capital profit', she explained to her husband Mike. 'It's far too dependent on our individual skills to be able to sell it on. But we can make a reasonable income from it, and we all share a common interest.'

'You mean healing', said Mike.

'Not just healing', replied Janet, 'we want to promote natural healing. We don't need to be pumped full of chemicals to get over the slightest ailment. We can offer a complete range of alternatives which work and have no harmful side effects. Neither do they need testing on animals. We've really a common cause, that we all believe strongly in, as well as a business.'

'Don't get too carried away with the cause', warned Mike, 'we still have the bills to pay.'

'Exactly', responded Janet, 'that's why I want to make it into a cooperative as I think it would fulfil our needs as an organization. We'd all have an equal vote in how things are done and equal pay, depending on how much profit we make and how many hours we work. Of course, we will need to pay you a fair rent for the use of the premises', she added.

'Of course', said Mike.

Activities

(a) What would be the advantage of Janet's proposed course of action?
(b) What could be the disadvantages?

Case study
Arjuna Wholefoods[26]

In 1970, three young people moved into a late-Victorian brick terrace shop, 12 Mill Road, and founded a rather different kind of food business. Patrick Boase, a 21-year-old architecture graduate from Cambridge University, had inherited a sum of money and wanted to do something creative with it. Sarah Eno, 23 and busy bringing up a young daughter, had inherited an interest in co-ops, communes and organic growing from her mother, the long-time anarchist activist Joan Harvey. The two of them decided to start Cambridge's first wholefood business; they were joined in this by Andrew Moffat, a 26-year-old engineering surveyor.

Andrew thought up the name, inspired by Pat's Balinese shadow puppet of Prince Arjuna from Hindu mythology. The name was not meant to be loaded with meaning, although a quote from the Bhagavad Gita is relevant: 'Foods that promote life and vitality, strength, health and joy and gladness, foods that are savoury, greasy, firm and cordial are dear to people on the path'. Arjuna began trading with a stall on the market in 1970. A few months later, the shop and restaurant opened at Mill Road. None of the three partners had much experience of running either kind of business, but all were highly motivated by a mixture of idealism and a great determination to have fun.

The combined shop/restaurant was very small. The restaurant consisted of four pitch pine tables, with benches and hand-made pottery. There were more seats in the garden. One customer remembers that 'you waited a long time and then some very strange food arrived'. Arjuna has always been almost completely vegetarian – non-vegetarian cheese was sold in the 1970s – but, at the start, wholeness was the key concept. The foods sold in the shop and restaurant were to be as unrefined and free from additives as possible.

Arjuna quickly established itself as a modestly successful business and a unique feature of Cambridge life. Pat proved to be a natural organizer, while Andrew looked after the finances. Sarah, as perhaps the most

(Continued)

politically orientated of the three, provided much of the ideological direction, and also put considerable energy into developing the cooking. Number 12 Mill Road became a focus for all kinds of different groups and individuals interested in new social, political or spiritual paths. For instance, Sarah hosted Cambridge's first Women's Lib meetings upstairs, there were also transcendental meditation classes and, for many years, meetings of the Strawberry Fayre committee. Wages were low – £10 a week – at a time when renting a bedsit cost £5 a week – and the work was often hard, but the level of job satisfaction was high.

Two things soon became apparent. First, the shop and restaurant were both too small, and everyone's energies would be best concentrated on one or the other. Second, the partners' goal of democracy at work would only be reached if all the workers were given a share in the ownership of the business. These two things were to determine much of Arjuna's future direction.

It was probably inevitable that the restaurant, highly labour-intensive as it was, would close. The shop was financially stronger, with a unique and interesting range of products, including home-made yoghurt and Cambridge's only selection of organically grown vegetables. Pat persuaded Maskell's to bake wholemeal bread – another first – and bought an old butter churn in which to mix muesli.

Formation of the cooperative

Almost from the start, ideas were being discussed for ways of giving all the workers a full share in the ownership and control of the business. Partners and staff received equal wages – although the partners also had the considerable benefit of free lodgings upstairs – and all the workers were involved in decision-making. However, there was an obvious gulf between the two parties which Pat, as the owner of the building and the principal provider of capital, felt particularly acutely. The matter became urgent in 1973, when Pat and Sarah founded Crabapple, a commune and wholefood shop in Shropshire, and thus found their attention divided. At that time, a straightforward legal framework did not exist for the kind of organization Arjuna wished to evolve into. A new constitutional model developed by the Industrial Common Ownership Movement (ICOM) provided the solution. The workers would register themselves as a coop under the new rules established by the Industrial Common Ownership Act of 1976, and would buy the business from the partners over a period of several years. In 1976, Arjuna the cooperative was born.

The transition was in many ways a smooth one, as numerous aspects of the running of the business could proceed exactly as before. One of the first members of the coop describes the atmosphere of the shop at this time as 'folksy, slow and calm' – in some ways, old-fashioned. Paradoxically, the shop was also intimidatingly alien to many people. Wholefoods and vegetarianism were still tiny minority movements, and their proponents often seen as cranky or hippyish. The unfamiliar name with its Eastern connotations, the poor lighting and the poster-covered windows which made it difficult to see in, contributed to the sense of mystery and otherness. This image was not to change significantly until the 1980s, when wholefoods made a long, slow move into the mainstream, and Arjuna's customer base widened. And taking all those posters off the windows certainly helped.

As ever, the workers were interested in more than just food. At this time, the membership was roughly divided into spiritually and politically orientated camps. The former tended to want a quiet life so that they could concentrate on personal development. An acupuncturist was appointed to look after workers' health. Experiments with group therapy sessions also began: the British Legion next door complained about the shouting and crying.

The politically orientated members wanted to be more active externally, making links with other coops and various campaigning groups. Food was donated to the peace camps at Molesworth and Greenham Common, and a loan was offered to Infinity Foods in Brighton, who had been bombed by the National Front. Arjuna also received threats. Wholefood coops across the country gave a boost to the campaign to persuade Nestlé to stop promoting baby milk formula in developing countries. Led by Green City in Glasgow, coops decided not only to encourage a boycott of Nescafé, but to refuse to stock any product with Nestlé connections. The 'Arjuna Lectures', a series of talks in the university on environmental themes, were also a great success.

Arjuna has gone from strength to strength in a period that has seen small food shops of all kinds increasingly squeezed out by supermarkets. (It celebrated its 45th birthday in 2015). Whereas supermarkets sell the same products in the same way, in the same style buildings, from one end of the country to another, Arjuna believe in diversity. Despite increasing conformity in the size, shape and colour of fruits and vegetables, they are delighted to be able to sell Mr Baker's cucumbers – they are strangely shaped, cheap, organic and delicious.

Small independent shops offer a sense of community and are often central to local communities. Arjuna's customers like the fact that they will be recognized by the workers, are likely to bump into friends and can pick up information about local events.

The minutes book of Arjuna records that, at one meeting, there was a discussion on 'job dissatisfaction, alienation, communication and where we are all at'. Such meetings have been fairly regular occurrences in the history of Arjuna, as few of the members have come to the coop with much business experience, and even fewer with experience of collective working. Thus, Arjuna is described as representing a 'great and occasionally painful learning experience'. Nevertheless, most of the workers leave feeling enriched by their time at Arjuna with memories of the good times they have had and all that they have learned. They leave with increased self-confidence and lasting friendships.

As long as the product and price are right, Arjuna gives business to other coops over conventional businesses. For instance, the coop Suma Wholefoods is one of their major suppliers. And they have given work to other local coops including the Cambridge Free Press and the Cambridge Building Collective.

Activities

(a) Rate the success of the Arjuna cooperative:
   (i) on a lifestyle and personal values level; and
   (ii) on a financial and business strategy level.
(b) How easy would it be to replicate this type of business? What would be the required ingredients to make this type of business work compared to the normal small business?

The Inventors: creating a new system of power and transport

When we think of the 'railway' today, we have in mind trains, carriages and trucks that run on rails. This particular form of transport in fact evolved from three separate discoveries in different areas of knowledge: the wheel, the rail and power. The wheel has been used by man to assist in transporting goods and people for many thousands of years. Wheels running on rails can do more work and require less energy to move than wheels running on ordinary ground. The rapid increase in coal mining from the seventeenth century and the need to haul it around the country led to the extensive exploitation

(Continued)

of this knowledge. Coal initially used the widespread network of waterways on canals, rivers and seas, but, as the mines developed away from this network, coal had to be carried to the waterways in wagons. Horsedrawn wagon ways using wooden tracks soon criss-crossed the land between collieries and water ways. Thus, by the end of the seventeenth century the wheel and the rail were widely used, but still only using the power of animals and humans.

The development of steam power was the next step that revolutionized this system.

The name most widely associated with the development of the steam engine is James Watt, who is often quoted as the inventor of the first steam powered unit. But Watt only improved earlier steam engines and it has been argued that he actually stifled innovation because of the 25-year patent that he enjoyed for his own engine. One of the earliest machines was patented by Thomas Savery in 1698 with the intended application of pumping water from the tin and copper mines in Cornwall but, although the machine did work, it was never up to its intended job. He was granted a catch-all patent so that, when steam power was finally harnessed to draw water from the mines by Thomas Newcomen, he had to go into partnership with Savery. Newcomen's first machine (the so-called 'atmospheric engine', because it used a partial vacuum created by condensing steam) went to work in a coal mine in 1712, protected by patent until 1733. Although the Newcomen engine and derivatives became a relatively common sight in the coal mines of Europe, its application was limited as it used a lot of coal and was uneconomic for applications outside of the pits.

This is where James Watt came in. He developed a steam engine which was much more economical on coal through the use of a separate condensing unit. Watt teamed up with a Birmingham-based manufacturer, Matthew Boulton, and together they were granted a patent in 1775 that was to run until 1800. Boulton and Watt not only had an effective monopoly on early steam power, but they also developed a business model that made the take up of their equipment easier. Instead of selling a rather expensive machine, they created a form of lease in which the user paid them one-third of the savings in the cost of fuel that their engine produced over the earlier Newcomen machines. It proved a lucrative business, especially in Cornwall where there was no cheap, local coal. Understandably, several local Cornish inventors tried to improve on the system and claimed to have come up with more efficient engines. But they were prevented from exploiting their ideas by the Boulton and Watt patent.

The most prolific and energetic of these was Richard Trevithick, a headstrong Cornishman who created many inventions. He developed engines that worked with high pressure steam, rather than the low pressure of Boulton and Watt's engines; Boulton and Watt's machines were big, with large boilers to generate sufficient power from low pressure steam. At first, steam engines were used as stationary units positioned on top of a hill to winch wagons up and lower them down the other side. Trevithick's engines used 'strong steam' under higher pressure and thus enabled the development of much smaller, lighter units which could power themselves along. Watt criticized this development as dangerous, pouring scorn on the whole idea of 'propelling a carriage with an explosive kettle' (Weightman, 2007, p. 58). But this proved to be a vital breakthrough equivalent to the transformation in computer design when the original, large processors using valve technology were replaced with compact machines using microchips. The smaller steam engines did, indeed, have the capacity not only to pull other objects, but also to power themselves along at the same time. It was Trevithick, not George Stephenson as many suppose, who created the first full-sized steam engine which could power itself along on rails – the breakthrough invention that was to revolutionize transport systems around the world.

Trevithick's first prototype had an eventful but short life. Although the engine worked well travelling up a steep hill in 1801, it tipped over on its next outing because of its rudimentary steering. Trevithick and his companions retired to a nearby inn to consider what to do next, forgetting to extinguish the fire in the boiler. When the water finally evaporated, the engine caught fire and the first locomotive was destroyed. Undeterred, Trevithick built other locomotives to run on rails, including one that he took to London where he demonstrated it on a circular track in 1808. Naming his attraction 'Catch me who can', he charged one shilling admission to the enclosure, including a ride on the engine for anyone who dared. Unfortunately, the wooden track was not strong enough for the engine and the demonstration was regarded as the work of an eccentric, rather than the forerunner of a transport revolution. When his locomotive was not taken up quickly, Trevithick moved onto other things, including a steam hammer and a barge with paddle wheels driven by steam. It was left to George Stephenson to take forward his locomotive invention and apply it, first, to hauling coal from the mines and, secondly, passengers as well as freight on the world's first public railway to use steam locomotives – the Stockton and Darlington Railway that opened in 1825.

Richard Trevithick, inventor of the steam locomotive.

Activities

(a) The first locomotive came from three separate discoveries in different areas of knowledge: the wheel, the rail and steam power. What types of discoveries in different areas of knowledge led to the following transport revolutions:

　(i)　the automobile

　(ii)　the airplane

　(iii)　space travel.

(b) Did patents help or hinder the development of the industrial revolution in the eighteenth and nineteenth centuries?

(c) What other forms of intellectual property might apply today to these developments in steam power?

(d) Why did Watt make a fortune on his patent of a steam engine while Trevithick died a pauper? Which of these two contributed more to the industrial revolution?

Use the internet to conduct searches into company names and patents.

Conduct a name search. First, think of a name you might want to call a company. Go to the website of Companies House (www.gov.uk/government/organisations/companies-house) and use their database to see if the name is already registered, or if there are similar names. Try to come up with a name that is not registered.

Conduct a patent search. Try looking at patents in a particular area of technology or expertise of a business through the UK Intellectual Property Office database (www.gov.uk/government/organisations/intellectual-property-office). Try to establish what competitive products there are in the technology and if the patents have been turned into commercial products, through further internet searches. Alternatively, take an existing patented product with which you are familiar (e.g. Dyson's products) and search for the relevant patents on the website.

Extended activity
Name and patent search

Summary of what is required

- Decide on the appropriate business form for your organization.
- Consider how to protect any actual and potential intellectual property of your enterprise.
- Analyze the feasibility of your opportunity as a viable business.
- Decide on modifications to the opportunity.

Planning a new venture
Feasibility study

Decide the legal form

The appropriate business form of limited company, sole trader, partnership or cooperative will be conditioned by the route you have selected. For example, if you have decided to buy an existing business, it may be that you will be acquiring shares in a limited company, which dictates your choice.

A franchisor may also prescribe the legal form you adopt. If the business is to be co-owned, you obviously cannot operate as a sole trader. Use the checklist for choosing the appropriate form (Table 10.1) to assess the advantages and disadvantages of each form open to you against each of the categories shown. Are there other conditions which are not listed?

If you are forming the business outside of the UK, investigate local legislation.[18] Decide on the most appropriate form of organization for your small business and note your reasons.

Protect actual or potential intellectual property

Consider how to protect any intellectual property that has arisen or may arise in the future in relation to the opportunity. This should include: trademarks including business names, logos and domain names, patents, copyright and designs.

The feasibility study

Summarize the opportunity as defined and researched in previous chapters as *a feasibility study*.

Before moving on to refining the details of your business, you need to review previous steps taken in planning your new venture and check that your idea is a feasible opportunity for you to undertake.

Define the proposed business or enterprise – the elevator pitch

You should now be in a position to write down, in simple terms, the nature of your proposed business or enterprise. While this should be a brief statement in a few sentences, it should be precise and not vague, covering the main features of the business. It should encapsulate the essence of the opportunity and the objectives of what you are trying to do. It should answer such questions as:

- What will you sell?
- Who will be your customers?
- What are the unique benefits?
- What are the aims and objectives of the business?
- What is the main route to market?

For example, a manufacturer might describe their business as:

The design and manufacture of electronic components for specialized scientific instruments using patented technology to improve precision and increase the speed of use of the final product. The purchase of an existing business will provide immediate economies of scale and industry credibility so that sales of £5 million and net profits of 10 per cent of sales can be achieved by year three.

A service business might describe themselves thus:

The provision of high-quality education in business management to micro firms in the creative industries that will reduce high closure rates in this sector. Experienced business associates using the latest communications technologies will limit the time taken out of the workplace by course participants. In year three, franchising will be used to expand the concept from the north-east to other regions and countries.

The value of this exercise is to look at the scope and objectives of your idea again so that you understand more precisely what you are trying to do. It should also allow you to summarize your idea succinctly and clearly in a few minutes so that external supporters or potential investors can understand what you are trying to do very quickly. This has been referred to as an 'elevator pitch', as you should be able to communicate the essence of your business while travelling between floors in an elevator – or a lift, in the UK (Southon and West, 2008).

The 3 Ms of feasibility

From Chapter 7, we know that survival strategies for small business rely crucially on three factors:

Management – dealing with the influences of the small business environment.
Marketing – matching customer needs to the strengths of the enterprise.
Money – financial foresight to ensure sufficient ongoing resources.

You need to analyze yourself and your business in relation to these three crucial areas using the checklists below.

Management: Objectives – Strengths – Weaknesses

* What are your personal objectives? What are the objectives of the enterprise?
* What are your own, and your team's, strengths in relation to the opportunity you have identified?
* Which weaknesses need to be addressed and how?
* How will you deal with the influences of the small enterprise environment?
* How will your chosen route to market and legal form help your management of the business?
* How will you protect the ideas that you have developed?

Review your work in previous sections of 'Planning a new venture' in Chapters 2 and 3 to ensure that there is a good match between your own strengths and the opportunity identified. Review the objectives specified in Chapter 7 to ensure they are aligned to your personal objectives. Ensure that the chosen route to market (Chapters 8 and 9) takes account of any weakness in the management team.

Market: Opportunities – Threats – Barriers

* What are the opportunities and threats posed by your chosen marketplace?
* Who is your intended customer (precisely) and what is your competitive edge?
* What are the competitive threats?
* What are the barriers to market entry?

Review 'Planning a new venture' in Chapters 4 and 5 to summarize the market position of your venture. Review the route to market (Chapters 8, 9 and 10) in relation to competitive threats and overcoming barriers to market entry.

Money: Sources – Rewards – Risks

A rough financial appraisal of your business idea is necessary at this stage, which should include a break-even analysis from initial estimates of costs and sales. Your analysis should answer the following questions:

* What are the financial rewards or benefits of your idea likely to be in the short and medium term?
* How quickly will you make a profit?

(Continued)

- What are the financial risks?
- What is the break-even point of the business: the level of sales required to cover the ongoing costs of doing business?
- What is the probability of a viable long-term business?

At this stage, costs and sales can be approximate estimates. More detailed planning comes later, in putting together a full business plan. Here, you need a first appraisal of how feasible your new enterprise looks in practice.

Review the sales turnover forecast made in Chapter 5. Consider both the ongoing costs of running the business and the one-off costs involved in setting it up. Compare the ongoing costs to the sales forecast over three years. If the costs are only covered by your optimistic levels of future sales, then the risk of failure is obviously high. If your pessimistic level of sales covers costs, the risk looks much smaller.

From this assessment, you can determine whether the chances of success are high enough to merit taking it to the next stage.

Decide on modifications to the opportunity

If your conclusions are that the idea is not worth taking further, then consider what modifications can be made to make it more feasible. First ideas are often changed, sometimes radically, in the light of further information and analysis. If you consider that you need to start again because your idea now seems highly unrealistic, even with modification, then this in itself is a valuable learning experience.

10.10 Notes, references and recommended further reading

Notes and further information

1 Many government and official association websites contain much valuable information related to company formation, including lists of responsibilities of directors and guides to good governance of companies.
- In the UK, see the gov.uk portal (www.gov.uk/business-legal-structures; www.gov.uk/browse/business/limited-company) and Companies House (www.gov.uk/government/organisations/companies-house).
- Internationally, the Institute of Directors offers good information through www.iod.com or separate websites in countries where they operate directly, for example: Australia at www.companydirectors.com.au; New Zealand at www.iod.org.nz; South Africa at www.iodsa.co.za.
- In the USA, the National Association of Corporate Directors at www.nacdonline.org contains information and news.

2 The Insolvency Service (accessible through the gov.uk portal: www.gov.uk/government/organisations/insolvency-service) is the UK government department that deals with insolvency matters. Their website has useful information on directors' responsibilities and liabilities in this respect.

3 Companies House have an excellent website that lists directors' responsibilities including the statutory returns that a company is required to make: www.gov.uk/government/organisations/companies-house.

4 See notes 1 and 3.

5 In the UK, pension contributions free of tax changed in 2006 from banded annual allowances to a single annual limit subject to a lifetime allowance (£40 000 per annum subject to a lifetime allowance of £1.25 million in 2015/16). See www.gov.uk/tax-on-your-private-pension.

6 Like all businesses, sole traders need to conform to the law in relation to various aspects of their activities, such as health and safety and trading standards. A useful summary of the trading and other laws can be found on the gov.uk web portal (www.gov.uk/browse/business/sale-goods-services-data).

7   A summary of this Act and other relevant legislation is on the HM Revenue and Customs website at: www .gov.uk/government/organisations/hm-revenue-customs. The National Archives also have a database of all the UK primary legislation including those that affect businesses at www.legislation.gov.uk/.

8   Cooperatives[UK] have a website (www.uk.coop) that details many of the support mechanisms available for social enterprises in a cooperative form.

9   See note 8.

10 For more information on FC United of Manchester, see www.fc-utd.co.uk; Footprinter Co-operative Printers, see www.footprinters.co.uk; Zed Books, see www.zedbooks.co.uk.

11 For more information on Greyston Bakery, see greyston.com; Green Works, see www.londonreuse .org; Divine Chocolate, see divinechocolate.com.

12 The website of the Intellectual Property Office (formally the Patent Office), the official government body responsible for IP in the UK, can be found at www.gov.uk/government/organisations/intellectual -property-office. The site contains a wealth of information on protecting intellectual property and a pathway to searching IP databases of existing patents and other IP.

13 Intellectual Property agencies around the world include:
    • World Intellectual Property Organization, part of the United Nations – www.wipo.int; this site contains a listing of worldwide IP Offices;
    • European Union, ec.europa.eu /internal_market/intellectual-property/;
    • Australia: Intellectual Property Australia – www.ipaustralia.gov.au;
    • India: Office of Patents, Designs and Trademarks – www.patentoffice.nic.in;
    • New Zealand: Intellectual Property Office of New Zealand – www.iponz.govt.nz;
    • South Africa: Companies and Intellectual Property Commission – www.cipc.co.za/;
    • Sweden: PRV – the Swedish Patent and Registration Office – www.prv.se;
    • UK Intellectual Property Office – www .gov.uk/government/organisations /intellectual-property-office;
    • United States Patent and Trademark Office – www.uspto.gov.

14 See note 13.

15 Advice on business names can be obtained from Companies House (www.gov.uk/government /organisations/companies-house) where a register of company names is kept.

16 See www.dailychanges.com which has a daily update on domains registered, deleted and transferred. On 7 January 2016, 152 000 domains were registered, 130 000 deleted, and 190 000 transferred to give a total of 160 million website domain names.

17 Nominet (www.nic.uk) is the internet registry for .uk domain names. It holds a database of domain registrations with over 7 million domain names and provides neutral advice on registering and maintaining a name.

18 For example, Norid is the .no registry: www.norid .no/domreg.html. It also lists domain name registries around the world.

19 A good description of the UK process of patent application is on the website of the Intellectual Property Office – www.gov.uk/government/organisations /intellectual-property-office.

20 See note 19.

21 The British Library (www.bl.uk) offers an information service for intellectual property including patents through its website (www.bl.uk/collection-guides /patents). This provides access to over 60 million patent specifications from 40 countries worldwide (added to at a rate of about 2 million each year), and official gazettes on patents, trademarks and registered designs. It also has other information useful to start-ups.

22 There is a European Patent Convention which allows you to obtain protection in a number of European countries without the need to apply for registration in each state through the European Patent Office (EPO) (www.european-patent-office.org). There is also the World Intellectual Property Organization (WIPO) (www.wipo.int).

23 The 1988 Copyright, Designs and Patents Act reformed much of British law in this area. The Copyright (Computer Programs) Regulations 1992 extended the definition of literary work to include computer programming. Copyright regulations in the EU were harmonized by the EC directive Copyright and Related Rights in the Information Society, 2001. Worldwide protection can also arise from the agreement on Trade-Related Aspects of Intellectual Property Rights (TRIPS), which forms part of the World Trade Organization (WTO) Agreement.

24 See note 13.

25 See note 23.

26 For more information on Arjuna Wholefoods, see www.arjunawholefoods.co.uk/.

References

Barrow, C. (2006) *The Complete Small Business Guide,* Capstone Publishing, see sec. 7.

BIS (2011) *A Guide to Legal Forms for Business*, Department for Business Innovation & Skills, www.gov.uk/government/uploads/system/uploads/attachment_data/file/31676/11-1399-guide-legal-forms-for-business.pdf, accessed 16 January 2016.

Blackburn, R. (2007) *Intellectual Property and Innovation Management in Small Firms*, Routledge.

Carlberg, J. G., Ward, C. E. and Holcomb, R. D. (2004) *Success Factors for New Generation Cooperatives,* Oklahoma State University Cooperative Extension Fact Sheets, Department of Agricultural Economics, University of Manitoba, July, osufacts.okstate.edu.

Cooperatives^UK (2008) *Annual Report and Financial Statements,* Cooperatives^UK Ltd, Manchester.

Cooperatives^UK (2015) *The Cooperative Economy 2015: An Ownership Agenda for Britain*, Co-operatives^UK Ltd, www.uk-coop.

Cornforth, C. (1986) Worker Cooperatives: Factors Affecting their Success and Failure. In: Curran, J., Gibb, A., Lewis, J. and Faulkner, T. (eds) *The Survival of the Small Firm,* Gower.

De Rassenfosse, G. (2012) How SMEs exploit their intellectual property assets: Evidence from survey data, *Small Business Economics*, 39(2): 437–452.

Duening, T. N., Hisrich, R. A. and Lechter, M. A. (2014) *Technology Entrepreneurship: Taking Innovation to the Marketplace*, Academic Press (2nd edn).

Eisenhardt, K. (1989) Agency theory: An assessment and review, *Academy of Management Journal*, 14(1): 57–74.

Ferguson, N. (2009) *The Ascent of Money: A Financial History of the World,* Penguin Books.

FC United of Manchester (2016) *A History of FC United of Manchester,* www.fc-utd.co.uk/m_history.php#intro, accessed 6 January 2016.

Footprint Workers Cooperative (2016) *About Footprint Workers Coop*, www.footprinters.co.uk/, accessed 6 January 2016.

Frietsch, R., Neuhäusler, P. and Rothengatter, O. (2013) *SME Patenting: An Empirical Analysis in Nine Countries*, Fraunhofer ISI Discussion Papers Innovation Systems and Policy Analysis, 36: 1–27.

Goss, D. (1991) *Small Business and Society,* Routledge, ch. 5, Alternative forms of small business.

Harrison, R. (ed.) (2013) *People Over Capital: The Cooperative Alternative to Capitalism: Essays and Insights on a New Global Awakening,* New Internationalist.

Jensen, M. C. and Meckling, W. H. (1976) Theory of the firm: Managerial behaviour, agency, costs and ownership structure, *Journal of Financial Economics*, 3(4): 305–360.

Keating, R. J. (2013) *Unleashing Small Business Through IP: Protecting Intellectual Property, Driving Entrepreneurship*, CreateSpace Independent Publishing Platform.

Kitching, J. and Blackburn, R. (1998) Intellectual property management in the small and medium enterprise (SME), *Journal of Small Business and Enterprise Development*, 5(4): 327–335.

Mason, C. M. and Harrison R. T. (1999) Informal Venture Capital and the Financing of Emergent Growth Businesses. In: Sexton, D. L. and Landstroem, H. (eds) *The Blackwell Handbook of Entrepreneurship,* Blackwell.

McManus, J. P. (2012) *Intellectual Property: From Creation to Commercialisation: A Practical Guide for Innovators & Researchers*, Oak Tree Press.

Micklethwaite, J. and Wooldridge, A. (2003) *The Company: A Short History of a Revolutionary Idea,* Weidenfeld & Nicolson, London.

Nyberg, A. J., Smithey Fulmer, I., Gerhart, B. and Carpenter, M. A. (2010) Agency theory revisited: CEO return and shareholder interest alignment, *Academy of Management Journal*, 53(5): 1029–1049.

Richards, G. (2009) *Spin-outs: Creating Businesses from University Intellectual Property*, Harriman House Publishing.

Southon, M. and West, C. (2008) *The Beermat Entrepreneur,* Pearson Business.

Van Puyvelde, S., Caers, R., Du Bois, C. and Jegers, M. (2012) The governance of nonprofit organizations: Integrating agency theory with stakeholder and stewardship theories, *Nonprofit and Voluntary Sector Quarterly*, 41(3): 431–451.

Weightman, G. (2007) *The Industrial Revolutionaries: The Creators of the Modern World 1776–1914,* Atlantic Books, London.

Zed Books (2016) www.zedbooks.co.uk/about, accessed 6 January 2016.

Recommended further reading

Bainbridge, D. (2012) *Intellectual Property*, Pearson (9th edn).

Government department websites on company formation including: www.gov.uk/business-legal-structures; www.gov.uk/government/organisations/companies-house.

Cooperatives^{UK} website www.uk-coop, for more information on co-operatives including the *The Cooperative Economy 2015: An Ownership Agenda for Britain*.

Government department websites on intellectual property including: www.gov.uk/government/organisations/intellectual-property-office. See note 13 for other international examples.

Johnson, S. (2015) *The Economist Guide to Intellectual Property: What it is, How to protect it, How to exploit it*, Economist Books.

Micklethwaite, J. and Wooldridge, A. (2003) *The Company: A Short History of a Revolutionary Idea*, Weidenfeld & Nicolson, London. A fascinating history of the development of the company as a legal form and its effects.

Harrison, R. (ed.) (2013) *People Over Capital: The Cooperative Alternative to Capitalism: Essays and Insights on a New Global Awakening*, New Internationalist.

Stokes, D., Wilson, N. and Mador, M. (2010) *Entrepreneurship*, Cengage. See ch. 12 The creation and protection of knowledge.

Weightman, G. (2007) *The Industrial Revolutionaries: The Creators of the Modern World 1776–1914*, Atlantic Books, London. If the case study of the development of steam power fires your imagination, then read this excellent history of the many innovators who underpinned the industrial revolution. It is more appropriate to entrepreneurship than many industrial history texts as it describes the entrepreneurs behind the inventions.

Managing the entrepreneurial small business

PART III

- Part III comprises Chapters 11 to 14. It considers how small businesses are managed in practice, focusing on successful strategies for start-up and growth, particularly in the areas of the management of people and resources, marketing and money. It concludes by investigating business exits and succession strategies.

- It is important to continue to undertake the activities that are either in the text, or at the end of each chapter, as these are designed to stimulate your thoughts and experiences of the topic under discussion.

- At the end of each chapter, you will find the relevant step in 'Planning a new venture'. In this section, the four steps represent a process of taking an opportunity from a position of reasonable prospects with a known route to market, to that of planned, acceptable risk. By the end of Chapter 14, you will be able to complete the business plan.

11 Management of people and resources

Introduction

Managing in a small business is not like managing part of a large organization. However, it is difficult to say precisely what the differences are, other than having fewer resources to do things. In this chapter, we examine, first, the impersonal resources that are managed in the small firm such as premises, equipment and business processes. The management of people, and the development of a management team, is often the crucial owner-manager role, particularly in a growing firm, and this is evaluated from a practical and a more theoretical perspective. It is widely thought that working for a small business is somehow more interesting and fulfilling, with less in the way of office politics than working in a large corporate concern. The reality is not this simple and conflicts are common. Many owners who exit from a business say that their most important learning experience in the entrepreneurial process was dealing with issues of relationships and trust (see also Chapter 14). This chapter investigates some of these issues and ways of dealing with them.

Activity 1
Is there a difference?

Is management of a small business intrinsically different to management in a large organization? If so, in what ways?

11.1 Total management

11.1.1 THE INFLUENCE OF SMALLNESS

How does managing a small firm differ from that of a larger organization? We have already seen that the small business environment exerts some pressures that can be different to the influences on larger organizations. Problems of the availability or cost of finance, and the burden of government regulations and paperwork are examples of the preoccupations that might concern the manager of a small enterprise but possibly do not concern many corporate managers in larger organizations (see Chapter 3, The small business and entrepreneurial environment).

However, differences in the environment are probably as great between sectors defined by products or markets as they are between those delineated by size of company. For example, the external influences on an engineering company manufacturing capital equipment for industrial customers will be very different to those on a retailer offering fashion garments to domestic markets. Such differences in the business environment can be just as significant as those between a large and a small company.

The small scale of a business does bring some common management problems and influences (Gibb, 1983), such as:

- small management team (often a solo manager);
- no specialist personnel or support functions, so managers are multifunctional;
- potentially autocratic leadership by owner-manager;
- informal control systems;
- closeness of working group;
- limited leverage in obtaining resources required, including finance;
- limited research and control of the business environment.

Some of these influences relate to the lack of specialist management in the firm. 'Total management' of an autocratic style and the use of informal control systems often arise from the very real pressure of time in a small business environment. Other influences reflect a sense of helplessness in the face of external forces, with no real resources to research the environment, let alone control it.

What sets small business management apart is the enormity of the range of issues confronting owner-managers, which they have to deal with personally. The internal structure of a small business creates the need for a different management approach. In a larger company, the chief executive is head of a team of specialists in production, finance, marketing, human resources and other functions. There will be a clear distinction between those planning the future of the business in the longer term and those implementing the strategy on a day-to-day basis. Small business owner-managers have to do it all. They are generalists who will have to turn their hand to all functions, from sales to production. They are the planners and the implementors, responsible for deciding strategy and making it happen, and also filling out the tax returns while they are about it.

This scale and diversity of issues to be dealt with is a unique feature of small business management.[1] Of course, no manager can hope to be expert in all fields, and advice or training is often needed. However, the required skill is not always the problem for an owner-manager faced with a multitude of problems demanding attention simultaneously. Having the experience and understanding necessary to know how to choose which problem to deal with first is often the difficulty. It is tempting always to tackle the most immediate issue first. For a small business, this may mean overlooking a less obvious, but more significant, problem which has a critical impact.

The juggler and the conductor

The analogy has been drawn between the owner-manager and the entertainer spinning dozens of plates on poles, all of which need attention to keep them going. One false move, one touch out of sequence and they all crash down.

By contrast, the chief executive of a larger company is likened to a conductor of an orchestra; their leadership can profoundly influence the result, but their attention can wander without stopping the orchestra from playing.

In contrast to the conductor of an orchestra, who can walk away for a while without the players stopping, the owner-manager is involved in many functions which require constant attention. The next section reviews some of the resources which are part of this difficult juggling act.

Activity 2
Management issues

The small business manager is responsible for many decisions in the early days of a new venture. How many specific decisions can you think of? List as many as possible under the headings of operations, people, marketing and finance.

11.1.2 MANAGING RESOURCES

Management is about using resources efficiently and effectively in order to meet the objectives of the enterprise. An important part of the entrepreneurship process is the ability to pursue opportunities without regard to the resources currently controlled, and to make decisions on how to obtain and use resources (see Chapter 2, Section 2.2). As research by Wilson and Martin (2015) demonstrates, not everyone has an equal chance to pursue entrepreneurial opportunities. Access to resources is certainly one necessary condition for an individual to have 'entrepreneurial capability', or the freedom to pursue an entrepreneurial opportunity.

The Resource-Based View (RBV) of organizations argues that they are made up of bundles of resources: human, financial, physical, tangible and intangible (see Kamasak, 2013; Rousseau, 2014). These are combined in different ways to create the great diversity of enterprises that we can observe around us. The resource-based concept considers that a successful enterprise competes for and wins resources before deploying them in unique ways. The strategic choices open to entrepreneurs are therefore dependent on having or acquiring new resources. Their choices are constrained by the availability, quality or style of resources within the enterprise and its environment. They are also affected by previous decisions to use and build resources into particular configurations, as it can become difficult to re-configure resources in order to change the direction of the enterprise.

Most entrepreneurs start with an idea and insufficient resources to pursue it. With determination, some gradually accrue what they need, designing an enterprise around the resources that they leverage from external sources. Others may start with clear plans and a view of the resources that they need to achieve them, and specifically seek those resources in order to proceed. This depends on whether the entrepreneur is following an emergent strategy or a more deliberate one (see Chapter 7.1.3). The resource-based view of enterprises underpins both of these approaches as, in different ways, entrepreneurs bring together a bundle of resources to create something new.

MAKING RESOURCES COUNT

James Dyson took five years to take his idea from concept to working prototype. He became frustrated with the performance of his vacuum cleaner and concluded it was down to the bag, which clogged up with dust after a certain amount of use. After thousands of experiments, he created a new type of cleaner that used a revolutionary, cyclonic process without bags. Unfortunately, he had used all his resources getting this far, and so had to peddle his invention around vacuum cleaning companies such as Hoover and Electrolux, offering them a licence to manufacture his break-through product. They all turned him down, possibly because his system threatened their lucrative business of selling bags. All except one that is, a small Japanese company that began to make a luxury version, the G-force, that soon developed a cult following nationally. The royalties from Japan gave Dyson sufficient resources to set up a manufacturing plant in the UK and he launched the DC01 in 1993. Within two years, it was the best selling cleaner on the market.

Ambitious to broaden his range by designing more breakthrough products, Dyson later decided to optimize his resources by moving his manufacturing operation to a lower-cost base overseas while retaining a design function in the UK. By setting up production in Malaysia, he calculated he saved 30 per cent on manufacturing costs that he could re-invest into the R&D of new products. By 2016, the Dyson product range had expanded to include bladeless fans, heatless hand driers and robotic cleaners, with more promised (see www.dyson .com.au/community/about-james-dyson).

Jeff Besos began the concept of **Amazon** in a deliberate, planned way. He became aware of the potential of the internet for retail sales in the early 1990s but could not decide on which products would most benefit from online marketing. He researched a list of over 20 products which he then refined down to a shortlist of 5: CDs, computer hardware, software, videos and books. Taking into account the resources immediately at his disposal and the potential of the market, he decided on books. He began trading online from his garage in 1995 under the Amazon brand. Sales were encouraging and reached $20 000 per week after a few months. Whereas the resources of traditional, 'bricks-and-mortar' booksellers ran to a stock of maybe 200 000 books, Amazon's stock was almost unlimited, as he could use the virtual stock of all his suppliers and publishers. However, his ultimate business model needed more resources than he had available. He planned to make a small percentage on sales of many product types to a very large customer base and that required an interna-tional platform with an infrastructure to match. In 1997, only two years after launch, he raised more finance through an initial public offering (IPO) on the NASDAQ, the US stock exchange for high-tech companies. Unlike many of the companies that crashed in the dot-com bubble, Bezos's business plan was uncompromis-ingly realistic. He did not aim to make profits for four to five years and he did exactly that, declaring his first surplus in early 2001. The IPO gave him the resources to last that long. Amazon has since accumulated the resources to add almost every type of consumer good to their range, from grocery deliveries to streaming movies, and have become the world's largest online retailer of almost everything (see Stone, 2014).

Until a management team has developed, the entrepreneur is responsible for all significant decisions regarding resources including:

- what resources are needed;
- where they will come from;

- how they will be used;
- how their use will be controlled and monitored.

Figure 11.1 Management of resources in a small firm: some issues to be resolved

Operations	**People**
▪ Premises	▪ Personnel policies
▪ Equipment	▪ Recruitment and dismissal
▪ Materials	▪ Employment contracts
▪ Processes	▪ Personal records and systems
▪ Systems	▪ Statutory and other regulations
▪ Legal and insurance	▪ Performance and pay reviews

Marketing	**Money**
▪ Research	▪ Cash management
▪ Product development	▪ Banking
▪ Pricing	▪ Purchasing
▪ Distribution	▪ Tax
▪ Communications and promotions	▪ Sourcing finance
▪ Sales administration	▪ Management accounts

This adds up to an almost endless combination of different responsibilities and activities. Some examples of the areas these cover are shown in Figure 11.1, which breaks the issues down into four main areas: operations, people (human resources), marketing and money. The remainder of this chapter evaluates two of these functional areas – operations and people; Chapters 12 and 13 consider the management of marketing and money.

11.2 Premises

In a start-up situation, or at critical growth points of a business, the location and type of premises become important decisions. The owner-manager has to answer some critical questions that are evaluated in the following sections.

Activity 3
Where is the best location?

What factors do you think the owner-manager should take into account in locating the premises of their business?
Which do you think is the most common deciding factor in practice?

11.2.1 WHERE IS THE BUSINESS TO BE LOCATED?
Kitchen tables – and even a telephone kiosk, in the case of Richard Branson[2] – have provided many new ventures with a first, low-cost working facility. Once independent premises become necessary, there are many considerations to be taken into account,[3] such as:

- ease of communication (e.g. road and rail);
- availability of labour, especially for any process requiring specific skills;

- availability of industry-specific resources such as high speed broadband for online companies (see De Clercq *et al.*, 2015);
- proximity to centres of population: this is a key factor for retail, catering and hotel businesses;
- costs of rent and rates: these still vary considerably even within relatively short distances;
- government and local authority assistance: there are a variety of ways in which specific geographic regions try to stimulate the growth of small business;
- proximity to the home of the founder of the small business. Research has indicated that, in practice, this is the most important consideration in deciding the location of a small firm (Falk, 1982; McCann, 2006). Very few founders move their homes in order to set up a new business.

11.2.2 WHAT TYPE OF PREMISES ARE NEEDED?

The legal and financial implications are usually the most important factors in deciding on the type of premises. Taking on a lease is often a major commitment for a small business, especially for an owner-manager who may have to give personal guarantees. As well as the obligation to pay rent and rates, the tenant will normally be obliged to pay for the insurance, maintenance and repair of leasehold property (for fuller details of the implications of acquiring freehold and leasehold premises, see Chapter 9, Buying an existing business). This can be a major obligation on a new business, although the costs become a smaller percentage of income as the business grows because the costs of premises are relatively fixed.

The nature of the business will largely dictate the type of premises required. Considerations include:

- building features such as the size of office, workshop and visitor waiting areas;
- facilities including loading areas, reception service, lifts, meeting rooms and network cabling;
- security features including locks, window grilles, alarms and CCTV;
- physical environment of the premises including lighting, washrooms, air cooling and open or partitioned space;
- exterior appearance of the buildings.

11.2.3 ARE THE RIGHT PREMISES AVAILABLE?

Finding suitable premises has been a major problem for many small firms. In the 1970s and early 1980s, several surveys showed that difficulties over premises, particularly in inner city areas, were a constraint on the development of small businesses (Falk, 1980). Armed with one study that clearly demonstrated that the shortage of premises had constrained the establishment and development of small firms (Coopers & Lybrand, 1980), central government became increasingly critical of local government planning policies in the UK.

Public authorities and private developers have now provided many more units suitable for small businesses. Small firms tend to relocate frequently as they grow. Requirements can change quite rapidly from a small space in a fully serviced, shared unit to larger, more independent premises. Flexibility of tenure is therefore needed, in addition to the right size of premises in a good location with appropriate facilities. These needs have been increasingly met by local councils, enterprise agencies and private sector companies offering flexible leases with short-term break clauses.

The premises available to small businesses include the following options:

- *Home.* Many businesses operate successfully from home as this is low-cost and convenient (see, for example, the multi-award winning online shopping site: notonthehighstreet.com, which was founded round a kitchen table in 2006). Disadvantages include balancing work and home life, tax complications and meeting clients.

- *Innovation/incubation centre.* These are usually furnished, offering a working space with communal facilities such as meeting rooms and reception. Sometimes, they offer additional business support in conjunction with a local agency or university. Some universities have their own incubation facilities for commercial spin-outs from their research base, or for student entrepreneurs and alumni. As they offer short-term contracts (usually one month's notice), they are easy to move into and leave, and therefore offer a good starting point for many new businesses.
- *Flexible lease.* More business premises are now offered with a flexible lease, often with a three-month break clause. Such an arrangement allows an owner the freedom to change premises as needs arise, although the rental costs are usually higher than comparable property on longer-term leases.
- *Traditional lease.* Longer-term leases of five years or more give a business security of tenure and lower costs. For an established, viable business ready to invest in infrastructure and the fitting out of premises, this is a popular option.
- *Buying property.* The purchase of suitable premises can provide the necessary security and return on investment for an owner who is certain of the long-term propects for their business, and who believes that commercial property is a good investment (and might be part of their pension arrangements).

11.3 Materials and equipment

Purchasing of materials and equipment is a key management activity in many small firms, especially manufacturers and retailers.

Materials

Materials purchased fall into two basic types:

- *Goods to be sold, either modified or unchanged.* This includes the stocks of raw materials for a manufacturer, retail stocks in a shop, food ingredients in a restaurant and building materials in the construction industry.
- *Consumable items, indirectly supporting the business.* This includes stationery, publicity material and reference catalogues.

Larger manufacturing companies and retailers will normally employ specialist buyers; the owner-manager usually fulfils this role in the formative years, perhaps handing over routine ordering to an office manager or assistant as the business develops. Good management of this function can assist the small firm in a number of ways:

- ensuring that the right material for the job is always purchased;
- reduction in costs: time spent on researching and negotiating with suppliers can result in lower buying prices;
- availability of stock: poor purchasing systems can easily lose sales because a manufacturer cannot produce on time, a retailer runs out of a popular line, or a construction company develops a reputation for delays;
- reduction in stock: just-in-time purchasing policies ensure adequate availability, while minimizing stock levels to keep down the working capital requirements of the small firm.

Despite these benefits, many owner-managers neglect the purchasing function, and fail to build good relationships with suppliers. The demands of other activities which may have more immediate effect often take precedence; for example, the visiting representative from a supplier is put off or not seen at all, as the owner-manager struggles to keep up with other demands on their time. Alternative supply sources are often not followed up because it is easier not to change from the existing supplier.

Equipment

The infrastructure of a small firm is made up principally of various categories of equipment, representing a key resource to be managed. These categories include:

- *Production machinery and equipment:* this is obviously specific to the type of manufacturing process.
- *Communication equipment:* information and communications technology (ICT) now offers systems that are increasingly sophisticated at a cost that a small business can afford.
- *Office or retail furniture:* image as well as functionality will influence the selection of furniture for public areas of a small firm.
- *Systems equipment:* this category represents an area of increasing expenditure for small businesses, as it includes computer hardware and software for a variety of applications, including document processing, accounts, databases and stock control. Cash registers and tills for retail outlets are also often part of a wider computerized system, capable of generating accounting, sales and stock control information as well as performing the basic function of monitoring cash intake.
- *Personal equipment:* cars, mobile telephones and portable computers are the main items of equipment that a small business manager may consider, especially if their work involves travelling to visit customers or suppliers.

Finance

Owner-managers often buy equipment on lease or lease purchase at real rates of interest above those applying to normal bank borrowing. Commentators have therefore been critical of small firm management for its use of financial resources to acquire equipment. While there are, no doubt, cases where small firms do pay more in finance costs than they need, there are often valid objections to looking beyond lease or lease purchase. It is often easier and less time-consuming to arrange leasing, and owner-managers may wish to keep their bank borrowing potential available for other purposes, such as the funding of expansion or losses, for which there are fewer alternatives (see Chapter 13).

Activity 4

What insurances are needed?

When a new venture begins to trade, insurance is required to cover certain eventualities. Which insurance do you think is needed:

(a) because it is obligatory; and
(b) because it is discretionary?

11.4 Insurance

The purpose of insurance is to minimize the impact of mishaps. As small firms are particularly vulnerable to one-off disasters, an important management issue will be the choice of appropriate insurance policies to mitigate the effect of misfortune.

Obligatory insurance

In some areas there is no choice. Insurance is obligatory in the UK for:

- *Employers' liability:* insurance against claims by employees who suffer injury or illness as a result of their employment is required by law.
- *Third-party vehicle insurance:* company vehicles are subject to the same legal requirement as private vehicles, and need at least third-party insurance.
- *Specified insurances:* some contracts will stipulate a requirement for insurance. Leases for premises normally require the tenant to take out property insurance. Lease or lease purchase agreements for equipment usually insist on a specified insurance cover.

Discretionary insurance

Other insurance is not obligatory, but is more or less desirable according to the circumstances of the business and the owner-managers. They include:

- *Fire, theft and other disasters:* covering premises and their contents, stock and goods in transit.
- *Engineering breakdown:* equipment can be insured for the costs of repair in the case of breakdown or damage.
- *Loss of profits:* in the event of fire, theft, breakdown and other misfortunes, a small firm can suffer not just the costs of replacement or repair, but the loss of profits while it is out of action. Insurance can cover these other costs of disruptions.
- *Public and product liability:* in the event of injury to members of the public, or damage to their property. Due to the size and frequency of claims in the USA, this insurance is particularly advisable for companies exporting to North America.
- *Professional indemnity:* against claims of misconduct or negligence in performing a professional service.
- *Legal costs insurance:* provides cover in the event of a legal dispute with customers, suppliers or employees.
- *Key man insurance:* a small firm is usually heavily dependent on one person, or a small number of people, whose death would jeopardize the future of the enterprise. Key man insurance helps by paying a large sum so that, at the very least, a business can cover its debts if a key person dies.
- *Personal insurance:* owner-managers are usually advised to take out life, permanent health and pension policies to protect their family and themselves.

Activity 5
Functions that require business processes

Processes and information needed in a small firm do not just relate to accounting. Which other functions in a small business require business processes and systems?

11.5 Business processes and ICT

11.5.1 COMPUTERIZED BUSINESS PROCESSES

To help the owner-manager in their seemingly impossible task of juggling all the important tasks in the day-to-day running of their firm, computerized business processes using ICT have become increasingly available and affordable. While manual systems are still used, ICT systems increasingly help small firms to develop processes, records and controls.

The economies of scale available to larger firms in computerization of important processes and operations have been eroded by the availability of hardware and software which has reduced in price, while it has increased in scope, power, flexibility and user friendliness. Quite sophisticated systems are now available to a small business to cover all major management processes and functions. These include:

- accounting and financial management
- personnel records, administration and payroll
- sales order systems
- customer relationship management (CRM)
- sales tracking, management and administration
- marketing communications and promotions
- production management or service delivery
- purchasing and stock control
- asset management
- internal communications.

Many owner-managers, however, have learned the lesson that it is more important to keep basic records in a methodical way right from the start of a new business, than to spend time installing sophisticated systems while overlooking more fundamental paperwork flows and information requirements.

Another common error is to assume that systems and record keeping are primarily financial in function. While accounting records are at the heart of any small firm's systems, every management function and business process can benefit from a systematic approach. Administration, especially that generated by government regulations, is a constant source of complaint by many owner-managers.[4] Unfortunately, these complaints often overlook the real benefits which can result from the use of information and formalized processes in all areas of small business management.

Before embarking on setting up computerized processes, it is important to consider the benefits expected from the new processes and technology, and how these contribute towards meeting the objectives of the business. Computerized business processes can deliver the following benefits:

- cutting costs through the automation of routine tasks;
- improving customer service levels; for example, by using a server-based customer database system;
- attracting new customers through the reach of the internet;
- increasing profit margins by helping employees work more productively.

It is important to ensure that computer hardware and software in the business are fully compatible. On upgrading or replacing existing equipment, it can sometimes be as cost-effective to install a whole new system, especially if this ensures compatibility. It is important to ensure that purchases take full account of plans for the future and any expansion they might involve. Most hardware only lasts between three and five years.

11.5.2 BUILDING A WEBSITE

The internet has become a vital resource for the small business for information gathering and communications to internal and external audiences. In setting up a new business, the entrepreneur can make use of countless websites to find help and advice (see Chapter 5), and the creation of a website is usually an important part of a communication strategy with key stakeholders (see Chapter 12, for the use of the internet for marketing communications).

There are a number of basic steps to take in order to build a website (Turban *et al.*, 2004, p. 608):

- *Select a web host.* Selecting where your website should be located on the internet is one of the first decisions. For example, you may choose to locate it within a network of other business sites. Most small business owners prefer to build stand-alone websites.
- *Register a domain name.* A stand-alone website will have a unique domain name (e.g. mybusiness.com), and key decisions need to be made about whether the domain name includes the business name or some other description of the business type (see also Chapter 10, Section 10.7.2, Trademarks and business names). It is also important to think about how the site will be 'future-proof' in respect of the international reach of the business – setting up with '.co.uk' could be potentially restrictive as compared with a '.eu' or '.com' address, for example (see Daryanto *et al.*, 2013).
- *Create and manage content.* The site will require a variety of content (e.g. text, images, sound and video) ranging in complexity according to the business's needs. Getting the right content, making it easy to find, delivering it effectively and keeping it up-to-date are all crucial steps in ensuring the success of the online business.
- *Design the website.* This is the critically important and creative part of the process that determines what the site will look like and how visitors will use it. To become noticed, businesses are using innovative designs so customers' expectations are rising. There is normally a fine balance between providing a professional and inviting site and controlling expenditure at this point.
- *Construct the website and test.* Websites are increasingly designed informally either by the entrepreneur themselves, or with the help of friends and colleagues. There are also a growing number of web design firms, many of whom specialize in small businesses. Once the look and feel of the site is approved, it can be transferred to the website host. At this point, the website is open for business. However, final testing is required to ensure all links and processes function as expected (including ensuring credit card transactions are secure, if this is a required function).
- *Market and promote the website.* The location (or URL) of the website can now be widely promoted by the business on products, business cards, letters and promotional materials. Search engine optimization is needed in order to maximize external visibility (see Chapter 12, Section 12.5).

Activity 6
Harmony or conflict?

Some people believe that small businesses tend to make a happier working environment than larger organizations.

Do you agree? Which factors may help a small business to become a more harmonious place to work? Which may cause more conflict?

11.6 Management of people

Although more than 75 per cent of small businesses employ only the owner, there are 1.3 million that do have employees in the UK, and their role as an employer is becoming increasingly significant. Over 15 million employees, 60 per cent of the workforce in the UK, work for SMEs (see Chapter 1, Section 1.3, for a more detailed discussion).

In these small firms, people are the key resource. The management of people is often the most important role played by the owner-manager. Like all other functional areas in a new start-up, the owner-manager will tend to take control of the human resources function. It is also the role which the owner-manager is least likely to give up as the firm grows. Rarely is a trained human resources (HR) manager appointed from outside, as even high-growth small firms tend to make do in this area. It is also the function in which owner-managers assess themselves as having the lowest level of expertise (Stanworth and Gray, 1991).

The job of managing people does not lie just within the small business itself. Managing people *outside* of the firm – investors, suppliers, customers, distributors – is also a key function for the owner-manager. They will need to express the business concepts in their head in such a way that will convince, rather than alienate, those who are needed to support the enterprise. In an international context, this requires an understanding of local customs and rituals, such as how people talk to each other, introduce one another, and 'break the ice' in a social situation.

FIRST IMPRESSIONS COUNT

Take the example of doing business in Kenya. On meeting business contacts for the first time, it is important you greet everyone present, starting with the most senior person. If you don't shake hands with everybody, this may well come across as stand-offish or rude. It is good practice to address all people with their full name or title at first; only as the atmosphere becomes more informal could you switch to a first-name basis. Don't be surprised if nobody jumps straight into business matters, though; small talk is expected. Enquiring after co-workers' or business contacts' families, their hometowns (but not their politics), is as important as talking about your own relatives and home country.

Managing a small business successfully requires being able to manage yourself and your relations with others. It can be nerve-racking meeting a new and potentially important business contact for the first time; the more you know about them and their way of working before you meet them, the better.

Adapted from blog post: Form a Kenyan Company Ltd, 24 October 2014, (bmskenya.wordpress.com/author/bmskenya/) (accessed 23 January 2016).

11.6.1 EMPLOYMENT LAW

One reason for the low level of confidence of owner-managers in a human resources management role is the complexity of employment law. In the UK, an employee gains rights according to the length of time they are employed by a firm. The obligations of the owner-manager as an employer include the following areas:

- recruitment – no discrimination on grounds of race, gender, sexual orientation, age, religion or belief, or disabilities;
- contractual arrangements – provide written statement of conditions of employment;
- administer and pay statutory maternity pay and statutory sick pay;
- dismissal – give written warnings and reasons;
- administer and pay redundancy money;
- conform to equal pay and minimum wage legislation.

Although at first sight these legal rights may seem weighted towards the employee, in practice, owner-managers can employ who they want, and remove those they do not want, provided they behave reasonably. This involves abiding by the regulations and giving employees the opportunity to explain themselves in the event of a problem.[5]

In other countries, employment regulations are equally complex and can be even more burdensome, particularly in continental Europe (Observatory of European SMEs, 2003).

11.6.2 HARMONY VERSUS CONFLICT

The case for harmony

Traditionally, it was a widely held view that the small firm provided a more motivational and happier working environment than the larger firm. This was certainly endorsed by the Bolton Report (1971), which stated:

> 'In many aspects, the small firm provides a better working environment for the employee than is possible in large firms. Although physical working conditions may sometimes be inferior in small firms, most people prefer to work in a small group where communications present fewer problems; the employees in the small firm can easily see the relation between what they are doing and the objectives and performance of the firm as a whole.'

This opinion was based largely on earlier work, which had suggested that better personal relationships between employer and employee were made possible by the low level of bureaucracy in the small firm.[6] This picture of harmony within a small enterprise was contrasted to the confrontational industrial relations in larger firms – the 'all one happy family' environment of the small firm, versus the 'them and us' attitudes in larger companies.

Some evidence did seem to support this view. There are lower levels of unionization and industrial action in smaller firms. One survey found that a large organization (1000+ employees) is 40 times more likely to experience industrial action than a micro firm (fewer than 10 employees), and that trade union recognition was much lower in smaller enterprises.[7]

Less idealistic views

However, there are several important challenges to this representation of harmonious working relations in the small firm. The lack of unionization and strike activity cannot be taken as synonymous with lack of conflict. There is considerable evidence that conflict expresses itself in different ways within the smaller firm.[8]

Employees in small firms are difficult to organize into unions, because of the fragmentation of their workplaces, the larger numbers of part-time employees and higher labour turnover rates. Unions, therefore, find it difficult to establish communications to encourage membership in the first place, especially as this is often hindered by owner-manager antipathy to unions. Where they are successful, unions then find that maintenance of membership is expensive. Conspicuous disputes and strikes may be relatively rare because of this lack of organization of labour in small firms, but it does not mean that the incidence of grievances is any less.

Research has confirmed that not only do small business employees feel as much discontent as those in larger organizations, but that employers also have high levels of dissatisfaction. Owner-managers frequently complain of the difficulties of finding and retaining staff with the right attitudes, behaviour and skills.

Other research has noted that working relationships are as much dependent on the type of industry and individual circumstances of a firm as they are on its size.[9] In this, as in other aspects, generalization is difficult because of the huge variety of contexts in which small firms exist (Chin-Ju, Sengupta, and Edwards, 2007). Employment conditions in a high-tech service firm (e.g. a small firm dependent on individual expertise, such as a design consultancy) are likely to be very different to those in a more traditional manufacturing company (e.g. a small firm dependent on its production line, such as a bottling plant).

At the extreme, the small firm can be reduced to a sweatshop working environment with employees suffering low pay, autocratic management and poor conditions. Some research has concluded that market forces largely determine the likelihood of adverse working conditions. Rainnie (1984) studied small firms in the clothing industry and observed the dependence of small garment manufacturers on large high street retailers. The buying power of large retailing chains, combined with intense rivalry among suppliers, who tended to be small firms because of the low barriers of entry into a fragmented industry, created intense cost-cutting pressures on the owner-managers. They, in turn, tended to use autocratic methods, exploiting a captive labour market to keep down their employment costs and maximize their output.

Other circumstances also influence behaviour (Hasle *et al.*, 2012). Friendly relationships can be destroyed by external pressures exerting stress on employers and employees. A cash crisis can ruin the good intentions of all parties to enjoy their work. Partners often know each other socially before joining forces in a small business, and they believe their excellent relationship will continue to the benefit of the enterprise. While this may be true in good times, the stress of less successful periods of trading can ruin relationships (including marriages) to the detriment of partners, managers and employees alike.

Expressions of conflict in small firms are more likely to take the form of employees leaving a firm, or a partnership breaking up, than the conventional form of disputes in larger firms. The higher than average level of labour instability in small firms, which experience higher employee turnover rates than larger firms, bears witness to the less than ideal working situation which often exists beneath the surface in a small firm.

Despite the possibility of problems, lower than average pay and less than ideal working conditions, many employees do still prefer to work in small, rather than large, organizations. Their experience will undoubtedly be conditioned by the type of management control exercised by the owner-manager.

11.6.3 TYPES OF MANAGEMENT CONTROL

The way in which an owner-manager exercises control over their workforce will depend not just on the personality of the manager, but also the disposition of power in the employer-employee relationship. Some circumstances will give the owner-manager, as the employer, relatively high levels of control over employees; in other situations, employees may be able to call more of the tune. For example, the owner-manager of a small firm requiring unskilled labour in an area of high unemployment is in a much more dominant position than the manager of a small enterprise reliant on employees with specialist skills which are in short supply.

To illustrate this relationship Goss (1991) identified four types of management control – fraternalism, paternalism, benevolent autocracy and sweating – in small firms. These are shown in Figure 11.2.

Figure 11.2 **Types of management control in small firms**

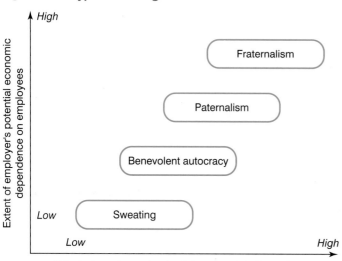

Fraternalism

This describes a situation where the owner-manager is heavily dependent on the skills of the employee(s) to get the job done. They, in turn, are relatively independent of the small firm because their expertise is in demand elsewhere. Employer and employee work alongside each other, with decisions made from a position of mutual respect. Fraternalism is common in the construction and building industry and in cultural and craft-based companies.

For example, the owner-manager and the craftsman who work in a small joinery, specializing in the restoration of old window frames and doors, were so dependent on each other that a harmonious working relationship evolved with no formal hierarchy for decision-making. This management style is also common in some professional and high-technology small businesses. For example, a private health practice, a training company or a software development business will be dependent on the skills of individuals, who can only be managed by mutual consent.

Paternalism

Where the alternatives for employees are more limited and the employer is less dependent on specific workers, then a paternalist management style may emerge. A clear distinction between employer and employee exists, but owner-managers are still sufficiently aware of the importance of their workforce to encourage common ties and personal relations. Farming has been typified as paternalistic because of the economic situation of small farms and the traditional role of the landowner in society.[10] Farm workers often have little choice of alternative employment and are poorly paid. Yet, the farmer is dependent on their commitment and experience, as they will be working for long hours with little supervision. While maintaining a clear social and economic distance, the small farmer will encourage mutual identification of aims among their farm labourers by gifts and wider community involvement.

Benevolent autocracy

This is the most common situation for a small firm; the owner-manager is less dependent on the employee, and able to exercise their influence from a position of power as an employer. However, employees are not so economically dependent on the small firm that they become totally subservient. Close links exist between employer and employee, and friendly relations exist, often on a first name basis, but this rarely extends beyond the workplace (except for an annual outing or Christmas festivity).

BENEVOLENT BOSSES

The founder of a small electronics company chose the location of the factory to ensure a ready supply of skilled and semi-skilled labour. Although able to hire and fire more or less at will, the owner-manager was anxious to keep employee turnover to a minimum because the selection and training of new staff was expensive and time-consuming. The firm developed a name in the area as a good employer, a reputation the owner was anxious to preserve by acting fairly, paying the market rate and providing reasonable working conditions.

In another example, the well-known conductor of a chamber orchestra (run as a small business, but employing freelance musicians) was referred to, albeit affectionately, as a 'benevolent dictator' by the orchestra members – many of whom became his close friends. For his part, the conductor was acutely aware of his responsibilities to his players, 'I was very aware that because we had fixed places and we'd had this tremendous loyalty, them to me and me to them, and no job security, it was my job to provide enough work...' (Wilson, 2014, p. 161).

Sweating

There are some circumstances which conspire to give the employer all the power and the employee virtually none. We have already described the environment of parts of the clothing industry in which fragmented suppliers, dependent on powerful buyers, exploit their labour force in order to provide a low-cost, flexible service. The 'sweat shop' emerges in conditions such as these. Some workers, especially immigrant female labour, are particularly vulnerable to exploitation because they lack relevant skills in an area of high unemployment. They have little alternative but to accept low pay and erratic employment dependent on the workload of the small firm. Their employers trade in marginal, highly competitive industries, subject to sudden rushes of orders and then gluts of production. They survive by keeping overheads down, using poorly equipped premises, and hiring and firing workers at the first indication of growth or contraction of the business.

For example, many top clothing brands and retailers, including Victoria's Secret, Disney, Gap, Lands' End, Levi's and Marks & Spencer, have, over recent years, been criticized in the press for using Asian sweatshops to manufacture their garments (*The Guardian*, 2011).

These four examples of the types of management control are not meant to be exhaustive; there are many variations on the theme. Neither are the types mutually exclusive. In some small firms, two different modes of relationship can exist side by side. An electronics design and manufacturing company, for example, may employ highly skilled technicians, who enjoy an egalitarian, fraternal relationship with the owner-manager, who is very dependent on their design expertise. The semi-skilled production operators also employed are more easily replaced, and may be treated in a more autocratic, although still benevolent, fashion.

What does emerge from looking at these types is that there is a highly varied pattern of management of people in the small firm. Central to them all is the owner-manager, whose personal style will be conditioned by the external forces prevalent in the industry.

THE SUGAR STYLE OF MANAGEMENT

Alan Sugar has always been a controversial entrepreneur and his management style has been exposed to public scrutiny through the television series *The Apprentice*. He claims this only shows his tough side, as softer management approaches do not make good television. His appointment in 2009 as a government adviser to promote entrepreneurship, with elevation to the House of Lords as Baron Sugar of Clapton, surprised some, who felt his robust style would not be an appropriate role model for the young people he was meant to inspire. He aimed to introduce the concept of entrepreneurship into primary schools so that children are taught from a very early age to have a work ethic. He wanted them to learn how to trade in the playground with lessons about profit and '*how to buy an apple for £1 and sell it on for £1.50*'. He claimed that, in the 1950s and 1960s, people needed to work but state benefits made them lazy, claiming that they are more expert in their entitlements than in their jobs. He is not a fan of flexi-time either, as he believes that it encourages employees to stay at home and pretend to work. However controversial his views, graduates and others are still queuing up to work with him. His personal fortune was estimated at £1 billion in 2015. (For a fuller portrait of Alan Sugar with details of his earlier life, see Chapter 2, section 2.4.1).

11.6.4 HUMAN RESOURCE PRACTICES

Good practice in human resource management in larger firms relies on formalized, written procedures and longer-term planning. Small firms tend to manage people through informal, unwritten and ad hoc practices. Much will depend on the management qualities of the owner-manager to make them work effectively.

Recruitment

Recruitment theory advocates several formal stages to ensure the selection of the right person for the job:

- A job description, which carefully analyzes the work to be done and details the responsibilities and levels of authority of the job.
- A person specification, which attempts to match the ideal candidate to the job, reflecting essential and desirable qualifications, experience, skills and characteristics.
- A promotional campaign advertising the vacancy to attract the best possible candidates, using website, social media, advertising and possibly recruitment agencies.
- A shortlisting and interviewing process, which is designed to find out as much as possible about the applicant and also allows them the opportunity to find out as much as possible about the employer.

In practice, the small firm tends to follow a much less structured approach.

Job descriptions and person specifications may not exist, except for management positions. Several studies have concluded that word of mouth is the most commonly used advertising medium for job vacancies in small businesses. Agencies and advertising are regarded as expenses to be avoided if at all possible, particularly as small firms are big employers of part-time staff. Interviews tend to be with owner-managers, who will be more concerned to see how well the person fits into the team than with their formal qualifications and experience. There is evidence of some sectoral differences in this general pattern, with high-technology firms, for example, more likely to follow more formal procedures.

Training

Small firms have a much lower incidence of formal training, relying mainly on training on the job (Blackburn, 1990; OECD, 2002). Owner-managers are reluctant to pay the price of external training, particularly the cost of losing staff for the time needed.

Although owner-managers tend to retain control over personnel matters, they also complain that people management is one of their biggest problems. Some avoid the issue altogether by remaining a one-person business, often by subcontracting work to other self-employed people. This has the added attraction of only incurring costs when necessary. In other cases, small enterprises grow by using labour within the family, rather than employing others (see Chapter 14, for more discussion on the family business).

11.6.5 ENTREPRENEURIAL TEAMS

Successful owners develop entrepreneurial teams that create value through entrepreneurial behaviour and decision-making. The solo owner-manager cannot maintain personal control over every aspect of an enterprise once it has grown to a certain size (see Small and Rentsch, 2010, on shared leadership in teams). If a small firm is pursuing a strategy of growth, it needs to develop an entrepreneurial management team. The size at which a management structure is required will vary; some commentators have suggested that, once a firm reaches 20 employees, it should begin to employ managers. We have already examined some of the implications of this (see Chapter 7). The failure of the owner-manager to build a management team and carefully define their own role within it can seriously threaten the growth, and even the survival, of a small firm. A team is essential if the business is to have value on the exit of the founder (see Chapter 14).

The non-owner-manager

Despite this, the role of the non-owner-manager has been neglected by researchers in the past. A review by Curran (1986) of small business research in the 15 years after the Bolton Report failed to reveal a single reference to the non-owner-manager. More recently, research has focused on the development of entrepreneurial teams, either from the very beginning of a new venture, or at critical stages in its growth.[11] Although the majority of new ventures are founded by one person, there is evidence that many high-growth successful businesses are run by a team of entrepreneurs from the beginning (Vyakarnam and Handelberg, 2005). In other cases, teams are built in layers whereby the founders form a nucleus around which an outer team develops as the business grows (Stockley, 2000). These may or may not be integrated successfully as the business matures. A key leadership role is to keep everyone working together so that more recently joined team members do not feel isolated from the inner nucleus.[12] One study suggested that managers with larger company experience are more likely to help a small firm grow than those with more limited experience.[13]

Team roles

Teams exhibit characteristics that can cause problems and conflict while social pressures can undermine their decision-making effectiveness. Teams tend to make decisions that are either more conservative or riskier than the average of their individual members' decisions. 'Groupthink' may distort opinions in favour of a few opinionated members.

The pressure to achieve consensus in groups can also contribute to poor decision-making. Conflict or healthy disagreement over tasks can help overcome this. However, when conflict is rooted in interpersonal or relationship issues, it is less helpful and likely to have adverse effects on the effectiveness of the team.

For a team to be fully effective, it needs to have a balanced mix of certain characteristics among the team members. Nine different roles that individuals frequently play in a team have been identified from studies of behaviour in both effective and ineffective teams. Belbin (1981) developed this into the model of team roles, as summarized in Figure 11.3. Everyone has a preferred role in a team situation, although one person can play two or three of the roles depending on the circumstances and needs of the group. For an effective team to exist, all of the roles need to be present.

The virtual or 'doughnut' organization

Teams can include outsiders as well as insiders and are often more effective when they do. Technology and other developments mean that businesses no longer need to have all the people working in the same place at the same time. Particularly in non-manufacturing firms, people can, in theory, work anywhere, at any time, providing that the necessary outputs are achieved. Neither do they have to be directly employed by an organization to work for it. Businesses increasingly pay others to deliver what they need done, rather than employ their own workforce to do it for them. Outsourcing means that teams of people working on a project for a business may not be employees but, instead, suppliers of services. According to Charles Handy (2002), these developments have revolutionized the way that organizations can operate. He likens effective modern businesses to 'doughnuts' in which the centre is filled in and the doughy part is empty. The solid core represents the central requirements of the job that needs doing at all costs. The empty outer ring is the opportunity for creativity and innovation, and for adding extra value to an organization. Leaders of firms that outsource many of their functions need to treat outsiders as insiders if they are to contribute creatively and to add value over and above delivery of the core outputs for which they have been contracted.

Virtual teams can be international in scope, with members operating from different bases around the world (Matlay and Westhead, 2005). They tend to split into core and peripheral members; some people are brought in and out of the operation on an ad hoc basis while others remain core to the business and enjoy greater privileges and control as a result.

Entrepreneurial teams include virtual members who support the entrepreneur with external services such as finance, supplies and specialist advice. The virtual team therefore expands to include banks, manufacturers, consultants, accountants and professional advisers.

Figure 11.3 The Belbin model of team roles

Coordinator or chairman e.g. Richard Branson	Controls and organizes the activities of the team, making best use of resources. Clarifies goals, promotes decision-making and delegates well. Calm and self-confident. Can be seen as manipulative.
Shaper e.g. Alan Sugar	Gives shape and form to activities. Dynamic, seeking ways to overcome problems with drive and courage. Sometimes unpopular due to their bullying tactics and irritability.
Plant e.g. James Dyson	Prime source of ideas and creativity for the team. Inventive, imaginative and unorthodox. Sometimes distant, uncommunicative and impractical.
Resource investigator e.g. Anita Roddick	Investigates and attracts resources – the 'fixer'. Extrovert networker, good under pressure. Loses interest rapidly so can have poor follow-through.
Implementer e.g. Queen Elizabeth II	Translates concepts into practical actions – the team workhorse. Conservative and disciplined, but can be inflexible and unresponsive to new ideas.
Monitor evaluator e.g. Jeremy Paxman	Analyzes and evaluates ideas in relation to team objectives. Introverts who are rarely wrong. Lacks drive and charisma. Can be overly critical and cynical.
Team worker e.g. David Beckham	Supports individual team members and fosters team spirit. Adept at counselling and conciliation. Social and perceptive but indecisive. Avoids pressure and may compete for status with ostentatious behaviour.
Completer/finisher e.g. Clive Woodward	Makes sure everything gets finished. Conscientious sticklers for detail who keep deadlines and follow through relentlessly. Perfectionists who worry too much and can be obsessive, non-delegators.
The specialist e.g. Raymond Bogaerts, the chef in Kimberley's restaurant case study (see Section 11.8.1)	Repository of technical knowledge or skills. Single-minded, dedicated self-starters. Only contribute in their area of specialism.

SHE WHO DARES

Rachel Lowe founded her business on the principle of a virtual team – and has seen the best and worst of one. In order to fund her university education, Rachel got a job as a taxi driver in Portsmouth. While driving the streets, she had the idea for a board game, 'Destination London', in which players assume the role of cab drivers in London. When it was first launched for Christmas in 2004, this outsold the established market leader, Monopoly, in one of the world's prestigious toy stores, Hamleys. Rachel went on to build the range of products by adding new locations such as Portsmouth, New York and San Francisco, and she built up international distribution channels.

She did all this while employing virtually no one. The initial impetus and resources to develop the idea came when she entered a university innovation competition and won £2000. This helped her to subcontract the development of a prototype. She also joined a business club for students and found a mentor among Portsmouth University entrepreneurship academics. Her business was based in a university **incubator** unit and the game is manufactured by a subcontractor.

One attempt to fill out her '*doughnut*' further and attract more support and funding failed dramatically in public. She appeared on BBC2's The Dragons Den (a show in which entrepreneurs pitch their idea to a panel of experts who decide if they wish to invest in it). After a traumatic grilling, Lowe's idea was rejected by the panel. She initially confounded the disbelievers by making her venture work, with over 20 editions of 'Destination' selling internationally.

Then, in 2009, everything went wrong. Part of her virtual team let her down so badly that they were criticized in the media. The delayed launch of a Harry Potter film on which she had based a new game left her with stock that she could not sell. Her bank controversially refused to support her and she was forced to put the company into administration.

Rachel's world fell apart, as she explained: 'When you're an entrepreneur you put everything on the line. If things don't work out, you can very quickly lose everything you've ever worked for, which in my case I did: my home, my car, my savings.' She felt let down by the banking system which, in the early days of the financial crisis, failed to help her. As a consequence, her plight featured in a BBC Panorama documentary 'Banks Behaving Badly'.

Neither did she give up on her business. She bought back the rights to 'Destination' from the administrator in 2010 and successfully re-launched the range, featuring the 2012 London Olympics in her 'Destination London' product. She has also developed a range of fragrances and accessories branded 'She Who Dares'. The strapline is 'nothing is impossible', reflecting her personal belief in self-determination. As part of that philosophy, her problems have strengthened, rather than reduced, her belief in the value of a team: 'As an entrepreneur you have to accept that there is only one of you, and people make successful companies, and I've got a great team.'[14]

(See Destinationboardgames.com and *The Business Magazine*, 2013.)

Not bosses but leaders

Developing a strong team is a key leadership skill. According to Adair (2002), leaders are concerned with three primary functions:

- the achievement of the task;
- the building and maintenance of the team;
- the support and development of the individual.

Our earlier portrayal of management in the small firm, using the analogy of the entertainer balancing plates on the ends of poles, seems to imply concentration on the achievement of the task if the plates are to be kept up. As the owner-manager takes on all the key roles in a small firm, the management style can become very task-oriented. There seems little time for the team, or the individuals within it, who are supporting the small enterprise. The team may not all be employed by the small firm.

People within a small firm may also be neglected, particularly as relationships tend to rely on informal structures. The owner-manager can become so engrossed in managing the impersonal resources that they neglect the people resources. They can become preoccupied and distant, appearing as more of a boss than a leader. The appointment of managers at an early stage may be expensive (and therefore risky) but it may also represent the only way an owner-manager can fulfil the functions of leadership and provide support for the team, as well as achieving the task (Burns, 2001; see also Basadur, 2004; and Ibbotson (2008), who suggests that many leaders assume their responsibility more by accident than by design).

As Adair (1987, p. 168) points out:

'Self-leadership comes before leading others. That means setting aims and objectives for yourself as well as high standards of conduct and communication.'

Entrepreneurs become 'not bosses but leaders' only if they can set out their vision clearly and achieve the respect of those that work for and with them.[15] As the founder and owner of the venture, the entrepreneur is looked upon to provide the example for others to follow.[16]

11.7 Summary and activities

Managing a small business is different to managing in a large company. Entrepreneurs need total management to juggle their many responsibilities in running a small firm. Premises are a key resource requiring decisions on location, physical and environmental features, and types of lease or purchase. Other operational resources to be managed include materials and equipment. Obligatory and discretionary insurance minimizes risk to resources. Computerized business processes and systems are now available that even small firms can afford and manage. These can yield cost, efficiency and customer satisfaction benefits.

People are the key resource in most enterprises. Many entrepreneurs feel inadequate to deal with the legal issues and conformity to employment laws that are required today. Despite the widely held belief that working in a small firm can be harmonious and motivational, relationship conflicts do often arise. Four types of management control have been identified in small firms: fraternalism; paternalism; benevolent autocracy; and sweating. Although small firms are most frequently managed by solo owners, some high-growth firms are managed by an entrepreneurial team, either from the outset or at a later stage. The Belbin model identifies nine different roles that individuals play in teams. A successful team is well-balanced between the various roles required. Modern organizations have been likened to a doughnut in which the centre represents core functions and tasks, but the outer ring adds value to a business while having a peripheral attachment to it. The entrepreneurial leader not only achieves the tasks required, but also builds teams and supports the individuals within them.

Consider a small business where you have recently been a customer which employs staff other than the owner-manager (e.g. a food or drinks outlet such as a restaurant, wine bar or public house).

How would you rate the service provided by the staff, and their general attitude to the customer?

Write a short analysis of the motivation of the staff and the type of management control which you feel this illustrates.

If you were the owner-manager of this business, how could you change staff attitudes and motivation for the benefit of the customer?

Extended activity
Staff assessment

Case study
Kimberley's restaurant: Part 1

THE OWNER VERSUS THE CHEF

Kimberley Lawson was feeling disillusioned. Her vision of running her own happy business, removed from the hierarchy and restrictive rules of her previous employer, was rapidly crumbling. When she had bought her own restaurant a year earlier, her main aim was to get away from the politics of big business and concentrate on making her own enterprise work, with a group of like-minded people. Her background seemed ideal to make the venture successful. She had trained with an international hotel group, and had gained experience in almost every aspect of catering management, from kitchen hygiene to cost accounting. She felt, after her five years' employment there, that she knew how to manage all the various functions that were needed to run a restaurant.

She had soon found, however, that this was not enough. She just didn't seem able to cope with all the demands on her when she had first acquired the restaurant.

'It's not that I don't know what to do', she had explained to her husband Matt, when he had enquired after noticing that Kimberley seemed particularly harassed. 'It's just that I don't know what to do first. When I worked for Milton International, everything was organized for you. When I was managing the coffee shop, for example, the menu had already been worked out between the marketing and the finance departments, the staff were employed by personnel and the food ordered through purchasing. Now I have to do all that myself and manage everything on a daily basis as well. I don't have time to think, let alone plan ahead, and there is no one I can ask to help. Everyone else is far too busy serving customers.'

These normal problems of a small business manager were no longer her big worry, however. She had eventually learned how to put priorities on her activities, and to distinguish between the most important and the most immediate jobs, which were not always the same thing.

The real issue now was that she didn't enjoy her work any more. 'I thought running my own business would be fun not just for me, but for everyone else involved. I used to dream of working in a small firm where everyone would have the same aims, we would all know what was going on, and we wouldn't have to put up with any of the bureaucratic nonsense that we had at the Milton. What do I get instead? Hassle from him, each and every day.'

Matt nodded. He had heard similar complaints before, so he knew that the source of the trouble was one Stefan Bogaerts, master chef. He had been with the restaurant when Kimberley had bought it, and seemed like a major asset at the time. His high standards of innovative cuisine made the restaurant different to its more traditional neighbours and had helped it to a position of high popularity.

'What's he done this time?' asked Matt.

'This time he has gone too far. He has refused to do what I asked, and demanded a written statement of his terms and conditions of employment. He's driving me back to the old bureaucracy just because he doesn't agree with my methods. As you know, I've suspected for some time that our waste levels in the kitchen are too high. Well, now I can prove it. I've spent a lot of time analyzing our food costs in relation to our prices. In theory, they should be no more than a third of the menu price. They're actually over 40 per cent, simply because we are using too much food. The portions are too big; customers just cannot eat all we give them. You should see what we throw away.' Kimberley raised both hands and clenched them in frustration.

'But aren't your generous portions part of the attraction of the place?'

Kimberley rounded on Matt. 'You sound like Stefan. He believes that we can't reduce portion sizes without losing customers. I told him that was my affair, and nothing to do with him. All he has to do is to cook what I ask. That's when he asked for a written description of his responsibilities. He says he's entitled to one, and

(Continued)

that he doesn't like the way I've changed his job. He claims that he was always involved in any menu changes before I took over.'

'Isn't it wise to consult him anyway? He does have to run the kitchen after all', suggested Matt.

'I don't mind consulting him, as long as he doesn't just refuse to do anything he doesn't agree with. The previous owner didn't understand menus. I do. Besides, he doesn't run the kitchen. He may think he does, but I can't trust him to hire the staff any more. He fills the kitchen with part-timers that he can shout at and give work to on a favour basis as he pleases. I want professionals in my kitchen.'

Matt had heard of the chef's slave-driving tactics in the kitchen, but nevertheless tried one last effort to support him. 'Yes, but what about the costs? Aren't your staff costs a lot higher than they used to be?' he asked.

Kimberley let out a long breath before replying. 'Yes. Which is why the food costs have to come down. His way of making money is to employ inexperienced part-timers, female of course, for a pittance. My way is to pay a proper wage for trained people, who will save their extra costs by reducing waste and generally being more professional in their work. If Stefan isn't going to accept it, he will have to go. I will make him redundant and work in the kitchen myself for a while.'

Activities

(a) Many people would share Kimberley's original vision that a small business could provide a happier working environment than a larger organization. Is this a realistic view in this particular environment? If not, why not?

(b) Kimberley's management style is evidently different to her predecessor's. How do you think Stefan likes to be managed? What do you think Kimberley should do? Assess her current management style, and the appropriateness of her decision to make Stefan redundant.

(c) Stefan's method of running the kitchen, with low pay and poor conditions, could be likened to the sweatshop. Which circumstances make it possible for these conditions to prevail in this restaurant?

(d) Use the Belbin model to decide the type of team role that Kimberley plays.

Part 2 follows later in the Chapter.

Case study
Eocha Ltd: Part 2

TWO-AND-A-HALF YEARS LATER

At the beginning of its third year in business, Eocha seemed on course to meet its original objectives. Turnover had risen quickly to over £450 000, and the company had made a small profit as forecast in the original business plan. The three shareholders seemed to make a good team. The executive management of Charles Appleton and Edwina Oaks was complemented by Robin Poques as a non-executive director and 40 per cent shareholder who advised on financial and administrative matters.

The crisis

Halfway through the third year, the loss of one significant customer prompted a crisis. Two key customers accounted for more than 60 per cent of sales and, when one of them decided to take the design of new products in-house rather than subcontract the work to Eocha, the planned expansion of the business was threatened. There were insufficient short-term sales to justify the overheads, which had been built up on expectations of higher levels of turnover. The bank, which had been very supportive earlier, made it clear that further loans or an increased overdraft would not be considered without personal guarantees from the directors.

Personal issues

To make matters worse, Robin Poques found that he was caught increasingly in the middle of a running battle between the two executive directors. Appleton blamed Oaks for not foreseeing the loss of an important customer and for failing to take the necessary steps to replace the lost sales ahead of time. Behind the business argument, Poques knew that there was a personality problem. Appleton found Oaks's thorough, but time-consuming, efforts to build relationships with their customers increasingly frustrating, especially when the need for new business became urgent. He also became irritated by her habit of taking time off to look after her young children when they were ill and away from school. After his own marriage had broken up a year earlier, he had thrown himself into the business with even greater intensity and had a lack of tolerance for those that did not share his long working hours. Poques admired his commitment and expertise but, like others in the business, he found him increasingly difficult to work with. He recalled the last board meeting at which Appleton had directly challenged Oaks's sales methods:

'You need to spend more of your time out there, knocking on doors and finding new customers, not visiting the ones we have already got.'

Edwina Oaks had grimly defended her strategy: 'I know we need to find new business, but that takes time. If we treat our existing customers properly, we will not only get more sales from them, but also new business through their recommendations to other firms.'

'It's too late for that. We need new sales now. If we wait any longer, there will be no Eocha for your customers to recommend', Appleton had said.

Poques tried to arbitrate between them, but now he felt he had to take sides. The internal wrangling was distracting them from the real issues. The drop in sales had drained their cash to the point where they had exceeded their overdraft limit. The bank had declined to extend it without personal guarantees from the directors. Appleton had refused to give such guarantees, or invest any new funds in the business, on the basis that he did not have enough confidence in the board. Oaks was threatening to leave unless she received the full backing of at least a majority of shareholders. Poques was beginning to think that the business could only afford one of the two executive directors right now – both financially and emotionally. As the shareholder with the casting vote, he had to decide on the next steps.

Appendix: Summary of results

End of year	Yr 1 Actual £000s	Yr 2 Actual £000s	Yr 3 Forecast £000s
Sales	110	459	384
Gross profit	77	312	307
Overheads	121	290	339
Net profit	(44)	22	(32)
Cash flow			
Accounts paid	190	430	410
Capital spend	148	34	55
Received	(230*)	(380)	(395)
Funding required**	108	84	70

*Includes £140 share capital in year 1.
**Currently met by bank overdraft (£50 000) and hire purchase.

Activities

Advise Robin Poques what to do next. In particular:

(a) Analyze the situation of Eocha after two years of trading compared to its original business plan (see Chapter 6). Draw up a list of current strengths and weaknesses, compared to those in the plan. In which areas do they seem to have succeeded? Where have they been less than successful? (It is useful to reconsider Chapter 6 in answering this.)

(b) List the critical resourcing problems that need addressing.

(c) Draw up a list of possible options to tackle the problems.

(d) Recommend a course of action.

Part 1 of this case is in Chapter 6.

Case study
Kimberley's restaurant: Part 2

KIMBERLEY VERSUS THE KITCHEN MANAGER

Kimberley had made progress in resolving the management problems in her restaurant. Stefan Bogaerts, the chef, had not appeared for work one day, and later telephoned to say he would not be back. Conflicts in small firms are often resolved by one person leaving the organization.

After a moment of panic, Kimberley had breathed a sigh of relief. 'At least I can make a fresh start now that he is gone', she had thought. After a period working in the kitchen herself, she had decided that the only way to develop the business was to recruit another person to manage the kitchen. Kimberley followed the personnel practices of her previous large employer, and carefully drew up a job description and a person specification before advertising the new job. The good response enabled her to select someone she felt was the ideal candidate who was experienced and motivated by the thought of working in a small firm. Laura, the new head chef, was given wider responsibilities than just preparing food, so Kimberley was not too surprised when she asked to see her one morning. But the meeting was not routine; Laura had problems.

'I'm sorry to burst in on you like this, but I don't think I can manage on my own any longer', she blurted out.

'On your own?' queried Kimberley. 'I thought we had agreed to work as a team. What's the problem?'

'In a word, communications, or lack of them', said Laura. 'I need you to tell me more about what is going on. I know we agreed that teamwork is important, but I feel as though I'm working alone most of the time until something happens I don't know about, that is, like the meat delivery changing from Friday to Thursday.'

Kimberley, checking her watch as she was due to visit a customer that morning, said 'Yes, we've been over that, and I have apologized. Look, I'm not sure what you're getting at exactly, but if this business is to develop the way I thought we both agreed we wanted, then I will have to leave you to manage your area. I don't have time to do my job now that we've taken on these commercial catering contracts, let alone help you with yours. You know what to do, and you have staff of your own; can't we just get on and do it?'

'I know you're busy', said Laura, 'but I need your help now and again, and I need you to tell me what you're doing, as it does affect my work you know. I can't just get on and do it unless I get feedback from you. Besides, it's nice to talk to someone now and again other than the wash-up staff.'

Kimberley smiled. 'Ok, I get the message, but not today. I have appointments to keep. I'll make a point of looking in tomorrow.'

Activities

What is your assessment now of Kimberley's management?

(a) Has she made a mistake in her choice of kitchen manager, who does not seem very independent?
(b) Is she right to insist that, now they have agreed their responsibilities, they should get on and do it?
(c) Is there is anything missing in her leadership of the business?
(d) Kimberley seems to have changed the role she plays in her team since Part 1. Using Belbin's model, which role do you think Kimberley is now playing? Which role do you think Laura is playing? Are these appropriate in this context?

Complete the management section of the business plan by:

- planning operations
- formulating a people plan.

Summarize your operations plan

Outline your plans for premises, materials, equipment, business processes and systems and other appropriate operating resources. See Chapter 6, Planning in practice: *giftsmania* for an example of an operational plan.

Managing the resources and the people

Summary of what is required

Summarize your people plan

- Outline how you plan to manage other people within your new venture, at the beginning and as it grows.
- Consider how you will recruit, retain and motivate staff. How will you ensure a team spirit emerges and endures?
- What will be your employment practices, and how will you operate payroll and personnel systems?
- How will you develop an entrepreneurial team with all the required roles filled?

See Chapter 6, Planning in practice: *giftsmania* for an example of planning for people and describing the team.

11.8 Notes, references and recommended further reading

Notes and further information

1 See also Marlow, S., People and the Small Firm. In: Carter, S. and Jones-Evans, D. (eds) *Enterprise and Small Business,* Financial Times/Prentice Hall, 2000. This has a useful summary of the influences on small firms that generate particular management styles.

2 Richard Branson's first venture was a magazine, *Student,* which he published while still at school with the help of a telephone kiosk to make contact with the outside world – see Brown, M. (1992) *Richard Branson: The Inside Story,* Headline Book Publishing, London.

3 A useful guide containing a checklist of what is important in choosing premises and the options available is produced by the Workspace Group plc, *The Small Business Guide to Choosing Your Office Space,* www.workspace.co.uk/the-workspace-offer /support/moving-advice (accessed 11 January 2016). Their website, www.workspace group.co.uk has other

useful information on business premises in London and south-east England, including incubator space.

4 See, for example, the Small Business Research Trust's *Quarterly Survey of Small Business in Britain,* Open University Business School, accessible via www.open .ac.uk/business-school/research/quarterly-survey (accessed 12 January 2016). This regularly records significant levels of problems with government regulations and paperwork (see also Chapter 3 this volume, The small business environment).

5 For advice on good practice in employment, see ACAS (Advisory, Conciliation and Arbitration Service), www.acas.org.uk. This site also has useful information on employment regulations.

6 Most notably that of Ingham, G. (1970) *Size of Industrial Organization and Worker Behaviour,* Cambridge University Press.

7 See, for example, Daniel, W. and Millward, W. (1983) *Workplace Industrial Relations in Britain,* Heinemann.

8 See, for example, Scott, M., Roberts, I., Holroyd, G. and Sawbridge, D., (1989) *Management and Industrial Relations in Small Firms,* Research Paper No. 70, Department of Employment.

9 See Chin-Ju, T., Sengupta, S. and Edwards, P. (2007) When and why is small beautiful? The experience of work in the small firm, *Human Relations,* 1 December 60: 1779–1807. This and other articles update earlier work with similar conclusions by Curran, J. and Stanworth, J. including, Some reasons why small is not beautiful, *New Society,* 14 December 1978 and Size of workplace and attitudes to industrial relations, *British Journal of Industrial Relations,* XIX, 1981.

10 See Newby, H. (1977) *The Deferential Worker,* Penguin, and Hasle, P., Limbourg, H. J., Kallehave, T. and Andersen T. R. (2012) The working environment in small firms: Responses from owner-managers, *International Small Business Journal,* 1 September, 2012 30: 622–639a.

11 See *International Small Business Journal,* 23(3), June 2005. This is a special edition on entrepreneurial teams with several articles of interest on this topic.

12 Kirby D. A. (2003) *Entrepreneurship,* McGraw-Hill Education. Chapters 7 and 8 deal with motivation, leadership and team building.

13 Stanworth, J. and Gray, C. (1991) *Bolton 20 Years On: The Small Firm in the 1990s,* PCP, see ch. 11, Managers and management within small firms.

14 For more information on Rachel Lowe, see destinationboardgames.com and www.swdfashion .com

15 See Northouse (2012), for detailed discussion of leadership theory, including trait and skills approaches, contingency and path-goal theories, transactional, behavioural, transformational and authentic leadership.

16 Much of the research on leadership in small firms emphasizes its 'transformational' (Matzler, Bauer and Mooradian, 2015) and 'creative' (Bilton and Cummings, 2010; Puccio, Mance and Murdock, 2011; Sternberg, Kaufman and Pretz, 2003) character, allowing entrepreneurs to steer their businesses successfully through innovation.

References

Adair, J. (1987) *Not Bosses But Leaders,* Talbot Adair Press.

Adair, J. (2002) *Effective Leadership,* Pan Macmillan.

Basadur, M (2004) Leading others to think innovatively together: Creative leadership, *The Leadership Quarterly,* 15: 103–121.

Belbin, R. M. (1981) *Management Teams – Why They Succeed and Fail,* Heinemann Professional Publishing.

Bilton, C. and Cummings, S. (2010) *Creative Strategy: Reconnecting Business and Innovation*, Wiley, see ch. 11, Leading from the middle, 145–155.

Blackburn, R. (1990) Job quality in small businesses: Electrical and electronic engineering firms in Dorset, *Environment and Planning, A,* 22: 875–92.

Bolton Report (1971) *Committee of Inquiry on Small Firms,* p. 21, HMSO Cmnd. 4811.

Burns, P. (2001) *Entrepreneurship and Small Business,* Palgrave.

Chin-Ju, T., Sengupta, S. and Edwards, P. (2007) When and why is small beautiful? The experience of work in the small firm, *Human Relations,* 1 December 60: 1779–1807.

Coopers & Lybrand (1980) *The Provision of Premises for Small Firms,* Department of Industry.

Curran, J. (1986) *Bolton Fifteen Years On: A Review and Analysis of Small Business Research in Britain 1971–1986,* Small Business Research Trust.

Daryanto, D., Khan, H., Matlay, H. and Chakrabati, R. (2013) Adoption of country-specific business websites: The case of UK small businesses entering the Chinese market, *Journal of Small Business and Enterprise Development*, 20(3): 650–660.

De Clercq, D., Thongpapanl, N. and Voronov, M. (2015) Explaining SME engagement in local sourcing: The roles of location-specific resources and patriotism, *International Small Business Journal*, 33(8): 929–950.

Falk, N. (1980) Small Firms in the Inner City. In: Cribbs, A. and Webb, T. (eds) *Policy Issues in Small Business Research*, Saxon House.

Falk, N. (1982) Premises and the Development of Small Firms. In: Watkins, D., Stanworth, J. and Westrip, A. (eds) *Stimulating Small Firms*, Gower.

Gibb, A. (1983) The small business challenge to management education, *Journal of European Industrial Training*, 7(5): 3–16.

Goss, D. (1991) *Small Business and Society*, Routledge.

Handy, C. (2002) *The Elephant and the Flea: Looking Back Towards the Future*, Arrow.

Hasle, P., Limbourg, H. J., Kallehave, T. and Andersen T. R. (2012) The working environment in small firms: Responses from owner-managers, *International Small Business Journal*, 1 September 30: 622–639a.

Ibbotson, P. (2008) *The Illusion of Leadership*, Palgrave Macmillan.

Kamasak, R. (2013) *Resource-Based View in All its Aspects: Why Small Firms Outperform Others?*, Scholars Press.

Matlay, H. and Westhead, P. (2005) Virtual teams and the rise of e-entrepreneurship in Europe, *International Small Business Journal*, 23(3): 279–302.

Matzler, K., Bauer, F. A., and Mooradian, T. A. (2015) Self-esteem and transformational leadership, *Journal of Managerial Psychology*, 30(7): 815–831.

McCann, P. (2006) Regional Development: Clusters and Districts. In: Casson M. *et al.* (eds) *The Oxford Handbook of Entrepreneurship*, pp. 671–693, Oxford University Press, Oxford.

Northouse, P.G. (2012) *Leadership: Theory and Practice*, 6th edn, Sage.

Observatory of European SMEs (2003) *SMEs in Europe*, Observatory of European SMEs 2003, No. 7, European Commission.

OECD (2002) *Management Training in SMEs*, Organisation for Economic Co-Operation and Development (OECD), Paris.

Puccio, G. J., Mance, M. and Murdock, M. C. (2011) *Creative Leadership: Skills that Drive Change*, Sage, see ch. 1, Change, Leadership and Creativity: The Powerful Connection, pp. 3–30.

Rainnie, A. (1984) Combined and uneven development in the clothing industry, *Capital and Class*, 22: 140–168.

Rousseau, D. M. (ed.) (2014) *Oxford Handbook of Evidence-Based Management*, Oxford University Press.

Small, E. E. and Rentsch, J. R. (2010) Shared leadership in teams: A matter of distribution, *Journal of Personnel Psychology*, 9: 203–211, Special issue: Shared Leadership.

Stanworth, J. and Gray, C. (1991) *Bolton 20 Years On: The Small Firm in the 1990s*, ch. 10, PCP.

Sternberg, R.J., Kaufman, J.C. and Pretz, J.E. (2003) A propulsion model of creative leadership, *The Leadership Quarterly*, 14: 455–473.

Stockley, S. (2000) Building and Maintaining the Entrepreneurial Team. In: Birley, S. and Muzyka, F. (eds), *Mastering Entrepreneurship*, Financial Times/Prentice Hall.

Stone, B. (2014) *The Everything Store: Jeff Bezos and the Age of Amazon*, Corgi Books, Transworld Publishers.

The Business Magazine (2013) *Rachel Lowe – She Who Dares*, www.businessmag.co.uk/entrepreneur/rachel-lowe-she-who-dares (accessed 14 January 2016).

The Guardian (2011) *Sweatshops Still Supplying Top Brands*, 28 April, www.theguardian.com/global-development/poverty-matters/2011/apr/28/sweatshops-supplying-high-street-brands (accessed 13 January 2016).

Turban, E., King, D., Lee, J. and Viehland, D. (2004) *Electronic Commerce: A Managerial Perspective*, Pearson/Prentice Hall.

Vyakarnam, S. and Handelberg, J. (2005) Four themes of the impact of management teams on organizational performance, *International Small Business Journal*, 23(3): 236–56.

Wilson, N. (2014) *The Art of Re-enchantment: Making Early Music in the Modern Age*, Oxford University Press.

Wilson, N. and Martin, L. (2015) Entrepreneurial opportunities for all? Entrepreneurial capability and the capabilities approach, *International Journal of Entrepreneurship and Innovation*, 16(3): 159–169.

Recommended further reading

Anderson, A. R. and Ullah, F. (2014) The condition of smallness: How what it means to be small deters firms from getting bigger, *Management Decision*, 52(2): 326–349.

Birley, S. and Muzyka, F. (2000) *Mastering Entrepreneurship*, Financial Times/Prentice Hall. ch. 5, People, families and teams.

Edwards, P. (2012) Employment rights in small firms. In: L. Dickens, *Making Employment Rights Effective: Issues of Enforcement and Compliance*, Bloomsbury, ch. 8, 139–158.

International Small Business Journal, 23(3), June 2005 – a special edition on entrepreneurial teams.

Kirby, D. A. (2003) *Entrepreneurship*, McGraw-Hill Education, chs 7 and 8.

Kotley B. and Slade, P. (2005) Formal human resource practices in small growing firms, *Journal of Small Business Management*, 43(1): 16–40.

Marlow, S. (2006) People and the Small Firm. In: Carter, S. and Jones-Evans, D. (eds) *Enterprise and Small Business*, 2nd edn, Financial Times/Prentice Hall.

Stone, B. (2014) *The Everything Store: Jeff Bezos and the Age of Amazon*, Corgi Books, Transworld Publishers. The remarkable story of the building of Amazon over two decades.

Workspace Group plc, *The Small Business Guide to Choosing Your Office Space*, www.workspace.co.uk /the-workspace-offer/support/moving-advice (accessed 11 January 2016). An excellent guide to choosing business premises.

12 Marketing

Learning objectives

By the end of this chapter you will be able to:

- Recognize the typical marketing issues faced by small businesses.
- Understand differences between traditional marketing and entrepreneurial marketing.
- Evaluate the marketing strategies and methods available to an entrepreneur.
- Identify word-of-mouth marketing strategies that can be used by small enterprises.
- Assess the impact of the internet and social media on entrepreneurial marketing.
- Evaluate the marketing channels available to a small business.

Introduction

In Chapter 4, we made the distinction between the process of creativity, or *invention*, and the process of putting creative ideas into practical use, or *innovation*. The testing ground that determines whether an invention has become an innovation is the marketplace, in which customers have the final say. We therefore suggested that two questions are crucial in the early development of an enterprise: who will be my customers and why will they buy from me? This is the process of identifying and attracting customers – the domain of marketing. Marketing is a critical function under the control of the owner-manager that differentiates between the survival and closure of a business venture (see Chapter 7). The failure to identify customers, or the inability to stimulate sufficient numbers of them to buy, is the predictable cause of the downfall of many enterprises.

This chapter examines the theories of marketing and compares traditional marketing concepts to the marketing activities undertaken by entrepreneurs. The specific marketing issues that face smaller businesses are explored. Following an evaluation of traditional, or classical, marketing theory, a new model of entrepreneurial marketing is proposed. **Word-of-mouth (WOM) marketing** plays a special role in the attraction of customers to small enterprises. While this is commonly believed to be reactive in nature, ways of proactively implementing a word-of-mouth marketing strategy are evaluated. The use of social media marketing in recommendations, or 'word of mouse', has made this an even more crucial marketing method. Other marketing communication methods and distribution strategies appropriate to small business are analyzed.

Activity 1
Marketing issues

S mall firms face particular marketing issues because of inherent characteristics, such as size, resources and market share. Can you suggest what some of these specific problems might be?

12.1 Small business marketing issues

We established in Chapter 7 that marketing plays a major role in any successful small business strategy. Marketing is key to the survival of a young enterprise and an essential ingredient in the development of a sustainable business in the long term. However, small businesses have inherent characteristics that give rise to distinctive marketing issues and problems (Stokes, 2002; Sethna, Jones and Harrigan, 2013).

Customer base

Small firms are, by definition, relatively small in a given industry or market. This characteristic often leads to a dependency on a limited customer base, geographically and numerically. Small firms tend either to serve local markets or to have a low share of a wider market, unless the industry is very new. Various studies[1] have shown that a high percentage of small businesses are dependent on fewer than ten customers, and some on only one buyer.

Resource constraints

A small firm has less to spend on marketing as a percentage of its income than a larger organization due to the impact of fixed costs that take up a higher proportion of revenues. Financial constraints also restrict their ability to employ marketing specialists. This led Carson (1990) to conclude that the marketing constraints on small firms take the form of limited resources, limited specialist expertise and limited impact.

Personalized management style

Smaller enterprises tend to have a more personalized management style than larger firms, with the typical owner-manager involved in all aspects of management and not sharing key decisions with others (see Chapter 11). Marketing in small firms follows this pattern; owner-managers tend to assume responsibility not only for the development of marketing strategy, but also for the implementation of marketing programmes. One study found that 95 per cent of small business owners made marketing decisions either by themselves or in consultation with a partner in the firm (Stokes *et al.*, 1997). As owner-managers are such a dominant influence, so their competency and attitudes towards marketing are a major factor in the development of marketing programmes in a small enterprise (Carson *et al.*, 1995; Fraser, 2013).

Uncertainty and evolution

Small firms have to cope with an uncertain environment, which means that they have to adapt and evolve as a business to survive (see Chapter 3). Uncertainty stems from lack of control over the market, a small customer and product base, and the diverse motivations and abilities of the owner-managers. Those firms which do survive in this uncertain environment adjust to the new conditions in a continual process of evolution. The marketing implication is that short-term considerations take priority over longer-term planning. Research has

Table 12.1 Small business characteristics and marketing issues

Small business characteristics	Marketing issues
Relatively small in given industry	Limited customer base
Resource constraints	Limited activity, expertise and impact
Personalized management style	Dependent on owner's marketing skills
Uncertainty	Intuitive, reactive marketing
Evolutionary	Variable marketing effort
Role of innovation	Developing and defending niches

confirmed that planning is a problem for marketing in small firms as it tends to be reactive in style (Blankson and Stokes, 2002). However, marketing strategies are unlikely to remain the same during the lifespan of a business. Marketing activities evolve to reflect the experience and learning of the owner-manager and the needs of the firm as it adjusts to its environment (Carson *et al.*, 1995).

Innovation, niches and gaps

Although innovation is neither a unique nor a universal characteristic of small firms, entrepreneurs in small businesses have played a key role in the innovation of new products and processes due to their flexibility and willingness to try new approaches in some areas (see Chapter 4). Innovations and gaps in supply that allow small firms to occupy market niches, or to serve geographically isolated areas have proven to be an important way of gaining a competitive edge. The marketing problem for small firms is how to develop innovative products and services in the first instance, and then how to defend their competitive advantage and exploit innovations to the full with limited resources. Large firms may wait for smaller enterprises to open up markets and make the mistakes, before using their superior resources to capitalize on the opportunity. Exploiting niche markets to the full can be as big an issue as developing them in the first place.

A summary of these characteristics of small firms which tend to give rise to marketing problems, as discussed here and in earlier chapters, is shown in Table 12.1.

Activity 2
Entrepreneurial marketing

Small business owners follow a variety of strategies to overcome the marketing problems discussed above. Do you think that they should follow general marketing principles and practices in these attempts? Or is there a specific type of marketing more appropriate to small business?

12.2 Marketing defined

12.2.1 TRADITIONAL MARKETING

What does marketing theory have to offer as solutions to these issues faced by entrepreneurs and small business owners? Traditional, or classical, marketing theories constitute a structured approach to the marketplace that involves four elements: the overall philosophy or *orientation* of the business; the *strategy* used to relate to the marketplace; the *methods* used to win and keep customers; and the *intelligence* or information gathered to underpin these elements (Kotler and Keller, 2015).

Market orientation

According to classical marketing principles, the customer should be central to everything an organization does. The concept of **market/customer orientation** requires that a detailed understanding of customer needs should precede and inform the marketing of products and services. This applies to the development of new products and services (and therefore business ventures). Opportunities are recognized through research into customer needs that identifies gaps in the market that can, in turn, be translated into new products.

Marketing strategy

Guided by this principle of customer orientation, marketing strategy defines how an organization competes in the marketplace through the three stages of market segmentation, targeting and **positioning**. First, the marketplace is divided through research and analysis into meaningful groups of buyer types, or market segments, that have different needs. Second, one or a number of these segments is chosen as the most appropriate target market to become the focus of marketing effort. Third, an offer is made to this target market through an appropriately positioned product or service.

Marketing methods

Following the selection of the target market and the product/service position within that market, marketing methods implement the strategy through a combination of activities and techniques, such as product/service enhancement, pricing, advertising and selection of distribution channels. These are referred to as elements in the '**marketing mix**', commonly summarized as the **4 'Ps'** of product, pricing, promotion and place (extended to seven 'Ps' in services marketing theory by the addition of physical evidence, people and process).

Market intelligence

Gathering market intelligence underpins marketing strategy and activity throughout. It includes formal research and information-gathering activities in the internal and external environments that could influence the future of the business.

In summary, traditional marketing takes the orientation of the enterprise around customer needs as its starting point. It develops marketing strategies through a process of segmentation, targeting and positioning, and implements this strategy through the elements of the marketing mix. The whole process is underpinned by the formalized gathering of market intelligence.

12.2.2 MARKETING DEFINED BY SMALL BUSINESS OWNERS

Entrepreneurs and owner-managers of small businesses tend not to perceive marketing this way. They see marketing in terms of methods to attract new business – the tactical techniques and activities to win customers. They are less aware of the principles of customer orientation, marketing strategy and intelligence gathering (Hills, Hultman and Miles, 2008).

However, the perceptions of what the term 'marketing' means to small business owners does not always match what those same owners do in practice (Stokes, Blackburn and Fitchew, 1997). Many owners equate marketing with selling and promoting only, suggesting that they 'do not have to do any marketing' because their business is reliant on word-of-mouth recommendations. However, this narrow view of marketing is not borne out by what the business owners actually do. Their activities indicate a strategic marketing awareness, particularly in areas such as monitoring the marketplace, targeting individual market segments, and emphasizing customer services and relationships. When asked to rank their most important marketing activities, they do tend to rate recommendations from customers above other methods. But this reliance on recommendations is not necessarily an indication of minimal marketing effort, as such recommendations are often hard won. In other words, they spend considerable time and resources on marketing, but by another name.

Too often, the best practices among larger firms are automatically assumed to be what is required for smaller businesses, providing they can be given the resources to adopt them. However, the marketing methods used by owner-managers may point the way to different forms of marketing that are more appropriate to small firms and entrepreneurs (Stokes and Nelson, 2013).

Activity 3
Which should come first – idea or market analysis?

Innovations are inventions that have an established market need. But which would you do first: identify a new product or service and then find out if there is a need? Or look for a gap in the market and then develop a new product or service?

12.3 Entrepreneurial marketing

Marketing in small firms is not the simplistic, promotional activity that it appears at first sight. Nor is it traditional marketing according to the textbook. If we examine each of the four elements in the definitions of marketing as described earlier, we discover distinct variations between what successful small business owners actually do and what marketing theory would have them do. This indicates the need for a different approach to marketing in an entrepreneurial context (Hills, Hultman and Miles, 2008; Gilmore *et al.*, 2013).

12.3.1 MARKET ORIENTATION: FOCUS ON THE CUSTOMER OR THE INNOVATION?

Entrepreneurs tend to start with the idea, and then try to find a market for it. Ideas are often prompted by personal experiences, or the knowledge that something can be done in a different way. Entrepreneurial innovation tends to flow from inventions that find a home in the marketplace, rather than careful research into customer needs that is then translated into new products. Traditional marketing advocates that a thorough assessment of market needs should come before new product development. Entrepreneurs tend to do it the other way round, investigating customer reaction after the development of the product or service (Stokes, 2000a).

James Dyson, designer of the revolutionary vacuum cleaner and founder of the company that bears his name, is a prolific inventor. One of his earlier products that claimed to have 'improved on the wheel'[2] was stimulated by his personal experience at DIY building. While renovating an old farmhouse, he became frustrated by the limitations of a conventional builder's wheelbarrow. He perceived several, serious design faults: it had a narrow wheel and thin

(Continued)

tubular legs that were unstable for heavy loads and sank into soft ground, and it had a metal body with sharp edges that could damage buildings and did not carry cement efficiently. As an entrepreneurial designer, he set about improving on what seemed to him a primitive product that had scarcely improved since wooden barrows made centuries earlier. The result was the 'Ballbarrow', with a ball instead of a wheel and a round, softer container made from plastic with fatter feet. Unfortunately, the building trade did not share his enthusiasm to replace their traditional barrow for his new model and 'many of the advantages were simply not perceived by the builder as advantages at all'.[3]

Research among builders may have predicted this reaction before the product was developed. But Dyson's product did eventually succeed in the marketplace. It found a different type of customer – gardeners – who did perceive the advantages of the Ballbarrow as real benefits over the conventional wheelbarrow. (To find out more, see Section 12.3.2 below.)

Entrepreneurs like Dyson have a zeal for developing new concepts and products, demonstrating an orientation towards innovation, rather than a slavish acceptance of what customers say they want. This is not necessarily based on a disregard for customer preferences. Rather, it is accepting that sometimes customers do not know what they need because they do not know what is possible. Market research into new products or services always has this issue to overcome: how can existing customers specify new product developments when they have neither the vision nor the technological competence necessary to understand what is possible?[4] They will tend to be guided by what is already available and base their judgment of new ideas on what already exists. Market research among potential consumers is unlikely to have come up with many of the breakthrough inventions in telecommunications that have shaped our modern world because they were unimaginable before they were invented. Research and development based only on customer preferences is likely to lead to modifications to existing products, rather than radically different concepts (Trott, 2008). Most people are better able to visualize improvements to products with which they are familiar than to visualize totally new ones.

For this reason, many key innovations come from outside, rather than within, an existing industry. Marketing on the internet has been driven largely by new companies, not established ones. The leading dot-com consumer marketing companies such as eBay and Amazon have not been developed by the existing retail giants. Existing organizations do become over-focused on the way things are, rather than on the way things could be. According to Theodore Levitt (1991), an early management guru, innovation is 'unnatural' because it means letting go of what has been mastered and trying out the unknown. Inertia is a more natural state, as James Dyson discovered when he tried to licence his revolutionary Dual Cyclone bagless vacuum cleaner to the existing industry leaders such as Hoover and Electrolux, all of whom turned down the concept. He had to prove that his new product met customer needs more closely than the standard industry product by successfully manufacturing and selling his breakthrough product himself.

In fact, such revolutionary innovations are rare. Evolutionary innovation that gradually improves products is more common (Trott, 2008). Entrepreneurial marketing is more likely to start with incremental adjustments to existing products/services or market approaches, rather than large-scale developments. While a few small firms may make the big innovative breakthrough and grow rapidly as a result, the majority that survive do so by growing more slowly, through making small but regular improvements to the way in which they do business. This may mean stocking new lines, approaching a new market segment with a particular service, or improving services to existing customers – in other words, incremental, innovative adjustments which together create a competitive edge. For example, an innovative restaurateur could add creative dishes to the menu, offer distinctive services to the local business community (such as accounts facilities and a high-speed lunch service) and develop special events for regular customers (film nights, wine tastings). None of these may represent a big breakthrough individually but, together, they help to create an innovative approach to the marketplace.

Not surprisingly, the product idea selected by the new owner of a small business is most likely to be determined by their previous experience. Research indicates that a high percentage of new owners chose a product which was the same as or similar to those offered in their previous employment.[5] This leaves most small firms with a narrow base for future product development, implying that many businesses do not have innovative roots. Another theme, previously emphasized, is the variability of motives among owner-managers, which will affect their innovations policy. Although some will show highly innovative tendencies, many others will not have the desire or capability to introduce new approaches.

We have already discussed the relationship between the small firm and innovation (see Chapter 4). The problems of innovative development for a small firm are considerable. The rate of failure of new products is high; the resources for research and development will be limited, coming in most cases from internal sources.[6] Failure of new products can easily cause the failure of the small firm if the stakes are high. Innovation considerations in small firms' marketing strategy often point to a dilemma. Without new products, small firms cannot survive in most competitive markets. Yet, the costs of product development, and the risks of failure, are often too high for the limited resources of a small firm to accept. The way out of the dilemma will probably involve closer cooperation and networking in joint developments between small and large organizations, in the private and public sector alike. It also indicates the need for incremental, rather than radical, innovation to both market and product approaches for the majority of small firms.

Whether radical or evolutionary innovation is pursued, the entrepreneurial approach is to formulate ideas or opportunities intuitively and then look for market acceptance, rather than adopting the market-oriented approach of analyzing the market systematically for unfulfilled customer needs. Following a review of research into opportunity recognition among small firms, Hills, Hultman and Miles (2008) proposed that successful entrepreneurs are more opportunistic, in that they have a propensity to act once they see a potential opportunity, and immediately evaluate the attractiveness of this based on past experience and industry criteria, rather than formalized research. This supports the view that entrepreneurs prefer to pursue innovations first and seek market acceptance second, rather than follow a more structured investigation into customer needs that could either miss the real market or the competitive time frame.

This is linked to theories of opportunity recognition and *effectuation* that recognize that entrepreneurs explore opportunities in an iterative process which takes account of the resources at their disposal and the uncertain environment in which they operate (see Chapter 7, Section 7.2). Decision-making is not as simple as specifying a goal and assessing the options for achieving it, as both goals and information relating to them may change (Sarasvathy, 2001).

Activity 4
Non-customer markets for entrepreneurs

It has been suggested that entrepreneurs market their firms to groups other than just customers. Can you suggest who these other groups might be? Give some specific examples in each case.

12.3.2 MARKETING STRATEGY: TOP-DOWN OR BOTTOM-UP?

Many successful small firms occupy 'niche' markets in which they supply specialized products or services to a clearly identified group of customers. Others find a gap in a particular marketplace for the provision of more general services. Either way, success is dependent on identifying a particular group of customers who need the product or service on offer (as described in more detail in Chapter 4). Research has confirmed that entrepreneurs that successfully grow their businesses define their target markets more precisely than those running non-growth firms (Hills and Hultman, 2005). If a common weakness of small firms is their over-reliance on small numbers of customers, a corresponding strength is that owner-managers often identify closely with a specific group of customers whose needs are well-known to them. Although this result is in line with traditional marketing theories of target marketing, the ways in which entrepreneurs achieve it is not always according to the book.

Top-down theory

Marketing textbooks[7] advocate a process that takes a market overview as the starting point and narrows this down to specific target markets through the three stages of segmentation, targeting and positioning. This represents a 'top-down' approach:

- *Segmentation:* The division of the market into groups of buyers with different needs is achieved through research that profiles customers using demographic, psychological and other buyer-behaviour variables.
- *Targeting:* Evaluation of the attractiveness of each segment and selection of the target segment are based on the broad issues of market attractiveness and the company's ability to compete.
- *Positioning:* Finally, a market position is selected and communicated which differentiates the product/service from competitors. The company's offering needs to have meaningful differences to competitive products or services, so that it occupies a distinct position in customers' minds.

This process implies that an organization is able to take an objective overview of the markets it serves before selecting those on which it wishes to concentrate. This usually involves both secondary and primary market research with evaluation by specialists in each of the three stages.

Bottom-up practice

Although successful entrepreneurs do seem adept at carefully targeting certain customers, the processes they use in order to achieve this do not seem to conform to the three stages described above. Evidence suggests that successful smaller businesses practice a 'bottom-up' targeting process in which the organization begins by serving the needs of a few customers and then expands the base gradually as experience and resources allow. Research into niche marketing approaches indicates that targeting is achieved by attracting an initial customer base and then looking for more of the same (Dalgic and Leeuw, 1994; Toften and Hammervoll, 2013). The stages of entrepreneurial targeting are:

- *Identification of market opportunity.* An opportunity is recognized by matching innovative ideas to the resources of a small enterprise. The opportunity is tested through trial and error in the marketplace, based on the entrepreneur's intuitive expectations which are sometimes, but not often, backed up by more formal research.
- *Attraction of an initial customer base.* Certain customers, who may or may not conform to the profile anticipated by the entrepreneur, are attracted to the service or product. However, as the entrepreneur is in regular contact with these customers, they get to know their preferences and needs.
- *Expansion through more of the same.* The entrepreneur expands the initial customer base by looking for more customers of the same profile. In many cases, this is not a deliberate process as it is left to the initial customers who recommend the business to others with similar needs to their own. A target customer group emerges and grows, but more through a process of self-selection, and some encouragement from the entrepreneur, rather than through formal research and deliberate choice.

J ames Dyson developed his revolutionary wheelbarrow, the 'Ballbarrow' (see Section 12.3.1) – with the building trade in mind. But the negative reaction of his original target market made him decide to look elsewhere. Concluding that 'the entrenched professional is always going to resist longer than the private consumer',[8] he turned instead to newspaper advertising and was astonished by the positive results. Gardeners were ready to adopt his product in considerable numbers and so became the target market for his marketing efforts. Sales grew rapidly following articles in the gardening press and a stall at the Chelsea flower show. He may not have got the initial target right, but he rapidly adapted to exploit the customers who did arrive. Within a short time, he had taken a 50 per cent share of the market, selling 45 000 Ballbarrows a year.

A bottom-up targeting process has advantages over the top-down approach. It requires fewer resources and is more flexible and adaptable to implement – attributes which play to small business strengths. It has corresponding disadvantages. It is less certain of success and can take longer to penetrate the market to full potential – issues that characterize many small firms.

Identifying targets other than new customers

However, target markets need not be solely concerned with customers in the conventional sense of the term. Other groups of people, from suppliers to local planners, can directly and indirectly influence the fortunes of small firms, and they may need marketing consideration.

Small businesses survive in their changeable environment not only by successfully marketing to those who buy their products or services, but also by developing important relationships with other individuals and organizations. Suppliers, bank managers, investors, advisers, trade associations, local government and public authorities may be as vital as customers to a small business's success. Entrepreneurs may target marketing strategies at these other markets which go beyond conventional definitions of the term 'customer'. In this sense, entrepreneurial marketing resembles *relationship marketing*, which recognizes the need to create, develop and maintain a supportive network in which the firm thrives.[9]

In other words, marketing can target any organization or individual that can have a positive or negative effect on the small firm. Relationship marketing theorists have attempted to identify these other markets more specifically in the **six markets model**,[10] as illustrated in Figure 12.1.

Figure 12.1 The six markets model

In more detail, the six markets are as follows:

- *Internal markets* are made up of individuals within an organization whose behaviour and attitudes affect the performance of the business. Selling the aims and strategies of a small business to employees, shareholders and family members helps everyone concerned work towards common goals.

  For example, Perf-X, a small manufacturing firm, held informal events and social gatherings throughout the year for its 25 employees, who described the culture of the firm as that of an extended family to which they all belonged.

- *Recruitment markets* are made up of potential employees. The aim of marketing here is to attract a sufficient number of well-motivated and trained employees. Particularly in small service businesses, employees have become a key marketing influence on the competitiveness of the organization.

  In order to attract the skilled workforce he needed, the owner of Perf-X held a series of open days which anyone could attend to find out more about the company. He made a point of personally welcoming visitors to demonstrate his own commitment and style of working.

- *Supplier markets* can be crucial to a small business's ability to service its customers. Suppliers are often vital in providing goods and services on time and at the right price. They can also be influential in passing on recommendations to potential customers.

  Most of Perf-X's new business came from recommendations from customers, suppliers and other contacts. The directors of Perf-X always welcomed visits from suppliers and took the opportunity to show them the latest developments of their business so they would be well-informed in talking to others in the trade about it.

- *Influence markets* are made up of organizations and individuals that can influence the marketing environment within which the company competes. There are many such potential 'influencers' on small businesses, from local government planners to trade associations.

  The owner of Perf-X regularly attended meetings of the local Chamber of Commerce where he made useful contacts with people involved in local public services and the professions, as well as with other business managers.

- *Referral markets* are sources of word-of-mouth recommendations, other than customers. Small firms may be recommended by other local businesses, professional advisers (lawyers, accountants and consultants), and friends or acquaintances who may not be direct customers of the business. Referral marketing is a key entrepreneurial strategy that we will discuss in more depth below.

  Perf-X's largest order came as a result of an introduction through the local university, where the owner was regularly in touch with academics at the School of Electronic Engineering.

- *Customer markets* represent a continuum of relationships, rather than a continuous search for new business transactions. The emphasis shifts from customer acquisition to customer retention through the development of mutually beneficial, long-term relationships. The aim of this type of marketing is to turn new customers into regularly purchasing clients, who become strong supporters of the business and an active source of referrals. They help find new customers and may also contribute to the development of new business opportunities.

  This seems more in tune with the realities of entrepreneurial marketing, which relies on identifying important customer groups and developing meaningful and long-term relationships with them.

  The design engineer of one of Perf-X's customers joked that he spent more time in Perf-X's premises than he did in his own office. The owner of Perf-X knew that it was probably true.

Activity 5
Entrepreneurial marketing methods

Which particular marketing methods or techniques are entrepreneurs most likely to use? Write out a list of potential marketing methods with an assessment or rating of how useful each is likely to be for a small firm.

12.3.3 MARKETING MIX: THE 4 Ps OR INTERACTIVE, WORD-OF-MOUTH MARKETING METHODS?

A selling point for a small business often lies in its ability to stay in touch with customers. Owner-managers themselves usually spend a considerable part of their working day in contact with customers. This allows them to interact with their customer base in a way which large firms, even with the latest technological advances, struggle to match. Interactive marketing for small firms implies responsiveness – the ability to communicate and respond rapidly to individual customers. Entrepreneurs interact with individual customers through personal selling and relationship building approaches that secure not only orders, but also recommendations to potential customers. This can be contrasted to the mass broadcasting methods, such as large-scale advertising campaigns, traditionally used by larger organizations.

The entrepreneurial marketing mix

Marketing strategies are implemented through the marketing mix, or the 'set of tools' that an enterprise uses to pursue its marketing objectives in the target market (Kotler and Keller, 2015). As these tools are numerous, various attempts have been made to categorize them into a manageable form, the most famous being the 4 Ps of product, price, promotion and place, as discussed earlier.

Entrepreneurial marketing activities do not fit easily into these existing models of the marketing mix. However, one theme does seem to run through the marketing methods commonly used by entrepreneurs: they prefer direct interchanges and the building of reciprocal relationships and referrals between their customers and their business. Entrepreneurs prefer *interactive* marketing; they specialize in interactions with their target markets because they have strong preferences for personal contact with customers, rather than impersonal marketing through mass promotions. They seek conversational relationships in which they can listen to, and respond to, the voice of the customer, rather than undertake formal market research to understand the marketplace.

Interactive marketing methods imply one-to-one contact through personal selling and direct communications. Larger entrepreneurial firms may use more impersonal methods, such as advertising and PR to inform their markets, but they often rely on specific qualities of their founders to project a personal image. The personalities of Richard Branson, Anita Roddick and Mark Zuckerberg still colour our perceptions of Virgin, The Body Shop and Facebook. In smaller firms, the ability of the owner-manager to have meaningful dialogues with customers is often the unique selling point of the business.

Word-of-mouth marketing

Entrepreneurial marketing relies heavily on word-of-mouth (WOM) marketing to develop the customer base through recommendations. Research studies have, for some time, cited this as the number one source of new customers for small firms.[11] Such recommendations may come from customers, suppliers or other referral groups. WOM marketing has been defined as:

> 'Oral, person-to-person communication between a perceived non-commercial communicator and a receiver concerning a brand, a product or a service offered for sale' (Arndt, 1967).

This long-standing definition makes two crucial distinctions between WOM and other forms of marketing activity:

- *It involves person-to-person, direct contact between a communicator and a receiver.* Today, WOM marketing communications are no longer restricted to oral conversations with friends and neighbours. The telecommunications revolution means that people exchange views on their buying experiences across a number of media, including text messaging and email (Phelps *et al.,* 2004; Harrigan, 2013). Twitter, online discussion groups and blogs now involve millions of people around the world exchanging news and views over a huge range of topics on a daily basis. This often includes positive or negative stories about buying experiences, or a product's performance. The scope for uncontrollable WOM marketing communications on the internet and via mobile telephony is enormous, and entrepreneurs are developing ways to harness this informal communications channel to their advantage (Trusov, Bucklin and Pauwels, 2009). 'Viral' and 'buzz' marketing are modern variations of WOM marketing, pioneered by entrepreneurs (see Sections 12.4 and 12.5).
- *The communicator is perceived to be independent of the product or service under discussion.* Many organizations have attempted to influence recommendations by giving incentives to customers for recommending friends and family. 'Member Get Member' (MGM) schemes have become more common. However, recommendations based overtly on incentives may not be perceived to be truly independent, making such direct interventions less effective.

The importance of such communications is well-documented in the marketing literature, which suggests that WOM is often crucial to purchase decisions in many consumer and business-to-business markets (Bayus, 1985). For many small firms, reliance on recommendations is no bad thing as it is more suited to the resources of their business. Referrals incur few, if any, additional direct costs; most owner-managers prefer the slow build-up of new business that word-of-mouth marketing implies, because they would be unable to cope with large increases in demand for their services.

The disadvantage of word-of-mouth marketing is that, essentially, it is uncontrollable. As a result, owner-managers perceive there to be few opportunities to influence recommendations other than providing the best possible service. In practice, there may be ways of encouraging referrals and recommendations by more proactive methods which are overlooked by small business owners. New ventures usually need conventional marketing methods to make them noticed in the first instance, as recommendations cannot take place until there is a customer base. Those firms that wish to diversify their customer base into new markets have an additional issue: how to attract customers from the new target market who are probably not within an existing referral network of customers and supporters.

We discuss ways of developing proactive word-of-mouth marketing activities below (in Section 12.4).

Activity 6
Entrepreneurial intelligence

Entrepreneurs seem to have an instinctive feel for developments in their marketplace. What is the source of this? How do they keep themselves up to date?

12.3.4 MARKET INTELLIGENCE: FORMAL DATA GATHERING OR INFORMAL NETWORKING?

We noted in Chapter 5 that even successful entrepreneurs put a low value on formal market research and seldom plan systematic programmes of research. Instead, they personally maintain an external focus on their activities that alerts them to opportunities and threats in their environment (as outlined in Chapter 2). Their informal information-gathering techniques allow them to monitor their own performance in relation to that of competitors and react quickly to competitive threats. They are also open to new ideas and opportunities through a network of personal and inter-organizational contacts. This process restarts the marketing cycle by forming the basis for further innovative adjustments to the activities of the enterprise.

Networks

The dependence of marketing activities on the owner-manager makes the idea of networking particularly useful in the context of small business marketing. As owner-managers have limited resources within their organization, they must look elsewhere for advice and information on which to base marketing decisions. We know that successful entrepreneurs build up a rich mental map of their market environment by making regular, formal and informal contact with others in the trade, customers, suppliers, competitors, professional bodies and associations (see Chapter 2). They have extensive personal contact networks (PCNs) which they can tap into for market information, advice and competitive intelligence. Limitations on resources also make collaboration between organizations an important option for small businesses. Inter-organizational relationships (IORs) help supplement product development and other marketing activities which are constrained by money and other resources.

For example, a group of small retailers was particularly affected by the closure of a nearby multi-storey car park for structural repairs which had dramatically reduced passing trade to their shops. Not only did they coordinate their case for compensation to the local council, but they also mounted a joint promotional campaign offering incentives of subsidized alternative parking and a park-and-ride service.

12.3.5 A MODEL OF ENTREPRENEURIAL MARKETING PRACTICE

The above analysis of marketing as practised by successful entrepreneurs compared to classical marketing theories suggests the need for a new model of entrepreneurial marketing that is not to be found in current marketing textbooks (Hills, Hultman and Miles, 2008; Gilmore *et al.*, 2013). Successful entrepreneurial marketing consists of a circular process: innovative developments and adjustments to products and services are targeted at identified customer groups who are contacted through interactive marketing methods, while informal information gathering monitors the marketplace and evaluates new opportunities, which may, in turn, lead to further innovations. This suggests that '4 Is' may be more appropriate than the '4 Ps' traditionally used to summarize marketing activities (Stokes, 2000b), as illustrated in Figure 12.2.

Activity 7
Entrepreneurial word-of-mouth marketing

Consider your own experiences in using the recommendations of others when you purchase products and services. What prompts you to ask for, or receive, recommendations? What can small business owners learn from this process, and what activities can they undertake in order to attract more customers like you through word of mouth?

Figure 12.2 Strategic entrepreneurial marketing – the '4 Is'

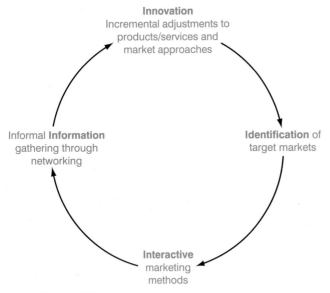

Source: Stokes (2002)

Particular marketing methods applicable to entrepreneurs and small business owners are evaluated in more detail in the sections that follow.

12.4 Word-of-mouth marketing methods

We have established that recommendations or referrals are the preferred way for almost all owner-managers to expand their customer base. Many are content to let recommendations work by themselves assuming that if they do a good job, people will recommend their business. Little may be done to find out about how recommendations take place, and what can be done to increase the flow of referrals. However, it is possible to take a more positive approach. There is increasing evidence that entrepreneurs do find ways of encouraging referrals and recommendations by proactive methods. Studies have demonstrated that entrepreneurs have successfully intervened to encourage WOM to achieve their aims in many sectors including graphic designers (Shaw, 1997), lawyers (File *et al.*, 1992), primary school head teachers (Stokes, 2002), social network builders (Trusov, Bucklin and Pauwels, 2009) and independent retailers (Stokes and Nelson, 2013). There is growing research-based evidence to support the anecdotal stories of practitioners such as Wilson (1996) and Sernovitz (2015) that it is just as possible to develop systematic word-of-mouth strategies as it is to organize more traditional advertising campaigns.

Today, 'word-of-mouth' communication is a misnomer. Although many recommendations are still made orally in face-to-face encounters, they often take place without face-to-face personal contact because of developments in communication technologies. The internet, smart phones and social media offer instant opportunities to pass on comments and advice about products and services to an international audience. 'E-tailers' such as Amazon invite customers to post comments on their websites about the goods they sell. Online groups and social networking and blogging services, such as Twitter and Facebook, are full of advice about products and services.

Although these new media have revolutionized the way in which recommendations or complaints are communicated, the basic principles of WOM marketing still apply.

12.4.1 THE PROCESSES OF RECOMMENDING AND COMPLAINING BEHAVIOUR

First, it is necessary to understand more about the processes that underlie recommending behaviour.

The power of impartiality

People take note of recommendations from friends, colleagues and, more recently, websites and social media about what they buy. Many turn regularly to particular acquaintances, experts, bloggers or favourite websites for advice because they are perceived to be knowledgeable in a specific field such as restaurants, hotels, films, fashion or computer equipment. Potential buyers act on this kind of advice because they believe it to be impartial, with no vested interest in the outcome of their recommendation. Researchers into buyer behaviour invariably cite 'friends' as the most trusted source of advice on what people purchase, for this reason. As consumers have become increasingly cynical about the true independence of third-party advice, hearsay has become more influential than well-researched sources of product information. Psychologists have even discovered that we are more prepared to believe what we overhear, rather than communications intended for us, because this reduces the possibility of a motive behind the message (Stokes and Lomax, 2002).

This is the fundamental principle on which WOM marketing is based: the receiver of word-of-mouth communications must regard the communicator as impartial, taking no commercial gain from the acceptance of the recommendation. If this basic condition is not fulfilled, the effectiveness of the recommendation is reduced.

Characteristics of WOM communications

It is important to understand the *volume*, *valence* and *direction* of WOM before developing a marketing strategy:

- The *volume* of WOM communications refers to the potential audience for recommendations and complaints, which can vary from one person to very many. This is important to the concept of viral marketing in which large international audiences can become involved (see Section 12.5.1). However, recommendations still tend to be most effective on a one-to-one basis from a known and trusted source, as this can guarantee impartiality.
- *Positive or negative valence* refers in psychology to the relative attractiveness of an event or person. Thus, the valence of WOM communications exists on a scale between very positive recommendations to extremely negative complaints. Often, customers who complain only do so to their friends, and not to the offending supplier. If negative word of mouth is rife about a business, the owner-manager could be the last to hear it. An important element of any word-of-mouth marketing strategy is concerned with damage limitation through an effective complaints procedure.

  There is some evidence that negative WOM is more common and is capable of higher volumes than positive WOM (e.g. Goodman and Newman, 2003). Research by East, Hammond and Wright (2007) refutes this, finding that positive WOM was three times more common than negative WOM across 15 product categories.
- The *direction* of WOM can change from *input* into a person about a buying decision to *output* from the same person concerning their purchase. This can affect the volume of WOM: if the person buys on a strong recommendation but has problems with the purchase, their negative WOM is likely to be loud; if the reverse happens and the person buys despite the input of negative WOM, they are more likely to praise their purchase publicly (Stokes and Nelson, 2013).

12.4.2 THE ELEMENTS OF A WOM MARKETING STRATEGY

Research among owner-managers who have carried out successful WOM marketing strategies suggests the following three stages to a referral campaign (Stokes and Nelson, 2013):

1 *Investigate how WOM processes operate in the industry and the business.* The key issue is to find out how to stimulate recommendations without appearing to exert some form of control over them and thereby breach the impartiality rule. In particular, an entrepreneur needs to find answers to the following questions:

- *Who* are the active groups that recommend the business? Although most owner-managers believe new business comes from recommendations, few know exactly which types of customer are the most active in making referrals. Intuitively, many believe it is their most loyal customers who recommend, implying a link between length of customer tenure and recommending behaviour. Theories of relationship marketing incorporating a 'ladder of customer loyalty' suggest that, as the relationship progresses over time, the potential for advocacy increases at each stage. However, research reported that *recent* customers were more likely to recommend than longer-term customers (East, Lomax and Narain, 2001). The rate of recommendation of the current supplier *declined* with the duration of customer tenure. This suggests that recently acquired customers may be a more appropriate target for WOM campaigns than long-standing customers.

   Although customers tend to be the number one source of recommendations (or complaints), suppliers, professional services and the local business community are often an undervalued source of referrals. Anyone who comes into contact with a business forms impressions that can lead to positive or negative comments and advice.

- *What* is being said about the business? It is obviously important to know whether customer comments are generally positive or negative. It is equally important to know exactly what is being talked about and what is being recommended. Even positive comments may not be in line with the expectations of the owner-manager. Which particular benefits stimulate customers to recommend? How many negative comments are being made, directly and indirectly, about the business? It is possible to prompt customers to talk about events or personalities in a business through giving them regular information in newsletters and visual aids.

- *When* are recommendations triggered? This is probably the most important and most difficult question to answer – what triggers a customer to make a recommendation and what might stimulate them to make them more often? Research indicates that customers who have a sense of *involvement* with a business, over and above normal commercial relationships, are more likely to recommend it. File, Judd and Prince (1992) concluded that increased participation levels between lawyer and client were indicative of increased numbers of referrals in the legal profession. Stokes (2002) found that parents who were more involved with their primary school through raising money or helping in the classroom had a higher rate of recommending than other parents. Telling stories and giving news about an enterprise through newsletters and articles may also stimulate satisfied customers to talk about an enterprise (Sernovitz, 2015). Visual aids such as free gifts have also been found to act in a similar way.

   Questions such as the above can only normally be answered by some form of research among customers to investigate their recommending and complaining behaviour.

2 *Intervene to influence the recommending process.* Informed by answers to the questions above, it is now possible to devise a campaign to increase referral rates. This may take the form of explicit requests for referrals and incentives, or subtle information in newsletters and social media that creates a discussion point. Often, the key is to give customers a reason to talk about the business by doing something exceptional or different.

ilson (1996) cites the example of an irate woman who complained to a general store about a set of tyres she had purchased. The store manager happily refunded her money. The twist was that they had not sold her the tyres – in fact, they didn't even sell tyres. But they recognized she firmly believed they had and that how they reacted to her demand for satisfaction would forever influence what she said about them – positive or negative. In the event, the story made the *Wall Street Journal,* so the refund paid for itself many times in free publicity.

3 *Defuse potential complaints.* Processes need to be in place, first, to find out about customer dissatisfaction and, second, to deal with complaints in an effective and generous way. Often, problems can be turned from potentially negative to positive word of mouth, as in the story cited above. Complaint handling is not just about damage limitation; it also creates opportunities for stories that generate referrals through a positive experience.

UNITED BREAKS MY GUITAR

One complaint that was not dealt with promptly led to a dip in the share price of a large American corporation. Dave Carroll, a professional musician with the group Sons of Maxwell, could not get any redress for damage done to his guitar on a United Airlines flight, so he wrote a song about the experience and posted it on YouTube. This is how he described the experience:

'In the spring of 2008, Sons of Maxwell were traveling to Nebraska for a one-week tour and my Taylor guitar was witnessed being thrown by United Airlines baggage handlers in Chicago. I discovered later that the $3500 guitar was severely damaged. They didn't deny the experience occurred but for nine months the various people I communicated with put the responsibility for dealing with the damage on everyone other than themselves and finally said they would do nothing to compensate me for my loss. So I promised the last person to finally say "no" to compensation (Ms Irlweg) that I would write and produce three songs about my experience with United Airlines and make videos for each to be viewed online by anyone in the world.' (www.davecarrollmusic.com)

The first song 'United Breaks Guitars' became an instant internet hit with over 2 million views in the first few days. United eventually offered compensation but the damage to their reputation had already been done, as a fall in their share price indicated. The power of negative WOM communications had been demonstrated yet again (see Carroll, 2012).

12.4.3 BUZZ MARKETING

'Buzz marketing' attempts to generate word-of-mouth messages by creating interesting stories about a product or service. But it is different to normal WOM in its deliberate use of consumers or paid professionals to spread a particular message about a product. For example, buzz marketing invites volunteers to try products, then encourages them to become 'buzz agents' by talking up their experiences with the people they meet in their daily lives. 'Live buzz marketing' makes use of an actual event or performance to create word of mouth (Foxton 2006). The performance may involve ordinary consumers or paid actors to create an impact in order to generate comment. This may be covert, in that the audience may not be aware that it is a pre-planned event, or overt, in that they are fully understanding of the marketing that is going on.

FILMS THAT BUZZ – THE BLAIR WITCH PROJECT

It has long been known that WOM recommendations from both friends and opinion-leading critics play a decisive part in the success or failure of films. Distributors now use buzz marketing techniques to promote new releases, particularly following the unexpected success of *The Blair Witch Project* (1999). This became the most successful independent film made, with box office receipts of $248 million worldwide despite a low cost budget for both production and marketing. It was marketed using buzz marketing techniques to generate interest through speculation over whether the film was real or not. The poster for the film deliberately encouraged people to think the film was an actual documentary, and that the three main characters had really disappeared in the woods. A fake documentary, 'Curse of the Blair Witch', investigated the 'legend' surrounding the film just before it's release, containing interviews with friends of the missing students, paranormal experts and local historians (all acted). The three main actors were listed for a short time as 'missing, presumed dead', partly because the producers put up 'missing' posters of the three stars of the film during the Cannes Film Festival. The Blair Witch Project created a new genre of 'fictional non-fiction' horror films as well as a successful, early example of buzz WOM marketing.

(See www.blairwitch.com)

Activity 8
Entrepreneurial marketing and the internet

In what ways can entrepreneurs, in particular, benefit from the internet in marketing their business? What benefits do other advances in telecommunications and social media give to the small business?

12.5 From word of mouth to word of mouse

Bill Gates (1995) famously forecast that the information highway would revolutionize business communications in ways that would particularly benefit small firms. Although the use of electronic mail, websites, social media and network systems can help entrepreneurs overcome some of the inherent problems of smallness, larger firms have also been using the new marketing methods made available by technological advances. Corporations have begun to interact more closely with individual customers in ways that mimic entrepreneurial marketing techniques.

There has been a convergence in the marketing approaches of large and small firms as the internet and social media have created a new communication channel: 'word of mouse'. For some businesses, it has opened up markets that did not exist; for others, there has been disillusion and despair.

THE BEST AND WORST OF TRIPADVISOR

Stephen Kaufer co-founded TripAdvisor in 2000 as a portal for professional reviews and official advice on travel. Embedded in the system was a button for visitors to the website to add their own comments. Consumer opinions rapidly outnumbered professional reviews so that the site was transformed into a collection of opinions from ordinary travellers. By 2010, TripAdvisor had grown to become the world's largest travel website, registering 40 million unique visitors in a single month.

Its popularity gave it considerable power over the fortunes of business owners and doubts grew over the authenticity of some of its reviews. The UK Advertising Standards Authority formally investigated complaints and ordered the website to remove its 'reviews you can trust' slogan. TripAdvisor tightened its policies and blacklisted 300 hotels for suspicious reviews, including one Cornish hotel that had bribed guests to leave positive reviews. Suspicions persisted and one reviewer was found to have visited over 50 Parisian restaurants while staying in 50 hotels in various countries in the same month. Some hotel owners who thought TripAdvisor was a good idea at first, because it publicized their business to an international audience, had cause to change their minds. They complained that business was being damaged by malicious reviews or that competitors were denigrating other hotels while their properties were achieving reviews that seemed impossible. There were calls for reviewers to be made to exercise restraint and to become more visible to readers.

However, the popularity of the site continues to grow, with research indicating that it is the most popular and trusted travel website.

12.5.1 SOCIAL MEDIA

The use of social media has changed the way that WOM communications work. Kaplan and Haenlein (2010) defined 'Social Media' as:

'. . . a group of internet-based applications that build on the ideological and technological foundations of Web 2.0, and that allow the creation and exchange of User Generated Content'

Originally, internet users were just consumers of information, until 'Web 2.0' developments allowed them to become involved in the creation of content ('User Generated Content'). Today, there is a wide variety of applications such as Facebook, YouTube, Twitter, Instagram, Snapchat and TripAdvisor that use these concepts. Individuals as well as large and small businesses have adopted social media to reach out to literally millions of people at a time. Barak Obama used social media (My.Barak.Obama linked to Facebook and Twitter) in his first and second US presidential campaigns. Large corporations such as Starbucks and Dell, in the USA, and Westpac Bank, in Australia, have adopted deliberate social media marketing strategies (Wamba and Carter, 2014). Recent research studies have found that SMEs around the world, from developed economies in the USA and Europe (Stokes and Nelson, 2013) to emerging African economies such as Kenya (Jagongo and Kinyua, 2013), are increasingly using social media both to increase their geographic coverage and to engage with customers on an individual level.

Some commentators (e.g. Ferguson, 2008) have warned against rushing into blogging and tweeting, as it can have negative as well as positive results – as the above example of TripAdvisor demonstrates. Owner-managers may be using social media because they are fearful of being left behind, rather than because they are convinced of its intrinsic merits; others may have unrealistic expectations through the 'social media hype' and become disillusioned when they are not met.

Social media may be just the latest in a long line of new channels for marketing messages, but it does exhibit significant differences to traditional WOM communications. Traditional WOM is passed orally from a sender to a receiver, as shown below in Figure 12.3. The message remains private to those directly involved unless it is either overheard, repeated by the sender, or sent on by the receiver to someone else, with opportunities for different interpretations and misunderstandings (Stokes and Lomax, 2008).

Figure 12.3 The communications process

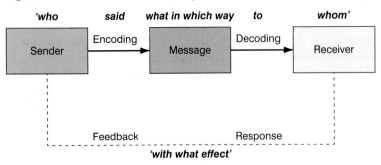

Source: Stokes and Lomax, 2008.

Social media communications work in a similar way but with a significant difference: they can be instantly 'overheard' by a large audience of other users who may pass the message on to others through other forms of social media or orally. This has two particular advantages:

- Business owners can reply to messages passed between customers about their products or services. This is particularly important if the comments are negative, as complaints that may have otherwise gone unnoticed can then be addressed;
- The reach of the message can be far greater, as one-to-one communications become one-to-many.

12.5.2 VIRAL MARKETING

The use of social media and the internet can, in some circumstances, combine the power of WOM with the reach and versatility of digital communications to create 'viral marketing' and 'viral advertising'. Viral communications can experience exponential growth as the message spreads rapidly though social networks created through internet applications such as Facebook or YouTube.

For someone to pass on such a message, it has to be interesting – for example, it is amusing or offers great value. Viral marketing often operates through funny or interesting videos that contain marketing messages, or rumours created on internet blogs. Behind viral marketing is the word-of-mouth principle that people like to pass on interesting stories about their experiences. The objective of entrepreneurial marketing is to harness this effect and ensure that interesting stories contain marketing messages that promote the entrepreneurial service or product.

THE HOTMAIL VIRUS

One of the first free web mail services, Hotmail, was launched to a small network of acquaintances by the founders Jack Smith and Sabeer Bhatia in 1996 with the message 'Get your free email at hotmail.com' attached to the bottom of every email sent. This had the effect of creating product champions out of existing users so that the service grew rapidly to over 10 million users.

It is important to remember, however, that viral marketing can act negatively on organizations as well as positively. Messages about bad experiences can also spread like a virus (see *United breaks my guitar* in Section 12.4.2 above).

12.5.3 SMALL BUSINESS AND WEBSITES

The internet seems to allow small businesses to communicate their message internationally at minimum expense. It does offer an incredible combination of international coverage with individual targeting; it was used by over 3 billion people in 2015, nearly half of the world's population,[12] yet it is also able to deliver messages tailored for one individual. Promoting a small business on the internet has other advantages: it can be relatively inexpensive to set up; visitors to websites can be tracked to provide market information; it has the potential for immediate impact; and it can be very creative and interactive.

Search engine optimization

The significant disadvantage is that it is very difficult for an advertiser to be noticed by their target market in a relatively disorganized, unstructured system of millions of websites. 'Visibility' of a website is at least as important as its design. For this reason, search engines that rank the list of sites according to their relevance to the user's search have become very important. Businesses need to ensure their site is ranked near to the top of relevant search lists because users rarely bother to look beyond the first page of names. This entails constant vigilance and management to ensure that websites are configured to the search engines' criteria for listing results ('hits') of the keyword search. As each engine uses different criteria to search its index covering millions of web pages, managing the visibility of a website has become a skilled job. Tips for such optimization include:[13]

- Create keywords the target audience is most likely to use.
- Use specific phrases, not general keywords.
- Optimize the title.
- Use meta tags.
- Use keywords early and often in page content.
- Do not 'spam' search engines.

Businesses also use a variety of offline promotional methods to increase traffic to websites because of the difficulties in raising and maintaining visibility online. These include main media advertising through television, radio and direct mail, as well as general publicity by including website addresses on letterheads and marketing literature. All of these factors mean that advertising on the internet may not be as cost-effective as it may at first appear. While sites can be designed and hosted relatively cheaply, maintaining sites and promoting their visibility can become more expensive.

In addition to its own website, a small business can also use **banner advertising** on other firms' websites. 'Ad banners' are the most common form of advertising on the web, so-called because they form a banner across the top of web pages, carrying promotional messages and links to the advertiser's website. The success rate of the advertisement is measured by the number of 'click-throughs' to the advertiser. Banners are also exchanged through reciprocal arrangements, under which two or more organizations agree to link their sites to increase traffic to each other.

The adoption of the internet as a marketing tool is affected by the nature of the customer base and market sector. The majority of small businesses trade in a local area and may not need the wide reach of the internet. This applies particularly to small retailers and local service companies. However, for manufacturers that need to reach a wide audience of both customers and suppliers, the internet has multiple benefits. Websites can be used not only to attract customers, but also to source components and equipment on a global basis. In sectors dominated by large companies such as food retailing and car manufacturing, the adoption of internet technology has become compulsory, as the large buyers insist on access to intranets to check the progress of orders and email communications with their suppliers.

12.6 Personal marketing communications

Entrepreneurs prefer direct, person-to-person marketing methods for two main reasons:

1 *A desire by the owner-manager to stay in touch with the market.* The competitive edge of some small enterprises is their rapid response to individual customer needs, which is facilitated by the owner-manager's regular contact with the customer base. As most small firms are in service industries, where a more flexible response is possible, this can be an important competitive consideration over larger organizations, whose reaction time is often longer.
2 *A belief that personal contact is the most cost-effective method of promotion.* Personal selling by the owner-manager is often the only available option in the start-up phase to keep costs to a minimum.

While personal promotional methods may be the preferred route, there is a common danger in this approach if the responsibility is always left with the owner-manager. Other pressures on the owner-manager's time may make this strategy into a purely reactive one; the internal management requirements of the small firm can leave insufficient time for long-term, planned sales approaches, and personal methods are only given sufficient attention when the business looks slack.

12.6.1 DIRECT SELLING

It is difficult to think of a small business owner-manager who does not have some involvement in selling, even though they may not recognize it as such. Even the self-employed plumber or builder makes a sales call when asked in for an estimate. Some owners may have a background in sales, but most owners have had no formal training in personal selling. Yet, the owner-manager is most likely to be the front line sales person for the small firm (Fraser, 2013).

There are alternatives to owner-managers performing the sales function directly themselves:

1 *A sales person(s)* can be employed by the small firm. The major barrier is cost. For example, a small firm operating on a 50 per cent gross margin would need extra sales of £100 000 just to cover the marginal costs of employing a sales person at a cost of £50 000 per annum before any contribution to general overheads or additional profit is made.
2 *Agents-on-commission* represent a way of overcoming this high fixed cost for a small firm. An agent will represent several manufacturers or distributors in a given trade, and sell their products to the relevant outlets in return for a commission (usually in the region of 10–15 per cent) on sales made. This is often an appropriate method for a new firm in a market where typically high volumes of relatively low-priced units are sold through a fragmented distribution. For example, a manufacturer of gift products might appoint regional agents to sell their products to gift shops, stationers and other specialist outlets.

   The advantage of this method is the rapid coverage of a large number of potential customers, at no risk to the manufacturer. The disadvantage is that there is no control over the effort in terms of amount or kind, and there is a loss of margin.

12.6.2 TELEPHONE AND ONLINE SELLING

Modern telecommunications are an essential part of the process of building customer relationships through direct contact, by making an appointment or answering an enquiry. Telesales or e-commerce can complete the whole process by taking the order. For a small firm with limited resources, telephone calls and emails have become an indispensible part of selling. Taking telephone or online orders is used particularly for existing customers who regularly place orders.

For example, a health food wholesaler first developed outlets for its products by direct sales visits. It was not economic to make further regular visits, so customers were telephoned once a week and asked if they needed to order further items. The phone call reminded retailers of the need to restock, and kept out competitive products as the shelves were kept full. Customers could also place orders online by visiting the company's website.

12.6.3 RETAIL SELLING

Small independent or franchised shops can be classified into two main types: convenience outlets, such as newsagents and confectioners, and specialist shops, varying from fashion-wear boutiques to art galleries. In both, there is a form of customer contact. In the convenience store, it will probably be no more than taking payment after customers have served themselves. In the specialist outlet, the contact is more likely to involve some selling.

The advantage of a retail outlet is that it represents a (hopefully) convenient, permanent place of contact between buyer and seller. The difficulty for the specialist retailer is in recognizing the line between the need to help the buyer make a decision, and maintaining a comfortable environment, in which the customer does not feel threatened or pressured.

The problem for all retailers is that online shopping is gaining an ever-increasing share of consumer spending. In some ways, this has been to the benefit of independent retailers that offer distinctive products and personal services that are less likely to be purchased over the internet. In 2014/15, the number of independent outlets increased in the UK, reversing the decline of previous years. Independent barbers, coffee shops, and nail parlours increased in number while garment and footwear chains declined (www .independent.co.uk).

12.6.4 EXHIBITIONS AND TRADE SHOWS

Trade shows and exhibitions cover every significant trade or industry, from lingerie (at LACE in Harrogate, UK), contemporary art (Frieze Art Fair, London and New York), to electronic equipment (at InterNepcon in Tokyo, Japan). There are also regional business-to-business exhibitions serving more varied industries on a local basis. These can represent a focused meeting place for a small business and an efficient way of seeing customers and competitors alike.

Exhibitions are expensive in stand costs and the time involved in preparation and attendance. They are essentially points of contact and, although orders are sometimes written during the exhibition, the key to productive use of this resource is usually in the follow-up to the introductions made.

12.7 Impersonal marketing communications

12.7.1 MEDIA ADVERTISEMENTS

There are two distinct types of media advertising used by small enterprises:

- *Directories and trade listings.* These are permanent references, outlining the products or services offered by firms which can be consulted by potential buyers. This form of advertising is widely used by owner-managers, who see the benefit of a permanent indication of their business in popular directories. These have changed recently in line with advances in telecommunications. For example, the well-known *Yellow Pages* has been superseded by Yell.com, an online directory.
- *Press, radio, television or website advertising.* There is a wide choice of media for a small firm to use on a more irregular basis, in the hope of creating or reinforcing awareness and demand for products or services.

Small enterprises are reluctant to commit expenditure on this kind of advertising. Although some measurement of the effects of advertising is possible (e.g. click-throughs from banner ads; direct response to press ads), the link between advertising and sales is difficult to establish, and frequently requires a long-term investment to be cost-effective. Small firms often therefore consider substantial expenditure on this type of promotion as a luxury they cannot afford.

12.7.2 DIRECT AND ONLINE MARKETING

Direct mail, now including **email**, has become an increasingly popular form of advertising for reasons that are particularly relevant to small business:[14]

- *It is targeted.* Small firms often trade in very narrow or fragmented markets, which traditional media over-hit or miss altogether.
- *Results can be quantified.* Unlike other forms of advertising, the results of a direct mail campaign, in terms of response back from the recipients, can be measured and valued. An entrepreneur can decide from the results whether the campaign justifies its costs.
- *It can be tested.* It is possible to test the response from direct mail on a limited basis, before extending the mailing to the full list. A small firm can thus reduce the risks involved in this type of promotional expenditure.

The issues associated with direct mail are:

- *The quality of the sending list is crucial;* the best-designed mailing sent to the wrong people will not produce results.
- *Response rates from direct marketing are usually very low, often less than two or three per cent.* While such responses may still meet the costs of the campaign, they limit the scope of the effort as the total volume of business generated may be small. There is increasing resistance to 'spam' internet messages and junk mail.

12.7.3 PUBLIC RELATIONS (PR)

Larger companies have long recognized the importance of good public relations, and the value that can be obtained by working with the media. **Public relations** (PR) departments and agencies can point to free advertising on TV or in the press to justify their costs to large corporations. Small firms can similarly benefit, but few make full use of the possibilities. Local media and the trade press consume large quantities of news, and small firm activities are often newsworthy, but unnoticed. The problems are familiar: owner-managers with no time or expertise to put together press releases, or make the necessary media contact.

12.7.4 LEAFLETS AND BROCHURES

Most small firms produce a leaflet or brochure describing their product or service. Digital publishing has encouraged many small firms to produce more literature about themselves which, at a relatively modest cost, can now be made to look professional and business-like. Many small firms have brochures that can be downloaded from their website, which minimizes costs and maximizes ease of access. Common issues in literature on small businesses include:

- *Unclear objectives:* a small firm's leaflet will typically try to be all things to all people. The impact of what is produced can be considerably reduced by the confusion or profusion of objectives.
- *Product-centred:* small firms often describe what they have to offer in terms of the technical specifications of their product or service, rather than by reference to what use this will be to a potential customer.

Activity 9
Reaching the market

In what ways can the small business owner involve others in the distribution of their products and services? What are the advantages and disadvantages of using such intermediaries?

12.8 Marketing channels

Marketing channels refer to how goods or services reach the marketplace. For any firm, there is a fundamental choice of channels: to distribute direct to end-users or through intermediaries. From this basic choice, other options then emerge, as illustrated in Table 12.2.

These options are self-explanatory, except for the last, 'multilevel' or 'network' marketing.

Multilevel marketing: this rather confusing term has been used to describe a variety of ways of reaching consumers through a chain of direct selling agents. At one extreme this includes 'pyramid selling', which is now legally regulated, as many self-employed people were duped into buying a stock of product which was being sold only to fill up the distribution pipeline and rarely to end-users.

However, it does have its more legitimate forms. 'Party plan', for example, is a method of distributing a variety of products, including plastic containers, books and cosmetics, by encouraging household gatherings at which the products are sold. This approach involves sales agents, usually operating on a part-time, self-employed basis, who organize the gatherings and earn commission on the sales.

In North America, a popular distribution system is sometimes referred to as multilevel or network marketing. It does involve setting up a pyramid structure of sales agents, who earn commission both on their sales to consumers and to other agents, but there is a crucial difference to the discredited pyramid selling. The agent does not need to buy stock in order to make a sale, other than for demonstration purposes. Thus, if final users are not buying the product, the system breaks down. The promoters of this system make extravagant claims about the level of sales now being achieved, and the growth they expect.[16]

Advantages of intermediaries

Small firms, with limited resources and expertise, can particularly benefit from using intermediaries. Specific advantages are:

- *Local knowledge and contacts of the intermediary:* small firms often base their business on the owner-manager's local know-how. Expanding into territories where it no longer applies can be risky without an intermediary to supply specific knowledge of the environment.

Table 12.2 **Distribution channels**

Direct to end-users	Through intermediaries
Direct sales	Agents and distributors
Retail and specialist outlets	Wholesalers
Online sales	Online/mail order companies
Mail order	Retail and specialist outlets
	Multilevel marketing

- *Reduced distribution costs:* a small producer can considerably reduce their distribution costs by using an agent or wholesaler, thereby eliminating the need for a large number of small deliveries direct to retailers.
- *Reduced stock holding:* by shifting the responsibility for stockholding down the *distribution* chain, a small manufacturer can reduce their own stockholding requirements and the associated financial and space considerations.

Disadvantages of intermediaries

There are disadvantages:

- *Loss of contact with the marketplace:* a small firm relying on intermediaries for their distribution and selling will be one or more steps removed from the consumer they are seeking to serve. Their customer becomes the distributor, wholesaler or retailer, and they have to rely more on them for information about customers down the chain, including the final consumer.
- *Less control over how the product is presented and delivered to the final customer:* an intermediary often provides information and advice, and the after-sales service.
- *Less influence over the levels of marketing effort:* most intermediaries represent more than one *supplier.* They therefore exercise choice over which products receive the most effort in terms of display, promotional effort and selling time. One of the strengths of the franchise system is that it avoids this issue, by insisting on the exclusivity for a franchisor's products or services with the franchisee.
- *Less revenue per item sold:* intermediaries cost money. Although this is a variable cost depending on the level of sales, loss of revenue can be substantial – commonly at least one-third of the final selling price if distributed direct to retail, or up to two-thirds where agents and wholesalers are used.

All of these disadvantages multiply as the distribution chain becomes longer.

12.9 Summary and activities

Small businesses have inherent characteristics that give rise to the following marketing issues: limited customer base, limited impact dependent on owner's marketing skills, reactive and variable marketing effort, and the need to develop and defend market niches. Although entrepreneurs interpret the term 'marketing' in a limited way, they implement more comprehensive strategies and activities under another name.

However, they tend not to follow traditional marketing principles but, rather, a more entrepreneurial form of marketing. This can be summarized as the 4 Is (rather than the 4 Ps) and consists of a circular process: innovative developments and adjustments to products and services are targeted at identified customer groups who are contacted through interactive marketing methods, while informal information gathering monitors the marketplace and evaluates new opportunities, which may, in turn, lead to further innovations.

Word-of-mouth marketing is the preferred way in which small businesses attract customers, enhanced today by use of the internet and social media. A proactive word-of-mouth marketing strategy has the following stages:

- Investigate how recommendations and complaints operate in the industry and the business: *who* is recommending; *what* are they saying; and *when* are they prompted to make a recommendation?
- Intervene to influence the recommending process by involving customers in the *business,* and stimulate referrals through visual aids and stories.
- Defuse potential complaints and use them as opportunities for positive recommendations.

The internet is having an increasing impact as word of mouth evolves into 'word of mouse' with the development of viral marketing and more sophisticated use of websites. Marketing communication options for small businesses include direct selling, telephone and online selling, retailing, exhibitions, media advertising, direct marketing, PR and literature.

The advantages of using marketing channels include: local knowledge, reduced distribution costs and reduced stockholding. They have the potential disadvantages of loss of customer contact, less control and less revenue per unit sold.

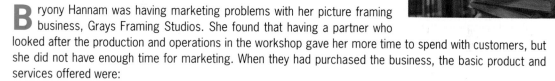

Case study
You've been framed: Part 4

MARKETING PROBLEMS

Bryony Hannam was having marketing problems with her picture framing business, Grays Framing Studios. She found that having a partner who looked after the production and operations in the workshop gave her more time to spend with customers, but she did not have enough time for marketing. When they had purchased the business, the basic product and services offered were:

1 *A bespoke picture framing service* Sixty per cent of sales were made by providing a framing service for customers' own images, ranging from photographs to fine art. As all the operations were carried out in their own workshop, this type of business generated a good gross margin of 70 per cent: in other words, the variable costs of the mouldings, board, glass and other materials involved in the framing process averaged 30 per cent of the final selling price.
2 *Framed and unframed pictures* As well as the framing service, a range of pictures, including inexpensive prints and posters, limited editions, original watercolours and oils, were offered through the three retail shops. Although these were usually sold framed, they could be purchased unframed. The gross margin on a framed picture averaged 50 per cent, as the cost of purchasing the image lowered the profit available on the framing. However, stock costs were not necessarily a problem, as some local artists were happy to leave their work on display on a sale or return basis.

She had managed to improve the turnover of each of their three shops by offering a comprehensive design service. Many regular customers were even happy to leave the choice of moulding and framing to Bryony, as they had learned to trust her judgment. However, after initial increases, sales had now reached a plateau once again and Bryony needed to consider her options for continued growth. Each of the three shops averaged approximately £12 000 turnover per month, with an average spend per customer order of £60. She studied the customer records and divided her customers into three main types:

- *Regulars* who visited the shops and made a purchase at least once every six months. She calculated there were about 50 of these each month, per shop.
- *Irregulars* who came back more than once, but only after an interval of six months or more. There were about 100 of these per shop, per month.
- *One-offs* who came into the shop to make a purchase but had not returned. There were about 50 of these per shop, per month.

(Continued)

Each shop was positioned between the local high streets and a car park so that convenience and passing trade were maximized. However, in one location, Bryony was particularly concerned about the effects of a new parking scheme proposed by the local planners which would reduce the number of parking places available to her customers. She had introduced new services to attract customers. Each shop now offered complimentary tea or coffee to customers prepared to linger, a concept Bryony had borrowed from a well-known book shop in New York. For larger orders, Grays Framing now made free home-deliveries, a service they were keen to offer because of increased parking problems at peak times.

'If we are to grow, we need more customers', she had explained to her partner, Tony Meeham, who ran the workshop, 'but it's like a leaky bucket. As fast as we fill up with new customers, we lose others who never seem to come back. None of the promotions we've tried have had any lasting effect. Most of our customers still come through recommendations.'

'Who do you think does the recommending?' Tony asked.

'Other customers mainly. But I have met customers who are sent to us from other local shops, particularly photographers – even the gallery in the high street. Some new customers come in simply because they are passing by, but prompted by what someone else has said to them.'

'Why do people recommend us? I presume our outstanding workshop quality is high up the list.' Tony smiled.

'Well, no actually,' said Bryony. 'They take that for granted, I'm afraid. They seem to like the personal service and design advice we offer in the shops. Customers get to know me or someone else in one of the shops, and trust us to advise them. The problem is that I can't be in all three shops at once, and staff tend to leave. If a customer comes in after six months or more, they might not recognize anyone and we have to build the relationship up all over again.'

'Do you think we should consult a marketing expert?' asked Tony.

'Mmm. Or I could go on a course. But will they know anything about the picture framing market – or the marketing problems of small businesses like ours?'

Activities

(a) What marketing problems does Bryony have? Consider the list of typical small business marketing problems in Table 12.1. Which of these does she share? Does she have any others?

(b) The six markets model in Figure 12.1 describes important markets other than customers. Which individuals or organizations might fall into the six categories in the case of Grays Framing? Which do you think require marketing approaches, and in what order of priority?

(c) Consider Bryony's analysis of her customer groups. How can she find out which ones are most likely to recommend her business, and what should she do with this information?

(d) Like many other small business managers, Bryony considers that most of her new customers come through word-of-mouth marketing. How can she actively encourage recommendations?

Case study

FIT FOR TALKING: THE CASE OF AN INDEPENDENT HEALTH CLUB

When Declan Williams first bought a specialist fitness club, his biggest problem was his best customers. A dedicated group of bodybuilders attended the club frequently, and used the equipment intensively. While they provided him with a core of good customers, they also blocked further expansion. These longstanding members only recommended new members if they were primarily motivated by bodybuilding, not general fitness. The owner knew that he had to reach the segment of fitness enthusiasts if he were to develop the business. He also knew that the existing clientele actually deterred new female members – only 16 per cent of the membership were women.

Deciding that the only way to cater for the different needs of these customer segments was to provide separate facilities, he converted the first floor of the club into a women-only gym. While this provided a talking point, it also gave him a particular problem in developing a word-of-mouth strategy: as so few customers were female, the base for making recommendations was very small. The owner tackled this issue by inviting fitness teachers to run their classes in the club. This provided him with the exposure to the new customer base that he needed. Female membership grew quickly to become over half of the membership.

A year or so later, the owner was ready for a further stage of expansion. In order to grow through word of mouth, he decided he first needed to know which members were currently recommending the club most frequently. He devised a simple questionnaire circulated to all members, encouraging response personally and through an incentive. From this, he discovered that there was a connection between the length of membership and referral behaviour: newer members were more likely to refer than the older members. The average length of membership for making a recommendation that resulted in a new client was 3.5 months. He also found that members who used the facilities most regularly were also most likely to recommend: 'The key to referral is involvement; they've got to be in there, using it, participating in the club'.

His strategy to stimulate referrals was therefore to concentrate on the new members, making sure they were given every reason to come in and use the club. He devoted considerable time to making sure they felt at home, had all the technical support and advice they needed, and were encouraged to join in club activities.

The results have been impressive. He doubled the membership and revenue of the club over a five-year period with little or no external advertising. His formula for this success was to break out of limiting membership networks by repositioning the club and to stimulate recommendations by ensuring new members became thoroughly involved in the club.

Activities

(a) What specific issues relating to word-of-mouth marketing does this case illustrate?
(b) How did Declan Williams overcome them? How does this illustrate more general theories of word-of-mouth marketing?
(c) Suggest other ways to develop a proactive recommendations strategy for health and sports clubs similar to this.

Case study

ALL MOUTH AND PLENTY OF ACTION: THE CASE OF AN ENTREPRENEURIAL HOTELIER

Alnur Dhanani had a problem. His hotel in Paddington, London, was caught in a marketing no man's land between the more expensive, well-known chains and budget, independent hotels. He did not have the brand name of the chains but wanted to rise above the undifferentiated, price-based approach of other independents. Most of his customers came as the result of recommendations but his occupancy rate was not high enough. He decided to give customers more to talk

(Continued)

about and restored some of the hotel rooms to exactly how they were in 1860 when the hotel opened, including furniture of the period. He believed this would encourage them to talk about 'something that was different about their holiday on their return home'.

As his customers were mainly overseas tourists, most of them booked through travel agents – it was before the days of TripAdvisor. Although he knew that recommendations played a key role in the selection of his hotel, he decided to conduct some market research among his customers to find out how the process worked. Using a simple questionnaire, he asked customers who had recommended the hotel to them and for what reasons, and what they, in turn, would say about the hotel and to whom. From this he discovered two weak links in the word-of-mouth chain:

- *Source of recommendations* Seventy per cent of guests said that recommendations from travel agents had been crucial in their decision to book the hotel, but only 30 per cent said they would pass recommendations back to the agents after their visit. Instead, customers said they would recommend the hotel mainly to friends and relatives, who were a relatively unimportant source of recommendations when customers were deciding to choose the hotel.
- *Types of recommendations* When customers chose the hotel, they said that the factors that influenced them most were location, price and facilities. However, when recommending the hotel to others, they tended to mention experiences such as the friendliness of staff and cleanliness of the hotel.

From the research, the owner concluded that he needed to close the loop between satisfied customers and travel agents in order to encourage the agents to make more recommendations on his behalf. He encouraged guests to fill in comments cards, summaries of which were sent to the original booking sources. Travel agents were sent visual reminders of the hotel location in the form of a Paddington teddy bear, followed by regular mailings of honey to feed it. Believing that such visual aids improved the likelihood of recommendations, the owner also gave a bear to each guest on departure to remind them of the novel aspects of the hotel.

The owner also encouraged customers to make recommendations that mentioned the key influences of location, facilities and price. Guests were given a detailed pocket-map of the vicinity of the hotel in relation to important tourist locations, including transport facilities and comparative costs. In addition to providing a service to guests, this acted as a visual aid for them to pass on to others, summarizing the key decision-making points as it also featured the hotel's facilities and prices.

To reduce negative word of mouth, the owner invested in a comprehensive complaints-handling procedure. Although it was normal industry practice for junior staff to handle problems, he gave responsibility to a senior manager so that guests had direct access to decision-makers. Generous compensations became standard. He believed that this helped not only to decrease the number of complaints, but also to enable the swift defusing of those problems that did arise.

Occupancy rates improved substantially over a period of 18 months, largely as a result of this word-of-mouth marketing strategy, according to the owner. By understanding more about how word-of-mouth recommendations worked in his particular business, he was able to make the process work more effectively on his behalf.

Activities

Analyze the marketing strategy adopted by Alnur Dhanani.

(a) How does it illustrate the stages for a word-of-mouth strategy (described in Section 12.4.2)?
(b) Evaluate and categorize the key activities and incentives that seemed to prompt word-of-mouth recommendations.
(c) Suggest other ways to develop a proactive recommendations strategy for hotels similar to this.

Case study

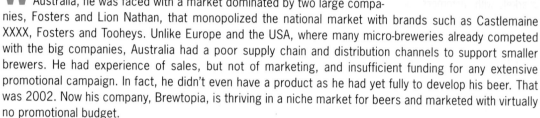

AN AUSTRALIAN WHO GAVE A XXXX FOR ANYTHING ELSE: A CASE OF BREWTOPIA

When entrepreneur Liam Mulhall wanted to launch a new beer in Australia, he was faced with a market dominated by two large companies, Fosters and Lion Nathan, that monopolized the national market with brands such as Castlemaine XXXX, Fosters and Tooheys. Unlike Europe and the USA, where many micro-breweries already competed with the big companies, Australia had a poor supply chain and distribution channels to support smaller brewers. He had experience of sales, but not of marketing, and insufficient funding for any extensive promotional campaign. In fact, he didn't even have a product as he had yet fully to develop his beer. That was 2002. Now his company, Brewtopia, is thriving in a niche market for beers and marketed with virtually no promotional budget.

His first idea was to buy a pub and put a small brewery into it. He did not know much about the beer industry and he soon found out that this simple concept was unlikely to work as it was almost impossible to put enough beer in front of consumers to get the economies of scale to make it work. However, it was the early years of 'Big Brother' and other TV reality shows that gained audience participation and loyalty through voting for participants in the programmes, so he was aware of the concept of involving potential customers in a new product as a way of generating awareness of the product before it was launched.

He decided to see if this could work in the context of the beer market by using the power of word-of-mouth recommendations from friends in order to compete with the large marketing budgets of the big breweries.

The launch campaign

He combined these two ideas into a new business concept. First, he invited about 150 friends and family to register on a website where they would get the opportunity to vote on the development and marketing of a new beer business. They were asked to vote on important aspects such as the name, style and taste of the beer, the type of bottle, pricing and sales outlets. He found it was important to give voters only two choices so that they felt really able to influence the decision. Second, he offered shares in the company for every vote cast, for buying the product and for referring friends. He felt that the physical involvement of owning shares would strengthen their emotional ties to the business and lead to more word-of-mouth communications.

The brewery was named 'Brewtopia' and the first beer product, 'Blowfly', was launched in January 2003. The initial plan was to market the beer direct to consumers via internet mail order, and then to expand into outlets such as pubs, restaurants and alcohol retailers once there was sufficient brand recognition to pull sales through the distribution. He believed that marketing Blowfly should not be about the beer but about entertainment and story telling. The company generated plenty of press and other interest through its unorthodox approach, particularly the offer of shares. It even tried to create 'buzz' from the delivery of its beer. Instead of delivering to licensed premises at off-peak times to minimize disruption, Blowfly was offloaded when the bars were full by delivery men in lab coats who arrived in a van disguised as an ambulance with siren wailing. The website on which the products were sold direct to consumers was equally controversial. It featured stories that challenged the mystique generated by the advertising of the big brands, with claims that beer was easier to make than bread as it only had four ingredients, and it published the actual costs of brewing.

(Continued)

Changing the strategy

Liam Mulhall admits that 90 per cent of what they tried did not work. What did work was what he calls their 'stick-at-it-ness' – they kept on trying new things until sufficient worked to represent a viable business. That business is not the one envisioned in the original plan. The business model that worked is 'mass customization', in that corporate or individual buyers can customize their own bottle of beer, wine or water by creating a personalized label and choosing from a variety of bottle sizes and product types. They stopped attempting to sell standardized beer such as Blowfly through retail outlets and focused more on the corporate and hospitality markets with customers such as Toyota and Sony. They sell own-brand products to restaurants and hotels. The products are retailed online aiming at the gift market, with own labeling or tribute beers such as 'Dudweiser' or 'Pooheys' (see Brewtopia.co.au).

Activities

(a) Describe how this case study illustrates each of the four stages of the entrepreneurial marketing process (the 'Four Is' – see Figure 12.2)

(b) Which types of word-of-mouth marketing methods did the company employ and how?

(c) Could these methods work in other markets to compete with dominant, established players? For example, how could you use some of the methods to enter the financial services market?

Extended activity
A marketing evaluation

Consider two small businesses (preferably involved in the food and drinks industry) with which you are familiar. (See the Extended activity in Chapter 1 and subsequently.) Compare and contrast the marketing strategy of these two businesses. List their strategies under the categories of the 4 Is of innovation, identification of markets, interactive marketing methods and information-gathering.

In what ways do you think they are good practitioners of marketing philosophy?

How could you improve upon their marketing strategies and their implementation of marketing methods?

Planning a new venture
Planning the marketing

Summary of what is required

Complete the marketing section of the business plan by:

- completing your analysis of the marketing environment;
- setting marketing objectives;
- outlining marketing methods;
- producing an example of promotional material, such as a flyer or web page.

The marketing environment

Marketing research should now be completed, so that the marketing environment is understood. Check that the following questions have now been answered:

- What is the market size and the discernible trends?
- What is the nature and extent of the competition?
- What other trends in the technological, economic and political environment will be important?

Marketing objectives

What are you aiming to do in marketing terms?

Specify marketing objectives for your enterprise. These should clarify the relationship you wish to achieve between your product or service, and the target market. In other words:

- They should summarize the product or service offered: for example, 'office equipment and supplies'.
- They should identify the target market: for example, 'offices in a 25-mile radius'.
- They should be measurable: for example, 'gain 10 per cent market share', or 'achieve sales of £500 000'.
- They should be time-specific: for example, 'within two years'.

Marketing strategies

Outline the marketing methods you will use to achieve these objectives using the 4 Is.

Innovation

- What are the products or services offered?
- What is different about what is offered compared with the competition?
- How will new products be found and protected?

Identification of target markets

- Who precisely is the customer?
- Why will they buy from you?
- What other market types are important?
- How will customer relationships be developed?

Interactive marketing methods

- What personal and impersonal promotional methods will you use?
- What incentives will be offered?
- How will you overcome traditional small business problems in relation to stimulating recommendations?
- Will you distribute directly, or through intermediaries?

Information gathering

- How will you find out more?
- What networks will you utilize?

Marketing communications

In order to illustrate the benefits of the product or service on offer, it is most helpful to produce an example of promotional literature, such as a draft flyer or web page. This need not be a graphic masterpiece, but should attempt to illustrate how the competitive edge of your business will be put across to the target customer group.

12.10 Notes, references and recommended further reading

Notes and further information

1   For example, Hall, G. (1995) *Surviving and Prospering in the Small Firm Sector,* Routledge; Department for Business, Innovation and Skills (2015) *Small Business Survey: SME employers*, March, BIS Research Paper no. 214.

2   See James Dyson's (1997) autobiography *Against the Odds,* Orion Business Books, in which he tells the story of his early inventions as well as the development and successful exploitation of the Dual Cyclone vacuum cleaner.

3   Ibid., ch. 4, Improving on the Wheel.

4   See Tauber, E. M. (1974) How marketing research discourages major innovation, *Business Horizons,* 17 (June): 22–26; Browlie, D. and Saren, M. (1992) The four Ps of the marketing concept: Prescriptive, polemical, permanent and problematical, *European Journal of Management,* 26(4): 34–47. These and other articles argue that customers cannot express needs beyond their own experiences, and therefore support the requirement for technology-driven product development as well as market analysis. See also Trott, P. (2008) *Innovation Management and New Product Development*, 4th edn, Pearson Education/ Prentice Hall.

5   See Binks, M. and Jennings, A. (1986) New Firms as a Source of Industrial Regeneration. In: Scott, M., Gibb, A., Lewis, J. and Faulkner, T. (eds) *Small Firms' Growth and Development,* Gower; Poutziouris, P. (2003) The strategic orientation of owner-managers of small ventures: Evidence from the UK small business economy, *International Journal of Entrepreneurial Behaviour & Research*, 9(5):185–214.

6   See Adams, A. and Wallbank, M. (1986) The Evaluation of New Product Ventures in Small Firms. In: Scott, M., Gibb, A., Lewis, J. and Faulkner, T. (eds) *Small Firms' Growth and Development,* Gower; Toften, K. and Hammervoll, T. (2013) Niche marketing research: Status and challenges, *Marketing Intelligence & Planning,* 31(3):272–285.

7   See, for example, Jobber, D. and Ellis-Chadwick, F. (2012) *Principles and Practice of Marketing,* 7th edn, McGraw-Hill; Kotler, P. T. and Keller, K. L. (2015) *Marketing Management,* 15th edn, Prentice Hall.

8   See note 4.

9   See Gummesson, E. (1987) The new marketing – Developing long-term interactive relationships, *Long Range Planning,* 20(4):10–20. Gummesson and another Scandinavian writer, Christian Grönroos, have been particular critics of the traditional 'warfare' approach of marketing in which the aim is to achieve a sales transaction at all costs.

10 See Payne, A., Christopher, M., Clark, M. and Peck, H. (1998) *Relationship Marketing for Competitive Advantage: Winning and Keeping Customers,* Butterworth-Heinemann. This book summarizes the principles of relationship marketing in a variety of different contexts.

11 For example: Barclays Review (1997) *Marketing and the Small Firm,* May, London, Barclays Bank Plc; Stokes, D., Blackburn, R. and Fitchew, S. (1997) *Marketing for Small Firms: Towards a Conceptual Understanding,* report to Royal Mail Consulting, July, Small Business Research Centre, Kingston University.

12 World internet users and population statistics are given on www.internetworldstats.com

13 For more details, see Turban, E., King, D., Lee, J. and Viehland, D. (2004) *Electronic Commerce: A Managerial Perspective,* Pearson/Prentice Hall, pp. 631–632.

14 There are several guides to direct marketing; for example, Bird, D. (2007) *Commonsense Direct and Digital Marketing,* 5th edn, Kogan Page.

15 For information (not necessarily objective) on multi-level or network marketing, see the many 'how-to' books on the subject, such as Thompson-Pinder, K. (2014) *10 Things You Absolutely Must Know Before Joining A MLM or Network Marketing Company,* CreateSpace Independent Publishing Platform.

References

Arndt, J. (1967) Word-of-Mouth Advertising and Informal Communication. In: Cox, D. (ed.) *Risk Taking and Information Handling in Consumer Behaviour,* Harvard University.

Bayus, B. L. (1985) Word-of-mouth: The indirect effects of marketing efforts, *Journal of Advertising Research,* 25(3), June/July.

Blankson, C. and Stokes, D. R. (2002) Marketing practices in the UK small business sector, *Marketing Intelligence and Planning,* 20(1): 49–61.

Carroll, D. (2012) *United Breaks Guitars: The Power of One Voice in the Age of Social Media,* Hay House.

Carson, D. (1990) Some exploratory models of assessing small firms' marketing performance, *European Journal of Marketing,* 24(11): 8–51.

Carson, D., Cromie, S., McGowan, P. and Hill, J. (1995) *Marketing and Entrepreneurship in SMEs,* Prentice Hall.

Dalgic, T. and Leeuw, M. (1994) Niche marketing revisited: Concept, applications and some European cases, *European Journal of Marketing,* 20(1): 39–55.

East, R., Hammond, K. and Wright M. (2007) The relative incidence of positive and negative word of mouth: A multi-category study, *International Journal of Research in Marketing,* 24(2): 175–184.

East, R., Lomax, W. and Narain, R. (2001) Customer tenure, recommendation and switching, *Journal of Consumer Satisfaction, Dissatisfaction and Complaining Behaviour,* 14: 46–54.

Ferguson, R. (2008) Word of mouth and viral marketing: Taking the temperature of the hottest trends in marketing, *Journal of Consumer Marketing,* 25(3): 179–182.

File, K. M., Judd, B. B. and Prince, R. A. (1992) Interactive marketing: The influence of participation on positive word-of-mouth and referrals, *Journal of Services Marketing,* 6(4): 5–14.

Foxton, J. (2006) Live buzz marketing. In: Kirby J. and Marsden, P. (eds) *Connected marketing: the viral, buzz and word of mouth revolution,* Butterworth- Heinemann.

Fraser, P. (2013) The Soloist in Entrepreneurial Marketing. In: Sethna, Z., Jones, R., and Harrigan, P. (eds) *Entrepreneurial Marketing: Global Perspectives,* Emerald Group Publishing, ch. 15.

Gates, B. (1995) *The Road Ahead,* Penguin.

Gilmore, A., McAuley, A., Gallagher, D. and Carson, D. (2013) Entrepreneurship and the Marketing Interface Research. In: Sethna, Z., Jones, R. and Harrigan, P. (eds) *Entrepreneurial Marketing: Global Perspectives,* Emerald Group Publishing, ch. 1.

Goodman, J. and Newman, S. (2003) *Understanding Customer Behavior and Complaints: TARP (Technical Assistance Research Programs),* available at asq.org.

Harrigan, P. (2013) Social Media, Customer Relationship Management, and SMEs. In: Sethna, Z., Jones, R. and Harrigan, P. (eds) *Entrepreneurial Marketing: Global Perspectives,* Emerald Group Publishing, ch. 12.

Hills, G. E. and Hultman, C. M. (2005) Marketing, Entrepreneurship and SMEs: Knowledge and Education Revisited, *Proceedings of the 10th Annual Research Symposium of the Academy of Marketing Special Interest Group on Entrepreneurial and SME Marketing,* Southampton University.

Hills, G. E., Hultman, C. and Miles, M. (2008) The evolution of and development of entrepreneurial marketing, *Journal of Small Business Management,* 46(1): 99–112.

Jagongo, A. and Kinyua C. (2013) The social media and entrepreneurship growth (A new business communication paradigm among SMEs in Nairobi), *International Journal of Humanities and Social Science,* 3(10): 213, Special issue, May.

Kaplan, A. and Haenlein, M. (2010) Users of the world, unite! The challenges and opportunities of social media, *Business Horizons,* 53(1): 59–68.

Kotler, P. T. and Keller, K. L. (2015) *Marketing Management,* 15th edn, Prentice Hall.

Levitt, T. (1991) *Thinking about Management,* Free Press.

Phelps, J. E., Lewis, R., Mobilo, I., Perry, D. and Raman, N. (2004) Viral marketing or electronic word-of-mouth advertising: Examining consumer responses and motivations to pass along email, *Journal of Advertising Research,* 44(4): 333–348.

Sarasvathy, S. (2001) Causation and effectuation: Toward a theoretical shift from economic inevitability to entrepreneurial contingency, *Academy of Management Review,* 26(2): 243–263.

Sernovitz, A. (2015) *Word of Mouth Marketing,* 3rd edn, Press Box Publishing.

Sethna, Z., Jones R. and Harrigan P. (eds) (2013) *Entrepreneurial Marketing: Global Perspectives,* Emerald Group Publishing.

Shaw, E. (1997) The Real Networks of Small Business. In: Deakins *et al.* (eds) *Small Firms and Entrepreneurship in the Nineties,* Paul Chapman Publishing.

Stokes, D. R. (2000) Entrepreneurial marketing: A Conceptualisation from qualitative research, *Qualitative Market Research: An International Journal,* 3(1): 47–54.

Stokes, D.R. (2000) Putting entrepreneurship into marketing: The process of entrepreneurial marketing, *Journal of Research in Marketing and Entrepreneurship,* 2(1): 1–16, Spring.

Stokes, D. R. (2002) Entrepreneurial marketing in the public sector: The lessons of head teachers as entrepreneurs, *Journal of Marketing Management,* 18(3–4): 397–414.

Stokes, D. R. and Lomax, W. (2002) Taking control of entrepreneurial marketing: The Case of an entrepreneurial hotelier, *Journal of Small Business and Enterprise Development,* 9(4): 349–357, Autumn.

Stokes, D. and Lomax, W. (2008) Marketing: A Brief Introduction, Thompson Learning.

Stokes, D. R., Ali Syed, S. and Lomax, W. (2002) Shaping up word of mouth marketing strategy: The case of an independent health club, *Journal of Research in Marketing and Entrepreneurship,* 4(2): 119–333.

Stokes, D. R., Blackburn, R. and Fitchew, S. (1997) *Marketing for Small Firms: Towards a Conceptual Understanding,* Report to Royal Mail Consulting, Small Business Research Centre, Kingston University, July.

Stokes, D. R. and Nelson, C. H. (2013) Word of Mouth to Word of Mouse: Social Media and the Entrepreneur. In: Sethna, Z., Jones, R. and Harrigan, P. (eds) *Entrepreneurial Marketing: Global Perspectives*, Emerald Group Publishing, ch. 13.

Toften, K. and Hammervoll, T. (2013) Niche marketing research: Status and challenges, *Marketing Intelligence & Planning*, 31(3): 272–285.

Trott, P. (2008) *Innovation Management and New Product Development*, 4th edn, Pearson Education/Prentice Hall.

Trusov, M., Bucklin, R. E. and Pauwels, K. (2009) Effects of word-of-mouth versus traditional marketing: Findings from an internet social networking site, *Journal of Marketing*, 73 (September): 90–102.

Wamba, S. F. and Carter, L. (2014) Social media tools adoption and use by SMEs: An empirical study, *Journal of Organizational and End User Computing*, 26(2) (April-June): 1–17.

Wilson, J. R. (1996) *Word of Mouth Marketing*, John Wiley & Sons.

Recommended further reading

James Dyson's (1997) autobiography *Against the Odds*, Orion Business Books.

Kirby J. and Marsden, P. (2006) *Connected marketing: The viral, buzz and word of mouth revolution*, Butterworth-Heinemann.

Sethna, Z., Jones R. and Harrigan P. (eds) (2013) *Entrepreneurial Marketing: Global Perspectives*, Emerald Group Publishing. This updates previous ground-breaking texts such as Carson, D., Cromie, S., McGowan, P. and Hill, J. (1995) *Marketing and Entrepreneurship in SMEs*, Prentice Hall, which were the first to combine the disciplines of entrepreneurship and marketing.

Stokes, D. R. (2000) Putting entrepreneurship into marketing: The process of entrepreneurial marketing, *Journal of Research in Marketing and Entrepreneurship*, 2(1): 1–16. This develops the conceptual '3 Is' model of the entrepreneurial marketing process in more detail.

Stokes, D. R. (2006) Marketing and the Small Firm. In: Carter, S. and Jones-Evans, D. (eds), *Enterprise and Small Business*, 2nd edn, Financial Times/Prentice Hall.

Wilson, J. R. (1996) *Word of Mouth Marketing*, John Wiley & Sons. A practitioner book with advice on how to stimulate WOM and interesting case studies.

13 Money matters for small business

Learning objectives

By the end of this chapter you will be able to:

- Understand the different funding sources available to entrepreneurs, and the circumstances under which these should be approached.

- Evaluate the extent to which market imperfections, including the finance gap and equity gap, act as a barrier to growth for small businesses.

- Recognize the financial problems that new and young small businesses are likely to encounter.

- Appreciate the importance of sound financial management, through reporting of profit and loss, cash flow and balance sheet.

- Identify key financial issues facing the entrepreneurial small business.

Introduction

This chapter is about another of the key strategic influences on a small business – money. It considers the financial needs of small firms, the sources of funds available to them and the appropriate control of those funds. Financial analysis is covered with some detailed instructions on how to construct profit/loss, cash flow and balance sheet forecasts in 21 steps. This is done using a worked example derived from a case study. The chapter also considers some of the key additional financial influences and factors relevant to those setting up and managing an entrepreneurial small business.

Activity 1
Financial requirements

A small business needs money to fund its operations that is not always covered by the cash flow from its sales. What types of funding needs are likely to arise? What are the main sources of finance available to meet these funding needs? For what purpose is each type of funding best suited?

13.1 The uses and sources of funds for SMEs

Small firms need money to finance a host of different requirements. These funding needs will vary according to the type and stage of development of the business, and the financial circumstances of the entrepreneurs involved.

In looking at the types and adequacy of funds available, it is important to match the use of the funds with appropriate funding methods. Using the wrong type of finance can cause unnecessary problems for a small business. For example, using an overdraft facility to fund new equipment to increase production will mean that there is less short-term finance available when the need to increase working capital arises.

Figure 13.1 illustrates the principal financial needs of a small firm and the main sources of finance that match those particular requirements.

13.1.1 PERMANENT CAPITAL – EQUITY CAPITAL

The permanent capital base of a small business frequently comes from some form of equity investment in shares in a limited company, or personal loans to or from partners or sole traders. It is used to finance the one-off start-up costs of an enterprise, or major developments and expansions in its life cycle. It may be required for a significant innovation, such as a new product development. In some cases, it is required to refinance a firm that has acquired borrowings which are inappropriate to its current situation; short-term borrowings, in the form of loans or overdrafts, may need to be converted into more permanent capital as a small firm grows,

Figure 13.1 The uses and sources of funds for a small business

A small firm needs...

£ Permanent capital	£ Working capital	£ Asset finance	£ Finance for international trade
• start-up	• debtor/creditor gap	• machinery	• growth through
• expansion and	• seasonal fluctuations	• equipment	international trading
development	• bridging finance	• software	
• innovation	• short-lived assets	• buildings and fittings	
• refinancing		• vehicles	

So it requires...

£ Equity capital	£ Short-term finance (up to three years)	£ Medium- to long-term finance	£ Specialist and export finance

For which the main sources are...

Personal investment	Clearing banks	Clearing banks	Clearing banks
Venture capital	Finance houses	Venture capital	Factoring companies
Business angels	Invoice discounting	Finance houses	Export houses
Crowdfunding	P2P lending	Leasing companies	Finance houses
Public sector sources	Public sector sources	P2P lending	
Public equity		Public sector sources	

or runs into problems. Equity from private investors (e.g. a **venture capitalist** or **business angel,** or through **crowdfunding**) may also be sought to take a small firm into the medium- or large-size category, or as an exit route for the original investors.

Ideally, permanent capital is only serviced when the firm can afford it; investment in equity is rewarded by **dividends** from profits, or a capital gain when shares are sold. It is not therefore a continual drain from the cash flow of a company, in contrast to a loan which needs interest and capital repayments on a regular basis. Equity capital usually provides a stake in the ownership of the business and, therefore, the investor accepts some element of risk in that returns are not automatic, but only made when the business generates cash surpluses.

13.1.2 WORKING CAPITAL – SHORT-TERM FINANCE

Most small firms need **working capital** to bridge the gap between when they get paid for their services or products and when they have to pay their suppliers and their overhead costs. Requirements for this kind of short-term finance will vary considerably by business type.

For example, a manufacturer or small firm selling to other businesses will have to offer credit terms and the resulting debtors will need to be financed; the faster the growth, the more the debtors, and the larger the financial requirement.

A retailer, a restaurant, a public house or other types of outlet selling direct to the general public will, however, often collect cash with the sale of goods. If they are paying their suppliers on credit terms, the cash flow will be advantageous. In some cases, this will be sufficient to finance the start-up of a small firm, so that suppliers are effectively financing the business. However, even these types of business may need working capital to fund temporary losses, caused by seasonal fluctuations, or to cope with prepayment of expenses such as rent payable in advance.

13.1.3 ASSET FINANCE – MEDIUM TO LONG-TERM FINANCE

The purchase of tangible assets is usually financed on a longer-term basis, from three to ten years, or more depending on the useful life of the asset. Machinery, equipment, major software developments, fixtures and fittings, company vehicles and buildings may all be financed by medium- or long-term loans from a variety of lending bodies. The term of the loan should match, or be shorter than, the expected life of the asset being acquired.

13.1.4 INTERNATIONAL TRADE FINANCE

Exporting brings its own set of money problems. Currency fluctuations, lengthy payment terms and security of payment all give rise to the need for some kind of specialist or export finance. According to the British Business Bank (2015), particular issues that can arise in export transactions are:

- The risk that an exporter will lose money due to a contract being frustrated or a contract bond (a guarantee that a contract will be fulfilled) unfairly called.
- The need for exporters to offer credit terms for larger contracts, rather than take payments as the contract is performed.
- The need for exporters to have sufficient working capital to perform large contracts, or to issue contract bonds that are required by their buyer.

13.1.5 INTERNAL FINANCE

The most important source of start-up capital comes from entrepreneurs and owner-managers themselves.

Research at the turn of the century showed that, on average, businesses in the UK received £20 000 in start-up finance: typically, £10 000 (50 per cent) from personal investments; £5000 (25 per cent) from family and friends; the remainder (25 per cent) from external sources (Harding, 2002, p. 5).

Although the costs of starting a new venture have since gone up, the reliance on internal sources of funding has also increased. The British Business Bank (2015) reported that, in 2014, the average amount of finance sought for a business start-up was £25 700. Over 75 per cent of businesses used personal savings, with only 12 per cent using a loan from a bank.

The level of personal owner investment is conditioned by two main factors:

- *Creditworthiness of the owner:* as homes are a major source of guarantee on loans and overdrafts, the higher values of properties and the rates of home ownership in prosperous regions will facilitate more borrowing to start-up ventures.
- *Experience and awareness of sources of funds:* people who are pushed into owner-management through redundancy or other problems tend to have limited financial expertise and lower awareness of possible sources of funds.

There is evidence of regional differences both across the UK and internationally.[1] There is also evidence of differences between male and female entrepreneurs – with the average start-up funding for men being nearly twice that for women (Harding, 2004).

Over and above the investments made by individual entrepreneurs and owner-managers themselves, the first port of call is usually to family, friends and 'fools' (otherwise known as 'the 3 Fs'). Although these can be a great source of finance for many starting out their new venture, it can lead to additional, personal complications if things go wrong.

The majority of small businesses also rely on internal funds to finance their business growth. Over 60 per cent of SMEs in the UK did not use external finance in 2014, preferring to use retained profits and cash flow to fund their development (British Business Bank, 2015).

13.1.6 EXTERNAL FINANCE

When internal funds are no longer sufficient, small businesses turn to a variety of external sources, as illustrated in Table 13.1

Table 13.1 **Funding flows to UK SMEs, 2014**

Types of funding	£ Millions
Bank lending	38 000
Asset finance	13 100
Private external equity	1 100
(of which Crowdfunding)	24
Peer-to-peer business lending	550
Peer-to peer invoice finance	220

Source: British Business Bank (2015)

During the global recession of 2008–11, SMEs scaled back their expansion plans and became cautious about taking on additional debt. As a result, the demand for traditional external finance by smaller businesses reduced and some turned to new online sources such as peer-to-peer finance and crowdfunding. The following sections examine each of these options in more detail.

Activity 2
Sources of funds

A small firm has several options for obtaining finance. For what purpose is each type best suited?

13.2 Debt finance

13.2.1 BANK LENDING

The main source of external funding is conventional bank lending, with over 60 per cent of external finance coming from overdrafts and term loans (BIS, 2015). Several trends in the nature of bank borrowing can be identified:

- **Personal guarantees vs business plans** In order to secure loans, SME owners traditionally had to provide some form of security (e.g. property and personal guarantees). This has now shifted towards an assessment of the enterprise through business plans and cash flow projections. But lack of security is still cited by some owners as a significant barrier to bank borrowing (BIS, 2015).
- **Overdraft vs loan** Historically, more businesses in the UK than in other countries relied on overdrafts, rather than loans. For example, in the 1990s overdrafts accounted for 56 per cent of small firm debt in the UK compared to 14 per cent in Germany (HMSO, 1994). The structure of bank lending in the UK (and across Europe) has shifted away from overdrafts, which could be called in by banks at short notice and towards loans with a fixed, guaranteed term. By the 2000s, the ratio of overdraft to term lending was almost equal at 48:52 (Bank of England, 2004); by 2014, the ratio had swung to 30:70 so that overdrafts represented less than one-third of bank borrowing (BIS, 2015 – see Table 13.2).
- **Qualitative vs quantitative assessments of creditworthiness** In the past, bankers claimed that small business credit was about 'lending to the person' (Berry *et al.*, 1993), with a personal interview and presentation of financial information being the key deciding factors (Berry, Citron and Jarvis, 1987). Small business owners

Table 13.2 Access to finance by SMEs: key trends 2014 vs. 2012

	2014%	2012%
Whether sought finance in last 12 months	19	24
Sought finance for working capital/cash flow	38	56
Sought finance for capital equipment or vehicles	24	23
Sought a bank loan	48	48
Sought a bank overdraft	21	35
Whether had difficulty from first source approached	39	47
Whether eventually obtained all finance needed	71	68

Source: Small Business Survey (2014); Department for Business Innovation and Skills (BIS, 2015)

were sometimes criticized for not managing this process professionally: the financial information supplied was often out of date (Egginton, 1982), unreliable (Tomlinson and Knight, 1978) and, in certain cases, difficult to obtain (Berry, Citron and Jarvis, 1987). More recently, banks' techniques for credit-assessing SMEs have undergone significant changes, with a shift away from qualitative techniques based around a bank manager's judgment and towards more impersonal, computer-based, quantitative analysis (Bank of England, 2004). Such analyses emphasize the ability of the bank to mitigate any risk involved in making an investment.[2]

- **Banks vs SMEs** Until the end of the 1970s, the major banks did not differentiate small businesses as a customer group, offering them two basic products: standard overdrafts and loans. The dramatic increase in the numbers of small businesses and the self-employed during the 1980s stimulated the main banks to develop services specifically targeted at small firms. In the early 1990s, a combination of high interest rates and the recession highlighted some tensions in the relationships between small firms and their banks.[3] Business owners complained that banks used highhanded and unfair practices in their dealings with small firms. Issues focused on the limited range of interest rates and excessive bank charges, as well as a perceived lack of support in problem times and poor advice. Things came to a head in 2002 when the Competition Commission found the major banks in the UK guilty of making excess profits from their SME banking operations (Bank of England, 2002, pp. 24–27). A range of price control initiatives was set in place, under the auspices of the Office of Fair Trading, and with the full support of the government and the banks.

Although the relationship between borrowers and lenders subsequently improved, the global finance crisis of 2008 once more plunged SMEs and banks into conflict. Falling global demand increased SMEs' need for cash support just when the banks tightened their lending rules to improve their own liquidity. At the peak of the financial crisis, it is estimated that 10 per cent of the total business stock was denied credit over a three-month period and that bigger and older firms fared much better than small businesses during this difficult time (Cowling, Liu and Ledger, 2012). Despite the UK government taking control of a significant part of the banking sector during the crisis, lending to small business remained stubbornly low. The government's response was to set up the British Business Bank in 2013, which was given the task of changing the structure of finance markets, so they worked more effectively for smaller business, and increasing the supply and types of funding available to them (British Business Bank, 2014).

In 2007/08, total lending to small firms in the UK was £53.2 billion compared with deposits made by small businesses of £54.5 billion (BBA, 2008). In other words, small businesses were net lenders to the banks. More surprisingly, the tough years of recession did not change this trend. In 2014, applications as well as renewals of borrowing facilities by SMEs declined further while cash deposits held by banks increased substantially. As a result, SME deposits exceeded borrowings by more than £48 billion (British Business Bank, 2015). Entrepreneurs' distrust of banks because of their unreliable support in the past may be a factor in their reduced reliance on the banking sector.

Research devoted to understanding the capacity of SMEs to ride out the storm of the global financial crisis highlights the apparent resilience of many owner-managers. As many as three-quarters of entrepreneurs had the desire to grow their business within 12 months of the crisis subsiding (Cowling *et al.*, 2015), and Davidsson and Gordon (2015) draw attention to the 'surprising persistence of nascent entrepreneurs through macroeconomic crisis'.

13.2.2 PEER-TO-PEER LENDING

Although traditional bank finance remains the most important source of external finance for small firms, it is declining in importance as owner-managers diversify their ways of raising money. Government intervention does not seem to be having much impact on banks' funding of SMEs, while new sources of finance facilitated by the internet and social media are playing an increasing role (see Bruton *et al.*, 2015).

Peer-to-peer (P2P) lending means that loans are arranged directly between the lender and the borrower, with no involvement by an intermediary institution such as a bank. It developed for personal loans through internet sites such as Zoopla but is also growing strongly in business-to-business markets using 'crowdfunding' platforms such as Funding Tree and Funding Circle. (For more on crowdfunding, see Section 13.3.3.)

By cutting out the bank as middleman through more direct contact between savers and borrowers, the P2P loan market offers savers a higher rate of interest on their cash, and businesses benefit from either a lower rate on their borrowings or less collateral for a loan. This sector claims that its technology also makes loan-making faster and easier.

It does, however, come with a warning to investors: P2P loan platforms do not comply with the same regulatory requirements as banks; they do not hold large capital buffers against loan defaults and there is no legal protection for lenders.

Growth in the UK is accelerating quickly. P2P business loans equalled £90 million in 2011, £1.2 billion in 2014 and is forecast to reach £12.3 billion in 2020 (Cebr, 2015). This is still a small percentage of business bank lending, which stood at £262 billion in 2014.

PEER-TO-PEER LENDING IN ACTION

ASM Organic Recyclates is a UK clean tech company that borrowed £94 000 in 2015 to help finance its expansion overseas. Using the crowdfunding site Funding Tree (fundingtree.co.uk), it achieved more than its target of £90 000, offering an interest rate of 9.89% over 24 months on the loan. ASM was launched in 2013, making eco-waste converters that recycle the recycling; it turns organic waste materials into products such as fertilizer pellets. With customers such as the London Zoo, it expects to expand revenues from £1.5 million currently to £4 million in three years. It needed the loan to fund international projects, including a deal in Canada.

13.2.3 MICROFINANCE

Microfinance is the provision of financial services to low-income people, often for business or self-employment purposes. Typically, the borrowers live in a developing country and need finance for activities in the 'informal' economy, such as street stalls, cottage industries or small-scale farming. The World Bank estimates that 2.5 billion people, the majority of the world's population, are excluded from financial services of any kind because their monetized income is too low (Ledgerwood, 2013). This also prevents them from undertaking entrepreneurial ventures that require money. Microfinance was developed in response to that need, pioneered in the 1970s as a way out of poverty. One of the earliest developments was the Grameen Bank set up in 1983 by Muhammud Yunus, who won the Nobel Peace Prize for his innovative methods of lending very small amounts of money that made a big difference to the poor and un-creditworthy of Bangladesh. Since then, the bank has lent more than £3 billion to 6 million people, mainly micro-entrepreneurs.

Microfinance has its critics. For example, when apartheid in South Africa ended in 1994, microfinance loans were made readily available to entrepreneurs keen to set up micro-enterprises. However, the easy availability of credit meant that much of the funding did not go towards increasing productive capacity but towards consumer spending. When unemployment rose dramatically, loans went unpaid and poverty was exacerbated not alleviated (Bateman, 2013). High rates of interest caused by the overhead costs and profit taking by the banks providing the microfinance has caused some to turn to P2P microfinance to overcome these problems.

Z **idisha.org** is one of the first P2P lending sites that crosses international boundaries, as the organization is based in the USA but makes micro-loans in Africa and Indonesia. Julia Kurnia, a US aid worker, saw how expensive microfinance had become in Africa once the overheads of expensive local offices were added. She launched Zidisha in 2009:

'We use technology to connect internet-capable young adults in the world's poorest places with a global market for person-to-person loans – an eBay-style marketplace where borrowers transact directly with lenders and raise the funding they need to grow their small businesses, limited only by their own track record of responsible repayment. Since we do not outsource loan management to local banks, the cost to borrowers is far lower than what has traditionally been possible for traditional microfinance. As a result, living in an unlucky part of the world need no longer put a ceiling on our members' ambitions. They can connect to Zidisha regardless, using technology to bypass hitherto insurmountable local obstacles' (www.zidisha.org/our-story).

Examples of loan requests (normally for around $100) include: dairy goats for a herdsman (Kenya); an electronic sewing machine for a clothes maker (Ghana); a power generator for a distilled water producer (Ghana); coffee making equipment for a vendor (Indonesia).

13.3 External equity finance

There has been increasing recognition of the role of external equity finance, particularly for growth businesses where the degree of risk and potential reward are high.[4] There are two main types of equity finance: private and public equity. The term 'private equity' is frequently used instead of 'venture capital', although the latter is actually a sub-set of private equity involving high-risk, early-stage deals.

Equity finance can be provided by banks, venture capital funds and private individuals acting as 'business angels' or, more recently, as 'crowdfunders'.

Banks also provide a limited range of equity investment products; for example, HSBC has offered a fund that invests in technology-based firms. Some banks (e.g. Lloyds) sponsor the UK Business Angels Association (UKBAA), which attempts to create links between firms that need investment and private individuals willing to provide finance in return for an equity stake (see more below). The liquidity problems resulting from the global financial crisis of 2008–11 have considerably restricted high street banks' activities in the equity funding market.

Secondary equity markets – the Alternative Investment Market (AIM)

While there are public equity markets available to small businesses in the UK, such as the Alternative Investment Market (AIM), they have not historically had the 'vibrancy and critical mass of NASDAQ' in the USA (Cruickshank, 2000, p. 173). Some commentators have gone further, suggesting that the lack of a large, pan-European equity market, focused on the needs of smaller companies, has acted as a barrier to the development of early-stage risk capital in Europe (see Lund and Wright, 1999; see also Revest and Sapio, 2012, who note the particular reliance of technology-based small firms in Europe on internal funds).

AIM has its origins in the unlisted securities market (USM) launched in 1980, which sought to give smaller companies access to a stock market. AIM followed in 1995 on the London Stock Exchange and it is now one of the most active markets in the world for growth companies, with more than 3000 companies being traded that, together, raised more than £96 billion at launch. Typically, AIM companies range in value from under £2 million to over £100 million. The costs for floating on AIM average out at 10 per cent of funds raised (the higher the funds raised, the lower the percentage).

13.3.1 VENTURE CAPITAL FUNDS

Venture capital provides finance for growing businesses, usually through equity capital with some loan element. Venture capital is a specific component of the private equity industry and refers to funds used to invest in companies in the seed (concept), start-up (within three years of the company's establishment) and early stages of development. There are currently nearly 250 private equity funds in the UK, who obtain investments from a variety of sources, including pension funds, insurance companies, investment trusts, regional development agencies and private individuals. The best-known is probably the 3i Group established in 1945 by the Bank of England and the clearing banks to provide finance to growing firms. There are also government backed venture capital funds known as Enterprise Capital Funds (ECFs), which were set up by the UK government (Department for Business, Innovation and Skills) to address weaknesses in the provision of equity finance to SMEs. In 2013, these ECFs became part of the British Business Bank (see Baldock, 2016, for discussion of the impact of the ECFs on business performance).

The UK venture capital industry is the largest and most developed in Europe, and recovered strongly after the recession; global investments by UK funds totalled £13.4 billion in 2014 (£10.1 billion in 2013) of which £4.7 billion was invested in the UK (£4.1 billion in 2013).[5]

However, it would be a mistake to assume equity finance is easy to come by. As Figure 13.2 shows, only 2 per cent of applicants succeed in raising funds.

As venture capitalists provide risk finance, their rates of return targets are high, varying from 25–60 per cent depending on the risk involved. The structure of any particular investment will vary, but usually involves any combination of three types of capital: equity shares, preference shares and loans. The level of share ownership required is normally less than 50 per cent, with a typical stake between 30–40 per cent; a seat on the board of directors is also common.

Venture capitalists seek exit routes, including a public listing on a stock exchange, such as the Alternative Investment Market in the UK or NASDAQ in the USA. However, the need for clearly visible exit routes restricts the types of company in which the venture capitalist is interested. While they do invest in start-ups, this is not particularly favoured, unless it already seems to be a substantial business in its early days, capable of generating substantial profits within four to five years; this often implies involvement in a new, high-tech industry. More commonly, venture capital funds are used for the expansion of already established, successful firms capable of sustained growth, or for management buy-outs. Venture capitalists manage portfolios of investments that

Figure 13.2 What are the chances of raising private equity?

Research indicates that, on average, this is what happens to business plans presented to investors:

- 60 per cent are rejected after a 30-minute review
- 25 per cent are rejected after a three-hour appraisal
- 10 per cent are rejected after a full-day evaluation
- 3 per cent are rejected following failed negotiations
- 2 per cent succeed in raising funds.

Source: Envestors LLP Guide to Raising Finance up to £2m www.envestors.co.uk. Reproduced with permission.

Figure 13.3 Stages of investment

Start-up: This relates to finance provided to companies for use in product development and initial marketing. Companies may be in the process of being set up, or may have been in business for a short time but have not yet sold their product.

Other early stage: Finance provided to companies that have completed the product development stage and require further funds to initiate manufacturing and sales. They may not yet be generating profits.

Expansion: Sometimes known as 'development' or 'growth' capital, provided for the growth and expansion of an operating company which is trading profitably. Capital may be used to finance increased production capacity, market or product development and/or to provide additional working capital (see Fraser, Bhaumik and Wright, 2015, for detailed discussion of the relationship between business growth and entrepreneurial finance).

Bridge financing: This is finance made available to a company in the period of transition from being privately owned to being publicly quoted.

Replacement capital: Minority stake purchase from another private equity investment organization, or from other shareholders.

Refinancing bank debt: This relates to funds provided to enable a company to repay existing bank debt.

PIPE: Private investment in public companies (minority stake only).

Rescue/turnaround: Financing made available to existing businesses which have encountered trading difficulties, with a view to re-establishing prosperity.

Management buy-out (MBO): This relates to funds provided to enable current operating management and investors to acquire an existing product line or business. Institutional buy-outs (IBOs), leveraged buy-outs (LBOs) and other types of similar financing are also common.

Management buy-in (MBI): These are funds provided to enable an external manager or group of managers to buy into a company.

Public to private: Purchase of quoted shares with the purpose of delisting the company.

Secondary buy-out: Purchase of a company from another private equity investment organization.

Source: BVCA (2009) Private Equity and Venture Capital Report on Investment Activity 2008. Appendix 3, p. 20.

spread the risks involved. Typically, two out of every ten investments made will be completely written-off, six will perform averagely well, and, at best, there might be two real stars (Barrow *et al.,* 2005, p. 95).

13.3.2 BUSINESS ANGEL INVESTMENTS

Business angels are private individuals with the means and desire to invest directly in small companies. Very often, their wish to invest is fuelled by their particular knowledge and interest in the market or industry, rather than purely for financial interests. This informal venture capital market is relatively invisible but a number of business angel networks (BANs) exists to provide an introduction service for owners seeking money and business angels willing to invest.

Business angel investments are an important source of equity finance for new and nascent businesses (Mason and Harrison, 2015). However, business angels typically make relatively modest individual investments. Research suggests that three-quarters of business angels make investments of less than £50 000; and 40 per cent averaged less than £20 000 per investment (C2 Ventures, 2003). However, they tend to co-invest in the same venture so, in total, business angels form a significant part of early stage investment.

The European Trade Association for Business Angels (EBAN) estimated that 271 000 business angels in Europe invested €5.5 billion in over 33 000 deals in 2013 (EBAN, 2014). The UK attracted the most investment at €84 million, followed by Spain at €58 million and Russia at €42 million. Total demand for this type of finance far exceeds supply, with research suggesting that more than 90 per cent of companies seeking angel funding are turned down in the early stages.[6]

13.3.3 CROWDFUNDING

Crowdfunding has been hailed as a new form of 'democratic finance', providing more accessible opportunities for funding new or developing ventures. Whereas traditional finance tends to raise large amounts of capital from a small number of lenders, crowdfunding does the opposite, raising small amounts of capital from a large number of people through internet platforms supported by social media marketing (Nesta, 2012).

Crowdfunding has grown rapidly since the launch of the first website, Artistshare in 2001. According to Nesta (2012), $1.5 billion was raised worldwide in 2011 through over 450 sites. By 2012, this had risen to $2.7 billion through 500 sites and, by 2013, to $5.1 billion from over 1000 sites. Three different categories of crowdfunding have emerged:

* equity-based platforms (e.g. syndicateroom.com) which give shares in a venture in return for investment, representing approximately 15 per cent of sites;
* debt-based sites (e.g. fundingcircle.com) which use P2P lending (see Section 13.2.3), representing approximately 18 per cent of sites;
* reward-based platforms (e.g. kickstarter.com) which exchange investment for gifts (e.g. product samples or launch parties) or recognition (acknowledgement in film credits or project publicity), representing 55 per cent of sites.

Reward-based crowdfunding has so far proven to be the most popular form. Leader in the field, Kickstarter.com, focuses on creative projects produced by musicians, film writers, artists and writers, and has raised globally over $2.2 billion from 10 million people for over 100 000 projects from its launch in 2009 to 2016 (kickstarter.com/press).

While this is impressive growth, market penetration is still low. Table 13.1 indicates that, in 2014, crowdfunding contributed £24 million of the £1.1 billion of equity finance raised in the UK, or around 2 per cent of the total.

A typical crowdfunding process involves:

* submission of the project to the crowdfunding platform;
* vetting by the platform host of suitability and legitimacy of the project;
* launch of the project on the site with a funding target to be reached within a time window (e.g. three months, seedr.com);
* funding closes and money is distributed if the target is met, or is returned to investors if not achieved. (On Kickstarter, 60 per cent of launches do not reach their target.)

Like P2P lending, crowdfunding can be a risky investment. From 2011 to 2013, one-fifth of companies that raised money on equity crowdfunding platforms went bankrupt. Crowdfunded investments are not part of the UK's Financial Services Compensation Scheme, so investors stand to lose all their money. However, there is a clear psychological attraction to the crowdfunding model when operating according to the principle of 'conditional commitment'. Funding from any individual is usually only taken when an agreed target is reached; this offers a form of reassurance to investors only to put their money behind ventures that are widely held to be worthwhile.

CROWDFUNDING CASES

The UK rock band **Marillion** are thought to have initiated the first crowd-funded event in 1997. Unable to afford to tour after the release of their seventh album, the band raised $60 000 on the internet from American fans to play in the USA.

In 2016, companies such as **Friday Beer Co.** hope to benefit from the same funding method but by offering equity, rather than concert tickets. The three founders hope to raise £150 000 for 25 per cent of the share capital of their company. The Friday Beer Company, 'official sponsors of the weekend' sell premium bottled beer to outlets around London, including Harrods. As of 13 February 2016, they had raised two-thirds of their target with four days to go. (Go to Crowdcube.com to find out whether they made their target.)

Positive News, a media cooperative, re-financed its operations in 2015/16 through crowfunding.co.uk by offering an equity stake with a difference. It invited supporters to buy community shares during a 30-day crowdfunding campaign, attracting investment of £263 000 from 1500 people in 33 countries. For a minimum investment of £50, each shareholder was offered an equal vote in the cooperative, no matter how much they invested. Positive News is an example of constructive journalism, publishing stories to 'spark the human spirit' (www.positive.news). The newspaper has stories of good news covering diverse topics from the provision of refugee safe-havens to the launch of ethical hedge funds.

Negative News

Although Crowdfunding has many success stories, it has also had some significant failures. In 2016, the claims management group Rebus went into administration after receiving over £800 000 from over 100 investors on the crowdfunding platform Crowdcube. Although it is the largest failure to date, Rebus follows other high-profile crowdfunded companies such as the takeaway company Hokkei and the shoe label Upper Street which raised £320 000 and £243 000 respectively in 2015 on equity crowdfunding platform Seedrs, both of which have since gone into liquidation.

13.3.4 OTHER FORMS OF FINANCE

The other main forms of finance for small firms are leasing, hire purchase, invoice discounting (factoring) and export finance.

- *Leasing* allows a small firm to obtain the use of equipment, machinery or vehicles without owning them. Ownership is retained by the leasing company, although in many cases there is a purchase option at the end of the lease period. Lessors often argue that their expert knowledge of the market for various assets increases their ability to offer flexible and competitive terms.
- *Hire purchase* provides the immediate use of the asset and also ownership of it, provided that payments are made in accordance with the agreement. There has been a steady growth in HP finance since the Bank of England began monitoring this aspect of small firms' finance in 1999 (Bank of England, 2004, p. 18).
- *Invoice discounting,* otherwise known as factoring, uses the value of invoices issued by the business to underwrite funding for working capital. The invoice discounting company (usually a bank subsidiary) releases the value of invoices immediately to the issuing company in return for a percentage of the total invoiced value. The company thus has immediate payment once an invoice is issued, although it pays for this service by not receiving the full value of the invoice. Although many companies rejected this type of approach in the past, taking the view that customers would see it as demonstrating some financial

weakness on their part, invoice financing has become more sophisticated and customers may not be aware at all of any discounting being involved.

- *Export finance* The most important step in financing international trade is in ensuring full and prompt payment. Many governments offer assistance with this because overseas trade is vital for a strong economy. For example, in the UK the Export Credits Guarantee Department (ECGD), through UK Export Finance, provides credit insurance that gives cover in the event of non-payment by an overseas customer. The ECGD offers a variety of insurance schemes which a small firm can assign to a bank, or other lending body, in order to obtain export finance.[7] *Export houses* offer a wide range of services to exporters, including finance.[8] In South Africa, the Export Credit Scheme provides financial and insurance support, sponsored by the government, to exporters, providing that over half of the content of the exports are made in South Africa.

Activity 3
Financial issues

Small firms are faced with a variety of financial issues, some of which are more common at different stages of their life cycle, such as during the start-up, growth or decline stages. Can you give some examples of these issues? At what life-cycle stages are they likely to be most common?

13.4 Access to finance – the issues

13.4.1 MARKET FAILURE

Central to our understanding of the difficulties or problems experienced by small business owners and entrepreneurs in accessing finance is the concept of market imperfection or failure. If the market for money is working 'perfectly', then all those businesses that require funds for a 'legitimate' use (i.e. an ethically sound project that will have a net positive financial return) will receive the money they need. Just like most markets, however, the market for money does not work perfectly. Market imperfections or market failures have been shown to arise for two main reasons:

- First, it is difficult for the financial markets to devise financial instruments that share the rewards between investors and small firms in a mutually beneficial manner (National Economic Research Associates, 1990). The key difficulty is making appropriate assessments of risk when possessing limited information about the particular project. This situation results from what is known as **information asymmetry** – where the lender is only partially informed about the prospects of the business (see Stiglitz and Weiss, 1981).
- Second, financial institutions have been shown *not* to be subject to 'normal' competitive forces. As we have already noted, the banking industry was referred to the Competition Commission in view of what was seen as 'the existence, or possible existence of a complex monopoly situation' (Cruickshank, 2000).

Two main types of market failure have received particular prominence in the literature on finance for small businesses: the finance gap and the equity gap.

13.4.2 FINANCE GAP

The **finance gap** has been described as an 'unwillingness on the part of suppliers of finance to supply it on the terms and conditions required by small businesses' (Storey, 1994, p. 239). It was first brought to wide attention by the MacMillan Committee (1931) on Finance and Industry. Three categories of information asymmetry have been identified in relation to the finance gap. These relate to:

1 the period immediately before any loan agreement for a particular specified project is signed (*adverse selection* – where the lender effectively invests in the 'wrong' project);
2 the period during which the project undertaken is actually running (*moral hazard* – where the lender does not know whether the money invested is actually being spent on the project chosen);
3 the period once the project has been completed (*opportunism* – where the investor does not know how the project performed and therefore may not be able to determine the exact rate of return accurately).

The evidence for the existence of such a finance gap in the UK has been debated for many years. The influential report *Competition in UK Banking* (Cruickshank, 2000) found little evidence of unmet demand for debt finance. Elsewhere, the Institute of Directors (IoD) found that 71 per cent of businesses stated that they did not think that it was difficult to access finance for their business (up from 69 per cent in 2002) (Wilson, 2004). By 2003, a NatWest SBRT survey (Small Business Research Trust, 2003) showed that only 1 per cent of small firms cited access to finance or the level of interest rates as their main problem. As we have seen (in Section 13.2.1), the impact of the financial crisis from 2008 was to make access to finance for SMEs more difficult. The 2014 Small Business Survey indicated that 39 per cent of small businesses were turned down at their first attempt to obtain finance and only 71 per cent raised the money they needed (see Table 13.2).

Activity 4
Researching the gap

Why not undertake your own research study to see whether the finance gap has been bridged? Ask your family, friends and other small business owners known to you through your personal networks, or situated in your local high street, whether they have experienced difficulties in accessing finance for their small businesses. What reasons were given for refusing finance, where this was the case?

13.4.3 EQUITY GAP
The information problems highlighted above are also relevant to the equity market. The structural causes of the **equity gap** are different, however, and can be categorized in terms of supply-side and demand-side issues.

Supply-side issues
The presence of information asymmetries means that equity investors can face significant costs in identifying suitable investment opportunities. These costs are likely to be prohibitive for the smaller, younger business. It is costly for the investor to undertake a search on the particular small, unquoted business seeking investment. In the case of a business with an unproven management team and track record, it can be difficult to assess the business's prospects of success. Equity investors will require a process of due diligence to gather appropriate information about the business, industry and market before any informed decisions are taken. There are likely to be expensive transaction costs involved in negotiating the terms of the agreement (Business Link, 2005; Mason and Harrison, 2015). In addition, the investor will need to monitor the ongoing performance of their investment. Such monitoring costs can also be relatively expensive.

Demand-side issues

On the demand side, research has highlighted a number of issues that deter the small business from seeking equity capital (HM Treasury and Small Business Service, 2003). Small businesses are fearful about seeking private equity as this might lead to more restricted management freedom. Loss of control is a genuine fear for many entrepreneurs and small business founders. In addition, however, many of the small businesses that do seek equity investments are constrained by a lack of **investment readiness**.

WHAT ARE THE MOST COMMON REASONS INVESTORS REJECT PROPOSALS?

- Lack of skills in the management team
- No track record or proof of concept
- Financial forecasts based on weak assumptions
- Too complex
- Inadequate financial returns
- Not scalable
- Lack of trust
- Lack of market awareness
- No clear exit route

Source: bba.org.uk

When it comes to assessing the evidence for the existence of the equity gap, the BVCA has refuted what they describe as 'the common misconception that the industry focuses only on the larger private equity investments' (BVCA, 2004). While only 4 per cent of the total invested in 2008 was at the 'early stage', this represented 34 per cent of the total number of companies receiving funding. This suggests that many of the 455 companies receiving early-stage investment would have been seeking relatively modest investments (see BVCA, 2009, p. 9).

However, there does seem to be difficulty in raising risk capital between approximately £250 000 and £2 million, with particular challenges facing those seeking sub-£1 million investments (HM Treasury and Small Business Service, 2003). In 2004, the Bank of England outlined the main challenge for the future in the financing of small firms to be accessing small amounts of risk capital, particularly those for early-stage businesses (Bank of England, 2004, p. 38).

13.4.4 THE LIFE CYCLE OF FINANCIAL PROBLEMS

If the first hurdle for a small firm is to ensure the availability of the appropriate amount and type of funds, the next step is to optimize the use of those financial resources by effective planning and control.

The Bolton Committee was critical of many aspects of the financial management of small firms, reporting that information was often so poor that management frequently learned of an impending crisis only with the appearance of the annual accounts, or following an urgent call from the bank manager (Bolton Report, 1971).

Fast-growing small businesses have particular problems in controlling their finances. Growth brings frequent changes to the internal structures and external environment of a small firm. It is often difficult to ensure that financial control systems keep pace with the changing circumstances.

Table 13.3 The financial life cycle of a small firm

Stage	Likely sources of finance	Financial issues
Conception	Personal investment	Under-capitalization, because of inability to raise finance
Introduction	Bank loans, overdrafts	Control of costs and lack of information
Development	Hire purchase, leasing	Over-trading, liquidity crisis
Growth	Venture capital	Equity gap, appropriate information systems
Maturity	All sources	Weakening return on investment
Decline	Sale of business/liquidation	Finance withdrawn; tax issues if business is sold.

For example, a small firm, which historically traded directly with consumer markets, expanded by setting up distributors both in the UK and overseas. This led to the development of debtors, as the distributors were given credit and a rapid increase in stocks which were needed to service the new outlets. The small firm did not have control systems in place to cope with these new demands and soon ran into liquidity problems.

The small business is likely to be confronted by a variety of financial problems as it advances through its life cycle (Hutchinson and Ray, 1986). Table 13.3 illustrates some of the potential issues in each stage.

In the early stages, the lack of track record can hinder raising the required **capitalization** and lead to an under-capitalized business.

As the business begins to trade, it will have little experience on which to base forecasts for planning purposes, and vital information may therefore be lacking. Costs will be incurred as the company finds its feet, for which there may be inadequate control systems at this stage.

Once full development gets under way and sales grow, over-trading can result, with debtors and stocks increasing rapidly as the negative cash flow builds up into a liquidity crisis. Research suggests that this is something that independent record labels have particularly suffered from (see Wilson, Stokes and Blackburn, 2001). In fast-moving industries, such as the music industry, the demand for new products can shift almost overnight. There is then the possible scenario of being forced out of business as a result of a previously unknown band obtaining a chart hit. The issue here is to ensure the good management of working capital. The costs of producing and marketing thousands of CDs may well have to be borne by the record company long before they receive the increased revenue from customers. The digital distribution of music can reduce production costs, but working with platforms such as Apple Music or Spotify inevitably involves the additional expense of working with labels, distributors and other artist aggregators.

If growth continues, and requires further funding through investment in equity it may be difficult to raise the required amount (as we have seen – particularly if less than £1 million), because venture capitalists shy away from these smaller investments.

Finally, the business matures and, although cash flow at this stage is positive, profitability levels off and return on investment may worsen. As maturity turns to decline, the business may be sold, or go into liquidation; new partners may buy into the business in an attempt to kick it back into growth. Overdraft facilities and other renewable finance may be withdrawn at this stage as confidence wanes. If the business is sold, taxation of any capital gain requires careful consideration by the vendor.

Is there any relief from this rather gloomy picture of a small firm staggering from one financial crisis to another? It would be easy to say that adequate forecasting and the appropriate control systems can minimize the problems. The reality is that small firms do experience financial stress at various moments in their history. It is also true, however, that these problems are often exacerbated by inadequate planning and control.

13.4.5 EUROPEAN COMPARISONS

Although the perspective taken in this chapter has so far focused primarily on the UK, many of the issues raised are common to small businesses across Europe and beyond (see European Commission, 2003). A number of the key themes include:

- Many SMEs have consistently considered access to finance to be a problem.
- The majority of SMEs still depend primarily on banks for their external funding, although this is changing.
- Across Europe, the cost of financing (interest rates and bank charges) tends to be higher for SMEs than for larger enterprises.
- Trade credit is a very important source of finance for SMEs, being more widespread than bank financing in some countries and sectors.
- Effective payment periods differ from country to country. In Italy, for example, it takes on average 87 days before payment is made, while Swedish firms collect their debts within an average of 34 days.
- There are considerable differences in the use of factoring or invoice discounting between countries. While 32 per cent of French enterprises use factoring, for example, this compares with only 2 per cent in Germany.
- Although more than 80 per cent of European SMEs do not make use of financial support measures (e.g. loan guarantee schemes), 14 per cent do not know about the existence of such financial support schemes in the first place.
- Across Europe, the most widespread suggestions for improving the availability of finance include reducing the taxation burden for businesses and investors, strengthening the equity base of firms and the promotion of loan guarantees (Commission of the European Communities, 2003; see also ec.europa.eu/growth/access -to-finance/index_en.htm).

Activity 5
A question of cash flow

It is often said that 'cash flow is king!' for small businesses. What is meant by this expression? List the main types of cash flow problem that small businesses encounter. How can these be avoided?

13.5 Managing finance

13.5.1 CASH FLOW, DEBTORS AND STOCKS

Financial control for small businesses starts with the management of cash flow. Cash is critical to survival, representing the lifeblood which enables all the activities of a firm to be undertaken.

It is easy for the fragile cash resources of a small business to become locked up in unproductive areas, such as debtors, work in progress and finished stocks. Any areas where funds can become trapped require effective management to minimize the extent of the lock-up.

13.5.2 DEBTORS' CONTROL

Debtors can hurt a small business in two major ways. First, they absorb cash and effectively increase the funding requirement of a small firm. Second, the longer a debt is alive, the greater the risk of a bad debt. Particularly in recessionary times, the risks of having invoices which go unpaid are high. The impact on a small firm can be disastrous, even causing the failure of the business in a domino effect as one firm falls after another.

These problems are not unique to small firms, but they can be accentuated by the smallness of an operating unit in any of the following ways:

- The costs of chasing slow payers or bad debts may be greater than the amount of money being pursued. This is a particular problem for companies with a large number of small customers.

  For example, a small mail order firm sold products priced under £50 on a 30-day trial basis as part of its marketing approach. It quickly generated over 1000 customers in this way, and found that considerable time and money had to be spent to control a sales ledger with this profile.

- The time taken to establish the creditworthiness of a potential customer may be longer than the sales process. Keenness to win an order, and not to jeopardize it by lengthy credit checks, may cause an owner-manager to accept imprudent credit risks.

  For example, the owner-manager of a small manufacturing firm was short of custom and losing money as production operatives and expensive equipment stood idle. A large order from a company not previously known to the owner-manager looked like their saviour: it returned the factory back to full capacity following a hasty negotiation. Unfortunately, the order increased the firm's cash problems, as the customer had liquidity difficulties of their own and proved to be an extremely reluctant payer.

  There is now a great deal that the small business can do to check up on prospective customers' credit. Credit reference agencies offer highly detailed payment and credit report services for relatively modest sums. Alternatively, references can be sought from the customer's bank.

- However, a small firm may not have the control systems to identify individual debtor problems before they become critical. An essential part of any management accounting system is an analysis of debtors by their age, as well as their amount, so that appropriate action can be triggered to chase up slow payers. This rigorous pursuit of payment, which gradually escalates the tone of requests from polite reminder to threat of legal action, is an unfortunate but essential element in small business management today. To be done effectively, accurate information on customers' indebtedness is required on a very regular basis.

  For example, a small business set up a debtor control system using a series of standard letters which were sent to customers once the age of their debt passed a certain number of days. These letters were triggered by information from the computerized accounting system, which produced an aged debtor analysis. The firm was not large enough to employ full-time accounting staff, and, therefore, used an external book-keeper who came in near the end of each month to process invoices and payments. Unfortunately, this system generated considerable confusion and aggravation, as the information on customer payments was invariably out of date. Customers became irritated by threatening letters after they had actually paid.

13.5.3 MANAGEMENT OF STOCK

Stock represents a poor investment for a small firm's financial resources. Stock surpluses earn no money, and risk deterioration if not used quickly. However, the consequences of running short of stock can be even more punitive; if orders go unfulfilled, or are even lost because of stock shortages, the effect on the cash flow can be disastrous. Stock management is therefore about balance, and the optimization of resources – weighing up the risk of running out versus the costs of playing it too safe. Stocks need controlling in three areas:

- *Raw material stocks* represent what a manufacturer needs to produce its own products and services.
- *Work in progress (WIP)* is stock which is currently being worked on, but is not yet saleable as finished items.
- *Finished stock* is ready for sale, but either awaiting shipment to a customer, or unsold.

Table 13.4 Liquid assets and current liabilities

	£000s	
	Current year	Prior year
Assets:		
Stock and work in progress	90	110
Debtors	220	270
Cash in bank	20	0
A. Total liquid assets	330	380
Liabilities:		
Trade suppliers	140	180
Other creditors (PAYE/VAT)	125	130
Overdraft	25	100
B. Total current liabilities	290	410
C. Total assets less liabilities (A–B)	40	–30

Keeping all these types of stock to an optimum level is a difficult balancing act, particularly in industries where demand is unpredictable and often short-lived. The fashion and toy industries, for example, are notorious for developing severe cash problems because of the difficulties of stock management. Fast-moving clothes can suddenly become virtually unsaleable as fashions change. Toy products still on the shelf after the Christmas rush may have to wait until the following Christmas season to be sold.

13.5.4 LIQUID ASSETS AND CURRENT LIABILITIES

A good measure of the health of a small firm's cash position comes from an estimate of its liquid assets and current liabilities: that is, such of its assets as can quickly be turned into cash, and liabilities which should be paid in the short term (12 months). Table 13.4 illustrates the items normally found in such an estimate. If a small business's current liabilities (B in Table 13.4) exceed the total of liquid assets (A in Table 13.4), then problems may be just around the corner unless corrective action is taken.

In the example above, the business was heading for a financial crisis as short-term liabilities exceeded liquid assets by £30 000 in the prior year. The owner-manager took remedial action by collecting money faster, thereby reducing debtors, and cutting back on stocks. This facilitated paying down some of the liabilities such as creditors and the overdraft, resulting in an improvement in the solvency of the business in the current year.

13.5.5 COSTS AND PRICING

Deciding prices by calculating costs and adding what is judged to be an adequate element of profit is probably the most common method in use by small firms. Marketing theorists frown upon this approach, as it does not always maximize the price that could be charged. Costs, they argue, should not be directly linked to prices, which should be determined by market forces; costs help to determine how well a business has done in terms of the profit generated by its pricing decisions, but this should be the extent of the relationship between the two. In practice, however, most small firms will use certain costs as an important element in their pricing decision. Pricing in small firms is more likely to be based on a compromise between an estimate of what the business needs to cover its costs and a view on what the customer expects and competitors are charging.

A common issue for small firms is to understand the costs they incur – not just their extent – but the different types:

- *Fixed costs* refer to business expenses which do not vary with the level of trading. They are the overheads of a small firm, such as rent, rates, insurance, heating, lighting and most salaries. A small manufacturer or retailer will have the same costs to pay for premises and full-time staff whether they have sales of £500 or £5000 per week. As all fixed costs have to be recovered eventually from sales, a crucial element in the pricing decision is the volume of sales that can be allocated to cover these overheads.

    If a small manufacturer or retailer has fixed overheads of £2000 per week, and sales estimates vary from 1000 to 5000 units per week, the allocation of fixed costs will range from £2 to 40p per unit.

- *Variable costs* are expenses which do change in direct proportion to the level of trading. They are the costs of raw materials for manufacturing, or the costs of stock that a retailer will sell, and are sometimes referred to as the cost of sales or cost of goods sold (COGS). Most small firms that use stock in significant quantity will have a clearer idea of what these costs are in terms of a mark-up or a gross margin (although the two terms are sometimes confused).

- *Mark-up* relates the selling price of an item to its variable costs. It takes the costs of the unit as the starting point, and represents how much is added to reach the selling price. It is often expressed as a percentage of the variable costs.

    If a retailer buys from a supplier for £20 + VAT and sells to the customer for £50 + VAT then the mark-up is £30, or 150 per cent (on top of the costs of £20). If the price is increased to £60 + VAT, the mark-up is £40 or 200 per cent.

    This can be expressed as:

$$\% \text{ mark-up} = \frac{\text{sales price} - \text{variable cost}}{\text{variable cost}} \times 100\%$$

Mark-ups are used particularly in the retail trade, where variable costs are usually a very significant but known factor in the price of an item. To ensure that its prices reflect up-to-date suppliers' prices, a small retailer may, for example, operate a standard minimum mark-up, which it simply adds on to suppliers' invoices as a first step in a pricing decision.

- *Gross margin* also relates the sales price of an item to the variable costs, representing the difference between the sales price and the variable costs. However, it takes the sales price as its starting point, and expresses how much of the sales price is left after deducting variable costs; it is often expressed as a percentage of the sales price.

    In our previous example, a small retailer selling an item for £50, which had been purchased for £20, would have a gross margin of £30, or 60 per cent of the sales price. If the sales price is increased to £60, the gross margin of £40 is 66 per cent, or two-thirds of the sales price.

    This can be expressed mathematically as:

$$\text{Gross margin} = \frac{\text{sales price} - \text{variable cost}}{\text{sales price}} \times 100\%$$

Gross margins are particularly useful where the variable costs of an item may be difficult to allocate precisely, but an average overall margin is targeted. For example, a small manufacturer or retailer, selling several products, budgets for a gross margin of 50 per cent. Each month, their management accounts report total sales and variable costs and, therefore, a gross margin. This will be an average of the margin of all products, which gives a first indication whether prices are in line with costs.

Figure 13.4 **Fixed and variable costs**

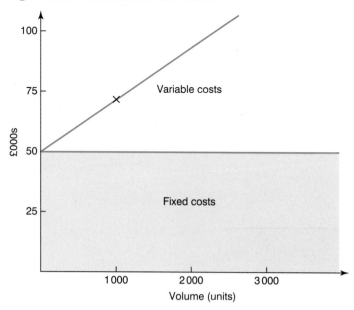

13.5.6 BREAK-EVEN ANALYSIS

A useful concept for the small firm which relates costs, prices and volumes is a **break-even** analysis.[9] This begins with an analysis of the fixed and variable costs, which can be illustrated graphically as in Figure 13.4.

In this example, the fixed costs of overheads and salaries are £50 000 per annum and variable costs are £25 per unit. If 1000 units are produced, the costs will be:

Fixed costs	£50 000
Variable costs (£25 × 1000)	£25 000
Total costs	£75 000
Therefore total costs per unit	£75

If 2000 units are produced, the costs will be:

Fixed costs	£50 000
Variable costs (£25 × 2000)	£50 000
Total costs	£100 000
Therefore total costs per unit	£50

Figure 13.5 Break even analysis

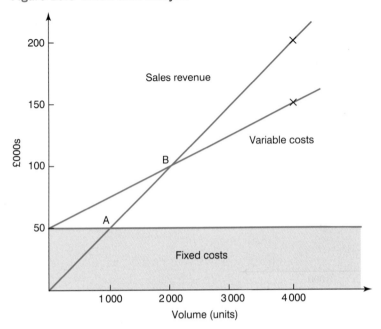

This information can be used in a number of ways:

1 A manufacturer, with the cost profile just described, looks at market prices and decides that £50 per unit is the maximum price obtainable.

A revenue line can now be added to the graph, as in Figure 13.5, to form a break-even analysis.

> A = Volume where fixed costs covered (1000 units)
> B = Break even volume (2000 units)
> X = Sales target for the product (£200 000 or 4000 units)
> XY = Profits (After deducting the fixed and variable costs, this equates to £50 000. After deducting only variable costs this is £100 000 or a 50 per cent gross margin)

This shows that, at a price of £50 per unit:

A break-even point can be calculated by using the following formula:

$$\text{Break-even volume} = \frac{\text{Fixed costs}}{\text{Gross margin per unit}}$$

$$\text{In our example, break-even} = \frac{£50\,000}{£25} = 2000 \text{ units}$$

2 Another small firm with the same cost profile is operating in a less competitive situation where there are no firm market prices. The firm believes it can make 2000 units per year and would like to make a profit of £50 000 on those sales. It can now plot what price to charge, as in Figure 13.6.

Figure 13.6 Price-setting analysis

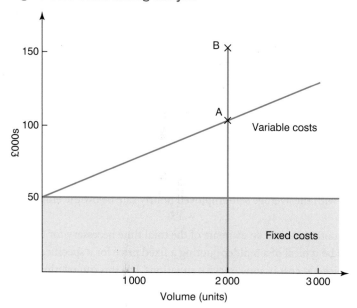

At 2000 units, A = total of fixed and variable costs (£100 000)
B = revenue needed to make £50 000 profit and therefore the price per unit (£75 per unit, or £150 000 divided by 2000 units).

3 A retailer is planning to open a new shop unit. As they buy their products from suppliers with known prices, they can predict a gross margin of 50 per cent on their current pricing policies. They also know that the fixed costs of the new shop in rent, wages, and so on will be £50 000 per annum. They have a break-even point of sales of £100 000 if they continue with their existing prices. If they believe this to be unlikely to be achieved, they have the choice of increasing their prices to achieve a better gross margin and therefore lower breakeven point, or of dropping the venture altogether.

13.5.7 CUSTOMIZED PRICING
Another variation of cost plus pricing is customized pricing. In this method, the customer effectively dictates the price, and the producer then works out what can be supplied for that price.

For example, a large supermarket chain is looking to buy a product which it will sell as an own-brand (i.e. under its own name). The end-user price has to be just lower than the brand leaders (say £2) and the supermarket has strict gross margin targets for this category of product (say, a minimum of 30 per cent). The supermarket buyer will be sourcing a product at a known price, therefore (no more than £1.40 in our example). A small firm wishing to bid for this business will attempt to tailor a product and a minimum order volume to match this price requirement.

13.5.8 TIME AND MATERIALS

Many small businesses are in a service sector business, where the key cost element will be the time spent on the job. These include domestic services such as plumbing, building and repair work, landscape gardening, tree felling and many more. Garages, freelance trainers, business consultants, solicitors and accountants also base their charges on time spent, plus any additional expenses incurred. The problems for a small firm in calculating time and materials include:

- *Hourly rate:* surprise is sometimes expressed by customers at the hourly rate charged by a service organization. Plumbers and mechanics charging £50 per hour, and partners in accountants and solicitors charging themselves at £350 per hour, all cause eyebrows to be raised. In fact, small firms often undercharge for their services, forgetting the hours of travelling, selling, administration or preparation that they will need to spend, which are unpaid and bring down their average hourly rate. Evidence that small firms under-price their labour has already been quoted, with the average self-employed hourly rate below the employed national average.
- *Time:* where a fixed price is required for a quotation, then an estimate of the total time necessary for the job becomes a key pricing decision. This would be typical of a builder quoting a fixed price for a specified job.
- *Materials:* materials are expected to be invoiced at cost in most service situations, but this can overlook some of the hidden costs in obtaining the materials, such as the time taken to source and buy the materials and the travelling costs involved in picking them up. To overcome this, materials are often charged at a full retail price, although discounts or wholesale prices were obtained.

13.5.9 DISCOUNTING

Discounts are a pricing mechanism commonly used by small firms. The use of discounts includes selling off old or damaged stock, rewarding customer loyalty, launching a new product or service and matching a competitor's price. These are often valid reasons for giving a discount which are to the benefit of the business. However, discounts, special offers and sales to help improve demand and cash flow are also misused by small firms, who overlook the real increase in volume that is required to make up for discounted prices.

For example, a retailer, averaging a 50 per cent gross margin on sales, offers a 20 per cent discount off all stock for a limited period. Sales volume jumps by 50 per cent from the normal level of 10 000 units for the month to 15 000 units; but the owner-manager would be mistaken to believe this has been a successful promotion, as the following calculation reveals:

	Normal trading	Special offer	Offer break-even
Sales units	10 000	15 000	16 666
Average price per unit	£1	80p	80p
Total sales	£10 000	£12 000	£13 333
Cost per unit	50p	50p	50p
Total cost	£5 000	£7 500	£8 333
Gross margin	£5 000	£4 500	£5 000

Although sales volume has increased considerably and sales revenue is also up by 20 per cent, the effect of the discount more than takes away this advantage, and less gross margin is made during the period. In fact, for the offer to break even at the gross margin, sales volume would need to increase by 66.6 per cent, or two-thirds up on normal trading. If small retailers calculated the real increase in volume they needed to recover the discounts they gave, then there would almost certainly be a drop in the number of 'Special Sales' that we see in our high streets today.

The corollary of this is that price increases can support relatively higher drops in sales volume before they have a negative effect on the gross margin. A small firm operating on a 40 per cent gross margin can support a 20 per cent loss of volume for a 10 per cent increase in prices before its realized gross margin is affected. It is more profitable to sell fewer items at a higher price.

13.6 Case studies and activities: Part 1

Case study
Calculating cash and profits: Part 1

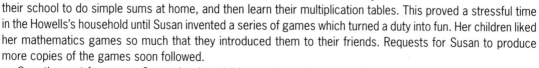

IT ALL ADDS UP FOR SUSAN

Susan Howells had found that mathematics homework in her household was a traumatic experience. It started when her children were asked by their school to do simple sums at home, and then learn their multiplication tables. This proved a stressful time in the Howells's household until Susan invented a series of games which turned a duty into fun. Her children liked her mathematics games so much that they introduced them to their friends. Requests for Susan to produce more copies of the games soon followed.

Over the next few years, Susan developed this experience into a small business. Working from home as a sole trader, she built up a respectable turnover in her children's activity games, based on making mathematics more fun. Towards the end of the third year, she decided it was time to set up her business on a more permanent basis in separate premises. Her family certainly agreed; they would be pleased to have their kitchen and living room back for their own use when the piles of Susan's products and literature left.

Susan explained her plans to her accountant. 'I want to set up from 1 January next year as a limited company, using Kal Kulate Ltd as my brand name. I have found some new premises for a small workshop and storage facilities, where I can employ the staff I need. But I will have to buy some new equipment. We need to become more organized and efficient in our production, which means buying more benches, tools and the like. I have had a preliminary talk with my bank manager, who was encouraging, but said I had to produce a cash flow forecast in order to apply for a larger overdraft. Unfortunately, I've no idea where to start, although he did give me some leaflets, with outline headings for a forecast. Can you help?'

'Yes, of course', replied the accountant, 'but you will have to do quite a lot of work to provide the information. A cash flow forecast is quite simple really. It tries to estimate how much cash will be coming into and going out of your business each month. From this we can judge what you can afford to invest in new equipment, and to risk in new overheads such as your premises.'

'Well, I've done a rough calculation of my profit for the year, and it looks as though I can more or less break even after paying myself some sort of salary. But that's not the same as a cash flow forecast is it?'

(Continued)

'No, it's different', replied the accountant, 'although one can be derived from the other. In fact it's usually easier to do forecasts of profit and cash at the same time. They use a lot of common information. The crucial difference is that a profit forecast looks at the difference between your sales and your costs at the moment those sales are made, or those costs incurred. It calculates a profit, or loss, based on invoices as they are sent, or received, not on when they are paid. The cash flow is only concerned with cash when sales and purchases are actually paid for.'

'Right, I think I see what you're getting at', replied Susan, 'but I'm sure it will be even clearer when we have the figures in front of us. Exactly what information do you need?'

'Here is a list of the headings we're looking at. I think you should spend a few days working on this information, and then we can talk about it again.'

A week later, Susan returned to see the accountant, and brought the information he had asked for with her.

'This is a very good start', replied the accountant, 'we should be able to produce a profit and loss, and cash flow forecast and balance sheet from this information. How are you going to finance your capital purchases of £21 150 by the way?' 'Well if I pay cash there are some real bargains at the moment', replied Susan, 'so I thought I would use an overdraft at the bank.'

Kal Kulate Ltd: profit and loss/cash flow input information

1   Sales forecast. Total net sales for year: £211 500

£s	Jan	Feb	March	April	May	June
	19 000	13 000	14 000	20 500	15 500	20 000

	July	Aug	Sep	Oct	Nov	Dec
	15 500	17 500	17 000	18 000	21 000	20 500

2   *Materials used:* raw materials purchased are estimated to represent 50 per cent of the net sales value sold in the month.

3   *Production wages:* wages of production operatives will be £3000 per month in total, including employer's NIC.

4   *Overheads:* overheads are estimated as follows:
   - Salaries of directors and administrative staff £2000 per month in total
   - Rent £12 000 per annum
   - Rates and insurances £500 per month
   - Publicity £500 per month
   - Other costs £1000 per month

5   *Bank interest:* it is assumed there will be an overdraft of £15 000 at 10 per cent per annum interest, plus bank charges of £1000 per annum.

6   *Depreciation:* depreciation will be based on fixed assets of £18 000 net costs depreciated over three years, or £6000 per annum.

7   *Receipts:* sales will be invoiced with VAT at 17.5 per cent and paid for in 60 days, or during the second month after invoice date (January invoices paid in March, etc.).

8   *Payment of overheads:* purchases will be paid for on the following basis:
   - Materials used, publicity and other costs 60 days from date of use, or during the second month after receipt of invoice. These costs will all be subject to VAT at 17.5 per cent.

- Rent will be paid quarterly (March, June, Oct and Dec).
- Rates and insurances will be paid monthly by standing order.

9 *VAT:* will also be added to some purchases when they are paid for. For the purposes of this exercise VAT is taken to be 17.5 per cent. (Historically, the standard rate of VAT in the UK has ranged between 8 per cent in 1974 and 20 per cent from 2011).

10 *VAT due:* Kal Kulate Ltd will be registered for VAT from 1 January and will need to submit VAT returns for each quarter, and pay any VAT due during the month following the quarter end. (The first quarter will be January to March with payments due in April.)

11 *Capital:* Capital assets which total £18 000 plus £3150 VAT will be paid for in January.

12 *Opening position:* Kal Kulate's opening cash balance will be nil, as it is not intended to bring any cash forward into the new limited company. Shares will be purchased for £5000 in December, which will be used to pay for any initial costs, such as prepayment of rent and legal charges.

   However, debtors and creditors will be brought forward as follows:

Debtors:	Nov sales £20 000 + VAT
	Dec sales £20 000 + VAT
Creditors:	Nov and Dec purchases at 50 per cent of the above sales + VAT
	Nov and Dec publicity and other costs at the monthly rate of £1500 + VAT.
Prepayments:	Rent will be paid for in advance, with the first quarter paid for in December, prior to incorporation.

13 *Stocks:* This will equate to one month's sales, i.e. the materials needed for one month's sales (50 per cent of the relevant month's sales value).

Activities: Financial forecasts

(a) Can you prepare the profit and loss and cash flow for Kal Kulate Ltd from this information?

(b) Looking at the profit and loss account, and the cash flow forecast, why is there only a small profit for the year, yet a larger positive cash flow?

(c) Using the cash flow forecast, make some recommendations for Susan's borrowing strategy. Is she right to want an overdraft to finance her new equipment?

(d) Can you produce a projected balance sheet for the end of the first year (December) from this information?

Kal Kulate's cash flow and profit and loss account are shown below. (It is obviously beneficial for you to attempt it on your own first.)

13.7 Financial analysis

13.7.1 MANAGEMENT ACCOUNTS AND FORECASTING

Small businesses differ greatly in their approach to the provision of accounting information, and the use of forecasts and budgets for planning and control of the business. Some studies suggest that there is a considerable gulf between small entrepreneurial companies aiming for high growth and firms which have no great ambitions to grow other than that required to survive (DTI, 1995). While there are fewer differences between the provision of historical accounting information, it is generally the case that entrepreneurial small firms make much greater use of forecasted financial information than more passive firms. This illustrates the greater perceived need for forecasting during times of change, than during periods of relatively stable sales.

The three most widely used financial summaries are the **profit and loss account**, the **cash flow** and the **balance sheet**. These terms are also known, respectively, as the income statement, statement of cash flow and statement of financial position.

- *The profit and loss account* shows how a business is doing in terms of sales and costs – and the difference between them of profit or losses. It is a moving picture and can be used to forecast and monitor results on a monthly basis, or for a longer period.
- *The cash flow* is perhaps the most important summary for a young firm, as it indicates the movement of cash into and out of the business. Similar to the profit and loss account, it differs in the important respect of reflecting credit given to customers and received from suppliers, as well as the amount of money invested in a business, or borrowed by it. Due to their importance, cash flows are used on a regular weekly or monthly basis.
- *The balance sheet* is a snapshot, rather than a moving picture, as it represents a summary of what money has been spent by a business, and what it has been spent on. It is usually an annual summary of the use and sources of funds in a company.

13.7.2 THE 21 STEPS TO PROFIT AND LOSS, CASH FLOW AND BALANCE SHEET FORECASTS

Although they are different forms of financial analysis, a series of steps can be used to build up a set of forecasts of profit and loss, cash flow and the balance sheet. This can be done manually, but a computer spreadsheet is a highly useful tool, as it allows for regular modifications and sensitivity analysis (e.g. to project the effect of a drop in sales or a rise in costs).

The following 21 steps are explained with a worked example of Kal Kulate Ltd, the company in the case study above.

Note: each step (on the following pages) can be related to the profit and loss, cash flow and balance sheets of Kal Kulate Ltd at the end of this section.

13.7.3 PROFIT AND LOSS

Step 1

Estimate *likely sales turnover* for the forecast period, based on historical precedent and research in the marketplace. Also work out any output VAT element on those sales (for the purposes of this exercise, VAT is taken to be 17.5 per cent. Historically, the standard rate of VAT in the UK has ranged between 8 per cent in 1974 and 20 per cent from 2011, with some goods being lower or zero – e.g. domestic fuel and power, children's car seats, contraceptives, smoking cessation products).

Step 2

Work out what *materials* will be used to make the goods needed to achieve the sales estimated in Step 1. This can only be accurately calculated by taking the opening stock, adding all the purchases in the period, and deducting the closing stock (see Step 14). Although this is done on a regular basis to verify actual profits, forecasts usually assume a percentage usage based on historical data.

Example: Kal Kulate Ltd – Step 1

Month	Net sales £	Output VAT £	Gross sale £
1	19 000	3 325	22 325
2	13 000	2 275	15 275
3	14 000	2 450	16 450
4	20 500	3 588	24 088
5	15 500	2 713	18 213
6	20 000	3 500	23 500
7	15 500	2 713	18 213
8	17 500	3 063	20 563
9	17 000	2 975	19 975
10	18 000	3 150	21 150
11	21 000	3 675	24 675
12	20 500	3 588	24 088
TOTAL	**211 500**	**37 015**	**248 515**

Example: Kal Kulate Ltd – Step 2

For example, Kal Kulate had an established pattern of materials costing 50 per cent of the net sales value. So sales of £19 000 in January would require £9500 (50 per cent) worth of materials to make them.

Step 3

Work out the *wages* and other employment costs of those involved directly in production.

This should include gross wages, plus employer s national insurance.

Example: Kal Kulate Ltd – Step 3

Kal Kulate employed three full-time and two part-time operatives who, together, were estimated to cost as follows:

	£
Gross wages	33 000
Employer's national insurance	3 000
Total (12 months)	36 000
Total (1 month)	3 000

Step 4

Workout the *overheads* of running the business. These will normally be the fixed costs and include:

- the salaries of directors and non-production staff;
- rent, rates, insurance and other premises costs;
- telephone, postage, printing, stationery, accounting and other office costs;
- advertising, exhibitions, selling, commissions and other publicity costs.

Example: Kal Kulate Ltd – Step 4

Kal Kulate grouped their fixed costs as follows:

	£
Salaries of director and office manager	24 000
Rent	12 000
Rates and insurance	6 000
Other costs including energy, stationery, postage, accounting and sundry costs	12 000
Publicity costs including advertising and exhibitions	6 000
Total (12 months)	60 000
Total (1 month)	5 000

(Salaries, rent, rates and insurance do not attract VAT for cash flow purposes.)

Note: some of these costs will attract VAT which needs to be added to the cash flow, but excluded in the profit and loss account.

For ease of calculation later on, it is wise to group costs where possible into those which do, and those which do not, attract VAT.

It is also easier to identify significant costs at this stage which may be on a different payments cycle to other costs, as this will make transference of those items to the cash flow simpler. (For example rent, which has no VAT, and which is often paid quarterly, can be identified separately from other premises costs, some of which include VAT, and are paid on a monthly basis.)

Step 5

Calculate interest on borrowings and other bank charges.

Interest and bank charges will clearly vary with borrowing levels, usage of the bank account and national interest rates, which will not be known at this stage. An estimate based on the likely average level of borrowing and known interest rates can be made, which should be kept pessimistic as change in this area can be swift.

Example: Kal Kulate Ltd – Step 5

Kal Kulate's overdraft was thought to average up to £15 000 with 10 per cent per annum interest, so that the following allowance was made:

	£
Interest	1500
Bank charges	1500
Total (12 months)	3000
Total (1 month)	250

Step 6

Depreciation is calculated by taking the expected life of the fixed assets of the business and writing them off progressively over that period, by making a charge to the profit and loss account.

Example: Kal Kulate Ltd – Step 6

Depreciation was based on new assets of £18 000 (plus VAT at 17.5 per cent of £3150). These were depreciated over three years, giving an annual depreciation charge of £6000, or £500 per month.

13.7.4 CASH FLOW
Step 7

Work out how quickly sales will be turned into cash; that is, when debtors are going to pay their invoices. Receipts from customers include any VAT which has been invoiced to them.

Example: Kal Kulate Ltd – Step 7

Kal Kulate's customers were invoiced on 30 days' credit. In practice, most took longer than this, and 60 days were allowed for payment in the cash flow. In other words, it was assumed that January's gross sales would be paid for in March, February's in April and so on. The receipts at the beginning of the year in January and February were November's and December's sales of the previous year, which were both £20 000 + VAT (£23 500).

Step 8

Work out when overhead costs and interest will actually have to be paid for. Some costs are paid for in the same month; for example, salaries and wages. Others are paid on a regular credit basis; for example, materials used and other overhead costs. Some important overheads are paid quarterly; for example, rent.

Example: Kal Kulate Ltd – Step 8

The pattern of Kal Kulate's payments was as follows:

- Materials purchased, publicity and other costs – 60 days
- Salaries and wages – same month
- Rent – quarterly (March, June, October, December)
- Rates and insurance – same month by monthly standing order
- Interest and bank charges – quarterly (March, June, October, December)

For example:

In January and February, purchases of materials used in November and December of the previous year are paid for. In March, purchases of materials used in January are paid for and so on.

Publicity and other costs are ongoing costs, estimated to be the same each month. In January, the costs incurred in November of the previous year are paid for; in February, the costs from December are paid for and so on.

Step 9

Work out the VAT paid on invoices for overhead costs. Some purchases attract VAT, which has to be added to the amount when it is paid. Although salaries, wages, rent, rates and insurance do not attract VAT, most other costs do.

Example: Kal Kulate Ltd – Step 9

Kal Kulate paid VAT on their purchases of materials and on their publicity and other costs. VAT paid on these purchases was therefore worked out at 17.5 per cent and included as a separate item.

For example, in January £10 000 of materials and £1500 of publicity and other costs were paid for. As the invoices would have had VAT added, the payments must include this amount (£11 500 × 17.5% = £2013).

(It can be added to the individual amounts, or, as in Kal Kulate's cash flow, noted as a separate line.)

Step 10

Work out how much VAT is due to be paid to HM Customs and Excise on the quarterly returns. This is calculated by totalling the *output* VAT added to sales invoiced in the quarter and totalling all the *input VAT* added to purchases invoiced to you in the same quarter. The difference between the total output VAT and the input VAT is paid to the government in the month following the end of the quarter.

Example: Kal Kulate Ltd – Step 10

Kal Kulate's VAT calculation looked like this:

	Jan/March	April/June	July/Sept	Oct/Dec
VAT outputs	8050	9801	8751	10 413
VAT inputs:				
Materials used	4025	4900	4375	5206
Publicity and other costs	788	788	788	788
Capital equipment (VAT element)	3150			
Total inputs	7963	5688	5163	5994
VAT due	87	4113	3588	4419
	(Due April)	(Due July)	(Due Oct)	(Due Jan of following year)

Output VAT represents the VAT element on the sales invoiced in the period. (For example, see Step 1 VAT: January = £3325, February = £2275, March = £2450, so the total for January–March = £8050.)

Input VAT represents 17.5 per cent on the costs of materials, publicity and other costs, on receipt of invoices, not when they are paid. (For example, see Step 2: materials used in January = £9500, February = £6500, March = £7000. Total for the period January–March = £23 000 × 17.5% VAT = £4025.)

VAT due represents the difference between output and input VAT. It is payable one month after the quarter's end, which in Kal Kulate's case was April, July, October and January (the following year).

(No VAT was payable in January of this year, as Kal Kulate only registered for VAT at this time.)

Step 11

Add in any capital purchases, including VAT, which are to be paid. If they are to be financed by hire purchase, then put the deposit and the repayments in the cash flow.

Example: Kal Kulate Ltd – Step 11

Kal Kulate, using its working capital, purchased £18 000 plus £3150 VAT worth of equipment, so this appears as a lump sum of £21 150 in the month of January.

Step 12

Calculate the monthly cash flow by subtracting total payments from total receipts for the month.

Then, work out an opening and closing balance for each month which represents the cumulative cash position of the business.

Example: Kal Kulate Ltd – Step 12

Kal Kulate starts with a clean sheet as it is a new limited company formed from the ongoing trading of a sole trader. The opening balance is nil, as no cash is transferred but, during the first month (January), receipts from debtors total £23 500. The total of payments out, including £21 150 on capital equipment, is £40 163. So, the cash flow for the month is negative (£16 663). The closing balance of January is the opening balance for February. There is a positive cash flow of £4487 during the month of February, so that February's closing balance is £12 176 (£16 663 – £4487 = £12 176). This negative position is effectively Kal Kulate's overdraft at the bank.

13.7.5 THE BALANCE SHEET END OF YEAR

Step 13

Work out the end of year value of fixed assets by taking away the depreciation charge from the total fixed asset costs.

Example: Kal Kulate Ltd – Step 13

	£
Fixed assets costs, excluding VAT	18 000
Depreciation during year	6 000
Net balance sheet value	12 000

Step 14

Stocks are entered into the balance sheet at cost, less any provisions for damaged, or slow moving and obsolete stock.

Example: Kal Kulate Ltd – Step 14

Kal Kulate valued their stocks at the beginning and end of the year to verify not only the closing value of stocks, but also the materials used during the year (in Step 2). The company's policy was to hold approximately one month's usage of stocks, and the forecast position was as follows:

Opening stock (Jan)	Purchases	Closing stock (Dec)	Materials used
£10 000	£106 000	£10 250	£105 750

Step 15

Estimate the total amount, including VAT, owed by customers at the end of the period. These debtors should be reduced by any debts where there is a good chance they will not be paid.

Example: Kal Kulate Ltd – Step 15

Kal Kulate assumed they would have two months, of debtors at the year end; that is, sales for November and December would not be paid, so that debtors would be:

	£
November sales	24 675
December sales	24 088
Total	48 763

Step 16

Estimate the total amount owing to trade suppliers, including VAT. This liability is entered as trade creditors.

> ### Example: Kal Kulate Ltd – Step 16
>
> Kal Kulate assumed they would pay for materials purchased two months after purchase; that is, at the end of December, they would owe for materials used in November and December + VAT, so that trade creditors would be:
>
> | | £ |
> |---|---|
> | November | 9 000 + VAT |
> | December | 8 500 + VAT |
> | Total | 17 500 + VAT = £20 562 |

Step 17

Estimate how much money is owed to other creditors for other supplies; for example, telephone, electricity, office supplies. Also include any tax collected but not yet paid; for example, VAT, PAYE and NIC.

> ### Example: Kal Kulate Ltd – Step 17
>
> At the end of December, Kal Kulate estimated they would still owe for November and December purchases and for the October/December VAT quarter.
>
> | | | £ | £ |
> |---|---|---|---|
> | Other costs: | November | 1500 + VAT | |
> | | December | 1500 + VAT | |
> | | | 3000 + VAT | = 3525 |
> | VAT October–December (see Step 10) | | = | 4419 |
> | Total | | | 7944 |

Step 18

Estimate any borrowings from banks and other sources, such as overdrafts or loans. For an overdraft, this should be the figure shown as the cash flow projection.

> ### Example: Kal Kulate Ltd – Step 18
>
> Kal Kulate's cash flow showed a negative cash position of £7714 at the end of December which effectively represented their overdraft.

Step 19

Calculate net current assets of the business by deducting current liabilities from current assets.

Current assets (Step 14 + Step 15) represent the assets of a business which can be realized in the short term, normally within 12 months.

Current liabilities (Step 16 + Step 17 + Step 18) represent what the business owes, and can be made to pay for in the short term, normally the amounts due within 12 months.

Example: Kal Kulate Ltd – Step 19

Kal Kulate's current assets of £59 013 (stock of £10 250 and debtors of £48 763), less their current liabilities of £36 220 (trade creditors of £20 562, other creditors of £7944, and a bank overdraft of £7714) gave net current assets of £22 793.

Step 20

Calculate net assets by adding fixed assets to net current assets. This represents one measure of the worth of a business.

Example: Kal Kulate Ltd – Step 20

Kal Kulate's fixed assets totalled £12 000 (£18 000 less £6000 depreciation) which, when added to the net current assets (£22 793), gave a net position of £34 793.

Step 21

Add in share capital – the amount paid for the shares of the company. Add in reserves of profits (or losses) retained in the company. (This figure should balance with the net assets when added to the share capital.)

Together, these make up the capital and reserves of the company, which represents what would theoretically be left to distribute to shareholders should the company be wound up at the balance-sheet date (it is therefore sometimes referred to as Shareholders' Funds).

Example: Kal Kulate Ltd – Step 21

Kal Kulate was set up with £5000 capital subscribed for shares. This does not appear in the cash flow forecast, as it was put into the company before the beginning of the forecast period.

The reserves carried forward represent this year's profit, plus profits retained in the business since it was started. In this forecast balance sheet, it is a balancing figure which, when added to share capital, equals the total net assets of £34 793.

Example: Kal Kulate Ltd: Forecast balance sheet

	Step no		£	£
FIXED ASSETS		Cost	18 000	
		Depreciation	−6 000	
	13	Book value		12 000
CURRENT ASSETS	14	Stocks	10 250	
	15	Debtors	48 763	
			59 013	
CURRENT LIABILITIES	16	Trade creditors	20 562	
	17	Other creditors	7 944	
	18	Bank overdraft	7 714	
			36 220	
NET CURRENT ASSETS	19			22 793
NET ASSETS	20			34 793
CAPITAL AND RESERVES	21	Share capital	5 000	
	21	Reserves	29 793	34 793
	21			

Kal Kulate Ltd: Profit and loss budget vs actual

12 months	Budget	Actual
Sales (net)	211 500	274 950
Materials used	105 750	154 970
Production wages	36 000	44 990
Gross profit	69 750	74 990
Overheads:		
Salaries	24 000	26 100
Rent	12 000	12 000
Rates and insurance	6 000	5 800
Other costs	12 000	12 850
Publicity	6 000	7 770
Total overheads	60 000	64 520
Interest and bank charges	3 000	3 790
Depreciation	6 000	6 000
Profit before tax	750	680

Kal Kulate Ltd: Debtors report summary (December)

	£
Current month	30 110
One month	30 840
Two months	13 219
Three months	4 990
Over three months	1 105
Total	80 264

(Continued)

Example: Kal Kulate Ltd: Profit and loss and cash flow forecast

Step no.	Jan	Feb	March	April	May	June
PROFIT AND LOSS						
1 SALES:						
1 Gross	22 325	15 275	16 450	24 088	18 213	23 500
1 VAT	3 325	2 275	2 450	3 588	2 713	3 500
1 Net	19 000	13 000	14 000	20 500	15 500	20 000
2 MATERIALS USED: (50%)	9 500	6 500	7 000	10 250	7 750	10 000
3 Production wages	3 000	3 000	3 000	3 000	3 000	3 000
Gross profit	6 500	3 500	4 000	7 250	4 750	7 000
4 OVERHEADS:						
4 Salaries	2 000	2 000	2 000	2 000	2 000	2 000
4 Rent	1 000	1 000	1 000	1 000	1 000	1 000
4 Rates and insurance	500	500	500	500	500	500
4 Other costs	1 000	1 000	1 000	1 000	1 000	1 000
4 Publicity	500	500	500	500	500	500
TOTAL OVERHEADS	5 000	5 000	5 000	5 000	5 000	5 000
5 Bank charges and interest	250	250	250	250	250	250
6 Depreciation	500	500	500	500	500	500
PROFIT/LOSS	750	−2 250	−1 750	1 500	−10 001	1 250
7 CASH FLOW RECEIPTS[A]	23 500	23 500	22 325	15 275	16 450	24 088
8 PAYMENTS:						
8 Purchase of materials	10 000	10 000	9 500	6 500	7 000	10 250
8 Salaries and wages	5 000	5 000	5 000	5 000	5 000	5 000
8 Rent	—	3 000	—	—	—	3 000
8 Rates and insurance	500	500	500	500	500	500
8 Publicity and other costs	1 500	1 500	1 500	1 500	1 500	1 500
8 Interest	—	—	750	—	750	—
9 VAT PAID	2 013	2 013	1 925	1 400	1 488	2 056
10 VAT DUE	—	—	—	87	—	—
11 CAPITAL	21 150					
TOTAL PAYMENTS[B]	40 163	19 013	22 175	14 987	15 488	23 056
12 CASH FLOW[(A−B)]	−16 663	4 487	150	288	962	1 032
12 OPENING BALANCE	—	−16 663	−12 176	−12 026	−11 738	−10 766
12 CLOSING BALANCE	−16 663	−12 176	−12 026	−11 738	−10 776	−9 744

Example: Kal Kulate Ltd: Profit and loss and cash flow forecast

July	Aug	Sept	Oct	Nov	Dec	TOTAL (12 months)
18 213	20 563	19 975	21 150	24 675	24 088	248 515
2 713	3 063	2 975	3 150	3 675	3 588	37 015
15 500	17 500	17 000	18 000	21 000	20 500	211 500
7 750	8 750	8 500	9 000	10 500	10 250	105 750
3 000	3 000	3 000	3 000	3 000	3 000	36 000
4 750	5 750	5 500	6 000	7 500	7 250	69 750
2 000	2 000	2 000	2 000	2 000	2 000	24 000
1 000	1 000	1 000	1 000	1 000	1 000	12 000
500	500	500	500	500	500	6 000
1 000	1 000	1 000	1 000	1 000	1 000	12 000
500	500	500	500	500	500	6 000
5 000	5 000	5 000	5 000	5 000	5 000	60 000
250	250	250	250	250	250	3 000
500	500	500	500	500	500	6 000
−1 000	—	−250	250	1 750	1 500	750
18 213	23 500	18 213	20 563	19 975	21 150	
7 750	10 000	7 750	8 750	8 500	9 000	
5 000	5 000	5 000	5 000	5 000	5 000	
—	3 000	—	—	—	3 000	
500	500	500	500	500	500	
1 500	1 500	1 500	1 500	1 500	1 500	
—	—	750	—	—	750	
1 619	2 013	1 619	1 794	1 750	1 838	
4 113	—	—	3 588	—	—	
20 482	19 013	20 119	21 132	17 250	21 588	
−2 269	4 487	−1 906	−569	2 725	−438	
−9 744	12 013	7 526	−9 432	−10 001	−7 276	
−12 013	−7 526	−9 432	−10 001	−7 276	−7 714	

13.8 Summary and activities (Part 2)

This chapter has explored three main aspects of finance for small businesses and entrepreneurs: (i) the sources of finance and needs of small businesses; (ii) the particular financial problems that small businesses can expect to face through the process of start-up and early growth and development; and (iii) the financial management tools available to a small business owner including break-even analysis, the profit and loss account, cash flow and balance sheet.

It is often believed that raising money is the hardest part of setting up a new business. It is true that it can be difficult to access external sources of finance (either debt or equity) without some personal assets that can be invested in the venture itself, or act as collateral. However, research presented in this chapter indicates that the principal barrier to new business development is probably more to do with individuals' attitudes to risk and their level of investment readiness (i.e. whether they have a well-prepared business plan indicating a clear understanding of all aspects of the prospective business). There is general agreement, however, that there are particular challenges in obtaining relatively small sums of risk capital (or private equity) which can be invested in the high-growth businesses of the future. Overcoming the equity gap is seen as a significant policy and industry-level goal. A range of public sector-driven initiatives has been developed to help meet this goal.

When it comes to managing finance successfully, the chapter highlights the importance of overseeing carefully all aspects of cash flow. Assessing break even and the time necessary for cash flow to turn positive are key indicators for the nascent entrepreneur. Negotiating deals with investors will necessarily turn on these critical aspects. The chapter presents advice on cash flow management and presents some guidance on how to compile a cash flow forecast alongside other necessary financial reports. Finally, it is suggested that good financial management requires a balance of strategic and tactical-level planning and control. While seeking advice from professional advisors can be very beneficial, it is incumbent upon the small business founder or entrepreneur to understand the financial model of their business as well, if not better, than anyone else.

Case study
Calculating cash and profits: Part 2

SUSAN MISCALCULATES

It had been a hectic year for Susan Howells. She had completed her first trading year as Kal Kulate Ltd and felt really proud of her achievements. She had exceeded her sales targets by 30 per cent in the year and had considerably increased her customer base.

She was therefore very disappointed when her accountant painted a very different picture. He showed her some preliminary accounts showing actual performance against the budget which they had put together at the beginning of the year.

'I can't believe it', said Susan, looking at the figures he showed her (refer back to Kal Kulate Ltd: Profit and loss budget vs actual).

'I've sold far more than I thought possible but made less money. What's gone wrong?'

'Before I answer that', said the accountant, 'perhaps we had better have the rest of the bad news. Your debtors have grown considerably in the last year. This aged analysis gives you the breakdown.' The accountant handed Susan the debtors report.

'I know the problem', sighed Susan, 'it's partly the big customers who never seem to pay on time, and partly the smaller ones who never seem to pay at all. Our small customers are a particular problem as some of them are very old debts now, and I'm worried they may even go out of business.'

'Yes, there is certainly that concern', said the accountant, 'and also your cash. You are very near your overdraft limit now. Apart from the interest costs, the bank will be getting nervous unless you can reduce your borrowing.'

'I have been trying to collect the money', said Susan, 'but some of these debts are such small amounts. I wonder if it's worth the cost of writing them letters and telephoning. I know they all add up to a lot of money, but each one individually is quite small.'

Activities: Understanding the accounts

(a) Why is Kal Kulate making less than budgeted profits when its sales are 30 per cent up? How can it improve profitability?

(b) The debtor issue is a common one for small firms who do not have the resources to pursue a large number of customers for payment. What steps could Susan consider to improve her cash flow?

Case study
Boogles adds up

Lisa Newton started Boogles Ltd at the age of 23, in the month she finished her Master's degree in investment management, with just £150. Never having had a full-time job in her life, Lisa's transition from full-time education to full-time entrepreneur was perhaps made slightly easier as she was (in her own words) 'still in student mode'. With so little start-up capital, there were no flashy offices, only a back bedroom and a kitchen table. Some businesses (including online businesses) are easier to start this way: Michael Dell began his computer company in his university dorm, Henry Ford started in a garage, and Facebook launched from a college campus. So, Boogles are in good company, although it was natural for them to keep a keen eye on the figures – they are bookkeepers who keep the accounts for other companies.

Lisa has stuck to being frugal and budgeting carefully. She decided that the clients' premises were the best place to carry out the work, as it reduced the outlay on premises costs. This was important, as they initially operated in Nottingham and London, where rents are not cheap.

The £150 was made up of £100 of Lisa's personal overdraft and a £50 investment from her mum. It takes personal sacrifice to begin a business in this way, but Lisa saw this as part of the challenge of entrepreneurship:

'I did not really miss having a regular pay cheque as I had never worked full time before. You don't need money to start a business. You just need passion and an idea, and other people will be drawn to help you on your mission. Entrepreneurial finance is different in that often the first people an entrepreneur will seek funds from are friends and family. They often raid their own resources before approaching the bank, and on the whole, women tend to be more cautious than men.'

The banks were not keen to take a risk with Boogles until it had proved itself. With a young entrepreneur at the helm who had no track record of even working in a full-time job, they were very restrictive. Lisa used credit cards, constantly transferring the balances to get those offering nought per cent interest rates. Initially, she did this in her own name but, as the business established a track record, banks became more willing to lend

(Continued)

finance to the company, although a director's guarantee always had to be signed. The first bank account was with the Bank of Scotland, but they would not give Boogles an overdraft, only a £500 credit limit on a credit card. After three years of struggling, Lisa switched to HSBC where she had had a personal account since her student days. HSBC immediately approved a loan of £10 000, an overdraft facility of £8500 and a credit card limit of £1500.

With so little start-up finance, Boogles experienced severe growing pains. In the first five years, turnover doubled year on year, and each time they had to find the money through careful juggling to pay the new staff as they came on board. Initially, Boogles would invoice clients monthly on 28-day payment terms and pay staff weekly. As the business grew, this become less and less feasible, so Lisa switched it around. Staff are now paid monthly, and clients are invoiced fortnightly on 7-day payment terms (extended to 14 days if they pay by direct debit). Expenses were paid by credit card, fully utilizing the credit terms on nought per cent finance wherever possible. Lisa explains the difficulties that she, and other entrepreneurs in these circumstances, experience:

'Cash flow is crucial to small businesses, particularly those underfunded from the outset. A growing business *needs* to have money spent and reinvested. Setting up staff contracts, client terms of business, the website, trademarks – all needs to be paid for initially. And then some costs, such as new product development, are constant. Despite being profitable, I have always had to manage the cash flow carefully, because the costs continue to rise through expansion. Having enough cash helps a business to grow more easily. It's like having enough blood in your body. The blood which is there has to pump around your system faster to keep all the organs functioning… and you can't do too much as you don't have the funds for it. As the business grew, it got too big for just me and the kitchen table, so I had to take on an administrator and premises – all fixed costs, which have to be met each month. The good thing is that businesses like Boogles don't waste money. They can't afford to. As long as a business remains lean and efficient, it will be profitable and in good order. When companies employ lots of staff, there is more room for them to hide and skive off.'

Boogles opted for debt finance all the way. As they have grown and made money, they have paid back debt … and then borrowed more, and then paid it back, and then borrowed more. Undoubtedly, the Boogles brand and business is worth more now than the original £150 investment, so Lisa believes she was right not to seek an outside investor:

'Interest payments on loans can be written off as an expense. But had I been funded by equity and not nought per cent credit card debt, then paying to buy out that investor would've been much more difficult and expensive because the value of the asset 'Boogles' would have increased over all the years we've been trading. And then I would still have to find the money to pay them out. So, using equity investment such as a dragon or an angel has its price. As the sole director, I have far more influence on the direction of my company, and perhaps an investor would not have agreed with me (rightly or wrongly).'

Boogles has constantly added new products and services since it began in 2004 as a bookkeeping service for small businesses and charities. Lisa soon added a division solely dedicated to solicitors' accounts and legal bookkeeping. She has also developed other income streams such as short courses on accounting software and weekend money courses for women.

She was keen not to limit the brand to just bookkeeping, but to establish her core theme as numbers and money. Through customer feedback, she recognized that there was a fun and child-friendly element to their brand name, and so added two other things to the product mix: the Boogles kids club, aimed at helping young people to understand the value of money, and a maths game called 'Making Numbers Fun!' aimed at 5–11-year-olds. Boogles now have a series of books, CDs and other products available from their online shop. Lisa has managed to fund this constant product development with partnerships, not cash:

> 'Sometimes entrepreneurial businesses don't need the money; they need the ability to get a job done. For example, I had students to illustrate my books. Sweat equity if you like but, in return, they get their name in print. So, forming win-win partnerships that exchange no cash is one way in which entrepreneurial businesses can get a job done plus generate goodwill in their local community by providing jobs for work experience.'

With a degree in accounting and marketing, Lisa not only had the finance skills; she also understood how to attract customers and keep them happy. She realized the importance of having a good brand and has always tried to develop its value. Again, she has managed to do this without the investment of much cash. Boogles has benefited from free PR through winning various awards. Lisa won the 'Young Entrepreneur of the Year Award' in 2007 and, in the following year, Boogles won an 'Enterprising Business Award' plus £1000 for new product development (which they used to get their maths game created). Through free publicity, she has raised awareness of her business, which has helped her raise funds from the bank. As Lisa says: 'Sometimes it's not "cash funding" that you need, but the end result in publicity, raised awareness, or an end product, which you can then sell and raise cash, and invest that money back into the business.'

Boogles latest project is to develop the bookkeeping service as a franchise. They were awarded funding of £3000 to test the feasibility of this as a business proposition. Lisa sees this initiative as a way of financing the business using other people's money:

> 'Franchising a business model brings income into the business which is reinvested to build the brand name and extend it further across the franchised territories. Plus, you get great, competent people who want to push the name further for you. And, arguably, a franchisee will work much harder than any employee. So, using other people's money and other people's time is how many entrepreneurs grow their business, regardless of whether they start out with cash or not.'

(To find out more about Boogles, visit: www.booglesltd.com)

Activities

(a) Boogles shows us that it is possible to start from next-to-nothing and make something out of it. But would Lisa have benefited from raising more money from external equity either at the beginning, or as the business grew?

(b) Were the banks right not to give Lisa an overdraft or loan when she first started when she had a convincing business idea and seemed well-qualified to develop it?

(c) Are there sources of funding for her business that Lisa has overlooked?

(d) Lisa has followed a policy of constant innovation, funded from reciprocal arrangements, grants and, most recently, franchisees who pay to set up a Boogles branch. Instead, Lisa could have concentrated on one core service until it became cash positive, and then used this cash to expand the business in different directions. Evaluate the advantages and disadvantages of these alternative approaches, and offer Lisa your advice on future strategy.

Try to find out the availability of various types of finance and its costs. For example, a local bank can usually provide information on commercial loans and overdrafts, with rates of interest and any fixed costs charged for the facility.

From the information you have gathered, why is it important to match the type of borrowing to the use of the funds? Can you give specific examples of what you would use the different types of finance for (e.g. loan, overdrafts, lease, and so on)?

Extended activity
The cost of money

Summary of what is required

Complete the money section of the business plan by:

- assessing the amount and type of funds required by your business;
- completing profit and loss and cash flow forecasts for the first year in detail, and for the second and third years in at least outline form;
- completing the balance sheet for the first year;
- considering the financial policies and control systems the business will need.

Planning a new venture
Forecasting the money

Financial requirements

You should now be in a position to assess the funding requirements of your business opportunity. In particular, you need to establish how much of the different types of finance you will require, and the likely sources:

- How much *permanent capital*, in the form of equity or personal investment, will be available?
- How much short-term, *working capital* is needed, and where will it come from?
- How much finance is required for *assets*, and what are the likely sources?
- If you are planning on *international trade*, how will this be financed?

Financial forecasts

Financial forecasts need to be undertaken to cover the first three years of the business:

- Profit and loss and cash flow forecasts:
  - **(a)** for year 1 by month;
  - **(b)** for years 2 and 3, as a summary for each year as a minimum. It is preferable to complete forecasts for these two years by quarters (and it may be easier to continue the monthly forecasts for year 1 if a spreadsheet is used).

- Projected balance sheet:
  - **(a)** an opening and closing balance sheet for year 1;
  - **(b)** end-of-year balance sheets for years 2 and 3 are optional, but very informative about the development of the business.

Financial policy and control systems

In your financial analyses, you will have made a number of assumptions which will effectively form policies for your business, covering such important areas as:

- Debtors: what will be your average debtor period?
- Creditors: how soon will you pay your suppliers?
- Margins and costs: what relationship will these bear to sales turnover?
- Stocks and work in progress: what levels will these run at in relation to your sales?

It is important to list these assumptions as an appendix to your financial forecasts.

How will you ensure these policies are implemented? Consider what financial control mechanisms and information you will require to ensure you can carry through your assumptions.

13.9 Notes, references and recommended further reading

Notes and further information

1   See, for example, Mason and Lloyd, (1986, p. 26). Research in Japan suggests that the cost of start-up is prohibitive for many would-be entrepreneurs (see Japan Small Business Research Institute, 2003). Research on access to finance for SMEs in deprived areas in the UK by Lee and Drever (2014) suggests that while owner-managers in these areas are more likely to perceive access to finance as a problem, there was no evidence to support the idea that it was, in fact, any harder. To this extent, geographic disparities appear to matter rather less than is often generally believed to be the case.

2   Note, for example, the CAMPARI model used by many banks: Character; Ability to repay; Margin to profit; Purpose of the loan; Amount of the loan; Repayment terms; Insurance against non-payment.

3   This and other aspects of the relationship between banks and small firms was reported in *The Guardian* (1991), 16 September, p. 12, and more recently by smallbusiness

.co.uk in September 2015 at www.smallbusiness .co.uk/news/opportunities/2493231/three-quarters -of-smes-have-no-contact-with-bank-relationship -manager.thtml (accessed 3 February 2016).

4   See DTI (2000); Bank of England (2000).

5   See the British Venture Capital Association (BVCA) for more details, available at www.bvca.co.uk.

6   Based on research by NBAN cited in Business Link (2005).

7   Further details available from the UK Export Finance website: www.gov.uk/government/organisations /uk-export-finance.

8   See The British Exporters Association (BExA) for more details, at www.bexa.co.uk/.

9   Sahlman (1997) suggests that the break-even analysis is a key component in the preparation of the entrepreneurial business plan (see ch. 6) alongside a clear estimate of the range of returns that the investor can expect to receive.

References and further reading

Baldock, R. (2016) An assessment of the business impacts of the UK's Enterprise Capital Funds, *Environment and Planning Government and Policy*, 18 January, published online before print. doi: 10.1177/0263774X15625995.

Bank of England (2000) *Finance for Small Firms – A Seventh Report*, Bank of England.

Bank of England (2002) *Finance for Small Firms – A Ninth Report*, Bank of England.

Bank of England (2004) *Finance for Small Firms – An Eleventh Report*, Bank of England.

Barrow, C., Burke, G., Molian, D. and Brown, R. (2005) *Enterprise Development*, Thomson Learning.

Bateman, M. (2013) Microfinance has been a disaster for the poorest in South Africa, *Guardian Professional*, 19 November, www.theguardian.com

BBA (2008) *Focus on Finance*, British Bankers Association.

BERR (2006) *Annual Survey of Small Business Opinions*, BERR.

BERR (2008) *Enterprise: Unlocking the UK's talent*, HM Treasury, available at webarchive.nationalarchives

.gov.uk/20081201222039/http:/www.berr.gov.uk/files
/file44993.pdf (accessed 23 February 2016).

Berry, A., Citron, D. and Jarvis, R. (1987) *The Informational Needs of Bankers Dealing With Large and Small Companies,* Research Report no. 7, Chartered Association of Certified Accountants.

Berry, A. J., Faulkner, S., Hughes, M. and Jarvis, R. (1993) Financial information, the banker and the small business, *British Accounting Review,* 25: 131–50.

BIS (2015) *Small Business Survey 2014, SME Employers,* Department for Business Innovation and Skills, Research Paper No 214, March.

Bolton Report (1971) *Committee of Inquiry on Small Firms,* HMSO, Cmnd. 4811.

British Business Bank (2014) *Strategic Plan, 2014,* Department for Business Innovation and Skills, June.

British Business Bank (2015) *Small Business Finance, 2014,* british-business-bank.co.uk/wp-content/uploads/2014/12/BBB_Small-Business-Finance-Markets-2014_Online_Interactive.pdf (accessed 1 February 2016).

Bruton, G., Khavul, S., Siegel, D. and Wright, M. (2015) New financial alternatives in seeding entrepreneurship: Microfinance, crowdfunding, and peer-to-peer innovations, *Entrepreneurship Theory & Practice,* 39(1): 9–26. Special Issue – Seeding entrepreneurship with microfinance.

Business Link (2005) *No-Nonsense Guide to Finance for High Growth Companies,* Business Link.

BVCA (2004) *Report on Investment Activity, 2003,* BVCA.

BVCA (2009) *Private Equity and Venture Capital Report on Investment Activity 2008,* available at: www.bvca.co.uk/Portals/0/library/Files/News/2008/2008_0003_report_on_investment_activity.pdf (accessed 23 February 2016).

C2 Ventures (2003) *InvestorPulse UK Angel Attitude Survey,* C2 Ventures.

Cebr (2015) *Future Trends in UK Banking, Cebr Report for Fiserv,* Centre for Economics and Business Research, February.

Commission of the European Communities (2003) *Summary Report: The Public Debate following the Green Paper 'Entrepreneurship in Europe',* EC.

Cowling, M., Liu, W. and Ledger, A. (2012) Small business financing in the UK before and during the current financial crisis, *International Small Business Journal,* 30(7): 778–800.

Cowling, M., Liu, W., Ledger, A. and Zhang, N. (2015) What really happens to small and medium-sized enterprises in a global economic recession? UK evidence on sales and job dynamics, *International Small Business Journal,* 33(5): 488–513.

Cruickshank, D. (2000) *Competition in UK Banking,* HMSO, 6.19.

Davidsson, P. and Gordon, S. R. (2015) Much ado about nothing? The surprising persistence of nascent entrepreneurs through macroeconomic crisis, *Entrepreneurship Theory & Practice,* article published online 26 February, doi: 10.1111/etap.12152.

DTI (1995) *Loan Guarantee Scheme,* DTI Small Firms Publications, URN 94/628.

DTI (1998) *Hire Purchase and Leasing,* DTI Small Firms Publications, URN 98/547.

DTI (2000) *Small and Medium Enterprise (SME) Statistics for the UK, 1999: Statistical News Release,* National Statistics Office, available from webarchive.nationalarchives.gov.uk/20070603164510/http://www.dti.gov.uk/SME4/pn2000.htm (accessed 23 February 2016).

EBAN (2014) *Statistical Compendium,* European Trade Association of Business Angels, available at www.eban.org/wp-content/uploads/2014/09/13.-Statistics-Compendium-2014.pdf (accessed 23 February 2016).

Egginton, D. A. (1982) *Accounting for the Banker,* Appendix E, Longman.

European Commission (2003) *SMEs and Access to Finance, 2003 Observatory of European SMEs,* No. 2, EC.

Fraser, S., Bhaumik, S. K. and Wright, M. (2015) What do we know about entrepreneurial finance and its relationship with growth? *International Small Business Journal,* 33(1) 70–88.

Harding, R. (2002) *Global Entrepreneurship Monitor United Kingdom 2002,* GEM.

Harding, R. (2004) *Global Entrepreneurship Monitor United Kingdom 2004,* GEM.

HMSO (1994) *Competitiveness: Helping Business to Win,* CM 2563, HMSO.

HM Treasury and Small Business Service (2003) *Bridging the Finance Gap: Next Steps in Improving Access to Growth Capital for Small Businesses,* December.

Hutchinson, P. and Ray, G. (1986) Surviving the Financial Stress of Small Enterprise Growth. In: J. Curran, J. Stanworth and D. Watkins (eds) *The Survival of the Small Firm,* Vol. 1, Gower.

Japan Small Business Research Institute (2003) *White Paper on Small and Medium Enterprises in Japan,* JSBRI.

Ledgerwood, J. (ed) (2013) *The New Microfinance Handbook: A Financial Market System Perspective,* International Bank for Reconstruction and Development/The World Bank.

Lee, N. and Drever, E. (2014) Do SMEs in deprived areas find it harder to access finance? Evidence from the UK Small Business Survey, *Entrepreneurship &*

Regional Development: An International Journal, 26(3–4): 337–356.

Lund, M. and Wright, J. (1999) The Financing of Small Firms in the United Kingdom, *Bank of England Quarterly Bulletin,* May: 195–200, available at: www.bankofengland.co.uk/archive/Documents/historicpubs/qb/1999/qb990207.pdf (accessed 23 February 2016).

MacMillan Committee (1931) *Report of the Committee on Finance and Industry,* Cmnd. 3897.

Mason, C. M. and Harrison, R. T. (2015) Business Angel investment activity in the financial crisis: UK evidence and policy implications, *Environment and Planning Government and Policy,* 33(1): 43–60.

Mason, C. and Lloyd, P. (1986) New Manufacturing Firms in a Prosperous UK Sub-Region: The Case of South Hampshire. In: Scott, M., Gibb, A., Lewis, J. and Faulkner, T. (eds) *Small Firms' Growth and Development,* Gower.

National Economic Research Associates (1990) *An Evaluation of the Loan Guarantee Scheme,* DfEE.

Nesta (2012) *Crowding in: How the UK's businesses, charities, government, and financial system can make* the most of crowdfunding. Dec., available at www.nesta.org.uk/sites/default/files/crowding_in_report.pdf

Revest, V. and Sapio, A. (2012) Financing technology-based small firms in Europe: What do we know?, *Small Business Economics,* 39(1): 179–205.

Sahlman, W. A. (1997) How to write a great business plan, *Harvard Business Review,* July–August.

Small Business Research Trust (2003) *NatWest Quarterly Survey of Small Business Customers,* December.

Stiglitz, J. E. and Weiss, A. (1981) Credit rationing in markets with imperfect information, *American Economic Review,* 73, June: 393–409.

Storey, D. J. (1994) *Understanding the Small Business Sector,* Routledge.

Tomlinson, G. B. and Knight, R. N. (1978) Unaudited financial statements – Boon or bane to lenders, *Journal of Commercial Bank Lending,* October: 38–41.

Williams, M. and Cowling, M. (2009) *Annual Small Business Survey 2007/8,* BERR.

Wilson, N., Stokes, D. and Blackburn, R. A. (2001) *Banking on a Hit: The Funding Dilemma for Britain's Music Businesses,* SBRC commissioned by the DCMS.

Wilson, R. (2004) *Business Finance 2004,* Institute of Directors.

Further reading

Entrepreneurship Theory & Practice, 39(1): Special Issue – Seeding entrepreneurship with microfinance (2015).

European Commission (2016) *Crowdfunding,* available at: ec.europa.eu/growth/access-to-finance/funding-policies/crowdfunding/index_en.htm (accessed 23 February 2016).

Jarvis, R. (2006) Finance and the Small Business. In: Carter, S. and Jones-Evans, D. (eds) *Enterprise and Small Business,* Pearson Education: pp. 338–356.

Mason, C. (2006) Venture Capital and the Small Business. In: Carter, S. and Jones-Evans, D. (eds) *Enterprise and Small Business,* Pearson Education: pp. 357–83.

Rigby, G. (2011) *Types and Sources of Finance for Start-up and Growing Businesses: An Instant Guide,* Harriman House.

Wiltbank, R. and Boeker, W. (2007) *Returns to Angel Investors in Groups,* Working Paper, available at SSRN: ssrn.com/abstract=1028592 (accessed 23 February 2016).

14 Business exits and realizing value

Learning objectives

By the end of this chapter you will be able to:

- Understand the difference between managing a business and adding value to it.
- Identify the possible outcomes from the closure of a business.
- Explore the options that business owners can take when they exit from a business.
- Evaluate the ways in which an enterprise creates value and how this can be realized.
- Assess the succession issues faced by business owners in a variety of contexts, including family businesses.
- Understand how small business management and entrepreneurship can create value for individuals and for society.

Introduction

Entrepreneurship and small business management can create value from which both individuals and society benefit. To achieve this, entrepreneurs take an opportunity through progressive stages from identification and evaluation to creating and realizing value (see Chapter 2). This chapter is concerned with the later stages of the entrepreneurial process – the exit of the owner and the realization of the value of an enterprise.

In previous chapters, we have considered how to identify, evaluate and exploit an opportunity (Parts I and II), and we have discussed the management of an entrepreneurial business (Part III). Here, we explore the completed business cycle by asking such questions as:

- What happens when a business closes?
- What is the fate of the owner?
- What helps create value in an enterprise?
- Once it is created, how do you harvest value?
- How does the business context influence the meaning of 'value' – for example, in family business and social enterprise?

Activity 1
Types of business closure

When a business closes, there are several types of outcome for the owners, some positive, some negative. What are these? Make a list of the different types of business exit from the point of view of the owner.

14.1 Business exits and closures

14.1.1 BUSINESS SURVIVAL AND ADDING VALUE: THERE IS A DIFFERENCE

A large number of enterprises – usually around 10 per cent of the business stock – close every year (see Chapters 1 and 3). Life spans of individual businesses vary greatly. A small number last a long time: the East India Company was set up to trade with the east in the reign of Elizabeth I and was dissolved 274 years later in the reign of Queen Victoria, having transformed itself along the way from a trading company to the ruling enterprise of India, an 'empire within an empire'; the Hudson's Bay Company, founded in 1670 to exploit the fur trade in North America and still trading today as HBC retailers in Canada, is the longest surviving multinational company (Micklethwaite and Wooldridge, 2003). Such longevity is rare. Ninety per cent of businesses last less than a decade and approximately half close within five years. As discussed in Chapter 3,[1] some patterns emerge from the statistics on business closure:

- Closure rates among small firms are very high. On average, around 10 per cent of the total numbers of small businesses cease trading each year.
- Young businesses are more likely to close than the old. Closure rates are highest in the early years and the chances of survival improve as the business ages.
- Small firms are much more likely to cease trading than large firms. Medium-sized and large firms have much lower closure rates than small firms. The most vulnerable are the very smallest micro firms.
- Those that grow are less likely to close than those that do not. Staying small is not a good survival strategy.
- Some sectors have higher closure rates than others. For example, manufacturing firms are less likely to close than those in construction.

These patterns indicate that the most vulnerable businesses are the very young, very small firms that exist in hostile, competitive environments. Chapter 7 investigated the factors within the control of the owner that were likely to lead to closure and the strategies that could be deployed to counteract this. We concluded that four key controllable factors particularly influence the survival and growth of a venture: the management of resources and people; marketing to customers; the availability and use of money; and the motivations of the owner-managers.

These are the factors that influence the longevity and development of a firm, but do they also create value? It is possible for a business to have a relatively long life but still have little value to a third party. For example, a consultant or a plumber who has been operating on their own successfully for many years would find it difficult to sell their business unless they continued working for it. Therefore, the factors that contribute to the survival of a business are not necessarily the same as those that add value to it in a way that can be realized when the owner exits.

14.1.2 WHAT HAPPENS TO BUSINESSES THAT CLOSE?

There is an unfortunate tendency to associate **business closure** with **business failure**, which implicitly assumes that little value is realized when a business closes. This is exacerbated by the use of other terminology such as business 'mortality' and 'deaths' that also have negative associations, implying that little of value is left (see Nummela, Saarenketo and Loane, 2016, for a contextualized definition of 'failure'; see also Yusuf (2012), for discussion of entrepreneurs' 'disengagement' from the start-up process). Entrepreneurs who close a business can still be stigmatized as failures and regarded with suspicion if they try to open a subsequent venture. Business closure is assumed to be a negative experience, rather than the inevitable consequence of business evolution. Fortunately, recent research has produced new insights into this final stage of the business life cycle, going some way towards correcting this imbalanced view. For example, Wennberg and DeTienne (2014) advise against a simplistic view of exit as 'negative' and survival as 'positive', drawing particular attention to the mix of founder intentions that lie behind exit strategies.

There is clearly a range of outcomes associated with the closure of a business from a lucrative sale at one extreme, to involuntary liquidation at the other (see Ucbasaran *et al.*, 2010; 2013). A business that closes even after a relatively short time may have served its purpose well and should not automatically be assumed to have failed. Some ventures only have a short-term purpose; for example, in the creative industries it is common for new ventures to have a natural, short existence that covers the timespan of a particular project, such as the making of a film or a theatre production. We also argue that you can learn as much, if not more, about how to run a business by experiencing difficulties and disaster as you can from the successful times. In this sense, the value of a closed business may be more in the learning experiences of the owner than in any financial gains.

The closure of a business takes several forms (Stokes and Blackburn, 2002). Using financial criteria, a **business exit** can be placed on a spectrum with large monetary gains for the owners at one end and significant losses at the other. Towards the financially positive end of the spectrum, around one-third of businesses are sold on by their owners for a monetary gain. However, the majority of sales are for modest amounts with the well-publicized, multi-million pound deals a rarity.

At the negative end of the spectrum, up to 20 per cent of businesses that close do so with debts that are left unpaid. In Western Europe, there are over 150 000 insolvencies each year of which approximately 40 000 are in the UK. This represents around 1 per cent of the total business population and 10 per cent of all the businesses that close. Therefore, they form only a small part of the total business activity in the economy, although they do represent very real problems for the individuals concerned.

This leaves a large number of businesses that simply close down with neither financial gain nor pain. Many businesses close simply because they no longer meet their owners' objectives. Some of these are undoubtedly ailing financially and are closed before they can cause too much damage. In other cases, owners have what they consider to be a better idea for a venture, or an attractive job offer. Businesses can also be closed for unfortunate, non-financial reasons, such as the breakdown in relationships between partners, or the ill health of the owner. Other business closures are purely technical; for example, when a sole trader enlarges their business to a partnership or limited company. Sometimes businesses are formed for a specific reason, such as the renovation of a property, and are closed when the project is complete.

These examples demonstrate the important distinction between closure and failure (see Figure 14.1). Many businesses do not really close at all as they have been sold on, or re-opened in another form. Either way, the underlying trade continues even if the original business entity does not. Together, they probably account for up to half of all closures. This can be seen happening visibly in many shopping areas and business estates with relatively frequent changes to trading names or appearances, but less frequent change to the underlying business conducted. The trade of many businesses carries on despite turbulent changes in the ownership and the structure of the organization.

Figure 14.1 What happens to businesses that close?

Sold-on
34%

Insolvent
18%

Closed-down
31%

Re-opened
17%

Source: Stokes and Blackburn 2002.

THE REINCARNATIONS OF STANLEY GIBBONS

The philatelic business of Stanley Gibbons has continued for over 150 years, yet it has been undertaken by a variety of different business entities. Edward Stanley Gibbons started a business as a sole trader dealing in stamps and philatelic items in the back room of his father's pharmacy in Plymouth in 1856. As one of the first into a growing market for collectible philatelic items, Gibbons succeeded both as a dealer and as a publisher, producing a catalogue of prices for the first postage stamps, such as the Penny Blacks. He retired at the age of 50, selling his business, Stanley Gibbons & Co., to Charles Philips. The new owner preferred to keep the Gibbons name not just as a brand, but also as the legal entity; he incorporated the business as Stanley Gibbons Limited in 1890. Over the following decades, the company became established as the leading philatelic authority through several changes of private ownership.

By 1968, it had grown sufficiently to gain a listing on the Stock Exchange. But turbulent times lay ahead. The market for stamps and collectibles boomed in the late 1970s and, at the peak of the market, the company shares were acquired by Letraset International, a graphic art business attempting to diversify. This proved a disastrous move for both companies. Letraset attempted to stimulate Gibbons into fast growth by pumping in cash for new stock, but the market had overheated and prices fell. As losses mounted at Gibbons, Letraset was itself taken over. In the fallout, Gibbons was acquired by dealers whose attempts to manipulate stamp markets tarnished a reputation built up over the previous century. Several owners, including Flying Flowers, have since attempted to bring back stability. In 2000, the Stanley Gibbons Group floated on the Alternative Investment Market (AIM) and an internet-based strategy was put in place in an attempt to revitalize the business. Through all this turbulence, the underlying trade has continued, and although the marketplace has changed substantially, Stanley Gibbons is still the business that is most commonly associated with stamp collecting around the world.

Stanley Gibbons, the world famous stamp business, has survived many changes to its ownership and to its premises in the Strand, London.

Edward Stanley Gibbons

Activity 2
Owners that exit from their business

When an owner leaves a business, they have a variety of options of what to do next. What are these and which ones do they tend to choose?

14.1.3 WHAT HAPPENS TO THE OWNERS OF BUSINESSES THAT CLOSE?

So far we have considered only what happens to the businesses that close. But what of the owners of those businesses? What do they do next? Some, like Stanley Gibbons, retire, as this was their motivation in selling or closing their business. Others go back into the employment of others, or at least seek to get a job. But a number of studies in Europe (e.g. Stam, Audretsch and Meijaard, 2005; Metzger, 2006), the USA (Headd, 2003) and Japan (Harada, 2005) have confirmed earlier UK research (Stokes and Blackburn, 2001) that the majority of entrepreneurs that exit one business continue as a business owner. Some already have other business interests; some start a similar business in a different form, while others try something different. Altogether, over half of owners that exit from one enterprise go back into business ownership.[2]

The world of business ownership has a revolving door, rather than a one-way exit. Most owners re-enter because they are sufficiently encouraged by their experiences the first time round. Even those who experience financial difficulties in one venture try again (see Figure 14.2). This is not usually an obstinate reaction to business closure, but a positive assessment that next time it could and should be better. They do not believe themselves to have been 'unsuccessful' because they tend to regard their experiences as a useful learning experience. Some may put a positive 'spin' on their experience and repackage their failure as a success to preserve their reputation (Coad, 2014). However, the attitude of the entrepreneur is the important factor in deciding whether or not they continue in business whatever their self-justification for past failures. Stokes and Blackburn (2002) classified and quantified entrepreneurs who leave a business according to:

- how their business performed financially; and
- their future intentions and attitudes towards running a business.

This resulted in a typology as illustrated in Figure 14.3.

Figure 14.2 What happens to the owners of businesses that close?

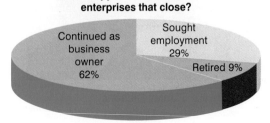

Source: Stokes and Blackburn, 2002.

Figure 14.3   A typology of business owners who have exited a business

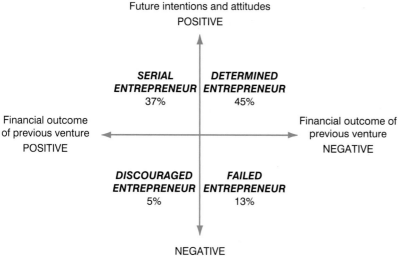

Source: Stokes and Blackburn, 2002.

1   Serial entrepreneurs (37 per cent). Having succeeded in a previous venture, they return with resources to invest in a new business. This group has probably sold one business and is keen to become involved in another.

2   Determined entrepreneurs (45 per cent of those who close a business). Despite problems in their previous venture, they return to business ownership determined to do better. This is the largest group, as it frequently takes more than one attempt to 'make a go of it'.

3   Failed entrepreneurs (13 per cent). The problems of a previous venture discourage them from re-entering into business ownership. This represents the group who can be said to have 'failed', in that they have closed a business in financial difficulty, often leaving bad debts, and returned to employment or unemployment. However, it is a relatively small percentage of those that do close down a business.

4   Discouraged entrepreneurs (5 per cent). Although their previous business venture succeeded, they do not wish to repeat the experience. Often, the strains of running a small business outweigh the financial rewards, so this relatively small group also withdraws from business ownership.

Owners that exit from one business usually believe that they have improved particular management and personal skills. Some even believe this is the best way to learn about running a business.

Entrepreneur Tony Allan (of the 'Tony and Giorgio' television series) claims that he prefers to recruit those who have experienced difficult times: 'When I choose teams of people I go for those who've failed before as they can apply that experience. I'm highly qualified to work for myself now.'[3]

His 'qualifications' come from a series of entrepreneurial ventures that he has closed or sold in relatively short periods. He developed his first business, Cutty Catering, by buying and selling fish into the catering trade in the 1990s. In 1997, he set up his first restaurant, Bank, a 'brash brasserie', that was quickly developed into a small chain of three and sold in 2001. By then, he had established the acclaimed chain Fish! as well as building a career as a TV cook and author. But rapid expansion of the chain through a stock market listing brought problems of over-expansion; the company collapsed and went into administration in 2002. Allan bought back seven of the restaurants and the name Fish! from the administrators and he was back in business.

The implication from such histories is that the process of closing a business can be beneficial, in that entrepreneurs ultimately learn how to run a successful business. Research has confirmed that the majority of owners view business closure as a positive learning experience (Metzger, 2006). When asked to rate their skills after closure compared to when they started, owners cited a number of improvements including business planning, building a customer base and financial record-keeping. But the area of greatest learning related to personal development, including coping with setbacks, self-management and dealing with change. Owners rated managing and motivating themselves through the changing fortunes of their venture as the most valuable learning experience. Trust and relationship issues were also important lessons, as a number of owners went into business with unsuitable partners, even though they were family or friends (Stokes and Blackburn, 2001).

In summary, the creation of value through an entrepreneurial venture can be in the personal development of the owner as well as in the venture itself.

14.1.4 SERIAL AND PORTFOLIO ENTREPRENEURS

Many entrepreneurs own more than one business either concurrently or sequentially as 'portfolio' or 'serial' entrepreneurs:

- A portfolio entrepreneur owns more than one business at the same time;
- A serial entrepreneur runs a business, sells it and moves onto another venture in a relatively short time.

While a **serial entrepreneur** tends to look for rapid growth, a **portfolio entrepreneur** compensates for lack of high growth in one venture by lower growth in many. Serial entrepreneurs thrive on the psychological reward of making an impact as well as the financial gain, and it is this that motivates some who are already relatively wealthy (Clancey, 2000). They also tend to regard failure as an experience that will make them stronger and bolder to take on new risks (Ryan, 2000). Some entrepreneurs seem to thrive on the gruelling early stages of starting and building a business, and prefer to hand it over for others to manage while they return to the start-up process (Fraone, 1999).

RISING FROM THE ASHES: MARC BRUNEL

The rise of Britain as the leading economic nation in the world was not without many business casualties, some involving well-known names. The achievements of Marc Brunel, father of Isambard Kingdom Brunel, are less well-known than his illustrious son, but also very significant. The Brunels were French, but Marc fled the excesses of the French revolution first to marry an English woman, Sophia Kingdom, in 1799. As well as ensuring his famous son was English, rather than French, he was also partly responsible for the defeat of France through his entrepreneurial activities. A prolific inventor, he became aware of one of the British navy's greatest needs during the Napoleonic wars – pulley blocks that controlled the rigging ropes of the sails. Each year, the fleet needed 100 000 of them and they could not get enough, as they were made laboriously by hand from a solid block of oak. Marc Brunel designed a system using machines to do the work, one of the first examples of automated manufacturing replacing craft-based production. He also designed a production line process to make boots for the army, many of which were worn at the battle of Waterloo when Napoleon's army was finally defeated. The end of the war also meant the end of a thriving business for Brunel, as neither the navy nor the army needed his mass-produced products in viable quantities. The penalties for failing to pay off debts were severe in the nineteenth century and, when his enterprises could no longer meet the bills, he was sent to debtor's prison as his businesses collapsed. Fortunately, the Duke of Wellington remembered the contribution of this French émigré to the English war effort and arranged for his release.

Sir Marc Isambard Brunel

Typical of many entrepreneurs, Marc Brunel was already planning his next venture while in prison, working on a problem that was threatening London even then – traffic congestion. As the city developed around the docks both north and south of the Thames, a major bottleneck for carts and coaches developed on London Bridge, but other crossings could not be built downstream without impeding shipping using the docks. Brunel realized that the only alternative was to build a tunnel under the Thames, but under-water tunnelling was an undeveloped skill at the time. First, he designed the 'Great Shield', a patented method that provides protection for workers who dig and build the walls at the same time. It was an innovation that formed the basis of modern tunnelling technology and was used during the construction of the Channel Tunnel that now links Brunel's country of birth with his country of adoption.

Next, he formed the Thames Tunnel Company, raised the necessary capital from private investors and began work in Rotherhithe in 1825 on a tunnel to Wapping, a quarter of a mile away on the north bank. He employed his son Isambard as one of the engineers. Three years later they had reached the middle of the Thames, but water burst through several times, precipitating a financial crisis that halted the work and temporarily closed the business. Marc Brunel had already demonstrated his reliance in the face of problems and, five years later in 1836, he had raised new capital from the government to begin the project again. He was aged 73 when the Thames Tunnel was finally completed in 1842, 17 years after he had begun the project. (See Brindle, 2006.)

Activity 3
Adding value to a business

Assuming an owner wishes to sell their business, how can they maximize its value? What practical steps can they take to ensure that their business is both easy and profitable to sell.

14.2 What adds value to a business?

So far, we have considered what happens to businesses that close and to owners that exit from a business. We have seen that the creation of value in this process comes from adding value both to the business and to the entrepreneur. But what makes some businesses worth buying while others are simply closed? The ultimate test that differentiates between the value of one business and another is the judgment of buyers in the marketplace. To value an enterprise, we can therefore ask: 'What is the business worth to someone else?' More importantly for those who wish to add value to an enterprise, we should also ask: 'Why is it worth this much – what gives one business a different value to another enterprise?'

14.2.1 METHODS OF VALUING A BUSINESS

We discussed the various ways in which businesses can be valued in Chapter 9, where we noted two basic valuation methods:[4]

- Market value of the tangible assets, such as property, equipment, stocks and debtors.
- Multiple of annual profits:[5] in order to give value to intangible assets, the annual earning power of the business is used.

The first of these measures is relatively straightforward as it reflects the value of assets that a business has accumulated during its lifespan. However, the full value of most enterprises is not in the assets they have acquired, but in the intangible assets and goodwill that contribute to its trading. These were summarized (in Chapter 9, Section 9.3.2) as image and reputation, employees, intellectual property and customers. Such assets only have real value while a business is still trading and so are normally measured by their ability to generate profits.

An important issue in using profits as the yardstick for valuation is how many years to take as the multiplier. Publicly quoted corporations are judged using a **multiple of profits** expressed as a **price–earnings (PE) ratio**. This is calculated by taking the total market valuation of the company's shares divided by the annual profits; it expresses how many years of current profits would be needed to buy all the company's shares at the current share price. PE ratios in excess of 10 are common in many sectors of the stock market and those perceived to be growing can achieve ratios in excess of 20. Private businesses, whose shares are not for sale publicly, normally achieve a much lower multiple of profits, usually lower than 10 and often in the three- to seven-year range.

Two factors influence this important multiple: interest rates and quality of earnings. High interest rates tend to lower valuations as borrowing to purchase the business becomes more expensive. **Quality of earnings** is a measure of the reliability of company profits; how long can they realistically be expected to continue at the current or higher levels? The answer usually depends on a number of factors, including competitiveness of the market sector, types and spread of customers, and the strength of the management team left to run the business.

14.2.2 THE FIVE KEY INGREDIENTS THAT CREATE VALUE

Thus, there are a variety of influences that create value in a business. These can be summarized into the five key categories discussed below: customer base and market position, knowledge and intellectual property, the entrepreneurial team, facilities and resources, and cash flow and profits growth.

Customer base and market position

With insufficient customers, a business cannot continue for very long, so a key measure of value is the quantity and quality of the customer base.[6]

- Quantity of customers: a key weakness of many businesses is their over-reliance on a small number of customers. Many small enterprises, particularly those in the business-to-business sector, trade principally with fewer than five customers. Problems with one key customer, either through competitive pressure or because the customer develops internal problems of its own, can rapidly change the profitability of a business. A high-value business has a spread of customers so that none are dominant, and downturns in one will be offset by a rise in business with others.
- Quality of customers: the quality of the customer base is determined by the loyalty of customers and the strength of their own businesses. A high-value enterprise has long-standing customers that keep coming back because they are satisfied, they continue to have a need for the product or service, and they are likely to stay in business themselves.

The market position of a business influences its value because this has an impact on the nature of the customer base. A company with a niche position in a market that has highly competitive barriers to entry can attract and defend its customer base more easily than a business in a highly competitive market in which price is the key purchase consideration.[7]

Embedded knowledge and intellectual property

A key asset of any small business is the knowledge of the entrepreneur(s) running it. A 'model entrepreneur' has all the relevant technical skills, management competencies and behaviours, and personal attributes to make the business work effectively.[8] These individual characteristics only add value to a business if they are transferable and embedded into the business in some way. If the entrepreneur exits from a business, the business loses value if key knowledge and expertise is not somehow left behind. An important ingredient in the valuation of a business is, therefore, the residual knowledge, know-how and intellectual property that exists independently of the owner-manager.

The identification and registration of intellectual property rights (IPR) add value to a business because they are transferable and can protect innovations from competition. IPR exists in four main categories: trademarks, designs, copyright and patents.[9] It is important to consider all of these categories as IPR resides not only in innovative products, but also in less tangible areas. Brand names, logos, designs and internal processes all add value to a business if they can be identified and protected in some way.

In some cases, it may not be possible to protect know-how. For example, the ability to deliver products and services according to customer demand may depend on expertise and systems that have evolved in a business over several years. They can still add value to the business because they represent a key aspect of customer satisfaction. To represent a permanent addition to the business value, they need to be embedded into structures, systems and processes that can operate independently of the owner-manager or key individual employees.

Knowledge is not just about the technology of making products or delivering services. It is also about the successful management practices of the business: the marketing activities used to attract and retain customers; the financial controls and systems used to manage the cash and profits; the ways in which employees are motivated and retained. In a successful, high-value business these represent a finely tuned set of management practices that have evolved in line with the growth of the business. They are understood widely throughout the business so that they do not exist solely in the owner-manager's head.

The entrepreneurial team

If the value of a business is not to be over-dependent on the expertise and knowledge of the owner, a management team capable of running the business on a day-to-day basis needs to be in place. A business that depends on the owner-manager alone to maintain customer relationships and run the operations of the business is very vulnerable. A high-value company has a well-developed and motivated management team with a broad base of expertise and experience.

Entrepreneurs are often painted as heroic individuals who single-handedly overcome all the obstacles in new venture creation and development. This notion of the entrepreneur as a 'lone hero' is encouraged by the promotion of individuals such as Branson and Sugar, with little mention of those around them who actually manage their enterprises. There is increasing evidence that successful entrepreneurs were part of a team throughout. Research into entrepreneurial teams indicates that fast-growth firms are more likely to have been founded by several owner managers, not just one (Cooney, 2005). Whether it is there from the beginning through multiple ownership, or develops through a management structure as the firm grows, a team of motivated managers is essential for a business to have enduring value beyond the exit of a founding entrepreneur.

People outside of the business as well as the team that manage it are also an important ingredient in value creation. A key personal attribute found in successful entrepreneurs is their ability to build a supportive team of external stakeholders including financiers, suppliers and support organizations such as government agencies or local universities (see Chapter 2).

Processes and facilities – the business model

Businesses create value by bringing together resources and processes in a way that constitutes a viable 'business model' (see Chapter 7, Section 3). A business model is the system that transforms an intangible business idea into products and services that have value in the market place (Hedman and Kalling, 2003; Osterwalder and Pigneur, 2010). It is how an entrepreneur exploits an opportunity by combining resources and facilities in a particular way so that products and services can be delivered that customers need them. These resources include:

- Tangible assets of a business: premises, equipment, stock.
- Processes and systems: these allow the business to continue no matter who is running it. They range from production and service delivery systems including quality control, to personnel processes such as annual reviews.
- Location: some business sectors such as retail outlets, hotels and restaurants, are crucially affected by location. Being in the right place is a key aspect of the value created in such businesses.

Without such resources, a business opportunity, however innovative or needed, cannot be realized and achieve value. The processes that run a business are sometimes its most valuable asset. A restaurant may need an innovative chef to make it stand out in a busy marketplace, but the business processes that control the taking and delivery of a customer order within a consistent timeframe are equally important – the most interesting dish is worthless if it is delivered too late and cold. Equally important are the processes that surround a business, such as the relationships with suppliers and other partners.

The resources themselves may have an intrinsic value and represent an asset in the balance sheet of the business. However, it is often their combined use through an effective process that represents the greatest value. The way in which the waiting staff and the kitchen of a restaurant link together to serve customers quickly and consistently is a valuable process that is worth more than the individual systems and tools needed to achieve it.

Cash flow and profits growth

The ability of a business to generate cash through profitable trading is a crucial part of its value. For this reason, a common way of valuing a business is profit multiples (see Section 14.2.1). The relationship between cash generation and profits will also affect the value of a business. Some types of business produce good profits but less cash because they require constant reinvestment to survive. For example, manufacturers in a competitive sector such as the car industry need to reinvest most of the cash they generate in the next generation of products. Profits are an important consideration, but the long-term ability to generate cash is the overriding factor in adding value to a business. High-value businesses tend to be those that have realistic objectives to grow their profits from a solid base, as standing still means going backwards in competitive markets.

Cash flow and profitability are, in effect, measures of how well the other four aspects of adding value are operating. A high-value enterprise will be cash positive because it has satisfied customers benefiting from the know-how of a business managed by a motivated team using good processes and adequate resources. If one of these factors is not optimized, the long-term profit potential is compromised, thereby reducing the value of the enterprise. This is illustrated in Figure 14.4, in which profits and cash represent the centre of the value system; a weakness in any one of the components will adversely affect the effectiveness and value of the whole structure.

Figure 14.4 Five factors that add value to a business

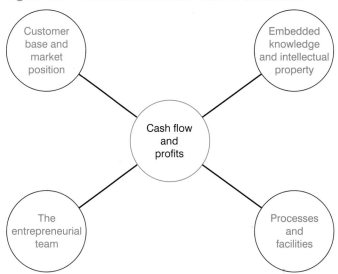

Activity 4
Selling a business

I n what ways can a business be sold?
Why are some owners unsuccessful at doing this?

14.3 Succession issues

Succession of the ownership of the business happens when the owner finds a way of exiting from the business by either selling or transferring the business to a new owner. This happens only in a minority of enterprises, even in family businesses. As we have discussed (in Section 14.1.2), around one in three of businesses that close are sold on to a third party. Only one-third of family businesses are passed on to the second generation, and only 16 per cent make it to the third generation (Janjuha-Jivraj and Woods, 2002).

14.3.1 SUCCESSION FAILURE

This highlights succession issues facing small business owners. **Succession failure**, in which a business has to be closed or broken up, is the result of unsuccessful attempts to sell or hand on a business. This is normally an age-related issue affecting owners in their late 50s or early 60s. As around 35 per cent of business owners in the UK are estimated to be over the age of 50, and 10 per cent are over 60, this is becoming a real issue for a large number of entrepreneurs.

The reasons for succession failure are primarily the converse of those that add value to a business. If a business has low value, it is difficult to sell or pass on to a successor. A study by Martin, Martin and Mabbett (2002) identified that the following factors contributed to vulnerability to succession failure:

- Lifestyle business goals that reflected the personal needs of the owners rather, than the need to grow the business.
- Poor business performance, unless the business had underlying tangible assets.

- Managerial dependence on the owner. Key dependencies included the owner's knowledge and customer relationships.
- No natural family or internal successor. Family members now have many more work alternatives than taking over the family business, so that succession is becoming rare. Few small firms have internal managers capable of taking on the business.
- Ignoring the need to plan succession. Although it can take several years to make an enterprise ready for exit, few owners develop an exit plan. A survey of SME owners in southern England recorded that two-thirds had no exit plan; even more surprisingly, less than half of those aged over 60 had an exit plan (Blackburn and Stokes, 2002).

In other cases, a succession takes place, with a different family member taking on the leadership role, but it does not work. The reasons for this include: the new leader is not up to the job; they do not have the support of other family members; the founder is not happy with a non-executive role and attempts to regain control (see DeTienne and Chiroco (2013) and Wilson, Wright and Scholes (2013), for related discussion of family business survival, the role of the board, and exit strategies).

14.3.2 METHODS OF SELLING A BUSINESS

There are two basic ways of realizing the monetary value of a business: an initial public offering (IPO), or a private sale.

Initial public offering

A medium-sized or high-growth business can make some, or all, of its shares available to the general public through an **initial public offering (IPO).** The shares of a public company are traded on a stock exchange and the owners can realize some of the value of the business by selling shares. The benefits to owners are that they receive cash for the initial sale of shares, and they can trade shares more easily in the future as there is a ready market. The company can finance growth more easily by issuing shares for cash, or for acquiring other businesses. The disadvantages are that the company has to conform to financial, regulatory and legal requirements that add considerably to the costs and complexity of managing the business. A public company has to make available quarterly information on business performance and operating details, such as directors' salaries. The increased audit, investment banking, public relations and information costs are normally over £100 000 per annum. In addition, the initial flotation of the shares will cost in excess of £250 000 (Sperry and Mitchell, 1999).

For most owners, the disadvantages outweigh the advantages and only a small percentage of firms become public companies. In the USA, there are less than 10 000 companies on the main stock exchanges and the London Stock Exchange lists less than 2500 companies. An IPO is not an appropriate route for owners who wish to retire because their continued involvement in the business is normally required.

Private sale

Businesses can be sold to third parties through private negotiations and deals. Potential buyers fall into several categories:[10]

- Investors such as private equity firms and business angels who are primarily looking for financial and strategic involvement, rather than day-to-day management.
- Individuals who wish to take an active role in the future running of the business.
- Trade buyers or other companies looking for an appropriate acquisition to develop their business.
- Managers within the business who buy out the owner, either on their own or in collaboration with other investors.
- Family members who take over the business from a relative.

Intermediary organizations exist that can help to facilitate this process. These include business transfer agents that tend to specialize in smaller businesses in specific sectors where private sales are more common, such as restaurants, hotels and retail outlets. Accountants and company brokers offer a more bespoke service to advise and sell larger businesses with higher values (usually over £250 000). Reliable information on the frequency and extent of business sales is rare, but the majority of sales of larger SMEs are to trade companies, while smaller businesses are more frequently sold to individual buyers.

Activity 5
Family issues

What are the advantages and disadvantages of having a business run by members of the same family?

14.4 The family business

Definitions of a **family business** vary (see Chua, Chrisman and Steier, 2003; Benavides-Velasco, Quintana-García and Guzmán-Parra, 2013). Some include any business that employs more than one family member, a very common situation that occurs in three-quarters of all businesses. Other definitions are more restrictive and include only those businesses passed on to a second generation, which happens less frequently, or in about one in three of family businesses (see Section 14.3 above).

Family businesses have particular issues in creating and realizing value. These relate to the motivations and methods for running the business that may differ from non-family firms:

- Strategic objectives and motives: the priority of a family firm may be to provide employment and income for family members, with less emphasis on commercial goals of profit generation and business growth. The founder's desire to perpetuate the family business to the benefit of their heirs is an important motive force in many family firms. This may influence their choices for value creation within the business, although research suggests there is little difference in business performance between family and non-family firms (Kuratko and Hodgetts, 2007).
- Management of people: the family hierarchy is an added complication to the normal issues of managing people. This may act as a constraint which sometimes contradicts business rationality when, for example, preference is given to family members in recruitment, training and remuneration. For this reason, some of the early literature in this field saw the role of the family in a negative light, with emotional issues and family ties competing with the demands of an efficient business (Fletcher, 2006). Commentators suggested the need to separate 'family' from 'business' as a way of overcoming these issues. Other studies have argued against such separation, emphasizing 'the family as business' that can perform a key integrating role (McCollom, 1992). On the one hand, the family can be seen as a resource that provides flexibility to a business and family workers who are loyal and trustworthy. On the other hand, the family can be seen as a constraint when, for example, it may be necessary to maintain a family member's job even if they are incompetent or disruptive.
- Ownership and control: issues relating to the ownership of the business, and responsibilities in running the business, are often less clear in a family firm than in a non-family business environment. However, many

family firms have the advantages of speedy decision-making due to the short lines of communication, and more long-term planning, because of the importance of the business to the family.

- Succession: it can be argued that succession issues are the most important defining feature of a family business. The impending departure or retirement of the founder or leader of a family business can be a profoundly destabilizing time. Conflict may easily arise when there is no natural successor and family members not normally involved in the day-to-day running of the business may become involved. The business may be seen as a monument to the founder and this feeling may override normal commercial judgement on how to realize the value of the firm. Succession more often becomes an emotion-laden issue in the family business (Kuratko and Hodgetts, 2007). However, some family firms develop a family culture of distinctive values and beliefs that provide a focused direction in running the business and clear policies for succession. Many of the world's most successful businesses were founded on family dynasties. Arthur Guinness not only founded a brewery in the eighteenth century, but also the family dynasty that was to control it for the next two centuries as the business was handed on from father to son for four generations before floating on the London Stock Exchange.

THE MURDOCH DYNASTY

Rupert Murdoch inherited a modest media business from his father, Keith, but the impact of death duties and taxes left him with nothing but a loss-making newspaper in Adelaide, Australia. He transformed this into the world's largest media empire, News Corporation, with assets of $56 billion and sales of $23 billion in films, newspapers and publishing around the world. But according to some reports, the problem of succession is threatening to destabilize his business.

Rupert Murdoch has six children from three marriages and, in 2016, he announced his intention to take a fourth wife, Jerry Hall. Three of his children, Elizabeth, Lachlan and James, have been particularly involved in his businesses. Lachlan, who managed the *New York Post* and the Fox television service, was initially favourite to head the family business. But, in recent years, first Elizabeth and then James have emerged as contenders for the succession.

Lachlan, a London-born American citizen, was sent to Australia in 1994, where he was chairman and chief executive of News Ltd, the Australian arm of News Corporation. He was deputy chief executive officer on the main board of News Corporation, a role that extended his reach well outside Australia and into the company's worldwide interests, but he abruptly resigned this post in August 2005. The family denied that he quit because of a rift with his father. Lachlan's elder sister, Elizabeth, came into the reckoning when she was given a senior job at BSkyB, Murdoch's UK satellite television company. This was a controversial appointment as she had less than two years' management experience and was described as a 'trainee' by the then chief executive (who left soon after making the comment). Elizabeth now seems intent on making her own way as she left Sky to set up her own film production business, Shine Entertainment. James worked his way up through the company's new media and newspaper interests in New York, before moving to Hong Kong to take charge of News Corporation's ailing Asian satellite service StarTV. Having turned this around, he was given the chief executive's role at BSkyB in 2003. Promoted to take charge of the News Corporation business in Europe and Asia in 2007, he became the bookies' favourite to take over when Rupert goes. He then became embroiled in the phone-hacking scandal by *News of the World* journalists and he was forced to resign as head of Sky in 2012; Lachlan re-emerged as the front-runner to succeed. James is not done yet, however. His return to Sky as chairman, announced in January 2016, began the process of his rehabilitation at the top of the Murdoch hierarchy.

Now that Rupert Murdoch is well into his 80s, we should not forget his grandchildren. James MacLeod, Rupert Murdoch's 25-year-old grandson, is making waves as a digital news entrepreneur as the co-creator of Clippet, a news app which delivers 60-second summaries of the main new stories to younger generation audiences. According to his mother, Murdoch's elder daughter, Prudence MacLeod, he is very much like his famous grandfather.

In 2013, Murdoch split his empire into two separate groups: Twenty-first Century Fox, which controls the media interests, and News Corporation, which has the publishing businesses. A strategy of dividing up the cake may be the only way to satisfy his hungry family.

14.5 Creating value for society

Entrepreneurship and successful small businesses create value for society, as well as for their owners. In Chapter 1, the contribution of small businesses to the national economy was examined which emphasized the role of entrepreneurship and small business management in the economic context of profit-making activities, job creation and regional development. In Chapter 2, the role of entrepreneurship in wealth creation was defined more broadly to include added value for society, as well as individuals. Social enterprises reinvest surpluses for the benefit of a particular community, rather than being driven by the need to maximize profit for shareholders and owners.

This potential contribution of entrepreneurship to economic and social well-being has been recognized in many government initiatives aimed at stimulating and encouraging entrepreneurial activities. Many initiatives and programmes now aim to encourage entrepreneurship and the development of small businesses. One particular focus is the role of youth, as increasing numbers of younger people are starting their own businesses. New Zealand leads the world in youth entrepreneurship with 43 per cent of business owners aged under 35, followed by Australia and the USA at 38 per cent, and the UK at 36 per cent, according to Frederick (2005). However, this is linked to concerns over the number of graduates that start their own business or become self-employed, as the UK and Europe lag behind the USA. Consequently, there are an increasing number of initiatives such as business plan competitions and extra-curriculum courses that actively encourage undergraduates to consider entrepreneurship as a career option.

Entrepreneurship can be seen as a philosophy of life that focuses on having the confidence and vision to make things happen, to see opportunities to do things differently and to act on those opportunities. In this sense, it can create value in a person through self-development. This is a key lesson from entrepreneurs that have closed a business: many exit with no financial gain or worse, but most regard it as a positive learning experience (see Section 14.1.2). Small business management and entrepreneurship is not only about creating value through successful new ventures; it is also concerned with adding value to individuals by developing their self-efficacy, leadership and personal effectiveness.

14.6 Summary and activities

Most businesses close within a few years of being started. Closure rates are highest among the very small and youngest firms, but they should not all be regarded as failures. One half of business closures are not really closures at all: around one-third are sold for some financial consideration, and 15 per cent close for technical reasons, such as a change from one legal form to another. A minority (around 20 per cent) do close with debts and therefore represent financial failures but the rest (30 per cent) are simply closed because they no longer meet their owners' objectives.

Over half of owners that exit from a business go back into business ownership. Even those who have suffered financially believe they have learned from the experience of business ownership. The most valued lessons are in personal development and self-management. Some owners become serial entrepreneurs, with a succession of businesses; others are portfolio entrepreneurs, owning more than one business at a time.

Five key factors influence the value of a business:

1 customer base and market position
2 embedded knowledge and intellectual property
3 the entrepreneurial team
4 processes and facilities working to a business model
5 cash flow and profits.

The value of a business can be measured by a combination of the market value of its tangible assets and a multiple of its annual profits. The monetary value of a business can be realized either through a private or trade sale, or through an initial public offering (IPO).

Succession failure occurs when an owner who wishes to exit cannot find a buyer or successor to run their business. A family business faces particular issues that differentiates it from non-family firms, and can become destabilized during the succession from one family member to another.

Entrepreneurship adds value to society as well as individuals by creating economic wealth and social enterprises that reinvest financial surpluses to meet social objectives. As a way of thinking and acting, entrepreneurship also creates value in individuals through personal development and effectiveness.

Case study
'Fogg's Failures': the entrepreneur who studied unsuccessful ventures

Christopher Fogg was invited to address a group of students that were interested in developing their entrepreneurial capabilities. This is what he said:

Since qualifying as a Chartered Accountant I have become a portfolio entrepreneur and have started over 50 businesses – alone and with others. But I am going to talk about my 'failures' not my successes, as I believe we can learn more from what doesn't work than from what does.

In 2008, I set up Connect London, a business incubator 'without walls', based on Connect San Diego, which is regarded as the best private model to help entrepreneurs start and develop high-growth businesses. This work involves assessing large numbers of new ventures. I have developed a simple methodology to help me carry out the first stage assessment based on 'Four Anchors' relating to the business itself and then a review of the business environment.

The **Four Anchors** are:

1 *Value – does the business create or add value to a customer or end user?*
2 *Clients' willingness to pay – is the customer or client likely to pay for this added value? Does the business solve a significant problem, or meet a want or need, for which someone is willing to pay a premium?*

3 *Money making characteristics – is the market large enough for sufficient money to be earned? Has it got high growth potential and early positive cash flow? Will it produce profits to satisfy investors? Will the rewards balance the risks?*

4 *People – is the business a good fit with the characteristics, knowledge and expertise of the founding entrepreneur and their management team?*

I recently asked myself whether my methodology would have helped predict my own failures. A review of my 'Top 10 business failures' against these Four Anchors went as follows:

Venture 1: Gambling with marbles

When I was 10-years-old, I encouraged fellow students to roll their marbles towards holes that I had cut into a shoe box. If they didn't get through one of the holes, I kept the marble. It was perhaps the highest rated business I have ever had, satisfying each and every one of the four anchors: it met a need – the excitement of gambling that clients were willing and able to pay for with their marbles. It had instant cash – or rather marble – flow, and I was the perfect entrepreneur with experience – I loved marbles and started gambling on horses with a postal tote service at a young age.

Why did it fail?

Children at my school quickly caught the gambling habit and soon began asking their parents for more money to buy marbles to replace the ones they had lost to me. I was reported to the headmistress who not only made me close my business, but also return all the marbles I had won because I fell foul of the rules of gambling in schools. I learned that although a new venture might meet all the business criteria, it also has to be legal.

Venture 2: Reproduction MG sports cars

Whilst travelling in Brazil, I noticed absolutely brilliant reproductions of old MG sports cars, based on the structure of VW Beetles. I started to import the kits, but for UK safety regulations these had to be built on the base of used right-hand drive VW Beetles imported from Europe.

Why did it fail?

Clients did not want to take the risk of a car based on an old VW Beetle – even though it looked beautiful. The entrepreneur (me) had no knowledge or experience of the import and sale of specialist cars (Anchor 4).

Venture 3: Chinese bicycles

I was in China endeavouring to sell very large-scale capital equipment for the manufacture of paper. Selling to China is very difficult so I tried a different tack – bartering. I was dealing with a Chinese trading company that also sold Chinese bicycles and I made the gesture of buying 1000 of their bikes. Everyone was delighted and I received a lot of publicity for the first sale of Chinese bikes to the UK.

Why did it fail?

I overlooked one thing – when the bikes arrived in the UK I discovered that I had not bought finished bikes but components for 1000 bikes – which is a lot of components. By the time I had paid for the assembly of these, the profit margin was low, especially as I could hardly sell old fashioned Chinese bikes at a premium. Obviously, the entrepreneur (me) had no knowledge or experience of bicycle importing, manufacturing or marketing (Anchor 4).

Venture 4: Second-hand Jumbo Jets

I was running an international trading company and received an enquiry (from my local Bangladesh restaurant) for three used Jumbo Jets for Bangladeshi Biman (the national airline). Having contacted other airlines and agents, I flew out for a meeting in Dhaka with a portfolio of eight used Jumbo Jets for sale in my briefcase. A group of about 20 people from government, banks, the air force and the airline grilled me with a barrage of technical, product and commercial questions.

Why did it fail?

I could not answer any of their questions! I was also very immature in understanding what 'individual commissions' would have to be paid to secure the business. Once again the entrepreneur (me) had come up short as I had no knowledge or experience of the business of selling used aircraft (Anchor 4).

Venture 5: Siemens vacuum pumps

Siemens market a vast range of electrical and electronic products, including a mechanical pump for producing a vacuum that was technically superior to competitive products. Its sales were almost zero. We persuaded Siemens to let us market the product through a network of 30 agents in the USA. We poached engineers and salesmen from the brand leader and the business was an amazing success with sales in excess of our most optimistic projections. At the end of six years, Siemens advised that they would not continue our contract. They were using too many of their own resources to service our clients, and, even more critically, they deemed it too risky to continue as they could not control us.

Why did it fail?

The business was too successful. If our sales were more modest, Siemens would have let us continue. (It met all four Anchors but failed on barriers to entry).

Venture 6: Hunt Wesson tomato products

On a visit to the USA in connection with Siemens, I looked out of my hotel window and saw an enormous factory with a name on the side that I just did not recognise – Hunt Wesson. Intrigued, I found out they were the largest producers of tomato-based products in the USA – bigger even than Heinz. I hadn't heard of them for the simple reason they did not sell to the UK. So, I approached them for the UK marketing rights. To my surprise, they gave it to me on the spot for a trial period of 18 months.

Why did it fail?

It proved too difficult to get the product introduced to UK supermarkets without massive marketing budgets that Hunt Wesson expected us to fund. We did not have the financial resources to establish a new brand to compete with Heinz. The entrepreneur (me) had no knowledge or experience in selling products to supermarkets (Anchors 3 and 4).

Venture 7: Orville Redenbacher's Gourmet Popping Corn

When Hunt Wesson acquired Orville Redenbacher's business, I used my contacts there to negotiate the rights to sell their Gourmet Popping Corn in the UK. We had a massive launch at the UK Trade Centre and attracted a lot of PR.

Why did it fail?

We could not interest retailers in stocking up-market, highly priced popcorn. The consumer was just not ready to pay the premium for this specialized product (Anchor 2).

Christopher Fogg

Venture 8: Honour snacks

This was another idea that I borrowed from the USA. You leave a tray of snacks and sweets in offices with an honest box for payment. Each week you top up the tray and, in theory, collect the cash. Today, in the UK, this is a successful business model operated by 'Snacks in the Bar' and a number of charities.

Why did it fail?

The trays and the cash boxes were both empty at the end of the week. At that time, office workers in the UK were not willing to pay for the product (Anchor 2) – but happily took advantage of my 'gifts'.

Venture 9: Fortune teller balls

An entrepreneur approached me to help him to import glass fortune teller balls into the UK. I did identify the dangers of this business in advance, but I have included it here as it led to a much bigger opportunity.

Why did it fail?

The entrepreneur gave up as he did not sell enough balls. The market in terms of size and profit margins in cash was not big enough to sustain the business and the entrepreneur (Anchors 2 and 3).

Venture 10: Waterless swimming

A director of Trust House Forte went to Blackpool beach and had his fortune told. He asked the fortune teller where he could find a supplier of plastic balls that he had seen in an amusement centre in the USA. The fortune teller said she did not know, but she gave him my details as I had supplied her fortune teller ball. I then received an enquiry for 100 000 plastic balls – which I took up immediately. The business was a massive success – I was even pictured in the Financial Times lying in a ball pond of balls. These 'ball ponds' – a tank or inflatable filled with 20 000 plastic balls – are still around today.

Why did it fail?

Once we had established the market, our supplier began to sell direct. If we had not been so successful, the ball manufacturer would have left us with the market. There were few barriers to entry, so we lost the market and withdrew. (Met all the Anchors but failed through very low barriers to entry.)

Should I have spotted my mistakes

I believe my assessment methodology of the four Anchors would have identified 8 out of 10 of my failures. The other two (Siemens pumps and Waterless swimming) needed higher barriers to entry to make them into viable long-term businesses. Their success meant that competitors, in the form of the manufacturers, entered the market. But note that four of what I call failures led directly to other opportunities.

Today, one of my most important roles is to facilitate 'good business failures'. That is, I help entrepreneurs to know when to quit, so that they do not leave debts behind nor suffer other trauma when one particular venture does not work out. Most importantly, I encourage them to learn from what went wrong.

(Continued)

Activities

(a) What is the most likely cause of 'Fogg's Failures'?

(b) Why does Chris Fogg believe that:
  (i) failure is an essential part of business success?
  (ii) the study of failures is a very important part of learning about entrepreneurship?

(c) Why does Chris Fogg have so many business ventures to his name? Should he have concentrated on researching just one of them to make it into a long-term success?

(d) Check a successful business that you know about against Fogg's Four Anchors. For example, how would you assess the business of text messaging from mobile phone operators against each of the four criteria?

Case study
Adding value to pizza

Peter Maldini, creator and owner of Maldini Pizza, refers to his restaurant concept as 'designer pizza and pasta'. He opened one restaurant in the centre of town two years ago that has been very successful, even developing something of a cult following. The food is not unusual – a variety of pasta and pizza dishes that can be found in other restaurants of this type. The prices are not expensive, with a variety of starters at around £3 to £5, and large pizza and pasta dishes at £7 to £10. What is different is the decor and the presentation. The food is presented on beautiful tableware with large white dishes and silver cutlery. The decor is modern Italian in style with much stainless steel and glass in evidence. Ceilings are high, which, linked to minimalist decorations and white walls, gives a feeling of spaciousness. The toilets summarize the tone of the place. The washbasins are steel set in a glass surround with walls of white Italian marble tiles – stunning! Some of the dishes reflect this style as the pasta comes in unusual shapes and colours, and there are authentic Italian oils and dressings on the tables. The food, like the decor, is simple but of high quality – what Peter Maldini describes as 'classically modern'.

Many of the waiting staff are Italian or French, adding to the continental feel, and wear large white aprons over black clothing. They are well-trained, welcoming and relaxed. However, they are also efficient. The owner insists they follow detailed instructions on the structure of their work with clear rules on customer service, such as maximum waiting times for orders and regular checks on customer satisfaction.

Peter Maldini was brought up in England, although he is a regular visitor to Italy. He describes his mother as 'very English' and his father as 'very Italian'. He is certainly proud of both backgrounds, which are reflected in his business. His aim is to merge Italian style and food under the 'Maldini' brand, and make it appealing to the UK market.

The exit plan

Although relatively young, Maldini recognizes that life is short in the catering trade and he wants to see a clear exit route from his business in five years so that he can pursue other projects. He plans to make at least £1 million from the sale of the business at that time. He has a number of ideas about how to add value to his business and make it more attractive to potential buyers:

1 He is considering opening another restaurant in a similar, mid-sized affluent town as a pilot for expansion. He is unclear whether any future outlets after that should be as a franchise operation or owned

outlets under management. The fitting out of the current restaurant cost £300 000 including equipment and refurbishment, so that expansion will require considerable capital. He believes he could grow quite rapidly to 10 or more restaurants, which would give him economies of buying and flexibility of staffing. However, he would not personally like to manage a chain bigger than that as he feels it would lose the 'personal touch'.

2 He believes he can offer other products under the Maldini label which emphasize Italian style and cooking. For example, he has investigated importing a range of cooking utensils and Italian food ingredients which he would sell by mail order to his restaurant customer base. He reckons his restaurant attracts over 40 000 paying customers per year, which, discounting children and those who come in more than once, equates to about 15 000 adults. He has collected a mailing list of around 5000 regular customers during the first two years' trading.

3 He is thinking of launching the 'Maldini Room Service', targeted at lunch/dinner parties and business entertaining. Busy people can order from the full menu and have the meal delivered in insulated containers, and served onto his Italian tableware, in their home or office. He developed the idea from catering firms operating in big cities that provide a corporate dining service without the need for in-house kitchens. He calculates that there are about 700 local businesses within a 10-mile radius that would be interested in eating on their own premises from time to time, at a cost of £15–£25 per head, including delivery.

The financials

He is quite familiar with the basic accounting information for his restaurant himself, although he does not produce regular, detailed management accounts. He would plan new restaurants on the same sales and cost profile as the first one.

Sales: the present restaurant had sales of £400 000 in Year 1 and £500 000 in Year 2. Maldini is expecting it to stay at this level, except for rises in line with inflation and new business developments. The average customer spend per head is £15. Seasonal fluctuations during the summer and at Christmas mean that August and December sales are usually two-thirds up on the average £40 000 per month turnover.

Costs of food and drink: he calculates a gross profit by subtracting costs of food ingredients and drink – wine, beer, soft drinks, and so on – from the sales total. The menu is priced to give an average 80 per cent gross profit on food dishes and 60 per cent on drink. The ratio of food to drink sales is normally 70:30.

Staff costs: he employs mainly part-time staff, on one daytime and one nighttime shift, each with a manager. As they open seven days a week, this adds up to a considerable number of staff. He thinks it is equivalent to about 15 full-time staff, although he has over 40 employees on his books. In total, staff costs are £17 500 per month including employment costs. Waiting staff keep their tips, so their earnings can be quite high at no extra cost to the restaurant.

Premises costs: rent, rates, insurances, heating, light and other costs relating to the premises are running at £5000 per month.

Office and publicity costs: accounting and administrative costs are not high, although they do have occasional publicity costs such as a mailing to their customer list, or the printing of a new menu – in all £2500 per month.

Cash: sales are paid for immediately, except for a slight delay on credit card sales. The biggest cost area, staff salaries, is also paid for in the same month in which it is incurred. Other costs – food and drink, premises, office and publicity costs – are paid for within 30 days on average; that is, the month after the cost is incurred. Although Maldini has to watch out for theft and non-payment, cash follows profits as he does not have much money tied up in stock or debtors. He does not have any substantial current borrowings as he funded the initial set-up costs from savings and a legacy. However, any expansion would have to be funded separately and finance costs built into the equation.

(Continued)

Marketing

Although Maldini has plenty of innovative ideas, and seems to know his target market well, he does very little to promote his business in traditional ways. Customers come to the restaurant by word-of-mouth recommendations, although he does mail a newsletter to his list of regular customers to inform them of special events and menu additions, especially at Christmas. His customers seem to come from a variety of age groups, but this is not really a family restaurant so younger children are rare. It attracts plenty of 25–35-year-olds, but also a slightly older group of over-50-year-olds. Plenty of women diners are in evidence, and the menu caters for vegetarians particularly well.

There is considerable competition. There has been a substantial increase in the number of local restaurants recently, especially of the less formal, cafe/diner type owned by national chains. However, people are eating out much more, a habit that seems set to grow.

Activities

(a) Estimate the current value of Maldini's business. If you were a buyer, how much would you be prepared to pay for it and why?

(b) How would you increase the value of the business in order to meet Maldini's exit plan?

    (i) How would you improve the existing business?

    (ii) Which development options would have the highest potential to add value?

Case study
Succession issues at Mackay Golf Ltd

Duncan Mackay founded Mackay Golf in 1958, when golf had emerged not only as a professional sport, but also as a lucrative, international business. He built up the company gradually over the years, specializing in high-quality clubs and accessories for the discerning player who was prepared to pay a little more for hand-made Scottish golf equipment. By the turn of the century, the company had grown to employ over 70 staff with a turnover of £4 million and net profits of £200 000. The company survived 50 years in business, but the founder did not. He died after a heart attack on one of his favourite courses, a month before the planned half-century celebrations. His widow, family and colleagues were left to contemplate the next steps for the business.

The family

For the first 35 years of the business, Duncan Mackay seemed a typical, family-business owner. He married his childhood sweetheart, Mary, and their only son, Malcolm, joined the company on completion of his business and finance degree. Malcolm proved an asset not only for his aptitude at sales and marketing, but also for his love of golf. A regular participant in amateur tournaments, Malcolm was a well-known figure in many clubhouses.

But 15 years before his death, Duncan turned his family and business world upside down by leaving his wife for his secretary, Isabel Stuart. After an acrimonious separation and divorce, Duncan remarried and had a second son, Kenneth, by Isabel. Although Malcolm stayed on in the business, he found relationships with his father difficult through the strain of these family pressures and he used every opportunity to spend more time on the golf course.

The shareholding of the business had become equally complicated. Duncan and Mary Mackay were the original shareholders in 1958, with 50 per cent of the shares each. When Malcolm joined the business, his mother transferred 30 per cent of the shares from her name to his in recognition of his contribution to the business and her own lack of involvement. Duncan's will came as a shock, particularly to Malcolm. He left 40 per cent of the company's shares to his second son Kenneth, to be held in trust by his mother, Isabel, until he was aged 18. The remaining 10 per cent of shares went to Bill Warren, General Manager of Mackay Golf.

The management

When Kenneth was born in 1995, Duncan Mackay was 60 years old. He promised his new wife that he would shorten his 65-hour working week to spend more time with his new family. He hired a manager, Bill Warren, to take over some of the responsibilities. Bill had enjoyed a successful career in the leisure industry in a variety of administrative and management posts. He was drawn to Mackay Golf for the quality of life offered by its location, the promise of shares in the business at some future date, and the opportunity to run a smaller company. He was happy to leave Malcolm to manage the sales effort with customers, as his own strengths lay in running an efficient operation back at base. Bill had been running the administrative, financial and production functions of the business for the last decade or more, advised by Duncan.

The market

The sports equipment market is still sufficiently fragmented to allow smaller companies such as Mackay Golf to survive in an increasingly competitive arena. Golf is a large market for personal sports equipment and grew quite strongly as the population aged and more golf courses were built. The UK market for golf equipment and supplies probably exceeds £800 million, with an estimated 3 million players. However, the financial downturn and a series of wet-weather years had caused a reduction in income into the sport. Golf is also one of the most competitive sports equipment sectors, with strong branding linked to high levels of promotional expenditure, particularly on endorsements. This has favoured the larger suppliers of well-known, international brands. Imports have increased substantially, mainly from the USA, Taiwan and Hong Kong. Traditionally strong European export markets for UK golf producers were undermined by the strength of the pound. Mackay Golf sales had declined for the two years prior to Duncan's death. Although their products were widely respected as quality leaders, their distributors in the USA and Europe were concerned at their high prices, lack of point-of-sale material and publicity in the retail outlets, and low investment in research and development for new products.

The shareholders' meeting

Soon after Duncan's death, the shareholders of Mackay Golf met to review the situation. After rather strained formalities, Bill Warren opened the meeting.

'I know we all have Duncan's passing on our minds, but I am sure he would have wanted us to take decisions based on what is best for the business. It seems to me we have two basic options: one is to carry on and hope we can fight our way through the difficult competitive situation we are in. The second option is to sell the business so that shareholders can realize what is still a valuable asset before it devalues any further.'

Isabel nodded her agreement to the second option. 'I for one would like to realize some capital. Duncan did not have many assets to leave in his will after the divorce settlement', she said, looking pointedly at Mary Mackay, 'which is why he left me and Kenneth the shares – it's all we have.'

'This is very defeatist talk.' Malcolm could restrain himself no longer. 'If you feel like out Bill, that's OK. I'll happily take over the helm totally now. It's what Dad wanted originally anyway. I strongly believe we can survive and grow. We have made good profits in the past and we can again – which will give you the money you need in dividend payments, Isabel. Selling now is admitting defeat, and we would not get the best price for the business.'

'And I know it's not what Duncan would have wanted. This was his life's work', said Mary.

(Continued)

Activities

You have been called in to give objective advice to the shareholders on what they should do.

(a) Summarize the problems faced by Mackay Golf Ltd. An analysis of strengths, weaknesses, opportunities and threats (SWOT) would be a good way of presenting the issues facing the company.
(b) Outline the options as you see them. Are there others that Bill Warren did not mention?
(c) Recommend a course of action that takes account of the management needs of the business, but also recognizes the family situation.

Summary of what is required

- Write an exit plan.
- Summarize the business plan.

Write an exit plan

- Consider a timetable for exit. How long do you wish to run and own the business?
- Consider what you want as a final value from your venture. How much money do you want your business to be worth at the stage you wish to either sell it, or take a less active role?
- Conclude your plan by listing the options for exit, especially if you are inviting others to invest in your business.

Planning a new venture
Exit and business planning

Summary of the business plan

You should now be in a position to write up your business plan. You may wish to review the structure of this in the light of the development of your ideas and information (see Chapter 6, Business planning). Presentation of your final business plan should take into account the need for:

- Conciseness: make your plan as concise as possible for an external audience, such as financiers. Keep the main body of the report for essential information only, using appendices where possible to enlarge on assumptions or research.
- Presentation: good presentation is seen as a sign of organized management, a quality you will need as an owner-manager.
- Enthusiasm: your plan should be interesting to read, as your enthusiasm for the project needs to show through. If you cannot be enthusiastic about it, then no one else will be!
- Realism: optimistic plans fool no one except the writer. Where there are major uncertainties, identify them. Do not try to cover them up, as they will look worse if discovered by the reader.
- Illustration: where possible show examples by use of sample web pages, flyers, photographs of products, locations, and so on Pictures speak a thousand words.
- Summary: you will need to make a short summary of your plan; this is commonly found at the front of the document.

14.7 Notes, references and recommended further reading

Notes and further information

1 See Chapter 3, Section 3.3, Sink or swim, for a fuller discussion of these issues.

2 Stokes and Blackburn (2001) categorized owners closing a business as 'Departing' from ownership – 29 per cent; 'retiring' – 9 per cent; 'returning' as business owners – 62 per cent. See also Figure 14.2.

3 Based on an article 'What is Tony Allan up to now?' in *Real Business*, Caspian Publishing, March 2003.

4 Chapter 9, Section 9.5, Basis of valuation of an existing business. See also Burns, P. (2010) *Entrepreneurship and Small Business*, 3rd edn, Palgrave, ch. 15, Exit: Failure and Success.

5 See Chapter 9, Section 9.5.2, Multiple of profits. Sperry, P. and Mitchell, B. (1999) *The Complete Guide to Selling Your Business*, Kogan Page/Institute of Directors, ch. 3, What is Your Company Worth?

6 See Section 12.1, Small business marketing issues. See also Hall, G. (1995) *Surviving and Prospering in the Small Firm Sector*, Routledge; Burns, P. (2010)

Entrepreneurship and Small Business, 3rd edn, Palgrave, ch. 15, Exit: Failure and Success.

7 See Chapter 3, Section 3.4, Hostile and benign environments. This uses Michael Porter's well-known Five Forces' model of industry competition to illustrate how some sectors are more volatile than others.

8 See Chapter 2, Section 2.5. This section analyzed the attributes of the model entrepreneur further to include: technical skills – product/market knowledge; management competencies – marketing, finance, human relations; and personal attributes – innovative, determined, external focus, team leader.

9 See Chapter 10, Section 10.7, Intellectual property rights. See also the IPO website, www.gov.uk/government/organisations /intellectual-property-office.

10 See Chapter 9, Buying an existing business, which considers the types of buyers and sellers of small businesses.

References

Benavides-Velasco, C. A., Quintana-García, C. and Guzmán-Parra, V. F. (2013) Trends in family business research, *Small Business Economics*, 40(1): 41–57.

Blackburn, R. and Stokes, D. (2002) *Who are the Entrepreneurs? A Survey of the Owners of Small and Medium Sized Enterprises*, Report for Kingston Smith, Small Business Research Centre, Kingston University, September.

Brindle, S. (2006) *Brunel: The Man Who Built the World*, Orion Books.

Burns, P. (2010) *Entrepreneurship and Small Business*, 3rd edn, Palgrave.

Chua, J. H., Chrisman, J. J. and Steier, L. P. (2003) Extending the theoretical horizons of family business research, *Entrepreneurship Theory and Practice*, 27(4): 331–338.

Clancey, H. (2000) Serial entrepreneurs, *Computer Reseller News*, 90(2): 74–75.

Coad, A. (2014) Death is not a success: Reflections on business exit, *International Small Business Journal*, 32(7): 721–732.

Cooney, T. (2005) What is an entrepreneurial team?, *International Small Business Journal*, 23(3): 226–235.

DeTienne, D. R. and Chiroco, F. (2013) Exit strategies in family firms: How socioemotional wealth drives the threshold of performance, *Entrepreneurship, Theory & Practice*, 37(6): 1297–1318.

Fletcher, D. (2006) Family and Enterprise. In: Carter, S. and Jones-Evans, D. (eds) *Enterprise and Small Business: Principles, Practice and Policy*, 2nd. edn, Pearson Education.

Fraone, G. (1999) Serial entrepreneurs, *Electronic Business*, 25(10): 56–62.

Frederick, H. (2005) *Educating GenerationE in Australasia: US Lessons, New Zealand Experience*, IntEnt Conference, University of Surrey, Guildford.

Harada, N. (2005) *Which Firms Exit and Why? An Analysis of Small-Firm Exits in Japan*, Department of Social Systems and Management, Discussion Paper Series, No. 1129, University of Tsukuba.

Headd, B (2003) Redefining business success: Distinguishing between closure and failure, *Small Business Economics*, 21(1): 51–61.

Hedman, J. and Kalling, T. (2003) The business model concept: Theoretical underpinnings and empirical illustrations, *European Journal of Information* Systems, 12: 42–59.

Janjuha-Jivraj, S. and Woods, A. (2002) Successional Issues within Asian Family Firms: Learning from the Kenyan Experience, *International Small Business Journal*, 20(1): 77–94.

Kuratko, D. F. and Hodgetts, R. M. (2007) *Entrepreneurship: Theory, Process, Practice*, South-Western College.

Martin, C., Martin L. and Mabbett, A. (2002) SME ownership succession – Business support and policy implications, *SBS Research and Evaluation*, April.

McCollom, M. E. (1992) Organizational stories in a family owned business, *Family Business Review*, V(1): 3–23.

Metzger, G. (2006) *Afterlife: Who Takes Heart for Restart*, Centre for European Economic Research (ZEW), No. 06–038.

Micklethwaite, J. and Wooldridge, A. (2003) *The Company: A Short History of a Revolutionary Idea*, Weidenfeld & Nicolson.

Nummela, N., Saarenketo, S. and Loane, S. (2016) The dynamics of failure in international new ventures: A case study of Finnish and Irish software companies, *International Small Business Journal*, 34(1): 51–69.

Osterwalder, A. and Pigneur, Y. (2010) *Business Model Generation*, John Wiley & Sons.

Ryan, V. (2000) Anatomy of an entrepreneur, *Telephony*, 238(15): 36–44.

Sperry, P. and Mitchell, B. (1999) *The Complete Guide to Selling Your Business*, Kogan Page/Institute of Directors.

Stam, E., Audretsch, D. and Meijaard, J. (2005) Entrepreneurial Intentions Subsequent to Firm Exit, *EIM Business and Policy Research*, SCALES-paper N200506.

Stokes D. R. and Blackburn R. A. (2001) *Opening Up Business Closures: A Study of Businesses that Close and Owners' Exit Routes: A Research Report for HSBC*, Small Business Research Centre, Kingston University, October.

Stokes, D. and Blackburn, R. (2002) Learning the hard way: The lessons of owner-managers who have closed their businesses, *Journal of Small Business and Enterprise Development*, 9(1): 17–27.

Ucbasaran, D., Westhead, P., Wright, M. and Flores, M. (2010) The nature of entrepreneurial experience, business failure and comparative optimism, *Journal of Business Venturing*, 25(6): 541–555.

Ucbasaran, D., Shepherd, D. A., Lockett, A. and Lyon, S. J. (2013) Life after business failure. The process and consequences of business failure for entrepreneurs, *Journal of Management*, 39(1): 163–202.

Wennberg, K. and DeTienne, D. R. (2014) What do we really mean when we talk about 'exit'? A critical review of research on entrepreneurial exit, *International Small Business Journal*, 32(1): 4–16.

Wilson, N., Wright, M. and Scholes, L. (2013) Family business survival and the role of boards, *Entrepreneurship, Theory & Practice*, 37(6): 1369–1389.

Yusuf, J.-E. (2012) A tale of two exits: Nascent entrepreneur learning activities and disengagement from start-up, *Small Business Economics*, 39(3): 783–799.

Recommended further reading

Barrow, C., Burke, G., Molian, D. and Brown, R. (2005) *Enterprise Development*, Thomson Learning. Chapter 16, What are your options for realizing value?

Burns, P. (2010) *Entrepreneurship and Small Business*, 3rd edn, Palgrave, ch. 15.

Cooney T. (2005) What is an entrepreneurial team? *International Small Business Journal*, 23(3): 226–235. This is a special edition on entrepreneurial teams and contains other articles of interest on this topic.

Fletcher, D. (2006) Family and Enterprise. In: Carter, S. and Jones-Evans, D. (eds) *Enterprise and Small Business: Principles, Practice and Policy*, 2nd edn, Pearson Education.

Stokes, D. and Blackburn, R. (2002) Learning the hard way: The lessons of owner-managers who have closed their businesses, *Journal of Small Business and Enterprise Development*, 9(1): 17–27.

Glossary of terms

Articles of Association legal document setting out the management arrangements of a limited company

Asset anything of worth owned by the business, including *tangible assets* such as cash, property, equipment and stocks and *intangible assets* such as image and customer goodwill

Asset parsimony using the minimum possible amount of assets to deliver the organization's outputs

Balance sheet a summary of what money has been spent by a business and what it has been spent on. It is usually an annual summary of the use and sources of funds in a company

Banner advertising advertising through promotional messages on websites

Base rate also called the Repo (repurchase transaction) rate, this is the borrowing and lending rate set by the Bank of England

Benevolent autocracy management style that combines a firm but friendly control

Big Five personality dimensions five traits that have been put forward as important influences in entrepreneurship: need for achievement, need for autonomy, locus of control, risk taking and self-efficacy

Break-even the level of sales required to cover the ongoing costs of doing business

Business angel a wealthy individual who contributes personal funds and expertise, usually at an early stage of business development

Business closure the closure of a business entity

Business exit the exit of an owner from a business

Business failure the closure of a business that has substantially failed to meet the owner's objectives, usually leaving financial problems

Business format franchise a continuing relationship in which the franchisor provides a licensed privilege to do business plus assistance in organizing training, merchandising and management in return for payments from the franchisee

Business plan a written document that identifies a business's goals and objectives and outlines how the firm intends to achieve these

Buy-in purchase of a business by managers from outside the company, often in association with existing managers

Buy-in management buy-out (BIMBO) purchase of a business by a combination of existing and outside managers

Buy-out purchase of a business by its existing management

Capital gains tax (CGT) tax on profit from the sale of an asset that was previously purchased at a lower price, e.g. the sale of stocks, bonds and property

Capitalization the total of a company's debt, stock (shares) and earnings

Cash flow the movement of cash into and out of the business

Competency underlying characteristics of a manager that result in an effective performance in the job

Competitive advantage a firm's relative market position and potential to differentiate what it sells from competitors' offerings

Cooperative enterprise jointly owned by its members. *Consumer cooperatives* are jointly owned by customers; *community cooperatives* by the community it serves; *worker cooperatives* are owned and controlled by all the people working for it for their mutual benefit

Copyright grant to the originator of a literary, musical, dramatic or artistic work, the exclusive rights of publication, production, sale or distribution

Core competence the skills that enable a firm to deliver a fundamental customer benefit

Corporate entrepreneurship the venturing and innovation activities of companies, particularly larger ones

Creativity the generation of a new and valuable ideas

Customer relationship management (CRM) integrated information system used to plan and control all aspects of dealing with customers and prospective customers

Design right grant to prevent copying of the appearance of a product including shape, colours, texture or materials

Direct mail/email marketing communications distributed through the post or the internet

Dividend a share in the company's profits. The size of the dividend depends on the profits being made by the company and their profit distribution policy

Domain name website address

Dominant design a design of product or service that achieves some dominance in the market, usually after a period of competitive activity between new entrants (e.g. the QWERTY keyboard)

Dynamic capability a learned and stable pattern of collective activity through which the organization systematically generates and modifies its operating routines in pursuit of improved effectiveness

Economy of scale significant cost reduction resulting from the high level of output in an industry

Electronic commerce transactions in which products, services and/or information is bought, sold, transferred or exchanged via computer networks, including the internet

Enterprise culture a way of thinking or philosophy that values and fosters the entrepreneurial spirit

Entrepreneur/entrepreneurial team an individual or group who mediates the process of entrepreneurship

Entrepreneurial alertness the ability to scan the external environment for opportunity

Entrepreneurial self-efficacy self-efficacy when viewed as a key antecedent to new venture intentions

Entrepreneurship the introduction of new economic activity. This requires the identification, evaluation and exploitation of an opportunity; the management of a new or transformed organization; and the creation of value through innovation

Entrepreneurship dynamic the role of teams or individuals who work collectively, either formally or informally, to found new organizations and to create innovations

Equity gap funding gap, held to be between approximately £250 000 and £2 million, which results from a combination of supply-side and demand-side issues, including information asymmetry and a lack of investment readiness

EU an economic and political union established in 1993 after the ratification of the Maastricht Treaty by members of the European Community, which forms its core. In establishing the European Union, the treaty expanded the political scope of the European Community, especially in the area of foreign and security policy, and provided for the creation of a central European bank and the adoption of a common currency by the end of the twentieth century

EU enlargement the growth in size of the European Union, from the six founding member states in 1952, to the 28 current member states, although in 2016 the UK voted to leave the EU

4 Is the four elements of strategic entrepreneurial marketing: innovation, identification of target markets, interactive marketing methods, informal information gathering

4 Ps the four elements of the classical marketing mix: product, price, promotion and place

Family business a business that employs more than one family member or a business that is passed on to the next generation of the same family

Finance gap unwillingness on the part of suppliers of finance (often banks) to supply it on the terms and conditions required by small businesses

Flexible specialization gives priority to value maximization and product differentiation in contrast to mass production of standardized goods that emphasizes cost minimization. Enabled by subcontracting, collaboration and inter-firm networks

Flotation when a company first sells its stock to the general public through a stock market

Focus group market research technique involving a small number of people, illustrative of a specific market, who are invited to discuss together topics of interest to the researchers

Forced sale sale of a business that is forced by circumstances, such as liquidation

Franchise a method for starting a new business within the framework of an existing larger business entity

Franchising a business arrangement in which one party (the franchisor) allows others (the franchisees) to use a business name, or sell products, in such a way that the franchisees can operate their own legally separate business

Fraternalism management style in which partners operate on an equal basis

Freehold tenure of land or property of indeterminate duration and with no fees

Free market a market economy based on supply and demand with little or no government control

GDP Gross Domestic Product. GDP is the grand total of all the consumer and government spending, investments and exports minus the value of imports

Gearing the percentage of borrowing compared to the percentage of assets. The gearing ratio measures the percentage of capital employed that is financed by debt and long-term finance. The higher the gearing, the higher the dependence on borrowings and the higher the level of financial risk due to the increased volatility of profits

Geodemographic database method of segmenting consumer markets by profiling the population in defined geographic areas using the census of population data

Goodwill arises when more is paid for a business than the value of its tangible assets. Includes the reputation, customers and skill base of a business

Green movement general trend towards protecting the environment supported by the Green parties and the ecology and conservation movements

Incubator organization that supports businesses with a range of services including provision of space, management coaching, business planning, administrative services and sources of financing

Industry the firms that produce and sell products and services that are close substitutes for one another (i.e. sellers)

Information asymmetry where the lender or investor is only partially informed about the prospects of the business

Initial public offering (IPO) making shares in a business available to the general public, usually through a stock exchange flotation

Innovation the successful exploitation of a new and valuable idea

Intellectual property rights (IPRs) ideas, inventions, designs, know-how and names associated with the business form intellectual property (IP) that can be protected to become intellectual property rights

Investment readiness refers to an entrepreneur's understanding of the motivations, needs and information requirements of potential investors

Leasehold land or property held under a lease

Liability of newness refers to the difficulties experienced by new firms simply as a result of being 'new'

Limited by guarantee a company limited by guarantee (i.e. a guarantee company) is a type of corporation used primarily for non-profit organizations that require a separate legal personality. A guarantee company has members who act as guarantors

Limited company a business that is organized in such a way as to give its owners limited liability

Limited liability partnership business form that limits the liabilities of the partners

Liquidation when a business is terminated or bankrupt, its assets are sold, the proceeds paid to creditors and anything left is distributed to shareholders

Locus of control the belief that we can influence the environment in which we find ourselves

Macro-environment consists of factors which have an impact on firms nationally and internationally

Manufacturer innovation when the developer expects to benefit by selling it

Market existing or potential customers for a given product or service (i.e. buyers)

Market customer orientation business philosophy that puts customer needs at the centre of all decision-making

Market information information about customers and competitors

Market intelligence information on customers, competitors and trends in the business environment

Market niche sub-segment of customers who require specialized products or services

Marketing channels the methods and distribution routes through which products/services reach the marketplace

Marketing information information about the influences on customers and market position of competitors

Marketing mix the marketing methods used by a business, including product development, pricing, promotions and distribution

Marxist theory following the work of Karl Marx and his successors in economic and philosophical theory

Memorandum of Association the charter of a limited company that sets out the company objectives and share structure

Micro-environment local factors which influence firms operating in particular markets and competing in certain industries

Multilevel marketing selling products through a chain of distribution agents selling direct to the consumer

Multiple of profits the annual profits of a business multiplied by a specified number for the purposes of valuation

Necessity-based entrepreneurship where individuals participate in entrepreneurial activities because all other employment options are either absent or unsatisfactory

Networking key management behaviour that produces a chain of interconnected persons and enables entrepreneurship

New Age consciousness-raising movements originating in the 1980s with a belief in spiritualism and reincarnation, and holistic approaches to health and ecology

New ideas often the meeting of two old ideas for the first time

Newsgroups online discussion groups

Objectives what is to be achieved (but not how)

Omnibus survey research conducted on behalf of a number of different clients

Opportunity a chance to progress a business proposition through 'a situation in which goods, services, raw materials and organizing methods can be introduced and sold at greater than their cost of production'

Opportunity-based entrepreneurship where individuals participate in entrepreneurial activities in order to exploit a perceived business opportunity

Partnership business form in which two or more individuals manage the business and are personally liable for its debts

Patent grant that confers upon the creator of an invention the right to prevent others from making or selling the invention without licence for a defined period

Paternalism management style that clearly differentiates between manager and employee

Path dependence where an organization can only develop as fast as its past (and current) position, paths and processes allow

PE ratio price-earnings ratio: the ratio of the market price of a share to the earnings per share

Pecking order theory theory which suggests that external funds are only necessary when internal funds are no longer adequate

Portfolio entrepreneur entrepreneur owning more than one business at the same time

Positioning how a business or product/service is perceived in the marketplace in relation to its competitors

Primary data new data specifically collected through field research

Product/service benefit the value of a product or service to a customer

Product/service feature a characteristic of a product or service

Productive churn the level of businesses opening and closing within a given period that stimulates competition

Profit and loss account shows how a business is doing in terms of sales and costs – and the difference between them of profit or losses

Public limited company a type of limited liability company in the UK and Republic of Ireland that is permitted to offer shares to the public

Public relations (PR) methods and activities used to promote favourable impressions and relationships with the public

Push and pull influences motivations for becoming self-employed

Quality of earnings a measure of how long the current levels of profitability of a business are likely to last

Receivership a type of bankruptcy a company enters when a receiver is appointed by bankruptcy courts or creditors to run the company

Recession a decline in the economy: if there is a decline for two quarters in succession then it is officially a recession; a severe recession is a depression

Resource-based view of the firm the approach that sees the firm's resources as the foundation for firm strategy

Sampling process of identifying a limited number of people or items that are representative of a larger population

Secondary data data that already exists, collected through desk research

Segmentation categorizing customers and consumers into groups with similar needs and expectations from their purchases

Self-efficacy an individual's belief in their ability to undertake and accomplish some particular task or activity

Serial entrepreneur entrepreneur who owns more than one business sequentially, owning and selling each business in a relatively short time

Service sector industries that offer services rather than producing goods – e.g. the retailing, entertainment and creative industries

Six markets model a relationship marketing concept of a supportive network of six stakeholder networks or markets: supplier, recruitment, internal, influence, referral and customer

Small business sector all of the small businesses active in the economy

SME small and medium-sized enterprise

Sole trader business owned and controlled by one person who is solely liable for its obligations

Strategy a plan, pattern, ploy, perspective or position relating to how a business is going to compete, what its objectives are and how these are to be achieved

Strong ties personal contacts with/through family and friends

Subcontracting assigns fulfilment services or production to a third-party organization or individual

Succession failure unsuccessful attempts to sell or hand on a business

Sweating management style that exploits a disadvantaged workforce

Switching costs one-off costs incurred by customers when switching from one supplier to another

Technology the combination of people, ideas and objects to achieve a particular goal; alternatively, it is the mix of physical appliances and human ways of doing things.

Trade mark sign or distinctive mark associated with a product/service of a business

User innovation when the developer expects to benefit by using it

Venture capitalist a person (usually working for a venture capital company) who invests money into risky but potentially very profitable businesses

Weak ties contacts made through indirect relations

Word-of-mouth marketing (WOM) recommendations for a product/service made through person-to-person communications perceived to be independent of the provider of the product/service

Working capital finance required to bridge the gap between when a small business gets paid and when it has to pay suppliers and overhead costs

Work-in-progress production or work that has not been completed but has already incurred some investment from the company and therefore is recorded as an asset

Index

Credit list